P9-AFY-260

AMERICAN LAW YEARBOOK 2008

AN ANNUAL SOURCE PUBLISHED
BY GALE AS A
SUPPLEMENT TO
WEST'S ENCYCLOPEDIA OF
AMERICAN LAW

ISSN 1521-0901

This Edition To: *Ref*
Forward Earlier
Edition To: *keep*
suppl. with
Encyclopedias

AMERICAN LAW YEARBOOK 2008

AN ANNUAL SOURCE PUBLISHED
BY GALE AS A
SUPPLEMENT TO
WEST'S ENCYCLOPEDIA OF
AMERICAN LAW

GALE
CENGAGE Learning

Detroit • New York • San Francisco • New Haven, Conn • Waterville, Maine • London

American Law Yearbook 2008

Project Editor: Jeffrey Wilson

Editorial: Amy Kwolek

Product Manager: Kate Hanley

Editorial Support Services: Selwa Petrus

Indexing Services: Janet Mazefsky

Rights Acquisition and Management: Robyn V. Young

Composition: Evi Abou-El-Seoud

Manufacturing: Rita Wimberley

Imaging: Lezlie Light

Product Design: Pam Galbreath

© 2009 Gale, Cengage Learning

ALL RIGHTS RESERVED. No part of this work covered by the copyright herein may be reproduced, transmitted, stored, or used in any form or by any means graphic, electronic, or mechanical, including but not limited to photocopying, recording, scanning, digitizing, taping, Web distribution, information networks, or information storage and retrieval systems, except as permitted under Section 107 or 108 of the 1976 United States Copyright Act, without the prior written permission of the publisher.

For product information and technology assistance, contact us at **Gale Customer Support, 1-800-877-4253.**
For permission to use material from this text or product, submit all requests online at **www.cengage.com/permissions.**
Further permissions questions can be emailed to **permissionrequest@cengage.com**

While every effort has been made to ensure the reliability of the information presented in this publication, Gale, a part of Cengage Learning, does not guarantee the accuracy of the data contained herein. Gale accepts no payment for listing; and inclusion in the publication of any organization, agency, institution, publication, service, or individual does not imply endorsement of the editors or publisher. Errors brought to the attention of the publisher and verified to the satisfaction of the publisher will be corrected in future editions.

ISBN 978-1-4144-0899-6
ISBN 1-4144-0899-4
ISSN 1521-0901

Gale
27500 Drake Rd.
Farmington Hills, MI, 48331-3535

This title is also available as an e-book.
ISBN-13: 978-1-4144-3748-4   ISBN-10: 1-4144-3748-X
Contact your Gale, a part of Cengage Learning sales representative for ordering information.

Printed in the United States of America
1 2 3 4 5 6 7 12 11 10 09 08

CONTENTS

The need for a layperson's comprehensive, understandable guide to terms, concepts, and historical developments in U.S. law has been well met by *West's Encyclopedia of American Law* (*WEAL*). Published in a second edition in 2004 by The Gale Group, *WEAL* has proved itself a valuable successor to West's 1983 publication, *The Guide to American Law: Everyone's Legal Encyclopedia.* and the 1997 first edition of WEAL.

Since 1998, Gale, a part of Cengage Learning, a premier reference publisher, has extended the value of *WEAL* with the publication of *American Law Yearbook* (*ALY*). This supplement adds entries on emerging topics not covered in the main set. A legal reference must be current to be authoritative, so *ALY* is a vital companion to a key reference source. Uniform organization by *WEAL* term and cross-referencing make it easy to use the titles together, while inclusion of key definitions and summaries of earlier rulings in supplement entries—whether new or continuations—make it unnecessary to refer to the main set constantly.

Understanding the American Legal System

The U.S. legal system is admired around the world for the freedoms it allows the individual and the fairness with which it attempts to treat all persons. On the surface, it may seem simple, yet those who have delved into it know that this system of federal and state constitutions, statutes, regulations, and common-law decisions is elaborate and complex. It derives from the English common law, but includes principles older than England, along with some principles from other lands. The U.S. legal system, like many others, has a language all its own, but too often it is an unfamiliar language: many concepts are still phrased in Latin. *WEAL* explains legal terms and concepts in everyday language, however. It covers a wide variety of persons, entities, and events that have shaped the U.S. legal system and influenced public perceptions of it.

FEATURES OF THIS SUPPLEMENT

Entries

ALY 2008 contains 156 entries covering individuals, cases, laws, and concepts significant to U.S. law. Entries are arranged alphabetically and use the same entry title as in *WEAL* or *ALY*—when introduced in an earlier *Yearbook* (e.g., September 11th Attacks). There may be several cases discussed under a given topic.

Profiles of individuals cover interesting and influential people from the world of law, government, and public life, both historic and contemporary. All have contributed to U.S. law as a whole. Each short biography includes a timeline highlighting important moments in the subject's life. Persons whose lives were detailed in *WEAL*, but who have died since publication of that work, receive obituary entries in *ALY*.

Definitions

Each entry on a legal term is preceded by a definition, which is easily distinguished by its sans serif typeface. The back of the book includes a Glossary of Legal Terms containing the definitions for a selection of the most important terms **bolded** in the text of the essays and biographies. Terms bolded but not included in the Glossary of Legal Terms in ALY can be found in the Dictionary volume of WEAL.

Cross References

To facilitate research, *ALY 2008* provides two types of cross-references: within and following entries. Within the entries, terms are set in small capital letters (e.g., First Amendment) to indicate that they have their own entry in *WEAL*. At the end of each entry, additional relevant topics in *ALY 2008* are listed alphabetically by title.

Appendix

This section follows the Glossary of Legal Terms and includes ten organization biographies, covering groups not previously included in prior editions of WEAL or ALY.

Table of Cases Cited and Index by Name and Subject

These features make it quick and easy for users to locate references to cases, people, statutes, events, and other subjects. The Table of Cases Cited traces the influences of legal precedents by identifying cases mentioned throughout the text. In a departure from *WEAL*, references to individuals have been folded into the general index to simplify searches. Litigants, justices, historical and contemporary figures, as well as topical references are included in the Index by Name and Subject.

Citations

Wherever possible, *ALY* includes citations to cases and statutes for readers wishing to do further research. They refer to one or more series, called "reporters," which publish court opinions and related information. Each citation includes a volume number, an abbreviation for the reporter, and the starting page reference. Underscores in a citation indicate that a court opinion has not been officially reported as of *ALY*'s publication. Two sample citations, with explanations, are presented below.

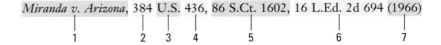

1. *Case title.* The title of the case is set in i and indicates the names of the parties. The suit in this sample citation was between Ernesto A. Miranda and the state of Arizona.

2. *Reporter volume number.* The number preceding the reporter abbreviation indicates the reporter volume containing the case. The volume number appears on the spine of the reporter, along with the reporter abbreviation.

3. *Reporter abbreviation.* The suit in the sample citation is from the reporter, or series of books, called *U.S. Reports,* which contains cases from the U.S. Supreme Court. Numerous reporters publish cases from the federal and state courts; consult the Abbreviations list at the back of this volume for full titles.

4. *Reporter page.* The number following the reporter abbreviation indicates the reporter page on which the case begins.

5. *Additional reporter citation.* Many cases may be found in more than one reporter. The suit in the sample citation also appears in volume 86 of the *Supreme Court Reporter,* beginning on page 1602.

6. *Additional reporter citation.* The suit in the sample citation is also reported in volume 16 of the *Lawyer's Edition,* second series, beginning on page 694.

7. *Year of decision.* The year the court issued its decision in the case appears in parentheses at the end of the cite.

Brady Handgun Violence Prevention Act, Pub. L. No. 103-159, 107 Stat. 1536 (18 U.S.C.A. § § 921-925A)

1 2 3 4 5 6 7 8

1. *Statute title.*

2. *Public law number.* In the sample citation, the number 103 indicates this law was passed by the 103d Congress, and the number 159 indicates it was the 159th law passed by that Congress.

3. *Reporter volume number.* The number preceding the reporter abbreviation indicates the reporter volume containing the statute.

4. *Reporter abbreviation.* The name of the reporter is abbreviated. The statute in the sample citation is from *Statutes at Large.*

5. *Reporter page.* The number following the reporter abbreviation indicates the reporter page on which the statute begins.

6. *Title number.* Federal laws are divided into major sections with specific titles. The number preceding a reference to the U.S. Code stands for the section called Crimes and Criminal Procedure.

7. *Additional reporter.* The statute in the sample citation may also be found in the *U.S. Code Annotated.*

8. *Section numbers.* The section numbers following a reference to the *U.S. Code Annotated* indicate where the statute appears in that reporter.

COMMENTS WELCOME

Considerable efforts were expended at the time of publication to ensure the accuracy of the information presented in *American Law Yearbook 2008.* The editor welcomes your comments and suggestions for enhancing and improving future editions of this supplement to *West's*

Encyclopedia of American Law. Send comments and suggestions to:

American Law Yearbook
Gale
27500 Drake Rd.
Farmington Hills, MI 48331-3535

SPECIAL THANKS

The editor wishes to acknowledge the contributions of the writers and copyeditors who aided in the compilation of *American Law Yearbook*. The editor gratefully thanks Matthew Cordon, Frederick K. Grittner, and Lauri R. Harding. Furthermore, valuable content review of entries came from: Matthew Cordon and Frederick K. Grittner.

PHOTOGRAPHIC CREDITS

The editor wishes to thank the permission managers of the companies that assisted in securing reprint rights. The following list—in order of appearance—acknowledges the copyright holders who have granted us permission to reprint material in this edition of *American Law Yearbook*:

Alex Ferrer, better known as TV's "Judge Alex," leaves the U.S. Supreme Court, Jan 14, 2008. AP Images—Fisherman Steve Smith and Alaska Governor Sarah Palin as a news conference, February 26, 2008. AP Images—Roy Englert, attorney for state of Kentucky, speaking to reporters, flanked by Kentucky Secretary of Justice and Public Safety Michael Brown, in front of US Supreme Court, January 2007. AP Images—Guantanamo demonstrator in prison garb and hood in front of US Supreme Court, December 2007. AP Images—James LaRue and his wife, Shannon, November 2007. AP Images—Dick Heller speaks to reporters outside US Supreme Court, November 2007. AP Images—NFL commissioner Roger Goodell speaks to reporters, Super Bowl trophy in foreground. AP Images—Conrad Black, attending sentencing for fraud in Chicago, December 2007. AP Images—David Chalmers of Bayoil outside court, April 2005. AP Images—US Sentencing Commission Chairman Judge Ricardo Hinojosa, December 2007. AP Images—FCC chairman Michael Powell speaks, January 2004. AP Images—Michael Mukasey. AP Images—President George W Bush and attorney general Michael Mukasey speak about the FISA wiretapping act, March 2008. AP Images—Marie Salvati with husband Joe (seated), August 2007. AP Images—Members of National Archives discuss and examine documents described as CIA "family jewels," June 2007. AP Images—Nebraska electric chair, April 2007. AP Images—Court artist portrait of Jose Padilla, January 2008. AP Images—Wreckage of Interstate 35W bridge, St Paul, Minnesota, August 2007. AP Images—New York governor Eliot Spitzer announces his resignation, with wife Silda at side, March 2008. AP Images—Protestors line street in Jena, LA, September 2007. AP Images—Serial killer Timothy Krajcir in undated photo. AP Images—2006 photo of mobster Joseph "the Clown" Lombardo. AP Images—Former Durham Cty NC district attorney Mike Nifong in court, August 2007. AP Images—Protestors demonstrate "water boarding" torture method on volunteer in front Justice Dept, Washington DC, November 2007. AP Images—Inside a Whole Foods Market store, August 2007. AP Images—Yorkshire terrier Pebbles, one victim of tainted pet food in March 2007. AP

Images—**Esther Miller holds a quilt with pictures of proclaimed sex abuse victims of priests in San Diego, California.** AP Images—**Former baseball player Roger Clemens testifying before Congress, February 2008.** AP Images—**Phil Spector leaving court, September 2007.** AP Images—**Bernie Kerik speaks to reporters, December 2004.** AP Images—**Former attorney general Alberto Gonzales announcing resignation, August 2007.** AP Images—**Dog kennels at convicted football player Michael Vick's Virginia home.** AP Images—**Sarah Phelps, left, and Sam Phelps, right, protest the funeral of soldier Charles Jones, September 2006. Westboro Church members protest military funerals to claim God is punishing US for condoning homosexuality.** AP Images—**Senator Larry Craig, February 2008.** AP Images—**Former NBA referee Tim Donaghy, April 2007.** AP Images—**Customers look at toys in Beijing, August 2007.** AP Images—**Norman Hsu, September 2007.** AP Images—**Reputed Klansman James Ford Seale, August 2007.** AP Images—**Detroit Mayor Kwame Kilpatrick, March 2008.** AP Images—**Deceased wrestler Chris Benoit, left, with WWF owner Vince McMahon, June 2007.** AP Images—**John McCain.** AP Images—**Barack Obama.** AP Images.

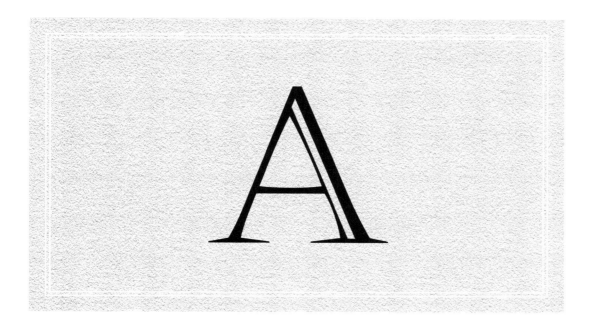

AGE DISCRIMINATION

Gomez-Perez v. Potter

The U.S. SUPREME COURT in May 2008 decided that a plaintiff can assert a claim under the Age Discrimination in Employment Act of 1967 when an employer retaliates against an employee for filing a complaint based on age discrimination. The Court reached this holding despite the fact that the federal **statute** on which the claim was based does not mention the word "retaliation." The case was noteworthy because the majority consisted of an unusual blend of conservative and liberal justices.

The Age Discrimination in Employment Act (ADEA), 29 U.S.C. §§ 621 **et seq.**, provides protection for employees of ages 40 and older from employment discrimination based on the age of the employee. The statute applies to both employees and applicants for employment. The ADEA proscribes discrimination against a person because of the person's age with regard to any term, condition, or privilege of employment. The statute applies to any employer who has 20 or more employees. It also applies to state and local governments, employment agencies, and the federal government.

The section of the ADEA that applies to federal government employee is 29 U.S.C. § 633a(a). Under this section, "All personnel actions affecting employees or applicants for employment who are at least 40 years of age . . . in the United States Postal Service and the Postal Rate Commission . . . shall be made free from any discrimination based on age." The agency authorized to interpret the statute, the EQUAL EMPLOYMENT OPPORTUNITY COM-

MISSION, took the view that the ADEA was designed to prohibit "retaliation for opposing any practice made unlawful by" the statute.

At least one **appellate court** previously held that the ADEA created a **cause of action** for retaliation when a federal employee complains about age discrimination. In *Forman v. Small*, 271 F.3d 285 (D.C. Cir. 2001), a curator with the National Museum of American History of the Smithsonian Institution brought suit under the ADEA, alleging that the Smithsonian Institution had retaliated against him when he alleged that he had been the victim of age discrimination. The court recognized that the ADEA allowed the plaintiff to bring the retaliation claim because a workplace, noting, "It is difficult to imagine how a workplace could be 'free from *any* discrimination based on age' if, in response to an age discrimination claim, a federal employer could fire or take other action that was adverse to an employee."

Myrna Gomez-Perez was first hired by the U.S. POSTAL SERVICE in New York in 1987. She was transferred in 1995 to the Caribbean District and began working in Puerto Rico. When she learned that her mother was ill, Gomez-Perez requested a transfer from the Dorado Post Office to the Moca Post Office so that she could be closer to her mother. Her supervisor approved this request, but one month later, she requested to be moved back to the Dorado Post Office. On the same day that she made this request, her supervisor converted her old position into a part-time job and hired another employee to fill it. Thus, the supervisor denied her request.

Gomez-Perez, then 45, subsequently filed an equal employment opportunity complaint with the Postal Service, arguing that her supervisor had discriminated against her on the basis of her age. After she filed the complaint, she alleged that she became the subject of various forms of retaliation, including suggestions that she had sexually harassed co-workers. Her work hours were reduced dramatically as well.

In 2003, Gomez-Perez filed suit against the Postal Service as well as John E. Potter, the Postmaster General, in the U.S. **District Court** for the District of Puerto Rico. She argued that her supervisor had retaliated against her for filing the EEO complaint, and she based her claim on 29 U.S.C. § 633a(a). In 2006, the district court held in favor of the Postal Service, finding that the ADEA did not allow private plaintiffs to bring retaliation claims under its provisions. *Gomez-Perez v. Potter*, No. 03-2236, 2006 WL 488060 (D.P.R. Feb. 28, 2006).

Gomez-Perez then appealed the decision to the First **Circuit Court** of Appeals. Before the **appellate** court, she argued that the Supreme Court in previous cases had recognized a cause of action for retaliation when the statute only refers explicitly to discrimination. More specifically, the Supreme Court in *Jackson v. Birmingham Board of Education*, 544 U.S. 167, 125 S. Ct. 1497, 161 L. Ed. 2d 361 (2005), the Court held that under Title IX, retaliation constitutes a form of discrimination that is prohibited by federal statute even though the statute does refer specifically to retaliation. The First Circuit was not persuaded, however, and ruled that the ADEA did not create a cause of action for retaliation. *Gomez-Perez v. Potter*, 476 F.3d 54 (1st Cir. 2007).

During oral argument, the justices focused most of their attention on the language of the statute. Justice ANTONIN SCALIA noted to Gomez-Perez's counsel that the plain language of the ADEA does not specifically cover retaliation claims. Justice RUTH BADER GINSBURG, on the other hand, suggested that an anti-discrimination statute must cover retaliation claims. "A person who is discriminated against will quite commonly say, 'I was not promoted because that was discrimination, and then because I complained about it, all these bad things happened to me.'"

In a 6–3 decision the Court reversed the First Circuit's decision. *Gomez-Perez v. Potter*, No. 06-1321, 2008 WL 2167189 (May 27, 2008). Justice SAMUEL ALITO, a conservative, sided with his more liberal counterparts and wrote the majority opinion. Alito focused much

of his attention on how the Court had treated retaliation claims under similar federal statute, including the Court's treatment of such claims under Title IX in *Jackson*. Much earlier, the Court had used a similar rationale in *Sullivan v. Little Hunting Park, Inc.*, 396 U.S. 229, 90 S. Ct. 400, 24 L. Ed. 2d 386 (1969) to find that a federal statute that prohibited discrimination based on race also prohibited retaliation.

Chief Justice JOHN ROBERTS wrote a dissent, which was joined in part by Scalia and Justice CLARENCE THOMAS. Roberts argued that the Court placed too much reliance on the precedent set forth in *Jackson* and *Sullivan*. Thomas also wrote a separate dissent where he argued that the Court should have decided the case based on the plain meaning of the statute's language.

Kentucky Retirement System v. Equal Employment Opportunity Commission

The Age Discrimination in Employment Act of 1967 (ADEA), 29 U.S.C.A. §§ 621 *et seq.*, was enacted to protect older workers from arbitrary employment practices, such as the setting up of age requirements unrelated to the ability needed for the job or creating a two-tiered benefits plan based on age. While similar in wording to Title VII of the Civil Rights Act of 1964, 42 U.S.C.A, §§ 2000e *et seq.*, the ADEA has some defenses and provisions uniquely applicable to age discrimination. The most important difference is that a person alleging age discrimination must prove that the employer intentionally discriminated on the basis of age. This standard of liability is called disparate treatment and is often very hard to prove. In contrast the standard of liability known as disparate impact only requires the plaintiff to show that the employer used a facially neutral test or other employment practice that unjustifiably resulted in discrimination against members of a protected group. Because the Supreme Court disallowed disparate impact in ADEA cases, plaintiffs have had a harder time prevailing. Such was the case in *Kentucky Retirement System v. Equal Employment Opportunity Commission*, __U.S.__, 128 S. Ct. 2361, __ L. Ed. 2d __ (2008), where the Court ruled that a state and county retirement plan that gave different levels of **pension** benefits to "hazardous position" workers based on their ages did not violate the ADEA.

Charles Lickteig, who worked in the Jefferson County, Kentucky Sheriff's Department, became eligible to retire at age 55. Classified as a hazardous position worker, Lickteig continued to work, became disabled, and then retired at age 61 after 18 years of employment. He discovered that he was treated differently than younger workers who became disabled before they reached the age of 55 or had served 20 years. The disability plan awarded benefits based in part on how close a disabled worker was to reaching normal retirement. The plan sought to provide disabled workers with the same retirement benefits they would have had if they continued to work until eligible for normal retirement. Lickteig filed a complaint with the EQUAL EMPLOYMENT OPPORTUNITY COMMISSION (EEOC), alleging that because older workers who became disabled after the age of 55 did not receive the same amount of benefits as younger workers, the same the plan affects older workers differently than younger workers.

The EEOC sided with Lickteig and filed suit in Kentucky federal **district court** alleging that the plan violated the ADEA. The district court and a panel of the Sixth **Circuit Court** of Appeals ruled in favor of the state, finding that the disability retirement benefits program, while taking age into account, did not attach any stigma based on age itself. The entire Sixth Circuit reheard the case and reversed itself, holding that the act of treating younger disabled retirees more generously than older retirees was sufficient to establish an ADEA violation.

The Supreme Court, in a 5–4 decision, reversed the Sixth Circuit ruling. Justice STEPHEN BREYER, writing for the majority, noted that Lickteig had to prove that the state intentionally discriminated on the basis of age when it created the two-tier disability retirement system. He concluded that Lickteig and the EEOC had failed to meet that burden of proof. The benefit at issue was offered to all employees working in hazardous positions on the same nondiscriminatory terms. Moreover, Congress had approved programs that calculated permanent disability benefits using a formula that expressly took age into account. The Kentucky plan reasonably took age and length of service into account when structuring benefits for disabled workers who were eligible for retirement. The differences in treatment were "not motivated by age."

Justice ANTHONY KENNEDY, in a dissenting opinion joined by Justices ANTONIN SCALIA, RUTH BADER GINSBURG, and SAMUEL ALITO, argued that the decision undercut the framework of the ADEA. Kentucky's motivations did not matter when assessing the benefits plan. Kennedy stated that "By explicit command of Kentucky's disability plan, age is an express disadvantage." It made no sense to force plaintiffs to prove intentional discrimination when the plan was discriminatory on its face.

Meachum v. Knolls Atomic Power Laboratory

The Supreme Court issued an important ruling in June 2008 involving burdens of proof under the Age Discrimination in Employment Act (ADEA), 29 U.S.C. §§ 623(a)-(c). Under the **statute**, an employer may avoid liability for age discrimination if the employer's business practices were based on a "reasonable factor than age." The Court determined that the employer bears the burden of proving that an action was for a reason other than age, rather than requiring an employee to prove that the action was not based on such a factor. The decision reversed a ruling from the Second **Circuit Court** of Appeals.

The ADEA establishes general prohibitions against age discrimination. The statute was based on an earlier version of the Civil Rights Act of 1964 but was drafted with an understanding that age presents unique problems for employers because an employer may need to terminate an older employee for a reason other than the employee's age. Accordingly, the statute provides, "It shall not be unlawful for an employer . . . to take any action otherwise prohibited [in the act] . . . where age is a **bona fide** occupational qualification reasonably necessary to the normal operation of the particular business, or where the differentiation is based on reasonable factors other than age. . . ." 29 U.S.C. § 623(f)(1) (2000).

In *Smith v. City of Jackson*, 544 U.S. 228, 125 S. Ct. 1536, 161 L. Ed. 2d 410 (2005), the Court recognized that a plaintiff can bring a disparate-impact claim under the ADEA, meaning that a plaintiff may prove a violation by showing that an employer's practice had the effect of discriminating against employees by age. A disparate-impact claim differs from a disparate-treatment claim in that the latter focuses on intentional discrimination based on age.

Both disparate-impact and disparate-treatment claims under the ADEA are governed by a burden-shifting scheme established in *Wards Cove Packing Co. v. Atonio*, 490 U.S. 642, 109 S. Ct. 2115, 104 L. Ed. 2d 722 (1989). Under this case, the plaintiff initially has the burden to prove that the employer's business practice has a significant disparate impact on older workers, meaning those over the age of forty. If the plaintiff can prove this, the burden shifts to the defendant to provide a legitimate business justification for the practice. Even if the employer can show this justification, though, the plaintiff may still prove a case under the ADEA by showing that the employer could have adopted an alternative that would have been just as effective as the discriminatory option.

Knolls Atomic Power Laboratory is one of several contractors employed by the federal government to maintain U.S. nuclear-powered warships. The United States Navy's Nuclear Propulsion Program, in consultation with Knolls itself, sets the staffing limit for the lab. Due in large part to the end of the COLD WAR, the demands for Knolls' services in the area of naval nuclear reactors decreased. Knolls thus had to reduce its workforce by a total of 143 people. The company made a buyout offer that about 100 employees accepted. However, the company was left with the need to eliminate about 30 other jobs.

To determine which of the remaining employees would be terminated, the company ordered its supervisors to list the employees on a matrix and ranking them in a number of categories. These categories included performance, flexibility, criticality of skills, and length of service. The performance category was based primarily on the average of previous evaluations, while the length of service was based on objective criteria. On the other hand, the flexibility and criticality categories were judged on subjective criteria based largely on the opinions of the supervisors. Of an estimated 2,063 company employees, 31 were selected for layoff based on these rankings. Thirty of the 31 employees who were laid off were over the age of 40.

Most of the employees brought suit, arguing that Knolls had violated the ADEA. The employees brought claims for both disparate treatment as well as disparate impact, arguing that the company "designed and implemented its workforce reduction process to eliminate older employees and that, regardless of intent, the process had a discriminatory impact on ADEA-protected employees." The workers produced a statistical analysis showing that the results achieved by Knolls' ranking process could rarely happen by chance in terms of the ages of the affected employees.

The trial court held in favor of the employees on the disparate-impact claim but held in favor of Knolls on the disparate treatment claim. *Meachum v. Knolls Atomic Power Laboratory*, 185 F. Supp. 2d 193 (N.D.N.Y. 2002). On appeal, the Second Circuit Court of Appeals affirmed. *Meachum v. Knolls Atomic Power Laboratory*, 381 F.3d 56 (2d Cir. 2004). Shortly after the Second Circuit's decision, though, the Supreme Court rendered its decision in *Smith*, and in 2005, the

Court vacated the Second Circuit's decision and remanded the case for further consideration.

On remand, a divided panel of the Second Circuit held in favor of Knolls, finding that the employees had failed to meet their burden of proof. *Meachum v. Knolls Atomic Power Laboratory*, 461 F.3d 134 (2d Cir. 2006). The dissent in the case, written by Judge Rosemary Pooler, argued that the majority had misinterpreted the standard for disparate-impact cases. According to the dissent, the **statutory** exemption in cases where an employer can establish reasonable factors other than age is an **affirmative defense** that the employer must prove.

In a 7–1 decision in which Justice STEPHEN BREYER did not participate, the Court reversed the Second Circuit. According to the Court, the exemption that applies when an employer gives reasons other than age provides an affirmative defense, and the **burden of persuasion** falls on the employer to prove this defense. This ruling is consistent with the Court's principle stating that "[w]hen a proviso . . . carves an exception out of the body of a statute or contract those who set up such exception must prove it." The ruling means that the treatment of this exception is the same as the exception where an employer imposes bona fide occupational qualifications, which is another exception that the Court treats as an affirmative defense. In issuing this ruling, the Court vacated the Second Circuit and remanded for further proceedings.

Justice ANTONIN SCALIA wrote a concurring opinion, where he argued that the question before the Court should have been answered by deferring to the Equal Employment Opportunity Commission's rule. Justice CLARENCE THOMAS dissented in part of the opinion because he disagrees that the ADEA allows disparate impact claims based on age.

Sprint/United Management Co. v. Mendelsohn

The admission of information at trial is governed by rules of evidence. The Federal Rules of Evidence govern all criminal and civil matters filed in **federal courts** and have been adopted, in large part, by state judicial systems. Whether certain information is admissible at trial can determine the outcome of a litigation, so lawyers are particularly interested in how the U.S. SUPREME COURT interprets evidence rules. This was the case in *Sprint/United Management Co. v. Mendelsohn*,__U.S.__, 128 S. Ct. 1140, 170 L. Ed. 2d 1 (2008), where the lower courts were divided over whether to admit testimony in age discrimination lawsuits from employees who were not supervised by the alleged company wrongdoer. The central issue was whether a *per se* rule applied admitting or excluding such evidence. A *per se* rule instructs the parties that the court will not examine the details of the proffered testimony or documents to determine admissibility; instead, the rule acts as a bright line that either admits or bars the introduction of that type of evidence. Such rules are disfavored by the courts, as relevance and prejudice are determined in the context of the facts and arguments in a particular case. Seen in this light, the announcement of a *per se* rule by the Supreme Court is a major development. In this case the Court pulled back from such a ruling, finding that the trial court's basis for its ruling was unclear and warranted clarification from that court.

Ellen Mendelsohn was employed in the Business Development Strategy Group pf the Sprint/United Management Company from 1989 until 2002. Mendelsohn was terminated in 2002 as part of a company-wide reduction in force. She filed suit in federal **district court** under the Age Discrimination in Employment Act of 1967 (ADEA), 29 U.S.C. §§ 621 *et. seq.*, alleging she was laid off because of her age.To help prove her claim, she wanted to introduce testimony by five former Sprint employees who claimed that their supervisors had discriminated on the basis of their age. Three of the employees alleged that they had heard one or more Sprint supervisors or managers make remarks denigrating older workers. One employee alleged that an intern program was a scheme for age discrimination and that she had seen a spreadsheet suggesting that supervisors could consider age in making layoff decisions. Another witness was prepared to testify that he had been given unwarranted negative performance evaluations because of his age and that he had witnessed another employee being harassed because of her age. The last witness alleged that the company had required him to get permission before hiring anyone over the age of 40. After he was terminated Sprint hired a younger employee to replace him and the company rejected his later job applications.

All of this proposed testimony suggested a hostile work environment based on age discrimination. However, none of the witnesses worked with Mendelsohn in the Business Development Strategy Group and none had worked under her supervisors in her chain of command. Sprint moved to exclude the testimony, contending

that it was irrelevant to the central element in Mendelsohn's claim that she was fired by her direct manager because of her age. Sprint said the testimony would only be relevant if the witnesses were "similarly situated" in that they shared the same supervisors. Finally, it argued that the testimony should be barred under Rule 403 of the Federal Rules of Evidence, as its **probative** value was substantially outweighed by the danger of unfair prejudice, confusion of the issues, misleading of the jury, and undue delay. The court agreed with Sprint and issued a brief order that stated Mendelsohn could only introduce evidence of discrimination against Sprint employees "who are similarly situated to her." The court defined "similarly situated to her" as requiring proof that her direct manager was the decision-maker in any adverse employment action and actions were in "temporal proximity." Beyond that, the district court provided no explanation for its ruling.

As the trial proceeded, the court orally clarified this ruling, stating that Mendelsohn could introduce testimony going to a totally different question as to whether the reduction in force was a pretext for age discrimination. In the end, Sprint prevailed at trial. The Tenth Circuit of Appeals interpreted the written order as the application of a *per se* rule barring evidence from employees with other supervisors as irrelevant to proving discrimination in ADEA cases. The appeals court concluded the lower court had abused it discretion because in this case the issue was not discriminatory discipline or actions but rather a company-wide policy of discrimination. Therefore, Tenth Circuit found the evidence relevant and reversed and remanded the case for a new trial.

The Supreme Court, in a unanimous decision, vacated the lower court decisions and returned the case to the district court to clarify its evidentiary ruling. Justice CLARENCE THOMAS, writing for the Court, ruled that the Tenth Circuit should not have ruled on the **relevancy** of the evidence and instead, should have remanded the case for clarification. The appeals court had failed to give the great deference to district court evidentiary rulings that the Court has required. It was unclear if the district court had used an incorrect precedent in making its ruling. Because of this ambiguity it was incorrect for the appeals court to conclude the district court abused its discretion. If in fact the court had applied a *per se* rule, the appeals court would have been correct to conclude the court had abused its discretion.

AGRICULTURE DEPARTMENT

Pollinator Protection Act of 2007

Following intense media coverage in 2007 that noted the drastic decline of pollinating bees in North America, both the House and the Senate in the U.S. Congress corroborated respective versions of their bills into one comprehensive Pollinator Protection Act of 2007. This, in turn, was intended to work in conjunction with the 2007 Pollinator Habitat Protection Act, all of which was then incorporated as part of the renewable **omnibus** "Farm Bill," (the Farm Security and Rural Investment Act), slated to expire March 15, 2008 but extended while Congress hammered out final language. The main objective of the new legislation was to combat "colony collapse disorder (CCD)" and North American native/managed bee pollinator decline.

The intense and substantial decline of bee populations within the Unites States over such a short period of time took even the experts by surprise. Nearly 80 percent of the world's crop plants require pollination, which is vital to plant production. Without pollinators, human, animal, and plant life cannot survive. Biodiversity threats such as pesticide poisoning, pollution, and land development has caused the loss of pollinators (which primarily include bees but also birds, butterflies, beetles, mosquitoes and even bats) at an alarming rate. However, the European honey bee remains the most important single crop pollinator in the United States. Scientists from the Xerces Society for Invertebrate Conservation and Cornell University have estimated the value of services provided by honey bees and native bees to be worth $15 billion and $3 billion annually in the United States, respectively. In addition to pollinating crops responsible for approximately one third of all food consumed by humans, pollinators are responsible for keeping the entire ecosystem alive. Fruits and seeds dependent upon pollination are the major part of diets for birds and mammals ranging from small mice to grizzly bears.

In urgent response to the plea of agricultural experts, farmers, and landowners across the country, the U.S. House of Representatives responded with its Pollinator Protection Act, a modified version of Congressman Hasting's H.R. 1709. Shortly thereafter, the U.S. Senate passed its version, the Pollinator Protection Act of 2007 (S. 1496/1694, which incorporated Senator Barbara Boxer's bill with the Pollinator Habitat Protection Act introduced by Senators Baucus and Chambliss).

The provisions contained therein addressed not only Colony Collapse Disorder in honey bees (the most important and urgent issue) but also the general decline of native pollinators in North America. The final bill enhanced funding for research on parasites, pathogens, toxins, and other environmental factors that affect both native and honey bees, and supported research into the biology of native bees. It also included a provision to fund, over five years, the Cooperative State Research, Education, and Extension Service to fund research grants investigating honey and native bee immunology, ecology, genomics, and bioinformatics, as well as the sublethal effects of insecticides, herbicides, and fungicides. It is known that in addition to outright bee deaths associated with these factors, reproductive and reproductive cycle failures are also blamed on them.

Under the Pollinator Protection Act, funds were allocated generally to four major areas of concern: agricultural research, cooperative state research and education, animal and plant health inspection services, and annual reporting. Reporting on the status and progress of bee research projects was to be directed to the Congressional Committee on Agriculture of the House of Representatives, and the Senate's Committee on Agriculture, Nutrition, and Forestry.

Incorporated provisions of Senator Baucus' Pollinator Habitat Protection Act (of which Senator Boxer was a co-sponsor) addressed that part of CCD and the general decline of pollinators which could be blamed on the continued loss of pollinator habitat, mostly resultant of land development and loss of wide tracts of natural landscape. The habitat protection provisions utilized existing Farm Bill conservation programs by now including pollinators as conservation targets in the Environmental Quality Incentives Program, Conservation Security Program, and the Conservation Reserve Program. Without taxing or increasing costs or creating specific new programs, the provisions dealing with habitat simply required existing conservation programs to acknowledge pollinator habitat as a conservation resource, and they rewarded producers whose conservation practices were beneficial to pollinators.

Section 2404 of the Senate Ag 2007 Farm Bill Conservation Title, still not finalized as of April 2008, would amend Section 1244 of the Food Security Act of 1985, 16 U.S.C. § 3844. The new provisions would require the Secretary of Agriculture, in carrying out any conservation program, to consider "(1) increasing native habitat to native and managed pollinators, and (2) establishing cropping systems, integrated pest management regimes, and other practices to protect native and managed pollinators." Section 2407 requested the Secretary to "continue efforts to make nurseries and land managers aware of pollinator-friendly native plants" and requested that Plant Materials Centers under the DEPARTMENT OF AGRICULTURE "emphasize pollinator-beneficial native plantings for native and managed pollinator habitat." Provisions also authorized the Secretary to create incentive payments and cost sharing initiatives for producers who focused or enhanced their practices on increasing or conserving pollinator-friendly habitats.

As of April 2008, the final version of an amended Farm Bill combining Senate and House pollinator bills was still being negotiated in committee. The delay was directed more at final funds allocations rather than legislative language or provision.

Researchers and scientists remained unable to blame a single causative factor for the rapid decline of bee pollinators, but were able to identify several disease, illness, and environmental factors (as outlined above) that substantially contributed to the problem. Meanwhile, the Xerces Society, an international non-profit advocacy organization, continued to push for media coverage and other educational awareness efforts to enhance knowledge and understanding of the urgency of the plight of pollinators. Several states and private organizations, no longer willing to wait for final federal action, began independent efforts to create pollinator protection statutes and incentives on their own.

ARBITRATION

The submission of a dispute to an unbiased third person designated by the parties to the controversy, who agree in advance to comply with the award—a decision to be issued after a hearing at which both parties have an opportunity to be heard.

Hall Street Associates, L.L.C. v. Mattel, Inc.

The use of arbitration has increased in part because state and **federal courts** have abandoned their hostility to this form of dispute resolution. The Federal Arbitration Act, (FAA), 19 U.S.C. §§ 1 *et seq.*, has encouraged the use of arbitration by providing expedited **judicial re-**view to confirm, vacate, or modify arbitration awards. The act also greatly restricts the grounds that a court can use to vacate or modify an award, limiting these to address egregious departures from the parties' agreed-upon arbitration. The U.S. SUPREME COURT, in *Hall Street Associates, L.L.C. v. Mattel, Inc.,__U.S.__*, 128 S. Ct. 1396, 170 L. Ed. 2d 254 (2008), ruled that the grounds for modifying, vacating, or correcting an arbitration award contained in the FAA are the exclusive grounds for using expedited judicial review.

Hall Street Associates L.L.C. leased property in Oregon to the Mattel, Inc. toy company for many years. Mattel used the property as a manufacturing site. The lease provided that Mattel would pay Hall Street for any costs resulting from the failure of Mattel or its predecessor tenants to follow environmental laws while using the property. In 1998 tests on the property's well water revealed high levels of a toxic chemical that was the residue of manufacturing discharges by Mattel's predecessor between 1951 and 1980. After more pollutants were discovered in well water by Oregon's Department of Environmental Quality (DEQ), Mattel and one of its predecessors signed a consent order with the DEQ, agreeing to clean up the site.

Mattel gave notice of intent to terminate its lease in 2001. Hall Street filed suit in federal court, claiming that Mattel did not have the right to vacate on the date it gave and that Mattel was required to pay Hall Street for the costs of cleaning up the pollutants. A **bench trial** was conducted (a judge rather than a jury acts as fact-finder) and Mattel prevailed as to the right to terminate the lease. As to Hall Street's demand for clean-up money, the parties failed to settle the claim through **mediation**. It was then agreed that the parties would arbitrate this issue. The **district court** was in favor of this process and it approved the arbitration agreement the two companies drew up. The court entered the agreement as an order, with one paragraph permitting the court to vacate or modify the arbitration award if it found the arbitrator's findings of fact were not supported by substantial evidence or if the arbitrator's conclusions of law were erroneous.

The arbitrator ruled in Mattel's favor, finding that the lease obligation to follow all applicable environmental laws did not require compliance with Oregon's Drinking Water Quality Act. The arbitrator said this act dealt with human health contamination, not environmental contamination. Hall Street filed a motion with the district court, asking it to vacate the decision because the arbitrator committed legal error by failing to find the water act was environmental in nature. The court agreed, vacated the award, and remanded the case to the arbitrator. In the order the court noted that the standard of legal review was the one chosen by the parties. On remand the arbitrator ruled for Hall Street. This time the court upheld the ruling and modified the arbitrator's calculation of interest. Both parties appealed to the Ninth **Circuit Court** of Appeals, with Mattel now claiming that the application of the standard of review contained in the agreement was invalid and unenforceable. The appeals court agreed, holding that the award could only be reviewed using the grounds contained in the FAA.

The Supreme Court, in a 6–3 decision, upheld the Ninth Circuit interpretation of the FAA. Justice DAVID SOUTER, writing for the Court, noted that the circuit courts of appeals were split over the exclusiveness of the **statutory** grounds for a court's review of an arbitration award. Some courts thought them exclusive, while others saw them as threshold provisions that could be expanded by agreement of the parties. Justice Souter concluded that the FAA provisions were the exclusive set of categories, which included corruption, **fraud**, evident partiality, misconduct, misbehavior, evident material mistake, and several other serious issues. There was no comparison between fraud and a **mistake of law**. The FAA provisions dealt with serious matters that went to the integrity of the arbitration process. The provisions were elements of a "national policy favoring arbitration with just limited review needed to maintain arbitration's essential virtue of resolving disputes straightaway." Any other interpretation of the **statute** would pave the way for full-scale, time-consuming judicial review. Therefore, parties to arbitration under the FAA may not change the scope of judicial review.

Preston v. Ferrer

The Supreme Court in 2008 ruled against the star of the syndicated television show "Judge Alex" by holding that his case should have been decided by an arbitrator. The case presented an issue of whether a California state law could require the parties to bring the case before the state's labor commission before requesting arbitration. In *Preston v. Ferrer*, 522 U.S. ___ (2008) (No. 06-1463), the Court in an 8–1 vote determined that the Federal Arbitration Act preempted the state law.

Alex E. Ferrer is a former state judge from Florida. He was originally born in Havana, Cuba, but his family migrated to the United States when he was a young child. While serving as a police officer, he earned a law degree from the University of Miami, and he later served as an administrative judge in Miami. In 2005, he became the star of a nationally syndicated television show named "Judge Alex."

In March 2002, Ferrer entered into a management agreement with Arnold Preston, an attorney who represents clients in the television and motion picture industries. The parties entered into a contract that included a standard clause, which required arbitration for "any dispute . . . relating to the terms of [the contract] or the breach, validity, or legality thereof . . . in accordance with the rules" of the American Arbitration Association.

The Federal Arbitration Act, 9 U.S.C. §§ 1 *et seq.* establishes a national policy that favors arbitration proceedings when commercial contracts call for this form of dispute resolution. In addition to providing a procedural framework for **federal courts**, it requires that both state and federal courts apply federal **substantive law** to the resolution of arbitration disputes. The Court in *Buckeye Check Cashing, Inc. v. Cardegna*, 546 U.S. 440, 126 S. Ct. 1204, 163 L. Ed. 2d 1038 (2006) ruled that when parties agree to arbitrate all of their disputes arising out of the validity of the contract, these questions should be resolved by the arbitrator instead of a state or a federal court.

In 2005, Preston sought to recover fees under his agreement with Ferrer and demanded arbitration. Ferrer responded with a petition to the California Labor Commission where Ferrer argued that the contract was invalid and unenforceable under the California Talent Agencies Act, Cal. Lab. Code Ann. §§ 1700 (West 2003 & Supp. 2008). According to Ferrer, Preston had acted as a talent agent without a license as required by California law, and thus the contract between Preston and Ferrer was entirely void.

A California Labor Commissioner hearing officer heard the case in November 2005 and determined that Ferrer had stated a "colorable basis" for the exercise of the Labor Commissioner's exercise of jurisdiction. However, the officer decided that the Labor Commissioner could not stay the arbitration. Ferrer subsequently brought an action in the Los Angeles Superior Court, where he sought a ruling that the action was not subject to arbitration and also requested an injunction that would prevent Preston from moving to compel arbitration.

The Superior Court in December 2005 determined that the Labor Commissioner was the proper decision-maker in the case. Thus, the court denied Preston's motion to compel arbitration. Preston appealed the decision to the California Court of Appeals. While the appeal was pending, the Supreme Court decided *Buckeye Check Cashing*, concluding that an arbitrator, rather than a court, should decide whether a contract is valid. In Preston's appeal, however, the state court determined that *Buckeye Check Cashing* did not apply because the case did not address an instance where an administrative body had exclusive jurisdiction over a disputed issue. The California Court of Appeals ruled that the state **statute** gave the Labor Commissioner "exclusive original jurisdiction" over the case. *Preston v. Ferrer*, 145 Cal. App. 4th, 51 Cal. Rptr. 3d 628 (Ct. App. 2006).

After the California Supreme Court declined to review the case, Preston sought to appeal the decision to the U.S. SUPREME COURT. The Court granted **certiorari** in September 2007. In his briefs to the Court, Preston argued that a series of cases, including *Buckeye Check Cashing* and *Gilmer v. Interstate/Johnson Lane Corp.*, 500 U.S. 20, 111 S. Ct. 1647, 114 L. Ed. 2d 26 (1991), the Court clearly established that the arbitrator is the first decision-maker who should resolve a question of the validity of the contract. Ferrer argued that the prior cases were distinguishable because they did not involve a state law that required exhaustion of administrative remedies prior to bringing a case before an arbitrator.

In an 8–1 decision, the Court sided with Preston and reversed the California **appellate** court's decision. An opinion by RUTH BADER GINSBURG determined that the Federal Arbitration Act and the cases interpreting it had established that contracts containing arbitration clauses should be interpreted by arbitrators not by administrative bodies, no matter what the California law said. In so ruling the Court disagreed with Ferrer that the case was at all distinguishable from a long line of prior Supreme Court precedents. "[W]e disapprove the distinction between judicial and administrative proceedings drawn by Ferrer and adopted by the appeals court," wrote Ginsburg. "When parties agree to arbitrate all questions arising under a contract, the FAA supersedes state laws lodging primary jurisdiction in another forum, whether judicial or administrative."

Justice CLARENCE THOMAS, in a lone dissent, argued that the Federal Arbitration Act does not apply to state court proceedings. He also dissented in several other decisions, including *Buckeye Check Cashing*, by making the same argument.

Alex Ferrer, better known as TV's "Judge Alex," leaves the U.S. Supreme Court, Jan 14, 2008.

AP IMAGES

ARMED ROBBERY

The taking of money or goods in the possession of another, from his or her person or immediate presence, by force or intimidation.

O.J. Simpson Indicted for Kidnapping and Armed Robbery

On September 16, 2007, famed football legend O.J. Simpson was arrested by police and booked on several **felony** charges following a confrontation with a sports memorabilia dealer at the Palms Casino-Hotel in Las Vegas on September 13. If convicted on the felony kidnapping and armed **robbery** charges, he again faced the possibility of life in prison. Simpson, 60, had been acquitted more than a decade previously for the murder of his ex-wife, Nicole Brown Simpson, and her friend, in a media-sensationalized trial that lasted for months. However, he was later found liable in a civil lawsuit for **wrongful death** filed by the murder victims' families.

Simpson was booked on two counts of robbery with a deadly weapon, two counts of assault with a deadly weapon, conspiracy to commit **burglary** and burglary with a firearm. He later posted $250,000 bail and was released from jail to await trial.

Simpson's version of the facts surrounding the arrest included a statement that no guns were involved and that he went to the room at the casino only to get personal mementos and sports memorabilia that were stolen, including his Hall of Fame certificate and a picture of him with J. EDGAR HOOVER. Simpson told reporters that auction house owner Tom Riccio had called him several weeks earlier to advise that several collectors were selling some of his items. According to Simpson, Riccio set up a meeting with the collectors, under the ruse of having a private collector interested in purchasing the items. Simpson said he and several men (whom he previously met at a wedding cocktail party) then went to the hotel room set up for the meeting and took the items. He told the Associated Press that he and co-defendants Charles Ehrlich and Clarence "C.J." Stewart were merely retrieving those items that belonged to him. He stated that he did not contact police or request their help in reclaiming the items because he found the police unresponsive to him ever since his wife and her friend were killed in 1994.

On the evening prior to Simpson's arrest, police had already arrested Walter Alexander, whom they say accompanied Simpson with a gun in the holdup on the night in question (September 13, 2007). Police did not allege that Simpson personally carried a weapon in the incident, but stated they had seized two firearms involved in the robbery. Pursuant to three search warrants at private residences, they also seized sports memorabilia signed by Simpson, as well as collectible baseballs and Joe Montana cleats. Whether Simpson was the owner of the seized items was a factual issue for trial.

At pretrial evidentiary hearings (similar to **grand jury** hearings, intended to establish whether sufficient evidence existed to warrant the charges), witnesses conflicted with one another in their testimony. A key issue was whether Simpson knew that a gun or guns would be used, and/or whether he had requested his accomplices to appear with guns. Simpson had stated on several occasions following the incident that he did not see any guns in the hotel room at the time of the confrontation. But Riccio, the man who set up the meeting, testified that he saw at least one gun waving near his face. Notwithstanding, Riccio testified it was possible that Simpson, who was standing several feet in front of the accomplice who had a gun, did not see it. Other witnesses who were expected to testify had previously stated that Simpson not only saw the guns, but suggested that firearms be brought to the hotel room.

According to Riccio, the group did not enter the hotel room in a "military style invasion," as previously suggested by another witness. He said that Bruce Fromong, one of the collectors, was loudly "scolded" by Simpson for possessing items that Simpson declared were his. But, said Riccio, things changed when the men started taking items not claimed by Simpson, such as Fromong's cell phone and the Joe Montana lithographs. "Things went crazy" after that, testified Riccio, and once the weapon was brandished, "there was no turning back." A contemporaneous recording of the event was played in court at the hearing. In it, Simpson and others could be heard cursing and yelling. Toward the end, a male voice was heard saying, "We were just robbed at gunpoint, man. We were just robbed at gunpoint by O.J. Simpson."

Simpson's attorney, Yale Galanter, vowed a vigorous defense, based on "conflicting witness statements, flip-flopping by witnesses and witnesses making deals with the government to flip." Alfred Beardsley, one of the collectors in the hotel room at the time, stated he wanted the case dropped and that he was "on O.J.'s side." He blamed the entire incident on Tom Riccio, saying that Riccio had lied to Simpson and gotten him "all pumped up."

In March 2008, Clark County **District Court** Judge Jackie Glass agreed to postpone Simpson's trial from April 7 until September 8, 2008. She anticipated a maximum six-week trial, and also noted the difficulty in selecting an appropriate unbiased jury. Earlier in the year, lawyers and court officials were preparing jury screening questionnaires that contained more than 100 questions and were expected to be sent to more than 400 potential jurors. The judge further decided that Simpson and co-defendants Charles Ehrlich and Clarence "C.J." Stewart would be tried together. She refused to dismiss any of the 12 charges against them. The defendants entered "not guilty" pleas at their arraignments.

ATTORNEY GENERAL

Gonzales Resigns as Attorney General Amid Controversies

Faced with calls for a no-confidence vote on his position as Attorney General, Alberto Gonzales in August 2007 resigned from the position after less than three years in office. The fallout

Former attorney general Alberto Gonzales announcing resignation, August 2007.
AP IMAGES

from his handling of the dismissal of eight federal prosecutors in 2006 was a major cause that led members of Congress to express their doubts in his leadership.

The son of a migrant farm worker and later a graduate of Harvard Law School, Gonzales spent much of his career as a corporate lawyer. In 1994, Gonzales joined George W. Bush's administration when Bush served as governor of Texas. About three years later, Bush appointed Gonzales as the Texas secretary of state. Bush in January 1999 appointed Gonzales to fill a vacancy on the Texas Supreme Court.

Gonzales joined Bush when the latter was elected President in 2000. Gonzales became the first Hispanic to serve the role as White House counsel. During this time, he wrote a number of memos that later sparked controversy. In January 2002, he wrote a memo to Bush suggesting that the Geneva Conventions were "quaint" and "obsolete" and that the protections for prisoners outlined in those documents did not apply to "enemy combatants" who were captured in Afghanistan. Also in 2002, Gonzales wrote a memo that narrowed the definition of torture, such that the memo justified controversial interrogation tactics that were being used by the DEFENSE DEPARTMENT and the CENTRAL INTELLIGENCE AGENCY. The White House later rescinded this memo.

When JOHN ASHCROFT resigned as Attorney General following Bush's presidential elec-

tion victory in 2004, Bush nominated Gonzales to fill the position. Gonzales' appointment met with immediate resistance as Democrats on the SENATE JUDICIARY COMMITTEE vigorously opposed his nomination. Nevertheless, Republicans viewed him as more moderate than Ashcroft, and the Senate as a whole approved his appointment by a vote of 60–36.

In 2005 and 2006, Gonzales led an eventually successful effort to advocate the reauthorization of the USA Patriot Act. However, his position with regard to civil rights in relation to national security continued to cause a stir. The *New York Times* in 2005 reported that Bush had authorized the National Security Agency (NSA) to conduct warrantless searches on individuals within the United States. Gonzales responded to the report by noting that the program was supported by the broad war powers given to Bush following the 2001 terrorist attacks. In July 2006, Gonzales testified before the Senate that Bush had blocked the JUSTICE DEPARTMENT from investigating the spying program. Gonzales was one of the government officials who had authority to review the program every 45 days. Facing pressure from Congress, Gonzales in 2007 announced that the NSA's warrantless eavesdropping program would be reviewed by a secret national intelligence court.

In addition to the controversy surrounding Gonzales' handling of the eavesdropping program, Gonzales became embroiled in a dispute over the dismissal of eight U.S. attorneys. He reportedly met in November 2006 to discuss the dismissal of seven prosecutors, a plan that was approved by the White House about a week later. On December 7, 2006, the Justice Department dismissed these seven attorneys, providing no reason for the firings. Reports later showed that the majority of those who were dismissed were given favorable evaluations during the periods of time that they held their positions. As the controversy continued to heat up, Deputy Attorney General Paul McNulty testified that the attorneys were dismissed due to poor performance rather than political reasons.

Senator Charles Schumer (D.-N.Y.) led an investigation into the attorneys' firings. He criticized the Justice Department for what he concluded were politically motivated decisions. He noted, "As we feared, the comprehensive evaluations show these U.S. attorneys did not deserve to be fired. To the contrary, they reveal they were effective, respected and set appropriate priorities." Justice Department officials countered that the reviews did not "take into account whether the U.S. attorneys carried out departmental priorities," apparently meaning that the prosecutors did not follow priorities established by the Justice Department. However, the reports themselves indicated that the prosecutors had indeed established the goals that the Justice Department had set as high priorities.

Calls for Gonzales' resignation became more prevalent in March 2007. Schumer stated that Gonzales "either doesn't accept or doesn't understand that he is no longer just the president's lawyer, but has a higher obligation to the **rule of law** and the Constitution, even when the president should not want it to be so." Arlen Specter, the top Republican on the Senate Judiciary Committee, openly questioned whether Gonzales' tenure as Attorney General had run its course. Gonzales lost more support on March 14 when Senator John Sununu (R.-N.H.) became the first Republican to call for Gonzales' resignation.

Gonzales responded to allegations about the dismissal of the attorneys by noting that though he should be held accountable, he was not involved with seeing memos or with other discussions about the proposed firings. About two months later, evidence surfaced that Gonzales indeed saw memos about the firings and had consulted with aides prior to the dismissals. Moreover, former Deputy Attorney General James Comey testified that in 2004, Gonzalez had pressured then-Attorney General Ashcroft to approve the eavesdropping program. This occurred while Ashcroft was in an intensive-care unit.

Congressional Democrats stepped up their efforts to pressure Gonzales to resign. House and Senate members introduced no-confidence votes in both chambers of Congress. Nonetheless, Bush continued to express support for Gonzales. Amid accusations of perjury for his earlier testimony, however, Gonzales finally gave in and announced his resignation on August 27. Bush claimed that Gonzales' name had been "dragged through the mud for political reasons," but even some Republican lawmakers said that the time for the resignation had come.

In November 2007, the Senate approved the nomination of former federal judge Michael Mukasey as the new Attorney General. During the time after his resignation, Gonzales has spoken at such institutions as Washington University in St. Louis, Ohio State University, and the University of Florida. However, according to a report in the *New York Times*, he has had difficulty finding a job at a law firm.

ATTORNEY

A person admitted to practice law in at least one jurisdiction and authorized to perform criminal and civil legal functions on behalf of clients. These functions include providing legal counsel, drafting legal documents, and representing clients before courts, administrative agencies, and other tribunals.

Prosecutor Disbarred in Duke LaCrosse Case

In January 2008, disgraced and disbarred Durham County, North Carolina former prosecutor Mike Nifong was removed from a civil lawsuit filed by three Duke University lacrosse players who were falsely accused of rape. Three weeks earlier, he had filed for bankruptcy, citing more than $180 million in liabilities, mostly for estimated damages from pending civil litigation. The removal from the civil lawsuit was anticlimatic, considering the media-sensationalized rape story that monopolized front-page headlines across the nation for several weeks in 2006. Nifong already had been disbarred from practicing law by the North Carolina Bar Association in June 2007 as a result of pursuing the case against the three Duke students even though DNA evidence had cleared them months earlier. Five months later, in October 2007, Nifong and 13 other were sued for their role in the malicious prosecution.

The three Duke students, Reade Seligmann, Collin Finnerty, and David Evans, were indicted by a Durham County grand jury in 2006 on charges of rape, kidnapping, and sexual offense. The charges stemmed from a party thrown by members of the lacrosse team who allegedly hired a stripper. However, the stripper later accused the three of attacking her in a bathroom and raping her. The fact that she was an African-American and the three accused students were white "privileged" Duke students further sensationalized the case and placed Nifong in the forefront of media coverage.

But the case began to unravel early on, riddled with flimsy evidence and an accuser who frequently changed her story. The three students strongly maintained their innocence from the beginning and fully cooperated with police. When two DNA tests failed to find a match between any of the three accused players and evidence in the case, Nifong, who was up for reelection at the time, pursued the case anyway. In fact, the DNA testing found genetic material from at least four other men in the accuser's underwear and body, but none of them was a Duke lacrosse team member. Notwithstanding, Nifong did not release this exculpatory information to defense counsel for several months.

Evidence presented at his State Bar disciplinary trial showed that prior to the rape case, Nifong was trailing another candidate by 20 percent to 37 percent in his political bid for reelection as county prosecutor. However, following his press coverage in the case, he was reelected by a 45 to 42 percent margin. He had liberally granted press interviews at the time and his public comments during press briefings had touched nerves of race, class and privilege, using loaded words such as "reprehensible," "unconscionable," and "deep racial motivation" (in the students' alleged conduct).

Following his reelection in November 2006, Nifong dropped the rape charges in December after the accuser again changed an important detail in her story. He announced that he would proceed against the students on other related charges. However, North Carolina's attorney general took over the case and in April 2007 determined that all the charges were unfounded. Near simultaneously, he announced that Nifong would undergo investigation by the state bar association.

Fourteen months after being charged, the three students were fully exonerated and all charges dropped. However, in the protracted interim, they had been forced from the lacrosse

Former Durham Cty NC district attorney Mike Nifong in court, August 2007.

AP IMAGES

team, dropped out as students, and at least one of them suffered the rescission of a job offer after the prospective employer learned of the indictment.

At Nifong's disciplinary trial, the panel of the North Carolina Bar concluded that no discipline short of disbarment would be appropriate. The panel found Nifong guilty of violating more than 12 ethics rules in prosecuting the case against the three young men. The most serious charges were that Nifong withheld the key DNA evidence from the players' defense attorneys that likely would have cleared them early on. Even more disturbing was the substantiated charge that he lied to the presiding judge in the rape case, after the judge asked him if he knew of any evidence that might exonerate the defendants. He also later lied to state bar investigators. The panel, in renouncing Nifong's conduct, concluded that Nifong practiced "dishonesty, fraud, deceit, and misrepresentation."

The disciplinary panel also concluded that the motivation for Nifong's misconduct was political and intended to further his political career. This was particularly evident in the racially-inflammatory remarks Nifong made during press conferences during the early days of the case. After a recess in the hearing, Nifong's attorney surprised the panel and stated that his client believed he deserved to be disbarred and would waive all right of appeal in the proceedings.

In October 2007, a 150-page civil suit was filed against Nifong and several local officials, including former police chief Steven Chalmers,

THE VIRTUAL LAWYER AND THE ETHICS OF LAW BLOGS

The image of being led by a secretary down a richly-paneled corridor to an attorney's well-appointed office in a downtown law firm is fast becoming a thing of the past. An increasing number of attorneys (as are other professionals, including physicians) are relying on electronic communications to execute many of their routine and ministerial tasks of law practice. But now, law practice itself has taken on a new dimension. In July 2008, Craig Johnson, a lawyer-entrepreneur, along with 14 partners, announced the start-up of Virtual Law Partners, "an idea whose time has come." He hoped to employ hundreds of stay-at-home lawyers across the country, who would retain a high percentage of their billings in return for contributing the remainder to handle overhead and administrative costs of the virtual law office. While this, in and of itself, is not new, the idea of establishing an attorney-client relationship entirely by electronic contact may be.

Between 2006 and 2008, the Internet was flooded with Web pages and new Web sites belonging to practicing lawyers or law firms with conventional law offices. Initially, they were formatted to appear as online advertisements, but increasingly they provided links to more substantive Web sites, both internal and elsewhere on the Web. Within a very short time, the entire idea appeared out of control, with bogus lawyers offering legal advice, real lawyers discussing their pending cases or puffing their credentials, and, increasingly, law blogs (often dubbed as "blawgs) that offered not only a forum for the presentation of informa-

tion, but also superior marketing potential for law professionals.

A blog, or Weblog, is a simplistic online publishing platform or Web page that allows the posting/sharing ("self-publication") of information easily accessible to anyone with Internet access. Blog sites also allow viewers to click on "links" to other related Web sites or Web pages from the initial blog site.

Critics of legal blogs believe they are essentially unprofessional and provide excessive opportunity for self-promotion. They also express concern for the potential (by general Internet users accessing legal blogs) of inducing reliance on legal information contained therein, without the benefit of fact-specific analysis. Without one-on-one communications with legal professionals, site users may attempt to apply the "general rule of law" to their own specific circumstances, and to their own peril or disadvantage. Other non-legal persons may attempt to use information gleaned from a legal blog to engage in dissemination of such information to others, possibly constituting the unauthorized practice of law.

Less palpable fallout also accompanies the major concerns. For example, in May 2008, the *Wall Street Journal*, in a story about lawyer blogging, made note of a juror who was dismissed from a panel in a 2007 securities fraud case after admitting to having read a San Diego lawyer's blog about the trial. The lawyer, who was posting day-by-day updates on the progress of the trial at his firm's Web site, was reportedly hired to write the blog by a law firm

involved in some of the subject litigation. Also of concern is the opportunity for lawyers, using anonymous blogs, to spin their own cases. The *Wall Street Journal* article also reported the professional demise of lawyer Richard Fenkel, who was sued for defamation by two Texas attorneys after he used his blog to allege irregularities in a patent infringement case. (Patent attorney Raymond Niro, of Chicago, had offered a $15,000 bounty for anyone willing to expose Frenkel's identity.)

Lawyers and law firms, on the other hand, increasingly view legal blogs as an ideal forum to disseminate free information about developments in the law, and to provide the public with easy access to basic legal information without waiting for the availability of a lawyer. The fact that the lawyer or law firm may gain new clients or positive visibility from the exchange is viewed as an added benefit.

Lawyers and law firms make use of blogs for multiple reasons, although all of them are essentially intended to enhance the standing and visibility of the lawyer/law firm. For example, through the use of blog sites, lawyers are able to gain more superior clients, increase visibility among other legal peers, earn respect as subject matter experts (SMEs), obtain speaking engagements, or simply enhance their credibility. For these reasons, lawyer and law firm blogs have generally been treated as electronic forms of advertising. Clearly, they offer alternatives to television commercials and yellow-pages advertising.

The U.S. Supreme Court has long-since settled the issue that attorneys could "advertise" their services, in the form of protected commercial speech

police investigators, and Brian Meehan, the director of DNA Security, Inc., which had conducted the DNA tests that proved key in unraveling the case. The lawsuit sought unspecified punitive and compensatory damages, attorneys' fees, and several legal reforms to the Durham Police Department's procedures and investigations. The suit followed failed negotiations between the parties.

In the complaint, defendants were accused of withholding evidence; intimidating witnesses; making public statements to smear the lacrosse players and cast them in an unfavorable light as privileged and spoiled white male students; and using a photo lineup that only featured Duke lacrosse players, so that the accuser would name only the players as her attackers.

under the First Amendment of the U.S. Constitution *Bates v. State Bar of Arizona*, 433 U.S. 350 (1977). But law blogs create their own unique set of concerns. Law blogs are often used for more substantive dissemination of legal information, such as general articles of interest in certain areas of practice, e.g., probate, or discussions about cases. Clearly, not everything in law blogs is commercial speech, i.e., advertising. The legitimate exercise of legal journalism, enjoying a higher standard of First Amendment protection, must also be acknowledged. Accordingly, some state bar associations have modified attorney advertising rules to include computer access communications, while others have issued ethical opinions regarding online advertising and blogging. Since any person with Internet capability can access a legal blog, the propriety of blogging by law professionals raises multiple issues of ethics, liability, and regulation, just to name a few. As state bar associations scramble to update their rules for practicing attorneys within their respective states, most have come to realize early on that much more than just regulation of advertising is at stake.

In a majority of states, lawyer solicitation of prospective clients through real time communications like chat rooms are prohibited, such as outlined in the state bar ethical opinions of Florida A-00-1, Illinois 96-10; Michigan RI-276; Virginia A-0110; and Utah 97-10. The Illinois State Bar Association went even further, prohibiting any computer communication succeeding chat room interventions (like e-mails).

A majority of state bar associations have amended and/or are in the process of amending their advertising rules to generally classify attorneys' websites as advertisement tools subject to regula-

tion. (Florida was considered the first state to address lawyer advertisements online.) Most bar associations require attorneys to submit a copy of their proposed advertising, along with a fee, to a state bar committee for approval. The trend has been to subject the main Web site page to advertising regulation, along with any testimonials (about past performance in cases) or biographical material on the attorneys.

However, legal blogs, especially those that are linked to the main Web page, are not subject to such regulation if they represent the legitimate exercise of legal journalism. That having been said, it is incumbent upon law professionals to post disclaimers that no attorney-client relationship is established by virtue of users gleaning legal advice and/or information from posted blogs. Moreover, any blogs that contain biographical information about lawyers or law firms are generally subject to regulations relating to advertising, as are blogs that discuss cases handled by the lawyers/law firms, and/or testimonials about results attained. Again, disclaimers explaining that no representation of same or similar results is intended by such discussion should be contained in the Web page.

In summary, the general rule is that attorney's websites are considered "communications," but there is now a fundamental premise that legal blogs are permissible exercises in journalism. Therefore, blogs by law professionals, initially controversial, are now well within the realm of acceptable law practice in most jurisdictions. The general trend in regulating such blogs is that it is the substance of the communication, and not the form of transmission, that dictates any controls. Legal professionals who relay false, deceptive, or misleading information are subject to discipline, whether the communication takes the

form of oral statements or written statements, including blogs.

According to the American Bar Association (ABA), "extrajudicial comments" made by lawyers during pending litigation have always been subject to discipline. The current rule already assesses whether statements "will be disseminated by means of public communication and will have a substantial likelihood of materially prejudicing an adjudicative proceeding in the matter," regardless of the medium used for dissemination. Therefore no change to the ABA's Model Rules is currently contemplated to address extrajudicial statements made by lawyers on their Internet blogs.

Restrictions to legal blogs generally fall within three main categories. First, blogs that may contain statements regarding quality of services provided, biographical information, or information relating to past results are generally subject to state bar association rules on advertising. Blogs that explain areas of law, summarize recent cases, or offer opinions regarding the state of the law are considered legal journalism and as such, are protected by the First Amendment. Third, all blogs should contain disclaimers, not only warning viewers/users of the absence of an attorney-client relationship, but also warning viewers/users that past results do not guarantee similar results in prospective cases.

False, deceptive, misleading, or defamatory communications have always been subject to discipline, and the fact that they take the form of "blogs" does not alter that result. Users and viewers of legal blogs use the information at their own risk, as they would medical advice or information, and it is incumbent upon them to verify the credentials of the lawyer or law firm posting the blog.

Among the demands for reform included in the suit was the request for an independent committee to publicly review complaints of police misconduct, improved police training, and a 10-year ban on Meehan or DNA Security Inc.'s involvement in any cases requiring a report or expert testimony. All defendants were accused of conspiring to keep the case alive while

Nifong faced a tightly-contested election in the Democratic primary.

The three exonerated students and their families attended the disciplinary trial for closing arguments and the penalty phase. Their attorneys stated that they "were not done yet" with Nifong and hinted at criminal charges and a request for independent federal investigation into Nifong's conduct. In addition to losing his job as prosecutor and being disbarred from practicing law, Nifong also spent a night in jail after the trial judge found him in contempt of court.

Seattle Law Firm Requests Attorney Fee Award in Pro Bono Case

In 2007, the non-profit group Parents Involved in Community Schools (PICS), representing several Seattle-area parents of high school students, won its civil rights court battle against Seattle Public Schools when the U.S. SUPREME COURT ruled in its favor. PICS v. Seattle School District No. 1, 127 S.Ct. 2738. In that case, the high court ruled that the school district's admissions policy (which used race to assign high school students to popular schools) violated the **Equal Protection** Clause of the U.S. Constitution (under the 14th Amendment).

The parents/PICS were represented at all levels (U.S. **District Court** for the Western District of Washington, Ninth **Circuit Court** of Appeals, and U.S. Supreme Court) by the large Seattle-based law firm of Davis Wright Tremaine (DWT), which took the case on a "pro bono" basis. However, following the successful outcome at the Supreme Court level, DTW then filed a petition to receive nearly $1.8 million in attorney fees, such fees being expressly authorized by federal **statute** in CIVIL RIGHTS CASES (42 USC 1988). The law firm's efforts to recover attorney fees were met with national media coverage debating the true meaning of "pro bono" legal work.

Technically, "pro bono publico" means "for the public good," and state and federal bars consistently encourage practicing attorneys and law firms to perform as much "pro bono" representation of parties in need of legal services as possible. The general understanding of **pro bono** legal services is that they are performed free of charge, or at least without the expectation of compensation. In the Seattle case, had the parents lost their legal battle, DWT would not have charged legal fees for the nearly 6,000 hours of time and effort, expended over seven years, in pursuing a case it deemed meritorious.

But after winning the case for its clients at the highest level, DWT petitioned the court to collect the attorney fees, to which it argued it was entitled. Notwithstanding, DWT argued that its work on the case should still be considered "pro bono work" because its attorneys did not charge their client, PICS, but rather the losing party. Under 42 USC 1988, prevailing parties in civil rights litigation may petition a court for an award of attorney fees and associated costs against governmental entities found to have violated constitutional rights. In this case, the governmental **entity** was the Seattle Public School District.

For its part, Seattle Public Schools argued that such a large, powerful law firm as DWT did not need the funds to sustain the firm. Shannon McMinimee, assistant general counsel for Seattle Public Schools, remarked to Amanda Bronstad, reporting for the *National Law Journal*, that DWT's request for attorney fees was "disingenuous," given that the law firm accepted the case on a pro bono basis.

But Mark Usellis, spokesman for DWT, opined that the school district was attempting to transform the fee request into a criticism against the law firm, rather than a remedy for wrongful conduct. Moreover, attorney Harry Korrell, who worked extensively on the case, opined that this would not even have been an issue had it been the AMERICAN CIVIL LIBERTIES UNION (ACLU) or the Lawyers Committee for Civil Rights Under Law, that was requesting fees, both of which often petitioned for and received awards of attorney fees for similar cases and causes.

This was not the first time that a high-profile case challenged the fees collected by law firms in pro bono representation. Also in 2007, a federal judge in New York awarded nearly $1 million in attorney fees, costs, and interest to a law firm which had represented (on a pro bono basis) workers at a New York restaurant in an attempt to collect their unpaid tips. Although the law firm won the case, its request for attorney fees raised concerns, especially since the fees amounted to more than the workers received ($700,000). The judge in that case noted that the law firm had already discounted its legal fees and that only a large firm could have taken such a large case. *Chan v. Triple 8 Palace*, 03-CV-06048 (S.D.N.Y. 2007). Going back into the 1990s, attorneys who represented the woman who sued the State of South Carolina and The Citadel for refusing to admit her to the military school also petitioned for attorney fees under 42 USC 1988, even though they had taken her case pro bono. They were awarded $4.6 million. Esther Lardent, president of the Pro Bono Institute at Georgetown University Law Center, encouraged firms to seek legal fees in pro bono cases involving major public interest cases, if for no other reason than to serve as a deterrent to others.

In the Seattle case, according to DWT attorney Korrell, DWT filed a motion in the trial court in December 2007 for entry of a final order, pursuant to the Supreme Court decision and remand, declaring that the school district's admissions policy plan violated the Constitution. DWT also sought a narrow injunction against the school's returning to a similar policy at a later date, and finally requested attorney fees. The school district opposed, filing a cross-motion to dismiss the entire case as moot, since it alleged it had dropped its "illegal" plan. Responsive and reply briefs were due in late June 2008.

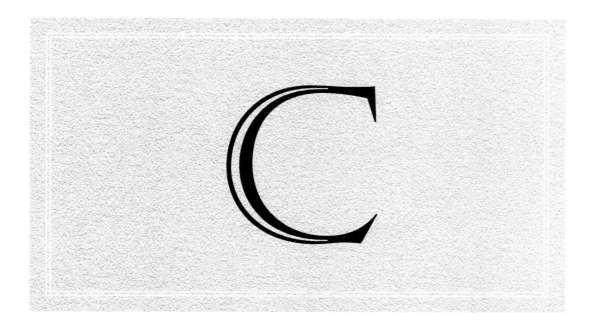

CAPITAL PUNISHMENT

The lawful infliction of death as a punishment; the death penalty.

Report Renews Call for a Nationwide Moratorium on the Death Penalty

Following a study in eight states, the AMERICAN BAR ASSOCIATION in 2007 issued a report that called for a nationwide moratorium on capital punishment in the United States, which would last until the states make improvements in their systems. According to the report, most of these states operate with capital defense systems that are underfunded and staffed with lawyers who are unqualified and who lack the resources to provide adequate defenses for death row inmates.

This is not the first time that the ABA has called for a stoppage in executions. Believing that jurisdictions that allow the death penalty operate with neither fairness nor accuracy, the ABA on February 3, 1997 issued a moratorium on capital punishment similar to the one issued in 2007. The ABA has focused primarily on two key points: first, that states ensure that death penalty cases are handled fairly and impartially, in accordance with due process; and second, that the states minimize the risk that innocent persons may be executed.

During the fall of 2001, the ABA established the Death Penalty Moratorium Implementation Project, which has engaged in a number of studies related to capital punishment since its establishment. During the same year, the ABA's Section on Individual Rights and Responsibilities issued a publication entitled *Death Without Justice: A Guide for Examining the Administration of the Death Penalty in the United States*. This publication establishes protocols for seven aspects of death penalty administration, including: (1) defense services; (2) procedural restrictions and limitations on state post-conviction and **habeas corpus** proceedings; (3) **clemency** proceedings; (4) jury instructions; (5) an independent judiciary; (6) racial and ethnic minorities; and (7) mental retardation and mental illness. The ABA's Death Penalty Moratorium Implementation Project also reviews five additional areas, including preservation and testing of DNA evidence; identification and interrogation procedures; crime laboratories and medical examiners; prosecutors; and the direct appeal process.

In 2004, the ABA established teams of state-based legal experts to review capital punishment systems in eight states. The ABA established these teams in the states of Alabama, Arizona, Florida, Georgia, Indiana, Ohio, Pennsylvania, and Tennessee. The teams generally consisted of judges, state legislators, prosecutors, defense attorneys, state bar association leaders, and law professors. Five of these eight teams asked their own state government leaders to temporarily halt executions until the teams could complete their analyses. None of these states did so, however.

These teams prepared independent assessments of the capital punishment systems in these states and determined whether these states complied with criteria that the ABA had established. In many instances, the teams could not find sufficient information to determine whether these states indeed complied. In several other areas, however, the teams found a number of problems that the ABA characterized as serious concerns. After releasing reports covering the various states, the ABA on October 28, 2007 released a report that called for the nationwide moratorium.

The preservation of DNA evidence was cause for concern in several of the states. The ABA recommends that states preserve all biological evidence through the entire legal process and after release from prison or execution. The purpose of this recommendation is to reduce the possibility that evidence that could prove a defendant's innocence could be destroyed. However, fewer than half of the states that were studied complied with this recommendation. A second concern regarding DNA is that states draft DNA testing statutes too narrowly, requiring applicants to comply with strict filing deadlines and other procedures.

The ABA teams were also troubled by actions of law enforcement personnel and policies regarding crime labs. The report concluded that most states do not require law enforcement agencies to record custodial interrogations, which could reduce problems related to false confessions. Crime laboratories also received criticism, as most that were studied failed to utilize state-of-the-art DNA testing techniques. In fact, most of the states in the study had at least one "serious incident" of mistake or **fraud** occurring in a crime lab. According to the report, many states do not sufficiently fund crime labs, and states in general do not require accreditation of the crime labs or medical **examiner** offices.

The report found a number of problems with prosecutors and the role of defense counsel in capital cases. The teams determined that states generally do not have policies requiring prosecutors' offices to establish policies on the exercise of prosecutorial discretion. Moreover, states have not adopted policies pertaining to the evaluation of cases "that rely on eyewitness identification, confessions, or the testimony of jailhouse snitches, informants, and other witnesses who receive a benefit." The report noted that on the defense side, the judiciary remains primarily responsible for appointing defense counsel, and that capital defense attorneys who are appointed by the courts are paid less than $50 per hour, a sum the report described as "woefully inadequate."

The ABA teams were critical of the procedures used in post-conviction proceedings. Many states make it difficult for defendants to obtain discovery materials after the convictions and also make it difficult for a defendant to obtain an evidentiary hearing during the post-conviction phase. The report was likewise critical of the procedures and policies pertaining to direct appeals in capital punishment cases and in the clemency processes of most of these states. The clemency process is the final stage of review that is available, but in most states, the person making clemency decisions is not required to give reasons for the decisions.

In addition to concerns related to jury instructions, judicial independence, and mental retardation and mental illness, the report cited racial problems related to capital punishment cases. Although all of the states have racial disparities in their capital systems, especially as those statistics relate to the race of the victims, these states have not kept data necessary to analyze or quantify the problems with bias or identify the causes of this bias. The report concluded that these states are doing little, if anything, to rectify problems with racial bias.

The ABA's calls for a halt to executions has not met with uniform support. In 2006, when a 21-member team concluded that Georgia's death penalty system was inadequate, the state refused to do so. A spokesperson for the state's attorney general said, "Our office continues to review the ABA report, but this appears to be a lobbying packet put together in an effort to have the Legislature make changes to the state process." Other critics focused their attention on the ABA's politics. According to William "Rusty" Hubbarth, the vice-president for legal affairs for Justice for All, a Texas victims' advocacy group, "The ABA has always been a very, very liberal organization. They have spent much more time worrying about the rights of the defendant, rather than the rights of the victims, or the rest of society."

ABA leaders have stood by their conclusions. "We just do not have confidence in the capital justice system after studying it," said Stephen Hanlon, chair of the Death Moratorium Project. "In determining who gets the death penalty, all too frequently, it seems to be not the person who has committed the worst crime, but the person who has the worst lawyer."

Death Penalty Developments

The debate over capital punishment in the United States and in the international community continued unabated in 2007 and 2008. The Supreme Court stayed the execution of 18 inmates and other states placed a moratorium on executions while the Court considered whether death by lethal injection constituted **cruel and unusual punishment**. In April 2008 the Court upheld the legality of lethal injections and executions resumed. However, only one of the several states that debated eliminating the death penalty—New Jersey—formally abolished it in 2007. On another front the Nebraska Supreme Court ruled that death by electrocution constituted cruel and unusual punishment, becoming the last death-penalty state to use the electric chair as the sole means of execution. Finally, the UNITED NATIONS adopted a non-binding resolution in December 2007 calling for a worldwide moratorium on capital punishment.

After the Supreme Court accepted review in 2007 of *Baze v. Rees*, which challenged the constitutionality of lethal injections, it received petitions from death-row inmates seeking stays of their executions until the issue could be resolved. The Court granted 18 stays and, by doing so, signaled to all death-penalty states that they should stop executions as well. The states complied and there began a seven-month moratorium on executions. The Supreme Court issued its decision in *Baze* on April 16, 2008. The Court, in a 7–2 decision, rejected the challenge by two inmates that the three-drug combination used to execute prisoners was unconstitutional. However, the Court could not issue a majority opinion as to the reasons why the method passed constitutional muster. Seven separate justices wrote their own opinions. Within hours of the decision's release 11 states announced that they would immediately resume executions. On May 6 the state of Georgia ended the moratorium by executing William Earl Lynd by lethal injection.

In December 2007 the state of New Jersey repealed its death penalty, becoming the first state to abolish capital punishment since the Supreme Court restored it in 1976. The law replaces the death penalty with life imprisonment without parole. Though advocates of abolition pointed to numerous cases where condemned inmates had been exonerated by DNA evidence, an added reason was that no inmate had been executed since the state reintroduced the death penalty in 1982. In addition, the state could save money by making the change. Keeping an inmate on death row cost the state $73,000 per year, while inmates in the general population cost $40,000 per inmate per year. Repealing the death penalty was expected to save New Jersey as much as $1.3 million per inmate over his lifetime. The eight prisoners on New Jersey's death row had their sentences changed to life imprisonment with no parole.

In February 2008 the Nebraska Supreme Court ruled that under its state constitution the use of the electric chair constituted cruel and unusual punishment. Nebraska had been the last state that mandated electrocution as the sole method of execution. The court concluded that there had never been a thorough and scientific examination on whether electrocution inflicts intense pain on the inmate. Reviewing the evidence of competing expert witnesses, the justices found that there was a strong probability that the prisoner did not lose consciousness and brain function immediately. The court believed the defense experts' testimony that high voltage caused pain in several ways apart from "the electrical burning that is occurring in the body." It dismissed the trial court's claim of instantaneous and irreversible brain death as a "myth." The court gave the legislature the opportunity to propose another means of execution. The Nebraska legislature rejected the **repeal** of capital punishment in March 2008 but did not consider a new means of execution. Nebraska Governor Dave Heineman directed the state attorney general to determine whether the Nebraska Supreme Court ruling should be appealed to the U.S. SUPREME COURT, try to convince the legislature to enact lethal injection as the method of execution, or both.

In December 2007 the General Assembly of the United Nations voted 104 to 54, with 29 abstentions, to adopt a non-binding resolution supporting a moratorium on capital punishment. The vote culminated a 1-year campaign that seeks to identify capital punishment as a human rights issue rather than a **criminal law** issue. According to AMNESTY INTERNATIONAL, 133 countries have abolished the death penalty in law or practice. In 2006 only 29 countries carried out executions, of which 91 percent took place in China, Iran, Iraq, Pakistan, Sudan, and the United States. The number of executions worldwide declined from 2,148 in 2005 to 1,591 in 2006.

Missouri Law Shields Identity of Executioners

On June 30, 2007, Missouri Governor Matt Blunt signed into law a bill (HB820/SB 258, 94th Gen. Assem., 1st Reg. Sess.) that required the identities of execution team members to remain confidential, and made all records that could identify a team member "privileged," i.e., neither subject to discovery or subpoena in litigation, nor subject to release in response to requests by the public at large. Although several other states also shielded the identity of team members, Missouri's law was considered the first to impose civil penalties for disclosure in violation of its provisions. It further provided members of the execution team the right to sue for compensatory and **punitive damages** from anyone who disclosed the member's participation in an execution. However, the new law also established Missouri's lethal injection protocol as an open record.

The law was prompted in part by a *St. Louis Post-Dispatch* story the previous summer that disclosed the identity of a Missouri doctor who oversaw state executions and whose professional record included revocation of staff privileges at two hospitals and twenty pending malpractice lawsuits against him. Although the doctor was captioned "Dr. Doe" in a related lawsuit, the *Post-Dispatch* investigated and then identified him by name. The doctor had originally come under scrutiny after admitting that he sometimes altered the amount of anesthetic given to condemned inmates in response to discovery **interrogatories** in a pending lawsuit.

Following the *St. Louis Post-Dispatch* story, three St. Louis-area state legislators who were members of a committee that oversaw the Department of Corrections were interviewed by the newspaper. The committee had the authority to investigate the department as well as compel testimony from officials. The legislators advised that they intended to raise questions within the committee, but the chairman advised that an official inquiry was unlikely, citing the limited information against the male nurse, including the absence of any disciplinary action taken against him by the state board of nursing.

This conflict between the public's right to oversee how government implements capital punishment, and the need to protect the identity of members of an execution team resulted in a judicial compromise in *Taylor v. Crawford*, 05-4173-CV (W.D. Mo. 2006). In that case, in response to discovery requests (interrogatories), the court ordered that the state disclose "the qualifications of any medical personnel who have participated in executions, without disclosing their identities or any confidential information." (The State had argued that disclosure of individual identities would be inappropriate because of security concerns for them as well as for the prison.)

The new Missouri law went into effect on August 28, 2007. However, that did not stop five death row inmates from filing papers in January 2008 to learn about their would-be executioners. The petition was part of an ongoing lawsuit challenging not only the shielding of personal information of the execution team members, but also the state's lethal injection protocol in general. *Clemons v. Crawford*, No. 573636-4015 (W.D. Ct. Missouri).

The petition, filed by attorneys in federal **district court** in Kansas City, Missouri, cited yet another *Post-Dispatch* revelation that a male nurse on the execution team had been on criminal probation for an incident of stalking. The petition alleged that such circumstances raised questions about the state's screening procedures as well as the nurse's "temperament and suitability" to be on the execution team. The petition further alleged that, in light of Missouri's new law protecting such disclosure, the petitioners'/inmates' right to such information in a federal lawsuit superceded state law. It argued that the inmates should not have to rely on the new media to learn about executioners' backgrounds.

Responsive pleadings by attorneys in the Missouri Attorney General's office (which represented the Department of Corrections) nonetheless invoked Missouri's 2007 law as substantively barring all requested disclosures. The responsive pleadings also argued that the requested information was subject to **attorney-client privilege**. But lawyers for the convicted killers represented in the suit, Reginald Clemons, Richard Clay, Jeffrey Ferguson, Roderick Nunley, and Michael Taylor, stated they were willing to accept anonymous depositions, keeping the names of the executioners out of court records.

In March 2008, the district court granted part of the inmates' motion to compel evidence, allowing the inmates to submit written interrogatories to two Department of Corrections executioners, regarding their background and training. It denied the request for live depositions. It also ordered the release of documents involving the recently revised lethal injection protocol.

In May 2008, the court granted Defendants' (the Department of Corrections, et al) Motion for Reconsideration of the court's previous (March) order compelling discovery. It also ordered the scheduling of dispositive motions, in light of the U.S. Supreme Court's April 2008 decision that rejected a similar Kentucky-based challenge to lethal injection as an execution method. *Baze v. Rees*, No. 07-5439. The death penalty was effectively on moratorium in all states pending the high court's decision. Following the release of that decision, part of the Missouri case became moot, but the challenge regarding release of information pertaining to the executioners remained. The district court noted that the requested documents might shed light on the Department of Correction's "mental state" regarding the revised protocol provisions.

State v. Mata

The means of executing individual for their crimes has changed over the past four centuries, as succeeding generations come to believe certain methods are inhumane, and, in the case of the United States, cruel and unusual punishments. In the late nineteenth century in the U.S., hanging was the preferred method of execution. However, with the introduction of electricity, advocates of the new technology claimed that death by electrocution in an "electric chair" was more humane than breaking a person's neck. In In 1890 the U.S. SUPREME COURT allowed the state of New York to use the electric chair, which led many states to adopt this method. In the Twentieth Century electrocution and death by poisonous gas were the most popular means of capital punishment until the 1990s, when death by lethal injection became the dominant method. By 2008 only the state of Nebraska mandated the use of the electric chair as the sole method of execution, but the Nebraska Supreme Court, in *State v. Mata*, 745 N.W.2d 229 (Neb. 2008), ruled that under its state constitution electrocution was **cruel and unusual punishment**. Seven states still allow inmates to choose the electric chair over lethal injection.

Raymond Mata, Jr. was convicted of murder in 2000 and sentenced for death. Mata appealed both his conviction and the means the state would use to execute him. The Nebraska Supreme Court upheld Mata's conviction but in a lengthy opinion ruled that the time had come to end the use of the electric chair. In a 6 to 1 decision the court held that "electrocution inflicts intense pain and agonizing suffering." Justice William Connolly, writing for the majority, noted that Mata was not challenging the constitutionality of the death penalty but whether the method of execution mandated by state law was constitutional. Nebraska, like all other states, has adopted the U.S. Constitution's provision against inflicting cruel and unusual punishment.

Justice Connolly acknowledged that the Nebraska Supreme Court had previously ruled that electrocution was not cruel and unusual punishment. However, the court now had the opportunity, for the first time, "to review a factual record showing electrocution's physiological effects on a prisoner." Likewise, the U.S. Supreme Court's 1890 decision was not based on objective evidence but state courts' "factual

Nebraska electric chair, April 2007.
AP IMAGES

assumptions" based on "untested science." This new factual record, coupled with the reality that only Nebraska used electricity as the sole means of execution, directed the court's analysis.

In reviewing previous U.S. Supreme Court rulings on electrocution, the court identified three shortcomings in this **jurisprudence**: (1) limited knowledge about electrocution's effects on the human body; (2) the states' desire to find a more human way of execution than hanging; and, (3) the Court's view, when electrocution was first introduced, that the Eighth Amendment's bar on cruel and unusual punishment was not intended as a restraint on the states' determinations of punishment. As to the last point, the Supreme Court has now applied the EIGHTH AMENDMENT to the states through the FOURTEENTH AMENDMENT.

Justice Connolly stated that the "baseline criticism in a challenge to a punishment is whether it imposes torture or a lingering death that is unnecessary to the mere extinguishment of life." Because it is impossible to know with certainty that electrocution causes unnecessary pain, courts must deal with probabilities. Evidence introduced at trial by the state and the defendant dealt with the probable effects of electricity on the human body. The state argued that prisoners lose brain function and consciousness instantaneously, thereby making them incapable of feeling unnecessary pain. Defense experts, however, persuasively showed that this was not the case and that there was no medical evidence of mass damage to the brain. In fact, there as evidence that 20 percent of the prisoners electrocuted in Nebraska between 1920 and 1977 were still breathing or alive after the initial application of current. Moreover, the court believed the defense experts' testimony that high voltage caused pain in several ways apart from "the electrical burning that is occurring in the body." Justice Connolly dismissed the trial court's claim of instantaneous and irreversible brain death as a "myth."

Having ruled electrocution unconstitutional, the court stayed Mata's death sentence. It gave the state legislature the opportunity to propose a new method of execution and be prepared to demonstrate that is is constitutionally acceptable. In March 2008 the Nebraska legislature defeated a bill that would have repealed capital punishment but it had yet to take up the issue of what would replace the electric chair as the method of execution.

New York Senate Passes Bill to Reinstate Death Penalty

In early 2008, the New York State Senate introduced and passed bills to reactivate the death penalty in that state. No executions had been effected in that state since 2004, based primarily on two developments. First, New York's general death penalty **statute** had been declared unconstitutional by the state Court of Appeals in 2004 (regarding a problematic jury instruction). Second, while various legislative attempts to rewrite the state law had been made, those efforts were interrupted by a U.S. SUPREME COURT stay on executions in October 2007, pending its further determination in *Baze v. Rees*, No. 07-5439 (2008), which challenged certain lethal injection procedures as **cruel and unusual punishment**. The Court's stay effectively created a **de facto** moratorium on all pending state executions nationwide. As of September 2007, a vast majority of states (at least 36 of 50) and the federal government had death penalty statutes/laws in effect.

Meanwhile, in October 2007, the New York State Court of Appeals, in *People v. Taylor*, refused to make an exception to its 2004 ruling (in *People v. LaValle*, 817 NE2d 341) that New York State's death penalty statute was unconstitutional. The state law was struck by the court because of a flawed jury instruction that appeared to advise capital jurors that if they did not choose the death penalty, the judge would sentence the defendant to life with the possibility of parole in 20 to 25 years. It was successfully argued that this law effectively coerced jurors into meting out death sentences rather than risking the chance that convicted killers might be freed on parole in the future.

Following the April 2008 U.S. Supreme Court's decision in *Baze*, (ruling that the subject lethal injection was constitutional and valid), state prosecutors around the country sought to move forward with executions for death row inmates that had been stayed for several months pending the Court's decision.

Also following the *Baze*, decision, the New York State Senate passed S. 6414 in May 2008 (previously S. 319), reinstating the death penalty in New York for the intentional murder of a police or peace officer or any employee of the Department of Correction Services. Joining it was a **correlative** bill, S. 4632, a general death penalty law that was actually passed in June 2007 to replace the existing one (struck in October), but put on hold pending the Supreme Court's ruling in *Baze*.

This time around, the new legislation in both New York bills was carefully drafted to address the concerns that had caused the previous **statutory** provision to fail. The new wording in both bills made certain that if a jury were deadlocked and unable to agree on a death penalty sentence, a sentence of life without parole would be imposed, and juries would know this prior to their sentencing deliberations. Further, the general death penalty bill, S. 4632, required that juries be given a third option when sentencing convicted killers, a sentence of life in prison with the possibility of parole. As of June 2008, both bills had been passed in the state senate and sent to the state's legislative assembly.

Despite media coverage implying an aversion to the death penalty by New York juries, the state senate, in a June 20, 2007 press release, noted that the majority of New Yorkers consistently supported the death penalty. In that press release, State Senate Majority Leader Joseph L. Bruno recognized the death penalty as a strong deterrent to crime. "When the death penalty was reinstituted, the number of murders and violent crimes in New York decreased dramatically," he stated. Also noted in the press release was a 2003 study by Emerson University in Boston that concluded an average of eighteen murders were deterred for each execution. The press release also cited a 2006 study by the University of Houston which showed that a moratorium on executions in the state of Illinois in 2000 led to 150 additional homicides over the following four years.

But the non-profit organization, New Yorkers Against the Death Penalty (NYADP) argued the opposite. It claimed that over ten years, the death penalty in New York wasted $200 million in taxpayer dollars, was not imposed fairly or reliably, and created risk of innocent persons being executed. It also stated that New York had more than 50 death-eligible federal cases awaiting **disposition** by the U.S. Attorney General's office, potentially more than any other state. In arguing that New Yorkers were hesitant to impose death penalties, NYADP noted that records compiled by the Federal Death Penalty Resource Counsel Project showed that federal prosecutors in New York State had asked juries to impose death sentences 19 times since 1988, but in only one case did a jury sentence the defendant to execution.

As of June 2008, the newly-worded general death penalty bill, now identified as state assembly No. AO8157, was still pending final vote.

Different Results for the Mentally Ill in Tennessee and South Carolina

Theoretically, mentally-deficient capital criminals have been protected from death penalty sentences for sometime. In 1986, the U.S. SUPREME COURT ruled as unconstitutional the execution of an insane person. *Ford v. Wainwright*, 477 US 399. More recently, the high court also ruled as unconstitutional the execution of a mentally retarded person. *Atkins v. Virginia*, 536 US 304 (2002).

Between these two extremes lies the sentencing of persons who are neither insane nor retarded but nonetheless seriously mentally ill, and for whom there is no constitutional bar against execution. In March 2008, the Tennessee Court of Criminal Appeals reversed the death sentence of Richard Taylor and remanded for a new trial, in lieu of which Taylor agreed to enter a guilty plea in return for life imprisonment. In June 2008, the State of South Carolina executed David Hill. Both men suffered from extreme mental illness.

For Taylor, the case was more clear-cut. The record on appeal indicated that Taylor, at the age of 21, was serving a sentence in 1981 'for joy-riding and **robbery** convictions when he stabbed a prison guard at the Turney Center Correctional Center in Tennessee. Eyewitnesses described him as raving, with wild eyes and a facial expression "like a wild horse," and trembling and shaking. The prison guard died. An already-incarcerated Taylor was then tried and convicted for killing the prison guard and sentenced to death. Prison records showed that

during his incarceration, Taylor had previously tried to kill himself by swallowing glass.

During his 18 years on death row, Taylor's attorneys (from the Office of the Tennessee Post-Conviction Defender and the AMERICAN CIVIL LIBERTIES UNION, ACLU) continued to appeal his sentence, arguing that his mental illness had affected every step of his case, from offense through trial. In summary, they argued that he had a long, documented history of severe mental illness, was denied psychiatric treatment at various times during his incarceration, and had not received his anti-psychotic medication for the two months preceding the crime (the attack on a prison guard) that resulted in his death sentence.

Although Taylor was granted a new trial in 2003, he was permitted to represent himself, despite a prison record replete with notations of his severe mental illness. He was again convicted and sentenced to death. It was this conviction and death sentence that was overturned in the March 2008 decision of the Tennessee Court of Criminal Appeals. The **appellate court** found numerous substantive errors requiring reversal, five of which were cited in its decision. *Tennessee v. Taylor*, No. M2005-01941-CCA-R3-DD, March 7, 2008.

The court, in reversing and remanding the case, stated,

> Upon review, we conclude the trial court failed to consider the full panoply of evidence relevant to whether the Defendant knowingly and voluntarily waived his right to counsel. He is thus entitled to a new trial. Additionally, the Defendant's constitutional right to counsel was denied at a competency hearing, the trial court erred in failing to hold a competency hearing during trial, and the trial court erred in failing to appoint advisory counsel. These errors also entitle the Defendant to a new trial. We also conclude that the trial court erred when it instructed the jury at the sentencing phase, and the Defendant is entitled to a new sentencing hearing. In accordance with the foregoing reasoning and authorities, we vacate the Defendant's conviction and sentence of death and remand for a new trial.

But in South Carolina, the state Supreme Court, in upholding the decision of a trial court, found death row prisoner David Hill "competent" to waive his right to further **appellate** review and other post-conviction relief, and found his waiver to be knowing and voluntary. *South Carolina v. Hill*, No. 26477, April 28, 2008. Hill and his wife had their three children removed from them by the STATE DEPARTMENT of social services because of concern about the parents' abuse of prescription drugs. Hill was convicted of three counts of murder after he walked into a county social services office and shot three employees dead. A massive manhunt followed, and Hill was found the following morning, lying on railroad tracks directly behind the building where the murders took place. He had a [presumably self-inflicted] bullet hole through the roof of his mouth and an exit wound through the top of his skull. He recovered from his wounds and later admitted to the killings.

The South Carolina Supreme Court affirmed his convictions and death sentence. *State v. Hill*, 361 S.C. 297 (2004); *cert. denied*, 544 U.S. 1020 (2005). Then in May 2007, Hill sent a letter to the State Solicitor requesting assistance to "drop the rest of my appeals and have an execution date set." On June 21, 2007, counsel for Hill submitted an affidavit indicating that Hill had changed his mind and did *not* wish to drop his appeals. A little more than three weeks later, Hill again advised the court that he wished to withdraw his pending post-conviction relief application and any remaining appeals. The trial court ordered a competency evaluation and thorough examination of Hill. Following a hearing, the trial court found Hill competent to waive his appeals and also found that his decision was made knowingly and voluntarily. On April 28, 2008, the South Carolina Supreme Court, upon full review of the trial court's record in addition to another thorough examination of Hill during oral arguments before the Court, affirmed the trial court's findings that Hill was competent to waive his rights, and did so knowingly and voluntarily. Hill was executed on June 6, 2008.

No First Amendment Right to View Executions

In January 2008, U.S. **District Court** Judge Susan Webber Wright of the Eastern District of Arkansas dismissed a lawsuit that had been filed in July 2007, demanding that witnesses be allowed to see and hear all phases and stages of the lethal injection process for capital defendants. Judge Wright ruled there was no FIRST AMENDMENT right of access to executions. The suit had been filed by the AMERICAN CIVIL LIBERTIES UNION (ACLU) on behalf of the Northwest Chapter of the Society of Professional Journalists, the *Arkansas Times*, a weekly newspaper, and

Max Brantley, its editor. *ACLU, et al, v. Larry Norris*, No. 5:07-CV-195 (E.D. Ark. 2008).

The lawsuit had argued that witnesses should be able to view everything from the time a condemned inmate enters the execution chamber until he/she is pronounced deceased, including "strapping the condemned down and the insertion of needles." It premised this right as being grounded in the First Amendment, akin to a Freedom of Information (FOIA) Act request. The lawsuit's articulated reason was that such access would help educate the public about how the state effects an execution, and would let witnesses see if anything goes wrong.

But the STATE DEPARTMENT of corrections and its director, Larry Norris, responded that the state was merely following state law, which provided that state executions were private and not public proceedings. Under state law, curtains were generally opened once an inmate was already strapped to a gurney and closed once the inmate was pronounced dead. Department spokesperson Dina Tyler stated to the Associated Press that keeping the curtain closed while an inmate entered the chamber allowed the condemned person some dignity. In its legal response, the department of corrections had countered, "Whether Arkansas should keep the curtain open from the time a condemned prisoner enters the execution chamber is a question of policy for the Arkansas General Assembly and state officials and not a question governed by the First Amendment."

The district court agreed. In its 10-page decision, the court noted that "The Supreme Court has never recognized a First Amendment right of access to executions." District Judge Wright also noted that the high court had previously held that, while conditions in jails and prisons were matters of great public concern and importance, access to penal institutions was a question of policy for a legislative body. The judge noted that executions had "moved from the public square to inside prison walls." An execution, noted the opinion, "bears little resemblance to a criminal judicial proceeding, where public participation plays an indispensable functional role in the process itself, and where public access enables citizens to judge whether our system of criminal justice is fair."

The district court further held that in this case, the prison director "has the responsibility to determine the substances to be administered and the procedures to be used in any execution." The law already provided for the director or an assistant to be present, as well as "a number of respectable citizens numbering not fewer than six ... nor more than twelve ... whose presence is necessary to verify that the execution was conducted in the manner required by law." The court also noted that state law additionally provided for the inmate's attorney and spiritual adviser to attend as well, along with any other spectators designated by the director, with a maximum overall attendance limited to 30 persons.

After release of the court's opinion, plaintiff editor Max Brantley told the Associated Press, "Even if constitutionally we don't have a right to be there at every step of that process, public accountability demands that we should be." He added that he and the other parties would confer with legal counsel to decide whether to appeal the ruling.

The ACLU had filed similar suits in other states previously, also citing First Amendment violations by state departments of corrections. In 1999, the Oregon Supreme Court struck as invalid certain state rules that barred execution witnesses from viewing the insertion of needles. As of early 2008, only the Ninth **Circuit Court** of Appeals has held (in a 2002 decision, *California First Amendment Coalition v. Woodford*) that the First Amendment provided a right of access to view executions from the beginning of the process. Following that remanded decision, in 2003, the California Department of Corrections ended its legal battle and decided to permit media personnel to witness the executions in full. Only states within the Ninth Circuit (including California and Oregon) were bound by that decision. Arkansas is under the jurisdiction of the Eighth Circuit Court of Appeals.

CENTRAL INTELLIGENCE AGENCY (CIA)

CIA Releases its 'Family Jewels'

The American public had known for a long time that the CENTRAL INTELLIGENCE AGENCY (CIA) kept secrets. But it was not until 2007 that the intricate details of many of the most covert—and sometimes illegal—CIA operations were released to the general public for review. Pursuant to a 15-year-old FREEDOM OF INFORMATION ACT (FOIA) request from Tom Blanton of the National Security Archive (NSA) made in 1992, 700+ pages of long-sealed documents were finally declassified and tendered to the NSA on July 26, 2007. Over the years multiple FOIA requests had been filed, but only a few dozen heavily-censored pages had previously been declassified and released.

Out came the "family jewels"—hundreds of decades-old documents that provided insight and detail into CIA activities including assassination plans, illegal wiretapping and attempts to discover "spies" at political conventions. The released documents comprised not a comprehensive or orderly chronicle of CIA activities, but rather a collection of various internal memoranda, communications with Congress, and newspaper clippings, some of which contained deletions, and a number of blank pages.

Many of the documents stem from the 1970s and the troubled time surrounding WATERGATE, the scandal involving CIA officers E. Howard Hunt and James McCord who allegedly broke into and wiretapped the Democratic National Committee headquarters. The scandal caused then-president RICHARD M. NIXON to resign from office.

Senior CIA official William E. Colby apparently struggled to determine how much to reveal as he prepared agency testimony for congressional committee hearings investigating Watergate in 1973. According to internal memoranda, he was advised by a senior colleague to lean toward "candor" rather than "minimal factual response." His then-boss, former CIA Director James R. Schlesinger, issued an internal order drafted by Colby to "report to me immediately on any activities now going on, or that have gone on in the past, which might be construed to be outside the legislative charter of this agency."

Responses came in from various division heads, lower-level bureaucrats, and some retired operatives, outlining or explaining various incidents of illegal surveillance and other questionable activities. In the end, Colby's loose-leaf collection contained 693 pages of memoranda.

By September 1973, Colby had succeeded Schlesinger as CIA Director. On December 22, 1974, a front-page story leaked in the *New York Times* ("Huge C.I.A. Operation Reported in U.S. Against Antiwar Forces, Other Dissidents During Nixon Years") reporting on some of the CIA's activities. The article intimated that "a check of the CIA's domestic files ordered last year ... produced evidence of dozens of other illegal activities ... beginning in the fifties, including break-ins, wiretapping, and the surreptitious inspection of mail."

Nine days later, on New Year's eve, 1974, Colby and the CIA general counsel John Warner met with the U.S. deputy attorney general and his associate to brief the JUSTICE DEPARTMENT about incidents alluded to in the

Members of National Archives discuss and examine documents described as CIA "family jewels," June 2007.

AP IMAGES

Times story that presented "legal questions." Colby also briefed President GERALD FORD about Schlesinger's directive to compile the CIA's "skeletons" in the agency's closet. Weeks later, in February 1975, Colby and Schlesinger met with then Secretary of State/National Security Adviser Henry Kissinger, who had previously advised President Ford that leaking of CIA secret activities was "worse than the days of McCarthyism." Kissinger had already been warned by Director of Central Intelligence Richard Helms that "these stories are just the tip of the iceberg," citing, for example, Robert F. Kennedy's role in assassination plans.

Ultimately, the CIA internally combed its files for what it referred to as "delicate information" with "flap potential." These became the "family jewels." Some of the more controversial and intriguing examples of closeted jewels included:

—detention and confinement of Soviet defector Yuri Nosenko "that might be regarded as a violation of kidnapping laws;"

—surveillance and/or wiretapping of journalists, including syndicated columnists Robert Allen and Paul Scott and *Washington Post* reporter Michael Getler;

—break-ins and/or warrantless entries into the homes or apartments of former CIA employees;

—mail opening from 1953 to 1973 of letters to and from the Soviet Union;

—mail opening from 1969 to 1972 of letters to and from China;

—behavior modification experiments on unknowing U.S. citizens;

—assassination plots against Fidel Castro, Congo leader Patrice Lumumba, and inactive connections to plots against Trujillo;

—surveillance of dissident groups between 1967 and 1971;

—secret files kept on over 9,900 Americans related to the anti-war movement (the VIETNAM WAR) including Beatles singer John Lennon;

—testing of electronic surveillance equipment on U.S. telephone circuits.

Michael V. Hayden, the CIA director in 2007 (appointed in 2006), decided to release the "family jewels" in response to the 1992 FOIA request as a measure of **good faith** to show critics that the agency embraces openness when and where possible. In a note to agency employees, he referred to the release as part of a "social contract" with the American public "to give those we serve a window into the complexities of intelligence." He also noted that the released papers included "reminders of some things the CIA should not have done" and pointed out the internal reforms and increased oversight that has occurred since Watergate.

The contents of released documents may be reviewed by the general public through the National Security Archive, and/or the National Security Archive Electronic Briefing Book No. 222, edited by Thomas Blanton.

Protestors line street in Jena, LA, September 2007.
AP IMAGES

CIVIL RIGHTS

Personal liberties that belong to an individual owing to his or her status as a citizen or resident of a particular country or community.

The Jena 6

A major civil rights protest march took place in Jena, Louisiana on September 20, 2007. Over 10,000 marchers walked through the town to protest the treatment of six black teenagers known as the Jena 6. The teenagers had been charged for the beating of a white teenager in December 2006. Protesters claimed the prosecutor had acted in a racially discriminatory way because he leveled serious **felony** counts, including attempted murder against five of the young men, while the white teenagers were treated much less severely. Though the protesters returned to their homes following the march, the legal efforts to free one the teenagers, Michael Bell, continued.

Racial tensions between white and black students at Jena High School began to heighten on August 31, 2006. Several black students asked to sit beneath a large tree located on the school's grounds, which was known in the community as traditionally reserved only for white students. A school administrator granted the request and they sat beneath the tree. The next day students arrived at school to find three nooses dangling from the large tree. A few days later the principal called an assembly in coordination with the Jena police department. La Salle Parish District At-

torney, J. Reed Walters, attended and spoke at the assembly. The students believed to be responsible for hanging the nooses were identified, and the principal recommended that they be expelled. However, the local school board, which was represented by Walters, concluded that the noose hangings were a "prank," rather than a **hate crime**. Walters, in his role as prosecutor for the parish, declined to charge any students with a criminal offense. The white students found responsible received only a three days in-school suspension.

The mild punishment received by the white students sparked a series of confrontations between black students and white students and heightened racial tensions in the town of Jena. On December 1, 2006, there was a private party where six black students were refused entrance to a party. An unknown white male and the black students got into a fight, and all were told to leave the party. Once outside, the black students were involved in another fight with a group of whites males who were not students. One white male was charged by police with simple **battery**. The next night there was an altercation between three black students and an older white male at a convenience store. Police charged the black students but not the white male. On December 4, 2006, a fight broke out at Jena High school, where Justin Barker allegedly received several contusions as a result of the altercation, and was sent to the local hospital for treatment. He was released from the hospital within three hours, and was able to attend a school ring ceremony that evening. Six black students—Robert Baily, Mychal Bell, Carwin Jones, Bryant Purivs, Theodoer Shaw, and Jesse Ray Beard—were arrested and charged with aggravated second-degree battery in connection with the school fight involving Barker, and all six students were expelled from the high school. District Attorney Walters elected to charge all six of the African-American students with attempted second-degree murder and conspiracy to commit second-degree murder in connection with the school fight. In June 2007, Mychal Bell was tried was convicted of aggravated battery and conspiracy and remained in jail, pending a September 20 sentencing hearing. The trial judge, **District Court** Judge J.P. Mauffray, threw out the conspiracy charge but upheld the battery conviction. Bell faced a maximum of 22 years in prison.

Local news media covered the events surrounding the Jena 6 but the national press did not become interested until the Bell trial and verdict. At the same time the story of the Jena 6 became a hot topic on the campuses of traditional black colleges and on the Internet. A rally was scheduled in Jena for September 20, the day Bell was to be sentenced. The week before the rally the state Third **Circuit Court** of Appeals overturned Bell's battery conviction but he was not released from jail. The march, which drew worldwide media attention, was peaceful. The line of marchers stretched for miles. At a rally the Rev. Jesse Jackson said "That's not prosecution, that's persecution."

Mychal Bell was released on $45,000 bail on September 27, placed on electronic monitoring, and supervised by a probation officer. On October 11 the judge revoked Bell's probation for a previous conviction and was sentenced to 18 months in a juvenile facility. A retrial was scheduled for December 3 on the original charges but Bell agreed to a plea bargain on December 7, 2007. He pleaded guilty to a reduced charge of battery and was sentenced to 18 months in a juvenile facility, with credit for the time he had served since October. Bell also agreed to testify against any of other members of the Jena 6 who might come to trial. Those members have not come to trial as of May 2008. Their cases are on hold pending a decision of the Third Circuit Court of Appeals as to whether the appeals court should order Judge Mauffray from hearing any of their cases. The defendants alleged that Mauffray has an unfair bias in the case.

CLASS ACTION

A lawsuit that allows a large number of people with a common interest in a matter to sue or be sued as a group.

Stoneridge v. Scientific Atlanta

Section 10(b) of the Securities Exchange Act of 1934, 15 USC § 78j(b) and **correlative** Rule 10b-5 of the SECURITIES AND EXCHANGE COMMISSION (SEC) both prohibit and provide remedies for securities **fraud**, i.e., **fraudulent** or deceptive conduct involving the promotion, sale, or exchange of publicly-traded stocks. The U.S. SUPREME COURT has previously held that Section 10(b) of the Act provides for, by implication, a "private right of action" for violations, in addition to actions brought by state prosecutors or the SEC. *Sup't of Ins. of N.Y. v. Bankers Life & Casualty Co.*, 404 U.S. 6. The Supreme Court has also held, in another previous case, that any private **cause of action** did not extend to conduct which could essentially be characterized as (merely) "aiding and abetting" a § 10(b) or Rule 10(b)-5 violation. *Central Bank of Denver, N.A. v. First Interstate Bank of Denver, N.A.*, 511 U.S. 164.

In *Stoneridge v. Scientific-Atlanta, Inc.* No. 06-43; 552 U.S. ___, ___ S. Ct. ___, ___ L. Ed. 2d ___ (2008), the Supreme Court affirmed a lower court decision, holding that the conduct of Defendant Scientific-Atlanta, Inc. did not rise to the level of a § 10(b)-5 or Rule 10(b)-5 violation, but rather constituted the "aiding and abetting" of such a violation by a co-defendant, Charter Communications, Inc. Therefore, Plaintiff/Petitioner Stoneridge Investment Partners, LLC, (Stoneridge), representing shareholders of Charter Communications, had no private cause of action against Scientific Atlanta. The significance of this case was to clarify that so-called "secondary actors," such as banks, accountants, lawyers, and others that may have peripherally participated in or contributed to a fraud may not be reachable as defendants (in private causes of action) in alleged § 10(b)-5 and Rule 10(b)-5 violations.

Stoneridge had brought a securities fraud action in federal **district court** against Charter Communications, Inc. (Charter), a cable television provider, for allegedly deceptive misstatements in its financial statements, designed to fraudulently inflate the price of its stock. According to the complaint, the alleged scheme involved a "sham transaction" in which Charter fraudulently overpaid its equipment vendor, Scientific-Atlanta, for television cable boxes, and Scientific-Atlanta then returned the excess payment amounts to Charter as "advertising fees." Charter then fraudulently accounted the returned excess payments as incoming revenue, allegedly designed to inflate its revenue by some $17 million. Stoneridge also charged Motorola Inc. with entering into the same sham transactions with Charter.

The federal district court dismissed the complaint for failure to state a claim, finding that the defendants had aided and **abetted** the fraud but had not violated anti-fraud securities laws themselves. The Eighth **Circuit Court** of Appeals affirmed.

In a prior similar case, the Fifth Circuit Court of Appeals ruled against a **class action** suit by former Enron Company shareholders against several investment banks (including Merrill Lynch Inc.) for their alleged role in Enron's misconduct. But the Ninth Circuit Court of Appeals held that under certain circumstances a "secondary actor" could be held liable. An example of such an instance under the Ninth Circuit's ruling is where the alleged conduct had "the principal purpose and effect of creating a false appearance of fact" in support of a scheme to defraud. This conflict between the nation's circuit courts of appeals prompted review by the U.S. Supreme Court.

The Supreme Court, in again affirming the decisions of both district and **appellate** courts, held that there was no private **right of action** under securities laws § 10(b)-5 or Rule 10(b)-5, against secondary defendants (such as Scientific-Atlanta and Motorola) because Charter's investors (Stoneridge) did not rely on any Scientific-Atlanta or Motorola statements or representations. "Detrimental reliance" (where plaintiffs allege that they relied upon fraudulent statements or misrepresentations, to their detriment) is an essential element in any action for fraud. Without such reliance, Scientific-Atlanta and Motorola could not have committed a fraud upon investors, but instead, at most, may have "aided and abetted" such fraud.

The Court also noted that it had already decided in its earlier decision in *Central Bank*, that no cause of action under the cited securities laws/rules existed for aiding and **abetting**. Justice Kennedy, writing for the 5–3 majority, further noted that although the *Central Bank* decision prompted calls for the creation of an express cause of action for aiding and abetting, Congress had failed to do so in the ensuing years.

Instead, in § 104 of the Private Securities Litigation Reform Act of 1995 (PSLRA), Con-

gress directed the SEC to prosecute such secondary actor aiders and abettors.

Stoneridge had argued that, although Scientific-Atlanta and Motorola may not have made public statements upon which the plaintiffs relied, plaintiffs nonetheless did rely upon their deceptive conduct. But the Court rejected the so-called "scheme liability," noting that if the scope of liability were to include not just statements but also the transactions reflected by those statements, an implied cause of action would essentially reach the whole marketplace and all players with which the issuing company did business. There was simply no authority under § 10(b) or Rule 10(b)-5 for such an expanded application.

Justice Stevens, joined by Justices Souter and Ginsberg, dissented, noting that Charter could not have carried out its fraudulent scheme to hide a $15-20 million cash flow shortfall without the knowingly fraudulent actions of Scientific-Atlanta and Motorola. The dissenting justices opined that the "deceptive devices" clause of the subject § 10(b) of the Act would have brought their conduct under the **purview** of the Act's requirements, and yet still distinguish this case from the decision in *Central Bank*.

COMMERCE CLAUSE

The provision of the U.S. Constitution that gives Congress exclusive power over trade activities between the states and with foreign countries and Indian tribes.

Department of Revenue of Kentucky v. Davis

The Constitution's **Commerce Clause** gives the federal government the right to regulate interstate commerce but the Supreme Court has all read into that provision what it has labeled a "dormant" Commerce Clause. The dormant Commerce Clause is the negative of the actual clause—it bars states from passing laws that improperly favor in-state economic interests by burdening out-of-state competitors. The Supreme Court has wrestled with how far this negative implication should be recognized, as it has balanced concerns about state economic protectionism against the system of federalism that gives states great independence. These concerns were again addressed in a case involving the taxation of municipal bonds, *Department of Revenue of Kentucky v. Davis*, __U.S.__, 128 S. Ct. 1801, 170 L. Ed. 2d 685 (2008). The Court ruled that the commonwealth of Kentucky could exempt its residents from paying tax on the interest of municipal bonds issued by the commonwealth and its cities, counties, and other political subdivisions, while taxing them for interest on municipal bonds issued by other states. This long-standing practice was justified in ways that did not implicate the dormant Commerce Clause.

George and Catherine Davis, Kentucky residents, paid state income tax on interest from out-of-state municipal bonds. They sued the state's department of revenue, asking for a refund of the bond interest, claiming that the differential taxation of municipal bonds violated the Commerce Clause, as it discriminated against the issuers and purchasers of out-of-state bonds. A Kentucky trial court rejected the Davis' claim, but the Court of Appeals of Kentucky reversed. The Supreme Court of Kentucky denied review of this decision but the U.S. SUPREME COURT agreed to hear the case because there was a conflict on this issue among the states and because "the result reached casts constitutional doubt on a tax regime adopted by a majority of the states."

The Court, in a 7–2 decision, reversed the Kentucky **appellate court**. Justice DAVID SOUTER, writing for the majority, reviewed the history and Court precedents involving the interpretation of the Commerce Clause, noting several doctrines that have shaped the Court's analysis. As to municipal bonds, he pointed out that the Kentucky taxation scheme was designed so the in-state bonds paid lower rates of interest than out-of-state bonds. The tax exemption for state residents made the lower interest rates acceptable and raised in-state demand for Kentucky bonds without subsidizing other issuers. The amount of money raised by bonds was significant: between 1996 and 2002, Kentucky and its subdivisions issue $7.7 billion in long-term bonds to pay for spending on transportation, public safety, education, utilities, and environmental protection. During that same time period all 50 states issued over $750 billion in long-term bonds, with 41 states employing differential tax taxation laws similar to Kentucky's.

Justice Souter concluded that Kentucky's law did not violate the dormant Commerce Clause because state and local governments have a responsibility to protect the health, safety, and welfare of its citizens. Laws that favor state and local government and which are "directed toward any number of legitimate goals unrelated to protectionism" do not violate the Commerce Clause. The issuance of bonds to pay for public projects "is a quintessentially public function,

with the venerable history" reaching back to the Seventeenth Century. Bonds, much like home mortgages, spread the costs over time. Moreover, a fundamental element of the dormant Commerce Clause states that "any notion of discrimination assumes a comparison of substantially similar entities." In this case the Kentucky tax scheme benefits Kentucky while treating all private issuers exactly the same. There was no forbidden discrimination because "Kentucky, as a public **entity**, does not have to treat itself as being 'substantially similar' to the other bond issuers in the market."

Finally, the effects of ending the preferential tax scheme would be devastating to states and their subdivisions. Many single-state funds that issued bonds would disappear, replaced by national mutual funds, because the loss of the tax preference would make the state fund less financially viable. Single-state markets serving smaller municipal borrowers would suffer, thereby reinforcing the conclusion that the state's objectives did not lie in "forbidden protectionism for local business."

Justice ANTHONY KENNEDY, in a dissenting opinion joined by Justice SAMUEL ALITO, objected to the "explicit, local discrimination" that the majority ratified. Though this decision would not have any great impact on the national economy or national unity, the protectionist trade laws and policies that the Framers sought to bar when writing the Commerce Clause were given new life. Laws with either "the purpose or the effect of discriminating against interstate commerce to protect local trade are void."

COPYRIGHT

An intangible right granted by statute to the author or originator of certain literary or artistic productions, whereby, for a limited period, the exclusive privilege is given to the person to make copies of the same for publication and sale.

United States Loses Copyright Protections to Antigua

The small Caribbean nation of Antigua won its case before the World Trade Organization (WTO) in December 2007, being awarded $21 million in U.S. dollars for what the WTO determined was a violation by the United States of its international trade agreements. This final ruling, which was not subject to appeal, ended a very protracted and convoluted battle between the countries over online gambling. Specifically, the WTO ruled that the United States had wrongfully blocked online casino gambling operators on the island of Antigua from the American market, while allowing online wagering for horse-racing. The dozens of online casinos operating within Antigua's borders constituted the small country's second-largest employing industry and was important to the country's economy. Antigua had asked for $3.44 billion in damages.

As background, the U.S. government, during world trade negotiations in the early 1990s, had agreed not to impose special restrictions on online gambling, but then ostensibly did exactly that. The subject agreement, General Agreement on Trade in Services (GATS), was one of more than 20 trade agreements negotiated among WTO members. In 2003, Antigua filed a complaint for U.S. unfair trade practices, in violation of GATS, with the WTO. The WTO consistently sided with Antigua, starting with the first WTO panel decision in 2004. Its **appellate** body upheld that decision in 2005, and gave the United States one year to comply with the ruling.

The deadline passed without U.S. concession; in fact, a statement from Washington declared that the United States had determined it was in compliance with GATS. It asserted that it had never intended to allow free cross-border gambling or betting, instead restricting those activities within the United States. In 2006, the U.S. government began to enforce other, previous laws against online gambling through the Unlawful Internet Gambling Enforcement Act of 2006. The stated rationale for the Act was the protection of U.S. citizens against the moral vice of gambling. The problem with that argument, according to Antigua's petition, was that U.S. citizens enjoyed full access to online wagering for horse racing. Instead, argued Antigua, the United States was merely attempting to keep online gambling "in-house," for economic gain and in violation of Antigua's rights as a member of WTO.

In March 2007, the adverse ruling was upheld for a second time, and WTO declared the United States as out of compliance with its rules. At that point, to comply with the ruling, the United States needed to either reverse itself and permit Americans to place bets online with offshore casinos, or in the alternative, make all forms of online gambling illegal, including the lucrative online wagering on horse-racing. With the latter, the United States would need to compensate GATS members for the so-called loss of market access.

The GATS allowed members to modify or withdraw commitments, provided they negotiated offsetting compensation (for the loss of market access), i.e., the overall level of GATS market access had to remain the same. In May 2007, two months after the WTO upheld its previous ruling, the United States announced that it was rewriting/withdrawing its trade rules to remove gambling from the jurisdiction of the WTO. In the ensuing months, it successfully renegotiated agreements with other WTO members such as Canada, Australia, Japan, and India. However, Caribbean nations had more difficulty with renegotiations, as the U.S. withdrawal of its GATS commitments represented a more severe impact on their smaller national economies.

In a final attempt to pressure the United States to not withdraw its GATS commitment and open up its market to cross-border gambling services, Antigua initiated another WTO procedure. Article 22 DSU provided for the right to request compensation or the temporary suspension of concessions until the member (in this case, the United States) brought the measure deemed out of compliance into compliance, or the member otherwise complied with the rulings and recommendations. In other words, Antigua asked for the right to retaliate.

On December 17, 2007, the European Union (EU) announced its agreement with the United States on a compensation package offered by the United States pursuant to its withdrawal in WTO of previous GATS commitments on gambling and betting services, including online gambling. Four days later, on December 21, 2007, the WTO issued its final ruling against the United States and in favor of Antigua. In its ruling, it granted to Antigua the requested right, under Art. 22 DSU, to retaliate against the United States (in this case, by violating U.S. intellectual property/copyright protections on goods like music and videos). However, it awarded the right to do so for an amount not exceeding US $21 million, not the $3.44 billion Antigua had claimed in damages. (The United States had argued that its behavior had caused approximately $500,000 in damages).

Following the ruling, the United States trade representative to Antigua issued a stern warning to avoid any acts of piracy, counterfeiting, or other violations of intellectual property rights while talks continued with that country. Otherwise, such behavior would "undermine Antigua's claimed intentions of becoming a leader in legitimate electronic commerce, and would severely discourage foreign investment."

CCIA Report on 'Fair Use'

The Fair Use exception to U.S. copyright law, codified in Section 107 of the U.S. Copyright Act of 1976 (17 USC § 107), refers to certain permitted uses of copyrighted material that will not invoke violations of copyrights, i.e., will not constitute infringements of copyright law. According to that section, "The fair use of a copyrighted work for . . . purposes such as criticism, comment, news reporting, teaching, scholarship, or research is not an infringement of copyright."

According to the U.S. Copyright Office, fair use of copyrighted material, i.e., use not requiring license from the copyright owner, is generally determined by applying four criteria: "the purpose and character of the use, including whether such use is of a commercial nature or is for nonprofit educational purposes; the nature of the copyrighted work; amount and substantiality of the portion used in relation to the copyrighted work as a whole; and the effect of the use upon the potential market for or value of the copyrighted work."

Over the years, numerous court decisions at all **appellate** levels have eked out the meaning and parameters of these exceptions, as applied to fact-specific cases before them. But, as a practical matter, an objective overview of the use of fair use and its effect and benefits upon national and global economies was lacking.

In September 2007, the nonprofit Computer and Communications Industry Association (CCIA) released its commissioned study that quantified, for the first time ever, the contributions that "fair uses" of copyrighted material made to the U.S. economy. Entitled, *Fair Use in the U.S. Economy*, the study was conducted in accordance with World Intellectual Property Organization methodology. According to its findings, four main groups of industries depended upon or greatly benefited from the fair use doctrine (along with other limitations and exceptions to a lesser degree). They were (1) manufacturers of consumer devices that allowed individual copying of copyrighted programming; (2) educational institutions; (3) software developers; and (4) internet search and web hosting providers.

According to the report, fair use exceptions were responsible for more than $4.5 trillion in 2006 annual revenue for the United States (representing a 31 percent increase from 2002). Another statistical finding in the report measured "value added," or a measure equal to a firm's total output minus its purchases of intermediate inputs. This was considered the best measurement of an industry's economic contribution to national GDP (gross domestic product). In this case, the report found that in 2006, fair use-related industry value added was $2.2 trillion, equal to 16.6 percent of total U.S. current dollar GDP. According to CCIA, this made the fair use economy greater in worth than the copyright economy.

The report cited digital technology as the main contributor to the importance of fair use, fair use industries comprising more than 18 percent of U.S. economic growth (one-sixth of the U.S. GDP) and nearly 11 million American jobs. Clearly, the expansion of the Internet as a tool for both commerce and education remained dependent upon the user's ease of ability to locate and access useful information through search engines. This created new businesses, such as Google and Amazon, which in turn fueled demand from other hardware sectors such as the fiber optics, routers, and consumer electronics industries. Notwithstanding, the study indicated that the fair use exception was critical to nontechnology industries as well, such as legal services, insurance, and newspapers.

CCIA president and CEO Ed Black, in an interview for *Information Week*, said, "Much of the unprecedented economic growth of the past 10 years can actually be credited to the doctrine of fair use, as the Internet itself depends on the ability to use content in a limited and non-licensed manner." Google, Microsoft, Yahoo, and the media in general were members of CCIA and clearly benefited from fair use. Without this exception, search engine firms and others would face greater liability for infringement, which would manifest as a significant deterrent to providing those services. It would also thwart educational exchanges of information. Moreover, members of the general public could not download or print copyrighted material from a Web page, email copyrighted material to another person or **entity**, or use a recording device to capture copyrighted audio or video works. They also could not make digital copies of copyrighted media programming to enjoy at a later time (such as Tivo time-lapsed recording), or transfer copyrighted material from one medium to another (for personal use). The manufacture and sale of consumer devices such as digital video recorders, PCs, or MP3 players would all but disappear.

Black stated that CCIA's purpose in releasing its study was to encourage lawmakers to recognize that copyright legislation required a balance of interests. "Copyright was created as a functional tool to promote creativity, innovation, and economic activity," Black went on. "It should be measured by that standard, not by some moral rights or abstract measure of property rights." Black also stated, via CCIA's organizational website, that he believed, in order to stay on the edge of innovation and productivity, fair use needed to be kept as one of the cornerstones for creativity and an engine for growth for the country.

First Person Held Civilly Liable for Illegal Music Downloading

The major U.S. record companies, through its trade group the Recording Industry Association of America (RIAA), have sought to eliminate or drastically reduce the amount of music that is illegally downloaded from the Internet. Attempts to encode their CDs with anti-theft programs proved ineffective and the use of Digital Rights Management (DRM) restrictions on the redistribution of downloadable music formats appeared to be nearing an end when Apple announced in 2007 that it would cease to encode songs with DRM that it sold through its iTunes sales site. Though the technological efforts have proven ineffective, the RIAA has had some success in using copyright law to sue alleged infringers. Since 2003, RIAA has filed 26,000 lawsuits over file sharing of music. The lawsuits have led to settlements with infringers but it was not until 2007 that one of these lawsuits went to trial. A federal jury in Duluth, Minnesota found Jammie Thomas liable for violating the copyrights of six recording companies and awarded those companies $222,000 in damages.

The RIAA and the recording companies employ experts to identify Internet addresses of illegal music uploaders and downloaders. In this case they alleged that Thomas, a 30-year-old single Brainerd, Minnesota mother of two who works for the Mille Lacs Band of Objibwe, copied or distributed 24 songs by placing them on the Kazaa file-sharing network. The companies actually believed she had, under the user name "Terestarr," shared over 1700 songs online, but **chose** to focus on just 24. The RIAA first warned Thomas through a computer instant message and then by sending her a cease-and-desist letter. When she did not agree to comply the RIAA then asked for financial compensation "($4,750) to settle the matter. When she again refused, the RIAA took the case to trial in federal court.

In early October 2007 a jury of six women and six men heard the evidence. Richard Gabriel, lead attorney for the record companies, relied on technical experts to prove Thomas had

illegally shared copyrighted files. An Internet provider testified that the address used by "Terestarr" belonged to Thomas. A computer **forensic** expert testified that he had identified and linked Thomas' IP address and cable modem to pirated music on Kazaa in 2005. However, he conceded on cross-examination that he could not determine if Thomas was the person who had done the sharing. Thomas' lawyer, Brian Toder, contended that she has not shared the music but instead was a victim of an Internet hacker who used her computer without her knowledge. On redirect by Gabriel, however, the expert testified that he had seen no evidence that someone had taken over Thomas' computer and Internet connection.

Another contested piece of evidence was the hard drive in Thomas' computer. She had replaced her hard drive soon after the RIAA told her she was under investigation, which Gabriel suggested to the jury was a way to destroy evidence that proved she had the songs on her computer. This theory was weakened when a Best Buy Geek Squad employee testified that the hard drive was replaced under warranty and that Best Buy would not replace a hard drive unless it was not working properly.

The jury deliberated less than five hours before deciding that Thomas has distributed the songs illegally. The jury awarded the plaintiffs $222,000, which worked out to $9,250 per song. The RIAA and the record companies hailed the verdict as a warning that the financial consequences for illegal file sharing could be steep.

In a surprising development, U.S. District Judge Michael Davis, who had presided at the trial, notified lawyers in the case that he was weighing whether to grant Thomas a new trial. Davis stated that he may have improperly instructed the jury on what constitutes distribution of copyrighted music on the Internet. David had instructed the jury that simply placing songs on a file-sharing network could be considered illegal distribution. No proof was required to show that anyone received the song files. This contradicted an appeals court precedent which stated infringement of the distribution right required that someone received the songs. A hearing was scheduled for July 2008 but both sides were discussing a settlement of the case.

"The Family Guy" Subject to Three Lawsuits Filed in 2007

Producers of the television show, "The Family Guy," became the subject of three separate lawsuits filed in 2007. The show is well-known for its parodies regarding pop culture topics as well as for its satire directed at celebrities. According to the plaintiffs, the parodies and satires went too far and infringed on the plaintiffs' copyrights

The first suit resulted from the show's parody of a distinctive elements that were featured on the "Carol Burnett Show," a popular variety series that aired from 1967 through 1978. Burnett invented a character known as "Charwoman," which was an animated caricature of Burnett herself and which appeared during the show's closing credits. Burnett was also famous for tugging on her ear during each show's final moments in a sign to her grandmother.

In April 2006, the Family Guy aired an episode that featured several male characters entering a porn shop. The Burnett character appears as a maid in the porn shop, and the music that plays sounds similar to the theme song from Burnett's show. "The Family Guy" characters then referred to Burnett's trademark ear tug, with one asking crudely, "I wonder what she tugged to say goodnight to her dad."

Burnett's show was well-known for its own parodies and spoofs. Nevertheless, the 73-year-old actress was less than amused and filed a $2 million suit against 20th Century Fox. She has claimed that the use of her character as well as the music constituted copyright infringement. Moreover, Burnett sought damages for violation of her publicity rights. According to her pleadings, Burnett had previously denied a request for "The Family Guy" to use her theme song because she reserves its use for personal appearances. Because of this denial, she said, the show demeaned her character in an act of revenge.

A spokesperson for 20th Century Fox said that the company was taken aback by the suit. "Family Guy, like The Carol Burnett Show, is famous for its pop culture parodies and satirical jabs at celebrities," said Chris Alexander, a spokesman for the producer. "We are surprised that Ms. Burnett, who has made a career of spoofing others on television, would go so far as to sue Family Guy for a simple bit of comedy."

A parody of the song "When You Wish Upon a Star" gave rise to a second lawsuit that was filed in October 7, 2007. An episode of "The Family Guy" that was initially produced in 2000 was entitled "When You Wish Upon a Weinstein." It focused on the main character's belief that because he could not manage his own money, he needed to hire a Jewish person to do so. During the episode, he sings a song entitled, "I Need a Jew," which became the subject of the lawsuit. Due to the offensive nature of the episode, it did not originally air. However, the show appeared on the Cartoon Network in 2003.

The song entitled, "When You Wish Upon a Star" was first written by Ned Washington and Leigh Harline and appeared in the 1940 motion picture, "Pinocchio." The song won the Academy Award that year for Best Original Song. The song's current copyright owner, Bourne Co., filed suit against several defendants, including companies associated with 20th Century Fox as well as the Cartoon Network. According to Bourne, the song "I Need a Jew" was a "thinly veiled" copy of the "When You Wish Upon a Star", and the parody infringed on the plaintiff's copyright. "With its theme of wholesome hopefulness, the song has gained worldwide status as a classic," the pleadings said of the plaintiff's song. "By associating Bourne's song with such offensive lyrics and other content in the episode, defendants are harming the value of the song."

According to the allegations in the lawsuit, the plaintiff attempted to negotiate a resolution with 20th Century Fox, but these efforts allegedly failed. Bourne sought actual damages and the defendants' profits from the infringement, as well as injunctive relief to prevent the show from airing. The plaintiff filed the suit in the U.S. **District Court** for the Southern District of New York.

The third lawsuit filed against "The Family Guy" in 2007 arose due to a parody or rendition of a comedy skit of comedian Art Metrano. In 1969, Metrano created a character known as "The Amazing Metrano." During his skit, he performed funny, simple tricks using his hands and feet while mimicking the actions of a magician. His act first appeared on the Lohman and Barkley Show in 1969, and he appeared periodically on other programs, including The Tonight Show with Johnny Carson. Metrano claims that this is his trademark routine.

In 2005, Fox produced a motion picture entitled "Stewie Griffin: The Untold Story," which focused on the exploits of the son of the main character in "The Family Guy." During this film, the animated character appears to go back in time to the era of Jesus Christ and shows Christ performing a comedy routine. According to Metrano's pleadings, the routine that was shown was identical to "The Amazing Metrano," including use of the theme song." Fox released a DVD of "Stewie Griffin: The Untold Story" in September 2005.

Metrano brought suit against 20th Century Fox as well as the creators of the "Family Guy," including Seth McFarlane, Steve Callaghan, and Alex Borstein. The suit, filed in the U.S. District Court for the Central District of California, seeks damages in excess of $2 million. In addition to **compensatory damages**, Metrano also seeks **punitive damages** and attorneys fees.

Metrano was known for his roles in several of the "Police Academy" movies, but he suffered a spinal cord injury in 1989 and became disabled. He currently performs in a show entitled "Jews Don't Belong On Ladders. . . . An Accidental Comedy," which raises money for those suffering from spinal cord injuries.

11th Circuit Sides with National Geographic in Copyright Dispute

The Eleventh **Circuit Court** of Appeals on July 2, 2008 sided with *National Geographic* in a case that has been in litigation for more than a decade. The case marked the second time that the Eleventh Circuit has issued a ruling on the dispute, which involves the question of whether *National Geographic* may transfer published archives to computer disks and sell them commercially without violating the copyrights of free lance contributors to the magazine. The court concluded that the magazine was not required to pay additional royalties on material that was reproduced on a computer disk.

Section 201(c) of the Copyright Act of 1976 provides as follows:

> *Contributions to Collective*—Copyright in each separate contribution of a collective work is distinct from copyright in the collective work as a whole, and vests initially in the author of the contribution. In the absence of an express transfer of the copyright or of any rights under it, the owner of the copyright in the collective work is presumed to have acquired only the privilege of reproducing and distributing the contribution as part of that particular collective work, any revision of that collective work, and any later collective work of the same series.

In several cases, issues have arisen about how this section applies when a publisher uses a copyrighted work from a contributor as part of an electronic database. This issue has arisen before the U.S. SUPREME COURT, but the lower **federal courts** have continued to struggle with these issues.

Jerry Greenberg was a freelance photographer who had photographs published in *National Geographic* issues dating January 1962, February 1968, May 1971, and July 1990. Like other contributors, Greenberg retained the copyright of his photographs and received royalties from *National Geographic* for the photos. The magazine as a general business practice reproduced back issues of the magazine in other forms, such as bound volumes, microfiche, and microfilm. In 1997, *National Geographic* created an archive of every monthly issue of the magazine from 1888 through 1996.

This collection was added to 30 CD disks, and the magazine issues appear digitally just as they did when they were originally published. The disk collection features a computer program that compresses and decompresses every image in the database. A user of the system may search photos that are contained in the CD set. Moreover, when a user first inserts a disk, the program displays a sequence of images as an introduction, and one of the images featured was Greenberg's photograph from the January 1962 issue. *National Geographic* registered a copyright for the disk set in 1998, claiming that the work had not been copyrighted before.

Greenberg filed suit in 1997 in the U.S. **District Court** for the Southern District of Florida, arguing that the CD disk set violated his copyrights to his photographs. The case paralleled litigation that was taking place in federal court in New York. In *Tasini v. New York Times Co.*, 972 F. Supp. 804 (S.D.N.Y. 1997), the U.S. District Court for the Southern District of New York concluded that publishers could place the contents of their periodicals onto CD-ROMs without obtaining permission of the writers whose contributions were part of the content of the CD-ROMs. Relying on the reasoning of this decision, the Florida district court held that *National Geographic* had not infringed on Greenberg's copyright.

On appeal in 2001, the Eleventh Circuit reversed the district court's ruling. The court in that case considered different parts of the CD set separately and concluded that while some parts were privileged under section 201(c) of the Copyright Act, other parts were not. More specifically, the court determined that the digital replicas of the photographs and the sequence of photographs were separately copyrighted elements. *Greenberg v. Nat'l Geographic Soc'y*, 244 F.3d 1267 (11th Cir. 2001). The U.S. Supreme Court denied **certiorari** to review the case.

Shortly after the Eleventh Circuit issued its opinion, the Supreme Court reviewed *Tasini*. The Court questioned how the articles in a database were "presented to, and perceptible by, the user of the [d]atabases." The Court's conclusion was that the databases presented the articles in a manner "clear of the context provided either by the original periodical editions or by any revision of those editions." Thus, the Court held that the newspaper that created the database owned the copyright in the database that used individual contributions from other copyright holders. *N.Y. Times Co. v. Tasini*, 533 U.S. 483, 122 S. Ct. 2381, 150 L. Ed. 2d 500 (2001).

Four years after *Tasini*, the Second Circuit Court of Appeals reviewed another challenge to the *National Geographic* CD collection. The Second Circuit rejected the Eleventh Circuit's original opinion because the Second Circuit concluded that *Tasini* effectively abrogated the original decision in *Greenberg*. The Second Circuit thus held in favor of *National Geographic*. *Faulkner v. Nat'l Geographic Enters. Inc.*, 409 F.3d 26, 36 (2d Cir. 2005).

The Eleventh Circuit revisited the dispute in 2007. A three-judge panel concluded that *Tasini* allowed *National Geographic* to reproduce print magazines in digital format under section 201(c). *Greenberg v. Nat'l Geogrpahic Soc'y*, 488 F.3d 1331 (11th Cir. 2007). On August 30, 2007, however, the court vacated the panel's decision and reviewed the case en banc.

The court issued its opinion on July 1, 2008. In a majority opinion by Eleventh Circuit Judge Rosemary Barkett, the court agreed with the Second Circuit's reasoning in *Faulkner* that the Supreme Court's decision in *Tasini* meant that *National Geographic* could reproduce and distribute the photographs in the CD set a "revision of that collective work" under section 201(c).

National Geographic hailed the decision. "These opinions [in the Second and Eleventh Circuits] obviously have been a long time coming and have been considered quite thoroughly, briefed quite thoroughly, and argued quite thoroughly," said Terry Adamson, executive vice president of *National Geographic*. He continued by saying that the prolonged litigation "has been all about preserving 120 years electronically, so it would be preserved for all time," compared with print publication that "will be lost."

Author Sues Jerry and Jessica Seinfeld Over Cookbook

Actor Jerry Seinfeld and his wife, Jessica, became the subject of a lawsuit filed by the author of a cookbook with a theme similar to a book written by Jessica. Claiming that the Seinfelds acted with "arrogance" and "greed," Missy Chase Lapine sued the Seinfelds for copyright and trademark infringement as well as slander.

In her pleadings, Lapine says that she is "certified in the master techniques of healthy cooking and was training in classical cooking techniques by the Institute of Culinary Education." She is the former publisher of a magazine entitled *Eating Well*, and she also worked at *Gourmet* magazine. She has worked with a number of associations as a specialist in nutrition techniques.

In 2002, Lapine began to conduct research to identify methods that would encourage children to eat healthy foods. During this research, she conducted tests and consulted with experts in nutrition, pediatrics, and cooking. She claims that during this time she developed "original methods for combining ingredients, including specially-selected purees of vegetables that children typically resist, such as spinach and cauliflower, with dishes that children typically crave, such as brownies, pizza and pancakes." These ideas formed the basis of her book, which she wrote over the next several years.

In February 2006, Lapine sent a 139-page proposal to HarperCollins Publishers. The proposal included several chapters from the complete manuscript. Four days after she sent the manuscript, though, a representative of HarperCollins sent Lapine a letter indicating that the publisher had decided to reject the proposal. About three months later, Lapine resubmitted her proposal and again included chapters from the book's manuscript. The publisher once again rejected it. The publisher's letter stated that "the children's food segment of the market is a tough one to navigate during a particularly tough time in the cookbook category in general. The influence of the food network and the availability of recipes online have really hurt this area." Accordingly, the publisher said it would pass on the book project.

Lapine then turned to another publisher, Perseus Books Group, which accepted her proposal in June 2006. The parties entered into an agreement in August 2006. In April 2007, the publisher released the book through its imprint, known as Running Press. *The Sneaky Chef: Simple Strategies for Hiding Healthy Foods in Kids' Favorite Meals* became a *New York Times* best seller within three weeks of its publication. Lapine and her agents filed appropriate paperwork with the U.S. Copyright Office and the U.S. PATENT AND TRADEMARK OFFICE.

Lapine actively marketed her book, appearing on such television programs as the "Today Show" and "Fox and Friends." She also appeared on national and local radio programs, as well as national magazines such as *Parenting* and *Women's Day*. She traveled throughout the country on a book tour as well.

About a month after her book was released, Lapine learned that HarperCollins planed to publish a cooking book by Jessica Seinfeld. An eight-page brochure showed similarities between the Seinfeld book and Lapine's book, including similarities in the cover design. Lapine's publisher attempted to halt publication of the Seinfeld book but was unsuccessful. According to HarperCollins, Seinfeld's book was "entirely original," and the publisher refused to make any changes to her book.

Seinfeld's book was published in October 2007 with the title *Deceptively Delicious: Simple Secrets to Getting Your Kids Eating Good Food*. The publisher made a few modifications to the cover of the book, changing the illustration. The subtitle from Seinfeld's book was changed from "Sneaky Secrets to Get Your Kids Eating Good Food" to "Simple Secrets to Get Your Kids Eating Good Food." The subtitle of Lapine's book is "Simple Strategies for Hiding Healthy Foods in Kids' Favorite Meals."

In her complaint, Lapine points out a number of other similarities. Both books, for instance, contain introductions written by doctors that address the problem of obesity among children in the United States. Both of the authors also provide personal anecdotes about their own children's picky eating habits. Neither of the authors is a professional chef, a fact that is pointed out in both books. Many of the recipes in both books are similar as well.

Jessica Seinfeld engaged in a promotional campaign for her book shortly after its release. She appeared on such programs as "The Oprah Winfrey Show" and "Live with Regis and Kelly." However, rumors began to circulate that she had plagiarized her book by using ideas from Lapine's book. In response to these allegations, Jerry Seinfeld referred to Lapine's claims when he appeared on the "David Letterman Show" on October 29, 2007. During the interview with David Letterman, Seinfeld referred to Lapine as a "wacko" and compared her with a woman who had previously stalked Letterman.

Seinfeld repeated his comments in an interview with E! News.

Lapine sued the Seinfelds in the U.S. **District Court** for the Southern District of New York. She has claimed that Seinfeld's book infringed on her copyright and also that the Seinfeld book infringed Lapine's trademark due to similarities in the artwork that appears on the covers of both books. In addition, Lapine sued Jerry Seinfeld for slander for his public statements about Lapine. Legal commentators have suggested that Lapine has a weak case regarding the copyright and trademark cases but that she may have a better chance to prove her slander action. The lawsuit does not specify the damages that Lapine seeks.

Heirs Reclaim Share of 'Superman' Copyright

After years of litigation, the heirs to the original co-creator of the comic hero character 'Superman' were able to regain ownership and control of a share of the copyright associated with the Superman character. In the March 2008 case of *Siegel v. Warner Bros. Entertainment Inc*, No. CV-04-8400-SGL, federal district judge Stephen Larson ruled in favor of the heirs. The decision did not void a copyright agreement executed by co-creator Jerome Siegel in 1938 for $130, but rather, affirmed the validity of a termination of copyright grant that was effected by Siegel's heirs in the latter 1990s. The status of the copyright and the respective parties' interests had been in quasi-litigation for years.

As teenagers at Glenville High School in Cleveland, Jerome Siegel, an aspiring writer, and his friend, Joseph Shuster, created their now-famous character in the 1930s as part of a comic book, "The Superman." Unable to find a publisher interested in their comic book, they embellished the main character into a secret-identity-possessing superhuman newspaper reporter named Clark Kent. Shuster was the budding artist who illustrated Siegel's idea, giving the character a cape, leotard, "S" emblazoned on his chest, and a distinctive curl lock of dark hair on his forehead. Together, the co-creators tried to market their comic strip, and finally in 1938 submitted their work to Detective Comics. In February 1938, Detective Comics sent Siegel a check for $130, along with a written agreement that assigned the rights to "Superman" to the publisher. Both Siegel and Shuster signed and returned the agreement.

A few weeks later, Detective Comics (DC) debuted its first volume of "Action Comics," starring the new character Superman. It was an instant success. Nine years later, in 1947, Siegel and Shuster filed suit in New York's Supreme Court to **rescind** and annul the 1938 agreement as void for lack of mutuality and consideration. They lost. The validity of the agreement was affirmed, but Siegel and Shuster nonetheless settled the claim for $94,000 in return for signing a new stipulation that DC owned all the rights to the character Superman.

In 1969, Siegel and Shuster again filed suit in federal **district court**, seeking a **declaratory judgment** that they were the owners of the renewal rights to the Superman copyright upon expiration of the original term of years. Again, they lost after both district and **appellate** courts concluded that they had assigned both initial copyright term and renewal terms in 1938. However, amid publicity that both men were living in squalor, publisher DC (which later became DC Comics) signed a second agreement with them in 1975, in which they expressly assigned to DC Comics and its affiliates "all right, title and interest in" Superman, "including any and all renewals and extensions of . . . such rights." In return, they were provided with an annual **annuity** of $20,000 to $30,000 for the remainder of their lives.

This probably would have been the end of the matter, but for the fact that shortly thereafter, Congress enacted the Copyright Act of 1976. This Act gave artists and their heirs the ability as well as a window of opportunity to terminate any prior grants of copyrights in their work(s) that were executed prior to January 1, 1978, regardless of the terms contained in those assignments, if certain requirements were met. Those requirements included a provision that the individual seeking to exercise the termination right "must specify the effective date of the termination, and that effective date must fall within a set five-year window which is at least fifty six (56) years, but no more than sixty-one (61) years, from the date the copyright . . . was originally secured, and such termination notice must be served two to ten years before its effective date." This meant that Siegel could exercise his right to terminate prior copyright grants any time during a five-year window starting in 1994 (1938 + 56). Of course, his interest in the copyright was limited to 50 percent (shared with co-creator Shuster's 50 percent interest, also assigned to DC).

Siegel died in 1996. In 1997, his heirs, including his spouse and a daughter, served copyright termination notices upon DC Comics and several other parties that had profited from the Superman character, such as Warner Bros. and Time-Warner, Warner Communications. It was the validity of those termination notices that was affirmed in the 2008 case.

Still, there were complex issues. Section 304 of the Copyright Act, governing terminations of copyright transfers, did not affect derivative works created during the period of the copyright grant. Clearly, during the years from 1938 through the 1990s, many derivative works were created, including the 1950s television series, the Christopher Reeves movies, and the majority of comic and cartoon programs. The court's ruling left intact these derivative rights, meaning, no monies were owed to the heirs for these works created during the grant period. The majority of these works were protected by separate copyrights retained by Time Warner until they expired. These, as well as the Superman character, were projected to enter the **public domain** on/around 2033.

Viacom v. YouTube

In an important case testing the parameters of online privacy and discovery, Viacom Inc. filed suit in federal district court against Internet giants YouTube and Google for copyright infringement involving some 160,000 "unauthorized" clips of Viacom programming made available on YouTube. According to the suit, these clips were viewed 1.5 billion times by visitors to YouTube. The complaint was filed in March 2007 in the U.S. District Court for the Southern District of New York. *Viacom International Inc. v. YouTube*, No. 07 Civ. 3582. Joining Viacom as Plaintiffs in the action were the Football Association Premier League Limited "and all other others similarly situated." The named Defendants were YouTube Inc., YouTube LLC, and Google Inc. The search engine giant Google was YouTube's parent company.

The crux of the case involved Viacom's claim of ownership of copyrights in specified television programs, motion pictures, music recordings, and other entertainment programs. YouTube originally established its name in the industry as a free service and video-sharing website for home videos or "amateur" works seeking visibility on the Internet. Virtually anyone could post a short video "clip" at the site, which had an international audience. Viewers logging onto the site could then access these clips, free of charge, by entering key terms in a search request, the result of which would be an inventoried list of video clips matching the search request. Viewers could then "click on" a selected video and view it as many times as desired, and as many video clips as desired. YouTube then publicly "performed" the chosen video by sending streaming video content directly from YouTube's servers to the user's computer, while simultaneously downloading a copy of the chosen video from the YouTube website to the user's computer where it could be viewed at will.

In the lawsuit, Viacom alleged that:

> Defendants encourage individuals to upload videos to the YouTube site, where YouTube makes them available for immediate viewing by members of the public free of charge. Although YouTube touts itself as a service for sharing home videos, the well-known reality of YouTube's business is far different. YouTube has filled its library with entire episodes and movies and significant segments of popular copyrighted programming from Plaintiffs and other copyright owners, that neither YouTube nor the users who submit the works are licensed to use in this manner. Because YouTube users contribute pirated copyrighted works to YouTube by the thousands, including those owned by Plaintiffs, the videos "deliver[ed]" by YouTube include a vast unauthorized collection of Plaintiff's copyrighted audiovisual works. YouTube's use of this content directly competes with uses that Plaintiffs have authorized and for which Plaintiffs receive valuable compensation.

The lawsuit went on to discredit YouTube's claim that it was merely "providing storage space, conduits, and other facilities to users who create their own websites with infringing materials." To the contrary, Viacom argued, "YouTube itself commits the infringing duplication, distribution, public performance, and public display of Plaintiff's copyrighted works, and that infringement occurs on YouTube's own website, which is operated and controlled by Defendants, not users."

The lawsuit sought $1 billion in damages (for lost royalty compensation and value) and injunctive relief. Viacom had previously requested that 100,000 videos be taken down in February 2007, as detailed in the Digital Millennial Copyright Act of 1998 (DMCA), 17 USC § 501 *et seq.* and YouTube complied.

By way of defense, YouTube and Google argued that they were protected under § 512(c)-(d) and (i)-(j) of the DMCA, which, among other things, limited the terms of injunctions and barred copyright-damage awards against online service providers who met certain criteria. Those criteria included that the provider (1) performed a qualified storage or search function for online users; (2) lacked actual or imputed knowledge of infringing activity; (3) received no financial benefit directly from such activity; (4) acted promptly to remove or disable access to infringing activity; (5) adopted and publicized a policy of terminating repeat offenders; and (6) accommodated and avoided interference with standard measures employed by copyright owners to identify or protect their works.

In July 2008, an important 25-page Order was issued by the court in the case. It concerned Plaintiff's motion to compel discovery of certain electronically stored information and documents, including a critical trade secret: the computer source code that controlled both YouTube's search function and Google's internet search tool, "Google.com." Both YouTube and Google cross-moved for a protective order, claiming that disclosure of the search code would irreparably harm their business, in that the search code was responsible for Google's growth from its founding to its present international status "with more than 16,000 employees and a market valuation of roughly $150 billion."

On July 1, 2008, the district court partially granted Viacom's discovery motion, ordering Google to produce the contents of YouTube's logging database, which was all data concerning each time a YouTube video was viewed on the YouTube website or through embedding a a third-party website. The Logging Database apparently recorded "for each instance a video is watched, the unique 'login ID' of the user who watched it, the time when the user started to watch the video, the internet protocol address, other devices connected to the internet and used to identify the user's computer ('IP address') and the identifier for the video."

The court rejected Google's argument that disclosure of this information would violate users' privacy, and cited Google's own "Public Policy Blog," which stated that IP addresses could not be used to identify individual users without more information. The court also rejected YouTube's argument that the information was protected by the 1988 Video Privacy Protection Act, 18 USC §2710. But the ruling stated that the Electronic Communications Privacy Act, 18 USC § 2510 *et seq.*, did prevent YouTube from disclosing any video that users had labeled as "private." The court protected these videos by limiting compelled disclosure to non-content information, such as the usage history.

The court denied Viacom's request for Google's trade secret, its search source code, accepting Google's argument that it would be devastating to its business. It likewise denied discovery of the source code for YouTube's new "Video ID' program, with which copyright owners may search the site for infringing materials by providing a sample clip of the copyrighted material for reference. Notwithstanding the denial of these requests, the court did allow that Viacom may have access to them if it could make a "plausible showing" to demonstrate that the search code was intentionally designed to facilitate the viewing of infringing content.

The effect of the ruling on the future of online privacy was unclear, as final adjudication of the case on the merits was still pending.

CORRUPTION

The Rise and Fall of Bernie Kerik

In November 2007, federal prosecutors unsealed an indictment against former New York City police commissioner Bernard B. "Bernie" Kerik, charging him with 16 counts of corruption, **mail fraud**, tax **fraud**, obstruction of justice, and lying to the government. The charges against Kerik carried a maximum sentence of 142 years and more than $5 million in fines.

Bernie Kerik became a household name as a onetime close aide to Republican presidential candidate Rudolph W. Giuliani; both men became national heroes for their leadership during the September 11, 2001 terrorist attack on New York City, when Kerik was serving as police commissioner under then-Mayor Giuliani. Kerik was also nominated to head the U.S. Department of Homeland Security under President GEORGE W. BUSH. In 2003, Kerik was appointed by the Pentagon to serve as interim minister of the interior in Iraq, under the Coalition Provisional Authority set up by the U.S. Department of Defense to run Iraq after the fall of Saddam Hussein.

The 30-page indictment charged, among other things, that within months of Kerik's appointment by Giuliani as New York City's prisons commissioner, he was already accepting payments from a New Jersey company eager to earn lucrative contracts with the city. The company, not identified in the indictment, allegedly

provided $250,000 in marble bathrooms, a whirlpool tub, and a grand marble rotunda in Kerik's Bronx apartment. That same company was under investigation for ties to organized crime at the time. In exchange, Kerik set up meetings with city officials as recently as 2005 to vouch for the company's reputation and help it get city contracts. The indictment further alleged that both Kerik and the company concealed their relationship.

The indictment charged Kerik with "selling his office" for hundreds of thousands of dollars when he was prisons commissioner and police commissioner, then lying to cover up the schemes. Eight unnamed and un-indicted co-conspirators were alluded to in the charges, including the owners of the contracting company, an Israeli industrialist, and a Brooklyn businessman whose loan was repaid in 2005. Investigators later obtained e-mails and recorded hundreds of hours of phone calls to which Kerik was a party, among other things, capturing his complaints about feeling like he was living on "welfare" compared with the contractors who were pushing money to him.

Significantly, the indictment further charged that over a six-year period, Kerik failed to report $500,000 in income to the INTERNAL REVENUE SERVICE, and falsely claimed several thousands of dollars in tax deductions. He was charged with coaxing witnesses to lie to investigators about payments he received and with providing false information to a state **grand jury** that was investigating similar charges.

Kerik's initial fall from grace occurred after President Bush nominated him to succeed Tom Ridge as Secretary of Homeland Security. During the vetting process, Kerik insisted that while completing documents required for Senate confirmation, he discovered that he had not paid required employer taxes for his nanny. Upon then discovering that the nanny, an illegal alien, was using a friend's social security number, he notified the White House that he needed to withdraw from consideration. Although President Bush expressed great disappointment to media reporters the following day, an avalanche of damaging tabloid and mainstream stories flooded the news media. Most linked Kerik to organized crime or accused him of misusing an apartment at Ground Zero (the site of the 2001 New York attack). Kerik insisted that the media had distorted his past, and told ABC News that he did not regret being nominated, in fact, it "was the greatest honor of [his] lifetime."

Even as late as May 2008, more criticism or negative media coverage followed Kerik. In May, Lt. General Ricardo Sanchez, the top U.S. military leader in Iraq from June 2003 to June 2004, referred to Kerik's role and work there as "a waste of time and effort." Kerik was ostensibly responsible for training Iraqi police while there, but Sanchez told the New York *Daily News* that Kerik spent more time on "conducting raids and liberating prostitutes." Sanchez also told reporters that when Kerik left Iraq, Sanchez checked the Interior Ministry's inventory and was "shocked" to discover that the only thing on the books were 50,000 Glock pistols.

Born to an alcoholic prostitute, Kerik dropped out of high school but rose above his peers as a decorated New York policeman and later police commissioner under his mentor, Guiliani. After both of them led the city through the September 11, 2001 crisis, he and Guiliani retired to form a prestigious consulting firm together.

Kerik, 52, pleaded not guilty at his court arraignment and vowed to fight the charges. He was released on a $500,000 bond after surrendering his passport and personal firearms. In January 2008, the **district court** disqualified Kerik's longtime personal attorney, Kenneth Breen, citing conflict of interest because Breen might be called as an adverse witness in the trial against Kerik. Meanwhile, in June 2008, two brothers were charged with perjury for providing Kerik free apartment renovations in return for favorable treatment/approval before local governmental regulatory authorities, and then lying about the transactions. The renovations were at the heart of the federal case against Kerik. In 2006, Kerik pleaded guilty to state **misdemeanor** charges for accepting those renovations between 1998 and 2000 (when he was the city's corrections commissioner), and for failing to report a $28,000 loan to him.

COURT

A legislative assembly; a deliberative body, such as the General Court of Massachusetts, which is its legislature. An entity in the government to which the administration of justice is delegated.

California Supreme Court is Nation's Most Influential, According to Report

A report published in the University of California, Davis Law Review in December 2007 concluded that the California Supreme Court is the nation's most influential court. The report

Bernie Kerik speaks to reporters, December 2004.

AP IMAGES

provides statistical analysis showing that the authors' claim is backed up by numbers that weigh heavily in favor of California's highest court. Critics, though, question the legitimacy of the report due to the positions of its authors.

Legal scholars for several years have engaged in a study known as "citation analysis." This type of study involves the review of the number of times that authorities have cited to one another in an effort to determine how influential various sources are. The first author to publish reports of citation analysis was John H. Merryman, a longtime professor at Stanford Law School. He published a report entitled "The Authority of Authority" in *Stanford Law Review* in 1954, and since that time, dozens of other authors have published their own reports utilizing citation counts. Many studies focus on judicial cases, while others focus on academic articles. The principle behind citation analysis is that the more times that authorities have cited an article or case, the more persuasive that article or case is likely to be.

The primary tool used for citation analysis is *Shepard's Citation Service*, which has been a tool used by lawyers for more than a century. It is available in print and electronic form. This tool analyzes every published decision filed by the **appellate** courts of every state and the federal system. Editors of *Shepard's* analyze an authority's treatment, such as whether a case has been "overruled," "criticized," "questioned," "distinguished," or "followed." According to this source, a case has been "followed" when "[t]he citing opinion relies on the case ... as controlling or persuasive authority."

In 2006, the California SUPREME COURT HISTORICAL SOCIETY held a panel program entitled "California—Laboratory of Legal Innovation." In preparation for this program, two lawyers who work with the California court system decided to conduct a study to determine how the legal community could assess or measure the level of a state court's innovation. This led these attorneys to engage in citation analysis of all fifty states. The authors of the study included Jake Dear, Chief Supervising Attorney for the California Supreme Court, and Edward W. Jessen, Reporter of Decisions for California.

Dear and Jessen concluded that their efforts should focus on how many times state court decisions "followed" decisions of the courts of other states. According to these authors, "Our court's library contacted LexisNexis, the current provider of *Shepard's Citation Service*, and asked if LexisNexis might be willing to undertake a novel and somewhat extensive research assignment: (1) identify all opinions since 1940, for each of the fifty state high courts that *Shepard's* has designated as having been followed in a published opinion by a state court outside the originating jurisdiction; (2) note the number of times each case has been followed; and (3) provide the raw data for our analysis."

LexisNexis complied with the authors' request, providing information about nearly 24,400 state high court decisions that were followed at least one time by out-of-state courts. The results showed that with 1,260 such instances, California easily had the highest number of cases that were followed by at least once other state high court. The next two highest courts were Washington (942) and Colorado (848). The three least followed courts were Kentucky (177), Louisiana (242), and South Carolina (261). A somewhat surprising aspect of the study was that several larger states did not rank especially high on the list. For example, Florida (21st, with 508 citations) and Texas (23rd, with 463 citations) ranked far below such smaller states as Kansas (6th), Maine (7th), and Montana (16th).

The report also provided data about the number of times that the states' high court decisions have been cited at least three times as well as the decisions that have been cited five or more times. According to the data, California cases were cited three or more times in 160 instances, dwarfing the number of cases from Washington that were cited three or more times (72). During the period of 1986 to 2005, however, the Washington cases closed the gap in this category. California still leads the nation with 61 such cases, while Washington had 50.

The fact that two employees of the California courts system wrote this report led to criticism of the report's results. Wrote one such critic, "Not to be petty about it, but a report by the chief supervising attorney of the Supreme Court of California and the reporter of decisions of California that concludes—voila!—that California is the most 'followed' jurisdiction in the nation is presumptively suspect." Other critics of citation analysis in general have noted that the practice often relies on the classification given by the attorneys who provide the analysis for *Shepard's*, stressing that such analysis is an inexact science.

Some judges noted, though, that California has taken the lead in several areas of the law, such as personal injury. The most followed decision of those included in the study was *Dillon v. Legg*, 441 P.2d 912 (Cal. 1968), which allowed a woman to recover for the emotional distress caused when she witnessed her own child's death.

CRIMINAL CONSPIRACY

An agreement between two or more persons to engage jointly in an unlawful or criminal act, or an act that is innocent in itself but becomes unlawful when done by the combination of actors.

NFL Star Michael Vick Sentenced to 23 Months on Dogfighting Charges

Atlanta Falcons quarterback Michael Vick was sentenced to 23 months in prison by a federal judge in 2007 after Vick pleaded guilty to charges that he ran a dogfighting operation in southeastern Virginia. The case shocked the nation as one of the most exciting athletes in the world went to prison during the prime of his career. Advocates for animal rights have condemned Vick's actions, which may have cost him his career.

Vick emerged as one of the most talented football players in the nation when he debuted as a freshman quarterback at Virginia Tech University in 1999. During that season, he led the team to an undefeated record and a berth in the national championship game against Florida State. He also led the Hokies to a bowl appearance in his second season in 2000 before deciding to turn pro in 2001. The Atlanta Falcons selected Vick with the first overall selection that year, as he became the first African-American quarterback to be selected with the first overall pick in the NFL draft.

Vick became a Pro Bowl quarterback in the NFL and had a number of endorsement deals, including a lucrative agreement with Nike. Three years into his career, he signed a 10-year, $130 million with the Falcons, which was the most lucrative contract ever signed by an NFL player. The contract included a $37 million signing bonus. Other NFL stars, including Payton Manning and Donovan McNabb, both subsequently agreed to contracts for less money than the deal Vick reached with Atlanta.

In April 2007, about three months after Vick appeared in the NFL Pro Bowl, police in Surry, Virginia served a warrant to search Vick's property one day after Vick's cousin, Davon Boddie, was arrested on drug charges. During their search, police officers found 66 dogs, including 55 pit bulls, in what appeared to be a dog-training facility behind the house. The officers also found blood stains on the walls of a room as well as a bloodstained carpet on the property. Officials conducted further searches in the two months that followed the original discovery.

After the original discovery by the officers, Vick denied that he was aware of any dogfighting activities on the property. However, on July 17, 2007, Vick and three other men were indicted by a federal **grand jury** on dog fighting charges. The indictment stated that Vick purchased the house in Surry in 2001 so that he and co-defendants Quanis Phillips and Tony Taylor could start a dogfighting operation. Vick originally paid $34,000 for the property and "used this property as the main staging area for housing and training the pit bulls involved in the dogfighting venture and hosting dog fights."

Vick, Phillips, Taylor, and a fourth defendant, Purnell Peace, named their enterprise "Bad Newz Kennels." They ran the operation from the Surry house, constructing a fence to block the real portion of the property from public view. The property had multiple sheds that were used to house injured dogs and hold training equipment. When Vick suffered a broken leg in 2003, he took a more active role in the operation. According to the indictment, Vick consulted with Peace in 2003 before Peace killed a dog by electrocution after the dog had lost one of the fights. The operation continued in 2007, when Vick, Peace, and Phillips executed eight dogs through such means as hanging, drowning, and "slamming at least one dog's body to the ground."

Because the indictment included allegations that Vick and other defendants transported dogs over state lines for dogfighting, the defendants

Dog kennels at convicted football player Michael Vick's Virginia home.
AP IMAGES

were charged in federal court. Vick was initially scheduled for arraignment on July 26 in Richmond on the same day that the Falcons were scheduled to open their training camp. NFL Commissioner Roger Goodell instructed Vick not to attend training camp, while Falcons' owner Arthur Blank decried Vick's behavior as "horrific." Within days of the indictment, Nike suspended Vick's latest line of shoes. Vick also lost endorsements from other companies, including Reebok, Upper Deck, Rawlings Sporting Goods and AirTran Airways. Protestors from PEOPLE FOR THE ETHICAL TREATMENT OF ANIMALS (PETA) picketed outside of the NFL's headquarters in New York City, asking the league to "Sack Vick."

Vick originally pleaded not guilty on July 26. However, Vick's co-defendants each pleaded guilty to the dogfighting charges and agreed to testify against Vick. On August 23, Vick signed a plea agreement and admitted in a statement of facts that he had participated in the dogfighting conspiracy and helped kill pit bulls. Though he admitted to bankrolling the operation, he denied betting on the dog fights.

Although commentators expected Vick to receive a sentence of between 12 and 18 months, news for the beleaguered quarterback became worse when co-defendants Phillips and Peace received sentences of 21 and 18 months, respectively. On December 10, 2007, Vick received his sentence of 23 months in prison. Federal law requires that a convict must serve at least 85 percent of a sentence, meaning that the earliest the Vick could be released would be May 2009. The more likely date of release would be July 2009, according to reports.

However, Vick faces still more legal problems. State prosecutors in Virginia have proceeded with a case alleging two state **felony** counts of beating or killing or causing dogs to fight other dogs or engaging in or promoting dogfighting. Vick could face up to five years in prison for each count. Vick's trial on state charges, which had been scheduled to start on June 27, was postponed on June 10. The state prosecutor said that the trial will not place until Vick is discharged from federal prison because the expense of transporting him to and from the prison would be too expensive.

In the meantime, Vick has been fighting with the Atlanta Falcons over his bonus money. The team tried to require Vick to return about $20 million bonuses that the team paid to him under the 2004 contract. A federal judge in February ruled that Vick could keep $16.5 million of the bonus money. The NFL said it would ask a federal court to vacate the judge's ruling.

CRIMINAL LAW

A body of rules and statutes that defines conduct prohibited by the government because it threatens and harms public safety and welfare and that establishes punishment to be imposed for the commission of such acts.

U.S. v. Kreisel

Law enforcement gained a powerful tool with the introduction of DNA testing. Because DNA has proved to be very effective in criminal prosecutions, Congress has enacted laws that require persons convicted of federal criminal offenses to provide a DNA sample that will go into a federal criminal database. By doing so, law enforcement will be able to match more easily DNA from offenders who go on to commit new crimes. The first federal law was enacted in 2000 and applied only to federal offenders who committed violent offenses. However, in 2004 Congress broadened the law to include all federal offenders. Offenders lost constitutional challenges to the 2000 act in **federal courts** but the 2004 law led to another round of challenges. The federal circuit courts of appeals have addressed these challenges and the Ninth Circuit, in *U.S. v. Kreisel*, 508 F.3d 941 (2007), followed the lead of other circuits in rejecting the challenge of a felon that the law violated his FOURTH AMENDMENT rights.

In March 1999, Thomas Kreisel, Jr. pleaded guilty to a federal drug charge involving the distribution of methamphetamine. He was sentenced to 30 months in prison and three years of supervised release. After Kreisel was placed on supervised release, his probation officer scheduled him for DNA testing. Kreisel objected in principle to the government's collection and permanent storage of his DNA. The probation department petitioned the **district court** to revoke Kreisel's supervised release because he failed to report for DNA testing. Under the DNA Backlog Elimination Act's 2004 amendments (42 U.S.C. § 4135a(d)), the conviction for conspiracy to distribute methamphetamine was a "qualifying Federal offense." At the revocation hearing, Kreisel's lawyer contended that the regulation promulgated by the Attorney General to govern the collection of DNA was procedurally defective and that the DNA act itself violated the Fourth Amendment's prohibition on unreasonable searches and seizures. The district court rejected both arguments and upheld the validity of the regulation and the law.

A three-judge panel of the Ninth Circuit voted 2–1 to uphold the district court ruling. Judge M. Margaret McKeown, writing for the majority, noted that the Ninth Circuit had, in 2004, upheld the original DNA act which covered only felons who had committee violent offenses. The 2004 amendment made anyone convicted of a federal **felony** subject to DNA collection. The Attorney General promulgated a regulation to carry out this new mandate, which requires that probation officers collect DNA samples from felons on probation, parole, or supervised release. The samples are furnished to the FEDERAL BUREAU OF INVESTIGATION (FBI), which analyzes the DNA and includes the results in CODIS (Combined DNA Index System), a centrally-managed database linking DNA profiles gathered from federal, state and territorial DNA collection programs. Both the 2000 and 2004 laws included privacy protection standards, making the unauthorized collection, use or disclosure of a DNA sample a crime. A person convicted of violating these standards is subject to a $25,000 fine and one year in prison.

Judge McKeown first considered whether the Attorney General had properly managed the way the regulation was implemented. Under federal administrative procedure law, a proposed regulation is published to give notice to the public and a comment period follows where objections can be made to the proposal. Kreisel argued that the Attorney General had failed to follow this process. McKeown pointed out that the notice and comment process applies to substantive or legislative rules but not to "interpretive rules." The 2004 regulation was a "classic interpretive rule: it is a rule 'issued by an agency to advise the public of the agency's construction of the statutes and rules which it administers.'" The 2004 amendment dictated the basis for the revision of the regulation, which mirrored the **statute** by designating "any felony" as a qualifying offense.

As to Kreisel's Fourth Amendment challenge, Judge McKeown noted that every **circuit court** of appeals that had considered the 2004 act had found it constitutional. The majority of the circuits used a "totality of the circumstances" test to review the constitutionality of the provision. This test pitted the degree to which the law intruded upon an individual's privacy against the degree to which the law is needed to promote legitimate governmental interests. Kreisel's privacy interest was severely diminished because he was a convicted felon on supervised release. The collection of the blood sample implicated his interest in bodily integrity but the court concluded it was no more intrusive than fingerprinting. In contrast, the government's interest in collecting DNA data from convicted felons was substantial. The data established a means of making releases comply with the conditions of their release, it acted as a deterrent to future crimes, and it helped solve past crimes. Therefore, the balance tipped in favor of the government's interest.

Judge Betty Fletcher dissented, arguing that the law was unconstitutional. In her view the law was too broad, as it mandated testing of felons regardless of their offense or their likelihood to re-offend. She pointed out that the Ninth Circuit decision upholding the 2000 act contained language that cautioned the ruling was of a "limited nature." Judge Fletcher believed that the "expediency" infected the majority's analysis. There seemed to be "no limiting principle beyond what the government says it needs."

Watson v. United States

Criminals who use firearms during the commission of their crimes are subjected to enhanced criminal penalties for doing so. Laws that reflect this policy seemingly are directed at a criminal who brandishes a firearm at a victim or who carries a weapon during a criminal transaction, such as a drug deal. However, the courts have been confronted with arguments from prosecutors who contend that such a law is applicable to a person who trades his firearm for drugs; he has "used" the firearm in the commission of the crime. This argument has proven successful,

leading prosecutors to seek enhanced sentencing penalties for a person who is given a firearm in exchange for illegal drugs. The U.S. SUPREME COURT, in *Watson v. United States*, __U.S.__, 128 S. Ct. 579, 169 L. Ed. 2d 472 (2007), rejected this argument, finding that the federal **statute** could not be stretched in such a way as to go beyond the ordinary meaning of the word "used."

Michael Watson told a government informant that he wanted to acquire a gun. The informant suggested that he would barter a gun in return for narcotics. Watson agreed and met the informant and an undercover law enforcement officer posing as a firearms dealer. Watson gave the informant 24 doses of the narcotic OxyContin and received a .50 caliber semiautomatic pistol. When officers later arrested Watson, they found the pistol in his car. He told officers he needed the firearm to protect his drugs and other firearms he kept at his house. Watson was charged distributing a Schedule II controlled substance and for "using" the pistol during and in relation to that crime in violation of 18 U.S.C § 924(c)(1)(A). This law sets a mandatory minimum sentence for a defendant who, "during and in relation to any crime of violence or drug trafficking crime . . . uses or carries a firearm." Watson pleaded guilty to all charges but reserved the right to appeal the gun charge. His sentence was enhanced by 5 years for using the gun. The Fifth **Circuit Court** of Appeals upheld the validity of the sentence, ruling that he had "used" the firearm but other circuits have taken the opposite view. Therefore, the Supreme Court accepted Watson's appeal to resolve the conflict in the circuits.

The Supreme Court, in a unanimous decision, overruled the Fifth Circuit's decision and its reading of the term "used" in § 924(c)(1)(A). Justice DAVID SOUTER, writing for the Court, noted that in a 1993 decision the Court had held that a criminal who traded his firearm for drugs "used" it within the meaning of the statute. In that case the Court relied on the "ordinary or natural meaning" of the verb "uses" in context. It was "both reasonable and normal" to say the person "used" his firearm by trading it for cocaine. However, Justice Souter pointed out a 1995 decision in which the Court held that merely possessing a firearm kept near the scene of drug trafficking did not amount to "use." There must be evidence sufficient to show an "active employment" of the firearm by the defendant.

Turning to Watson's case, Justice Souter found that the government's argument lacked authority in "either precedent or regular English."

As to precedent, the 1993 and 1995 decisions were not precedential. The 1993 case addressed the trader who swaps guns for drug, not the trading partner who ends up with the gun. The 1995 decision was of no value because it required that a gun be used actively as an "operative factor" to the drug offense. The question at issue before the Court was whether "it makes sense to say that Watson employed the gun at all." The 1995 decision did not answer that question.

Therefore, the case had to turn on the meaning of the language and the verb "uses" as "we normally speak it." With no **statutory** definition of the word, the Court was required to look for the "everyday meaning" of words, revealed in "phraseology that strikes the ear as 'both reasonable and normal.'" Viewed this way, the government did not, in Souter's view, have much of a case. In this case the informant or undercover agent "used" the pistol to get drugs, but "regular speech would not say that Watson himself used the pistol in the trade." The government had argued that such a conclusion would create "unacceptable asymmetry" with the 1993 decision, penalizing one side of a drugs-for-guns transaction but not the other. Justice Souter was unconvinced, noting that Congress has 14 year to resolve this asymmetry but had failed to do so. This long period of "congressional acquiescence" enhanced Souter's reading of the statute. Finally, if there was a tension between the 1993 case and Watson's, "respect for the language" would be furthered by amending the law rather than by "racking statutory language to cover a policy it fails to reach." Justice RUTH BADER GINSBURG filed a concurring opinion, agreeing with the result but finding the 1993 decision wrong. She concluded the Court should have overruled it.

CRIMINAL PROCEDURE

The framework of laws and rules that govern the administration of justice in cases involving an individual who has been accused of a crime, beginning with the initial investigation of the crime and concluding either with the unconditional release of the accused by virture of acquittal (a judgment of not guilty) or by the imposition of a term of punishment pursuant to a conviction for the crime.

Release of Department of Justice Interrogation Tactics Memos

What was previously considered legal during U.S. interrogations of foreign detainees held outside the United States was a fairly static understanding, at least until the terrorist attacks on the United States on September 11, 2001. In prior wars and battles, the United States had faced a palpable enemy, usually in the form of another country. Treatment of prisoners of war and detainees from countries at war with the United States was outlined in various international treaties and agreements, notably, the Geneva Convention mandates.

But after September 11, 2001, the United States was forced to face the reality of rogue nations or persons claiming to represent legitimate nations, and/or groups of international enemies united only by a common goal to destroy the United States. With such virtually faceless and nameless enemies, U.S. military and security officials sought new ways to identify and locate them before they could strike again.

Against this backdrop, a series of domestic "battles" among members of the Bush Administration, Congress, military officials, the U.S. Department of Justice (DOJ), the Central Intelligence Agency (CIA), and the American public tugged and pulled at competing interests in attempting to establish the boundaries of what was considered acceptable conduct by those who interrogated suspect or enemy detainees held outside the United States.

In April 2008, yet another major and controversial memorandum on the subject, written in 2003, was finally declassified and made available to the public. This was pursuant to an ongoing lawsuit filed by the American Civil Liberties Union (ACLU) against the U.S. Department of Defense (DOD) for release of documents under the Freedom of Information Act (FOIA), 5 USC 552. In the March 2003 memorandum, made public for the first time in 2008, the DOJ advised the DOD that military interrogators were free to employ a wide array of interrogation methods when questioning foreign detainees held outside the United States, without fear of criminal liability or constitutional violation.

The 81-page document, later rescinded by the chief at DOJ's Office of Legal Counsel (OLC), was authored by former deputy assistant attorney general and then-deputy at the OLC, John Yoo. The memo was in response to a request for guidance from William J. Haynes II, at that time serving as the Pentagon's general counsel. Haynes had asked the DOJ "to examine the legal standards governing military interrogation of alien unlawful combatants held outside the United States." Specifically, it was intended to give legal guidance to DOD lawyers wrestling with a list of interrogation methods for prisoners at the military prison at Guantanamo Bay in Cuba.

In substance, the memo paralleled earlier guidance provided to the CIA in 2002. It stated, in relevant part,

> [W]e conclude that the Fifth and Eighth Amendments, as interpreted by the Supreme Court, do not extend to alien enemy combatants held abroad . . . [S]everal canons of instruction apply here. Those canons of construction indicated that federal criminal laws of general applicability do not apply to properly-authorized interrogations of enemy combatants, undertaken by military personnel in the course of an armed conflict. Such criminal statutes, if they were misconstrued to apply to the interrogation of enemy combatants, would conflict with the Constitution's grant of the Commander in Chief power solely to the President. . . .

> [W]e examine the international law applicable to the conduct of interrogations . . . [and] conclude that . . . the United States' obligation extends only to conduct that is "cruel and unusual" within the meaning of the Eighth Amendment or otherwise "shocks the conscience" under the Due Process Clauses of the Fifth and Fourteenth Amendments. . . .

> [W]e discuss defenses to an allegation that an interrogation method might violate any of the various criminal prohibitions . . . We believe that necessity or self-defense could provide defenses to a prosecution.

In simpler terms, the memorandum gave the military broad latitude and discretion to use relatively harsh interrogation methods without fear of prosecution or violation of constitutional restraints. The legal logic contained within conveyed that federal laws prohibiting assault were not applicable to military interrogators dealing with members of Al Qaeda because of Presidential powers during wartime. The memo also opined that many American and international laws would not apply to interrogations overseas.

Despite the wide latitude provided to interrogators under the memo's guidance, Pentagon officials never authorized some of the more harsh interrogation methods used by the CIA, such as waterboarding, a simulated drowning

technique. Moreover, no Pentagon officials had since found any senior Bush Administration officials as having been complicit in any of the abuse at Abu Ghraib. However, their investigations did find that for several years following the September 11, 2001 attacks, the Pentagon admittedly failed to set uniform standards for military interrogations worldwide.

Following this and other internal guidance and the debate it caused at the time, Congress passed the Detainee Treatment Act in 2005, that required the DOD to restrict interrogation methods to those set out in the Army Field Manual, which banned coercive interrogations. In 2007, President Bush issued an executive order narrowing the list of approved techniques for the CIA. Although that list of authorized techniques remained classified, intelligence officials did state that waterboarding was not on the list of approved techniques, but that President Bush could authorize it during an emergency.

That having been said, in late 2007, leading Democrats in Congress demanded that the DOJ release two 2005 memos, circulated internally shortly after Alberto Gonzales became U.S. Attorney General, that purportedly reversed the DOJ's earlier rejection of severe interrogation techniques, and reinstated the option to use them where warranted. Senate Judiciary Committee Chairman Patrick Leahy (D-VT) told *The New York Times* that the Judiciary Committee had been trying to obtain the memos' contents for two years (since they were written). Frustrated members of Congress questioned attorney general nominee Michael Mukasey on his views of interrogation tactics during Senate confirmation hearings. While stating that he personally found them abhorrent, Mukasey offered no opinion on their legality without first reviewing them, he responded. Other officials, speaking to *The Times* on conditions of anonymity, said those 2005 opinions remained in effect.

Amid a new flurry of concern, White House Press Secretary Dana Perino responded to *The Times* report on October 4, 2007. Perino advised, "I am not going to comment on any specific alleged techniques. It is not appropriate for me to do so. And to do so would provide the enemy with more information on how to train against these techniques . . . but I will reiterate to you once again that we do not torture. . . ."

Danforth v. Minnesota

When the U.S. SUPREME COURT announces a new rule of **criminal procedure** or law, it soon finds itself with additional cases from inmates who were convicted under the old rule asking that the new rule be applied retroactively. The Court has established standards for determining whether those previously convicted, and whose direct appeals had been exhausted before the date of the ruling, may seek to reverse their convictions. If it is not a "watershed rule" that implicated the fairness and accuracy of criminal proceedings, those persons convicted under the old rule cannot collaterally attack their convictions using the new rule. However, there has been uncertainty over whether state supreme courts have the authority to give broader effect to new rules of criminal procedure. The Supreme Court, in *Danforth v. Minnesota*, __ U.S. __, 128 S. Ct. 1029, 169 L. Ed. 2d 859 (2007), held that states may give broader effect to new rules, opening up a new avenue for state court appeals from inmates.

In 1996 a Minnesota jury convicted Stephen Danforth of first-degree criminal sexual conduct with a minor. At his trial the 6-year-old victim appeared on videotape for the jury but she did not testify in court. Danforth appealed his conviction, arguing that the Sixth Amendment's Confrontation Clause prohibited the videotape from being introduced into evidence. The Minnesota Court of Appeals held under U.S. Supreme Court precedent the tape was admissible because it was sufficiently reliable. The Minnesota Supreme Court denied review and the case was closed. However, in 2004 the U.S. Supreme Court announced a new rule for evaluating the reliability of testimonial statements in criminal cases. In *Crawford v. Washington*, 541 U.S. 36, 124 S.Ct. 1354, 158 L.Ed.2d 177 (2004), the Court held that "statements of witnesses absent from trial" were admissible "only where the declarant is unavailable, and only where the defendant has had a prior opportunity to cross-examine [the witness]."

Danforth filed a post-conviction petition soon after this decision was announced. He argued to the trial court and to the Minnesota Court of Appeals that if *Crawford* had been applied to his case the victim's out-of-court statements would not have been admitted and the jury would not have convicted him. The trial judge dismissed Danforth's petition and the Minnesota Court of Appeals ruled that *Crawford* could not be applied retroactively to cases on **collateral** review. They both noted that the U.S. Supreme Court had ruled in a subsequent case that *Crawford* had not announced a "watershed" rule and therefore could not be invoked on collateral review. The Minnesota Supreme Court granted review this time and held that it did not have the authority to apply a broader retroactivity standard than that announced by the U.S. Supreme Court and it would not apply the *Crawford* even if federal law did not require it to do so.

The U.S. Supreme Court, in a 7–2 decision, reversed the Minnesota Supreme Court ruling, holding that states are not required nor are they prohibited from giving broader application to a new rule of U.S. Supreme Court criminal procedure. Justice JOHN PAUL STEVENS, writing for the majority, reviewed a long line of cases dealing with retroactivity from 1965 onward. He concluded that in the Court's last major review of this doctrine there had been no discussion concerning the authority of any state agency or state court to extend the benefit of a new rule to a broader class. Second, the Court's precedent had been based on federal **habeas corpus statute**. Third, the principle of federalism gives states the right to oversee their justice systems. States should be free to "evaluate and weigh the importance of" finality in their court decisions. Justice Stevens also pointed to Court decisions giving states the authority to craft their own civil retroactivity remedies. The absence of any precedent limiting the authority of state collateral review courts "to provide remedies for federal constitutional violations is sufficient reason for concluding that there is no such rule of federal law." Though this decision will lead to different rules in the fifty states, Justice Stevens noted that this nonuniformity "is a necessary consequence of a federalist system of government."

Chief Justice JOHN ROBERTS, in a dissenting opinion joined by Justice ANTHONY KENNEDY, contended that the Court is the final **arbiter** of federal law and state courts "are therefore bound by our rulings on whether our cases construing federal law are retroactive." He believed the decision contravened the **Supremacy Clause** and undermined the authority of the Court. Most troubling, under this precedent two criminal defendants, each convicted of the same crime, could face disparate treatment if the two states in which they were held applied different retroactivity standards. One may be executed while the other is set free.

DISCRIMINATION

In constitutional law, the grant by statute of particular privileges to a class arbitrarily designated from a sizable number of persons, where no reasonable distinction exists between the favored and disfavored classes. Federal laws, supplemented by court decisions, prohibit discrimination in such areas as employment, housing, voting rights, education, and access to public facilities. They also proscribe discrimination on the basis of race, age, sex, nationality, disability, or religion. In addition, state and local laws can prohibit discrimination in these areas and in others not covered by federal laws.

CBOCS West v. Humphries

In an important employment discrimination case, the U.S. Supreme Court has settled, in the affirmative, the issue of whether claims of race-based retaliation could be brought under 42 USC § 1981. The significance of this case was that it confirmed for plaintiffs an alternative cognizable cause of action for race-based retaliation, in addition to that under Title VII of the Civil Rights Act of 1964. This frees them from the administrative burdens associated with Title VII, including the short administrative statute of limitation. It also frees plaintiffs from the damages caps that Title VII imposed on jury awards.

In *CBOCS West, Inc. v. Humphries*, No. 06-1431, 552 U.S. ___, plaintiff Humphries, an African-American, was employed as an associate manager at a Cracker Barrel restaurant owned by CBOCS. He was ostensibly fired for leaving a safe in the restaurant unlocked overnight. How-

ever, in his complaint, he alleged that he was fired in retaliation for complaining to a district manager about another African-American employee who was fired for offenses that Humphries argued were tolerated from white employees. Humphries further alleged that a supervisor made overtly racial remarks about African-Americans and Mexican-Americans. He filed suit in federal district court under both Title VII of the Civil Rights Act of 1964, and 42 USC § 1981 of the Civil Rights Act of 1866. He alleged both racial discrimination for the firing, and race-based retaliation for having complained about the treatment of the other African-American employee.

The district court dismissed the Title VII claims for failure to timely pay filing fees; it also granted CBOCS summary judgment on the § 1981 claims. However, the Seventh Circuit Court of Appeals, while affirming the dismissal of the direct discrimination claim, remanded the case for a trial on Humphries' § 1981 claim of retaliation. The Seventh Circuit ruled that the statute did indeed encompass retaliation claims. CBOCS appealed to the U.S. Supreme Court, which affirmed the Seventh Circuit's opinion.

The relevant statutory language in 42 USC § 1981 (enacted in 1866, following the Civil War and end of slavery in the United States) provides that "[a]ll persons within the jurisdiction of the United States shall have the same right . . . to make and enforce contracts . . . as is enjoyed by white citizens." The following section, § 1982, provides that "[a]ll citizens . . . shall have the same right, . . . , as is enjoyed by white citizens . . . to inherit, purchase, lease, sell, hold, and convey real and personal property.

CBOCS, in defense, had argued that § 1981's plain text did not refer to retaliation, which generally occurred after the formation of an employment contract. While a contract of employment was covered under § 1981, argued CBOCS, any post-contract conduct was not. Further, Congress had failed to expressly include an anti-retaliation provision in its 1991 amendment to § 1981. CBOCS also argued that such an expansive interpretation overlapped Title VII and could therefore undermine the procedural mechanisms under that statute.

As background, it had long been held, in prior decisions, that 42 USC § 1982 (not § 1981) recognized and encompassed retaliatory actions, e.g., *Sullivan v. Little Hunting Park*, 396 U.S. 229 (1969), as later interpreted and relied upon in *Jackson v. Birmingham Bd. Of Education*, 544 U.S. 167. Another line of prior cases had consistently held that § 1981 and § 1982 were to be interpreted alike, having been enacted together, having common language, and serving the same purpose of providing black citizens the same legal rights as white citizens. See, e.g., *Runyon v. McCrary*, 427 U.S. 160. But there were no direct cases on point addressing § 1981's application to retaliatory conduct that *followed* the "making" of a contract (in this case, a contract of employment).

Congress eventually enacted the Civil Rights Act of 1991, which very explicitly defined the scope of § 1981 to include post-contract-formation conduct. Since that time, the federal Courts of Appeals had uniformly interpreted § 1981 as encompassing post-contract retaliatory conduct. All that was needed was an affirmation from the U.S. Supreme Court, and according to the Court, the present case provided that opportunity for clarification and affirmation.

In so holding, the Court relied heavily on the doctrine of *stare decisis*, or the willingness of the Court to abide by its own previous decisions (precedents). In the present case, finding that 42 USC § 1981 would in fact support Humphries' claim for retaliation, Justice Breyer wrote for the Court,

> We conclude that considerations of *stare decisis*, strongly support our adherence to *Sullivan*, and the long line of related cases where we interpret § 1981 and 1982 similarly. CBOCS' arguments do not convince us to the contrary. We subsequently hold that 42 USC § 1981 encompasses claims of retaliation. The judgment of the Court of Appeals is affirmed.

Justice Breyer was joined in the majority opinion by Chief Justice Roberts and Justices Stevens, Kennedy, Souter, Ginsburg, and Alito. Justice Thomas wrote a dissenting opinion, joined by Justice Scalia, in which he opined that because the Court's holding had no basis in the text of 42 USC § 1981, and was not really justified by *stare decisis*, (because no prior case had held exactly what was held in this case), there was no firm basis for the Court's decision in the present case.

DRUGS AND NARCOTICS

Drugs are articles intended for use in the diagnosis, cure, mitigation, treatment, or prevention of disease in humans or animals, and any articles other than food intended to affect the mental or body function of humans or animals. *Narcotics* are any drugs that dull the senses and commonly become addictive after prolonged use.

Burgess v. U.S.

The Supreme Court in 2008 resolved a conflict in federal law about the meaning of a "felony drug offense." The defendant in the case was convicted under a state law that defined a drug crime as a **misdemeanor**. The Court, however, concluded that the conviction amounted to a **felony** because the crime was punishable by more than one year's imprisonment. Accordingly, the Court affirmed the defendant's sentence under federal law. The case gained notoriety because a South Carolina felon successfully helped the defendant file his appeal.

Keith Lavon Burgess was arrested in 2002 in Florence, South Carolina for possessing a small amount of cocaine. Under South Carolina law, Burgess's crime for simple possession was classified as a misdemeanor, which was punishable by up to two years imprisonment. A state court gave Burgess a one-year **suspended sentence** along with two years probation and fifty hours of community service.

About one year after his arrest, Burgess was again arrested in a Florence, South Carolina shopping mall for selling 240 grams of crack cocaine. In 2003, he pleaded guilty to a single count of conspiracy to distribute 50 or more grams of base cocaine, which violated 21 U.S.C. § 841(a). Though the state law under which Burgess was convicted in 2002 was defined as a misdemeanor, prosecutors sought to enhance his sentence by classifying the first conviction as a felony. Under § 841(b)(1)(A), "[i]f any person commits [a drug violation] after a prior conviction for a felony drug offense after a prior conviction for a felony drug offense has become final," then the defendant is subject to a 20-year minimum sentence of imprisonment.

Under 21 U.S.C. § 802(44), a "felony drug offense" is defined as "an offense that is punishable by imprisonment for more than one year under any law of . . . a State . . . that prohibits or restricts conduct relating to narcotic drugs. Under another section, 21 U.S.C. § 802(13), a "felony" is defined as "any Federal or State offense classified by applicable Federal or State law as a felony." Burgess argued that the trial court should define "felony drug offense" by incorporating the definition of "felony." Under Burgess's argument, the court would have concluded that his 2002 conviction was not a felony drug offense because state law defined his crime as a misdemeanor.

The federal government, in turn, argued that his previous conviction was indeed a felony because federal law defined felony as a crime punishable by more than one year in prison. Prosecutors stressed that it did not matter how state law defined the crime, because federal law is clear that any crime punishable by more than one year in prison is a felony. The prosecution's argument prevailed at the trial court, as U.S. District Judge Terry L. Wooten sentenced Burgess to 156 months in prison.

Following Burgess's sentencing, two **federal courts** of appeals reached conflicting results about the meaning of felony drug offense under § 841(b)(1)(A) and § 802(44). In *United States v. West*, 393 F.3d 1302 (D.C. Cir. 2005), the U.S. Court of Appeals for the DISTRICT OF COLUMBIA concluded that the sentencing enhancement applied only in "those instances in which the prior drug offense is both punishable by more than one year and classified as a felony by the controlling authority." The First **Circuit Court** of Appeals, however, ruled that the enhanced sentence applied when the crime was punishable under state law by more than a year, irrespective of whether state law defined the crime as a felony.

Burgess appealed his sentence to a three-judge panel of the Fourth Circuit Court of Appeals. The **appellate court** agreed with the First Circuit that the language of the **statute** was unambiguous with respect to the definition of a felony drug offense. According to the court, "We discern no basis from the plain language or **statutory** scheme of the [Controlled Substances Act] to indicate that Congress intended 'felony drug offense' also to incorporate the definition

of § 802(13)." The court also ruled that Burgess was not entitled to a more lenient sentence because the court did not agree that the law was ambiguous.

While Burgess was serving his sentence in South Carolina, he enlisted the assistance of a felon named Michael R. Ray, a so-called jailhouse lawyer in the facility. Ray drafted a petition for **writ** of **certiorari** on Burgess's behalf and submitted it to the Supreme Court. Though the Court typically agrees to hear less than one percent of the cases presented to it, the Court granted certiorari to review Burgess's case. This made Ray something of a celebrity, even though he did not argue the case before the Court, nor was he released to see the argument in person. Stanford law professor Jeffrey L. Fisher instead argued the case before the Court.

A unanimous Court had little trouble affirming the Fourth Circuit's decision. In an opinion by RUTH BADER GINSBURG, the Court found no ambiguity in the federal sentencing law, noting that had Congress wanted to incorporate § 802(13)'s definition into § 802(44), the legislature could have done so rather easily. The Court also noted that the legislative history of the Controlled Substances Act suggested that Congress intended for enhanced sentencing to apply where the state law provided for a length of a sentence, no matter how the state classified the crime. "Before 1994, the definition of 'felony drug offense' depended on the vagaries of state-law classifications of offenses as felonies and misdemeanors," wrote Ginsburg. "The 1994 amendments [to the Controlled Substances Act] replaced that definition with a uniform federal standard based on the authorized length of imprisonment." Because Congress clearly did not intend the result that Burgess urged, the Court rejected his argument and affirmed the Fourth Circuit's judgment.

Ray was scheduled to be released from prison near the time that the decision was handed down. He claimed to have written about 75 appeals to the Supreme Court in the past. His success in the Burgess case, however, led the South Carolina Attorney General's office to consider taking action against Ray for practicing law without a license. Ray was at one time a paralegal but became involved with various **fraud** schemes that led to his imprisonment.

Purdue Frederick Pleads Guilty to Misbranding Oxycontin

Purdue Frederick Co. and three top executives in May 2007 pleaded guilty to charges related to the misbranding of OxyContin, a powerful painkilling drug. The company and the executives agreed to pay more than $634 million in damages, representing one of the largest fines imposed in a misleading marketing campaign.

OxyContin was developed as a painkiller that was supposed to be less dangerous than morphine. It was designed for patients with cancer as well as those with chronic pain. Purdue Frederick, a Connecticut-based subsidiary of Purdue Pharma, L.P., introduced the drug in 1995. The drug is an opium derivative and is prescribed to patients with moderate to severe pain. Promoted as a "miracle drug," the manufacturer earned $2.8 billion in revenue from the sale of OxyContin.

Despite its claims regarding the safety of the drug, evidence surfaced that OxyContin (which is the **trade name** for oxycodone) was anything but safe for its users. When the drug is crushed and injected, it gives users a powerful high. Use of the drug caused death in some cases, and law enforcement officials claimed that criminals broke into homes and robbed pharmacies for the drug. The drug earned the street name "hillbilly heroin."

Court documents in the case indicated that the company was aware that the drug was dangerous and yet Purdue Frederick continued to market the drug as a safer alternative to morphine. In fact, Purdue's market research department found as early as 1996 that "[t]he biggest negative of [OxyContin] was the abuse potential." These findings persisted through 2001. Nevertheless, Purdue continued to claim that the drug was "less addictive, less subject to abuse, and less likely to cause withdrawal than other pain medications," according to court documents.

Purdue Frederick misbranded OxyContin in several ways. The company trained its sales representatives to tell health care providers that the drug had a less euphoric effect and had less abuse potential than other painkilling drugs. Company supervisors used graphs that exaggerated the blood level effects that the drugs had. These graphs suggested that OxyContin had different effects than other opioids, the morphine-like substances used for pain relief. The sales representatives were trained to use the graphs during role-playing exercises at the company's Connecticut headquarters.

Several reports indicated that patients could become addicted to OxyContin. A 1999 study focused on patients who suffered from osteoar-

thritis. The study indicated that the patients showed withdrawal symptoms and that some patients showed signs of physical dependence on the drug. Other studies conducted in 2000 and 2001 provided further evidence that patients experienced withdrawal symptoms when taken off the drug.

Despite this evidence, supervisors and employees drafted a medical journal article regarding a study of osteoarthritis patients showing that those who took less than 60 mg of OxyContin did not display withdrawal symptoms even when their use was disrupted abruptly. The article also concluded that patients taking less than 60 mg of the drug would not develop a tolerance for the painkiller. Even though these statements contradicted the actual findings that studies had shown, sales representatives provided these articles to health care providers to show that OxyContin was a weaker alternative to morphine.

The warning labels that appeared on OxyContin packages also contained false information. The package indicated that "[d]elayed absorption, as provided by OxyContin tablets, is believed to reduce the abuse liability of the drug." This statement suggested that the delayed release of OxyContin meant that it was less likely to result in addiction than immediate-release alternatives. However, Purdue Frederick's own research showed that a drug abuser "could extract approximately 68% of the oxycodone from a single 10 mg OxyContin tablet merely by crushing the tablet, stirring it in water, and drawing the solution through cotton into a syringe."

The DRUG ENFORCEMENT ADMINISTRATION in a 2002 report determined that OxyContin had caused 142 deaths and had contributed to 318 others. Nevertheless, company executives did nothing to warn the public of the drug's possible harms. "Even in the face of warnings from health care professionals, the media, and members of its own sales force that OxyContin was being widely abused and causing harm to our citizens, Purdue, under the leadership of its top executives, continued to push a **fraudulent** marketing campaign that promoted OxyContin as less addictive, less subject to abuse, and less likely to cause withdrawal," said John Brownlee, U.S. attorney for the Western District of Virginia. "In the process, scores died as a result of OxyContin abuse and an even greater number of people became addicted to OxyContin."

As part of the plea agreements for their own actions as well as the company's actions, Purdue

Frederick's executives signed written agreements to pay a total of $634,515,475. More than $430 million of this amount went to the United States and to federal and state agencies. Another $130 million was set aside to resolve private claims. Heavy fines were also paid by top executives Michael Friedman, president and chief executive officer; Howard Udell, executive vice president and chief legal officer; and Paul D. Goldenheim, executive vice president for worldwide medical affairs. The three agreed to pay a combined $34.5 million as part of the plea agreement.Purdue Frederick's lead counsel in the case was former New York City Mayor Rudolph Giuliani, who was then a candidate for President. He helped to negotiate the plea bargain agreement. The fines paid by Purdue Pharma and Purdue Frederick were believed to represent 90 percent of the company's profits on the sale of the drug.

No Right of Access to Unapproved Drugs

In the United States, access to medication by private persons is limited to those drugs approved by the U.S. FOOD AND DRUG ADMINISTRATION (FDA). Acting as a gatekeeper, the FDA is tasked with ensuring that products are not only safe for human consumption, but also, that they perform and/or are as effective as indicated by the manufacturers, and that risks/side effects/untoward consequences are made known to end-users. In January 2008, the U.S. SUPREME COURT denied review of an **appellate court** decision finding no constitutional right of terminally ill patients to access drugs not yet approved by the FDA. By denying review, the high court let stand the lower court's decision. *Abigail Alliance for Better Access to Developmental Drugs and Washington Legal Foundation v. von Eschenbach*, 495 F.3d 695 (D.C. Cir. 2006 *en banc*)

Back in 1979, the Supreme Court had considered the merits of such an argument, and rejected a constitutional right to use unapproved drugs, i.e., drugs not yet having completed the rigorous testing needed to be approved by the FDA (in that case, laetrile). *U.S. v. Rutherford*, 442 U.S. 544. A growing number of advocates for the terminally ill had since sought to have the Supreme Court overrule that case, or at least, provide exceptions.

This was primarily because FDA approval may take years. Drug testing usually consists of three phases or "trials," each one involving a larger number of patients. Following completion of the drug trials, the FDA then evaluates both data received from the manufacturers on

efficacy and side effects, as well as Phase 3 results, which involve double-blind, placebo-controlled trials comparing actual efficacy and side effects with the data previously provided by the manufacturers.

In 2001, University of Virginia student Abigail Burroughs died of head and neck cancer at the age of 21. Her last months alive had been spent fighting to gain access to an ostensibly-promising new experimental anti-cancer drug (Iressa) recommended by her oncologist at Johns Hopkins University Hospital. (The drug Iressa was later approved by the FDA but shown to be relatively ineffective in most cancer patients.) Following her death, her father founded the Abigail Alliance for Better Access to Developmental Drugs and sued the FDA in federal **district court** in 2003. The Alliance was joined in its suit by the Washington Legal Foundation. The gist of the argument was that terminal patients had a fundamental right to access such medicines. The suit also proposed a new three-tier model for experimental drug regulation, arguing that such drugs should be available to certain legally-competent terminally ill adult patients "as early as the conclusion of the first of three phases of clinical trials." The constitutional arguments were couched in terms of depriving patients of their right of "self defense" and violating their FIFTH AMENDMENT right to life, liberty, or property without adequate due process.

The district court dismissed the case for failure to state a claim, but a three-member panel of the U.S. **Circuit Court** of Appeals for the D.C. Circuit reversed by a 2–1 vote, holding in part that the right to access unapproved drugs could be inferred from an individual's due process right to refuse life-sustaining medical treatment. Finding that plaintiff's argument deserved a constitutional strict-scrutiny review, the **appellate** court remanded the case to the district court to determine whether FDA's policy was "narrowly tailored to serve a compelling [governmental] interest."

Notwithstanding, Alliance's victory was short-lived. The entire D.C. Circuit Court, sitting *en banc*, vacated the judgment of the three-member panel in January 2008 and summarily dismissed all of Alliance's arguments. It essentially distinguished the right of access to treatment from a claimed right of access to unapproved treatments. The appellate court found no such fundamental right grounded in the Constitution.

Going back to the 1979 Rutherford decision, the issue was whether Section 505 of the

1938 Food, Drug, and Cosmetic Act (which the FDA oversees enforcement of) precluded terminally ill patients from obtaining Laetrile. At that time, the Supreme Court noted, "To accept the proposition that the safety and efficacy standards of the Act have no relevance for terminal patients is to deny the Commissioner's authority over all drugs, however toxic or ineffectual, for such individuals." In another relevant Supreme Court case, *Gonzales v. Raich*, 545 U.S. 1 (2005), the high court held that the dispensing of new, unapproved drugs (in this case Cannabis) was nonetheless subject to prior FDA approval, even if the State of California and individual physicians approved of its use.

Despite the adverse court decision, terminally ill patients still had four legal and readily available means to access unapproved drugs: (1) by enrolling in a clinical trial sponsored by a pharmaceutical company or clinic; (2) obtaining a compassionate or otherwise special exemption for treatment from an investigator in a clinical trial; (3) contacting a manufacturer or sponsor directly; and/or (4) requesting a single patient or emergency IND (investigational new drug) application through the FDA. The majority of patients enrolled in clinical trials are receiving drugs that are in either Phase 2 or Phase 3 testing. In "compassionate use" or other exceptions, Phase 2 drugs are generally used, but there is no hard fast rule precluding use of Phase 1 drugs.

EDUCATION

Schools Crack Down on Candy, Sweaters

Two East Coast schools made news in 2008 for suspending students for such acts as purchasing contraband candy and for wearing a sweater in violation of a school's dress code. Administrators in both cases later rescinded their original actions, but these actions left parents and others wondering about each school's priorities in initially making these decisions.

In New Haven, Connecticut, an eighth-grade honors student was suspended for buying a package of candy from another student at school. The student's actions violated a school policy adopted in 2003 that prevented the sale of candy and other junk food on campus. The school adopted the policy as part of a district-wide wellness policy. The school's policy states that "no candy or junk food fundraisers will be allowed on school grounds," and the school only permits health food to be sold in vending machines on the campus. The policy also disallows bake sales and other food sales during normal school hours.

New Haven superintendent Reginald Mayo said that the policy was designed in part for children's health and also for their safety. The school reportedly experienced an increase in illicit candy sales during the fall of 2007. Moreover, a student had his wallet stolen, prompting concerns that students who carried around cash after selling the candy were in danger.

The controversy arose when Michael Sheridan bought a bag of Skittles from a fellow classmate. The boy said that although he was unaware that school policy prohibited the sale of the candy, he noticed that the other student was acting suspiciously when the student sold Sheridan the bag of candy. "He was all just secretive, that's all I got from it," said Sheridan, who had transferred to the school just the year before.

Sheridan's punishment is what grabbed the media's attention. He was initially suspended from school for three days for the incident, though this was later reduced to one day. He was additionally stripped of his title as class vice president and was prohibited from attending an honors dinner. The boy had apparently never had any disciplinary problems at all, prompting his mother to protest, "It's too much. It's too unfair."

After receiving national attention, school officials changed their minds. Superintendent Reginald Mayo and Principal Eleanor Turner met with Sheridan's parents and reversed their decision regarding his post on the school's student council. The school also expunged the boy's record of the incident. "I am sorry this has happened," Turner said. "My hope is that we can get back to the normal school routine, especially since we are in the middle of taking the Connecticut mastery test." She added that she should have given written warnings against candy sales in additional to the oral notice.

Another school suspension of an honors student arose in Lawrence, Massachusetts, where a student was disciplined for wearing a sweater in violation of a school's dress code. Flormarie Figueroa is a 16-year-old student of the Business Management and Finance High School in Lawrence. She said she felt a draft in the school, and so she put on a sweater. Two of her teachers asked her to leave because she did not comply with the school's dress code, which does not generally allow students to wear sweaters. When Figueroa refused to take off her sweater, she was asked to leave class.

School principal Joseph McMilleon cited the girl for "insubordination to two teachers when asked to leave the classroom due to non-compliance with the uniform policy." Based on this charge, the principal suspended Figueroa for one day. According to superintendent Wilfredo Laboy, the school typically suspends 50 to 60 students per week.

The girl's mother, however, thought that this particular suspension was brought about because the mother had spoken out against school officials in the past. "[Flormarie's] being targeted because of my speaking out that there's no communication (by the school administration) with the parents," said Maria Figueroa. She also said that she planned to take a personal day to spend the day with her daughter while she serves the suspension. "I will be shadowing her for the day—giving her support—because she did absolutely nothing wrong," Maria said. "The fact of the matter is there is absolutely no sweater policy because it's still being brought before [a school committee]."

Maria Figueroa reportedly had criticized school officials in letters and at meetings. However, Laboy rejected the mother's statement that the girl was targeted for the mother's previous actions. "Ms. Figueroa is one of 8,900 parents in the district," he said. "She has the right to her opinion. But the inference we're singling out her daughter because she's vocal, I completely refute that idea."

Laboy also claimed that the school was not cold on the day that the girl refused to remove her sweater. According to him, the school will alter the dress code when necessary depending on the weather. "We've allowed kids when it's cold to wear sweaters," he said. "We've compromised, but we are not going to comprise to the point where kids capriciously and unilaterally use it as an excuse."

A local newspaper entitled *The Eagle Tribune* questioned the school's judgment in making the decision. "Is there anyone in this school system with a shred of reason?," the paper asked in an editorial "Absolutist policies deny educators the ability to make sound judgments. In fact, they put school leaders in the ridiculous position of suspending a student who earns mostly A's and a smattering of B's because she was cold."

About two weeks after Flormarie Figueroa served her suspension, the school approved changes to the dress code. Students under the new rule may wear certain approved sweaters over the top of their uniforms.

Board of Education of the City School District of the City of New York v. Tom F.

The Individuals with Disabilities Education Act (IDEA), 20 U.S.C.A. §§ 1400 *et seq.*, seeks to ensure that children with disabilities have available to them a "free appropriate education." The parents of children with disabilities have fought to place their children in private schools and have the school district pay the tuition. Because private school tuition can cost as much as private college tuition, school districts are reluctant to approve such requests. This has led to litigation in the **federal courts** and appeals that have reached the Supreme Court. The Supreme Court, in *Board of Education of the City School District of the City of New York v. Tom F.*, __U.S.__, 128 S.Ct. 1, 169 L.Ed.2d 1 (2007), confronted this issue but split 4 to 4, with Justice ANTHONY KENNEDY not participating (no reason was given) in the case. By evenly dividing the vote the Court upheld, without issuing a full opinion, the decision of the Second **Circuit Court** of Appeals. In that decision the appeals court held that parents could seek reimbursement even if their children never attended a public school.

The case was brought by Tom Freston on behalf of his son, Gilbert. Freston helped found the MTV Network and later became chief executive officer of Viacom, a prominent media corporation. When Freston was fired as CEO, he reportedly received an $85 million severance package. In 1995 Freston sent Gilbert to kindergarten at New York City's Stephen Gaynor private school on the Upper West Side, without seeking to enroll his son in public school. For the first two years of Gilbert's schooling, the New York City schools reimbursed Freston for the Gaynor school tuition, which amounted to $30,000 per year.

In 1997 the school district evaluated the boy and created an Individualized Education Program (IEP), as is mandated by the IDEA. Based on the evaluation and the plan the district recommended that Gilbert be placed in a public school with a 15-to-1 student-teacher ratio. Freston declined the recommendation and had his son return to Gaynor, where the student-teacher ratio was 10 to 1. He also asked that a hearing officer review the district's decision, a procedural right granted by the IDEA. The hearing officer concluded that the proposed public school did not meet the boy's academic needs. Beyond the higher student-teacher ratio, Gilbert would have been placed in a mathematics class with kindergarten students, though he had fourth-grade math abilities. The officer ordered the district to reimburse Freston for the tuition costs.

The school board appealed this order in federal **district court**. The board argued that the plain language of the IDEA allowed it deny reimbursement because Freston's son bypassed public schools. The IDEA provision in question stated that a parent could be reimbursed for private school tuition if the child "had previously received special education and related services under the authority of a public agency." In Freston's case the child had never received special education services from the school district before enrolling in the private school. The board believed this provision was designed to encourage parents to send their children to public schools before opting for private education. The district court agreed and overturned the hearing officer's decision. However, the Second Circuit Court of Appeals reversed. This led to the Supreme Court's review of the case.

At oral argument in October 2007, some of the justices questioned why local taxpayers should pay the private school tuition for a multi-millionaire's son. Freston argued that he was interested in preserving the rights of disabled children and their parents, regardless of income. He pointed out that there is no means-testing requirement in the IDEA and that the key question was whether children could have a "free appropriate education" according to their needs. It made no sense to force a child to attend a public school for a brief time merely to satisfy the right to reimbursement.

Shortly after oral argument the Supreme Court announced that it was evenly divided on the matter. Therefore, the circuit court of appeals decision was affirmed.

EIGHTH AMENDMENT

Baze v. Rees

In a widely followed case involving the future of the death penalty in the United States, the Supreme Court in April 2008 ruled that execution by lethal injection was a humane form of execution. Accordingly, the Court held that Kentucky's three-drug method of execution by lethal injection does not constitute **cruel and unusual punishment** in violation of the EIGHTH AMENDMENT to the U.S. Constitution.

The first state to adopt lethal injection as its method of execution was Oklahoma in 1977. Of the 37 states that impose the death penalty, 36 now use lethal injection as the means to do so. The states impose this by mixing a combination of drugs that result in death. Critics have argued that the states did not adopt this method of execution as a result of medical or other scientific studies, but rather simply fell in line with other states.

In 1998, Kentucky elected to use lethal injection as opposed to electrocution as the method of execution in the state. Nothing in the Kentucky **statute** pertaining to executions specifies the drugs that must be used, but rather provides that "every death sentence shall be executed by continuous intravenous injection of a substance or combination of substances sufficient to cause death."

After adopting lethal injection as its method of execution, the Kentucky Department of Corrections developed a written protocol for implementing this method. The protocol originally called for use of two grams of sodium thiopental, 50 milligrams of pancuronium bromide, and 240 milliequivalents of potassium chloride. The amount of sodium thiopental was increased from two to three grams in 2004 as a result of litigation. A certified phlebotomist and an emergency medical technician insert catheters and intravenous sites on the inmate's body. Another team mixes the lethal solutions. The sodium thiopental is designed to render the inmate unconscious before the team administers the pancuronium and potassium chloride. A physician stands by in the event that the governor calls a last-minute stay of execution. Since 1998, the only one person has been executed in Kentucky by way of lethal injection.

Two death penalty inmates, Ralph Baze and Thomas C. Bowling, **chose** by default lethal injection as the means to execute them. While awaiting execution, they filed an action arguing that this means of putting them to death constituted cruel and unusual punishment in violation of the Eighth Amendment to the U.S. Constitution as well as the Kentucky Constitution. Baze and Bowling specifically argued that the state's method of execution violated their right because the chemicals that the state uses causes more pain than either constitution allows.

The defendants in the action were officials with the Kentucky Department of Corrections and the Kentucky State Penitentiary, as well as Governor Ernie Fletcher. They argued that Baze and Bowling failed to demonstrate that the state's method of execution is, as the trial court

Roy Englert, attorney for state of Kentucky, speaking to reporters, flanked by Kentucky Secretary of Justice and Public Safety Michael Brown, in front of US Supreme Court, January 2007.
AP IMAGES

stated, "incompatible with evolving standards of decency or involves the unnecessary and **wanton** infliction of pain." Instead, the defendants argued that the evidence showed "no unnecessary pain inherent in an execution by lethal injection and chemicals utilized in the protocol according to the corresponding dosages would result in a quick and painless death."

Judge Roger Crittenden of the Franklin **Circuit Court** denied relief to Baze and Bowling, and the inmates subsequently appealed the decision to the Kentucky Supreme Court. The state court had previously considered an Eighth Amendment challenge to lethal injection and had rejected the argument that this method of execution was unconstitutional. *Wheeler v. Commonwealth*, 121 S.W.3d 173 (Ky. 2003). The court also noted that several other state and **federal courts** had rejected similar arguments. In its review of the case of Baze and Bowling, the court found no reason to change its mind. Accordingly, the Kentucky Supreme Court denied relief to the inmates. *Baze v. Rees*, 217 S.W.3d 207 (Ky. 2006).

The prisoners filed a petition for **writ** of **certiorari** to the U.S. SUPREME COURT in July 2007, and the Court in October granted the petition. The Court limited its review to the question of whether Kentucky's protocol for administering the death penalty violated the Eighth Amendment. Once the Court had agreed to review the case, several lower courts decided to effectively place a moratorium on the administration of lethal injections. The Supreme Court itself also blocked some executions after agreeing to hear Baze and Bowling's case.

The case represented the first time since 1879 that the Supreme Court had reviewed whether a certain method of execution violated the Eighth Amendment. The Court in *Wilkerson v. Utah*, 99 U.S. 130, 25 L. Ed. 345 (1879) ruled that a sentence of death by firing squad was not unconstitutional. The Court in 1890 also ruled that a sentence of death by electrocution did not violate a defendant's due process rights. *In re Kemmler*, 136 U.S. 436, 10 S. Ct. 930, 34 L. Ed. 519 (1890).

In a rather surprising 7–2 decision (albeit with several concurring opinions), the Court affirmed the Kentucky Supreme Court. Writing for a **plurality** of the Court, Chief Justice JOHN ROBERTS noted that the Court began "with the principle . . . that capital punishment is constitutional. It necessarily follows that there must be a means of carrying it out." Roberts rejected the inmates' arguments that Kentucky's method of legal injection was too painful. "Some risk of pain is inherent in any method of execution—no matter how humane—if only from the prospect of error in following the required procedure," Roberts wrote.

Other justices agreed with the result but offered other reasoning. For instance, Justice CLARENCE THOMAS, joined by Justice ANTONIN SCALIA, said that he would reject challenges to the means of execution unless a certain method was "deliberately designed to inflict pain." Justice JOHN PAUL STEVENS noted that though he thought the death penalty should be ended, he agreed with the conclusion that Kentucky's method of execution was not so badly flawed that it violated the Eighth Amendment.

Two only two dissenting justices were RUTH BADER GINSBURG and DAVID SOUTER. Ginsburg concluded that Kentucky's method "lacks the basic safeguards" that would ensure that a prisoner dies a painless death.

ELDER LAW

A relatively new specialty devoted to the legal issues of senior citizens, including estate planing, health care, planning for incapacity or mental incompetence, the receipt of benefits, and employment discrimination.

Jury Acquits Nursing Home Owners of Katrina Drownings

In September 2007, after only four hours of deliberation, a Louisiana state jury acquitted the two owners of St. Rita's Nursing Home in New

Orleans for the drowning deaths of 35 elderly and disabled residents during the flooding in the aftermath of Hurricane Katrina in 2005. The St. Rita trial was moved 100 miles to St. Francisville because only a small percent of St. Bernard residents had returned to the area.

In addition to the criminal charges of negligent homicide from those deaths, the owners also had been charged with (and acquitted of) 64 counts of cruelty to the infirmed, stemming from the same flood disaster. They were the only two persons ever criminally prosecuted for the numerous mistakes and errors of judgment made by many persons in the hours and days after Katrina struck, which ultimately claimed the lives of more than 1,400 persons (some estimates as high as 1,800) throughout Louisiana and the coastal states. (In July 2007, officials decided not to prosecute a doctor and two nurses for murder stemming from alleged euthanasia of four incapacitated patients in a flooded and non-functional New Orleans hospital.) The St. Rita's Nursing Home trial lasted three weeks, but the case raised larger questions about who, if anyone, should face liability or punishment for the massive Katrina failures.

The gist of the charges were premised on a mandatory evacuation order issued by local government authorities. Three other nursing homes in the area evacuated their patients/residents, but the owners of St. Rita, Sal and Mabel Mangano, made a last-minute decision to "shelter in place." (The Manganos did not testify in their own defense. They have never made a public statement explaining why they aborted evacuation efforts.) What is known is that on the day prior to Katrina hitting the area, the Manganos, who had stocked up on foods, generators, and medications, hunkered down at the nursing home with 59 elderly patients, other family members and staff. It is also known that Mabel Mangano did contact a nursing home in Baton Rouge to inquire about available beds if an evacuation "was necessary."

Once the local levees breached, water gushed into the one-story nursing home and rose to the ceiling within 20 minutes. Several of the residents floated on their plastic-covered mattresses to safety, although it is known that many of the drowning victims were bedridden. Others who made it to the roof were ferried away to a parish courthouse. Three other nursing homes in the same St. Bernard Parish were evacuated. Prosecutors argued this was a sign that defendant Manganos were too "cheap" to evacuate their residents, and instead decided

to gamble with their residents' lives. They further argued that the Manganos acted with "reckless disregard" for their patients' safety–one of the criminal elements they needed to prove in a negligent homicide case. "They stuck their heads in the sand, tails in the air and hoped that Mother Nature wouldn't kick them in the butt," the assistant attorney general told jurors in closing arguments.

Notwithstanding, evidence that financial considerations drove Manganos' decision was scant. One person testified that after a hurricane-preparedness meeting several years ago, Mabel Mangano allegedly said "Unless the hurricane is coming in my back door, I'm not putting my residents through an evacuation and wasting money." Other testimony indicated that the Manganos only had one nine-passenger van available to transport residents–woefully inadequate and further evidence of their "reckless disregard."

The defense arguments, on the other hand, focused on Manganos' decision to "shelter in place" as a sign of their concern for residents and fear of potentially lethal dangers associated with evacuating fragile and frail residents. This fear was well-grounded, defense experts testified. The Manganos also had survived 1965's Hurricane Betsy, and believed their facility had been built on a high spot that was less vulnerable to flooding. Finally, by all accounts, patient and resident care at St. Rita was good. In closing arguments, defense attorneys characterized the Manganos as victims themselves, "scapegoats" for a government responsibility that was performed ineptly and inadequately.

The levee breaches and overtopping of flood waters has been blamed, alternately and collectively, on the U.S. Army Corps of Engineers, Louisiana Governor Kathleen Babineaux Blanco (D), New Orleans Mayor Ray Nagin (D), and various federal, state, and local governments. Blanco and Nagin were criticized for their chaotic evacuation effort, which left many people behind, particularly the elderly and infirmed. (Blanco spent about three hours on the stand, in summary, explaining that she had left evacuations to local officials.) The FEDERAL EMERGENCY MANAGEMENT AGENCY (FEMA) and President GEORGE W. BUSH received negative press and criticism for slow response times.

Statistics later released by the Louisiana Department of Health and Hospitals indicated that 78 percent of the identified dead were over the age of 51, and 39 percent were over 75. Other reports indicated that many of the deaths were preventable; some persons were simply abandoned. Others died of chronic illnesses which were manageable under normal conditions but became lethal without medicine or continued treatment.

The Manganos still faced some 30 civil lawsuits filed against them by survivors and family members of residents. They, in turn, had filed several lawsuits against local and state officials, arguing that the governments should share liability.

ELECTIONS

The processes of voting to decide a public question or to select one person from a designated group to perform certain obligations in a government, corporation, or society.

Crawford v. Marion County Election Board

The U.S. SUPREME COURT in 2008 ruled that a voter identification system from Indiana was not unconstitutional. The basis of the ruling was that the state has a valid interest in protecting the integrity and reliability of the electoral process.

In 2005, Indiana enacted a **statute** that requires citizens who are voting on election day to present a piece of photo identification that is issued by the government. This "Voter ID Law" applies to those voting in person during primary and general elections, but it does not apply to those voting through absentee ballots. An indigent voter or someone who objects to being photographed on religious grounds must execute an appropriate affidavit before a **circuit court** within 10 days following the election for votes from those individuals to count. Likewise, a person who has photo identification but fails to present it on election day may vote, but that person's vote will count only if the person presents photo identification within 10 days of registering his or her vote. The state provides free photo identification to qualified voters.

Immediately after the Indiana Legislature passed the bill imposing the Voter ID Law, the Indiana DEMOCRATIC PARTY and the Marion County Democratic Central Committee brought suit in the U.S. **District Court** for the Southern District of Indiana against state officials responsible for enforcing the statute. The plaintiffs sought a judgment that the law was invalid and sought to enjoin enforcement of the statute. A second suit was brought on behalf of several nonprofit organizations that represent

groups of elderly, disabled, poor, and minority voters, as well as two elected officials who would be affected by the law. The State of Indiana intervened to defend the statute's validity.

The plaintiffs in the case argued that the Voter ID Law substantially burdens the right to vote, which would violate the FOURTEENTH AMENDMENT to the U.S. Constitution. The plaintiffs also argued that the law imposes an election method that is neither necessary nor appropriate for avoiding election **fraud**. Moreover, the lawsuit alleged that the law would effectively disfranchise qualified voters who do not possess required identification and will impose an unjust burden on those who could not easily obtain this identification.

An expert named Kimball W. Brace submitted a report to the district court indicating that at many as 989,000 registered voters in the State of Indiana do not possess a state-issued driver's license or photo identification. Brace's report also concluded that registered voters in groups of citizens with household incomes of less than $15,000 were twice as likely not to possess photo identification as citizens with incomes of more than $55,000.

In a lengthy opinion, U.S. District Judge Sarah Evans Barker decided to grant the defendants' motion for **summary judgment**. According to Barker, the plaintiffs did "not introduce evidence of a single, individual Indiana resident who will not be able to vote" as a result of the Voter ID Law. She also rejected Brace's report as "utterly incredible and unreliable," noting that the court lacked "the time and space to discuss the numerous flaws in Brace's report." Barker estimated that the number of Indiana residents who lacked a state-issued driver's license or identification card at the time of the statute's enactment was around 43,000. *Indiana Democratic Party v. Rokita*, 458 F. Supp. 2d 775 (S.D. Ind. 2006).

The plaintiffs appealed the ruling to the Seventh Circuit Court of Appeals. A divided panel of the **appellate court** affirmed the trial court's ruling. According to the majority, the absence of any plaintiffs who could claim that the voting law would deter them from voting was telling. The two-judge majority noted that "the motivation for the suit is simply that the law may require the Democratic Party and other organizational plaintiffs to work harder to get every last one of their supporters to the polls." The lone dissent written by Judge Terence T. Evans referred to the law as "hollow," concluding that the statute was "a not-too-thinly-veiled attempt to discourage election-day turnout by certain folks believed to skew Democratic." *Crawford v. Marion County Election Bd.*, 472 F.3d 949 (7th Cir. 2007).

The Supreme Court in 2007 agreed to review the case. At oral arguments, Justice ANTHONY KENNEDY made clear that he did not agree that producing a photo identification card imposed an unacceptable burden on voters. When addressing lawyer Paul M. Smith, Kennedy asked, "You want us to invalidate a statute on the ground that it's a minor inconvenience to a small percentage of voters?" Nevertheless, Kennedy and other justices expressed some concern about the effect that the law has on registered voters who do not have photo identification.

Several Republican-led legislatures have pushed similar laws, stressing that these are necessary to prevent voter fraud. Democrats have countered that the law would have an unfair impact on the poor, elderly, disabled, or urban dwellers. The justices, however, said little about these political undercurrents.

In a 6–3 decision, the Court affirmed the Seventh Circuit's decision. Justice JOHN PAUL STEVENS wrote a **plurality** opinion that was joined by Kennedy and Chief Justice JOHN ROBERTS. Stevens' opinion rejected the argument that the law benefits Republicans more than Democrats, noting that justifications for the law "should not be disregarded simply because partisan interests may have provided one motivation for the votes of individual legislators." *Crawford v. Marion County Election Bd.*, No. 07-21, 2008 WL 1848103 (April 28, 2008).

Justice ANTONIN SCALIA, joined by Justices CLARENCE THOMAS and SAMUEL ALITO, concurred with the Court's judgment. Scalia concluded that the law only imposed a minimal burden but that the law was justified. A dissent by Justice DAVID SOUTER, joined by Justices RUTH BADER GINSBURG and STEPHEN BREYER, found that the law "threatens to impose nontrivial burdens on the voting rights of tens of thousands of the state's citizens."

New York State Board of Elections v. Lopez-Torres

State judicial elections have been a part of U.S. politics since the 1820s. Unlike the federal system, where judges are given lifetime appointments, judicial candidates in many states must appear on the ballot if they wish to wear the judicial robe. During the course of U.S. history elected there have been many schemes for selecting and electing judges. New York state has one of the most complicated selection processes

in the nation, making it virtually impossible for judicial candidates not endorsed by the Democratic or Republican parties to get on the ballot. A group of judicial candidates, voters and a nonprofit organization challenged the constitutionality of the New York law, arguing that the scheme violated their political association rights, which are guaranteed by the First Amendments. Though the lower **federal courts** agreed, the U.S. SUPREME COURT, in *New York State Board of Elections v. Lopez-Torres*, __U.S.__, 128 S. Ct. 791, 169 L.Ed.2d 665 (2008), ruled that the New York law was constitutional.

New York state trial judges who work in the state's **general jurisdiction** trial courts are called "Supreme Court Justices." In 1921 the New York legislature revamped the electoral process for Supreme Court justices, enacting a three-part scheme that includes a primary election, a nominating convention, and a general election. Justices are elected from New York's 12 judicial districts. In each of the judicial districts are a number of assembly districts. During the first phase the state held a primary election at which rank-and-file party members elected judicial delegates. Judicial candidates needed to assemble a slate of delegates to run on their behalf, so these delegates could vote for their candidates at the judicial nominating convention. Small subgroups of delegates stood for election in each assembly district but before they appeared on the ballot they first circulated petitions within the district. Within 37 days each slate of delegates had to gather 500 valid signatures from party members residing in the assembly district.

Once a delegate slate was approved, it was placed on the primary ballot by the State Board of Elections. However, the ballot did not disclose the name of the judicial candidate that was linked to the delegates. Therefore, a candidate would have to run a voter education campaign in each assembly district. The political parties held their judicial nominating conventions one to two weeks after a slate of delegates was elected. In theory any judicial candidate could lobby the delegates for support but in practice only candidates who had the backing of the party's leadership would be nominated. The nominating conventions rubber-stamped the party candidates. Between 1990 and 2002 over 96 percent of nominations went uncontested and delegate absenteeism was high. The final phase of the process, the general election, was equally an uncontested affair, as one-party rule was the norm in most judicial districts. Between 1990 and

INTERNET BECOMES A MAJOR MEDIUM DURING 2008 CAMPAIGN

Roughly one month after the 1996 presidential election that saw **Bill Clinton** defeat **Bob Dole**, the Internet had an estimated 36 million total users, representing 0.9% of the world population. During that campaign, Americans received news about the campaign through the sources that they had for decades—television, newspapers, radio, magazines, and other more traditional media. According to a poll conducted in November 1996, two percent of respondents said that they received news about the campaign through the Internet.

The landscape of presidential campaigns has changed drastically since that time. The number of people indicating that they read campaign news on the Internet jumped to 26 percent in December 2007, according to Pew Research Center for the People and the Press, which polled 1,430 individuals as part of its quadrennial survey. Respondents indicated that they relied much less on the other, more traditional sources for this type of information. For example, in a November 1996 poll, sixty percent of respondents said that they

obtained their campaign news from newspapers, while only thirty percent said the same in December 2007.

Of course, in a number of instances, web sites serve the same basic function as newspapers, so some of these numbers may merely suggest that the some users prefer the same information in a different format. Thus, the most popular Internet sites for campaign news include MSNBC, CNN, and Yahoo News. Nevertheless, the Pew survey showed that a number of non-traditional sites have also become significant sources for this campaign news. This is especially true of social networking sites, which have exploded in popularity since the last presidential election in 2004.

"Substantial numbers of young people say they have gotten information on the campaign or the candidates from social networking sites such as MySpace and Facebook," the report concluded. "Overall, more than a quarter of those younger than the age of 30 (27%)— including 37% of those ages 18–24—have gotten campaign information from social

networking sites. This practice is almost exclusively limited to young people; just 4% of Americans in their 30s, and 1% of those ages 40 and older, have gotten news about the campaign in this way."

Another major development in the past four years has been the growth of online video sharing sites. The first of these sites was YouTube, which was developed in 2005 and has seen exponential growth since then. In 2006, Senator George Allen (R.-Va.) made an infamous racial slur when he called an Asian member of a competitor's staff a macaca, which translates into monkey. A member of the competitor's staff taped the reference, and the clip appeared on YouTube as well as other sites on the Internet. When Allen lost the 2006 election, many blamed the clip for his downfall.

Like the social networking sites, YouTube became a significant source of information for younger voters in the 2008 campaign. "At a time when a declining number of young people rely in television for most of their news about the campaign, a sizable minority are going online to watch videos of campaign debates, speeches, and commercials," the

2002 almost half of the elections for Supreme Court Justice were uncontested.

Brooklyn Civil Court Judge Margarita Lopez Torres first won election in 1992 but she was repeatedly unsuccessful in gaining support from Democratic officials to run for Supreme Court Justice. In 2004 she and others filed suit, alleging that the law violated her FIRST AMENDMENT political association rights. The federal **district court** agreed and the Second **Circuit Court** of Appeals upheld the ruling. The state then appealed to the U.S. Supreme Court.

The Court, in a unanimous decision, overruled the Second Circuit. Justice Anthony Scalia, writing for the Court, held that the New York scheme did not violate the First Amendment rights of prospective judicial candidates. He noted that a political party has a First Amendment right to limit its membership as it

pleases, and to "choose a candidate-selection process that will in its view produce the nominee who best represents its political platform." The real claim of Torres was not that she could not vote in the election for delegates or cannot run in that election but that the convention process does not give her "a realistic chance to secure the party's nomination." None of the Court's election law cases established a constitutional right to have a "fair shot" at the winning the party's nomination. It would be impossible for courts to judge whether a candidate got such a fair shot.

As for the allegation that one-party rule in the judicial districts required the Court to use the First Amendment to "impose additional competition in the nomination-selection process," Justice Scalia reasoned that as long as candidates have an "adequate opportunity" to report concluded. According to the Pew report, forty-one percent of those polled who are under the age of 30 watched at least one form of campaign video online. Of those ages 30 and older, twenty percent saw at least one of these videos.

In July 2007, Democratic presidential candidates held a debate that was the first of its kind when the debate was limited to questions submitted by YouTube users. Nearly 3,000 users submitted questions in the form of 30-second video clips, and the candidates responded to those questions. The debate was shown live on CNN, which co-sponsored the event. The debate was described as an effort to allow younger, Internet-savvy voters to ask direct questions to the candidates. While some of the users showed their youth—posting rhetorical questions such as "Wassup?"—the issues that that users asked focused on such current events as the Iraq war, gay marriage, health care, and global warming.

Due to the large number of Internet users interested in the 2008 campaign, nearly every candidate focused considerable attention on strategies to reach these potential voters. In fact, the two leading Democratic candidates, **Hillary Clinton** and Barack Obama, used the Internet to announce their candidacies in 2006. In the recent past, campaigns might have employed someone to run a candidate's website. In 2008, these peo-

ple have been at the center of the campaign's strategy, earning the nickname "Internet strategists."

"Four years ago, these people were called webmasters, not campaign strategists," said Carol Darr of George Washington University's Institute for Politics. "And they were complaining that they didn't have a seat at the table with the senior campaign strategists. Now they're front and center. Half of the articles are about the Internet strategists now."

The vast majority of the 2008 candidates established public pages, with most using both MySpace and Facebook to spread their messages. As of June 2007, Republican John McCain had more than 35,000 "friends" on his MySpace profile, while other candidates allowed users to peek into the candidates' private lives by sharing, for example, pictures, musical preferences, and habits. One aspect of these social sites in the context of a campaign is that a user can align himself or herself with a candidate or political belief by adding the candidate as a friend on the user's profile.

Although much of the focus of the Internet's audience has been on younger people, Internet users are certainly not limited to the young. An estimated 70 percent of adults in the U.S. use the Internet now, and candidates have used

the web during each phase of the various campaigns. Moreover, the Internet allows candidates to develop strategies to target different online audiences.

"[The Internet is] a place for people who tend to be news junkies and political junkies," Dodd said, noting that the numbers of potential online users continues to grow. "And it's the group of people most likely to volunteer, to donate, to get out and advocate on behalf of campaigns. So it really is this golden group of people [that candidates are trying to reach]. Even though it's small, it's exactly who you want to reach if you're a candidate."

Candidates also used the Internet for the important function of fund-raising. In 2004, Democratic hopeful Howard Dean relied in the Internet to raise funds. Although more than 60 percent of his donors gave less than $200, Dean nevertheless raised a total of $53 million for his campaign. While Dean was not successful in earning the nomination that year, other hopefuls took note. Democrats in the 2008 campaign have excelled at raising cash through small-scale donations, while Republicans have used email as a form of direct-mail campaigns in an effort to raise funds. Said Darr, "The Internet will allow a candidate to go in a fundraising stance from zero to 60. You could never do that before the Internet."

appear on the general-election ballot, the First Amendment was not at issue. New York did allow unsuccessful nominating-convention candidates to collect signatures and appear on the general-election ballot. Scalia concluded that the First Amendment created an open marketplace where political ideas compete. It did not call on the federal courts "to manage the market by preventing too many buyers from settling upon a single product." Therefore, New York could continue to use the 1921 law.

EMPLOYMENT DISCRIMINATION

Federal Express Corporation v. Holowecki

The EQUAL EMPLOYMENT OPPORTUNITY COMMISSION (EEOC) enforces federal civil rights laws dealing with employment discrimination, including the Age Discrimination in

Employment Act of 1967 (ADEA), 29 U.S.C. §§ 621 *et.seq*. Under the ADEA, when an employee files a charge alleging unlawful age discrimination with the EEOC, the charge triggers the ADEA's enforcement mechanisms. Once the charge is filed the employee cannot file a lawsuit for 60 days. Though the word "charge" is used several times in the law, Congress did not provide a definition. Over time the circuit courts of appeals have developed different definitions of "charge," leading to differences on when employees file a age discrimination lawsuit. The Supreme Court, in *Federal Express Corporation v. Holowecki*,___ U.S.___, 128 S. Ct. 1147, 170 L. Ed. 2d 10 (2008), was called on to decide if the completion of an EEOC intake questionnaire and an accompanying affidavit constituted a "charge." The Court concluded it did, finding that the detailed affidavit elevated the paperwork to a formal charge of discrimination.

Patricia Kennedy, an employee of Federal Express (FedEx), was one of 14 current and former employees who filed suit in federal **district court** in New York in 2002, alleging that the company had violated the ADEA when it instituted two programs in 1994 and 1995. The programs, which the company contended were designed to improve productivity, tied the couriers' compensation and continued employment to certain performance benchmarks, such as the number of stops a courier makes per day. The plaintiffs argued that the programs targeted employees over 40 years of age and were attempts to force older workers out of the company before they were entitled to retirement benefits. These programs were a pretext for harassing and discriminating older workers in favor of younger workers.

FedEx moved to dismiss Kennedy's complaint because it alleged that she had filed her charge with the EEOC at least 60 days before filing her federal lawsuit. Kennedy replied that she had filed a valid charge more than 60 days before filing suit. She completed an intake questionnaire, Form 283, and attached a signed affidavit describing the alleged discrimination in great detail. The district court agreed with FedEx, concluding that the documents did not constitute a charge and dismissing the case. The Second **Circuit Court** of Appeals reversed this decision and the Supreme Court accepted review to resolve the conflict on this issue in the lower courts.

The Court, in a 7–2 decision, ruled that Kennedy had filed a valid charge. Justice AN-THONY KENNEDY (no relation), writing for the majority, saw two distinct questions that had to be answered: What is a charge as the ADEA uses the term and were Kennedy's documents a charge? The ADEA did not define charge and the EEOC regulations fell short of providing a comprehensive definition. Kennedy noted that the pertinent regulation identified five pieces of information that a charge must contain: the names, addresses and telephone numbers of the person making the charge and the charged **entity**; a statement of facts describing the alleged discriminatory act; the number of employees of the charged employer; and a statement indicating whether the charging party has started state proceedings. However, the next section of the regulation seemed to qualify these requirements by stating that a charge is "sufficient" if it is in writing, names the prospective charged entity and generally alleges the discriminatory acts. Because of these conflicting provisions the circuit courts were divided over what constitutes a

charge. FedEx contended that an intake questionnaire cannot be a charge unless the EEOC acts on it, while the EEOC and some courts of appeals said it could be a charge if it expresses the filer's intent to activate the EEOC's enforcement mechanisms. Finally, Kennedy asserted that all completed questionnaires were charges.

Justice Kennedy agreed with the EEOC in rejecting Kennedy's argument, finding that not all documents meet the minimal requirements for a charge. The Court, under its precedents, is obliged to defer to **administrative agency** regulation if the regulation is reasonable. Justice Kennedy found the regulations reasonable, if not totally clear about what is need to constitute a charge. The EEOC's position in the case was that a filing was a charge when, taken as a whole, it could be construed as a request by an employee for the agency to take whatever actions is necessary to vindicate the employee's rights. The Court agreed with this middle ground, as it distinguished between filings from individual who have questions about their rights and want more information and those filings that seek action. Moreover, because people filing charges are usually not represented by a lawyer, the EEOC should have leeway to interpret documents as requesting that the agency take remedial action. A more detailed standard that required filers to state in explicit terms that they sought action would likely produce more consistent results but it was up to the EEOC to make that decision.

Turning to the filing in question, Justice Kennedy held that the EEOC acted correctly in construing the documents as a charge. Though the intake questionnaire might not be enough to constitute a charge, the inclusion of the detailed affidavit tipped the balance. In it she asked the EEOC to "force Federal Express to end their age discrimination plan." Therefore, Patricia Kennedy could remain part of the lawsuit.

EMPLOYMENT LAW

California and Oregon Rule on Employer Accommodation of Medical Marijuana

During respective 2007–2008 court term sessions, both California and Oregon courts rendered major decisions in the ongoing conflict of medical marijuana laws and employers' rights. In January 2008, the Supreme Court of California ruled that employers had a right to refuse employment to workers using marijuana for medical purposes. *Ross v. RagingWire Tel.* No. S-138130. But in June 2008, the Oregon Court of Appeals held that an employer must make reasonable accommodation for medical marijuana used for a disability. *Emerald Steel Fabricators v. Bureau of Labor and Industries*, No. 304-A130422. As of June 2008, 12 states had medical marijuana laws in place, with South Carolina the latest state to introduce legislation to the state senate for consideration (S.220)

In the California case, the Supreme Court of California ruled 5–2 against an employee who had argued that his employer violated the California Fair Employment and Housing Act by firing him after a drug test. The drug test was part of an employment physical examination for new employees. The plaintiff, Gary Ross, was a 46 y.o. disabled veteran fired from his new job as a systems engineer at RagingWire Telecommunications. Ross had asserted that a doctor had prescribed marijuana to treat his chronic pain. Under California's Compassionate Use Act, persons who used marijuana for medical purposes based on a physician's recommendation could invoke that as a defense in certain state criminal charges involving marijuana, particularly, the offense of possession. However, in its decision, the California court was quick to note that the Compassionate Act created only a narrow exemption for medical users who were criminally prosecuted. Nothing in the Act required an employer to accommodate medical use of marijuana by employees, the court ruled. Therefore, the employer was within its rights to terminate the employment of the new employee for violating its drug-free workplace policy.

In the weeks immediately following the January 2008 decision, California legislators worked to create a medical marijuana employment rights bill. While it would serve to reverse the California appellate decision, it would leave intact the existing Compassionate Use Act, which already prohibited marijuana use at the workplace or during working hours, and protected employers from liability by carving an exception for safety-sensitive positions. In June 2008, the state legislative assembly passed the measure, AB2279, and it moved to the state senate for consideration.

In Oregon, the state court of appeals was asked to review an earlier ruling by the state Bureau of Labor and Industries (BLI), which found that Emerald Steel Fabricators had violated state law when it discharged an employee who used medical marijuana. In a technical decision that focused more on procedural preservation of objections on appeal, the court affirmed the BLI's decision.

A key issue was the fact that the employee had not used marijuana at the workplace, which employers were not required to permit. But the Oregon Medical Marijuana Act of 1998 had been unclear about whether employers needed to accommodate workers who smoked medical marijuana off the job. Defendant Emerald Steel had argued that employees could be affected by medical marijuana use while on duty in "safety-sensitive positions." Emerald also argued that marijuana use remained illegal under federal law despite state law that allowed it for medical purposes. However, these were new issues raised on appeal, so the court did not address them. Again, the focus of the decision was on the fact that Emerald Steel had not entered evidence to support these defenses at the time of the administrative hearing, and therefore, did not preserve these issues for review. Accordingly, the appellate court affirmed the BLI's decision.

The Oregon Supreme Court had previously held, in a 2006 case, that a physical impairment corrected by mitigating measures (medical marijuana) did not rise to the level of a protected disability under employment accommodation laws. *Washburn v. Columbia Forest Products*, 340 Or 469. That case was premised on positive results in an employment-based drug urine test. However, the decision never reached the question of whether the employee had used marijuana in the workplace, which is how the Oregon Court of Appeals was able to rectify the two decisions.

As of June 2008, the 12 states with medical marijuana laws in place were: Alaska, California, Hawaii, Maine, Montana, Nevada, New Mexico, Oregon, Rhode Island, Vermont, and Washington. In three states, the bills were approved by legislatures, while in the remaining states, bills were approved through the voter initiative process. Vermont introduced a bill to expand the range of conditions for which it could be used. Michigan also introduced new measures under the previous HB4038. In South Carolina, S.221 would permit registered patients and their caregivers to possess six plants and up to one ounce of marijuana for an open-ended list of ailments. Senator William Mescher, who introduced the South Carolina bill, died of a stroke in April 2007 and the bill sat until early 2008, when it was reintroduced.

ENVIRONMENTAL LAW

An amalgam of state and federal statutes, regulations, and common-law principles covering air

ALL THINGS GREEN

Historically speaking, when economies sagged, creative projects and creative thinking about environmental issues tended to slump as well. This was due to the fact that any available funds or discretionary income needed to be channeled toward supporting only the bare essentials. But all that may have changed with the realization that global warming and $100/barrel oil prices could effectively be contained, if only more creative and environmental-friendly laws and policies were to be introduced. Suddenly, it seemed, the figurative Green Express was traveling across America, and some of its more prominent passengers were state and local governmental entities, major corporations, educational, and scientific entities. No longer was it Senator Al Gore's (D-TN) little pet project to raise the environmental awareness of young, bright university students. Now it was a Nobel-prize-winning presentation on global warming, along with heightened concern by everyday citizens that seemed to hasten the movement toward the Greening of America. As Dan Esty, a professor of environmental law and policy at Yale University, predicted, corporate America's "green" campaign would survive a tight economy. He told interviewers for the *Christian Science Monitor* in late 2007, "There could be stress in the next year or two, but I'm confident that investment in the environment will be higher."

To be sure, U.S. companies from General Electric to Wal-Mart have increased their announcements of initiatives intended to enhance the environment, from more efficient buildings to alternative energy to employee bonuses for carpooling or walking to work. Had it not been for the shortage in availability of hybrid vehicles, New York's formidable taxicab population would already have converted to all-green taxis. The massive Internet search engine Google dimmed its online screen lighting in recognition and celebration of Earth Day—something that, at least to the baby-boomer generation, sounded like a throwback to the 1970s. Even the slump in the housing market did not deter creativity; if anything, it created an opening. Several major mortgage lenders, including Bank of America, Citigroup, and JP Morgan Chase began rewarding homeowners with $1,000 off closing costs if they made energy-efficient improvements to their houses. Several states created programs to encourage energy efficient improvements for homes. Kansas, Pennsylvania, and New York all offered low- or reduced-interest loans for green home improvements.

In true capitalistic fashion, the quest for green became competitive. Companies called press conferences to announce new initiatives, while other companies plotted to make money off the movement. For example, as Sara Munoz reported in *The Wall Street Journal*, banks offering environmental-friendly mortgage loans had figured out that the annual estimated savings in utility bills could be added to borrowers' projected yearly incomes, thus making them eligible to borrow an extra $10,000 in a 30-year mortgage. All in all, even

talking the Green seemed to enhance stature among fellow-Americans, as many Green Party candidates discovered in the 2007–2008 election season.

Global warming played a key role in Green efforts worldwide. The United Nations' (UN) Intergovernmental Panel on Climate Change had announced in 2007 that greenhouse-gas emissions from human activity, particularly the burning of fossil fuels such as oil and coal, was "very likely" the main cause of global warming and issued a warning of dire consequences to the world if such intensified global action to curb emissions was not undertaken

One of the biggest and more controversial aspects of Green efforts involved the Voluntary Carbon Market, a global initiative that ran parallel with the Kyoto Protocol, the international global warming treaty. Signatories to the treaty, including both countries and companies, made commitments to curb their carbon dioxide emissions.

The United States rejected the Kyoto Protocol and instead opted for voluntary controls. Companies and individual entities in the United States made commitments to reduce their pollutants and carbon emissions incrementally over the next several years, in return for a voluntary rather than mandatory program. As Congress grappled with debates over whether the United States should instead impose mandatory caps on greenhouse-gas emissions or continue to rely on voluntary activity, another (and more controversial) alternative surfaced: carbon offsets. The voluntary offset market ultimately emerged as a way for companies or individuals not bound by the Kyoto agreement to

pollution, water pollution, hazardous waste, the wilderness, and endangered wildlife.

California Sues the EPA for Waiver on Car Emissions

In an effort to reduce the amount of greenhouse gas emissions, the state of California has sought to adopt tough emission standards for new cars. The proposed standards would force auto manufacturers to cut emissions by 25 per-cent from cars and light trucks, and 18 percent for SUVs, beginning with the 2009 model year. However, before California can enforce these standards it must obtain a waiver from the ENVIRONMENTAL PROTECTION AGENCY (EPA) because federal environmental law preempts state environmental laws. California submitted its regulatory standards to the EPA in December 2005, but by November 2007 the state had not received a ruling. California filed suit in November against still show that they were addressing global warming and thus respond to public or shareholder pressure.

Carbon offsets are essentially environmental passes. They represent cuts in global-warming emissions that have been made somewhere in the world. The idea behind them is that money raised from the offsets would fund projects to reduce emissions. Each carbon offset roughly represents the value of offsetting (avoiding) one ton of CO_2 or equivalent greenhouse gas pollution. Companies or individuals earning these credits may use them to qualify for governmental funds, grants, and special projects designed to develop new ways to reduce emissions.

The controversy surrounding these offsets centered around the fact that they could be bought and trades as commodities between companies and countries. As offset credits were earned by environmentally-friendly companies who did more than their share, they discovered they could sell their excess credits to a polluting company or individual. Overall, the objective of meeting decreased emissions would still be met; it was just that some entities continued to excessively pollute but could compensate by still claiming possession of carbon offsets. Projects began popping up from Texas to China, said *The Wall Street Journal.* They ranged from planting trees, which absorb high amounts of ambient carbon dioxide, to capturing methane, another harmful greenhouse gas that is emitted by rotting animal waste on farms.

The voluntary offsets differ from pollution permits traded under the Kyoto Protocol. The Kyoto-based pollution credit market, worth billions of dollars, is overseen by UN-sanctioned officials who must approve projects before credits could be sold. But the voluntary offsets lack regulation, raising doubts about whether claimed cuts in emissions are really taking place.

Critics claim that both systems are rife with abuse. In early 2008, Ecosystem Marketplace and New Carbon Finance released a report, *State of the Voluntary Carbon Markets: Forging the Frontier,* showing that the average price to offset one ton of CO_2 or equivalent gas rose 49 percent in 2007. Moreover, volume in the over-the-counter market for offset trading nearly tripled in 2007, from $97 million in 2006 to $331 million in 2007.

In November 2007, three groups representing some of the biggest sellers and buyers of carbon offsets announced the Voluntary Carbon Standard in an attempt to offer uniformity and credibility to the offset trade market. Although participation and compliance with the proposed standard remained voluntary, the drafters were hoping that public pressure would push many entities to participate. Since there still was no independent panel to approve or reject projects to earn offsets, critics believed the standard was too lax.

For example, forestry markets account for a large share of the voluntary offset market. Trees consume large amounts of carbon dioxide as they grow, a positive factor. But they emit as much if not more carbon dioxide when burned. The sale and/or trade of excess offsets between the two sectors of the industry may look good on paper, but result in zero advances in emissions reduction. To address this snag, under the new voluntary standards, offset sellers must have their forest projects vetted by trained entities to verify that the projects are accomplishing as much as claimed.

Meanwhile, the main thrust of green legislation around the country tended to focus on alternative energy. From local grassroots initiatives to state-funded programs, goals and objectives were incorporated into comprehensive plans that would reduce energy use and/or pollution by stated percentages over a stated number of years. For example, U.S. businesses spent approximately $3.5 billion on renewable energy in 2005, compared to about $132 billion in conventional oil and gas during the same year. Yale's Professor Esty projected the renewable energy investment to increase to over $100 billion by 2008. This would represent a conscious shift of interest and investment from one sector of the energy market to another.

Title IX of the much-touted House energy bill passed by the U.S. Congress in December 2007 included provisions for loan guarantees for renovation projects meeting articulated green building certification requirements. Other sections of the bill mandated, the Secretary of Energy to issue regulations prohibiting the sale of 100-watt incandescent light bulbs after January 1, 2012 (Sections 9021–9030); the raising of required energy efficiency for washing machines, dishwashers, refrigerators, etc. (Sections 9001-9020); the updating of state building codes to be more energy efficient (Section 9031); and additional financial assistance to consumers for home weatherization projects (Section 9034). In early 2008, House Democrats, led by Speaker Nancy Pelosi, pledged to back clean-energy rhetoric with real change, starting with the Capitol Dome, scheduled to get its electricity from wind power and heat from natural gas in the foreseeable future.

the EPA, asking a court to order the EPA to rule on the standards. Then, in December, the EPA finally ruled, denying the state request. The state filed suit in January 2008, seeking to appeal the EPA decision in a federal court. Sixteen other states joined California in the lawsuit, which drew congressional attention. A Congressional committee began a probe of the EPA decision to decide whether political pressures forced the agency to rule against the waiver request.

The California Air Resources Board (ARB) developed the regulations based on a 2002 law that required California to establish new standards for motor vehicle greenhouse gas emissions beginning in model year 2009. The 25 percent reduction on cars would, by 2016, increase to a 30 percent reduction. California claimed that these standards would eliminate greenhouse gases equivalent to taking 6.5 million cars off the road by the year 2020. If all 50 states with similar plans did the same, greenhouse gases equivalent to removing nearly 22 million vehicles off the road. California officials noted that 16 states, comprising about 45 percent of all U.S. auto sales, had adopted or were in the process of adopting, California's standards.

Governor Arnold Schwarzenegger became a strong advocate of the new standards, even though they conflicted with the approach taken by fellow Republican, President GEORGE W. BUSH. Schwarzenegger tried to prod President Bush to take action on the waiver, writing him letters in April and October 2006. In April 2007 the governor wrote EPA administrator Peter L. Johnson a stern letter, noting that 16 months had passed since the waiver application and warning him that the state would file a lawsuit within 180 days if no decision had been made in that time. Under the Clean Air Act and the Administrative Procedure Act, states have the right to seek a court order compelling agency action. The state proceeded to file a federal lawsuit against the EPA in November 2007 in the U.S. **District Court** for the DISTRICT OF COLUMBIA, arguing that Congress intended the EPA to rule on such waivers in weeks or months, but not years. Arizona, Connecticut, Illinois, Maine, Massachusetts, New Jersey, New Mexico, New York, Oregon, Pennsylvania, Rhode Island, Vermont, and Washington intervened in the lawsuit on behalf of California. The EPA replied that it had always planned to make a decision by the end of 2007 but that several factors had come into play that delayed its decision. It noted that it was a party to a lawsuit that was not resolved until the U.S. SUPREME COURT ruled in April 2007. In that case the Court ruled against the agency and found that the EPA did have the authority to regulate greenhouse gas emissions, which it had denied. Moreover, the EPA said it had received a large volume of public comments that needed to be reviewed.

On December 19, 2007, the EPA finally ruled, denying California's waiver application. Johnson explained to the press that the Bush Administration preferred a single, unified national standard to a state-by-state scheme of regulations. Johnson also referred to the Energy Independence and Security Act of 2007 that had been signed that same day. The law requires automakers to reach industry-wide fuel efficiency for cars, SUVs, and small tracks of 35 miles per gallon by 2020. Governor Schwarzenegger quickly announced that the state would appeal the ruling in federal court and an appeal

was filed in early January 2008. At the same time Rep. Henry Waxman, Democrat of New York and Chair of the House Oversight and Government Reform Committee, announced that his committee would investigate whether the decision was politically motivated. He asked that the EPA turn over all documents related to the decision.

Controversy erupted in late February 2008, when internal EPA documents were disclosed by California Senator Barbara Boxer, a Democrat, which showed that EPA agents had urged Johnson to approve the waiver. Agents said denying the waiver would compromise the integrity of EPA and another memo stated there was no "legal or technical justification" for denying the waiver application. At a Senate hearing, Johnson refused to say whether the White House has pressured the agency to deny the request. Several days later he issued a notice that provided an official explanation for his decision. In the notice, Johnson stated, "In my judgment, the impacts of global climate change in California, compared to the nation as a whole, are not sufficiently different to be considered 'compelling and extraordinary conditions' that merit separate state GHG [greenhouse gas] standards for new motor vehicles."

In March 2008 bills were introduced in the House and Senate that seek to overturn the EPA waiver denial and give the states the right to enact or implement higher greenhouse gas emission standards. A Senate committee approved the bill in late May, while Rep. Waxman's House committee issued a report that same week which concluded that the White House had played a "significant role" in the EPA decision. Though the waiver had unanimous support of EPA career staff, the waiver was rejected after Johnson met with unnamed White House officials.

ERISA

LaRue v. DeWollf, Boberg & Associates, Inc.

The federal EMPLOYEE RETIREMENT INCOME SECURITY ACT (ERISA) seeks to protect the rights of employees and the **solvency** of employer-administered retirement and investment plans. The aim of this complex federal act is to protect retirement plans rather than the individuals who have a stake in them. This is reflected in provisions that prohibit individual from suing their employers for ERISA violations. The ban on private rights of action is settled law, but the Supreme Court was confronted with a case where the employee did not seek damages but payment into his plan of the money he lost when the employer failed to follow his instructions on how his money was invested. The Court, in *LaRue v. DeWollf, Boberg & Associates, Inc.*, __U.S.__, 128 S. Ct. 2361, __ L. Ed. 2d __ (2008), held that the employee did have a private **right of action** because he sought to protect the entire plan from **fiduciary** misconduct. The decision also reflected the shift in employer-sponsored retirement plans since ERISA was enacted 1974, from defined benefit plans to the defined contribution plans that now dominate retirement planning.

James LaRue worked for DeWollf, Boberg & Associates and contributed to an ERISA-regulated 401(k) retirement savings plan that was administered by his employer. The plan permits participants to direct their contributions to different investment funds. In 2004, LaRue filed a lawsuit in federal **district court**, alleging that in 2001 and 2002 he directed DeWollf to make changes in the investment funds for his individual account but that DeWollf never made the changes. He claimed that this omission depleted his interest in the plan by approximately $150,000 and that DeWollf's inaction rose to the level of a breach of fiduciary duty under ERISA. He sought "make whole" or equitable relief, but did not ask for damages. DeWollf filed a motion with the court, asking it to dismiss the lawsuit because LaRue could not ask for monetary relief under ERISA. LaRue reiterated that he did not ask for damages but wanted the plan to "properly reflect that which would be his interest in the plan, but for breach of fiduciary duty." The court concluded that because DeWollf did not possess any disputed funds that rightly belonged to LaRue, he was seeking damages rather than equitable relief. Even assuming DeWollf breached its fiduciary duty, LaRue did not have the right to sue for damages under ERISA. The Fourth **Circuit Court** of Appeals affirmed the district court, finding that ERISA's provision allowing lawsuits only applies to protecting the entire plan, not the rights of an individual beneficiary. Though LaRue's remedy of having DeWollf pay into his plan account could be seen as being part of the plan, the appeals court was concerned that allowing such a recovery would undermine the "careful limitations Congress has placed on the scope of ERISA relief."

The Supreme Court unanimously voted to overturn the Fourth Circuit decision and to allow LaRue to pursue his claim. Justice JOHN PAUL STEVENS, writing for five of the justices,

James LaRue and his wife, Shannon, November 2007.
AP IMAGES

noted that ERISA does allow plan participants to sue employers to recover for improper administration and management of fund assets. The alleged misconduct by DeWollf fell "squarely within this category." A 1985 Supreme Court ERISA decision, which the Fourth Circuit had relied on, concluded that Congress was primarily concerned with remedies to protect the "entire plan" rather that with the rights of an individual beneficiary. Justice Stevens distinguished this case precedent, finding that it reflected "the former landscape of employee benefit plans." This landscape had changed, with defined contribution plans such as 401(k) plans replacing the defined benefit plans that were dominant when ERISA was enacted.

The benefit plan reviewed in the 1985 case did not have individual accounts but instead paid a fixed benefit based on a percentage of the employee's salary. Misconduct by administrators of a defined benefit plan would not affect an individual's entitlement unless it could lead to the risk of default by the entire plan. Congress enacted ERISA provisions to protect against this happening. Therefore, an individual would have no right to sue under this type of plan.

The defined contribution plan, on the other hand, was different. Fiduciary misconduct did not have to threaten the solvency of the entire plan to "reduce benefits below the amount the participants would otherwise receive." Because of the differences in the two types of plans, the 1985 precedent "was beside the point;" it only applied to defined benefit plans. Freed from this precedent, the Court held that ERISA authorizes recovery "for fiduciary breaches that impair the value of plan assets in a participant's individual account." LaRue had the right to pursue his recovery.

ESPIONAGE

The act of securing information of a military or political nature that a competing nation holds secret. It can involve the analysis of diplomatic reports, publications, statistics, and broadcasts, as well as spying, a clandestine activity carried out by an individual or individuals working under a secret identity for the benefit of a nation's information gathering techniques. In the United States, the organization that heads most activities dedicated to espionage is the Central Intelligence Agency.

No Standing to Challenge Government Spying

In July 2007, a split panel of the U.S. **Circuit Court** of Appeals for the Sixth Circuit vacated the judgment of a federal **district court** and ruled that plaintiffs challenging government spying under the National Security Agency (NSA) lacked legal standing to sue. The NSA operated a program providing for interception (monitoring, wiretapping) of communications involving any individuals with suspected ties to al Qaeda (a terrorist organization widely held as being a key player in attacks against the United States) without first getting a court-issued warrant. In February 2008, the U.S. SUPREME COURT denied review of the **appellate** court's decision. *ACLU v. NSA*, 493 F.3d 644 (6th Cir. 2007).

According to facts summarized in the Sixth Circuit's opinion, sometime after the terrorist attacks upon the United States on September 11, 2001, President Bush authorized the NSA to commence a counter-terrorism operation ultimately referred to as the Terrorist Surveillance Program (TSP). Specifics of the program were classified and therefore undisclosed. Notwithstanding, it was publicly acknowledged that the TSP included interception (e.g., wiretapping), without warrants, of telephone and Internet email communications, where one party to the communication "is a member of al Qaeda, affiliated with al Qaeda, or a member of an organization affiliated with al Qaeda, or working in support of al Qaeda." Another aspect of the program was "data-mining," or collecting tele-

phone call data, such as numbers called and length of calls, etc.

The original case was filed in federal circuit court in Detroit, Michigan by the AMERICAN CIVIL LIBERTIES UNION (ACLU), representing a conglomerate plaintiff group that included journalists, academics, and lawyers. Together, they charged that their writings and research often caused them to visit or search Internet Web sites that used keyword searches that could be construed as suspicious under government surveillance programs. Moreover, they often placed or received international telephone calls to and from clients or colleagues in geographic locations that would also flag their communications for possible interception or surveillance. As stated in the Sixth Circuit opinion, the persons to or from whom communications were carried on with, were those "who the plaintiffs believe are the types of people the NSA suspects of being al Qaeda terrorists, affiliates, or supporters, and are therefore likely to be monitored under the TSP." Importantly, noted the Sixth Circuit, the plaintiffs alleged that they had a "well-founded belief" that their communications were being tapped.

Plaintiffs sought a permanent injunction against the NSA's continued operation of the TSP program. They also charged that two aspects of the TSP, warrantless wiretapping and data mining, violated the First and Fourth Amendments of the U.S. Constitution, the Separation of Powers Doctrine, the Foreign Intelligence Surveillance Act (FISA), and several other cited legislative provisions.

The NSA had invoked the State Secrets Doctrine (established in previous and long-standing Supreme Court decisions) that barred the discovery or admission of evidence that would "expose [confidential] matters which, in the interest of national security, should not be divulged." *United States v. Reynolds*, 345 U.S. 1, 73 S. Ct. 528, 97 L. Ed. 727 (1953). The doctrine had two components, a rule of evidentiary privilege, and a rule of non-justiciability (where the subject matter of the lawsuit itself is a state secret, such that a claim cannot survive). In the present case, the NSA argued that, without the privileged evidentiary information, none of the plaintiffs could establish standing to sue. (The NSA did provide the district court an opportunity to review certain secret documents, **in camera** and under seal, in support of their invoking of the state secrets privilege.)

The district court, however, agreed with plaintiffs and condemned the government's position, stating, "There are no hereditary kings in America and no powers not created by the Constitution." The court ruled that the NSA program violated the Fourth Amendment's prohibition against unreasonable searches and seizures because it set up a system of warrantless interception entirely outside of **judicial review** or oversight. The district court also held that the program violated the FIRST AMENDMENT because such government spying tended to have a chilling effect on free speech. Individuals fearing government monitoring might curtail otherwise protected political or legal speech or activity. The district court also granted a permanent injunction against continued operation of the TSP.

But the Sixth Circuit vacated the decision, particularly noting that the district court had premised its entire ruling on the three publicly-acknowledged facts about NSA operations, (i.e., that it eavesdropped, without warrants, on international communications suspected of involving al Qaeda) without considering the individual plaintiffs. While acknowledging that the case presented "a number of serious issues," the **appellate court** further noted that none of these substantive issues could be addressed without a preliminary determination that the plaintiffs had standing to litigate those issues.

The appellate court went on to mention that standing was an aspect of justiciability, meaning that there must first be a careful judicial examination of whether any plaintiff (only one needed)had standing that would entitle him or her to an **adjudication** of the substantive claims. The court found that no plaintiff was able to show that he or she had actually been subjected to alleged NSA surveillance, but had merely premised the lawsuit on a subjective "well-founded belief." Therefore, the plaintiffs lacked standing to sue. Further, the court found the plaintiffs had not claimed any separate injury specifically tied to the alleged NSA datamining program, making that claim unjusticiable as well. Having found that plaintiffs lacked standing to sue, all claims fell and the appellate court vacated the district court's decision and remanded with instructions to dismiss plaintiffs' claims.

The Sixth Circuit did not reach the issue of whether the lawsuit was moot after the Bush Administration announced in January 2007 that a FISA court had approved the communication interception program. (The original district court decision was in 2006.)

EXCLUSIONARY DOCTRINE

Virginia v. Moore

The U.S. SUPREME COURT in 2008 issued a ruling that tested the constitutional limits of searches and seizures under the FOURTH AMENDMENT to the U.S. Constitution. The Court in *Virginia v. Moore*, ___ U.S. ___, 128 S. Ct. 1598, ___ L. Ed. 2d ___ (2008) ruled that the Fourth Amendment does not require exclusion of evidence obtained in search during an arrest following a stop of a motorist who was driving without a license. In an unanimous decision, the Court held that the Fourth Amendment does not provide a remedy for what amounts to a violation of a state **statute**.

The case arose from an incident on February 20, 2003. Detective B.J. Karpowski overheard a police radio conversation about a man nicknamed "Chubs" driving in the area. The person who went by "Chubs" was David Lee Moore, who had recently been released from the state penitentiary. Karpowski informed other officers in the area about the call and told the officers to stop Moore's car.

Two other detectives, Mike Anthony and T. McAndrew, heard Karpowski's message and then found Moore. They stopped Moore's car and determined that he was driving on a suspended license. After confirming the status of Moore's license, the officers arrested him, handcuffed him, and placed him in McAndrew's vehicle. Because of a miscommunication between the officers, they did not search Moore at the time of his initial arrest. The officer, though, had to wait 45 minutes for animal control services to pick up a dog that was riding in Moore's vehicle.

After animal control arrived, the officers drove Moore to a hotel where he was staying. They gave him *Miranda* warnings and obtained his signature to search the hotel room. McAndrew then searched Moore and discovered a packet of crack cocaine and $516 in cash. When asked why the officers initially decided to arrest Moore, Anthony said, "Just our prerogative, we **chose** to effect an arrest. Additionally, subsequent to that traffic stop, narcotics were eventually recovered."

Moore was stopped for what amounted to a Class 1 **misdemeanor**. Under Virginia Code § 19.2-74, the detectives should have issued Moore a summons and released him from custody after they secured his promise to appear to answer the summons. The officers could have arrested Moore if he were suspected of drunk driving, failed or refused to discontinue an unlawful act, gave the officers reason to believe that he would disregard the summons, or gave the officers reasonable belief that he was likely to harm himself or someone else. None of these exceptions applied to Moore, and so under state law, the officers should not have arrested him.

Moore argued before the trial court that the evidence found during the search of him following his arrest should be suppressed because the seizure of the evidence violated the Fourth Amendment to the U.S. Constitution. The trial court denied his motion to suppress, and after a **bench trial**, the court convicted Moore of possession with intent to distribute cocaine. Moore received a five-year sentence, with eighteen months suspended.

Moore appealed his conviction to the Court of Appeals of Virginia. A divided panel of the court determined that the officers' search of Moore violated Moore's Fourth Amendment rights. *Moore v. Commonwealth*, 609 S.E.2d 74 (Va. App. 2005). The **appellate court** reheard the case *en banc*, however, and affirmed the conviction, finding that the search did not violate the Constitution. *Moore v. Commonwealth*, 622 S.E.2d 253 (Va. App. 2005). The Virginia Supreme Court then decided to hear the case and reversed the Court of Appeals. *Moore v. Commonwealth*, 636 S.E.2d 395 (Va. 2006).

According to the Virginia Supreme Court, Moore's case was controlled by the U.S. Supreme Court's decision in *Knowles v. Iowa*, 525 U.S. 113, 119 S. Ct. 484, 142 L. Ed. 2d 492 (1998) and the Virginia Supreme Court's decision in *Lovelace v. Commonwealth*, 522 S.E.2d 856 (Va. 1999). In *Knowles*, an Iowa police officer had stopped a motorist for speeding and issued a citation. After issuing the citation, the officer conducted a full search of Knowles' vehicle and found marijuana. The Supreme Court determined that the search violated the Fourth Amendment because the officer had not conducted the search pursuant to a lawful arrest.

In *Lovelace*, the Virginia Supreme Court reviewed a case involving the search of man who had been arrested for drinking an alcoholic beverage. Officers in that case suspected that the defendant had been drinking and had thrown an empty beer bottle in the direction of the officers. During a search of the defendant following his arrest, the officers found crack cocaine and marijuana. The defendant was convicted of possession. After a series of appeals, the Virginia Supreme Court determined that the search was unconstitutional under the authority of *Knowles*,

largely because § 19.2-74 does not authorize officers to arrest a suspect but rather only issue a summons.

The U.S. Supreme Court unanimously reversed the Virginia Supreme Court. In an opinion by Justice ANTONIN SCALIA, the Court determined that neither the history of the Fourth Amendment nor traditional reasonableness standards supported the conclusion that the Fourth Amendment required exclusion of evidence pursuant to this type of arrest.

The Court specifically rejected the argument that the result in *Knowles* controlled the outcome in the case. "The Virginia Supreme Court may have concluded that *Knowles* required the exclusion of evidence seized from Moore because, under state law, the officers who arrested Moore should have issued him a citation instead," Scalia wrote. "This argument might have force if the Constitution forbade Moore's arrest, because we have sometimes excluded evidence obtained through unconstitutional methods in order to deter constitutional violations. But the arrest rules that the officers violated were those of state law alone, and as we have just concluded, it is not the province of the Fourth Amendment to enforce state law. That Amendment does not require the exclusion of evidence obtained from a constitutionally permissible arrest." Justice RUTH BADER GINSBURG wrote a concurring opinion, where she argued that Moore's position had more historical support than the majority concluded. However, she otherwise agreed with the rationale of the Court's opinion.

EXECUTIVE PRIVILEGE

The right of the president of the United States to withhold information from Congress or the courts.

White House Visitor Logs are Public

Presidents of the United States have claimed that certain information is privileged and cannot be disclosed to Congress or to the public. The administration of GEORGE W. BUSH has asserted **executive privilege** a number of times when Congress has sought documents or testimony from high-ranking Executive Branch officials. The Bush Administration successfully turned away a lawsuit that sought information about which energy company executives met with Vice President Richard Cheney to discuss energy policies. In 2008 two pending lawsuits proceeded that sought White House visitor logs. One action seeks to determine how often several conservative religious leaders visited the White House for meetings. A second action seeks to determine the number of times Jack Abramoff, a corrupt and now convicted lobbyist, visited the White House. In both cases the Bush Administration asserted executive privilege, arguing that the logs were not public records. Moreover, the White House used a 2006 agreement between it and the SECRET SERVICE to bolster its argument.

In the first case the Citizens for Responsibility and Ethics in Washington (a liberal advocacy group) asked to see the visitor logs to determine how many times the Rev. Jerry Falwell, Focus on the Family's James Dobson, and other conservative religious leaders met with the Bush Administration. Under the federal FREEDOM OF INFORMATION ACT (FOIA), citizens are entitled to all public records unless the government can assert an exception. The White House declined to release the logs, claiming they are presidential documents. (During the Clinton Administration the visitor logs were used by political opponents to document the visits of political donors, pardon-seekers, and former White House intern Monica Lewinsky.) This argument, which had not been made by previous administrations, was buttressed by a 2006 agreement between the White House and the Secret Service. Under this agreement the Secret Service, which maintains the logs, turns over the logs to the White House, which are labeled presidential documents. This label means that the logs cannot be released under the FOIA. However, this agreement was not made until after the litigation in this case had begun.

After the White House asserted its FOIA exception and denied release of the logs, the advocacy group asserted its right under FOIA and appealed the decision to federal **district court**. Judge Royce Lamberth ruled in December 2007 that the visitor logs were public records. The judge grounded the decision on the fact that the Secret Service and not the White House directly maintained the logs. Lamberth stated that "Because the Secret Service creates, uses and relies on, and stores visitor records, they are under its control. Knowledge of these visitors would not disclose presidential communications or shine a light on the president's or the vice president's policy deliberations." The fact that the 2006 agreement between the White House and the Secret Service came after the litigation in this case had begun made it, in Lamberth's view, "self-serving."

The Bush Administration appealed the order to the U.S. **Circuit Court** of Appeals for the DISTRICT OF COLUMBIA. The three-judge appeal panel conducted oral argument in April 2008. The government's lawyer argued that releasing lists of visitors would hurt the president's right to seek advice privately and confidentially. Though the White House called the logs presidential documents the appeals panel was skeptical. One judge noted that the only information given was the name of the person visiting the White House. A person could stand outside the White House and observe who goes in and who goes out. Another judge raised concerns about giving the president blanket powers to make records of White House agencies presidential documents that are currently public records. Moreover, persons who visit the White House, such as social planners and caterers, would be treated the same as persons who give advice to the president privately.

The appeals court recognized the need for the president to receive advice privately and suggested that a compromise should be reached by both sides that balanced the rights in question. However, the government said it would be impossible to screen the visitor lists to determine which meetings might be sensitive. Though the court did not immediately rule, whatever decision that it made would certainly be appealed to the Supreme Court.

FALSE CLAIMS ACT

Allison Engine Co. v. United States

In June 2008, the U.S. SUPREME COURT resolved a question of whether the False Claims Act applies to any **fraudulent** claim paid for with government funds rather than only those fraudulent claims directly submitted to a government official. The Court determined that the act can be used if the false claim is intended to be paid by the government. In so ruling, the Court sent the case back to the Sixth **Circuit Court** of Appeals to apply the appropriate standard.

The False Claims Act was originally enacted during the CIVIL WAR to prevent **fraud** perpetrated by defense contractors. The modern version of the **statute** has both a civil and a criminal portion. The civil portion provides as follows:

> Any person who: (1) knowingly presents, or causes to be presented, to an officer or employee of the United States Government or a member of the Armed Forces of the United States a false or fraudulent claim for payment or approval; (2) knowingly makes, uses, or causes to be made or used, a false record or statement to get a false or fraudulent claim paid or approved by the government; [or] (3) conspires to defraud the Government by getting a false or fraudulent claim allowed or paid in full[,] . . . is liable to the United States Government for a civil penalty of not less than $5,000 and not more than $10,000, plus 3 times the amount of damages which the Government sustains because of the act of that person.

31 U.S.C. § 3729(a). Section (c) of the Act defines "claim" as "any request or demand, whether under a contract or otherwise, for money or property which is made to a contractor, **grantee**, or other recipient if the United States Government provides any portion of the money or property which is requested or demanded, or of the Government will reimburse such contractor, grantee, or other recipient for any portion of the money or property which is requested or demanded."

The U.S. Navy in 1985 entered into contracts with two shipbuilders to construct a fleet of missile destroyers. The shipbuilders included Bath Iron Works and Ingalls Shipbuilding. The companies needed to construct a total of 90 generator sets to supply the electrical power to the ships. The shipbuilders contracted with Allison Engine (formerly a division of General Motors) to build these generators. Allison Engine, in turn, subcontracted with General Tool Company to assemble the generator sets, and General Tool Company (GTC) subcontracted with Southern Ohio Fabricators, Inc. (SOFCO) to manufacture parts of these sets.

The shipbuilders were paid a total of $1 billion for each destroyer, while Allison Engine was paid $3 million per generator set. GTC and SOFCO were paid $800,000 and $100,000, respectively, for each generator set. The generator sets were constructed according to specifications established by the Navy, and all of the funds used the pay the contractors and subcontractors were eventually paid for by the Federal Treasury.

Two former employees of GTC who had worked on the generator set assembly teams brought actions under the False Claims Act, alleging that the subcontractors had committed fraud in the construction of the generator sets. According to these employees, the subcontractors knew about several defects in the construction of the generator sets in violation of the Navy contracts, yet these companies submitted their invoice anyway. The employees argued that the invoices were "false or fraudulent claims" paid for with government funds and that this action violated the False Claims Act. The employees brought the suit as a *qui tam* action, which allows a private party to recover some of the amount that is due to the government under the Act.

At trial, the employees failed to introduce invoices that the primary contractors had submitted by the companies to the Navy. The subcontractors moved for judgment as a matter of law, arguing that the employees had not provided evidence that the subcontractors had violated the False Claims Act since the employees had not proven that the invoice had been presented to the Navy, since the invoices had been sent to the primary contractors instead of to the Navy itself. The **district court** agreed with the subcontractors, holding that the employees were required to show proof that false claims were presented to the government.

On appeal to the Sixth Circuit Court of Appeals, a divided panel agreed that proof of presentation of a false claim is required under the statute. However, the court concluded that §§ 3729(a)(2) and (3), unlike § 3729(a)(1), does not require proof that a claim was presented directly to the government for payment. Rather, the panel determined that proof of intent for a false claim to be paid by a private **entity** using government funds was enough to sustain a claim under the act. Accordingly, the Sixth Circuit reversed the district court. *United States v. Allison Engine Co.*, 471 F.3d 610 (6th Cir. 2006).

The U.S. Supreme Court agreed to hear the case, though during oral argument it appeared as if the case may be derailed. An attorney representing one of the employees told the Court that though the subcontractors had not directly billed the Navy, Allison Engine had sent a "certificate of conformance" to the Navy. This prompted statements from Justices ANTONIN SCALIA and JOHN ROBERTS, who thought the case did not present the same issues that they had originally thought. However, counsel for Allison Engine responded that no such certificate had been presented, and the Court did not dismiss the case.

A unanimous Supreme Court disagreed with much of the reasoning used by the Sixth

Circuit. In an opinion by Justice SAMUEL ALITO, the Court determined that the Sixth Circuit's interpretation deviated impermissibly from the **statutory** language. Under the Court's interpretation, the party submitting the false claim must intend for the government itself to pay the claim. This does not mean, though, that a **subcontractor** must bill the government directly for the subcontractor to be liable under the statute. Where a subcontractor intends for the government to pay a bill that the subcontractor submits to the contractor, then the subcontractor may be liable if the claim is false.

Since the Sixth Circuit had based its decision in a faulty interpretation of §§ 3729(a)(2) and (a)(3), the Court vacated the panel's opinion and remanded the case to the court of appeals.

FEDERAL COMMUNICATIONS COMMISSION

Fox Television Stations, Inc. v. Federal Communications Commission

The FEDERAL COMMUNICATIONS COMMISSION (FCC) has the authority to police the use of obscene, indecent, and profane language on broadcast television and radio programming. In the past, the FCC has used this authority sparingly, rarely sanctioning networks or local stations for the utterance of common swear words. This restrained enforcement policy changed in 2003 when the rock star Bono uttered the F-word at the Golden Globes Award Show broadcast by NBC. The FCC shifted its policy, declaring that any use of the F-word was indecent, no matter how fleeting or in a non-sexual context. In addition, the commission held that the use of the word was profane. Broadcasters were put on notice that any broadcast of the F-word would subject them to monetary penalties. The FCC also suggested that broadcasters implement a delay technology that would give them the time to "bleep" out indecent and profane words from live broadcasts. In 2006 the FCC backed its new position by ruling that several live broadcast utterances of the F-word or the S-word violated this policy. The FCC declined to assess monetary penalties because the broadcasts occurred before the Golden Globes decision, but its shift in policy alarmed broadcasters. The FOX, CBS, NBC, and ABC television networks appealed the FCC order, contending the new policy was arbitrary and capricious and that it raised FIRST AMENDMENT censorship issues.

In a 2–1 decision, a three-judge panel of the Second **Circuit Court** of Appeals agreed with the television networks that the policy change was arbitrary and capricious. *Fox Television Stations, Inc. v. Federal Communications Commission*, 489 F.3d 444 (2d Cir. 2007) It declined to rule on the First Amendment issue because the first ground was sufficient to settle the matter. Judge Rosemary Pooler, writing for the majority, reviewed the FCC's history of policing indecent speech. Pooler noted that the FCC had not aggressively pursued isolated utterances of obscenity and **profanity**. Instead, it concentrated on material that was explicitly sexual or excretory and was patently offensive as measured by contemporary community standards.

The FCC's Golden Globe decision illustrated the abrupt shift in policy. The FCC's Enforcement Bureau denied complaints filed about Bono's offensive language because the word, viewed in context, did not describe sexual or excretory organs or activities and the utterance was fleeting and isolated. The FCC, in overruling its Enforcement Bureau, held that any use of any variant of the F-word inherently had sexual connotations and therefore fell within the FCC's indecency definition. The commission also stated that the use of the F-word was patently offensive under contemporary community standards and that the isolated or fleeting use of the word was irrelevant. In doing so, the FCC overruled all prior decisions in which the fleeting use of an expletive was held not to be indecent. In addition, the commission found that the use of the F-word was profane. Prior decisions had interpreted "profane" to mean **blasphemy** but the current members saw no basis for limiting the definition to this meaning.

Turning to the 2006 decision by the FCC, Judge Pooler pointed out that the utterances in dispute took place on two awards shows and a morning news show. The application of the commission's new "fleeting expletive" policy had to be considered in light of its previous policy and the reasons justifying the new one. The court set aside the policy because it was arbitrary and capricious. Judge Pooler acknowledged that administrative agencies should be accorded great deference in managing their responsibilities but they when they make policies there must be a "rational connection between the facts found and the choice made." The networks contended that the FCC had acted arbitrarily because it made a complete about-face on its treatment of "fleeting expletives" without providing a reasoned explanation that justified its action.

FCC chairman Michael Powell speaks, January 2004.

AP IMAGES

The court agreed, finding no compelling reasons to justify the change. The FCC's primary reason for the crackdown was a so-called "first blow" theory. Because the airwaves entered the privacy of the home uninvited and without warning, allowing isolated or fleeting expletives "unfairly forces viewers (including children) to take "the first blow." Judge Pooler rejected this as a "reasoned basis" for overturning the prior policy for several reasons. First, the FCC did not provide a reasonable explanation for why it had changed its perception, after 30 years, that a fleeting expletive was not a harmful "first blow." Moreover, the first blow theory had no rational connection to the commission's actual policy toward fleeting expletives. The FCC had ruled that it would excuse an expletive if it occurred during a "bona fide news interview," and it had told the court during oral argument that the news exception was a broad one. For example, a broadcast of the oral argument, where the offending expletives were spoken in **open court**, would be permissible. In addition, the FCC had permitted the airing of the film "Saving Private Ryan," which had numerous expletives, because censoring the words would have detracted from the power and realism of this artistic work. These scenarios would not have prevented viewers, including children, from taking the "first blow" caused by the expletives. Therefore, this theory could not justify the change in policy.

Judge Pooler also found even less analysis to support for the change in the definition of profanity. The FCC had not set forth any independent reasons to expand the definition of profane speech. It merely stated that its prior precedent did not prevent it from setting a new definition. In addition, the commission could not explain why the change was necessary, as prior to 2004 it had never attempted to regulate profane speech. To the court there appeared no reason why profane language couldn't be addressed through the commission's indecency and obscenity enforcement.

In early 2008 the Supreme Court agreed to hear the FCC's appeal of this decision, with oral argument taking place in its 2008–2009 term.

FCC Changes Media Ownership Rules

The FEDERAL COMMUNICATIONS COMMISSION (FCC) has the administrative authority to set rules on media ownership in the United States. Until the 1990s there had been consensus within the FCC and Congress to prevent large media companies from controlling television stations, radio stations, and newspapers in large cities. From a **public policy** perspective, consolidated ownership would rob localities of a diversity of information choices. However, in the 1990s, as the Internet grew and newspapers saw advertising revenues begin to decline, the major media companies began lobbying for a change in media ownership rules. They argued that economic realities required such changes. The FCC changed its ownership rules in 2003 but they were eventually tossed out by a federal appeals court in 2005. In December 2007 the commission again enacted rules to allow broadcasters in the 20 largest U.S. cities to also own a newspaper. Members of Congress have objected to the changes and have introduced legislation to overturn the new rules.

The Telecommunications Act of 1996 made major changes in mass media regulation. It sought to increase competition in local, long distance, can cable TV markets. The act repealed cross-ownership rules for telephone/cable, cable/broadcast, and cable/network. It also increased the percentage of households that a single broadcaster could reach from 25 to 35 per cent. Another provision required the FCC to review media ownership rules every two years to determine whether they were "necessary in the public interest as a result of competition. When GEORGE W. BUSH became president in 2001 he appointed several FCC commissioners, including Chairman Michael Powell. Powell advocated greater competition and used the mandated biennial review to put forward regulations that would relax restrictions on media ownership.

In June 2003 the FCC approved, on a 3–2 vote, three major changes. First, a single media company would be permitted to own TV stations that reached 45 per cent of U.S. households, an increase of 10 percent. Second, the FCC lifted the ban on a single company owning both a broadcast outlet and a newspaper in the same market. This change affected all but the smallest markets, which were defined as having less than nine TV stations. Third, the rules allowed companies to own more than one TV station. In markets where there were at least five stations, a company could own two stations; a company could own three TV stations where there were 18 or more stations. There was substantial opposition to the rules in Congress but it was the Third **Circuit Court** of Appeals that decided their fate. In 2004 the appeals court overturned the rules, finding that the FCC had not "sufficiently justified its particular **chose** numerical limits for local television ownership, local radio ownership, or cross-ownership of media within local markets."

The Republican majority on the FCC then began a new rulemaking process. In 2005, Commissioner Kevin J. Martin succeeded Michael Powell as chair of the commission and conducted public hearings around the U.S. concerning media ownership rules. However, Martin was criticized by the two Democratic commissioners for allegedly calling public hearings without adequate notice and rushing the review process. The matter was finally brought to the FCC for a vote on December 18, 2007, where Martin's proposal won approval on a 3–2 vote.

The new proposal eliminated the national audience cap on television broadcasters that proved very controversial in the 2003 rules, leaving the other two 2003 changes for consideration. At the commission meeting, Martin noted the steady decline in revenue for newspaper companies and argued that the new proposal "strikes a balance" between a changing media marketplace and the preservation of competition and diversity in broadcasting. The FCC approved a rule that permits a media company to own a newspaper in one of the 20 largest media markets if, after the transaction, at least eight independently-owned-and-operated television stations remained. The FCC also granted permanent waivers 42 newspaper-broadcast combinations in large and small markets that had been given temporary waivers as they awaited the commission's decision. The commission also approved the local television multiple ownership limits that were part of the 2003 rules.

Some members of Congress denounced the changes. On March 5, 2008, Senator Byron Dorgan, Democrat of North Dakota, introduced a "resolution of disapproval" that would invalidate the commission's vote. Dorgan argued that the FCC had succumbed to "corporate interests" and that without a congressional vote blocking the changes, the nation would see even more concentration of media ownership by a few large corporations. On May 15 the Senate approved the resolution, while a companion bill awaited a hearing in the House of Representatives. The resolution must be approved within 60 legislative days or else the rules go into effect. However, commentators pointed out that even if the resolution passes, President Bush could veto it.

FOOD AND DRUG ADMINISTRATION

Merck Settles Vioxx Lawsuits

The FOOD AND DRUG ADMINISTRATION (FDA) is charged with regulating prescription medications, assessing the effectiveness of new drugs and their safety. The FDA has come under fire after heavily-marketed drugs by large pharmaceutical companies were taken off the market because of dangerous side effects. Vioxx, a drug developed and marketed by Merck & Co., promised arthritis-sufferers relief from joint inflammation and pain without the side-effects of stomach problems which can be triggered by aspirin and other types of painkillers.

In May 1999, the FDA approved rofecoxib, the actual name of the drug, as safe and effective. In September 2004, Merck withdrew Vioxx because of concerns about increased risk of heart attack and stroke associated with long-term, high-dosage use. The FDA estimated that Vioxx might have caused over 27,000 heart attacks, 30 to 40 percent of which were probably fatal, in the five years it was on the market. The withdrawal of the drug did not end matters; individual and **class action** lawsuits were filed against Merck by individuals who claimed personal injury. In addition 29 states and the DISTRICT OF COLUMBIA began investigations of Merck's advertising of Vioxx. In November 2007 Merck reached a $4.85 billion agreement that would allow the company to settle more than 95 percent of Vioxx lawsuits. In May 2008 the company entered into a $58 million multi-state agreement over alleged deceptive advertising.

Merck withdrew Vioxx in September 2004 after it discovered that taking the drug for 18 months or longer could double the risk of patients suffering a heart attack or stroke. An FDA study issued a few weeks later confirmed these findings. Withdrawing the drug was a financial blow to Merck, as annual sales of Vioxx totaled over $2.5 billion annually. The financial exposure from lawsuits soon became apparent. The first trial took place in 2005 in a Texas state courtroom, where Carol Ernst sued Merck for the heart attack and death of her husband Robert, a Vioxx user. Ernst's lawyers alleged that Vioxx caused the fatal cardiac arrhythmia and that Merck had suppressed information about the dangers of the drug. Merck denied that Vioxx caused deaths, on the grounds that these charges have never been proven. The company also denied allegations that it concealed information, pointing out that it voluntarily withdrew Vioxx from the market. Ernst prevailed, with the jury awarding her $24.5 million for **mental anguish** and economic losses and $229 million in **punitive damages** after finding that Merck acted recklessly in selling Vioxx despite having knowledge of the drug's heart risks.

At the time of the Ernst verdict, 4,000 Vioxx lawsuits had been filed. By late 2007 over 27,000 lawsuits were pending. Merck had vowed to fight all Vioxx lawsuits and had won some favorable verdicts. Jurors had decided in favor of the company 12 times and for plaintiffs five times, with five mistrials. In a major reversal, Merck announced on November 8, 2007 that it had reached a $4.85 billion deal to settle most of the Vioxx lawsuits. The company agreed to set up two funds. The first fund of $4 billon would cover claims for hear problems and the second fund of $850 million would cover stroke claims. Amounts to individuals will vary and all claims would be reviewed on an individual basis. The settlement was reached after securing approval from three of the four federal judges overseeing the coordination of more than 95 per cent of the litigation. Merck also said that it would continue to fight those individuals who do not agree to a settlement. The change in thinking by Merck reflected financial realties. The company had reserved $1.9 billion since 2004 to defend itself and it appeared litigation would go on for many years. Plaintiffs lawyers and their clients agreed to file their claims by early 2008, with the expectation that interim awards would be issued by August 2008.

The investigation of Merck's advertising of Vioxx by over half the states was triggered by the massive amounts of money Merck spent to promote the new drug and by its alleged concealment of health risks in its print and television ads. Merck spent hundreds of millions of dollars during the five years Vioxx was on market, focusing on direct-to-consumer televisions ads. This led to hundreds of thousands of consumers demanding prescriptions before Vioxx's side effects could be fully assessed. In May 2008 Vioxx entered into settlement with the states, paying $58 million. In addition, it agreed to submit all new television commercials for its drugs to the FDA for review and revision. In both settlements Merck did not admit to any wrongdoing.

FIRST AMENDMENT

Washington State Grange v. Washington State Republican Party

The regulation of election must balance the FIRST AMENDMENT right of political association against the right of the people to determine how they want to select candidates for office. Political parties are especially protective of their desire to choose their candidates. From 1935 to 2003 the state of Washington selected nominees for state and local offices using a blanket primary that placed candidates from all parties on one ballot and allowed voters to select a candidate from any party. The candidate who won a **plurality** of votes within each party became that party's nominee in the general election. In 2003, however, the Ninth **Circuit Court** of Appeals struck down this primary system, finding that it unconstitutionally burdened a political party's associational rights by forcing it to associate with voters who did not share their beliefs. In response the Washington State Grange, a fraternal, social, and civic organization, proposed a ballot initiative, I-872, as a replacement. The voters approved the plan and it became effective in December 2004. It was promptly challenged by the Washington State REPUBLICAN PARTY. The Supreme Court, in *Washington State Grange v. Washington State Republican Party*, __U.S.__, 128 S. Ct. 1184, 170 L. Ed. 2d 151 (2008), ruled that the new primary system on its face was constitutional and did not violate the First Amendment rights of political parties. The Court left open the possibility that it might rule differently if in practice it produced results that were plainly discriminatory.

Under I-872, all elections for partisan offices are conducted with a primary and a general election. Primary candidates must file a "declaration of candidacy" form on which they declare their "major or minor party preference, or independent status." The candidates' names and party

preferences are designated on the primary ballot. A political party cannot prevent candidates who are unaffiliated or even repugnant to the party from designating it as their party of preference. In the primary election voters may select any candidate, regardless of the party preference of the candidates or the voters. The candidates with the highest and second-highest vote totals advance to the general election, regardless of their party preferences. Under this system it would be possible for the two general election candidates to share the same party preference. Each candidate's party preference is listed on the general election ballot and this preference may not be changed between the primary and general elections.

The system did not go into effect because the Washington State Republican Party filed a federal lawsuit challenging the law "on its face." A facial challenge meant that the party believed the law as unconstitutional as written and that it would be pointless to see how it worked in practice. The party contended that the law usurped its right to nominate its own candidates and forced it to associate with candidates it did not endorse. In its view these problems violated its First Amendment associational rights. The federal **district court** agreed and ordered that the system not be implemented. The Ninth Circuit Court of Appeals agreed, finding that I-872 severely burdened the party's associational rights because the system created a risk that primary winners would be seen as the party's nominees even when the party did not want to be linked to the candidate.

The Supreme Court, in a 7–2 decision, reversed the Ninth Circuit decision and found the law, on its face, constitutional. Justice CLARENCE THOMAS, writing for the majority, noted that a facial challenge is more difficult because it can only succeed if it established that "no set of circumstances exists under which the Act would be valid." The Court could not go beyond the law's facial requirements and speculate about hypothetical cases. As to the law itself, the Constitution grants the states broad powers to conduct their elections. To overturn an election law it must be shown that the law severely burdens associational rights.

Justice Thomas said that overturning Washington's plan would be an "extraordinary and precipitous nullification of the will of the people." The law did not refer to the candidates as nominees of the any party and it did not treat them as such. Party preference under the law was minimized because the top two candidates from the primary could be from the same party.

Moreover, whether "parties nominate their own candidates outside the state-run primary is simply irrelevant." The heart of the party's argument was that voters would be confused by the candidates' party preference designations. The voters would incorrectly assume that the candidates had been nominated, associated, or approved by the party. Justice Thomas rejected this argument as "sheer speculation." In his view "there is simply no basis to presume that a well-informed electorate will interpret a candidate's party-preference designation to mean that the candidate is the party's chosen nominee" or that the party approves of the candidate. Under a facial challenge the Court could not strike down a law based on the "mere possibility" of voter confusion.

Chief Justice JOHN ROBERTS concurred in the decision but stated that if the state could not design a ballot that made clear the party designation was not an endorsement but a preference, then the law would not survive an "as applied" First Amendment challenge. Justice Anthony Scalia, in a dissenting opinion joined by Justice ANTHONY KENNEDY, protested that the decision and the law undermined the rights of political parties to control their own destinies. A party's message may become distorted if, for example, a racist candidate stated his preference for the party. A party would have no way to repudiate the candidate and risked having its identify and goodwill "hijacked." Justice Scalia believed there was no way for the state to write a ballot under the law that would pass First Amendment muster. Therefore, the Court should have ruled the law unconstitutional as written.

U.S. v. Williams

Congress has sought to criminalize the possession, distribution, and **solicitation** of child pornography since the mid-1990s. A first attempt, the Child Pornography Protection Act of 1996, was ruled unconstitutional by the Supreme Court on FIRST AMENDMENT grounds. This act focused on prosecuting individuals who possessed "any visual depiction" that "is or appears to be, of a minor engaging in sexually explicit conduct." The Court struck it down because it was overbroad, ensnaring possessors of images of youthful-looking adult actors or virtual images of children generated by a computer. Congress responded with new legislation that addressed the problems identified by the Court. The Prosecutorial Remedies and Other Tools to End the Exploitation of Children Today Act of 2003, 117 Stat. 650. focused on the pandering of child pornography—i.e., the offer-

ing or soliciting of supposed pornographic images. The Supreme Court, in *U.S. v. Williams*, __U.S.__, 128 S. Ct. 1830, 170 L. Ed. 2d 650 (2008), upheld the law, ruling that Congress had succeeded in narrowing the breadth of the law to avoid intruding on an individual's First Amendment rights.

Michael Williams, a Florida resident, pleaded guilty in federal court of pandering child pornography and of possessing child pornography. Williams and an undercover SECRET SERVICE agent struck up a conversation in an Internet chat room after Williams posted a message that he had "good" pics of his toddler daughter that he was willing to swap for similar photos. After a few conversations, Williams became suspicious that the agent was a law-enforcement agent. He posted a public message in the chat room that called out the agent and contained a hyperlink to seven photos of actual children between the ages of 5 and 15 engaging in sexual acts. The Secret Service then obtained a search warrant and found at least 22 images of child pornography on Williams' computer hard drives. Though Williams pleaded guilty to both counts, he reserved the right to challenge the pandering conviction. The challenge would not effect his 5-year prison sentence, as both sentences ran concurrently. The Eleventh **Circuit Court** of Appeals agreed with Williams that the 20034 pandering law violated the First Amendment because it was overbroad and impermissibly vague.

The Supreme Court, in a 7–2 decision, overruled the Eleventh Circuit. Justice ANTONIN SCALIA, writing for the majority, noted that a law is overbroad and invalid on its face for First Amendment purposes if it "prohibits a substantial amount of protected speech." The **overbreadth doctrine** seeks to balance competing social costs. The threat of enforcement of an overbroad law that inhibits the free exchange of ideas must be balanced against a law that seeks to deter antisocial behavior that has "obvious harmful effects."

Scalia reviewed the **statute** itself and pointed out that it only "prohibits offers to provide and requests to obtain child pornography." The law did not require the "actual existence" of child pornography. Rather than focusing on the underlying material the law targeted the "collateral speech that introduces such material into the child-pornography distribution network." The material or purported material that could not be pandered tracked the holdings of the Court on material that lacked First Amendment protection: obscene material depicting actual or virtual children engaged in sexually explicit conduct. The statute also required a defendant to "knowingly" **pander** material that the defendant believes was child pornography. Therefore, if a defendant, through misdescription leads another party to believe that the material is child pornography, and the defendant does not have the subjective belief that the material is child pornography, then there is no violation of this part of the law.

Justice Scalia found that there was no First Amendment right to request or offer to provide child pornography. Therefore, a person offering material as child pornography can be convicted on either of two grounds: for believing that the material depicts real children, or for intending to convince a would-be recipient that it does. As to objections that the law could ensnare the unwary or the innocent, Scalia dismissed them as "an endless stream of fanciful hypothesis." For example, some claimed that advertisements for Hollywood movies that depict underage characters having sex would violate the statute. Scalia rejected this claim, stating that the "average person understands that sex scenes in mainstream movies use nonchild actors" and "depict sexual activity in a way that would not rise to the explicit level necessary under the statute." He concluded that the law was "a carefully crafted attempt to eliminate the First Amendment problems we identified" in the decision striking down the 1996 law.

Justice JOHN PAUL STEVENS, in a concurring opinion joined by Justice STEPHEN BREYER, said the majority's construction of the statute had removed "any constitutional concerns that might arise." Justice DAVID SOUTER, in dissenting opinion joined by Justice RUTH BADER GINSBURG, was not as sanguine. Souter did not object to making it a federal crime to mislead others by offering alleged pornographic material that did not in fact exist. That was a case of **fraud** that did not implicate the First Amendment. He was concerned that a person had a First Amendment right to possess pornographic images that did not depict real children but still could be prosecuted for offering them. The loss of the "real child" requirement implicated protected First Amendment expression.

FRAUD

A false representation of a matter of fact—whether by words or by conduct, by false or misleading allegations, or by concealment of what should have been disclosed—that deceives and is intended to deceive another so that the individual will act upon it to her or his legal injury.

Seventh Circuit Upholds Criminal Convictions of Conrad Black

On June 25, 2008, the U.S. **Circuit Court** of Appeals for the Seventh Circuit unanimously affirmed the convictions of former media giant Conrad Black and three others found guilty in July 2007 of mail and wire **fraud** (and Black, in addition, of obstruction of justice). *U.S. v. Black, Conrad*, No. 07-4080 (7th Cir. 2008). The focus of the appeal was on the sufficiency of evidence as well as the use of a certain jury instruction. The 62-year-old British Baron, formally known as Lord Black of Crossharbour, was already serving his six and a half year sentence in a Florida federal prison at the time of the Seventh Circuit's decision.

In its 16-page decision, the **appellate court** summarized relevant findings at the trial court level, including the jury's 2007 verdict that Black was guilty of mail and wire fraud in violation of 18 USC § 1341 and of obstruction of justice under 18 USC § 1512(c). The charges stemmed from his (and the other defendants') roles as senior executives (Black was chairman and CEO) of Hollinger International, which, through its subsidiaries, owned a number of domestic and international newspapers. The defendants were found to have engaged in a multimillion-dollar corporate fraud scheme that shorted both the company and its shareholders of several million dollars.

Hollinger was controlled by a Canadian company, now defunct, called Ravelston, which in turn was controlled by Black, who owned 65 percent of its shares. The evidence at trial established that Black was able to control Hollinger through his majority stake in Ravelston.

Hollinger had a subsidiary called APC, which owned several newspapers and was in the process of selling out. When APC had only one remaining newspaper, a small weekly community paper in Mammoth Lake, California, Hollinger's corporate counsel (another defendant) drafted and executed (on behalf of APC) an agreement (covenant not to compete) to pay Black and the other defendants $5.5. million in return for their promise not to compete with APC for three years. The trial established that the money was paid. The trial also established that neither Hollinger's audit committee (required for all transaction approvals) nor

Hollinger's board of directors was informed of this transaction.

The defendants had argued that the $5.5 million actually represented management fees owed to Ravelston, but had been characterized as compensation for the non-compete covenant in the hope that Canada might not treat the fees as **taxable income**. Notwithstanding, evidence at trial showed that Hollinger, a large and sophisticated public corporation, had no documents to indicate either that the $5.5. million was credited to management fees accounts or, for that matter, approved by the corporation at all. The payment checks were also backdated to a time when APC had sold most of its newspapers, a scheme that the jury found to make the ostensible non-compete compensation less suspicious. Additionally, the checks were made out to Black and the other defendants personally. None of the defendants disclosed the money in the 10-K reports required annually by the SECURITIES AND EXCHANGE COMMISSION (SEC). The defendants also caused Hollinger to falsely represent to its shareholders that the payments had been made "to satisfy a closing condition." As to Black, a corporate security camera caught him on video as he hauled 13 boxes of documents from his Toronto office after learning they were being sought as part of an investigation into his financial dealings. There was additional evidence showing that Black had tried to avoid the security cameras. That evidence led to the obstruction of justice charge and conviction.

Black also defended that he did no harm to the company, because the purpose of the "for private gain" criminal element in this case was to achieve a gain at the expense of the Canadian government, not Hollinger. But the Seventh Circuit's opinion noted, "They are making a no harm-no foul argument, and such arguments usually fare badly in criminal cases ... [There was] no doubt that the defendants received money ... and very little doubt that they deprived Hollinger of their honest services." The **appellate** court also rejected Black's argument that the jury was improperly given the "ostrich" jury instruction, which provides that a jury can find a defendant guilty for intentionally avoiding knowing the truth about criminal behavior. Said Justice Posner in the appellate opinion, "If you receive a check in the mail for $1 million that you have no reason to think you are entitled to, you cannot just deposit it and when prosecuted for theft say you didn't know you weren't entitled to the money."

Conrad Black, attending sentencing for fraud in Chicago, December 2007.
AP IMAGES

Ultimately, the Seventh Circuit opinion, in affirming the convictions, held that (1) there was no error in the jury instruction which directed jurors to convict upon proof that defendants had schemed to deprive a corporation or its shareholders "of their intangible right to the honest services of the corporate officers, directors or controlling shareholders ..."; (2) the obstruction of justice charge (against Black) did not require proof of materiality; all that was required was a showing that documents were concealed in order to make them unavailable in an official proceeding; (3) the "ostrich instruction" was proper; and (4) the court did give inadequate limiting instructions with respect to the jury's use of the false filings with the SEC (not affecting the ultimate verdict).

Counsel for Black did not indicate whether an appeal to the U.S. SUPREME COURT was forthcoming. Moreover, Black and his parent Canadian company, Hollinger, Inc. had additionally faced lawsuits by the SEC (*SEC v. Black*, No. 04-7377), and by *Sun-Times Media*, (*Hollinger International v. Hollnger Inc*, No. 04-698).

David Chalmers and BAYOIL Companies Sentenced

In March 2008, the U.S. Attorney for the Southern District of New York in Manhattan announced the sentencing of David Chalmers, of Houston, Texas, and two corporations operated by him, BAYOIL INC. (American) and BAYOIL SUPPLY & TRADING LTD. (Bahamian) (collectively, BAYOIL COMPANIES), for their roles in illegal kickbacks to Iraq under

David Chalmers of
Bayoil outside
court, April 2005.
AP IMAGES

its Oil-for-Food Program. *U.S. v. Chalmers*, No. S1-05-CR-59(DC). Chalmers, 54, was sentenced to two years imprisonment and payment of **restitution** in an amount over $9 million. The corporations were each sentenced to three years probation and payment of restitution in conjunction with **joint and several liability** with another defendant, Oscar Wyatt, Jr.

While the sentencing was unremarkable, the crimes were not. They involved a set of defendants who tendered secretive illegal **surcharge** payments directly to the former Saddam Hussein regime of the former Government of Iraq, in exchange for crude oil, and in circumvention of the United Nations' sanctions and the Oil-for-Food Program.

As background, in August 1990 (about four days after Iraq invaded Kuwait), the UNITED NATIONS (UN) imposed economic sanctions on the Government of Iraq. Specifically, it prohibited UN member states from trading in any Iraqi commodities or products. UN Security Council Resolution 986 authorized the Government of Iraq to sell a limited quantity of oil, but the proceeds from sales were deposited in an **escrow** bank account managed by the UN. The money in the account could only be used for humanitarian purposes approved by the UN, including food and medicine for the Iraqi people and reparations to victims of the Hussein regime's 1990 invasion of Kuwait.

On/about 2000, the Hussein regime developed a way to circumvent this sanction and obtain free money directly without UN supervision. It began to condition the right to purchase oil under the Oil-for-Food Program (i.e., to prioritize prospective purchasers) on their willingness to make secret surcharge payments directly to the Hussein regime. Chalmers, working with and through BAYOIL COMPANIES, elected to participate and began paying the illegal kickbacks between 2000 and 2003. This diverted millions of dollars otherwise available for humanitarian purposes intended to benefit the Iraqi people under the Oil-for-Food Program.

With a pending September 2007 trial, in August 2007, Chalmers and the BAYOIL COMPANIES each pleaded guilty to "participating in a conspiracy to commit wire **fraud** related to the payment of secret illegal surcharge payments to the former Government of Iraq." Another defendant, Ludmil Dionissiev, an associate of Chalmers, pleaded guilty to facilitating the transportation and sale of Iraqi oil in January 2001. He was charged with facilitating the smuggling of Iraqi oil by sending a message to a Russian political figure that an agent of the BAYOIL COMPANIES had promised to pay an illegal surcharge on the oil on behalf of the Russian political figure. On December 13, 2007, Dionissiev was sentenced to a fine of $5000 and two years probation.

In addition to guilty pleas from Chalmers, Dionissiev, and the BAYOIL COMPANIES, the Oil-for-Food investigation led to several additional convictions. In October 2007, Oscar Wyatt, Jr., the founder of the Coastal Corporation, pleaded guilty (four weeks into his trial) to conspiring to make illegal kickback payments to the Saddam Hussein Regime. In 2006, Tongsun Park, a Korean national was found guilty by jury trial of conspiring to, among other things, serve as an unregistered agent of the Hussein regime in the United States; Samir Vincent, an Iraqi-American businessman, pleaded guilty to the same charge the year before. Vincent, not yet sentenced, had cooperated and testified for the U.S. government. Wyatt and Park both received prison sentences and fines.

Federal charges related to the Oil-for-Food Program were also filed against several other persons and entities, including Ephraim Nadler and Benon V. Sevan. At the time, Sevan was the Executive Director of the UN office that operated the Program. The charges alleged that Sevan received more than $150,000 from Nadler on behalf of the Government of Iraq, as a result of an oil transaction under the Program.

Those funds remitted to the U.S. Attorney's Office in connection with its investigation of abuses in the Oil-for-Food Program have been substantial: more than $11 million from Wyatt; $20 million from Chevron Corporation; and more than $5 million from El Paso Corporation, the latter two being publicly-traded companies that obtained Iraqi oil under the Program through third parties who paid the illegal kickbacks to the former Iraqi government. The monies collected were transferred to the Development Fund of Iraq (established by UN Security Council Resolution 1483 in 2003) as restitution for the benefit of the people of Iraq.

Democratic Fundraiser Norman Hsu Sentenced and Charged Again

Democratic fundraiser Norman Hsu, a Chinese businessman who was convicted of grand theft in the United States more than 15 years ago but fled to Asia before sentencing, was sentenced in January 2008 in a San Mateo, California court for the 1992 no-contest conviction. (He was charged in 1991 but entered his plea in 1992). Immediately thereafter, he was transferred to federal custody in New York to face **fraud** charges involving political fundraising totaling more than $20 million.

Hsu was a major contributor and fundraiser for Senator Hillary Rodham Clinton (D-NY), and it was widely reported that she would return at least $850,000 in donations because of the fraud charges. According to Lee Cary in his April 2008 article for *American Thinker* ("Norman Hsu Who?"), the three highest benefactors of Hsu's funds were three New York politicians: Hillary Rodham Clinton, state Attorney General Andrew Cuomo, and then-state Governor Elliot Spitzer, in descending order. "The second highest [Cuomo] might have been the man that a Governor Spitzer would have appointed to complete a President Hillary Clinton's unexpired Senate term [on the assumption of her winning]," Cary opined.

After fleeing to Asia while on bail following his 1992 conviction, Hsu resurfaced in the United States years later as a political fundraiser. When media coverage of Hillary Rodham Clinton's presidential campaign exposed Hsu's fugitive status, he surrendered to San Mateo authorities in August 2007. Free on $2 million bail, he again fled, but was caught a short time later in a Colorado hospital after injuring himself aboard an Amtrak train leaving the area.

Hsu's attorneys had attempted to have the 1992 case dismissed, or at least to allow Hsu to

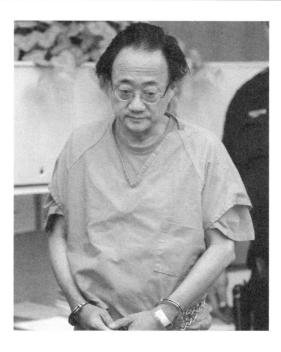

Norman Hsu, September 2007.

AP IMAGES

withdraw his no contest plea, arguing that his right to a speedy trial had been violated. The argument was premised on alleged facts that authorities were passive in attempting to locate him, despite his visibility, being photographed with political candidates and attending major fundraising events. The judge rejected that argument and Hsu was sentenced to the three years he faced under his original plea deal for the 1992 conviction. More importantly, the new charges Hsu faced involved more than $20 million dollars federal prosecutors alleged he bilked from political campaign donors.

Little was publicly known about Hsu until numerous old storage files were opened at various courts and from former partners and friends, in light of the more recent fraud charges. The collage of information revealed several failed businesses and bankruptcy filings, lawsuits, a kidnapping, and an unexplained financial recovery from each of his financial failings. He was said to have charmed people into investments in real estate, restaurants, and apparel businesses. According to court documents filed in the federal fraud case, several people lost their life savings.

Norman Yuen Hsu was born in Hong Kong in October 1951, according to his own statements to acquaintances, although a former college friend and business associate, Pedro Woo, stated that Hsu's roots were in Shanghai. In any event, he moved to California and received a Social Security Card in 1969 when he enrolled as a student of computer science at the University of California, Berkeley. According to public records, he married at 22 in 1974, shortly after graduating.

In 1976, Hsu received a California license to sell real estate. After completing a degree program at the University of Pennsylvania's Wharton School in 1981, he dabbled in various retail and restaurant enterprises and maintained a long list of businesses registered under his name. Known for dressing well, he apparently built trust by establishing himself as a successful businessman. He had impeccable educational credentials, was seen in popular political and social circles, and was often quoted in trade magazines.

Hsu and two college friends, including Pedro Woo, started a retail men's wear enterprise, from which Woo suffered a $50,000 loss (the third partner returned to Hong Kong). Woo, who was angry and felt Hsu abused his trust, could not track Hsu down for recourse. In fact, Hsu began to develop a reputation as long as the list of false addresses he left behind, much to the wonderment and chagrin of longtime **bona fide** occupants of those addresses who had never heard of him and were frustrated by mail from bill collectors.

In retrospect, it appeared that Hsu was building the classic pyramid-type investment scams, particularly one in the 1980s involving latex glove products. When several investors sued, Hsu filed for bankruptcy protection. Hsu vanished again just prior to his sentencing hearing in 1992, only this time, to Asia. According to Hong Kong business records, he began setting up two vague businesses with broadly-worded charters; both went bankrupt in 1997 and 1998. It is believed that shortly thereafter he returned to California, where he again dabbled in real estate and retail clothing businesses. As Hsu's California business contacts appeared to have tapered off, he reemerged in New York, this time in political circles. It remained unclear just how, why, or specifically when that happened.

Hsu became heavily involved in political fundraisers for the DEMOCRATIC PARTY and tendered hefty donations, as well as threw lavish parties, for several of them. In 2004, when the Democrats succeeded in Congress, Hsu hosted a large party at a swank New York Club, during which he reportedly grabbed the microphone and ordered anyone not supporting HILLARY CLINTON to "get out!" Hsu also was a member of the Clinton Global Initiative, for which he paid an annual $15,000 donation membership fee.

Hsu's life began to crash again when media persons following political fundraisers began de-

scribing discernible patterns between Hsu's contributions and those of people with no prior history or means of contributing. Federal investigators began probing into whether donors were reimbursed and/or donation money from one individual was spread out among many donors to slide in under the maximums allowable per contributor. Amid these new probes, Hsu, who was to surrender his passport and discuss bail reduction, disappeared again only to be caught in Colorado.

FREEDOM OF RELIGION

First Circuit Upholds Teaching About Same-Sex Families

In January 2008, the First **Circuit Court** of Appeals upheld the dismissal of a lawsuit filed by parents protesting the elementary school teaching to their young children of gay lifestyles and same-sex marriages. In *Parker v. Hurley*, 514 F.3d 87 (1st Cir. 2008), the **appellate court** found that the parents' right to exercise their religious beliefs under the Free Exercise Clause of the FIRST AMENDMENT to the U.S. Constitution was not violated when their children were exposed to contrary ideas in school.

In April 2006, Tonia and David Parker filed suit against elementary school officials in Lexington, Massachusetts, after their son brought home a book from his kindergarten class that depicted a same-sex family. Two other parents, the Wirthlins, joined the suit after a second-grade teacher read a story to the class about two princes falling in love.

The parents asserted violations of their own as well as their children's rights under the First Amendment. They further asserted violations of their substantive parental and due process rights, protections of which were binding upon states under the FOURTEENTH AMENDMENT. The parents specifically alleged that they should have been given prior notice by the elementary public school, which would have given them the opportunity to exempt their young children from exposure to books that they found religiously repugnant. In support of this claim, the parents cited Mass. Gen. Laws ch. 71, § 32A, a state law that required parents to be given notice and the opportunity to exempt their children from curriculum which primarily involved human sexual education or human sexuality issues. The parents did not object to the use of these materials as part of a non-discrimination curriculum in the public schools, but rather, challenged the school district's failure to provide them with prior notice. They requested future relief until their children reached seventh grade.

The school declined to apply the **statutory** exemption to these parents because it asserted that the materials to which the children were exposed did not primarily involve human sexual education or human sexuality issues.

In February 2007, the federal **district court** dismissed the case for failure to state a federal constitutional claim. The parents appealed to the First Circuit Court of Appeals.

But the **appellate** court affirmed the lower court's dismissal. It found that a child's exposure to alternative or gay lifestyles did not constitute "indoctrination" or "discussion of human sexuality" as the parents claimed, thus invoking the Massachusetts 'prior notice' **statute**. Rather, the court opined, the activities complained of merely exposed the children to an age-appropriate acknowledgement of the existence of same-sex families in a state where gay marriage was legal. "Public schools are not obliged to shield individual students from ideas which potentially are religiously offensive, particularly when the school imposes no requirement that the student agree with or affirm those ideas, or even participate in discussions about them," the court held.

The appellate court noted that it found no federal case under the Due Process Clause which permitted parents to demand an exemption for their children from exposure to certain books in public schools. The court characterized the due process right of parental autonomy as a subset of a broader substantive right of familial privacy. But the appellate court noted that other cases establishing such privacy rights under the Due Process Clause were more fundamental in nature, such as the right to marry or the right to procreate. "In sum," said the court, "the **substantive due process** clause by itself, either in its parental control or its privacy focus, does not give plaintiffs the degree of control over their children's education that their requested relief seeks."

The court then turned to whether a combination of substantive due process and First Amendment free exercise interests could give rise to a **cause of action**. But again, looking to the facts, the court found that there was insufficient conduct on the part of the school to establish a claim of indoctrination (the court made note that the children were not forced to read books on pain of suspension). Nor were the children subjected to a constant stream of similar material. There was no allegation of a formalized curriculum requiring students to read books affirming gay marriage.

In summary, the court found that the facts alleged in the complaint did not rise to the level of "claims of constitutional magnitude." Therefore, the district court did not err in dismissing the claims under the U.S. Constitution. The appellate court acknowledged that the school's choice of books for young students offended the plaintiffs. But, noted the court, the plaintiffs could seek recourse through the political process at the local level. Their objections to the educational materials did not mean they were entitled to a federal remedy under the Constitution.

Connecticut Supreme Court Upholds Denial of Buddhist Temple

The Connecticut Supreme Court on February 12, 2008 upheld a denial of a permit by a town **zoning** and planning commission to deny a Cambodian Buddhist society the right to construct a 7,600-square-foot temple in the town. In so ruling, the court rejected arguments that the zoning commission had violated state and federal law in denying the application. The Buddhist society claimed that the denial was the result of racial bigotry, due in large part to the Asian design of the proposed temple.

In 2000, Congress passed the Religious Land Use and Institutionalized Persons Act of 2000 (RLUIPA), 42 U.S.C. §§ 2000cc **et seq.** This **statute** provides, in part, as follows:

> No government shall impose or implement a land use regulation in a manner that imposes a substantial burden on the religious exercise of a person, including a religious assembly or institution, unless the government demonstrates that imposition of the burden on that person, assembly, or institution—(A) is in furtherance of a compelling governmental interest; and (B) is the least restrictive means of furthering that compelling governmental interest.

The statute also prohibits implementation of a land use regulation in a manner that "treats a religious assembly or institution on less than equal terms with a nonreligious assembly or institution." Moreover, the statute proscribes a city from imposing a land use regulation that "(A) totally excludes religious assemblies from a jurisdiction; or (B) unreasonably limits religious assemblies, institutions, or structures within a jurisdiction." 28 U.S.C. § 2000cc.

The State of Connecticut also enacted a statute that prohibits discrimination on the basis of religion. Under section 52-571b of the Connecticut General Statutes states that neither the state government nor a political subdivision of the state may "burden a person's exercise of religion" under the state Constitution. Exceptions under the state statute are similar to those under the RLUIPA in that the state may burden a person's exercise of religion only if the state demonstrates that the burden furthers a compelling governmental interest and that the burden is the least restrictive means of furthering that interest.

In 1999, a Cambodian Buddhist society purchased a ten-acre lot in Newtown, Connecticut. The property is located in a farming and residential zone where the operation of a place of religious worship is allowed under a special exception. In August 2002, the society applied for a special exception that would allow it to build a 6,000-square-foot meditation temple and meeting hall on the property. The proposal also called for off-street parting for about 100 vehicles. The society later revised the application to indicate that the building would be 7,618 square feet, featuring both a **mediation** temple and a meeting hall. The plans also called for 148 parking spaces to accommodate the society's 450 members who would meet at the temple on an annual basis.

Newtown's zoning commission constructed public hearings on the application in October and December 2002. At a special meeting on February 20, 2003, the commission voted to reject the society's application. The reasoning for the rejection was that the application did not comply with standards set forth in the city's zoning regulation. The commission concluded that the temple was inconsistent with the "quiet single-family residential neighborhood with a rural setting" and was thus out of harmony with the general character of the neighborhood.

The commission also stated several other reasons for its denial. The commission discovered evidence that the U.S. Department of Commerce had awarded a grant for a health care facility that was reportedly located on the society's property. Unconvinced the society's representations that the property would not be used for health care purposes, the commission concluded that the proposal did not satisfy the city's regulations. Moreover, the commission expressed concern about the increase in traffic volume in the neighborhood as well as whether the septic system and water supply system proposed in the temple's plans would comply with the state's public health code.

The society, along with society president Pong Me, appealed the commission's decision to a Connecticut superior court. Among the society's arguments were that the commission's decision violated both the RLUIPA and section 52-571b of the Connecticut statutes. Several owners of property either adjacent to or near the society's property intervened as defendants in the case. The trial court concluded that the commission's denial of the society's application did not substantially burden the society's exercise of religion under either the federal or the state law. However, the court agreed with the society on issues of whether the society's proposed use comported with the city's zoning regulations. Nevertheless, the trial court determined that it was within the commission's discretion to deny the society's application.

The society appealed the decision to the Connecticut Supreme Court. Among its arguments before court, the society claimed that the trial court had erred in concluding that the commission had violated the society's rights under RLUIPA or section 52-571b. Judge Richard N. Palmer, writing for a unanimous court, rejected the society's arguments. The court concluded that the commission had "substantial evidence" on which to deny the application. According to the court, RLUIPA "does not apply to neutral and generally applicable land use regulations that are intended to protect the public health and safety, such as those at issue in the present case." *Cambodian Buddhist Society of Conn., Inc. v. Planning & Zoning Comm'n of the Town of Newtown*, 941 A.2d 868 (Conn. 2008).

Commentators noted that the decision was consistent with others nationwide holding that the federal law has limited application in cases where there is no evidence of religious discrimination. Spokespeople for the Buddhist society said they were "extremely disappointed" in the decision, noting that the society needed the temple to prevent its religion and culture from declining or dying off.

FREEDOM OF SPEECH

The right, guaranteed by the First Amendment to the U.S. Constitution, to express beliefs and ideas without unwarranted government restriction.

Ninth Circuit Upholds Online Vote-Swapping

In *Porter v. Bowen*, 496 F.3d 1009 (9th Cir. 2007), a three-member panel of the U.S. **Circuit Court** of Appeals for the Ninth Circuit held that vote-swapping Web sites were legal and protected by the FIRST AMENDMENT to the U.S. Constitution. (In March 2008, a petition for rehearing *en banc* [before the entire court] was denied.) Even so, this was the second time the matter was before the Ninth Circuit. In 2003, it had rendered another similar decision, involving essentially the same parties, but had remanded the case back to federal **district court**. *Porter v. Jones*, 319 F.3d 483 (9th Cir. 2003). It was the district court's decision on remand that became the subject matter of the 2007 decision.

The 2000 presidential election was one of the closest in U.S. history. In addition to two neck-in-neck frontrunners (GEORGE W. BUSH and AL GORE) from the two major political parties, there were also third-party candidates on both the left and right ends of the political spectrum who were vying for votes, especially from independents and voters in "swing-states," or states without a dominant party affiliation associated with their voters. Bush and Gore supporters became worried that in such a tight race, votes for third-party candidates could be significant in "throwing" a swing state. They also became concerned about the quirks of the American electoral system, under which small numbers of third-party votes could become decisive in winner-take-all states (the majority). (Winner-take-all systems allocate all of a state's electoral votes to the candidate who receives the most popular votes in that state, even if that share of votes is less than an actual majority.)

During this highly-charged 2000 presidential pre-election period, San Francisco resident Alan Porter created a Web site, VoteSwap2000.com, and eventually teamed up with William Cody, owner of VoteExchange2000.com. The undisputed objective of the two Web sites was to provide a forum for voters to trade their votes via e-mail. Essentially, the web sites would facilitate third-party supporters in a swing state (such as Florida or Ohio) to agree to be paired with major-party supporters in states where the major-party's candidate really didn't need the vote because the margin was so favorable, i.e., "safe states." The swing-state voters would then promise to vote for the major-party candidate and, in exchange, their counterpart "safe-state" voters would promise to vote for the third-party candidate. The point of all this was ostensibly to ensure that major-party candidate Al Gore would improve his odds in swing states, while third-party candidates (such as Ralph Nader) would still garner enough national popular votes

to qualify the third-party for federal funding in future elections (five percent minimum).

Four days after the Web sites opened for operation, Porter and Cody were served threatening "cease and desist" letters from then-California Secretary of State, Bill Jones, for alleged violations of various state election and penal code (criminal) provisions, including Code provisions 18521 and 18522 (prohibitions on brokering the exchange of votes). Immediately, the owners shut down/disabled their respective Web sites, fearing prosecution. Ultimately, they ended up filing suit against Jones and the state, alleging that the threatened prosecution violated the First Amendment and the Dormant **Commerce Clause**, and further, that Jones' actions exceeded the scope of his authority under California's election code. They sought both injunctive and declarative relief.

In the 2003 decision, the district court dismissed Porter's and Cody's claims as moot, but stayed their claims for prospective relief. The Ninth Circuit reversed, finding the case ripe for decision and not moot, and remanded (the 2003 decision).

Notwithstanding that decision, the district court, on remand, granted **summary judgment** in favor of Jones, again deciding that Porter's/Cody's claims for prospective relief were moot, but for a different reason than previously held: a new letter sent from Jones's successor, Shelley, to then-Speaker of the California Assembly, asking for "legislative clarification" of the provisions cited by his predecessor Jones against the two vote-swapping Web site owners. In the letter, Shelley stated, "Until such legislative clarification is made, I will not seek to prevent the operation of websites such as voteswap2000.com and voteexchange2000.com." The district court found this new letter to "clearly and unequivocally indicate that the laws will not be enforced in the same manner against future conduct by [Porter, Cody] or others until the legislature provides further clarification." The district court entered its decision in March 2006.

Again, Porter and Cody appealed, and again, the Ninth Circuit reversed the district court on the matter of mootness. The court held that Shelley's letter did not make it clear that California would not threaten such websites in the future, and therefore, the appeal was not moot.

Moving on to the merits of the case, the Ninth Circuit held that the website's vote-swapping mechanisms were protected activities under the First Amendment. Accordingly,

Sarah Phelps, left, and Sam Phelps, right, protest the funeral of soldier Charles Jones, September 2006. Westboro Church members protest military funerals to claim God is punishing the U.S. for condoning homosexuality.

AP IMAGES

California needed to meet a high-scrutiny test to overcome the presumption of First Amendment protection. Although California did articulate its valid interests in preventing election **fraud** and corruption, "and perhaps in avoiding the subversion of the Electoral College," those interests did not justify the complete disabling of the Web sites or vote-swapping mechanisms. In other words, Jones's actions were not sufficiently narrowly-tailored to advance the State's legitimate interests.

The court also found that Jones was entitled to qualified immunity from damages. This was because the constitutionality of stopping vote-swapping was not clearly established in 2000.

Westboro Baptist Church Held Liable for Protesting Military Funeral

A federal jury in Baltimore in October 2007 ruled that the controversial Westboro Baptist Church of Topeka, Kansas was liable for $10.9 million. The church has become infamous for protesting military funerals under the pretext that the soldiers have died because God is punishing America for supporting homosexuality. A father of one of the deceased soldiers sued the church when church members protested at his son's funeral.

Fred Phelps, formerly an attorney, founded Westboro Baptist Church in 1955. For many years, Phelps represented black clients in civil rights suits. He was disbarred during the early 1990s amid a conflict with state investigator and

state judges. He has since focused his efforts on his church. Eleven of Phelps' 13 children are also lawyers. Westboro has about 75 members, most of whom are members of Phelps' family. Four of Fred Phelps' children have rejected his ministry.

The church first gained notoriety in 1998 when members decided to protest the funeral of Matthew Shepard, a gay college student who was beaten to death after being lured from a bar by two men. Church members showed up to display signs that read "God Hates Fags" and shouted that Shepard was in hell for being a homosexual. The group also attempted to post a plaque in Wyoming that suggested Sheppard was in hell.

Since the Shepard incident, Westboro members claimed that God has caused such incidents as the SEPTEMBER 11TH ATTACKS, Hurricane Katrina, and mining deaths in West Virginia in 2005. Church members also threatened to protest at the funeral of actor Heath **Ledger**, who was straight but played a gay character in the movie "Brokeback Mountain." The church maintains several websites that spread messages of hatred. According to Phelps, "God promised dire outpourings of very painful wrath, and there's nothing more painful than killing one of your children and that's what's going on in Iraq. That's what we're preaching and the forum of choice to deliver such a message, obviously, is the funeral of the kid that's been blown to smithereens."

Church members have focused their attention on many funerals of fallen soldiers. The soldiers are not gay nor are they accused of being gay. Instead, the church believes that they died because God is punishing the United States for its tolerance of homosexuality. The members argue that the soldiers have died while earning their paychecks and that they are not true heroes. In addition to the signs focusing on homosexuality, protestors also display signs with such statements as "America is Doomed" and "Don't worship the dead."

A motorcycle group named Patriot Guard Riders began to attend funerals at the request of families to shield those in attendance at the funerals from the protests. The organization claims that its membership exceeds 100,000, many of whom are veterans. During funerals, members of the Patriot Guard Riders display flags that block families from having to see the Westboro protestors. The bikers also attempt to drown out the protests by singing patriotic songs or revving their motorcycle engines.

The Westboro protests have led several states to enact legislation that would prohibit protestors from picketing within a certain distance (300 to 500 feet) of the funeral. According to the National Conference of State Legislatures, forty states have enacted these types of laws. Westboro members claim that these statutes are unconstitutional. Nevertheless, because of this legislation, the members have moved their efforts to other venues, such as military hospitals.

The family of one fallen soldier fought against the Westboro church by turning to the courts. Marine Lance Cpl. Matthew A. Snyder died on March 6, 2006 in the Al Anbar province in Iraq. His body was returned home for burial two weeks later. Westboro church members showed up to protest, displaying their typical signs and also the signs reading "*Semper Fi* Fags*,*" which is especially offensive to Marines. The church also posted an item to its website, indicating that Matthew Synder's father, Albert, had "taught Matthew to defy his Creator, to divorce, and to commit adultery," as well as "raised him for the devil."

Albert Snyder filed suit against Westboro in a U.S. **district court** in Baltimore. He claimed that the protests were emotionally damaging to him, as he was already grieving from his son's death. The suit also alleged that the church violated Synder's privacy, defamed him, and caused intentional infliction of emotional distress. Snyder sought compensatory and **punitive damages**. According to the suit, punitive damages were appropriate because they would serve as a deterrent against future protests. In addition to the church, other defendants included Fred Phelps and two of his daughters.

On October 31, 2007, the federal jury returned a verdict, awarding Snyder $10.9 million. Of this amount, $2.9 million was for **compensatory damages**, $6 million in punitive damages for invasion of privacy, and $2 million in punitive damages for emotional distress. Snyder pledged that he would continue to fight the Westboro church's protests. "I hope it's enough to deter them from doing this to other families," said Snyder. "It was not about the money. It was about getting them to stop." Despite the ruling, the church said that it would carry on with its protests.

FIRST AMENDMENT experts expressed some concerns with the ruling, noting that judgments such as these could curtail protected speech.

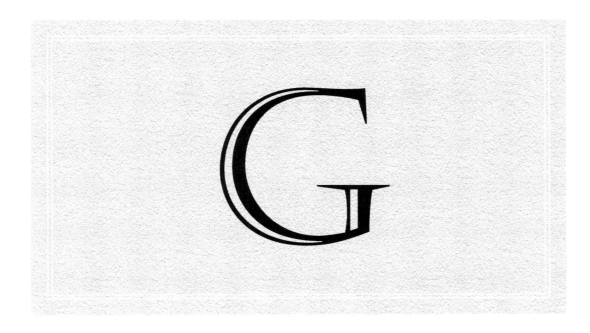

GAMBLING

NBA Referee Admits to Betting on Games

Veteran pro basketball referee Tim Donaghy pleaded guilty in August 2007 to charges that he bet on National Basketball Association games, including games that Donaghy officiated. Donaghy's actions were part of a conspiracy where he received payments for providing tips about teams on which his coconspirators should place bets. As of April 2008, Donaghy still awaited his sentence.

The NBA employs 60 referees to work preseason, regular season, and playoff games. The referees are prohibited under league rules from betting on NBA games or from providing information to others that would assist in making bets on NBA games. The league creates master release schedules that establish the officiating crews for upcoming games. However, the league does not publicly release the identities of the referee for a particular game. NBA referees are prohibited from disclosing which games they are scheduled to work. In fact, the referees may not engage in other outside employment without league permission.

Donaghy began his service as an NBA referee in 1994 and served in that capacity for 13 seasons. Donaghy was one of the officials during an infamous 2004 game between the Indiana Pacers and the Detroit Pistons, when Pacer players began fighting with Detroit fans. Between 2005 and 2007, Donaghy served as a referee for 131 regular season games as well as 20 playoff games.

Around 2003, he began to place bets on NBA games, including those that he officiated.

In December 2006, he began to provide inside information about NBA players, referees, and coaches to a professional gambler named James Battista. Battista attended the same high school in Springfield, Pennsylvania as Donaghy. According to allegations, Donaghy provided information to supplement his income. He received $2,000 if his information was correct and Battista won his bets. However, if Battista lost, Donaghy received nothing. After a certain period of time, Battista increased his payment for information leading to winning bets to $5,000.

The FEDERAL BUREAU OF INVESTIGATION traced hundreds of telephone calls from Donaghy

Former NBA referee Tim Donaghy, April 2007.
AP IMAGES

STATES CONTINUE TO LOOK TO GAMBLING TO SOLVE BUDGET WOES

Lawmakers in many states began the new year in 2008 faced with significant budgetary problems. The housing market in many areas had stalled, resulting in lower home sales and reduced housing prices. This reduction caused a drop in other purchases, such as appliances, carpeting, and related home improvement items. States that rely heavily on sales taxes suffered due to the reduced sales. Officials in a number of states, including Florida, were left scrambling to find ways to bridge the gaps between spending and revenue.

When budget crunches hit, states have looked more and more to gambling to provide a boost in revenue to solve their problems. While lotteries and other forms of gambling have existed in American since long before the founding of the country, the legalization of the various forms of gaming, including permanent, land-based casinos in major cities, is a relatively new phenomenon. When a state is faced with a budget crunch, pro-gaming politicians will argue that their state needs a privately-run casino to keep gamblers from spending money in other states. Others, often anti-tax advocates, will say that legalizing gambling is sensible way to generate new state revenues without raising taxes.

After most states had outlawed lotteries by the turn of the 20th century,

IN FOCUS

the lotteries began to see a resurgence in the 1960s and 1970s. In the 1950s and early 1960s, the New Hampshire state legislature considered a number of bills that would allow the state to run a sweepstakes, which was the forerunner to the modern state lottery. The state finally approved this legislation in 1963, and during that year, the state appointed its first sweepstakes commission. Supporters touted the promise that the sweepstakes would bring to schools, for revenues from the lottery would fund education. Even today, the New Hampshire Lottery Commission website notes, "Since the inception of the New Hampshire Lottery in 1964, more than $930 million has gone to aid education, making the children of New Hampshire the biggest winners of all."

Other states began to follow suit, with many states approving their state lotteries in the 1980s. In nearly every case, the legislators and/or voters approved the lottery systems with the understanding that the revenues would be used to bolster state education funds. The state of Florida provides an example that was similar in many states. In 1986, the Florida state legislature allocated 62 percent of its annual budget to education. With pro-lottery supporters stressing that lottery funds could be used to enhance education

without raising taxes, the state approved a lottery in 1987, and the lottery went into effect in 1988.

Unfortunately, the **allocation** of the revenues from the Florida lottery also provides a representative example of how funds from these revenues have been expended. The percentage of the Florida budget dedicated to education has dropped steadily since 1988, and lottery money has been used more to maintain schools rather than to enhance education. In fact, when schools experienced an increase in enrollment but the state saw lottery sales flatten, spending-per-student in the state dropped below the levels from prior to 1988, and the state routinely ranks in the bottom ten percent nationally in per-pupil spending. According to Randy Bobbitt, author of *Lottery Wars*, "If the lottery has bad sales one year, schools lose out."

As states continued to approve lotteries, American Indian tribes began to promote development of casinos on Indian lands. In 1987, the *U.S. Supreme Court* opened the door to Indian gaming when it ruled in *California v. Cabazon Band of Mission Indians*, 476 U.S. 1168, 106 S. Ct. 2888, 90 L. Ed. 2d 975, that where a state allows a form of gambling, a tribe in that state may also engage in that form of gambling. The following year, Congress approved the Indian Gaming Regulatory Act, 25 U.S.C. §§ 2701 **et seq.**, which provides that a tribe

to Battista's messenger, who was a man named Thomas Martino. The phone records indicated a pattern of phone calls that occurred just prior to games, and officials were able to correspond these calls with bets that were made. The FBI's investigation also showed that Battista made cash payments to Donaghy when the information led to winning bets. Commentators noted that the betting may not have affected which team won or lost games where Donaghy was involved, but the FBI concluded that Donaghy "compromised [his] objectivity as a referee because of [his] personal financial interest in the outcome of NBA games."

The FBI first revealed its investigation in Donaghy in July 2007. As news of the investigation leaked, researchers immediately began to review tapes of games that involved Donaghy to determine whether he had made calls that could have influenced the outcome of games. Although no conclusive evidence arose, the investigation called into question whether fans could trust that NBA games were not compromised. For example, in one game in February 2007 between the Miami Heat and the New York Knicks, the Knicks shot 39 free throws compared to eight by the Heat. The Knicks were favored in the game by 4½ points and won the game by six.

may have casinos if the tribes negotiate a compact with their respective states. These compacts generally dictate the percentage of gaming revenues that the tribes must share with the states. By the mid-1990s, revenues from Indian gaming were estimated to be between $6 billion and $8 billion. The success of these ventures led more Indian tribes in more states to negotiate for more casinos. In 2008, the National Indian Gaming Commission, a federal agency charged with regulating Indian gaming, indicates that there are 360 Indian gaming facilities in the United States operated by 220 tribes.

As the Indian tribes experienced their success, lawmakers were tempted to expand gambling to bring in greater revenues. In the 1990s, a number of Midwestern and Southern states that were hit with hard economic times approved the development of riverboat gambling. Because of popular opposition to these casinos, early regulations had strict limitations on the number of hours these riverboats could be open, and some states had limitations on losses. However, as competition became more intense, states that feared losing revenues began to lift these restrictions. By the 2000s, a few states allowed the casinos to move from the riverboats to the land on the riverfronts. As of 2008, eleven states permit casinos, and more are considering allowing casinos.

In Florida, Governor Charlie Crist response to the budget crisis led him to begin negotiation with the Seminole Indian Tribe to allow state-sanctioned casinos on the tribe's lands. According to Crist, "There are some other opportunities we're looking toward to help us with the budget challenges we have today. We're negotiating with the tribe. I want to be open-minded, and I want us to be innovative." Critics, however, were quick to pounce on Crist for his decision making. One editorial in the *Palm Beach Post* noted, "Uh oh. One little financial thirst, and Gov. Crist is already reaching for the gambling Kool-Aid." In November 2007, Crist signed an agreement with the tribe that permitted it to have Las Vegas-style slot machines, baccarat and blackjack at its casinos. In return the state would receive a share of the increased revenues. However, in July 2008 the Florida Supreme Court ruled the agreement illegal, finding that Gov. Crist did not have the authority to make such a deal.

Opponents of state-sponsored gaming, including critics in Florida, have stressed that casinos often fail to bring in promised revenues and can increase costs due to higher rates of crime, bankruptcy, and mental illness. Researchers at Baylor University and the University of Georgia estimated that casinos in the United States cost states about $40 billion thanks to additional law enforcement and prison space. Professor Earl Grinols of Baylor notes, "If it was just harmless entertainment, it wouldn't be a **public policy** question." However, Grinols' research suggests that casinos have a 3.1-to-1 cost-to-benefit ratio, meaning that the cost of a casino to society is roughly three times the benefit.

Moreover, some data suggests that though states may bring in revenues from gambling, the casinos often cause other forms of revenue to decrease. Those who spend their money at casinos spend less money elsewhere, and so sales taxes can decrease. Gambling critics stress that when a state allows casinos to open, it typically means that the state will become dependent on the gambling, because the casinos will likely make non-gambling businesses suffer. And due to this dependency, lawmakers may become more inclined to allow expansion of gambling thanks to promises of even more revenues.

In 2007, Kansas went further than most other states when the state legislature approved a bill that allows the state to own casinos and allows counties in the state to vote whether casinos should be allowed. Supporters touted the increased revenue opportunities, which could be used to fund education, transportation, and other state-sponsored projects. Although some areas such as Sedgwick County (which contains Wichita) rejected casinos, others have approved the casinos and have begun to consider bids for casino projects from developers willing to pay hundreds of millions of dollars for the construction of these facilities.

With more states considering proposals to allow expanded gambling in their states, the debate is far from over. And while some state and local leaders are starting to become more skeptical about the economic benefits of the casinos, many depressed areas have become hard-pressed to find better alternatives.

NBA commissioner David Stern pledged to help in the investigation in any way possible. Stern said, "We would like to assure our fans that no amount of effort, time or personnel is being spared to assist in this investigation, to bring to justice an individual who has betrayed the most sacred trust in professional sports, and to take necessary steps to protect against this ever happening again."

Stern later called the situation the worst he had experienced as NBA commissioner. He expressed concern that Donaghy could have provided information to others that could have compromised games in which Donaghy was not involved. "Not only aren't [referees] permitted to either gamble or provide information to people," said Stern. "They may not even provide other than to their immediate family the details of their travel schedules or the games they are going to work."

The federal government charged Donaghy on two counts, including conspiracy to commit wire **fraud** and conspiracy to transmit wagering information. With regard to the wire fraud charge, the government relied on a rather arcane legal theory known as an "intangible right of honest services." This concept means that the NBA had a right to honesty and integrity for the work of its officials and that Donaghy had conspired to violate this right. The second charge related to Donaghy's acts of transferring gambling information across state lines, which violates federal law.

On August 15, 2007, Donaghy pleaded guilty to the charges. Standing before Judge Carol Bagley Amon of the U.S. **District Court** for the Eastern District of New York, Donaghy admitted that his actions affected the games that he officiated. "By having this nonpublic information, I was in a unique position to predict the outcome of NBA games," said Donaghy. He was released on a cash bond of $250,000 but faced a maximum of 25 years in prison and fines of more than $500,000.

Donaghy was originally schedule to be sentenced in January 2008, but his sentencing was postponed. He has reportedly been cooperating with investigators who are tracking gamblers. In April 2008, both Battista and Martino pleaded guilty to gambling charges. Martino could face 18 months in prison, while Battista could face 16.

GAY AND LESBIAN RIGHTS

Martinez v. County of Monroe

State courts continue to wrestle over the question of whether to legally recognize same-sex marriages from other states and countries that permit such unions. The financial benefits conferred upon married couples, including health care benefits and tax statuses, can be considerable, so same-sex marriage partners have been eager to claim them. A division of the New York Supreme Court, **Appellate** Division, in *Martinez v. County of Monroe*, 850 N.Y.S.2d 740 (App. Div. 2008), ruled that a community college must grant spousal health care benefits to an employee whose Canadian same-sex marriage was valid under the laws of Canada and the province of Ontario.

In July 2004 Patricia Martinez married Lisa Ann Golden in the province of Ontario, Canada. That province's court had determined that same-sex couples were entitled to marry. In 2005 the Canadian Parliament passed a **statute** ratifying that court's ruling and similar ones from several other provinces. Martinez, an employee of Monroe Community College (MCC), immediately applied for spousal health care benefits for Golden. MCC, while recognizing that their marriage was legally valid in Canada, denied Martinez's benefits application in November 2004. Martinez filed suit in New York state

court, alleging that the denial of spousal health care benefits violated her rights under the **Equal Protection** Clause of the New York State Constitution and the New York law that bans discrimination in employment based on sexual orientation. The trial court ruled in favor of MCC's motion to dismiss the complaint, finding that Martinez's marriage was not entitled to legal recognition in New York and that the college did not violate the Equal Protection Clause or the employment discrimination law when denied the benefits application. Martinez then appealed to the Appellate Division of the New York Supreme Court.

The five-judge appeal panel, in a unanimous decision, overruled the lower court. Judge Erin Peradotto, writing for the court, noted that for over a century New York had recognized marriages solemnized outside of the state unless they fell into one of two categories: a marriage prohibited by the "positive law" of New York, or marriages involving incest or **polygamy** which were prohibited by "natural law." Therefore, if a marriage is valid in another state or country, it must be recognized by the state unless contrary to the two categories of prohibition. New York had in the past recognized a marriage between an uncle and his niece "by the half blood," **common law** marriages valid under the laws of other states, proxy marriages from the DISTRICT OF COLUMBIA, and a valid Canadian marriage of a man and a woman both under the age of 18. All of these marriages would have been invalid if solemnized n New York.

In the present case the marriage between Martinez and Golden did not fall within either of the two exceptions to the marriage-recognition rule. The state legislature had not enacted a law prohibiting the recognition of same-sex marriages entered into outside of New York. Therefore, the appeals court concluded that the **positive law** exception did not apply. The **natural law** exception did not apply because it had been generally limited to marriages involving polygamy or incest. MMC had argued that recognition of the same-sex marriage was contrary to New York state **public policy**. It pointed to a 2006 New York decision that held that the state constitution did not compel recognition of same-sex marriages solemnized in New York. Judge Peradotto did not find this decision controlling because that court also held that the state legislature may enact a law recognizing same-sex marriage. This meant that the the appeals court in 2006 did not find same-sex marriages against public policy. It was also noteworthy that New

York was one of the few states that did not, pursuant to the federal Defense of Marriage Act, 28 U.S.C. § 1738C, enact legislation denying full faith and credit to same-sex marriages validly solemnized in another state.

Having concluded that the Martinez-Golden marriage must be recognized by the state of New York, Judge Peradotto ruled that MCC's denial of benefits violated the law against discrimination in employment on the basis of sexual orientation. The only reason for the denial of benefits was Martinez's sexual orientation. The court ruled that case should be returned to the lower court where Martinez could offer proof that she was entitled to monetary damages because of the denial of benefits in 2004 and 2005. Those damages were not lessened by the fact that on January 1, 2006, Golden began receiving health care benefits under a new provision in the college's employment contract.

Chambers v. Ormiston

The 2004 decision by Massachusetts's highest court to permit gays and lesbians to marry has generated legal controversies inside and outside that state. Non-resident same-sex couples went to Massachusetts, obtained marriage licenses, and were married there. Upon returning to their home states some couples sought legal recognition of their unions. These attempts have generally been unsuccessful. However, as some of these same-sex unions have ended, gays and lesbians have sought to use state divorce laws to protect their legal rights. The Rhode Island Supreme Court, in *Chambers v. Ormiston*, 935 A.2d 956 (R.I. 2007), rejected such an attempt by a lesbian couple to use state divorce laws, ruling that state legislature never contemplated the word "marriage" to include same-sex unions. Therefore, the state family courts did not have jurisdiction to grant divorces to same-sex unions.

In May 2004, Rhode island residents Margaret Chambers and Cassandra Ormiston traveled to nearby Massachusetts and applied for a marriage license. After they received the license the couple was married by a Massachusetts **justice of the peace** in Fall River. The couple returned to Rhode Island and lived together. In 2006 they decided to dissolve their relationship that Massachusetts recognized as a marriage. Chambers filed a petition for divorce in state family court, and Ormiston filed an answer and counterclaim. The chief judge of the family court, recognizing that this was a case of **first impression**, certified a question to the Rhode Island Supreme Court, asking it to decide whether or not the family court

had subject-matter jurisdiction to grant a petition for divorce to a same-sex couple. The Supreme Court reviewed the question in January 2007 and decided that it needed more findings of fact from the family court. In addition, the court directed the family court to reword the certified question to clarify that the issue was whether the family court "could recognize the purported marriage for the purposes of entertaining a divorce petition."

The family court responded to this request in February 2007 and the Supreme Court heard oral argument in October 2007. In December 2007 the court issued its decision by a vote of 3–2, ruling that the family court did not have jurisdiction to hear a divorce petition from a same-sex couple married in another state. Justice William Robinson III, writing for the majority, based his analysis on **statutory** interpretation. The fundamental tenet of statutory interpretation is whether the language in question has a plain meaning and is unambiguous. If so, a court must acknowledge this meaning and go no further in examining the **statute**.

At issue was the meaning of the word "marriage" in the statute authorizing state family courts to "hear and determine all petitions for divorce from the bonds of marriage." Justice Robinson concluded that the statute was not ambiguous and that the job of the court was to "determine what the words in this statute were intended to mean." Though the current state legislature might have a different understanding of what the term "marriage" means, the court was required to examine what the word meant when the law creating family courts was enacted in 1961. The word "marriage" was not defined in the statute, leading the court to review contemporary dictionaries. Using the definition from Webster's Third New International Dictionary of the English Language, published in 1961, the court ruled that the legislature would have understood the word marriage to refer to a state of union with a person of the opposite sex. Therefore, the plain meaning of the word led the majority to conclude that the family court did not have jurisdiction to entertain the Chambers/Ormiston divorce petition. The role of the judiciary was not to make policy but determine the legislative intent as expressed in statutes. If the people of the state wanted to confer jurisdiction for same-sex unions, it was up to the legislature to act.

Justice Paul Suttell, in a dissenting opinion, argued that the family court did have jurisdiction to hear the divorce petition because the issue of what constituted a legal marriage was not before the court. The Massachusetts marriage was valid under that state's law, and there was nothing in Rhode Island law that expressly prohibited same-sex unions. The family court law specifically stated that the courts have the authority to entertain a divorce petition whether or not the marriage itself is valid. Second, Justice Suttell pointed out that it was well-settled law in 1961 that the "validity of a marriage is determined by the law of the place where celebrated." The marriage was valid under Massachusetts law. Therefore, the family court had jurisdiction to hear a petition dissolving the this marriage.

HABEAS CORPUS

[*Latin, You have the body.*] A writ (court order) that commands an individual or a government official who has restrained another to produce the prisoner at a designated time and place so that the court can determine the legality of custody and decide whether to order the prisoner's release.

Allen v. Siebert

When Congress passed the Anti-Terrorism and Effective Death Penalty Act of 1996 (AEDPA), Pub. L. No. 104-132., it sought to reduce the number of habeas filings by imposing strict timelines on petitions. However, the procedural rules governing petitions for writs of **habeas corpus** from **federal courts** have grown complicated since AEDPA's enactment. The **statute** did not cover all time limit issues, resulting in a steady stream of cases that had to be considered by the federal **appellate** courts. There have been conflicts among the circuits on many technical issues that ultimately govern whether a prisoner has waited too long to file a federal habeas action. The Supreme Court has issued decisions on these technical legal issues to help resolve these circuit conflicts, but variances in state laws have meant that the Court has had to revisit issues time and again. In *Allen v. Siebert*, __U.S.__, 128 S.Ct. 2, 169 L.Ed.2d 329 (2007), the Court again confronted a dispute over whether an inmate failure to file a timely state postconviction petition took away his right to file a federal habeas petition. The key issue was whether the untimely state petition was not "properly filed" as required by AEDPA.

Daniel Siebert was convicted of first-degree murder and sentenced to death by an Alabama state court. His conviction and sentence were affirmed on direct appeal and the certificate of judgment was filed in May 1990. The U.S. SUPREME COURT denied Siebert review in November 1990. In 1992 Siebert filed a petition for postconviction relief in Alabama state court, but the court dismissed the petition as untimely because it was filed three months after the expiration of the two-year **statute of limitations**. The Alabama Supreme Court denied review of the dismissal in September 2000, and Siebert did not seek review from the U.S. Supreme Court. One year later, in September 2001, Siebert filed a petition for a federal **writ** of habeas **corpus** in Alabama U.S. **district court**.

AEDPA established a 1-year statute of limitations for filing a federal habeas petition but this time period can be tolled (suspended) while a "properly filed" application for state postconviction review is pending. Because Siebert's direct became final before the passage of AEDPA, the one-year limitations period began running in April 1996, when AEDPA became effective. Therefore, if Siebert could not show that he had a **state action** pending at that time, the federal petition would be untimely by four years. The district court concluded that his petition was untimely because his state petition had been dismissed as untimely and therefore it was not "properly filed" for AEDPA purposes. The Eleventh **Circuit Court** of Appeals reversed this decision, ruling that Siebert's state petition for postconviction relief was "properly filed" because the state court rejected it on a nonjurisdictional ground.

The Supreme Court, in a 7–2 decision, reversed the Eleventh Circuit. In a *per curiam* opinion (no justice takes credit for writing the decision) the majority held that the appeals court had misread its recent decision, *Pace v. DiGuguglielmo*, 544 U.S. 408, 125 S.Ct. 1807, 161 L.Ed.2d 669 (2005). In *Pace*, the Court ruled that a state postconviction petition that was rejected by the state court as untimely was not "properly filed" within the meaning of § 2244(d)(2) of AEDPA. Because it was not properly filed, the one year statute of limitations on filing a federal habeas corpus petition was not tolled and the prisoner's federal petition had to be rejected. To hold otherwise would allow a state prisoner to toll the AEDPA's statute of limitations "at will simply by filing untimely state postconviction petitions." That would turn the AEDPA tolling provision into an "extension mechanism" that was contrary to congressional intent and "open the door to abusive delay." Therefore, when a petition is untimely under state law, "that is the end of the matter" under § 2244(d)(2).

In the Alabama case the Eleventh Circuit had sought to distinguish *Pace*, reasoning that the Alabama procedural rule operated as an "affirmative defense" that was different from the statute of limitations in *Pace*. The Supreme Court rejected this reading, noting that *Pace* "turned not on the nature of the particular time limit relied upon by the state court, but rather on the fact that time limits generally establish 'conditions to filing' a petition for state postconviction relief." It made no difference if a time limit is "jurisdictional, an **affirmative defense**, or something in between, it is a 'condition to filing.'" The *Pace* ruling was meant to prevent federal courts from delving into the intricacies of state **procedural law**. Therefore, the Court restated its conclusion in *Pace*: "When a postconviction petition is untimely under state law, 'that [is] the end of the matter' for purposes of § 2244(d)(2)."

Boumediene v. Bush

For a third time the Supreme Court rejected the efforts of the Bush Administration and Congress to detain and try foreign terror suspects at the Guantanamo Bay naval base without providing suspects with the right to seek a **writ of habeas corpus** challenging their confinement. In *Boumediene v. Bush*, __U.S.__, __S.Ct.__ , __L.Ed.2d__ 2008 WL 2369628 (2008), the court rejected arguments that the protections afforded the detainees under the Detainee Treatment Act of 2005 (DTA) and the Military Commissions Act of 2006 (MCA)

were adequate. Specifically, the Court ruled that the Commissions Act's provision that stripped the **federal courts** of jurisdiction to hear habeas **corpus** petitions filed by the detainees was unconstitutional. The decision, which came on a 5–4 vote, placed in doubt whether the government will continue to keep the detainees at Guantanamo and whether many of the detainees will ever come to trial. The ultimate decision on many of these issues will likely have to be made by the next presidential administration, which comes into office January 20, 2009.

In 2002 Lakdahr Boumediene and five other Algerian natives were seized by state police in Bosnia after U.S. intelligence officers suspected they were plotting an attack on the U.S. Embassy there. Bosnian authorities turned over the suspects to the U.S. government, which classified the suspects as enemy combatants. The suspects were sent to the Guantanamo Bay naval base, where they have been held in solitary confinement. Boumediene filed a petition for a writ of habeas corpus through his defense lawyer but the federal **district court** dismissed his petition. The court concluded that, as an alien detained at an overseas military base, he did not have the right to file a habeas petition. The U.S. Court of Appeals for the D.C. Circuit upheld the dismissal but the Supreme Court reversed this decision in *Rasul v. Bush*, 542 U.S. 466, 124 S. Ct. 2686, 159 L. Ed. 2d 548 (2004). The Court ruled that the federal habeas **statute** applied to non-citizen detainees held at Guantanamo.

Congress became involved in the dispute when it sought to overturn the *Rasul* decision by passing the DTA. The act stripped the federal courts of jurisdiction over habeas petitions filed by the Guantanamo detainees. The detainees challenged the DTA, arguing that it did not apply to their pending habeas petitions. The Supreme Court, in *Hamdan v. Rumsfeld*, 548 U.S. 557, 126 S. Ct. 2749, 165 L. Ed. 2d 723 (2006), sided with the detainees. This led Congress to enact the MCA in 2006, which stripped jurisdiction from the courts to hear pending habeas petitions. The D.C. Circuit heard Boumediene's case for a second time, with the detainee contending that the MCA was unconstitutional because it violated the Constitutions' Suspension Clause. This clause states that the "Privilege of the Writ of Habeas Corpus shall not be suspended, unless when in Cases of Rebellion or Invasion the public Safety may require it." The appeals court again found in the government's favor. The court said the Suspension Clause only protects the writ of habeas corpus as it was

Guantanamo demonstrator in prison garb and hood in front of US Supreme Court, December 2007.

AP IMAGES

conceptualized in 1789. The Framers would not have believed the writ applied to an military base leased from a foreign government. Moreover, U.S. constitutional rights do not apply to aliens held outside the United States.

A divided Supreme Court overturned the appeals courts. Justice ANTHONY KENNEDY, writing for the majority, held that the detainees had a constitutional right to challenge their confinement in federal courts. Kennedy stated that "The laws and Constitution are designed to survive, and remain in force, in extraordinary times." Moreover, these cases "lack any precise historical parallel. They involve individuals detained by executive order for the duration of a conflict that, if measure from September 11, 2001, to the present, is already among the longest wars in American history."

The Court concluded that the Suspension Clause had full effect at Guantanamo. It made no difference that Cuba maintained sovereignty over the base and leased it to the U.S. government, as habeas petitions had extraterritorial application. As to the government's argument that the federal courts should be restricting military authority during a war on terror, Justice Kennedy cited the 1803 ruling in *Marbury v. Madison*, 5 U.S. 137, which established the authority of the Supreme Court to review congressional legislation: "To hold that the political branches may switch the Constitution on or off at will would lead to a regime in which they, not this court, say 'what the law is.'"

Justice ANTONIN SCALIA, in a dissenting opinion joined by Chief Justice JOHN ROBERTS and Justices CLARENCE THOMAS and SAMUEL ALITO, called the decision an "incursion into military affairs." In his view the country was at war "with radical Islamists" and the decision would "almost certainly cause more Americans to be killed."

Munaf v. Geran

In *Munaf v. Geran*, 553 U.S. ___, 128 S.Ct. 2207, ___ L. Ed. 2d ___ (2008), the U.S. SU-PREME COURT was again faced with another case testing the scope of habeas within the context of the international war on terror. In this case, the Supreme Court held that a U.S. citizen may file a petition for **habeas corpus** to challenge his detention by American military forces taking part in a multinational force (MNF) overseas.

Munaf was born in Iraq, but became a U.S. citizen in 2000. Shortly thereafter, he married a Romanian woman and moved to Bucharest. In 2005, he accepted an assignment as a translator for three Romanian journalists working in Iraq. The foursome (Munaf and the journalists) was kidnapped in Iraq but released two months later to the Romanian Embassy in Baghdad. Upon release, Munaf was arrested by U.S. military forces participating in the MNF-Iraq, after being implicated himself in the kidnapping.

After fifteen months in custody, Munaf's sister petitioned on his behalf for a **writ** of habeas **corpus**. She filed it with the U.S. **District Court** for the DISTRICT OF COLUMBIA in Washington. Three weeks after she filed, Munaf received notification that he would be tried in an Iraqi court and transferred to Iraqi custody if he was convicted. Munaf then filed for a temporary restraining order against transfer of custody until his habeas petition was resolved.

The U.S. government opposed, arguing that Munaf had confessed his involvement both in writing and on camera. The government further argued that the district court lacked jurisdiction over the habeas petition.

On the other hand, Munaf's attorney argued that Munaf was not advised of the charges against him until he appeared in court. His attorney also argued that, since Iraqi courts require a formal complaint from the injured party before a prosecution will commence, it was a U.S. Coast Guard officer who filed the complaint, claiming Munaf was acting at the behest of the Romanian government. The attorney alleged that Romania consistently denied authorizing the arrest.

Prior to the district court's decision, Munaf was convicted in the Iraqi court and sentenced to death. One week later, the federal district court dismissed his case, concluding it did not have jurisdiction over the matter. Munaf appealed to the U.S. **Circuit Court** of Appeals for the D.C. Circuit, which granted a temporary injunction on his transfer to Iraqi authorities pending its decision.

The D.C. **appellate court** affirmed the district court's conclusion that it lacked jurisdiction. It cited a 1948 *per curiam* (written by all judges, not just one) decision by the U.S. Supreme Court, *Hirota v. MacArthur*, 338 U.S. 197, as controlling in this case. In *Hirota*, the Court ruled that Japanese citizens held in Japan by U.S. troops could not invoke habeas corpus to challenge their sentences by a multinational military **tribunal** sitting in Japan but including American military personnel. The D.C. **appellate** court reasoned that this case was similar because, like *Hirota*, neither the present MNF nor the Iraqi court were U.S. tribunals subject to U.S. law (particularly U.S. law regarding habeas).

But the U.S. Supreme Court decided otherwise, in an unanimous opinion reaffirming the rights of U.S. citizens to seek habeas review. Chief Justice JOHN ROBERTS wrote the opinion reversing the appeals court below. The Court unequivocally held that the habeas **statute**, 28 USC § 2241(c)1, extended to U.S. citizens held by American forces overseas where the American forces were operating subject to an American chain of command. (The government had argued that the district court lacked jurisdiction because the American forces holding Munaf were operating as part of the MNF.) But in rejecting that argument, the Court noted that the language of the statute applied to all persons held "in custody under or by color of the authority of the United States." According to the Supreme Court, the word "or" in the statute made clear that actual government custody sufficed for jurisdiction, even if that custody could be construed as custody "under or by color of" another authority, such as the MNF.

The Court further rejected *Hirota* as controlling. The Court reasoned that in *Hirota* justices may have found it significant that the government had argued that General MacArthur was not subject to United States authority and that his duty was to obey the Far Eastern Commission and not the U.S. War Department. Therefore, no process issued by a U.S. court would have affected his actions. In contrast, in the present case, the government had acknowledged that U.S. commanders answered to the President. Finally, the Court noted that Munaf was a U.S. citizen, and further noted that habeas jurisdiction could depend on citizenship. *Johnson v. Eisentrager*, 339 U.S. 763.

Despite the affirmation of habeas rights for U.S. citizens held by American forces overseas, the Supreme Court also found that federal district courts lacked authority to interfere with or bar the transfer of those persons alleged to have committed crimes within the territory of foreign sovereigns and/or detained in those territories for prosecution. Therefore, the appellate court had erred in granting injunctive relief for transfer of Munaf to Iraqi custody.

IDENTITY THEFT

Fourth Circuit Upholds Verdict Against Equifax

The Fourth **Circuit Court** of Appeals in December 2007 affirmed a sizable verdict against one of the major credit agencies, Equifax, for the damages caused by the company's failure to correct errors that resulted from an identity theft incident. Although the court reduced the award for emotional distress caused to the victim, the $395,000 total verdict after appeal, including attorneys fees, was one of the largest in this type of case.

Suzanne Sloane on June 25, 2003 gave birth to her second child at Prince William Hospital in Virginia. While she was there, a hospital employee named Shovana Sloan noticed that Suzanne had a similar name and birthday. Shovana obtained Suzanne's social security number and began to obtain credit cards, loans, cash advances, and other goods and services in Suzanne Sloane's name. In two months, Shovana ran up $30,000 in debt in Suzanne Sloane's name.

Suzanne discovered these transactions in January 2004 when Citibank contacted her about the company's cancellation of a credit card that had been issued in her name. Citibank informed her that she needed to contact Equifax to discuss any concerns. She immediately tried to call Equifax, but could not get through. Instead, she visited the company website and obtained her credit report. The information on the credit report allowed her to identify Shovana Sloan's crimes. Suzanne Sloane immediately contacted the police as well as Equifax.

Equifax placed a **fraud** alert on Sloane's file and told her to "roll up her sleeves" and start contacting creditors about the identity theft. She notified about 20 of them during two days she took off from work. At the direction of several of these creditors, she submitted notarized forms to them for the companies to correct the errors on her credit history.

Despite her efforts, Sloane continued to experience problems stemming from the identity theft for several months after her initial discovery. In March 2004, she was turned down for a pre-qualification letter that she and her husband, Tracey, had planned to use to purchase a vacation home. At this time, the loan officer told Suzanne that her credit score was "terrible" and that she would not be able to obtain credit until she corrected her score with Equifax. Suzanne stopped applying for credit for the next seven months. In October 2004, she and Tracey tried to buy a used car but was again rejected due to problems with Suzanne's credit score. She had further problems in January 2005 when a loan company would only agree to offer her an adjustable rate loan instead of a 30-year fixed loan.

Sloane in March 2005 sent a formal letter to Equifax where she disputed 24 specific items that appeared on her credit report. The company agreed to remove all but two of them from Citifinancial, though Equifax later admitted that it should have removed all of them. Two months later, the two Citifinancial items remained, and the company had also erroneously restored two Washington Mutual accounts that had been previously removed. Over the next several months, Equifax continued to make mistakes, including running a report that contained Shovana Sloan's name but Suzanne Sloane's social security number. More egregiously, in May 2005, Equifax mailed a letter to Suzanne's home that was addressed to the name of Shovana Sloan. The letter indicated that Sloan may have been the victim of identify theft and offered to sell her a service that could monitor her credit file. Suzanne's attorney, A. Hugo Blankingship III, referred to Equifax's actions as "a comedy of errors."

Suzanne presented evidence of the significant emotional distress that she suffered. Because she and her husband were constantly denied credit, they began to fight. Their marriage deteriorated to the point that Tracey was considering divorce as an option. They began to sleep in separate rooms, and Tracey refused to see a marriage counselor with Suzanne. Suzanne began to suffer from insomnia, and she had difficulty staying awake at work.

Sloane had also had problems with other credit reporting agencies, but those companies had corrected the problems relatively quickly compared with Equifax. On November 4, 2005, she filed suit against Equifax as well as Trans Union, Experian, and CitiFinancial. She alleged that the companies had violated the FAIR CREDIT REPORTING ACT, 15 U.S.C.A. §§ 1681 *et seq.* She also sued Prince William Hospital as well as the company that had placed Shovana Sloan at the hospital. Sloane settled against all of the other parties, but Equifax refused to settle the case.

A jury in the U.S. **District Court** for the Eastern District of Virginia rendered a verdict in favor of Sloane. The jury awarded her $106,000 for economic loss and $245,000 for **mental anguish**, humiliation, and emotional distress. The court also ordered Equifax to pay $181,083 in attorney's fees. Equifax subsequently appealed the judgment to the Fourth Circuit Court of Appeals, which only partially affirmed the district court's ruling. *Sloane v. Equifax Informatoni Servs., Inc.,* 510 F.3d 495 (4th Cir. 2007).

Equifax did not dispute the jury's findings but instead objected to the damage awards. According to the company, Sloane suffered only a single, indivisible injury, and that the court should have taken into account the settlements she had reached with the other credit reporting agencies. The company also argued that Sloane had not submitted evidence that supported her claim of economic loss. Moreover, Equifax stressed that the jury had made an unreasonable finding by awarding Sloane $245,000 for pain and suffering.

The court determined that the first two arguments were without merit. Though Sloane had suffered similar injuries due to the actions of the other credit reporting agencies, her problems with Equifax occurred both before and after she had problems with the other companies. The court also rejected Equifax's argument that Sloane had not suffered economic loss, for the denials of credit proved that she had suffered such harm.

The court agreed, however, that the jury's award for pain and suffering was excessive. On the other hand, the court had a difficult time identifying what amount would be appropriate. After reviewing published cases dealing with similar types of actions, the court reduced the pain and suffering award from $245,000 to $150,000.

IMMIGRATION

The entrance into a country of foreigners for purposes of permanent residence. The correlative term *emigration* denotes the act of such persons in leaving their former country.

Ninth Circuit Upholds Arizona's Ban on Hiring Illegal Immigrants

In July 2007, Arizona Governor Janet Napolitano signed into law HB 2779, Arizona's Fair and Legal Employment Act. The bill required employers to enroll in and utilize the federal E-Verify program to verify the legal status of their employees. If they failed to do so, or were found to knowingly or intentionally employ "unauthorized aliens" (illegal immigrants), suspension or revocation of business licenses was authorized. Moreover, Section 23-212(C)(1) classified a first violation as a Class 6 **felony**, for which offenders shall pay "an additional assessment of at least five thousand dollars but not more than fifty thousand dollars to be deposited in the immigration enforcement fund established by section 26-103." A second violation (revocation of license) could prevent a business from operating in the state. The law was considered the strictest in the nation for employer sanctions.

Federal law already criminalizes the hiring of illegal immigrants, but Arizona's Act was in response to what is perceived as lax federal enforcement. Governor Napolitano's signature was accompanied by a letter to Senator Harry Reid (D-NV) and Speaker Nancy Pelosi (D-CA), saying that Congressional inaction was forcing states to act on their own. Arizona's illegal population was estimated at 500,000.

Several employers and other interested organizations filed lawsuits challenging the Act. The complaints (later consolidated) essentially argued that the Arizona law was preempted by federal immigration law. Further, the plaintiffs argued that the law violated employers' due process rights.

But the **district court** dismissed the complaints on procedural grounds. *Arizona Contractors Association v. Napolitano*, CV-07-2496-PHX-NVW. The plaintiffs then filed new complaints correcting the defects, and also appealed the dismissal to the Ninth **Circuit Court** of Appeals. The new lawsuits and the appeal asked for temporary relief against the new law's implementation (**preliminary injunction**). *Arizona Contractors Association v.Candelaria*, CV-07-2496-PHX-NVW.

In December 2007, district court Judge Neil V. Wake denied temporary relief. More importantly, Judge Wake ruled that the plaintiffs were not likely to succeed in their new lawsuit or on appeal of the first lawsuit. The Ninth Circuit declined review on the temporary relief.

In February 2008, Judge Wake ruled on the merits of the challenged law, holding that it was not an unconstitutional effort by a state to regulate immigration. (Proponents of the law had argued that *enforcement* of immigration was not a federal responsibility.) Judge Wake concluded that the Arizona law did not conflict with federal preemptive law because federal law expressly permits states to regulate business licensing.

On February 29, 2008, a three-judge panel of the Ninth Circuit Court of Appeals upheld the decision of the district court to deny temporary relief. In a brief order issued by the court, the judges concluded that plaintiff-appellant employers and immigration groups had failed to show sufficient cause (adequate need) for delaying enforcement of the law. On the greater issue challenging the constitutionality of the law, oral arguments and briefs were ordered. A decision was not expected for several months.

Meanwhile, the new law was having the effect that proponents had hoped for. Illegal immigrants were leaving the state by the hundreds, and the state unemployment rate dropped to 3.7 percent. However, not all the news was positive. Critics feared a tightening labor market, resulting in higher wages but also higher costs for goods and services. Moreover, many feared that fleeing undocumented workers were merely relocating themselves in neighboring states with more favorable laws, and therefore only changing the demography rather than substance of the problem.

Judith Gans, program manager for immigration policy at the University of Arizona's Udall Center for Studies in **Public Policy**, feared that the loss of workers would result in an economic disadvantage for Arizona. Gans noted that several key industries in Arizona depended heavily on immigrants, both legal and illegal, to fill gaps in the workforce, in particularly low-skill jobs in the construction, manufacturing and agriculture sectors. In support of her conclusion, she cited, in an interview for the *Arizona Republic*, a study released by the Center concluding that the state's economic output would drop annually by at least $29 billion, or 8.2 percent, if all non-citizens were removed from Arizona's workforce. Approximately 14 percent of the state's 2.6 million workers were foreign-born, and about two-thirds to three-fourths of non-citizens were undocumented, she stated.

At least four other states were considering or working on bills modeled after the Arizona law. Notwithstanding, business groups and large companies continued to oppose the efforts, threatening that they would not expand business in states where the laws were enacted.

INSURANCE

A contract whereby, for a specified consideration, one party undertakes to compensate the other for a loss relating to a particular subject as a result of the occurrence of designated hazards.

Louisiana Attorney General Sues Insurance Companies

In November 2007, Louisiana Attorney General Charles C. Foti, Jr. announced that his office had filed suit against several insurance companies in New Orleans Parish Civil **District Court**. The petition alleged various ongoing schemes by the companies to avoid fair compensation to victims of Hurricanes Katrina and Rita, in violation of the Louisiana Monopolies Act (an anti-trust law). "But to be clear," Foti added in his announcement, "these abuses were not new to the recent hurricanes." Some insurance experts opined that Foti filed in state court, asking for a jury trial and citing state **monopoly** law rather than federal anti-trust law, in hopes of finding local sympathetic factfinders.

Named as defendants in the suit were Allstate Insurance Company; Lafayette Insurance Company; Xactware, Inc.; Marshall & Swift/

ILLEGAL IMMIGRATION WOES

As the final months of the Bush Administration's White House tenure neared the end, so also did the hope of any meaningful reform to immigration laws being enacted before a new president took office. Although the public remained eager for immigration reform, most Americans opposed any path to legal citizenship for the estimated 12 million illegal immigrants already in the United States as of 2008. Moreover, because 2008 was an election year, politicians were less eager to deliver plain talk to their constituents about the realities of passing legislation that could pass muster with all parties and competing interests at stake.

This was not to suggest that nothing was done to improve the control of illegal immigration. On the contrary, the Bush Administration responded to what many Americans had said all along: forget new legislation and just enforce the laws that already exist. To that end, during his State of the Union Address in January 2008, President Bush enumerated the steps taken by his administration to improve border security and other immigration challenges.

Bush told the nation that since he took office in 2001, funding for border security and immigration enforcement had increased by 159 percent, from $4.8 billion to 12.3 billion in 2008. The number of border patrol agents had also been increased from 9,000 in 2001 to 18,000 by the end of 2008. Moreover, Bush advised, the Department of Homeland Security (DHS) as on track to complete 370 miles of pedestrian fencing along the southwest border of the United States by the end of 2008. This, combined with vehicle fencing, gave the Administration credit for a total of 670 miles of fencing along the southwest border by the end of 2008. Other measures included the addition of three Unmanned Aerial Systems (UAS) and $100 million of dedicated funding for a new Southwest Border Enforcement Initiative in the 2009 budget. The DHS reported a 20 percent drop in apprehensions of illegal immigrants along the southwest border, supporting the argument that such efforts had indeed deterred illegal entries.

The Administration was also responsible for ending the decades-old practice of permitting U.S. and Canadian citizens to enter the country with merely oral declarations of identity and citizenship. Beginning in January 2008, all cross-border travelers needed documents to support their identities and citizenship. Starting in June 2009, the Western Hemisphere Travel Initiative will take effect, requiring passports or similar secure documents for all travelers.

Finally, in what the *New York Times* referred to as "the toughest crackdown on illegal immigration in two decades," employers found themselves increasingly subject to fines, convictions, losses of business licenses, and other sanctions if found to have knowingly engaged in the hiring of illegal immigrants. After years of lax enforcement, federal immigration agents increased the number and force of raids at workplaces, resulting in an unprecedented 4,970 arrests for 2007. Moreover, more than 175 state bills were introduced to address the employment of illegal immigrants. In 2008, Mississippi became the first state to make it a felony for an illegal immigrant to work. The state's measure also provided a cause of action for terminated employees to sue their employers if they were replaced by an illegal immigrant. Other states, well within their rights, began to deny college benefits, drivers' licenses, or other state perks to illegal immigrants.

But there was a darker side to these efforts. Employers started to push back, mobilizing and lobbying to make state laws more friendly to employers. Business groups across the country opposed the use of the federal E-Verify system of checking working papers of all new hires, complaining that the Social Security Administration's database was fraught with error. But the Bush Administration had an answer for the complaints: the crackdown on employers was the price they would pay until voters saw the light and agreed to open the gates to immigrant workers. The administration was referring to its failed immigration reform package that sparked national debate over a "guest worker" program that many considered cloaked amnesty.

On June 28, 2007, the U.S. Senate essentially "killed" the Bush Administration's comprehensive immigration reform bill intended to fortify

---

Boeckh, LLC; Insurance Services Office, Inc.; State Farm Fire and Casualty Company; USAA Casualty Insurance Company; Farmers Insurance Exchange; Standard Fire Insurance Company; and McKinsey & Company. The suit alleged that defendant insurers conspired to limit payments to policyholders after the hurricanes and engaged in elaborate **price-fixing** schemes. Some of the alleged illegal tactics included coercing policyholders into settling their damage claims for less than actual value, editing engineering assessment reports, delaying and forestalling payments, and

forcing policyholders into costly litigation to challenge their estimates. "The acts of this combination have seriously impeded the economic growth and disaster recovery of [Louisiana] and its citizens and effectuated an ongoing **fraud** on commerce in this state," stated one allegation in the 29-page lawsuit.

Although claims of price-fixing and antitrust conspiracies are generally harder to prove than other violations, in this case there was one common thread to bind the defendants into one common conspiracy, Loyola law professor Dane the nation's borders while creating a vehicle toward citizenship for an estimated 12 million current illegal immigrants. The bill had essentially failed three weeks prior, but was revived at the last minute by bi-partisan lobbying to reconsider a revised version. A *cloture* motion received a 64-35 vote to allow continued debate, but that success was short-lived. After considering three more amendments, the votes fell 14 short of the 60 needed for a final *cloture* (ending debate and clearing the way for final passage of the legislation). The topic was considered so volatile that it was unlikely to be revisited again before 2009, or at a minimum, until after 2008 elections. Senator Edward M. Kennedy (D-MA), the party's key negotiator, called the defeat "enormously disappointing for Congress and for the country," but added that, "[w]e will be back." He and others had worked hard to find common ground for an immigration compromise which they referred to as "an imperfect but necessary fix" to the current system.

The "current system," had not been seriously overhauled in 20 years, resulting in a sagging policy under which millions of illegal immigrants used forged and counterfeit documents or lapsed visas to live and work in the United States. Mr. Bush's proposed plan would have made those millions eventually eligible for legal status over time, while immediately focusing on tightening border security and creating an employee verification system intended to weed out illegal workers from jobs in the United States. The bill also would have created a temporary worker ("guest worker") program and a system that based future legal immigration on employment rather than family ties.

After Congress failed to rework immigration reforms, the Bush Administration stepped up its border and work site monitoring, resulting in a 61 percent increase in the average daily detainee population, which hovered around 28,700 by December 2007. As the detainee population grew, the American Civil Liberties Union (ACLU) found deficient medical care to be the primary complaint, and promptly filed suit alleging excruciating suffering and the deaths of several detainees at an detainee center in San Diego, one of more than 300 nationwide.

In July 2008, the Department of Homeland Security delivered another negative report. An internal investigation by DHS's inspector general revealed an alarming number of deaths of immigrants detained by the government. With the Bush Administration's aggressive enforcement policies, the number of jailed immigrants continued to rise. Detained illegal immigrants were generally housed in centers run by Immigration and Customs Enforcement (ICE) officials or private companies, as well as in state and local jails that had agreed to take them.

Although the report was limited, focusing on only two deaths of 74 that had occurred since 2004, it did commend officials at Immigration and Customs Enforcement, the agency tasked with overseeing immigrant detentions, for adhering to standards addressing follow-up procedures after detainees have died. The report recommended better access to health care for detainees, stronger oversight, and better detention standards to be drafted.

In another report released June 30, 2008, the United Nations documented "credible claims"(UN) of denied, inadequate, or incorrect care or delay in treatment at ICE facilities. Two new bills were introduced in Congress. One, introduced by Senator Robert Menendez (D-NJ) would require DHS to establish procedures for timely delivery of healthcare, as well as report all deaths to the DHS Inspector General and to Congress, and enhance the decision-making capabilities of medical professionals. Under the current law, on-site staff decisions could be overruled by off-site officials without further review.

In an election year, the word "amnesty" was sure to cause shudders in both Democratic and Republican circles. Even the experts could not agree on a palatable reform policy that could bring together some of the opposing forces. According to a report published in the *Christian Science Monitor*, Mark Krikorian, executive director of the Center for Immigration Studies in Washington, proposed shrinking the number of illegal immigrants gradually (attrition) through enforcement of existing laws. Another immigration expert, Joseph Chamie, research director at the Center for Migration Studies in New York, opined that legalization was the only viable path and long-term option that made any sense. At least both Republicans and Democrats agreed on the need for tightening U.S. borders. But even with enhanced border patrol, little had changed for the millions of illegal immigrants already inside the border.

Ciolino told CBS New Orleans' media affiliate, WWL. That was defendant McKinsey & Company, a New York-based consulting group that allegedly taught insurance companies how to reduce payouts and increase profits. The lawsuit alleged that McKinsey, called the "architect" of sweeping changes in the insurance industry starting in the 1980s, advised its insurer-clients to "stop 'premium leakage' by undervaluing claims using the tactics of deny, delay, and defend." The suit further alleged that all of the defendant insurance companies had used the services of McKinsey, and therefore, had conspired in a price-fixing scheme.

Likewise, defendants Marshal & Swift/Boeckh and Xactware were not insurance companies, but rather manufacturers and creators of claims-processing computer software that has helped the industry standardize claim processing. But according to the lawsuit, these defendants created a "tainted" database of claims settlement figures that the industry relied on to reduce figures quoted to policyholders as accurate or fair compensation for needed repairs or replacements. All the data was centralized by Xactware's **parent company**, defendant Insurance Service Office (ISO). Foti used these compiled alleged facts to support allegations of industry collusion.

Foti further alleged that insurers, by using such outside vendors to unify "power and control . . . under a shroud of secrecy," were able to systematically reduce the percentage of premium dollars returned to policyholders in the form of claims payments. The suit alleged that historically, the insurance industry had paid (in claims) 70 cents on every premium dollar, but in Katrina, it paid 50 cents per premium dollar.

The lawsuit's filing coincided with local media's investigation into insurance company policies and practices that resulted in record profits despite Katrina and Rita claims. For example, Allstate netted more after-taxes income than it had before dealing with losses from the 2005 hurricanes, according to Consumer Federation of America. In fact, in 2006 when it was still paying claims for Katrina and Rita, its profits jumped to $5 billion. The consumer group also found that between 1996 and 2006, the amount of each premium dollar that Allstate paid back to its policyholders fell from 73 cents per dollar to 59 cents. Such business practices were allegedly uncovered in internal Allstate presentation slides in which McKinsey demonstrated how the insurer could boost profits.

In defense, insurance companies asserted that profits were the result of millions of new policyholders, including auto insurance customers. Further, and in particular, Allstate responded that when Louisiana insurance officials conducted a market review of its response to Katrina and Rita, they concluded that it was compliant with state statutes, rules, and regulations. (But the state insurance commissioner ordered the company to change its "flawed" property inspection process, and to reinstate policyholders after Allstate cancelled the policies of more than 4,700 homeowners.)

Parallel with this news was the move by Judge Michael T. Parker of Federal District Court in Mississippi to extend an existing restraining order that prevented that state's attorney general from continuing a criminal investigation into State Farm's handling of Katrina claims. State Farm had sued Mississippi Attorney General Jim Hood in September 2007 and won its petition for a restraining order prohibiting Hood from reopening a criminal case or continuing **grand jury** hearings.

The Louisiana insurance commissioner, Jim Donelon, who was briefed on the lawsuit by an aide, said Mr. Foti was obligated to sue if he found evidence of collusion between the companies. The lawsuit was projected to continue in court over the next few years.

Tuepker v. State Farm Fire & Casualty Company

Anyone who has reviewed an insurance policy knows that these documents are typically long and complicated. The insurer provides details on what it is insuring, how much it will pay in the event of an incident, and what is excluded from the coverage. Insurance exclusion clauses take some insured owners by surprise when they file a claim, for a policy clause that suggests coverage may be taken away by a later exclusion clause. Not surprisingly, disputes over coverage lead to litigation. In the aftermath of Hurricane Katrina in August 2005, many homeowners where shocked to find that the hurricane coverage they purchased provided no protection. Insurance companies had included "flood" exclusion clauses that denied payment for damage caused by Katrina's storm surge. Homeowners sued but have for the most part been unsuccessful in overturning or limiting these flood exclusion clauses. The U.S. Fifth Circuit Court of Appeals, *Tuepker v. State Farm Fire & Casualty Company*, 507 F.3d 346 (5th Cir. 2007), upheld a flood exclusion clause, declining to find it ambiguous and refusing to apply the "efficient **proximate cause** doctrine."

John and Claire Tuepker's house on the Gulf Coast of Mississippi was destroyed by the combined effects of Hurricane Katrina on August 29, 2005. All that as was left was the concrete slab on which their home had sat. The Tuepkers filed a claim with State Farm but the company denied coverage. Though the policy contained a "Hurricane Deductible," which implied coverage, the policy also had a flood exclusion clause. This clause stated that the company excluded coverage for damages caused by "flood, surface water, waves, tidal water, tsunami, seiche, or overflow of a body of water, or spray from any of these, all whether or not driven by wind." The Tuepkers filed a lawsuit in Mississippi U.S. **district court**, seeking a **declaratory judgment** that the damage to their house caused by the storm surge was not excluded under State Farm policy.

The federal district court sided with State Farm on the flood exclusion clause, finding that it was a valid and enforceable provision. However, under Mississippi state law where there is damage caused by both wind and rain (covered losses) and water (losses excluded from coverage), the "amount payable under the insurance policy becomes a question of which is the proximate cause of the loss." The State Farm policy appeared to be inconsistent with this law. The court also found that an "anti-concurrent-causation clause" in the policy was ambiguous and ineffective to exclude damages caused by wind or rain. This clause stated that even if wind and rain caused damage, there could be no coverage if there was accompanying water damage. If the Tuepkers could prove that hurricane winds and rains entering the house through openings caused by hurricane winds proximately caused damage to their property, those losses would be covered under the policy. State Farm then appealed these questions to the Fifth **Circuit Court** of Appeals.

A three-judge panel of the Fifth Circuit unanimously found in favor of State Farm. Judge William Garwood, writing for the court, noted that the federal court must be guided by Mississippi state insurance law. As to the water damage exclusion clause, the court found the clause's recitation of events accurate in describing the "influx of water into the Tuepkers' home that was caused by the Katrina storm surge." Judge Garwood cited a previous Fifth Circuit decision that applied Mississippi law in which the term "storm surge" was "little more than a synonym for 'tidal wave' or wind-driven flood." The lack of a specific reference to a "storm surge" in the water damage exclusion did not make the policy ambiguous or allow the Tuepkers to recover for their losses caused by the storm surge.

Judge Garwood reversed the district court's ruling that the anti-concurrent causation clause was ambiguous. The Tuepkers argued that this clause conflicted with the policy's express coverage for losses attributable to wind. The appeals court found that the words of the anti-concurrent causation clause was unambiguous under Mississippi law. The clause clearly stated that policy did not cover "any loss which would not have occurred in the absence of one or more of the following excluded events." This clause, in combination with the water damage exclusion "clearly provides that indivisible damage caused by both excluded perils and covered perils or other causes is not covered." As to the application of the efficient proximate cause doctrine, Judge Garwood concluded that under Mississippi law an anti-concurrent causation clause will "circumvent" this doctrine. The appeals court decision closed the door on thousands of homeowners seeking insurance coverage for Katrina's storm surge.

INTERNATIONAL LAW

The body of law governing the legal relations between states or nations.

Canadian Supreme Court Refuses Asylum Appeal by US Army Deserter

During the VIETNAM WAR, over 50,000 American men avoided the draft by seeking asylum in Canada. The Canadian government permitted the Americans to stay. Some became Canadian citizens, while most returned to the United States after President Jimmy Carter issued on his first day in office, January 20, 1977, an amnesty order that pardoned draft resistors. The Canadian view of U.S. soldiers seeking asylum after deserting during the Iraq war has been decidedly different. In a November 2007 decision, the Canadian Supreme Court upheld prior decisions by an appeals court and the Immigration and Refugee Board of Canada (IRBC) that rejected a asylum applications by two U.S. Army deserters. The Court reaffirmed the conclusion of the IRBC that the deserters would not be at risk for their lives if they returned to the United States, nor would they be at risk of "cruel and unusual treatment or punishment."

The Iraq War has triggered the desertion and movement of approximately 400 U.S. servicemembers since 2003. All deserters are placed on the Federal Bureau of Investigation's (FBI) wanted list, and warrants exist for their arrest. Two U.S. Army members deserted in 2004 after learning their units were being deployed to Iraq. Jeremy Hinzman, a member of the 82nd Airborne Division, left Fort Bragg, North Carolina with his wife and son in January 2004, opposed to a war that he believed was illegal and immoral. They settled in Toronto. Brandon Hughey, a member of the 1st Calvary in Fort Hood, Texas, fled to Canada in March 2004, objecting to the Iraq War.

The two men applied for refugee status but were denied. They appealed to the IRBC, contending that serving in Iraq would require them to commit crimes against civilians. In addition, they argued that if they returned to the United States that they would be persecuted. Under the UNIFORM CODE OF MILITARY JUSTICE (UCMJ) they would face court martial and time in prison. In addition, Hinzman had applied unsuccessfully in 2002 to the Army to be discharged or reassigned as a conscientious objector. Their lawyer, Jeffry House, attempted to argue that the Iraq war violated international law and that the occupation of Iraq violated international human rights, as set out in the Geneva Conventions.

However, the IRBC ruled this argument inadmissible. In March 2005 the IRBC denied Hinzman and Hughey asylum. In the Hinzman case the board found that he did not qualify as a conscientious objector, as he had stated in the past that he was not opposed to all wars. Under the Geneva Conventions a deserter may be considered a refugee if it can be shown that he or she would suffer disproportionately severe punishment for the military offense on account of his or her race, religion, nationality, membership of a particular social group or political opinion. In Hinzman's case the treatment or punishment that he feared would be punishment for nothing other than a breach of a neutral law that did not violate human rights. Any punishment that Hinzman might receive for being absent without leave or desertion would be pursuant to the **articles** of the UCMJ, which was a law of general application that did not violate human rights or the Geneva Conventions.

The men appealed to the Federal Court, the Federal Court of Appeals, and, finally, the Canadian Supreme Court. Each time the court refused to review the case, with the Supreme Court ending Hinzman and Hughey's claims for refugee status. Though they lost their immigration appeals, the government had not deported them as of late May 2008. In December 2007, Parliament's Standing Committee on Citizenship and Immigration urged the government not to deport any war objectors without a criminal record, including their immediate families, if the military service they refuse is related to a war not sanctioned by the UNITED NATIONS.

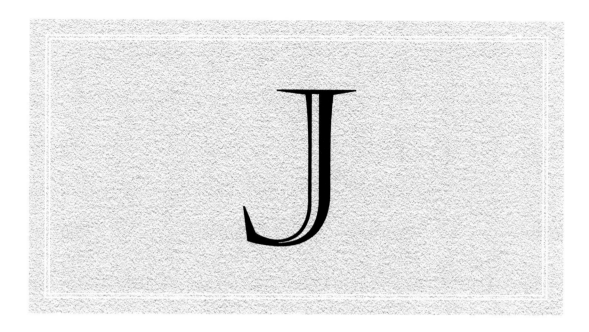

JURY

In trials, a group of people selected and sworn to inquire into matters of fact and to reach a verdict on the basis of the evidence presented to it.

Snyder v. Louisiana

The Supreme Court's landmark case, *Batson v. Kentucky*, 476 U.S. 79, 106 S.Ct. 1712, 90 L. Ed. 2d 69 (1986), states that prosecutors are forbidden from excluding prospective jurors on the basis of race through the use of peremptory challenges. A **peremptory challenge** permits a party to remove a prospective juror without giving a reason for his or her removal. This type of challenge has had a long history in U.S. law and has been viewed as a way to insure an impartial jury. However, under the *Batson* test, a defendant may object to a prosecutor's peremptory challenge based on an allegation of racial bias. The prosecutor then must come forward with a neutral explanation for challenging the prospective juror. If the prosecutor cannot offer a neutral explanation, the court will not excuse the juror. The Court has been called on over the past 20 years to decide whether a trial court judge acted correctly in accepting the explanation of the prosecutor. In *Snyder v. Louisiana*, __U.S.__, 128 S. Ct. 1203, 170 L. Ed. 2d 175 (2008), the Court stepped in again, ruling that the reasons offered by the prosecutor for striking a black prospective juror were a pretext for racial discrimination.

Allen Snyder was convicted of first-degree murder in a Louisiana court and was sentenced to death. He had killed the boyfriend of his wife, who was separated from Snyder at the time of the murder. Jury selection for his trial started the last week of August, 1996. The prosecutor and Snyder's lawyer struck prospective jurors for cause first and then moved on to exercising their peremptory challenges. Under Louisiana law, the parties were allowed to exercise "backstrikes." This meant they were permitted to use their peremptory challenges up until the final jury was sworn, striking jurors whom they had initially accepted when the jurors' panels were called. Of the 85 prospective jurors who were questioned, 36 survived challenges for cause. Five of the 36 were black and all five were eliminated by the prosecution through the use of peremptory challenges. The jury found Snyder guilty and sentenced him to death. Snyder appealed his conviction, contending that the selection of the jury was racially biased under *Batson*. The Louisiana Supreme Court rejected his claim. Snyder then took his case to the U.S. SUPREME COURT.

The Supreme Court, in a 7–2 decision, overturned the state supreme court ruling, finding that in the case of one black juror the prosecutor violated *Batson*. Justice SAMUEL ALITO, writing for the majority, noted that it was up to the trial court judge to determine if the defendant has shown purposeful discrimination by the prosecution. An **appellate court**, when reviewing *Batson* challenges, must sustain a trial court's ruling on discriminatory intent unless it is clearly erroneous. Great deference is given to the trial judge's decision because it must evaluate the prosecutor's credibility, which typically involves examining the demeanor of the prosecutor. Other factors, including a juror's demeanor, make the trial court's "first hand observations of even greater importance." Despite this recitation of deference to the trial court, Justice Alito questioned the judgment of the trial court judge in assessing discriminatory intent.

The case turned on the challenge of Jeffrey Brooks, a black man, to sit as a juror. Brooks, a college senior, was scheduled to begin his student-teaching obligation and initially expressed interest in not serving. However, the judge's law clerk talked with Brooks' dean, who assured the court that if the trial ended in a few days there would be no problem in Mr. Brooks making up the hours. Based on this finding Brooks made it to the final panel. The next day the prosecutor exercised a peremptory challenge against Brooks, thereby instituting a backstrike. Snyder's lawyer made a *Batson* objection. The prosecutor offered two reasons for his strike: (1) Brooks looked very nervous throughout his questioning the day before, and (2) His fear of missing his student-teaching assignment might lead to him vote for a lesser verdict to avoid the penalty phase, which determines if a defendant should be sentenced to death. Snyder's lawyer disputed these explanations. The trial judge offered an opaque ruling: "All right. I am going to allow the challenge. I'm going allow the challenge."

Justice Alito declined to give deference to the judge's evaluation of Brooks' nervousness because the judge did not explain his reasons for accepting either of the prosecutor's justifications. Because of this silence, Justice Alito concluded that "we cannot presume that the trial judge credited the prosecutor's assertion that Mr. Brooks was nervous." The second proffered reason, Brooks' student-teaching obligation, also failed to meet the Court's "highly deferential standard of review." Though Mr. Brooks at first expressed concern about serving on the jury, once his dean stated that this would not be a problem, he did not express any further concern. As for the prosecutor's claim that Brooks might not vote for capital murder, so as to avoid the penalty phase of such a verdict, Justice Alito found this scenario "highly speculative." Even if Brooks had favored a speedy conclusion to the trial, it would not have necessarily led him to reject a first-degree murder verdict. If the majority of the jurors had favored a finding of first-degree murder, Brooks' "purported inclination might have led him to agree in order to speed the deliberations." However, the most significant evidence pointed to the fact that the prosecutor had told the prospective jurors at the beginning of the process that the trial would be brief. Mr. Brooks would not have been concerned about his teaching obligation because the trial happened early in the semester and he would have had many weeks to make up a few lost hours. In fact, the trial lasted just two days, which confirmed that prosecutor's explanation was implausible. Finally, the fact that the prosecutor accepted a white juror who disclosed conflicting obligations undercut the concerns he cited about Brooks. Therefore, the prosecutor's pretextual explanations gave rise to an inference of discriminatory intent. The Court reversed Snyder's conviction and remanded the case for a new trial.

LEGAL AID

A system of nonprofit organizations that provide legal services to people who cannot afford an attorney.

California Joins States Expanding Legal Aid Funds

In October 2007, California Governor Arnold Schwarzenegger signed into law a state bar-backed bill to increase funds provided for **legal aid** programs under the Interest on Lawyer Trust Accounts (IOLTA) program. California joined about a dozen other states that have adopted similar changes by legislation or court rule. Assembly Bill No. 1723, by Assembly Judiciary Committee Chairperson David Jones (D-Sacramento) would raise additional funds for legal aid programs without spending tax dollars. The bill, like those in other states, essentially reformed the rules governing the interest that banks pay on IOLTA funds, which have been around for years. The changes involve new authority to invest IOLTA funds in higher-risk, but higher-earning securities.

State IOLTA funds are created when attorneys who handle money belonging to their clients (including settlement checks, fees advanced for services not yet performed, i.e., **retainer** fees and court costs, etc.) are required to deposit them in clearly identifiable bank trust accounts. Attorneys, when creating these bank accounts, are generally required to label them as a "trust account," "client funds account," etc. All fifty states currently have rules or statutes on creating IOLTA accounts. Prior to IOLTA, funds were either held in trust by law firms or deposited in non-interest-bearing checking accounts.

It became increasingly clear over the years that an opportunity to earn interest was lost when large funds or funds held for a long period of time (as when tied up in litigation) were kept in such non-interest-bearing accounts. When IOLTA accounts were created, they offered an opportunity for state bar associations to dedicate interest earned to pay for public legal aid programs without using taxpayers' money. Moreover, attorneys who deposited small sums or short-term funds could pool them into a single, interest or dividend-bearing trust account. The collective funds could earn far more income in excess of the costs that financial institutions charged to open small, individual accounts. Collected IOLTA funds could then be forwarded to the state bar associations in each state to be distributed for public programs in that state. In California, IOLTA interest income had supported approximately 100 nonprofit programs and organizations that provided legal aid to indigent and low-income persons, senior citizens, and persons with disabilities.

Prior to the passage of AB 1723, interest-bearing checking accounts were the only available option for California IOLTA funds. The interest earned on these accounts averaged less than one percent and was generally stagnant. Effective January 1, 2008, California's new law amended Business & Professional Code Sections 6091.2, 6211, 6212, and 6213. The new mandates required financial institutions to offer comparable bank investment products to their IOLTA customers as to other similarly-situated customers.

The new amendments updated the financial vehicles available for attorneys, who can now have IOLTA funds held in conservative, high-yield or other bank products. This was particularly advantageous for large-balance accounts, and was expected to double the yields of IOLTA account interest earned, and thus double the money available to legal services supported by IOLTA funds.

The success of the IOLTA accounts prior to the new changes was largely due to the interest paid on checking accounts in the 1990s, generally high. But since 1993, California's IOLTA funding dropped nearly 60 percent. According to statistics released by the California Commission on Access, IOLTA funds produced almost $19 million in interest in 1993, which, if adjusted for inflation, would amount to nearly $25 million. Conversely, IOLTA funds produced just $10.7 million in interest earned in 2005, generally just under one percent on average.

The U.S. SUPREME COURT has previously addressed the constitutionality of IOLTA accounts. In *Phillips v. Washington Legal Foundation*, 524 U.S. 156, 118 S. Ct. 1925, 141 L. Ed. 2d 174 (1998), the justices ruled, in a tight 5–4 decision, that interest earned from IOLTA accounts was in fact the private property of clients, and that re-appropriating it under IOLTA amounted to a "taking" under the FIFTH AMENDMENT. However, the Court did not address the argument that since clients would never see that money anyway (the banks would keep it on small accounts) without IOLTA, there was no loss for which "just compensation" was due.

In 2003, the Supreme Court agreed. In affirming a Ninth **Circuit Court** of Appeals decision, the high court ruled that IOLTA programs did not violate clients' right to compensation as long as the program was limited to small or short-term deposits that would not otherwise be placed in interest-bearing accounts. *Brown v. Legal Foundation of Washington*, 538 U.S. 216, 123 S. Ct. 1406, 155 L. Ed. 2d 376 (2003). Since the money would not have gone to clients anyway, but would go to the bank, the states did not owe "compensation." The Court further noted that even if the money appropriated from IOLTA to legal service programs amounted to a "taking" of clients' earned interest, such a taking was valid for a public purpose to save taxpayer dollars and did not violate the Fifth Amendment.

California's IOLTA accounts are administered by the Legal Services Trust Fund Program, a department within the State Bar of California. A 21-member Legal Services Trust Fund Commission oversees the Trust Fund Program, commission members being appointed by the State Bar's Board of Governors and the Chief Justice. The

Trust Fund Program also manages two other sources of funds that offer free civil legal services to low-income and indigent people, the California Equal Access Fund and the Justice Gap Fund.

LEWDNESS

Behavior that is deemed morally impure or unacceptable in a sexual sense; open and public indecency tending to corrupt the morals of the community; gross or wanton indecency in sexual relations.

Senator Larry Craig Disgraced in Airport Restroom Incident

Senator Larry Craig (R.-Idaho) became embroiled in a major controversy in 2007 when he was arrested in a Minnesota airport for allegedly soliciting sex from an undercover male police officer. Craig initially pleaded guilty to the charges, but when the incident became public, he attempted to recant. The controversy cost Craig his leadership positions in the REPUBLICAN PARTY and cost him his political career.

Craig grew up in an ranching family in Idaho, served in the Idaho NATIONAL GUARD for three years, and was a member of the Idaho state legislature during the 1970s. He first entered Congress in 1981 when he was elected to the House of Representatives from the first district in Idaho. In 1990, he was elected to the Senate for the first time and was reelected to the position in 1996 and 2002.

Craig has been an outspoken proponent for initiatives that would limit gay and lesbian rights. He has supported a federal constitutional amendment that would ban same-sex marriage, noting that he believes it is "important for us to stand up now and protect traditional marriage, which his under attack by a few unelected judges and litigious activists." Craig supported the Defense of Marriage Act in 1996, which would have prevented states from having to recognize same-sex marriage performed in other states. Craig in 1996 also voted against legislation that would have outlawed employment discrimination based on sexual orientation.

Craig was present at the Lindbergh Terminal in Minneapolis-St. Paul on June 11, 2007. According to the police report filed in the case, Sergeant Dave Karsnia entered one of the restrooms at the airport at noon. Karsnia was dress in plain clothes and had entered the restroom to investigate allegations of sexual activity there. About fifteen minutes after Karsnia entered the restroom, Craig appeared outside of the stall where Karsnia was sitting. Craig hovered outside of the stall for about two minutes, looking into Karsnia's stall several times through the crack in the doorway.

When a stall next to Karsnia's came open, Craig entered and placed his roller bag in front of the stall. This tactic is apparently used to block the view from the front of the stall in order to conceal sexual activity. Craig allegedly began to tap his right foot, which is another sign that he wanted to solicit sex. At one point, Craig moved his right foot so that it touched Karsnia's left foot. Craig then made gestures by running his hand underneath the divider between the stalls. This activity continued for about four minutes until Karsnia displayed his badge underneath the stall door and motioned for the exit to the restroom. Craig responded by shouting "No!" and left the stall without flushing the toilet.

Craig initially resisted going to the police operations center at the airport, but he finally agreed to do so. He was read his Miranda rights and then interviewed. At one point, he apparently showed the officer his Senate business card. Craig argued that the reason his foot touched the officer's was because he has a "wide stance" when using the restroom. The senator also said that he had bent over to pick up a piece of paper on the floor in an attempt to explain why the officer could see his hand motions.

Karsnia's report refuted Craig's claims, noting that there was no paper on the floor as Craig had stated. The senator said that he could not recall other events that the officer alleged. After the interview, Craig agreed to enter a guilty plea for his actions. He pleaded guilty to charges of interference with privacy and **disorderly conduct**, which were lesser offenses to the more serious public **lewdness** charges that could have been brought. Craig paid a $500 fine along with his guilty plea.

Craig's guilty plea came on August 8, and at that time his arrest was not public knowledge. News of his arrest was first published by the Washington newspaper *Roll Call*, and the story gained widespread interest afterward. Republican leaders immediately expressed their concerns regarding Craig's leadership. The *Idaho Statesman* stepped up its investigation of accusations regarding other incidents where Craig may have solicited sex from other men.

On August 28, Craig made a public statement that he did nothing wrong at the airport and instead claimed that he had pleaded guilty to

Senator Larry Craig, February 2008.

AP IMAGES

make the problem go away. "In pleading guilty, I overreacted in Minneapolis, because of the stress of the Idaho Statesman's investigation and the rumors it has fueled around Idaho," Craig said. "Again, that overreaction was a mistake, and I apologize for my misjudgment.

One day after making his first public statements about the incident, a number of Republicans called for him to step down. "I believe that he pleaded guilty, and he had the opportunity to plead innocent," said Republican senator and presidential candidate John McCain. "So, I think he should resign. My opinion is that when you plead guilty to a crime you shouldn't serve." Others echoed this opinion, noting that if he did not resign voluntarily the voters of Idaho could make their opinions known. Craig agreed to step down as the leading Republican on several Senate committees.

On September 1, 2007, Craig announced that he would resign from the Senate, effective September 30. However, less than a week later, he said that he would not resign, pending the outcome of his efforts to withdraw his guilty plea. His effort to remain in the Senate angered others in the G.O.P., who believed that they had contained the damage caused by the scandal. Craig did not step down as he announced, even though a Minnesota judge ruled that Craig could not withdraw his guilty plea. Craig appealed this decision to the Minnesota Court of Appeals. As of July 2008, briefing was completed and oral argument will likely take place in the fall.

MAGISTRATE

Any individual who has the power of a public civil officer or inferior judicial officer, such as a justice of the peace.

Gonzalez v. United States

In both civil and criminal cases, a trial court may conduct *voir dire*, or preliminary examination and questioning of potential jurors, to assess competency, bias, personal knowledge of or relationship to a party or witness, etc. A presiding judge has several options when conducting voir dire. The judge may conduct voir dire personally, using the court's own questions to prospective jurors. Alternatively, the judge may seek input from counsel for all parties, or the judge may permit all counsel to conduct their own voir dire with only court oversight. In *Gonzalez v. United States*, 553 U.S. ___, 128 S. Ct. 1765, 170 L. Ed. 2d 616 (2008), the U.S. SUPREME COURT held 8–1 that express consent by a defendant's attorney to permit a **magistrate** judge to personally conduct voir dire, without any record that the defendant was personally consulted, was nonetheless binding and valid.

Homero Gonzalez, a 45-year-old Mexican citizen residing legally in the United States, was charged in federal **district court**, along with a co-defendant, with several crimes associated with the possession of a large amount of marijuana. He appeared before a magistrate judge for a detention hearing and arraignment, but he did not speak English and required a court interpreter to translate the proceedings into Spanish. He also appeared before a district judge for four pretrial conferences. During the last conference, the district judge, through the interpreter, in-

formed Gonzalez that voir dire would start the following week, but the judge did not mention that a magistrate rather than federal judge would preside.

When voir dire began, the magistrate judge addressed Gonzalez personally, through his interpreter, introducing herself and advising him that she would be conducting jury selection. She then called counsel for both parties to the bench and obtained their consent to her presiding over the process. Both unequivocally consented. Following jury selection, a district judge then presided over the trial. Gonzalez was subsequently convicted and sentenced.

Gonzalez appealed his conviction to the U.S. Court of Appeals for the Fifth Circuit. He obtained new counsel for the appeal. The U.S. federal defender argued on appeal that since Gonzalez had not personally waived his right to have an Article III (of the U.S. Constitution, establishing a federal judiciary system) judge conduct jury selection, the consent by his then-counsel to the magistrate to select a jury was invalid. The Fifth Circuit rejected this argument, not only finding that the consent of trial counsel was valid, but also noting that Gonzalez never raised this argument prior to appeal.

In an older case, the Eleventh Circuit had ruled that a defendant must knowingly and personally consent to the magistrate's involvement in selecting the jury. *United States v. Maragh*, 174 F.3d 1202 (11th Cir. 1999) The conflict in **circuit court** rulings prompted acceptance for review by the U.S. Supreme Court.

The Supreme Court ruled, by 8–1, that express consent of trial counsel suffices as validly binding. The high court characterized voir dire as comparable to a "scheduling matter" and among those for which agreement **of counsel** generally controls. Justice ANTHONY KEN-NEDY, writing for the Court's majority opinion, noted that the Federal Magistrates Act, 28 USC § 636(b)(3) provided for district court judges to assign designated functions to magistrate judges. The Court had previously held, in *New York v. Hill*, 528 U.S. 110, 120 S. Ct. 659, 145 L. Ed. 2d 560 (2000), that counsel, acting without indication or particular consent from a client, could waive a client's **statutory** right to a speedy trial because such "scheduling matters" were plainly among those for which agreement by counsel generally controls." The Court further cited its decision in *Peretz v. United States*, 501 U.S. 923, 111 S. Ct. 2661, 115 L. Ed. 2d 808 (1991), holding that the Federal Magistrates Act authorized magistrate judges to preside over **felony** jury selection if the parties consented.

Justice Kennedy referred to the acceptance of a magistrate for jury selection as a tactical matter well suited for an attorney's decision. The Court rejected Gonzalez' argument that the decision to have a magistrate judge for voir dire was a fundamental choice raising a question of constitutional significance. Justice Kennedy noted that no serious concerns about the Act's constitutionality were presented, and further, Gonzalez had conceded that magistrates were capable of competent and impartial performance in presiding over jury selections.

Justice Thomas filed a lone dissent. He rejected the premise set forth in *Peretz v. United States*, indicating that decision should be overruled. He also opined that the failure of Gonzalez to raise a timely objection could be corrected.

MALICIOUS PROSECUTION

An action for damages brought by one against whom a civil suit or criminal proceeding has been unsuccessfully commenced without probable cause and for a purpose other than that of bringing the alleged offender to justice.

Framed Men Awarded $101.7 Million from Federal Government

Four men who were wrongly convicted of murder in 1968 were awarded $101.7 million by a federal **district court** in Massachusetts in July 2007. The case stems from the Federal Bureau of Investigation's mishandling of a killing of a smalltime mobster that occurred in 1965. The

case sparked interest in the Boston area because of its relationship to an era when the mafia had a powerful presence in the city.

In March 1965, the FBI learned that two of its informants, Vincent Flemmi and Joseph Barboza, murdered Edward "Teddy" Deegan in Chelsea, Massachusetts. Flemmi and Barboza had lured Deegan to an alley under the pretext that they planned to burglarize a finance company. Despite their knowledge of this, the Boston office of the FBI did nothing to stop the murder. Barboza later testified that he was joined in the killing by Peter J. Limone, Henry Tameleo, Louis Greco, and Joseph Salvati. Limone and Tameleo were allegedly mafia leaders, while Greco and Salvati had minor criminal records.

The case went to trial in 1968. Barboza said that Limone had offered him $7,500 to murder Deegan, and that Tameleo sanctioned the act. Barboza also implicated Greco and Salvati. In July 1968, a jury convicted all four men. The court sentenced Greco, Tameleo, and Limone to die in the electric chair, while Salvati received a life sentence. Massachusetts abolished the death penalty during the 1970s, and so the three who were designated for execution were sentenced to life in prison. Barboza was killed in 1976.

The case did not leave the public's consciousness. Fifteen years after his conviction, Greco appeared on the television show "Lie Detector," which starred lawyer F. LEE BAILEY. A polygraph test determined that Greco was telling the truth when he said he did not have any role in Deegan's murder. Greco died in prison in 1995 after serving 28 years. He was preceded in death by Tameleo, who died in 1985 at the age of 84. In 1997, Massachusetts governor William F. Feld commuted Salvati's sentence after Salvati had served nearly 30 years of his term.

The *Boston Globe* in 2000 uncovered evidence of corruption the Boston FBI office, including the FBI's knowledge of the plot to kill Deegan in 1965. According to a story published on December 21, 2000, "Secret documents recently discovered in a JUSTICE DEPARTMENT probe of FBI corruption appear to show that the bureau knew not only that the wrong men were convicted of a 1965 gangland murder, but also that agents were told about the plot two days before it happened and apparently did nothing to stop it." An FBI task force report confirmed reports that Barboza had framed the four defendants convicted in 1968.

In January 2001, Massachusetts Superior Court Judge Margaret Hinkle found a "substantial likelihood of a miscarriage of justice" in the murder cases. She determined that the four probably would have been acquitted had the jury in their case seen the FBI's documents. On January 18, 2001, Hinkle vacated Salvati's murder conviction and dismissed all of the charges against him. Greco's conviction was overturned posthumously in 2005. This action came two years after the House Committee on Government Reform condemned the FBI for failing to turn over the documents that could have allowed the four men to prove their innocence.

Salvati and Limone, along with the families of Greco and Tameleo, sued the federal government for their wrongful convictions and incarcerations. The trial began in November 2006 at the U.S. District Court in Boston. Lawyers for the plaintiffs asked for $1 million per year that the men were imprisoned, meaning that the government could have been forced to pay as much as $112 million.

During the trial, lawyers for the Justice Department argued that the FBI was not liable because the agency was not obligated to share internal documents with prosecutors or defense lawyers in the case. The federal government noted that the state had prosecuted the men after conducting an independent investigation. However, U.S. District Judge Nancy Gertner held that FBI "responsible for the framing of four innocent men."

The trial featured testimony from the families of the falsely convicted men. Children of Limone and Salvati had to visit their fathers in prison, while the wives had to find ways to support their families. Greco's wife divorced him in 1970 and moved to Nevada, leaving her teenaged sons with a relative. The plaintiffs showed photographs of the men during the five decades that they spent in prison.

In July 2007, Gertner ordered the federal government to pay $101.7 million to the men and their families for the wrongful conviction. She released a 223-page decision that detailed her findings. "FBI officials up the line allowed their employees to break laws, violate rules, and ruin lives, interrupted only with the occasional burst of applause," Gertner said. She also noted that the FBI gave bonuses and commendations to officers who helped send the men to prison in 1968.

The FBI never apologized for the actions of its officers, and the penalty is believed to be one of the largest ever imposed against the

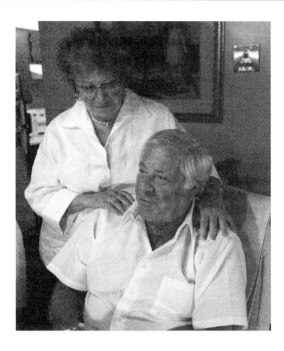

Marie Salvati with husband Joe (seated), August 2007.

AP IMAGES

federal government. The court awarded money to the spouses and children for loss of consortium and for intentional infliction of emotional distress. The case was brought under the FEDERAL TORT CLAIMS ACT, which allows private parties to sue governmental entitles in some circumstances.

"Sadly when law enforcement perverts its mission, the criminal justice system does not easily self-correct," Gertner said. "We understand that our system makes mistake; we have appeals to address them. But this case goes beyond mistakes, beyond unavoidable errors of a fallible system. This case is about intentional misconduct, **subornation of perjury**, conspiracy, and the framing of innocent men."

MALPRACTICE

The breach by a member of a profession of either a standard of care or a standard of conduct.

Revisiting the *Feres* Doctrine

In 1950, the U.S. SUPREME COURT decided, in *Feres v. United States*, 340 U.S. 135, 71 S. Ct. 153, 95 L. Ed. 152, that active-service military personnel could not sue military health care providers for medical errors. Over the years, the holding in this case became known as the **Feres Doctrine**.

Much of the reasoning behind the unanimous opinion in *Feres* rested upon the fact that the military already provides service members with medical care and coverage for service-connected injuries and illnesses, including future medical benefits for service-connected disabilities, in some cases amounting to lifetime medical care. The legal remedy for medical malpractice is generally a monetary award aimed at making the plaintiff/complainant "whole" again, (e.g., covering all medical costs as well as compensation for pain and suffering, scarring, etc., caused by the alleged error). Since the military already provides most of these benefits for service-connected injuries or illnesses (including Veterans Administration benefits), the Court reasoned, there was no need or entitlement to a duplicative remedy through litigation. The issue before the Court in *Feres* involved an interpretation of the FEDERAL TORT CLAIMS ACT, which permits citizens limited rights to sue the government for alleged wrongs committed by federal employees or agencies. Another major consideration in the *Feres* decision was the need to prevent military discipline problems that could stem from subordinates filing lawsuits against their superiors.

But a spate of newer incidents brought renewed fervor to overturn *Feres*. In September 2007, a former Navy pilot who became a medical malpractice attorney filed a $5 million lawsuit in U.S. **District Court** for the Middle District of Florida for the death of Navy 3rd Class Nathan Hafterson at Naval Hospital in Jacksonville. An affidavit by a state-certified expert witness in the case opined that Hafterson died as a result of the failure of Navy doctors to timely treat his medicine-induced hyperthermia (high fever) with the proper antidote, Dantroline. According to a 2006 report by *Military Times* citing federal court papers, medical malpractice at this facility between 2000 and 2005 resulted in 12 deaths and at least four patients left crippled or disabled.

Then in January 2008 came the death of Marine Sergeant Carmelo Rodriguez, whose military doctors misdiagnosed a deadly melanoma for a wart. Rodriguez, 29, was an Iraq war veteran and budding part-time actor originally from New York. Military medical records revealed that a doctor completing his enlistment "physical" (medical checkup) in 1997 noted Rodriguez' skin as "abnormal," in particular, noting a "melanoma on the right buttocks." There was no accompanying recommendation for further monitoring, follow-up, or treatment. Other military records referenced the same abnormal growth as a "wart," still without treatment or attention. It is medically well rec-

ognized that melanoma, a form of deadly skin cancer, can quickly metastasize and become fatal if left untreated. When a CBS News TV crew came to the residence of Rodriguez to interview him, the 80-lb. weakened man, diagnosed with stage-4 metastatic melanoma, died eight minutes later, holding the hand of his seven-year-old son.

His death prompted Rep. Maurice D. Hinchley (D-NY), in early 2008, to promise renewed effort in Congress to overturn *Feres*. Conversely, Rep. Duncan Hunter (R-CA), acknowledging renewed efforts to **repeal** *Feres*, publicly supported the doctrine as "a reasonable approach to ensuring that litigation does not interfere with the objectives and readiness of our nation's military," reported the *Los Angeles Times*. Several previous bills had easily passed in the House but later failed in the Senate.

Still, motivated by the notion that Congress will not act unless the public forces it to, Rodriguez' family was joined by several others who lost loved ones to alleged military medical malpractice. Barbara Cragnotti, whose son lost part of a lung and sustained neurological injuries from undiagnosed pneumonia while in the military service, became head of the organization VERPA (Veterans Equal Rights Protection Advocacy). The non-profit group was determined "to expose and remedy" what it refers to as "the un-American Feres Doctrine." In 2007, it renewed its VERPA LLC Renewed National Petition and 'Feres Doctrine' Mandate (FDM) & Right to Know (RTK) Project, circulated for signature among military families and headed for Congressional review.

Even the Supreme Court, in 1987, had come within one vote of overturning its 1950 decision. Justice ANTONIN SCALIA wrote the dissenting opinion for the four-member minority in *Smith v. United States*, involving a military sergeant unknowingly used in the LSD human experiments at Edgewood Arsenal, Maryland. Wrote Scalia, "*Feres* was wrongly decided and heartily deserves the 'widespread, almost universal criticism' it has received." (Despite the adverse Court decision, Congress passed a special law to compensate Sergeant Stanley.)

The original *Feres* decision encompassed three separate cases at the time. Rudolph Feres was a soldier who died in a barracks fire as the result of a faulty heating system. The other two cases involved military medical malpractice, including the discovery of a nearly three-foot-long towel left in the abdomen of one soldier following an operation by military surgeons.

MCCAIN, JOHN

United States Republican Senator John S. McCain III (born 1936) truly came to the public's attention with his failed bid for the presidential primary nomination against George W. Bush in 2000. Once in the spotlight, many found the blunt and feisty Vietnam War veteran's candor refreshing. Known for his bipartisan collaborative efforts in the Senate, McCain was equally bipartisan in his criticism. His national reputation, as an independent-thinking Republican who stood by his principles, led to his victory in the race for the 2008 Republican nomination for president.

McCain was born on August 29, 1936, in the Panama Canal Zone. After bouncing from school to school in the tradition of a child of a military family, McCain was sent to high school at the elite Episcopal High School in Alexandria, Virginia. After graduation McCain went off to follow the family trade at the United States Naval Academy in Annapolis, Maryland. However, disciplinary issues led to him barely squeaking by academically, as he graduated in the bottom five of his class in 1958.

McCain trained as a Navy pilot, and he volunteered for service in Vietnam in 1967. In June of 1967, McCain (by then a lieutenant commander) set out for Vietnam from Norfolk, Virginia aboard the USS Forrestal. The carrier was in the Gulf of Tonkin on July 29, its crew preparing for the second launch of the fifth day of striking enemy targets in North Vietnam, when one of its own bombs detonated on deck. McCain narrowly escaped the resulting conflagration that killed 132 crewmen, with two others missing and presumed dead, and injured 62 more. It was one of the worst military accidents of the war. A little less than three months later, on October 26, McCain was making his 23rd bombing mission over North Vietnam when his plane was hit by an antiaircraft missile. Forced to eject, breaking both arms and a leg in the process, he landed in a lake near Hanoi and was captured. He spent the next five and a half years as a prisoner of war (POW) at the sarcastically nicknamed "Hanoi Hilton."

The seven years following McCain's homecoming were uneven. He advanced professionally, attending the National War College in Washington, D.C. and receiving a promotion to captain in 1977. 1977 also saw his appointment as the Navy's liaison to the U.S. Senate, a position that laid the groundwork for his political ambitions. His personal life, however, was less than stellar. Carousing, womanizing, and a poor choice of companions led to some unsavory episodes, and ultimately resulted in a divorce from his first wife in 1980. McCain's life began to get back on the right track after his 1980 marriage to Cindy Lou Hensley, daughter of a prosperous Arizona beer distributor. He retired from the Navy the following year, and the newlyweds moved to Arizona to embark on McCain's new career. In 1982, he was elected to the United States House of Representatives as a Republican. A longtime admirer of then-President Ronald Reagan, McCain generally embraced the party line for his two terms in the House. In 1985, he was elected to the Senate seat vacated by retiring elder statesman Barry Goldwater. And before too long, McCain began to make waves.

McCain was reelected to the Senate for two more terms in the 1990s. During those years, his blunt approach, sharp temper, and unwillingness to toe the party line caused consternation among fellow Republicans. Then in 1999, he threw his hat into the ring for the 2000 Republican presidential primary and his singular style gained a much broader audience. Though McCain failed in his bid for the nomination against George W. Bush, many people from both political parties found his straight talk and disarming candor (complete with gaffes) refreshing. Indeed, McCain's popularity was such that he became one of the few senators that gained a national constituency.

During Bush's second term as president, McCain became an important voice on the war in Iraq and the fight against terrorism, in turn Bush's toughest critic and strongest ally. Citing his years as a prisoner of war, McCain severely criticized the Bush Administration in 2006 for its treatment of prisoners and led a

John McCain.
AP IMAGES

JOHN MCCAIN

1958	Graduated, U.S. Naval Academy
1967-73	Prisoner of war in Vietnam
1985	Elected to U.S. Senate
2000	Failed to win Republican presidential nomination
2008	Republican nominee for President

congressional effort to pass a clear ban on torture and inhumane treatment of war detainees. Bush resisted, but reluctantly signed a compromise bill. In early 2007, however, McCain supported Bush's decision to increase the number of American troops in Iraq, even though public opinion had turned against the war and the Democrats had won control of both houses of Congress in November of 2006 largely thanks to their anti-war stance.

In April of 2007, McCain launched his second campaign for president. Many political observers thought McCain would never win enough support from conservatives to win the Republican nomination. In January of 2008, McCain won the New Hampshire Republican primary, in an upset very similar to his 2000 victory there against Bush. He went on to win in Florida and in South Carolina. On February 5, when nearly half of the states held presidential primaries and caucuses, McCain scored several victories in large states, giving him a nearly insurmountable lead among the Republican candidates.

MEDICARE

A federally funded system of health and hospital insurance for persons age sixty-five and older and for disabled persons.

Merck Settles Whistleblower Suit for $659 Million

Without admitting liability or wrongdoing, Merck & Company (Merck) agreed, in February 2008, to pay more than $650 million to settle a seven-year-old lawsuit based on a whistleblower's claim of **fraudulent** billing involving federal **Medicaid** programs in several states. The whistleblower, a former Merck sales manager, was awarded $68 million as his share of the settlement. At the time of the settlement, the U.S. JUSTICE DEPARTMENT was reviewing 630 other healthcare-related whistleblower claims regarding unfair pricing practices affecting state and federal governments.

In "qui tam" whistleblower cases, as here, any amounts recovered as penalties/awards against the defendant(s) are shared between governments under whose statutes the violation(s) occurred, and the informers who brought the cases to light. The term "qui tam action" refers to the fact that the plaintiff sues for himself as well as for the government.

Merck, based in Whitehouse Station, New Jersey, was the maker of the arthritis drug Vioxx (pulled from the market in 2005 for safety reasons) and the cholesterol-reducing drug Zocor, and was the nation's third-largest pharmaceutical manufacturer. The settlement agreement included dismissal of a related but separate qui tam case alleging that Merck also overcharged for its antacid medicine Pepcid. (The doctor who challenged Merck in that case was also to receive a share of the settlement proceeds.) However, the agreement did not encompass a pending criminal **grand jury** investigation related to Vioxx marketing practices. It also left pending a separate contemplated multi-billion-dollar settlement of thousands of other products-liability civil lawsuits alleging that Vioxx-users suffered heart attacks after using the drug.

The Merck cases, *Steinke v. Merck & Co.*, No. 3:05-CV-00322-HDM-RA, and *United States ex rel. LaCorte v. Merck & Co.*, No. 99-CV-3807, had been quietly proceeding under court seal since 2000, when H. Dean Steinke, the whistleblower, voiced concern that Merck's sales tactics amounted to illegal kickbacks to doctors and hospitals. The case and **correlative** investigation expanded over time to include deeper allegations that Merck may not have complied with rules under the Medicaid Rebate Act that require drug manufacturers to offer federal and state agencies their "best price" on drugs.

Steinke's case against Merck, filed in U.S. **District Court** for the District of Nevada under the False Claims Act (and incorporating the earlier investigation by federal prosecutors in Pennsylvania), charged the company with over-billing the government for Vioxx and Zocor through the federal Medicaid program, as well as state public healthcare programs. The correlative case involving Pepcid was filed in federal district court in Louisiana. Both charged that Merck manipulated a legal loophole known as "nominal pricing," intended by Congress to give poor patients access to prescription medicine, to bilk governments out of millions of dollars.

The federal Medicaid Rebate Act (Medicaid Drug Rebate Program), Sec. 1927, 42 U.S.C. §§ 1396r–8 *et seq.*, was created by Congress as part of the **Omnibus** Budget Reconciliation Act of 1990 (OBRA'90), Pub. L. No. 101-508, 104 Stat. 1388, in response to increasing Medicaid expenditures for prescription drugs. Under the Act, drug companies that seek Medicaid payments must pay to each state in which they do business, on a quarterly basis, a rebate that is calculated upon what is known as the Best Price.

Establishing the "Best Price" and "nominal price" under the Act involves complicated formulae. In effect, rebates from drug companies to Medicaid programs are based on either the difference between what each state paid and any lower price paid by other purchasers, or a separate formula involving a 15.1 percent discount off the Average Manufacturing Price, whichever provides the greater rebate.

Merck was accused of giving medicine to hospitals and doctors at virtually no cost (an alleged 92 percent discount), in order to "hook" poor patients on expensive medicine. In return, the hospitals and doctors had to agree to favor the drugs when writing prescriptions and later purchase a set amount of the pharmaceuticals. Thus, when patients left the hospital, doctors most often kept them on the medicine, but the government now had to pay the higher bill for the drugs.

More specifically, the suit alleged that Merck fraudulently concealed three different discounts/give-a-ways that it gave hospitals to promote Zocor and Vioxx. If factored into either formula, these discounts would have significantly dropped the best or average price and raised the amount of rebates owed under the Medicaid programs.

In 2006, the Nevada district court ruled that Merck's "nominal pricing" give-a-ways had to be included in Merck's calculation of Best Price, and ultimately the rebates *Nevada ex rel. Steinke v. Merck & Co., Inc.*, 432 F. Supp. 2d 1082 (D. Nev. 2006). Since Merck did not dispute that it had concealed/excluded these give-a-ways in its calculations, the court's ruling left the company exposed to the possibility of massive rebate amounts owing to the Medicaid programs. This provided the incentive for settlement.

Under the agreement, the final terms of which were filed in the District Court for the Eastern District of Louisiana on February 7, 2008, Merck was to pay the federal government $218 million and various state governments $181 million in the consolidated Pennsylvania case. The portion of the settlement dealing with the related Louisiana case involving Pepcid required Merck to pay the federal government $137.5 million and the state governments $112 million. Added to these amounts were the awards allocated to the whistleblowers and legal fees.

Medicaid is the nation's national health plan for the poor. It is funded by federal and state dollars but primarily administered by state agencies. It operates under contracts between state governments and private health care providers, including hospitals. According to the or-

ganization Taxpayers Against **Fraud** (TAF), more than $20 billion has been recovered in federal civil actions under the False Claims Act since a 1986 amendment to the **statute** enhanced remedies for qui tam whistleblowers.

MERGERS AND ACQUISITIONS

Methods by which corporations legally unify ownership of assets formerly subject to separate controls.

Whole Foods CEO Trashes Competitor Prior to Take-over

In July 2007, Whole Foods Market Inc. acquired Wild Oats Markets, a leading organic and natural foods retailer, for $565 million. This might not have been particularly noteworthy in legal circles but for strong opposition to the merger (on antitrust grounds) by the U.S. FEDERAL TRADE COMMISSION (FTC). The last retail merger opposed by the FTC was more than ten years prior, in 1997, when it successfully blocked the takeover (for $4 billion) of Office Depot Inc. by competitor Staples Inc., citing the harm to competition in the growing market of office supplies.

Prior to filing suit in U.S. **District Court** for the DISTRICT OF COLUMBIA, the FTC internally voted 5–0 to authorize staff to seek a temporary restraining order. Because of its scant history of objecting to such mergers, the FTC's filing signaled to the court that it considered the transaction serious enough to warrant injunction.

In *Federal Trade Commission v. Whole Foods Market, Inc.*, 502 F. Supp. 2d 1 (D.D.C. 2007), the FTC first argued for a **preliminary injunction** staying the merger between the largest and second-largest natural foods grocers. As grounds for its request, it argued that the resulting merged company (successor) would control too great a share of the U.S. natural foods and organic market, leading to increased prices and fewer choices for consumers. FTC also cited Whole Foods' alleged bad-faith attempts to devalue Wild Oats stock to facilitate a cheap buy-out.

Commanding equal press coverage was the release to the media of court documents in the case, allegedly showing Whole Foods CEO John Mackey "trashing" Wild Oats on the Internet, under an assumed pseudonym and persona to conceal his true identity. Critics and the FTC alleged that Mackey was attempting to discredit Wild Oats and devalue its stock in order to then purchase the company at the lowest

Inside a
Whole Foods
Market store,
August 2007.

AP IMAGES

possible price. Using the alias "rahodeb," Mackey advised browsers visiting Internet financial forums that Wild Oats stock was grossly overpriced. He further predicted that the company would fall into bankruptcy and be sold after its stock spiraled to less than $5 a share.

For its part, Whole Foods acknowledged that the postings by "rahodeb" were indeed written by its CEO, John Mackey, but disassociated its company from his statements. Nonetheless, Whole Foods defended Mackey, saying his comments were taken out of context and were made between 1999 and 2006. It further defended that the FTC should not focus on just the two merging companies, but rather, should consider the merger's broader effect on the overall supermarket and grocery industry, many components of which were expanding their lines to include natural and organic food departments.

But the FTC countered by entering into evidence several internal Whole Foods memoranda that described Wild Oats as a critical competitor. That, in combination with the conflicting testimony and alleged motives of CEO Mackey in his Internet rantings, were substantively damaging to Whole Foods' defense.

Notwithstanding, on August 16, 2007, the district court denied FTC's motion for a preliminary injunction. The court's decision was not premised on a failure of FTC to present convincing evidence of foul play on the part of Whole

Foods. Rather, the decision was premised on the court's definition of the applicable relevant "market" that might be negatively impacted by the proposed merger. Was it a product market to be defined narrowly as one involving only organic and natural food products, or was it to be defined as the broader grocery food market in general? The court expressly noted that "[a]s with many antitrust cases, the definition of the relevant product market in this case is crucial. In fact, to a great extent, this case hinges on the proper definition of the relevant product market."

In pursuing its case, the FTC had relied on its earlier success in *FTC v. Staples*, 970 F. Supp. 1066 (D.D.C. 1997). In that case, the same court had accepted the FTC's position that the merger of Staples Inc. and Office Depot Inc. likely would have anti-competitive effects.

The FTC's arguments in *Whole Foods* were closely analogous to its previous arguments in *Staples*. However, dissimilar facts resulted in the court coming to a different conclusion. For example, in *Staples* FTC produced pricing data demonstrating that in cities where Staples was the only office superstore, its prices were 13 percent higher than in cities where it competed with another office superstore (Office Depot), and viceversa. But those price differences were not affected by the presence of other retailers (such as Wal-Mart Stores Inc. and Best Buy Co.) that carried some of the same products. Other evidence showed that Staples, Office Depot, Office Max, etc., considered each other competitors, but did not consider the general retailers as such.

Conversely, in *Whole Foods*, the court found no significant economic proof that prices were lower in cities where both Whole Foods and Wild Oats were present. The court also concluded there was no strong evidence that entry of a second premium natural and organic supermarket into an area had any effect on the incumbent firm's prices. Therefore, the court did not find the facts compelling enough to warrant such a narrowly defined product market as it had in *Staples*.

The U.S. **Circuit Court** of Appeals for the District of Columbia subsequent denied FTC's request to stay the merger pending appeal of the district court's decision, but the FTC signaled that it intended to pursue the appeal. The matter received significant press coverage, including editorials criticizing the FTC for bringing a case based on a narrow product market that was limited to premium natural and organic supermarkets.

In the interim, Whole Foods went forward with the merger, despite the fact that a favorable decision for FTC could void everything, even years down the road. By February 2008, Whole Foods' stock saw a rocky first quarter, with profits down 27 percent. Mackey, remaining CEO of the successor company, blamed "a slowing economy."

MONEY LAUNDERING

The process of taking the proceeds of criminal activity and making them appear legal.

Cuellar v. United States

In June 2008, the U.S. SUPREME COURT determined that a criminal defendant who had hidden several thousands of dollars in his car should not have been found guilty of violating a federal **money laundering statute**. The decision in *Cuellar v. United States*, No. 06-1456, 2008 WL 2229165 (2008), reversed the judgment of the Fifth **Circuit Court** of Appeals and resolved a split of authority among several lower federal **appellate** courts.

A Texas police officer named Kevin Herbert pulled over Humberto Fidel Regaldo Cuellar on July 14, 2004. Cuellar was driving south towards Del Rio, Texas in a Volkswagon Beetle. Del Rio is directly across the border from Acuna, Mexico. Herbert had observed Cuellar driving very slowly at 40 miles per hour in a 70 mile per hour zone.

Herbert also saw Cuellar swerve onto the shoulder of the highway, leading Herbert to believe that Cuellar was intoxicated.

After Herbert stopped Cuellar, the officer called in a state trooper named Danny Nunez for assistance because Herbert could not speak Spanish. While Herbert and Cuellar waited for Nunez, Herbert attempted to determine whether Cuellar had insurance. Cuellar handed Herbert some papers from the car's glove compartment. Cuellar then exited the car without Herbert asking him to do so and lifted the hood of the trunk at the front of the car. This act alerted Herbert that Cuellar might be trying to divert attention from another area of the car where contraband may be kept.

None of the papers that Cuellar handed were insurance. These papers instead consisted of such items as bus tickets and certain Mexican permits. When Nunez arrived, he questioned Cuellar about where he was traveling. Cuellar acted nervously and avoided making eye contact with Nunez, which made Nunez become suspicious. Several of Cuellar's stories contradicted one another. During the conversation, Nunez saw a bulge in Cuellar's pocket and asked Cuellar about it. It turned out to be a wad of cash that smelled like marijuana to the officers.

With Cuellar's consent, the officers conducted a search of the vehicle. They saw evidence of drill marks on the fender walls as well as evidence of tampering with the gas tank. This evidence suggested that someone may have hidden contraband in or around the gas tank. The officers also saw mud that had apparently been splashed on the car, which was also a sign that someone had tried to hide tool marks or other evidence of work done on a car in an effort to hide contraband.

The interior of the car was also suspicious. The officers noted that some of the carpet looked newer than other parts, which were faded and worn. Moreover, the officers found animal hair near the rear of the car but not towards the front. Some criminals evidently use animal hair to try to confuse dogs, though police experts note that this tactic does not work. Other items in the car, such as a receipt from a fast food restaurant, suggested that Cuellar was dishonest in telling the officers where he had been.

When the canine unit arrived, the dogs discovered money below the car's back floorboard area. In a hidden compartment the officers discovered $83,000 wrapped in bundles in Walmart bags and duct tape. The bags were marked with a Sharpie, indicating the amount in each bundle. The officers located a Sharpie, along with other tools, in the glove compartment of the car. After his arrest, Cuellar continued to tell conflicting stories to the officers regarding his travels.

Cuellar was prosecuted for violating the international money laundering statute at 18 U.S.C. § 1956(a)(2). Under this statute, the government was required to prove that the transportation used by Cuellar was designed to "conceal or disguise the nature, the location, the source, the ownership, or the control" of the money. A jury convicted Cuellar after a two-day trial, and the trial judge sentenced Cuellar to 78 months in prison.

A divided panel of the Fifth Circuit Court of Appeals reversed Cuellar's conviction. According to Judge Jerry Smith of the court, though the evidence may have shown that Cuellar had concealed the money for the purpose of transporting it, for the statute to apply, the purpose of the transportation itself must have been to conceal or disguise the unlawful proceeds. In other words, the transportation must have been undertaken to give the appearance of legitimate wealth, since this is the goal of someone attempting to launder money. *Cuellar v. United States*, 441 F.3d 329 (5th Cir. 2006).

The Fifth Circuit reheard the case **en banc** and reversed the panel's decision. Judge Eugene Davis, who had dissented in the panel opinion, wrote the majority opinion for the en **banc** court. According to Davis' opinion, Cuellar had violated the statute, in large part, due to his extensive efforts to hide the nature, location, source, ownership or control of the funds. Judge Smith dissented, stressing the difference between "concealing something to transport it, and transporting something to conceal it," with only the latter implicating the money laundering statute. *Cuellar v. United States*, 478 F.3d 282 (5th Cir. 2007).

The U.S. Supreme Court granted **certiorari** on October 15, 2007 and heard oral arguments on February 25, 2008. During the oral arguments, several justices posed questions based on hypotheticals, pondering how far criminal liability under the statute would extend. Some of the discussion focused on the title of the statute regarding money laundering, with several justices asking why that title would be appropriate if the statute also applied to a defendant concealing money to transport it. Justice RUTH BADER GINSBURG noted, "On the government's theory, anyone who transports hidden money to get it out of the country, who drives the car, just the driver, is a money launderer."

A unanimous Supreme Court agreed with the government's position to some extent but nevertheless reversed Cuellar's conviction. According to an opinion by Justice CLARENCE THOMAS, Congress had intended for the money laundering statute to cover a broader range of activities than the title might suggest. Thus, the Court agreed that it covers transportation that is designed to conceal or disguise the location, ownership, or control of the funds. With regard to Cuellar, however, the Court could not conclude that the merely hiding the funds was enough to violate the statute. Cuellar instead must have known that the design of his transportation was to conceal or disguise the nature, location, source, ownership, or control of the money. Since the government had failed to prove that Cuellar had the requisite purpose to violate the statute, the Court held that the conviction could not stand.

MORTGAGE

A legal document by which the owner (buyer) transfers to the lender an interest in real estate to secure the repayment of a debt, evidenced by a mortgage note. When the debt is repaid, the mortgage is discharged, and a satisfaction of mortgage is recorded with the register or recorder of deeds in the county where the mortgage was recorded. Because most people cannot afford to buy real estate with cash, nearly every real estate transaction involves a mortgage.

The 2007–2008 Subprime Crisis

In July 2008, President George W. Bush announced his plan to rescue the nation's two largest (and government-chartered) mortgage finance companies, Fannie Mae and Freddie Mac, in an attempt to stop or stay the sliding mortgage crisis and its effect on the nation's overall economy. The plan called for Congress to authorize up to 18 months' funds (in the billions of dollars) to buoy the companies through a critical period. This would be done by government investments, e.g., government-purchased company stocks and loans. Opposition from both parties in Congress was substantial: the prospect of again bailing out private companies went against the grain of their constituents and voters, and also could set off a larger taxpayer bailout.

But the reality of the companies' role in the national economy was indisputable. Together, Fannie Mae and Freddie Mac either held or guaranteed mortgages valued at more than $5 trillion dollars, and both companies were rapidly sinking into debt from defaulted mortgage loans. As of July 2008, Fannie Mae carried debt of $800 million, while Freddie Mac had about $740 million in debt. As their mortgagor-borrowers continued to default on mortgage payments, causing an even deeper slump in the housing market, the stocks of the two companies plunged and waves of foreclosures continued to erode the market. Every major bank, as well as many mutual funds and pension funds and foreign governments, held significant amounts of securities which began to decline in value. The stock market ebbed and flowed in response, as did the bond market. The slump in the mortgage industry affected both new and used housing markets, which in turn depressed the overall housing market, particularly in construction. The national economy appeared fragile and experts agreed that a default by either Fannie Mae or Freddie Mac could prove catastrophic for the entire financial system.

The July 2008 proposal followed a year of sliding home values and increasing mortgage defaults and foreclosures across the country. While experts agreed that there was really no single entity or individual to blame, all experts virtually agreed that the crisis was precipitated by a mixture of key participants: the world's largest investment banks, other lenders, credit rating agencies and underwriters, investors, and the homeowners themselves.

Clearly the role of Wall Street's investment banks was key to the problem. Authors Paul Muolo and Mathew Padilla, in their 2008 book, *Chain of Blame: How Wall Street Caused the Mortgage and Credit Crisis*, showed in detail how the downward spiral was created. According to them, from 2000 to 2007, executives from Merrill Lynch, Bear Stearns, Lehman Brothers, and other financed non-bank mortgage lenders began to aggressively sell mortgage products to consumers through "loan brokers." The selling line to consumers, to bait them into debt, was the generally-accepted assurance that home values had always historically gone up over the years, making the housing market one of the safest investments for the average consumer to offer sure-fire turn-around in profit.

As the housing boom created more competition in the mortgage industry, mortgage products became more creative. Loan-brokers, many of which ran boiler-room operations with employees at laptop computers being tasked with closing "one loan/hour," increasingly sought new customers from the "subprime" sector, meaning, consumers whose credit or financial resources would not qualify them for conventional, "prime" mortgage loans. Because subprime mortgages were relatively new in the market, there was limited information about their long-term performance. However, according to the International Monetary Fund (IMF), more than 90 percent of securitized subprime loans were turned into securities with the top rating of AAA.

One of the largest players in the subprime sector was Countrywide Financial, the nation's largest home mortgage lender. Its founder, Angelo Mozilo, conducted a now-infamous conference call in July 2007 with several top Wall Street equities analysts eager to turn profits. Together, they refined an overall system in which loan brokers would supply a steady stream of newcomer consumers to non-bank mortgage lenders. These consumers, who could not qualify for conventional mortgage products, were offered creative packages, many of which required no down payment and no up-front money toward the purchase of a house or the gaining of a mortgage loan. Many of them were given "adjustable rate" mortgage products with introductory low percent rates.

The subprime sector of the market would then mix its loans with *prime* loans, which would enhance the overall value of the mix and raise the overall credit scores to make the loan packages more attractive investments. These subprime packages were then sold to investors, who re-packaqed them as bonds to sell on Wall Street. Wall Street then sold the bonds, backed by subprime mortgages, to overseas investors in Europe and Asia (which ultimately led to financially-suppressed markets there as well). The Wall Street bonds and securities often ended up being purchased by large fund managers, such as those administering pension funds and mutual funds. Fannie Mae and Freddie Mac bought mortgages from banks and non-traditional lenders (e.g., Countrywide), held some and sold others in the form of mortgage-backed securities. In the end, like dominoes falling, few in the chain of mortgage and securities investments walked away unaffected.

According to the Mortgage Bankers Association, nearly four percent of prime mortgages were past due or in foreclosure as of September 2007,—the highest rate since the group started tracking prime and subprime mortgages separately in 1998. The default rate for subprime loans was almost one in four, or 24 percent. The combined rate of delinquency and foreclosure was 7.3 percent, higher than at any time since the group started tracking data in 1979. According to the IMF in its April 2008 *Global Financial Stability Report*, global losses could reach $945 billion once other related losses, such as in commercial real estate, were included.

MUKASEY, MICHAEL B.

U.S. Attorney General Michael Mukasey was born on July 28, 1941 in the Bronx borough of New York City. He graduated from the Ramaz School, an Orthodox yeshiva on Manhattan's Upper East Side, in 1959 and then received an undergraduate degree from Columbia University in 1963. In 1967, he was awarded a law degree from Yale University before heading back to New York to enter the private practice of law. Mukasey's first job as an attorney was with the firm of Webster Sheffield. He moved on to the U.S. Attorney's Office in Manhattan in 1972. During his four-year tenure there, he developed a friendship with another young prosecutor named Rudolph W. Giuliani. Giuliani would go on to become mayor of New York City and, in 2007, a Republican presidential hopeful. The two reportedly retained a close relationship throughout the years.

In 1976, Mukasey joined the New York firm of Patterson Belknap Webb & Tyler. His notable clients there included socialite Claus von Bulow, the Daily News, and the Wall Street Journal. Successful as his legal career had been thus far however, it was to reach still greater heights.

Mukasey was appointed to the bench of the U.S. District Court for the Southern District of New York by then-President RONALD REAGAN in 1987. The Manhattan federal court was so famously independent that it had acquired the moniker "Sovereign District of New York," and Mukasey promptly fit right in, quickly gaining a reputation as a tough and objective jurist. Indeed, while there was little doubt about his conservative character—he later endorsed provisions of the controversial Patriot Act, for instance, and supported Giuliani's presidential bid—his sense of fairness and adherence to the law garnered him many fans from the defense bar as well as the prosecutors. Good examples of this duality lay in Mukasey's rulings in the 2002/2003 trial of alleged terrorist Jose Padilla—on

Michael Mukasey.

AP IMAGES

MICHAEL B. MUKASEY

1967	Awarded law degree from Yale University
1976	Joined law firm of Patterson Belknap Webb & Tyler
1987	Appointed to bench of U.S District Court
2006	Retired from federal bench
2007	Appointed and confirmed as U.S attorney general

the one hand, he agreed with the government's view that Americans could be held indefinitely as enemy combatants. On the other hand, he ruled against the government's contention that such prisoners should be denied access to legal counsel and was considerably less than pleased when prosecutors continued to drag their feet in the matter. The Economist quoted the judge's response as, "Lest any confusion remain, this is not a suggestion or a request that Padilla be permitted to consult with counsel, and it is certainly not an invitation to conduct a further 'dialogue' about whether he will be permitted to do so. It is a ruling—a determination—that he will be permitted to do so."

Mukasey retired from the federal bench in 2006 and returned to his partnership position at Patterson Belknap. In September of the following year, he was again called to public service when President GEORGE W. BUSH nominated him for the position of U.S. attorney general following the resignation of Alberto Gonzales. The U.S. Senate confirmed him on November 8, 2007 in a 53-40 vote and sworn in the next day.

MURDER

The unlawful killing of another human being without justification or excuse.

Murder-Suicide Ruling in Pro-Wrestler Benoit Case

In late June 2007, the professional wrestling world was shocked to learn of the sudden deaths of champion wrestler Chris Benoit, his wife, and young son, all found in the family's suburban

Atlanta home. In the few days preceding the incident, Benoit left two strange e-mail messages to a wrestling friend, hinting that his wife and 7-year-old son were not doing well, and advising that his house was unlocked and his dogs were outside. The messages were forwarded to police when concern for Benoit increased.

Police entering the residence found the body of Benoit's wife, Nancy, rolled up in a blanket on the floor, hands and feet bound, and slightly bloodied from signs of struggle. The body of son Daniel was found face down in his bed, with no visible trauma. (Several needle marks were found in the boy's arm; it was later revealed that Benoit had been giving his diminutive son growth hormones for some time.) A copy of the Bible was next to each body. Benoit's body was found hanging from a cord attached to a weight machine in the basement. No suicide note was apparently written or found; neither was there any sign of forced entry or **burglary**. Police ruled the deaths as a double homicide-suicide and announced their findings at a news conference on the following day.

There was immediate speculation that heavy steroid use and its alleged manifestations (including what is called "roid rage") may have played a role in the tragedy. Officers found several types of prescription medication, including prescription anabolic steroids, in the home. They also found several receipts in the house, indicating that Benoit had received drug deliveries including human growth hormone from Signature Pharmacy in Orlando, Florida, and the Internet arm of the business, known as MedXLife.com. According to the District Attorney's Office in Albany, New York, which was investigating the company, six persons, including two owners, had pleaded guilty and 20 more were arrested, including physicians and pharmacists, as part of the investigation.

Toxicology results later revealed that Benoit's body contained ten times the normal level of testosterone, which appeared to have been injected shortly before he died, as well as the anti-anxiety medicine Xanax, and a painkiller, hydrocodone. His body tested negative for alcohol, and no other anabolic steroids were listed in the toxicology results. The state medical **examiner** also reported that steroids did not appear to play any role in the deaths of Nancy Benoit or Daniel Benoit.

CNN Medical Correspondent Dr. Sanjay Gupta noted, in his coverage, that the drugs found in Benoit's home are synthetic testoster-

Deceased wrestler Chris Benoit, left, with WWF owner Vince McMahon, June 2007.

AP IMAGES

ones used to build muscle mass, but there were "known relationships" between such steroids and roid rage. Symptoms included psychosis, anti-social behavior, and depression. Notwithstanding, Gupta stated that there was no way to conclude with medical certainty that they played a significant role in Benoit's behavior.

News of Benoit's death and surrounding circumstances prompted the World Wrestling Entertainment (WWE) to issue a media statement, in which it criticized press reports linking Benoit's alleged murder-suicide to roid rage. The statement further asserted that Benoit had tested negative for steroids in April 2007, as part of a two-pronged Talent Wellness Program started the previous year that also included "aggressive substance abuse and drug testing polic[ies]." Moreover, WWE's statement noted that details and reported findings surrounding the murder site, e.g., the placement of Bibles next to the bodies, and the binding of the wife's feet and hands, indicated that Benoit had acted with deliberation and not rage. Authorities also had concluded that a substantial period of time existed between the deaths of wife and son, followed by another substantial period of time before Benoit allegedly committed suicide. This further undermined any theory that he acted out of rage.

But the statement from the WWE was not enough to assuage family survivors (including two children from another marriage) and relatives. According to Mike Mooneyham of Charleston's *Post and Courier*, Benoit's estate offered WWE a deal under which it would waive any future claims against WWE in exchange for an up-front settlement of $2 million for Benoit's two surviving children. Liability was ostensibly premised upon autopsy results showing that Benoit's brain was so damaged from repeat concussions that it resembled that of an 85-year-old Alzheimer's patient. Medical experts claimed the damage was the result of a lifetime of chronic head trauma suffered while Benoit was in the wrestling ring. Through an attorney representing the estate, Benoit's father alleged that WWE knew of the head injuries but failed to provide treatment or rest for any of its performer wrestlers, causing a strain that ultimately contributed to the killings. WWE denied any involvement in the Benoit tragedy and rejected the settlement offer. It also reiterated its formal policy that "prohibits the non-medical use and associated abuse of prescription medications and performance-enhancing drugs."

Montreal-born Benoit, a 40-year-old, 5′10″, 220-lb. wrestler often called the "Canadian Crippler," was a 22-year veteran star on the WWE circuit. He won the world heavyweight championship in 2004. Nancy Benoit was a wrestling stage manager. They were married in 2000.

In March 2007, *Sports Illustrated* reported that eleven professional wrestlers were included in the list of athletes tied to a national steroid probe. At the time, WWE spokesman Gary Davis reiterated to magazine interviewers WWE's prohibitive policy, but refused to say whether any wrestlers had tested positive since the program was introduced. Vince McMahon, chairman of the WWE board, was indicted on steroid-related charges in the 1990s but was later acquitted.

New York Man Convicted of Murder in Internet Hoax Case

A New York jury in 2007 convicted a black man of killing a white teenager during a racially-charged confrontation in front of the man's house. The man claimed that he feared he was being attacked by a lynch mob, but the jury determined that he should be criminally liable for his death. In March 2008, the judge in the case sentenced the man to two to four years in prison for the crime, leading the father of the teenager to threaten the man's son.

John White moved his family into a 3,000 square foot home on Long Island in New York. His son, Aaron, became the new kid in the neighborhood. Aaron befriended a group of Ford Mustang enthusiasts known as The Blackout Club.

The group reportedly met a certain parking lot to show off their cars, and the boys in the group frequently gathered at each other's homes.

On August 9, 2006, however, a conflict between Aaron and the other boys turned deadly. At a birthday party held for one of the group members, Aaron showed up with another friend. During the alcohol-filled party, the 15-year-old sister of the party's honoree complained that Aaron had threatened to rape her on a MySpace profile. The profile turned out to be a fake, but the messages that appeared on the profile nine months earlier were repeated in a chat room. One of Aaron's friends later admitted to creating the phony profile as a hoax.

The girl told 17-year-old Daniel Cicciaro, a recent high school graduate who was a popular member of The Blackout Club. Cicciaro was in a drunken state when he decided to confront Aaron over the rape threats. Cicciaro gathered four friends and drove to Aaron's house. During the ride over to the house, Cicciaro called Aaron and engaged in a shouting match, at one point using a racial epithet. An armed John White confronted the group when the group arrived at White's house. White pointed a gun in Cicciaro's direction, but the accounts differed as to how the gun discharged. When the gun fired, Cicciaro was killed.

Attorneys for White, a 54-year-old asphalt foreman, stressed that he thought a modern-day lynch mob was approaching his home. Newspaper accounts of the incident noted that White had grown up in the Deep South and that his family had been the subject of racial hatred. During the 1920s, for instance, his grandfather's business in Alabama was burned down by the KU KLUX KLAN. White thought the same was happening to his family. "In my family history, that's how the Klan comes," said a tearful White. "They pull up. They blind you with their lights."

White's trial began during the fall of 2007. He claimed that the gun that shot Cicciaro had discharged accidentally and that he was sorry for the accident. Prosecutors, however, painted a different picture. They noted that White should have simply locked his doors and called the police instead of confronting the group armed with a weapon. Moreover, the prosecution stressed that White had said nothing about the lynch mob concerns until trial and that the attack on his grandfather's store had occurred 30 years before White was born. According to the police, when White was arrested, he said, "I did what

I had to do. You might as well put the cuffs on now. This is the end of me."

The jury deliberated for four days before reaching a verdict. On December 22, 2007, the court announced that White had been found guilty of **manslaughter**. The jury was reportedly in a deadlock during a significant part of their deliberations. At one point, they had met for 12 consecutive hours, but jury members were still deadlocked. The jury finally reached a conclusion after the judge told them to continue to meet.

Supporters for Cicciaro's family applauded the verdict, honking the horns of their cars and shouting "Dan-O! Dan-O! in memory of Daniel. Daniel's mother said that her son was "finally vindicated," stressing that the case "was never about race. It was about individuals and individuals' actions." Daniel's father also supported the verdict, saying, "Maybe now they'll stop slinging my son's name and stop accusing him of all this racism."

White's defense attorney, Fred Brewington continued to note that the case was about race, saying that the verdict was "disappointing for African-Americans." According to Brewington, "You have to survive in Suffolk County, where people can roll up on your house at 11:30 at night, threaten you, threaten your family, curse at you, call you a [N-word], and you've got to take it." About three weeks after the verdict was announced, the Reverend Al Sharpton joined White at a gathering of supporters. Sharpton said to a group of about 400 that the police focused too much attention on the shooting and not enough on the culpability of the teenagers who approached White's house.

White's sentence sparked more controversy. In March 2008, the judge sentenced White to two-to-four years in prison for manslaughter, far below the 15-year maximum sentence. The sentenced sparked outrage in Daniel Cicciaro Sr., who directed an obscenity at John White's wife and son immediately after the sentence was read. The father of the slain boy claimed that racial politics had played a role in the sentencing.

Cicciaro caused another major controversy when he suggested that Aaron White should be shot. Cicciaro's outbursts led John White to file a complaint for harassment two days after White was sentenced. White has remained free pending an appeal of his manslaughter verdict.

Serial Killer Krajcir Admits to Decades-old Killings

In December 2007, 63-year-old Timothy W. Krajcir, already in an Illinois prison for a rape conviction, confessed to the killings of at least nine women in four states between 1977 and 1982. He also confessed to several other decades-old rapes and related assault charges.

Krajcir had been in continuous state custody for other crimes since 1983. While imprisoned all those years, Krajcir had remained silent about his role in any murders. It was DNA evidence, taken from old tissue samples from a 1982 murder victim, that finally brought him down. Such testing was non-existent at the time of the murder.

After being confronted with the incriminating evidence, Krajcir admitted and/or pleaded guilty to that and other murders in a plea deal to avoid the death sentence. In January 2008, he received two 40-year sentences for two Illinois murders, and in April 2008, after pleading guilty in a Cape Girardeau, Missouri court, he was given five consecutive life sentences for five murders in that state. Krajcir was also indicted for a kidnapping and **burglary** in Paducah, Kentucky in 1979 (later allegedly murdering the kidnapped victim in Illinois). However, in light of the consecutive life sentences in the other cases, and the fact that the murder was likely committed in Illinois, Kentucky officials announced that they would decline to prosecute Krajcir for the Paducah crimes. Still pending was the indictment for rape and murder of a woman in Pennsylvania.

Krajcir had spent most of his adult life incarcerated as a repeat sex offender. Ironically, most of his killings were committed during brief non-incarcerated periods, and even more ironically, while studying psychology and criminal justice as a student at Southern Illinois University (SIU). He eventually graduated from SIU with a degree in law enforcement. Authorities believed that much of his ability to elude police after the murders was gleaned from what he learned at school.

For example, while at SIU, Krajcir lived in Carbondale, Illinois. But he committed most of his crimes in cities other than where he lived, resulting in detectives focusing on local suspects rather than him. Carbondale was approximately an hour's drive from the locations of several heretofore unsolved murders (dating back to the 1970s and 1980s) in Cape Girardeau, Missouri; Marion, Illinois; and Paducah, Kentucky. Krajcir later told authorities that he often would stake out potential victims in shopping center parking lots in Cape Girardeau. He then would follow them home to ensure that they lived alone, and return several days later to attack them.

Serial killer Timothy Krajcir in undated photo.
AP IMAGES

Police in Cape Girardeau found Krajcir's first victims on August 15, 1977. Mary Parsh, a 58-year-old woman, was found dead alongside her 27-year-old daughter, Brenda. Both were nude and lying side by side on a bed in their home, with their hands tied behind their backs. Both had been shot in the head. The crime went unsolved until Krajcir's confession in 2007.

In November 1977, Southern Missouri University student Sheila Cole's body was found at a rest stop in southern Illinois. She had been kidnapped from a Wal-Mart parking lot and shot to death. Again, the case remained unsolved. Likewise, 51-year-old Virginia Lee Witte's body was found in 1978 in Marion, Illinois Krajcir later admitted he randomly targeted her after both were driving side by side on a main road in the area. In 1979, 51-year-old Myrtle Rupp was similarly killed in her home in Reading, Pennsylvania. It later turned out that Krajcir, who is originally from Pennsylvania, was visiting in the area at that time. Investigators believe that 29-year-old Joyce Tharp was robbed and kidnapped from her home in Paducah, Kentucky in 1979, and killed in Illinois before her body was brought back to Paducah.

Eluding police who were investigating the murders, Krajcir was nonetheless jailed in Illinois in 1979 for having sex with his landlord's 13-year-old daughter. He was conditionally released in 1981.

A few months later, in January 1982, 57-year-old Margie Call was found dead in her Mis-

souri home, raped and strangled, with her hands apparently bound. Several weeks later, 65-year-old Milfred Wallace was found nude and shot in the head. Her hands were also tied. Police again focused on local potential suspects such as old friends, classmates, or past lovers of the women.

Later in 1982, area residents were frightened when Southern Illinois University student Deborah Sheppard was found raped and strangled in Carbondale. Shortly thereafter, Krajcir moved from Carbondale to Pennsylvania. He was arrested months later on yet another sexual assault charge, and served five year in prison there. In 1988, he was transferred back to Illinois to resume his previous prison term (for having sex with his landlord's daughter), having violated the parole terms of his original conditional release.

Meanwhile, Cape Girardeau investigators were piecing together key links in the various murders committed within a 50-mile radius. Although Krajcir had left some incriminating evidence at the crime scenes, no DNA national databases had existed in the early 1980s; neither could investigators find any of his fingerprints in a national database. Similarly, police found a palm print matching Krajcir's at one crime scene, but in the early 1980s, palm prints were not being tracked.

Fast-forwarding to 2007, advances in DNA technology led Illinois investigators to test a small DNA sample from Deborah Sheppard's Carbondale murder. It matched Krajcir, who by now was in a database and still incarcerated in Illinois. When questioned about Sheppard's murder, Krajcir denied his involvement. However, when confronted with the DNA results, he confessed on December 3, 2007.

The confession sparked the interest of the Cape Girardeau investigators, just 45 miles away. Another DNA test matched Krajcir's in samples taken from the Wallace murder (Missouri). Krajcir again denied involvement. It was not until Cape Girardeau prosecutors agreed to not seek the death penalty that Krajcir admitted killing Wallace and four other women in Missouri. He later admitted to killing Tharp, the Paducah, Kentucky woman. His indictment for the 1979 rape and murder of 51-year-old Myrtle Rupp of Reading, Pennsylvania, was still pending.

Klansman James Ford Seale Convicted for Role in 1964 Deaths

In June 2007, a federal jury convicted 71-year-old reputed Ku Klux Klansman James Ford Seale of kidnapping and conspiracy for his participation in the 1964 deaths of two black teenagers in southwest Mississippi. The beaten and badly decomposed bodies of 19-year-olds Charles Eddie Moore and Henry Hezekiah Dee were found in the Mississippi River near Tallulah, Louisiana, two months after they disappeared from Franklin County, Mississippi on May 2, 1964. The teenagers were found by random chance during an unrelated search by U.S. Navy divers for three missing civil rights workers (part of the "Mississippi Burnings" case which drew more media attention at the time). Their bodies were identified by personal effects, including a belt buckle given to Moore by his brother.

Old files and documents from the time show that Seale, along with Charles Marcus Edwards, had originally been identified by the FBI as suspects and were arrested. According to FBI interrogators, Edwards admitted that he and Seale had heard rumors that Black Muslims were bringing guns into the area and were planning an armed insurrection in rural Franklin County. Edwards further admitted that, after Seale picked up the two hitchhiking teens, he and Seale drove them into the woods for a beating. Edwards claimed both were alive when he left them.

An informant told FBI interrogators that Seale's brother and another Klansman took the unconscious men to the river, weighted them down with an old Jeep engine block and pieces of railroad track, and dumped them over the side of a boat. (The Klansman and informant have since died.)

At the time of the incident, the FBI was overwhelmed with a series of violent crimes related to the CIVIL RIGHTS MOVEMENT and general unrest in the South. Its resources had been heavily consumed by the search for the three missing civil rights workers, so it turned the case of the teens' deaths over to local Mississippi authorities. (The bodies of the three missing civil rights workers were later found in an earthen dam in Mississippi.)

Shortly thereafter, a local **justice of the peace** dismissed all charges against Edwards and Seale (who was a sheriff's deputy in the county and a reputed Klansman) without presenting evidence to a **grand jury**. This was notwithstanding 1960s FBI documents indicating that Seale, when confronted by authorities, was quoted as saying "Yes, but I'm not going to admit it. You are going to have to prove it."

In 2000, the U.S. Justice Department's Civil Rights Unit reopened the case, but en-

Reputed Klansman James Ford Seale, August 2007.
AP IMAGES

countered problems finding living witnesses and credible evidence. Moreover, for years, family members had repeatedly told reporters and investigators that Seale was dead. FBI files indicated that the case was again closed in 2003.

Then in 2005, Thomas Moore, brother to one of the victims, was contacted by a Canadian documentary filmmaker, David Rigden, about photos and documents in the "cold case." Although originally at arms' length, the two eventually bonded and agreed to continue efforts on their own to revive interest in the case and seek justice. They were able to locate both Edwards and Seale, old and sick but living just a few miles from the scene of the original abduction.

After finding the men, Rigden and Moore contacted authorities, and the case was again reopened by the JUSTICE DEPARTMENT in 2005. The resulting investigation represented the corroboration and incorporated work of current FBI agents working with five former FBI agents originally assigned to the matter during the 1960s, as well as the Franklin County Sheriff's Office and the Mississippi Highway Patrol. The FBI premised federal jurisdiction on information and documents indicating that the beating had occurred in the Homochitto National Forest, as well as the fact that the victims were transported over state lines.

In January 2007, U.S. Attorney General Alberto Gonzales held a Justice Department news briefing to announce the indictment of Seale by a federal grand jury on two counts of kidnapping resulting in death and one count of conspiracy. When asked why Seale and Edwards were not charged with murder, Gonzales responded that "... we looked at the evidence, we looked at the law, and we believe that the indictment reflects the charges that are appropriate here and the charges that we can prove." Seale, reported by his attorney to have cancer, pleaded not guilty and further denied being a Klan member.

At trial, the prosecution's key witness was Seale's cohort, Edwards, now 72 years old. Edwards testified, *inter alia*, that he and Seale belonged to the same Klan chapter that was led by Seale's father. According to his testimony, the beaten teens, still alive, were stuffed into the trunk of Seale's car and driven to a farm. Seale later told him that Moore and Dee were driven across the Mississippi River into Louisiana and dumped into the river with heavy weights attached to them.

In return for his testimony, Edwards was not charged. During closing arguments, prosecutors acknowledged to the jury that they made "a deal with the devil" but argued that it was necessary to achieve justice. Although Seale's public defender argued to the jury that Edwards was a "liar ... out to save his own skin," prosecutors reminded the jury (through the testimony of a retired FBI agent) of Seale's own prior words, taunting the FBI interrogators that they had to "prove it."

Seale was sentenced on August 24, 2007 to three life sentences in prison. David Rigden continued to work on his documentary film about the deaths, to be called *Mississippi Cold Case*.

Mistrial and Retrial in Phil Spector Murder Case

Following a jury deadlock in September 2007, Los Angeles Superior Court Judge Larry Paul Fidler declared a mistrial in the criminal case against music mogul Phil Spector, accused of killing Lana Clarkston at his California mansion on February 3, 2003. The jury had deliberated for twelve days before advising the judge that they were unable to reach a verdict. Media stations reported that the 10–2 split was in favor of conviction, and reporters later interviewed several jurors. Counsel for the Clarkston family, John C. Taylor, supported prosecution's decision to retry the case.

Clarkston was a 40-year-old aspiring B-movie actress (best known for her role in Roger Corman's cult film "Barbarian Queen"). She was working as a hostess at the House of Blues in West Hollywood when she met Spector, 67, in the lounge's VIP room. He invited her to go home with him that night. At approximately 5:00 a.m. the following morning, Clarkston died of a single gunshot wound fired inside her mouth while she was seated in the foyer of Spector's Alhambra mansion. During the trial, prosecution argued that Spector had a history of threatening women with guns, while the defense argued that Clarkston shot herself, either accidentally or by suicide.

A new trial was initially scheduled for early 2008, but was later rescheduled for September 2008. The primary reason for the delayed retrial was to accommodate Spector's new legal team, put in place after the September 26 mistrial. Only one attorney, Christopher Plourd, remained from the original defense team, the others having either resigned or been fired by Spector. Plourd was involved in two capital punishment cases and was unavailable for the Spector retrial until the autumn. Deputy District Attorney Pat Dixon, although eager to commence the retrial as soon as possible, conceded the necessity of reconciling any conflicts with Plourd's schedule. Moreover, new defense counsel from San Francisco, Doron Weinberg, advised the court that he would need several months to review and study 10,000 pages of the trial transcripts.

Another cause for delay was a 44-page motion filed by Weinberg to disqualify Judge Fidler from residing over the retrial. The motion listed numerous acts on the part of the judge during the first trial, which, according to Weinberg, constituted improper bias and prejudice to Spector. These included a **gag order** imposed upon both Spector's wife and a potential defense witness, and the judge's decision to withdraw a jury instruction in favor of a newly worded one, following the first announcement of a jury deadlock. Weinberg argued in his motion that these acts of bias, to Spector's detriment, evidenced Judge Fidler's desire to counter public perceptions that celebrities were often given special or deferential treatment in California courts. (Michael Jackson, Robert Blake, and O.J. Simpson were all acquitted in the same downtown criminal court.)

In his response, Judge Fidler declared the motion untimely because any objections to his decisions or rulings from the bench should have been raised when they occurred during the trial. Notwithstanding, the judge also addressed the merits of Weinberg's motion by signing a declaration that denied any bias or prejudice against any party in the case. Weinberg told reporters that he would seek appeal.

The original jury instruction in question, called "Special Instruction 3," advised the jury that prosecution must prove **beyond a reasonable doubt** that Spector pointed a gun at Clarkston and the gun ended up inside her mouth while in Spector's hand. After jurors sent questions to the judge, deliberations were suspended for two days while attorneys argued over new jury instructions explaining prosecutors' contention that Spector committed an act that resulted in Clarkston's death. Judge Fidler then provided the jury panel with updated instructions, which included a clause giving several scenarios in which Spector could be found guilty of Clarkston's murder, including "forcing her to place the gun in her mouth." This further angered defense counsel, who objected that no such evidence had been presented to the jury during trial. However, Judge Fidler ruled that the new language was reasonable based on evidence presented.

The flamboyant Spector, a gold-standard music producer famed for his "Wall of Sound" recording technique, was accused of shooting Clarkston in the mouth with his snub-nosed .38-caliber Colt Cobra in the wee morning hours of February 3, 2003. This followed a night of alleged heavy drinking, both at and after they left the House of Blues. Prosecutors presented evidence at trial that in the wee morning, Spector's chauffeur heard a loud pop, testifying that Spector then came to the back door with a gun in his hand and said, "I think I killed somebody."

Notwithstanding, three jurors who appeared at a news conference after the mistrial asserted that the hung jury was the result of doubts concerning prosecutors' ability to convince all 12

Phil Spector leaving court, September 2007.
AP IMAGES

jurors that Spector's hand was on the gun, and the failure of authorities to complete a psychological profile on Clarkston (the defense had argued that she was suicidal.) A few jurors also expected to see evidence of more blood on Spector, and were somewhat concerned about language barriers involving Spector's chauffeur, for whom English appeared to be a second language.

Although the prosecution declared its intention to retry Spector for murder, proescutors also had the option of offering him a plea bargain, as well as dropping the case entirely. If convicted of second-degree murder, he faced 15 years to life in prison, plus the possibility of an additional ten years for the use of a firearm. In the interim, Spector was free on $1 million bail.

NATIVE AMERICAN RIGHTS

Cobell v. Kempthorne

The federal government's policies involving the rights of Native Americans have led to many problems over the past 200 years. The government's attempt to dismantle tribes that began in the late 1800's with the Dawes Act and continued into the 1930s devastated Native American communities. In addition, this policy sought to instill the Anglo-American concept of private ownership in Native Americans by dividing reservation land into individually owned tracts or allotments of up to 160 acres. The government also allowed non-Indian settlement upon and exploitation of some reservation land. This resulted in the alienation of millions of acres from tribal ownership. The act also required the federal government to hold the alloted land in trust for the individual allotees and their heirs for 25 years, but this was extended over the years. Income generated from these allotments was to be placed in accounts for Individual Indian Money (IIM) account holders.

As of 1990, 11 million acres were held in trust for the heirs of the allottees. Many trust allotments are now owned in common by hundreds or even thousands of beneficiaries, each with undivided interests in the whole parcel. In 1997 a **class action** lawsuit was filed in federal court by a group of Native Americans, alleging that the Department of Interior, which oversees these IIM accounts, had violated federal **statutory** trust obligations. Since then the case has gone back and forth between the federal **district court** and the Federal **Circuit Court** of Appeals and led to the removal of district court judge

hearing case. In early 2008 the new judge assigned to the case, James Robertson, issued a voluminous decision in *Cobell v. Kempthorne*, 532 F. Supp. 2d 37 (D.D.C. 2008), ruling that the Department of Interior's 2007 historical accounting plan did not satisfy the department's obligation to produce an accounting of IIM trust accounts.

Judge Robertson conducted a 10-day **bench trial** in October 2007, seeking to find out if the DEPARTMENT OF THE INTERIOR had remedied or was remedying its breach of duty under the Indian Trust Fund Management Reform Act of 1994, 25 U.S.C. § 4011(a). This act reflected many years of congressional frustration over Interior's management of the IIM trust. It ordered Interior to provide an historical accounting to trust beneficiaries The 1997 lawsuit was filed after the plaintiffs concluded the department had not even begun this effort. The original judge, Royce Lamberth, divided the case into two phases, addressing the "to-be plan" that Interior would use going forward and another plan that would deal with the historical accounting. Judge Robertson, reviewing the nine published circuit court of appeals decisions on this case, noted that there had been "no definitive, undisturbed ruling on the core question" in this dispute: What is the scope or nature of the accounting required by the 1994 law?

Judge Robertson pointed out that the historical accounting project would have been "unthinkable" until the advent of powerful computers and software. The project would involve merging records and procedures that had been used for almost 100 years. The department's efforts in the past had been hampered by different practices in its regional offices and by the fact that most trust records had been destroyed on a regular basis until 1989. The department had an "abysmal" record of failing to prioritize the maintenance and preservation of trust documents and its attempts to perform the historical accounting in the late 1990s did not go well. After Judge Lamberth ordered the department to develop a better plan, Interior proposed a $2.45 billion plan. Congress objected to the cost and refused to fund the plan, leading Interior to propose a plan in 2007 that excluded accounts closed before 1994, transactions occurring after 2000, and transactions in closed accounts or in the accounts of deceased beneficiaries. This plan abandoned a total transaction-by-transaction approach in favor of a mixture of transaction-by-transaction and statistical sampling.

Though Judge Robertson gave Interior "substantial credit" for trying to strike a balance between "exactitude and cost." It made no sense to spend several billion dollars to account for a trust fund worth around the same amount. In addition, the department's efforts at improving the process for future beneficiaries were encouraging. However, these improvements could not remedy "the failures of the past." The judge found that the 2007 historical accounting plan would not result in an adequate accounting compelled by the 1994 act. The plan's major defect was its failure to provide a "verified opening balance and as asset statement." Without this information it would be "utterly impossible" for a beneficiary to determine whether the department had faithfully carried out the duties of the trust. Though Judge Robertson concluded Interior was unable to perform an adequate accounting, this did not mean "a just resolution of this dispute is hopeless." Although he believed the time had come to bring the lawsuit to a close, he ordered the parties to return to court later in the year to discuss a process for finding an appropriate remedy.

OBAMA, BARACK

Barack Obama was a state senator from Illinois when he won the Democratic nomination for the U.S. Senate in March of 2004. When he won the seat, the charismatic politician became only the third African American to serve in the Senate since Reconstruction. His selection as the keynote speaker at the Democratic National Convention that July confirmed his status as a rising star. That appearance also led to Obama running for and winning the Democratic nomination for president in 2008.

Obama was born in Hawaii. His father was a black man from Kenya, his mother a white woman from Kansas who had moved to Honolulu with her parents. Obama's father left the family to attend Harvard and eventually returned to Kenya, where he worked as a government economist. His mother's second husband was an Indonesian oil manager, and Obama lived in that country from the ages of six to ten. Afterward, he went back to Hawaii to live with his grandparents.

Although Obama's father only visited him once after he left, the son grew up with stories of his father's brilliant mind. Obama honed his own mind at Hawaii's top prep academy, Punahou School. From there, Obama went to Columbia University, where he became interested in community activism. After graduating in 1983, he moved to Chicago to spend three years as a community organizer on the city's poverty-stricken South Side. Obama's intellect, drive, and social conscience led to his decision to become a lawyer. He went to Harvard Law School, where he became the first African-American president of the

prestigious Harvard Law Review. Upon his graduation (magna cum laude) in 1991, Obama shunned offers of prominent law firms and impressive clerkships in order to practice civil rights law in Chicago. He also took a position teaching constitutional law at the University of Chicago Law School. Soon the idealistic young attorney became involved in politics.

Obama was elected to the Illinois Senate in 1996, representing the 13th District as a Democrat. His work there included writing landmark legislation to stop racial profiling and sponsoring a bill to expand medical coverage for uninsured children. He also developed a reputation for an inclusive style that eschewed mudslinging and gained the admiration of his opponents. In March of 2004, Obama took his efforts to connect with all kinds of people to the Democratic primary for the U.S. Senate. His message apparently resounded with voters, as he won a

Barack Obama.
AP IMAGES

BARACK OBAMA

1991 Graduated Harvard Law School

1996 Elected to U.S. Senate

2004 Keynote speaker at Democratic national convention

2008 Deomcratic nominee for President

surprising 53 percent of the vote—including support from white blue-collar workers. Obama explained his appeal across demographic lines to Bob Herbert of the New York Times. While admitting there are differences among people, Obama said there is also "a set of core values that bind us together as Americans." His message continued to resonate with voters, and Obama became only the third African-American U.S. Senator since Reconstruction.

Obama continued to attract attention while serving in the Senate, in no part due to his charisma, drive, and desire to find common ground with political opposites. From the nearly moment he entered the office, he was asked if he would run for president in 2008. Obama did not commit right away, but served his constituents and let all voters better understand him and his philosophy with his memoir *Dreams From My Father* (originally published in 1995, but re-published in 2004) and his 2006 best-seller *The Audacity of Hope*.

After announcing his candidacy for the Democratic nomination for president in February 2007, Obama immediately began campaigning in Iowa. Though he was still relatively unknown compared to Hillary Clinton and John Edwards, Obama made inroads and his campaign gained momentum throughout the year and into primary and caucus season. Obama won the Iowa caucuses, and though he lost in New Hampshire, he made steady gains throughout January 2008. By February 2008, Edwards had dropped out of the race, and Obama continued to win key primaries and caucuses over Clinton. He did well on Super Tuesday, then won at least ten straight primaries and caucuses held after that date. Obama succeeded on the fundraising front as well, averaging one million dollars in donations per day. While Obama had emerged as the frontrunner and was beating Clinton in the delegate count after February 19 primaries in Wisconsin and Hawaii, he had not yet sewn up the nomination and continued to campaign vigorously. On June 3, 2008, he finally won an insurmountable delegates lead over Clinton, and became the Democratic nominee for president.

PARALEGAL

A person, working under the supervision of a lawyer, qualified through education, training, or work experience to perform substantive legal work that requires knowledge of legal concepts and is customarily, but not exclusively, performed by a lawyer

Richlin Security Service Co. v. Chertoff

The U.S. SUPREME COURT in June 2008 resolved a question of whether paralegal fees incurred during an administrative dispute could be recovered under a federal **statute** that requires an agency to pay attorney's fees to a party that disputed a claim with the agency formerly known as Immigration and Naturalization Service (INS). According to the Court, the paralegal fees should have been included among other attorney's fees. The Court's opinion reversed a ruling from the U.S. Court of Appeals for the Federal Circuit, which had reviewed various aspects of the case a total of five times.

Richlin Security Service Company in 1990 and 1991 entered into two contracts with the INS to provide private security guard services at Los Angeles International Airport. Due to **mutual mistake** between the parties, the INS misclassified Richlin's employees as "Guard I" instead of "Guard II" under a wage classification scheme set forth in the Service Contract Act, 41 U.S.C. §§ 351 *et seq.*. This resulted in Richlin's employees being underpaid for several years.

The U.S. DEPARTMENT OF LABOR in 1995 recognized the misclassification and determined that the Richlin's employee were entitled to back wages. The Labor Department's conclusion at that time was that Richlin was responsible for payment of these wages. Richlin in turn filed a claim with the government, seeking to recover $1.5 in back wages and related taxes. Richlin argued that the original contract between the company and the INS should have included these amounts.

The contracting officer with the INS reviewed Richlin's claim and concluded in March 1996 that the claim should be denied. Richlin then appealed the claim to the Department of Transportation Board of Contract Appeals, where Richlin requested that the contract be reformed. The Board agreed in part but refused to reform the contracts until the LABOR DEPARTMENT took formal action. The Federal Circuit affirmed the Board's decision in 1998. *Meissner v. Richlin Sec. Serv. Co.*, 155 F.3d 566 (Fed. Cir. 1998).

Subsequent to the Federal Circuit's affirmation, Richlin and the Labor Department entered into an agreement pertaining to the wages. The agreements specified the following: (1) that Richlin's employees were owed $636,818.72 in back wages; (2) that the back wages were to be paid into an **escrow** account administered by Richlin's counsel; (3) that any excess funds were to be remitted to the Labor Department; and (4) that the Labor Department agreed that, by virtue of the obligations undertaken in the agreement, the obligations to the former employees of Richlin had been liquidated and satisfied. However, the Board of Contract Appeals denied Richlin's request to complete **reformation** of the contract notwithstanding the agreement with the Labor Department. On appeal, the Federal Circuit disagreed with the Board, holding that because Richlin did not stand to benefit from the payment of the back wages, the Board should award Richlin the amount of these wages according to the agreement. *Richlin Sec. Serv. v. Rooney*, 18 Fed. Appx. 843 (Fed. Cir. 2001).

In 2003, Richlin filed a claim for the attorney's and paralegal fees under the Equal Access to Justice Act (EAJA), 5 U.S.C. § 504 (2000). This claim focused on the work conducted by the law office of Gilbert J. Ginsburg, who had represented Richlin since 1994. The paralegal billing rates, which were based on **market value**, had increased from $50 per hour in 1994 to $135 per hour in 2003. Under the EAJA, if a party prevails in an adversarial action against an **administrative agency**, the agency must pay to the **prevailing party** "fees and other expenses incurred by that party in connection with that proceeding," unless the agency's adjudicative officer determines that the agency's position was substantially justified or that the circumstances of the case would make such an award unjust. "Fees and other expenses" by statute include "reasonable attorney or agent fees," and the statute specifies that the amount of fees should be based on "prevailing market rates for the kind and quality of the services furnished." However, attorney's fees are capped at $125 per hour in the absence of special circumstances that justify an amount above this.

The Board of Contract Appeals in 2005 determined that paralegal fees were not attorney's fees under the statute. The Board awarded the paralegal expenses at a rate of $35 per hour, which reflected the cost of the paralegal services to the law firm. Richlin had requested a total award of $51,901.10 for the paralegal fees. The Board instead awarded Richlin a total of $10,594 for these fees. Richlin appealed the Board's decision to the Federal Circuit, which affirmed. According to the majority of the panel, the paralegal costs should be considered "other costs" under the EAJA. The court thus allowed the determination of $35 per hour for these costs to stand. *Richlin Sec. Serv. v. Chertoff*, 472 F.3d 1370 (Fed. Cir. 2006).

Richlin appealed the decision to the U.S. Supreme Court, which granted **certiorari** in November 2007. In its briefs, Richlin stressed that the Federal Circuit's decision conflicted with at least four other circuits. Moreover, Richlin argued that the Court's decision in *Missouri v. Jenkins*, 491 U.S. 274, 109 S. Ct. 2463, 105 L. Ed. 2d 229 (1989) controlled the outcome of Richlin's case. In *Jenkins*, the Court determined that a litigant could recover paralegal fees under the Civil Rights Attorney's Fees Awards Act of 1976, 42 U.S.C. § 1988, which allows parties to recover attorney's fees but says nothing specifi-

cally about paralegal fees. In that case, the Court determined that the term "attorney's fees" also encompassed the paralegal fees.

In an opinion by Justice SAMUEL ALITO, the Court agreed with Richlin and reversed the Federal Circuit. According to Alito's opinion, the text of the statute differentiated between "fees" and "expenses," and the amounts billed for paralegal services should be considered fees and not expenses. Accordingly, the amount should not only reflect the cost for these services as incurred by the litigant, but should be calculated at prevailing market rates.

The Court was likewise persuaded by the decision in *Jenkins* to resolve the potential ambiguity in the EAJA. Moreover, the Court rejected the government's argument that the legislative history of the EAJA supported the position that the statute does not cover the paralegal's fees. *Richlin Sec. Serv. Co. v. Chertoff*, No. 06-1717, 2008 WL 2229175 (2008).

Justice ANTONIN SCALIA and CLARENCE THOMAS refused to join parts of the opinion, especially the parts pertaining to legislative history analysis. However, neither of the justices filed a dissenting opinion as to these parts.

PATENTS

Rights, granted to inventors by the federal government, pursuant to its power under Article I, Section 8, Clause 8, of the U.S. Constitution, that permit them to exclude others from making, using, or selling an invention for a definite, or restricted, period of time.

Microsoft and Alcatel-Lucent Battle Over MP3 and Other Patents in Court

Microsoft spent much of 2007 engaged in a legal dispute with Alcatel-Lucent in a patent infringement case that had wide-reaching implications regarding computer technology. Both sides have claimed victories during the litigation, which continued in 2008. The apparent victor has been Alcatel-Lucent, which was awarded a judgment of $367.4 million in April 2008.

MP3 (MPEG-1 Audio Layer 3) is a type of digital audio decoding which has become highly popular for use in portable audio devices as well as computers. In 1989, American Telephone and Telegraph (AT&T) and Fraunhofer Institute in Germany agreed to develop the technology. AT&T spun off one of its units, Bell Labs, which became Lucent Technologies. Lucent was later acquired by Alcatel in 2006 to form Alcatel-Lucent. Several companies, including Fraunhofer and Thomson Computer Electronic, claim ownership in MP3 patent rights.

In 2003, Lucent Technologies sued two of Microsoft's customers, Gateway and Dell, for patent infringement regarding the MP3 technology. According to Lucent, the companies committed the infringement through their use of features in the Microsoft Windows operating system. Microsoft filed a **declaratory judgment** action in San Diego against Alcatel-Lucent, claiming that Microsoft should be the defendant in the case. As a result of the action, Alcatel-Lucent sued Microsoft.

In February 2007, a jury in federal court in San Diego ruled that Microsoft was liable to Alcatel-Lucent in the amount of $1.5 billion for infringing patents on MP3 encoding and decoding technology. Prior to the decision, the judge in the case threw out two of the patent claims and separated the 13 remaining disputes into six groups. The February 2007 decision related to the first of these groups. Microsoft disputed the decision on several grounds, including the fact that the company had previously purchased a license for the technology at issue from Fraunhofer for much less than the amount of the verdict.

"We think this verdict is completely unsupported by the law or the facts," said Microsoft corporate vice president and deputy general counsel Tom Burt. "Like hundreds of other companies large and small, we believe that we properly licensed MP3 technology from its industry recognized licensor – Fraunhofer. The damages award seems particularly outrageous when you consider we plaid Fraunhofer only $16 million to license this technology."

Microsoft was not the only company concerned about the outcome of the case. The issue in the dispute focused on how the Windows Media Player software plays MP3 files. Other companies, such as Apple, also use the same technology and had purchased licenses from the same **entity** as Microsoft. Thus, if the verdict against Microsoft stood, Alcatel-Lucent could then target these other companies. Commentators at the time of the decision expected that an appeal would take a year or two.

About one week after the jury verdict in the first patent dispute, U.S. District Judge Rudi Brewster threw out one of Alcatel-Lucent's claims related to speech recognition software. Burt applauded the decision, noting, "This ruling

reaffirms our confidence that once there's **judicial review** of these complex patent cases, these Alcatel-Lucent claims ultimately won't stand up,"

In July 2007, Microsoft asked Brewster to reduce the $1.5 billion verdict from February, believed to be the largest in U.S. history. The jury had determined this amount by taking 0.5 percent of the average sales price of an infringing computer and multiplying that amount by every copy of Windows. According Microsoft's lawyers, the trial court had miscalculated the damages by basing the award on the cost of an entire computer instead of the cost of a copy of the Windows software. Alcatel-Lucent lawyers countered that the damage calculation was correct. "Substantial evidence exists to support a royalty base of the entire computer system," said lawyer Paul Bondor. "The infringing product here is the computer system."

In August 2007, Brewster issued a ruling where he sided with Microsoft. According to Brewster, the jury's decision could not stand for two reasons. First, Brewster determined that one of the two patents in question had not been infringed. The second patent was co-owned by Fraunhofer, from whom Microsoft had a license. The judge therefore concluded that the "jury's verdict was against the clear weight of the evidence." Brewster also denied Alcatel-Lucent's request for supplemental damages, prejudgment and post-judgment interest, and a permanent injunction against Microsoft.

Microsoft was less successful in October 2007 when the company, along with Dell and Gateway, failed to convince Brewster to dismiss a $2 billion claim regarding technology used to play DVD, Internet videos, and computer games. Alcatel-Lucent in 2003 joined a technology group known as MPEG-LA, which controls the MPEG-2 computer video standard. Microsoft and the other plaintiffs argued that the move was designed to avoid having to share technology with the 1,000 other companies that belong to MPEG-LA. Brewster's decision meant that a jury would need to resolve the issues that Microsoft and the other companies raised.

In April 2008, a jury determined that Microsoft was liable for $367.4 million for infringing patents related to a user interface found in Microsoft's software. Burt said that the company would move to have the awards overturned, just as was the case with the jury verdict from February 2007. "We will move immediately to have the two verdicts against Microsoft overturned. We feel confident the verdicts will

Detroit Mayor Kwame Kilpatrick, March 2008.

AP IMAGES

be overturned, just as the court overturned a verdict last year by a San Diego jury," said Burt.

PERJURY

A crime that occurs when an individual willfully makes a false statement during a judicial proceeding, after he or she has taken an oath to speak the truth.

Detroit Mayor Kwame Kilpatrick Charged with Perjury

Kwame Kilpatrick, the embattled mayor of Detroit, Michigan, was indicted in March 2008 on charges of perjury, obstruction of justice, misconduct in office, and several other **felony** charges. The charges stem from false testimony given in August 2007 about a relationship that Kilpatrick had with his former chief of staff.

Kilpatrick is the son of U.S. Congresswoman Carolyn Cheeks Kilpatrick (D.-Mich.). He earned a law degree from Michigan State University (though he did not practice law) before being elected to the Michigan House of Representatives in 1996. Five years later, Kilpatrick became the youngest mayor in the history of Detroit when he was elected to the position at the age of 31 in 2001. His terms in office have been filled with a series of controversies.

During 2002 and 2003, Kilpatrick and his chief of staff, Christine Beatty, had a sexual affair while both were still married. During this relationship, they shared thousands of text mes-

sages. Kilpatrick for several months denied that he had a relationship Beatty, emphasizing that he is a strong family man with a wife and three sons. Beatty divorced her husband in 2006.

Two former police officers filed suit against the city in a whistleblower suit. Harold Neithrope was a former police bodyguard who alleged that the mayor and other bodyguards had misbehaved. Former deputy police chief Gary Brown investigated the claims. A jury award Neithrope and Brown $8 million in damages, including interest.

Kilpatrick and Beatty both testified at Neithrope's and Brown's trial in August 2007. Both denied having a romantic or sexual relationship. According to the *Detroit News*, Beatty denied the affair at least ten times on the witness stand. Moreover, Kilpatrick and Beatty both said that they did not engage in a plot to fire Brown.

Text messages between Kilpatrick and Beatty became the focal point of a subsequent investigation. During Kilpatrick's first term in office, he issued a directive indicating that electronic communications submitted on city equipment should not be considered private or personal. These messages were thus stored electronically and could be retrieved. City attorneys argued, though, that the messages between Kilpatrick and Beatty were private and could not be released to the public.

The attorney for Neithrope and Brown obtained the text messages during the litigation. The *Detroit Free Press* fought through FREEDOM OF INFORMATION ACT litigation to obtain these exchanges, but Kilpatrick fought diligently to prevent the release of the messages. Documents revealed that Kilpatrick approved a payout of $8.4 million to the officers so that the messages would not become public.

Nevertheless, in January 2008, the newspaper obtained copies of 14,000 messages between Kilpatrick and Beatty. Many of the messages were highly personal in nature and revealed that they had both a romantic and sexual relationship during the period of time that the messages were sent. In one exchange, both indicated that one was "madly in love with" the other, and the messages indicated that they had arranged numerous trysts. Moreover, the messages indicated that they had discussed dismissing Brown, which stood in contrast to their sworn testimony that they had not plotted to fire the deputy police chief.

On March 18, 2008, the Detroit City Council approved by a vote of 7–1 a resolution calling for Kilpatrick's resignation. Kilpatrick said that the resolution was irrelevant and that he would not resign. The resolution cited 33 grounds for Kilpatrick's resignation, noting that he "repeatedly obfuscates the truth." The statement concludes that "there is an overwhelming and growing sentiment amongst citizens of Detroit that the City Council should stand firm against Mayor Kilpatrick and seek his resignation." Kilpatrick stood firm, however, saying that he would continue to work with the city council as mayor.

About a week after the city council passed its resolution, Kilpatrick became the first mayor in the history of Detroit to face criminal charges. A twelve-count complaint charged Kilpatrick and Beatty with perjury, conspiracy to obstruct justice, obstruction of justice, and misconduct in office. Wayne County Prosecutor Kym Worthy announced the decision to prosecute Kilpatrick during a 34-minute speech.

"Even children understand that lying is wrong," Worthy said. "Honesty and integrity in the justice system is everything. This is what this case is about." She continued, "Some have suggested that the issues before us are personal or private. Our investigation has clearly shown that public dollars were used, people's lives were ruined, the justice system was severely mocked, and the public trust trampled on." Worthy noted that the two had ruined the lives of Neithrope and Brown, as well as a third officer who had also filed suit in a related case.

Kilpatrick responded that he was "deeply disappointed" in Worthy's decision to prosecute him. "This has been a very flawed process from the very beginning," he said. "I look forward to complete **exoneration** once all the facts surrounding this matter have been brought forth. In the meantime, I will remain focused on moving the city forward."

On May 9, state representative David Law introduced a resolution calling for Michigan Governor Jennifer Granholm to remove Kilpatrick from office. According to the statement, "Public trust is the cornerstone of a democracy and the city of Detroit is crumbling. The mayor's refusal to leave office is affecting the city's ability to run effectively, and I am calling on the governor to make a change for the best interests of Detroit and its neighboring communities." Kilpatrick responded by reiterating that he will not step down. He faces up to 15 years in prison per count.

Scooter Libby Convicted of Perjury in CIA Leak Case

The prosecution of I. Lewis "Scooter" Libby, former chief of staff to Vice President Dick Cheney on charges including obstruction of justice, false statements, and perjury culminated in a Washington, D.C. jury convicting Libby of these crimes on March 6, 2007. The case, which centered on the Bush Administration's efforts to discredit ambassador Joseph C. Wilson, involved leaking to the press the fact that Wilson's wife, Valerie Plame, was an intelligence agent for the CENTRAL INTELLIGENCE AGENCY (CIA). Though early in the investigation of the leak President GEORGE W. BUSH stated he would fire anyone involved in disclosing Plame's identity, he did not fire his trusted political advisor Karl Rove. Instead, Bush commuted Libby's 30-month prison term. On another front, Wilson and Plame's civil lawsuit against Cheney, Libby, Rove and ten other unnamed government officials was dismissed by a federal district judge in July 2007.

The case grew out of President Bush's 2003 State of the Union address, in which he tried to bolster support for invading Iraq. During his speech, he state that "The British government has learned that Saddam Hussein recently sought significant quantities of uranium from Africa." This claim became the subject of extensive debate after reporters learned that the statement contradicted the findings of former ambassador Joseph Wilson, who had visited Niger in February 2002 at the direction of the government. Journalists pursued this story for months and on July 7, 2003 Wilson published an op-ed piece entitled "What I Didn't Find in Africa." In the piece he said that "some of the intelligence related to Iraq's nuclear weapons program was twisted to exaggerate the Iraqi threat." Soon after publication of this article the White House began an effort to discredit Wilson, telling selected reporters that Wilson's wife, Valerie Plame, was a CIA operative and that she was involved in sending her husband to Africa. On July 14, syndicated columnist Robert Novak revealed Plame's identity as an intelligence agent, attributing the information to two "senior administration officials." Three days later, three reporters for *Time* wrote that government officials had disclosed Plame's identity to them.

In September 2003 the Department of Justice named U.S. Attorney Patrick J. Fitzgerald to conduct an independent investigation of the leak of Plame's identity. A federal law makes it a crime to knowingly reveal the name of a CIA undercover operative. In addition, individuals given access to classified information are prohibited from sharing it with unauthorized persons.

In late October 2005, Libby was indicted by a federal **grand jury** on one count of obstruction of justice, two counts of making false statements, and two counts of perjury. He resigned as chief of staff and pleaded not guilty to the charges on November 3. Fitzgerald said that Libby had intentionally deceived authorities. Karl Rove, who appeared before the grand jury five times and who was named as another leaker of Plame's identity, was not indicted.

Prior to the start of Libby's trial in January 2007 trial, former Deputy Secretary of State Richard Armitage admitted that he was the one who leaked Plame's identity to Washington Post report Bob Woodward and columnist Novak. After this disclosure Novak revealed that Rove had contacted him about Plame as well. Shortly before the beginning of the trial Libby's lawyers indicated that Vice President Cheney would testify in Libby's behalf. At trial the defense sought to cast doubt on the credibility of reporters who testified that Libby had contacted them about Plame and it suggested that the White House had sought to protect Karl Rove and make Libby the fall guy. Neither Libby or Cheney testified at the trial. On March 6, 2007 the jury convicted Libby of four of the five charges, including perjury and obstruction of justice. On June 5 U.S. District Judge Reggie Walton sentenced Libby to 30 months in prison, a $250,000 fine, and probation. The judge also ruled that Libby could not remain free on bond while he appealed this conviction. On July 2 President Bush commuted Libby's prison term but left the fine and probation components untouched. Libby also remained a convicted felon. Though Libby did appeal his conviction, he dropped it in December 2007. His lawyers stated that continuing the appeal would unduly burden Libby and his family.

Plame and Wilson were outraged over the commutation and received more bad news when their federal civil lawsuit was dismissed two weeks later. The lawsuit accused Vice President Dick Cheney and others of conspiring to leak Plame's identity, which violated her privacy rights and was illegal retribution for her husband's criticism of the administration. U.S. District Judge John Bates dismissed the case on jurisdictional grounds and declined to express an opinion on the constitutional arguments made by the plaintiffs. Bates concluded Cheney, Rove, Libby, and Armitage were acting within their job duties. Plame had argued that what they did was illegal and outside the scope of their government jobs. "The alleged means by which defendants chose to rebut Mr. Wilson's comments and attack his credibility may have been highly unsavory, " Bates wrote. "But there can be no serious dispute that the act of rebutting public criticism, such as that levied by Mr. Wilson against the Bush administration's handling of prewar foreign intelligence, by speaking with members of the press is within the scope of defendants' duties as high-level Executive Branch officials." Plame and Wilson appealed the decision, which was heard by the U.S. Court of Appeals for the DISTRICT OF COLUMBIA Circuit in May 2008. Plame also published in 2007 *Fair Game: My Life as a Spy, My Betrayal by the White House*, a book describing her view of the entire affair.

PREEMPTION

A doctrine based on the Supremacy Clause of the U.S. Constitution that holds that certain matters are of such a national, as opposed to local, character that federal laws preempt or take precedence over state laws. As such, a state may not pass a law inconsistent with the federal law. Alternatively, a doctrine of state law that holds that a state law displaces a local law or regulation that is in the same field and is in conflict or inconsistent with the state law.

Chamber of Commerce v. Brown

The U.S. SUPREME COURT in June 2008 ruled that a federal labor law preempted a California **statute** that prohibited employers from using state money to influence unionization. The law was passed in 2000 by California and had been upheld by the Ninth **Circuit Court** of Appeals sitting **en banc**. With backing from the administration of GEORGE W. BUSH, business groups and the U.S. CHAMBER OF COMMERCE challenged the law before the Court, which reversed the Ninth Circuit and invalidated the statute.

The National Labor Relations Act (NLRA) does not contain an explicit provision stating that the law preempts conflicting state law. However, the Supreme Court has held that the NLRA implicitly contains two types of **preemption** that are necessary to implement federal labor policy. The first type based on the Court's decision in *San Diego Building Trades Council v. Garmon*, 359 U.S. 236, 79 S. Ct. 773, 3 L. Ed. 2d 775 (1959). This preemption, known as *Garmon* preemption, "is intended to preclude state interference with the National Labor Relations Board's interpretation and active enforcement of the 'integrated scheme of regulation' established by the NLRA." Under this standard, a state may not regulate activity that the NRLA "protects, prohibits, or arguably protects or prohibits."

The second type of preemption under the NLRA stems from the Court's decision in *Machinists v. Wisconsin Employment Relations Commission*, 427 U.S. 132, 96 S. Ct. 2548, 49 L. Ed. 2d 396 (1976). *Machinists* preemption prohibits either the National Labor Relations Board (NLRB) or the states from regulating conduct that Congress intended to be unregulated because this conduct was left to be "controlled by the free play of economic forces." The basis of this type of preemption is that Congress sought a balance of concerns regarding union organization, collective bargaining, and labor disputes.

The NLRA, 29 U.S.C. § 157-158, gives employees the right to organize, to bargain collectively, and to engage in concerted activity for their mutual aid and protection. Another provision prohibits an employer from interfering with, restraining, or coercing employees in exercising their rights under the NLRA. In 1941, the Court addressed an issue regarding the speech rights of an employer. In *NLRB v. Virginia Electric & Power Co.*, 314 U.S. 469, 62 S. Ct. 344, 86 L. Ed. 2d 348 (1941), the Court ruled that nothing in the NLRA prevents an employer from "expressing its view on labor policies or problems," unless the employer's speech amounts to coercion under the terms of the statute.

Congress further expanded on the speech rights of both employers and unions in a 1947 amendment to the NLRA. Under this amendment:

> The expressing of any views, argument, or opinion, or the dissemination thereof, whether in written, printed, graphic, or visual form, shall not constitute or be evidence of an unfair labor practice . . . if such expression contains no threat of reprisal or force or promise of benefit.

In September 2000, the California Assembly passed A.B. 1889 (codified at Cal. Gov't Code § 7sect; 16645-16649), which was designed to protect an employee's right to choose whether to be represented by a labor union. Under this statute, a private employer that receives state funds could not use those funds to "assist, promote, or deter union organizing." Another provision barred a "private employer receiving state funds in excess [of $10,000] in any calendar year on account of its participation in a state fund" to use those funds influence employees in their decision to organize. The statute defined the phrase "assist, promote, or deter union organizing" broadly to include "any attempt by an employer to influence the decision of its employees in this state or those of its **subcontractor** regarding . . . [w]hether to support or oppose a labor organization that represents or seeks to represent those employees . . . [or] [w]hether to become a member of any labor organization." The statute also prohibited other related actions by the employer.

In 2002, the U.S. Chamber of Commerce and a number of other organization brought an action against several state officials in California. The AFL-CIO intervened in the case. In September 2002, the U.S. **District Court** for the Central District of California issued a partial **summary judgment** in favor of the Chamber of Commerce, holding that the NLRA preempted the state statute under *Machinists*. The district court enjoined the state and the AFL-CIO from taking any actions against an employer subject to the NLRA. *Chamber of Commerce v. Lockyer*, 225 F. Supp. 2d 1199 (C.D. Cal. 2002).

Although a divided panel of the Ninth Circuit Court of Appeals affirmed the district court's judgment, the Ninth Circuit sitting en **banc** reversed the decision. The **appellate court** determined that though the state of California acted as a regulator in enacting the **statutory** provisions, Congress had not intended for the NLRA to prevent states from imposing restrictions on the use of their own funds. Accordingly, the court reversed the district court's ruling. *Chamber of Commerce v. Lockyer*, 463 F.3d 1076 (9th Cir. 2006).

At oral argument, the justices appeared to be sharply divided. Counsel for the Chamber of Commerce argued that the California law directly conflicted with the goals of the NLRA and national labor policy. The justices asked several seemingly hostile questions in response to this argument, with many of these questions coming from Justice RUTH BADER GINSBURG. Nevertheless, seven of the justices ruled in favor of the Chamber in a judgment that reversed the Ninth Circuit's decision.

In an opinion by Justice JOHN PAUL STEVENS, the Court determined that the pertinent sections of the California statute were preempted under *Machinists* because the statute attempted to regulate a "zone protected and re-served for market freedom." The Court noted that the NLRA contains provisions that are de-signed to protect non-coercive speech by both employers and employees regarding the organi-zation of labor. California's attempt to regulate employer speech in the manner that it did con-tradicted the goals of the NLRA's provision that allows free debate on unionization. Therefore, the Court held in favor of the Chamber of Com-merce. *Chamber of Commerce v. Brown*, No. 06-939, 2008 WL 2445420 (June 19, 2008).

Justice STEPHEN BREYER, joined by Ginsburg, dissented. According to Breyer, the California statute imposed a spending limitation that did not amount to a regulation that the NLRA preempted. He argued that the Court should have vacated the Ninth Circuit's decision to allow the lower court to resolve more ques-tions about the application of the California law.

Riegel v. Medtronic, Inc.

Congress has charged the FOOD AND DRUG ADMINISTRATION (FDA) with regulating, among other things, the marketing of prescrip-tion drugs and medical devices. The Federal Food, Drug, and Cosmetic Act (FDCA) has long required FDA approval of new drugs, but the states were left with the responsibility of regu-lating medical devices. In 1970s, in the wake of serious injuries and death caused by the Dalkon Shield, an intrauterine birth control device, pressure grew to have the federal government regulate medical devices. Congress responded by passing the Medical Device Amendments of 1976 (MDA), 21 U.S.C. §§ 360c *et seq.* The MDA directed the FDA to construct a new reg-ulatory regime, which included the classification of devices into three classes. The first two classes, which include elastic bandages and wheel chairs, did not require much oversight. Most attention was given to Class III devices, which include replacement heart valves, im-planted heart pacemakers and heart stents. Be-fore Class III devices can be sold they must gain premarket approval from the FDA. One part of the MDA preempts the states from regulating medical devices if the requirements are different from, or in addition to, any federal requirement contained in the MDA. In *Riegel v. Medtronic, Inc.*, _U.S._, 128 S. Ct. 999, 169 L. Ed. 2d 892 (2008), the U.S. SUPREME COURT ruled that the MDA **preemption** requirement means that a patient cannot sue the maker of medical devices for alleged defects in the product using state common-law grounds of negligence, **strict**

liability, or breach of an **implied warranty** of fitness.

Charles Riegel underwent underwent coro-nary angioplasty in 1996, after suffering a heart attack. His doctor inserted Medtronic's Ever-green Balloon Catheter (a Class IIII device) into Riegel's diseased and heavily calcified right ar-tery in an attempt to clear the blockage in the artery. Medtronic warned on the label that the catheter should not be used on patient's with calcified arteries. It also warned against inflating the catheter beyond 8 atmospheres of burst pressure. Despite these warnings the doctor in-flated the catheter five times to a pressure of 10 atmospheres. On its fifth inflation the catheter ruptured. Riegel developed a heart block, was put on life support, and underwent emergency coronary bypass surgery. He and his wife filed a lawsuit in New York federal **district court** in 1999, alleging that the design, labeling, and manufacturing of Medtronic's catheter violated New York **common law** and that these defects caused Riegel to suffer severe and permanent injuries. The district court ruled that the MDA preempted the common law causes of action raised in the complaint. These included strict liability, implied warranty of fitness, and negli-gence in the design, testing, inspection, labeling, distribution, marketing and sale of the Ever-green catheter. The judge found that none of the Riegels' claims were based on the theory that Medtronic violated federal law. The Second **Circuit Court** of Appeals upheld the dismissal of the lawsuit based on federal preemption.

The Supreme Court, in an 8–1 decision, up-held the lower courts and held that the MDA preempts state common-law damages lawsuits. Justice ANTONIN SCALIA, writing for the major-ity, reviewed the FDA's premarket approval pro-cess. He noted that it is a "rigorous" process, with the manufacturer submitting a multi-volume ap-plication that covers all aspects of the medical device. An FDA may refer the application to a panel of outside experts and may request addi-tional information from the manufacturer. The agency spends an average of 1,200 hours re-viewing each application. After it completes its review it may grant or deny premarket approval. If the application is denied, the FDA may send a letter that states the device could be approved if the applicant submitted specified information or agreed to certain conditions and restrictions. Af-ter premarket approval, the devices are subject to reporting requirements. The Medtronic catheter had received premarket approval in 1994. When changes were made in the labeling of the device, the FDA granted supplemental approvals in 1995 and 1996.

Based on this premarket approval process, Justice Scalia concluded that the federal government had established requirements applicable to Medtronic's catheter. This was important because the MDA preempts only state requirements that are different from, or in addition to, any federal requirements. The question then turned to whether the Riegels' common-law claims were based on such New York requirements relating to safety and effectiveness. Justice Scalia noted that the Court had ruled that federal statutes governing insecticides and cigarette smoking preempted state common-law actions. It made no difference if a state **tort law** or a state law regulating medical devices was employed, as the effect would be the same: the disruption of the federal regulatory scheme. The Riegels' had argued that the duties underlying negligence, strict liability, and implied warranty were not preempted because they they were not requirements "with respect to devices." Justice Scalia rejected this contention, finding nothing in the MDA preemption provision to suggest that "the pre-empted state requirement must apply *only* to the relevant device, or only to medical devices and not to all products and all actions in general."

Finally, Justice Scalia held that not all state requirements are preempted under the MDA. The act did not prevent a state "from providing a damages remedy for claims premised on a violation of FDA regulations." The state duties "in such a case 'parallel,' rather than add to, federal requirements."

PRIVACY

In constitutional law, the right of people to make personal decisions regarding intimate matters; under the common law, the right of people to lead their lives in a manner that is reasonably secluded from public scrutiny, whether such scrutiny comes from a neighbor's prying eyes, an investigator's eavesdropping ears, or a news photographer's intrusive camera; and in statutory law, the right of people to be free from unwarranted drug testing and electronic surveillance.

Fifth Circuit Strikes Down Texas Ban on Sex Toys

The Fifth **Circuit Court** of Appeals in February 2008 struck down a Texas **statute** that banned the sale and other promotion of sex toys.

According to the court, the statute violated the Fourteenth Amendment's protection of the right to privacy. After the decision, only three states continue to ban these types of sales.

Texas first enacted its obscenity statute in 1973, although its goals were relatively modest at that time. The legislature redefined what constitutes "obscene material" in 1979 so that the term was more in line with the Supreme Court's definition of obscenity in *Miller v. California*, 413 U.S. 15, 93 S. Ct. 2607, 37 L. Ed. 2d 419 (1973). The revised statute prohibited the "promotion" and "wholesale promotion" of "obscene devices." Under the new statute, an obscene device was one "designed or marketed as useful primarily for the stimulation of human genital organs."

The statute was the subject of a constitutional challenge in 1985, when a party argued before the Texas Court of Criminal Appeals that the statute did not violate an individual's right to privacy. More specifically, the court concluded that there is no constitutional right to "stimulate . . . another's genitals with an object designed or marketed as useful primarily for that purpose." *Yorko v. State*, 690 S.W.2d 260 (Tex. Crim. App. 1985). In 1993, the legislature amended the statute to include an **affirmative defense** that applied when use of the device served some **bona fide** purpose other than sexual stimulation.

Similar statute exist in three states, including Mississippi, Alabama, and Virginia. Mississippi's statute has withstood a constitutional challenge, while the other two have not been challenged in court. Other states previously enacted statutes with these bans, but state and **federal courts** have struck those down on privacy grounds.

Two companies that own businesses engaged in the sale of these sexual devices brought a declaratory action in the U.S. **District Court** for the Western District of Texas. The defendants in the case were Ronnie Earle, the Travis County District Attorney, as well as the State of Texas. The companies represent such businesses as Dreamer's, Le Rouge Boutique, and Adam & Eve, Inc. The complaint said that the statute violated substantive liberty rights that were protected by the FOURTEENTH AMENDMENT as well as commercial speech rights that are protected by the FIRST AMENDMENT.

According to these companies, many married and unmarried couples use sexual devices as part of their sexual relationship. For some couples, these companies maintained, one partner may not be able to engage in intercourse due to physical impairment or contagious, sexually-transmitted disease. In these circumstances, a sexual aid may be the only means to engage in a safe, sexual relationship. Other courts have noted the extensive review of the medical uses for sexual devices, with one commentator noting that "it is common for trained experts in the field of human sexual behavior to use sexual aids in the treatment of their male and female patients' sexual problems." Moreover, others may use these devices to avoid engaging in premarital sex.

The district court determined that the statute did not violate the Fourteenth Amendment because the Constitution does not protect the right to promote these obscene devices. Accordingly, the court granted the government's motion to dismiss. The companies then appealed the decision to the Fifth Circuit. The government argued that the case could not proceed because the companies did not have standing to bring the suit by asserting the constitutional rights of their customers. The court rejected this argument, noting that "(1) bans on commercial transactions involving a product can unconstitutionally burden individual **substantive due process** rights and (2) lawsuits may be brought by providers of the product."

The court next turned its attention to the privacy argument. According to the plaintiffs, an individual has a substantive due process right to engage in private intimate conduct that is free from intrusion by the government. The government countered that that right does not apply to the stimulation of "one's genitals for non-medical purposes unrelated to procreation or outside of an interpersonal relationship." The court noted, however, that the government's argument did not take into account the dictates of the Supreme Court in *Lawrence v. Texas*, 539 U.S. 558, 123 S. Ct. 2472, 156 L. Ed. 2d 508 (2003).

"The right the Court [in *Lawrence*] recognized was not simply a right to engage in the sexual act itself, but instead a right to be free from governmental intrusion regarding 'the most private human contact, sexual behavior'," the court said. The state argued that the decision in *Lawrence* should not apply to the sale of sexual devices because the Court in *Lawrence* was more concerned about how the statute in that case targeted a specific class of people. The Fifth Circuit rejected this argument, noting that the *Lawrence* court rested its decision on substantive due process grounds and not on **equal protection** grounds.

"Just as in *Lawrence*, the State here wants to use its laws to enforce a public moral code by

restricting private intimate conduct," the court said. "The case is not about public sex. It is not about controlling commerce in sex. It is about controlling what people do in the privacy of their own homes because the state is morally opposed to a certain type of consensual private intimate conduct. This is an insufficient justification for the statute after *Lawrence*."

Those engaged in the sale of sexual devices applauded the decision. "I think the courts are finally listening to the people," said Sherri Williams, an Alabama resident who owns stores that sell these devices. "You have 'Sex in the City', 'Desperate Housewives', and other shows promoting what society is doing. I think the courts have finally opened their eyes and looked around, which is a miracle in the South."

PRODUCT LIABILITY

The responsibility of a manufacturer or vendor of goods to compensate for injury caused by a defective good that it has provided for sale.

FDA Issues Warnings About Botox and Myobloc

The FOOD AND DRUG ADMINISTRATION (FDA) in February 2008 issued a warning about potential dangers associated with the use of the popular anti-wrinkle drug Botox, as well as the Botox competitor, Myobloc. The warning came after a consumer group issued a petition to the FDA asking the agency to increase its warnings about the drugs. The FDA's actions stopped short of what the group asked in the petition.

Botulinus toxin is a poisonous substance that can cause paralysis or even death. Researchers in the 1890s discovered that this bacteria is connected with a form of spore-forming bacteria. Near this same time, additional research revealed that the botulinum toxin consists of seven strains, lettered A through G. At least four of them, including A, B, E, and F, can cause illness in human beings.

Although some research in during WORLD WAR II focused on means to use botulinus toxin as a biological weapon, by the 1950s, some scientists had also discovered that the toxins could have beneficial uses. A physiologist named Vernon Brooks in 1953 found that a small amount of the toxin injected into a hyperactive muscle could cause temporary relaxation of that muscle. Later studies showed that the muscle-relaxing effects of the drug could help those who have crossed eyes.

Research on botulinum toxin continued in the 1970s, when Dr. Alan B. Scott received FDA approval to inject small amounts of the toxin into human volunteers. Early in the 1980s, he published a paper where he concluded that the botulinum toxin appeared to be safe for treatment of strabismus (cross-eye). Additional research showed that this treatment could also be effective for those suffering from various types of spasms. Drug manufacturer Allergan received FDA approval in 1988 to distribute type A of the botulinum toxin for treatment of several conditions. Shortly after receiving this permission, Allergan changed the name of the drug to Botox.

More uses of this drug emerged in the 1990s. An ophthalmologist named Jean Carruthers discovered that patients using the drug for spasms temporarily lost their frown lines. She and her husband published a paper in 1992 concluding that use of the toxin was a "simple, safe" procedure for treating brow lines. Use of Botox for this purpose became popular in the late 1990s and finally obtained official government approval in 2002. In 2003, *USA Today* dubbed the drug the "little neurotoxin that could," and Botox sales reached more than $1 billion by 2006. The competitor to Botox is Myobloc, a Type B strain of botulinum toxin that is produced by Solstice Neurosciences.

Not all of the reports about the safety of Botox or Myobloc have been favorable. The European Medicines Agency (EMEA), which is the counterpart to the FDA, posted information about adverse effects that the toxins could have. In March 2005, EMEA indicated that of 552 reported cases of adverse events related to Botox or Myobloc, more than 30 percent were serious. As of November 2005, in fact, 17 deaths had resulted from use of the drugs, including six due to aspiration pneumonia. Information posted on March 2007 indicated that "[d]istant reactions, including muscle weakness, dysphagia, and aspiration represent a significant portion of all reported serious events associated with the use of botulinum toxin containing products ... fatal cases have been reported." The FDA has not issued warnings to patients or doctors about the use of these drugs.

The public interest group Public Citizens researched FDA data about use of Botox and Myobloc during a nine-year period. According to their studies, there were 658 reported cases of people suffering adverse effects from use of the drugs. Of these, 180 patients had fluid in their lungs (aspiration) or difficulty swallowing (dysphagia). Dysphagia could have led to food or liquid entering the respiratory tract and lungs, which could cause aspiration pneumonia. The study of the FDA data only included information voluntarily given, which accounts for only about 10 percent of the actual cases.

Public Citizens recommended that the FDA issue a warning letter to all doctors, indicating the health risks associated with Botox and Myobloc. The group also suggested that the FDA label the drugs with a "black box" warning, which is the strongest warning that the agency can give. "These significantly improved warnings to doctors and patients would increase the likelihood of earlier medical intervention when symptoms of adverse reactions to botulinum toxin first appear and could prevent more serious complications, including death," said Sidney Wolfe, director of the Public Citizen's Health Research Group. "Nobody should be dying from injected botulinum toxin. Educating physicians and patients about what adverse symptoms to look for and when to seek immediate medical attention will save lives."

The FDA responded to Public Citizens' petition by issuing an early communication regarding the drugs. "FDA has received reports of systemic adverse reactions including respiratory compromise and death following the use of botulinum toxins types A and B for both FDA-approved and unapproved uses," the FDA report said. "The reactions reported are suggestive of botulism, which occurs when botulinum toxin spreads in the body beyond the site where it was injected. The most serious cases had outcomes that included hospitalization and death, and occurred mostly in children treated for cerebral palsy-associated limb spasticity."

Though the FDA only announced that it would begin an inquiry, the announcement caused Allergan's stock to drop by six percent in one day. The company responded to the concerns by stressing that the reported incidents of problems associated with Botox occurred when patients used the drug as part of an aggressive and high-dosage treatment for certain conditions. Analysts suggest that while the FDA may require revisions to the packaging of Botox and Myobloc, the action will not affect sales of the drugs.

Contamination Leads to Massive Pet Food Recall

During March 2007, contamination in certain brands of pet food led to illness and death in potentially thousands of household pets. This led to a massive recall of nearly 100 brands of pet foods, followed by an investigation by the FOOD

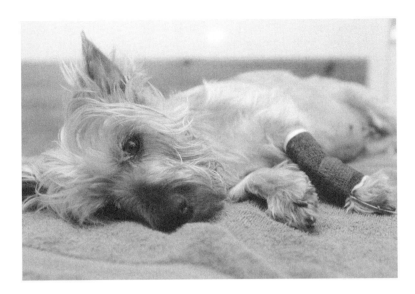

Yorkshire terrier Pebbles, one victim of tainted pet food in March 2007.
AP IMAGES

AND DRUG ADMINISTRATION (FDA). The investigation led to the indictment of several individuals who may have been responsible for the contamination. More than year after the recall, however, few procedures have been adopted that would prevent a recurrence of such an event.

The FDA, operating primarily through the Center for Veterinary Medicine (CVM), regulates the manufacture and distribution of pet food, in addition to feeds, feed ingredients, and animal drugs. According to the CVM's website, "One of CVM's highest priorities is assuring the safety of the food supply. And, because of the Center's work and the cooperative efforts of all FDA employees, the American food supply is among the safest in the world."

The first signs of the pet food contamination in 2007 came when scores of pets began to suffer kidney failure, and initial reports indicated that at least 16 pets had died. By mid-March, nearly 100 brands of the "cuts and gravy" style of pet food were recalled by Menu Foods of Canada, the largest producer of pet foods in North America. Pet owners reported that their animals showed certain symptoms, such as vomiting, lethargy, and extreme thirst. For several weeks, neither the company nor other researchers could determine the cause of the illnesses, although some suspected that contaminated wheat gluten could be the cause.

The FDA first learned of the possible contamination when it received the news of the recall by Menu Foods. One day after this recall was announced, the FDA sent investigators to Menu Foods' plant in Emporia. From there, government officials reportedly worked with the company to identify the contaminated products and to ensure that these products were removed from store shelves. The FDA also began to receive calls from veterinarians and pet owners about the illnesses. Within four weeks, the FDA received more than 14,000 calls about these illnesses, representing more than twice the total number of complaints that the agency usually receives in a year about pet foods.

FDA inspectors gathered samples from the contaminated pet food to send to the FDA labs. Analysis of these samples ruled out several known causes of kidney failure, including vitamin D and ethylene glycol (antifreeze). The tests also revealed no evidence of toxic metals that are sometimes known to cause kidney problems in pets. Although at least one laboratory found the presence of aminopterin, a former of rat poison, additional tests could not confirm this as the cause for the animal deaths.

The FDA discovered that a possible cause of the contamination was the presence of melamine, which is a molecule that has a number of industrial uses, such as the manufacture of cooking utensils. Melamine is also used as a fertilizer in some countries, though this is not permitted in North America. The FDA's **Forensic** Chemistry Center discovered melamine in both the pet foods as well as wheat gluten, which is used as an ingredient in the gravy of many of the varieties of the contaminated pet foods. Scientists at Cornell University found traces of melamine in the urine and kidneys of cats that were used as part of a taste-testing study by Menu Foods.

Despite the evidence of melamine in the contaminated foods, little research had been done regarding melamine's effect on dogs and cats. "While the levels we've found to date in both the finished pet food product and the wheat gluten are below what would be considered toxic in rodents, there is extremely little data in the scientific literature on melamine exposure in dogs and cats," said Stephen F. Sundlof, director of the CVM. "Regardless, the association between melamine in the kidneys of cats that died and melamine in the food they consumed is undeniable."

The FDA was able to trace the contaminated wheat gluten back to ChemNutra, a distributor in Las Vegas, Nevada. Through its work with ChemNutra, the FDA determined that the source of the contamination was a Chinese supplier. Federal inspectors at that point began to sample 100 percent of wheat gluten shipped for import from China. Of 400 samples taken from Chinese imports within a month of the initial recall, 21 tested positive for melamine.

By this time, several other companies had recalled certain pet products, including those produced by Del Monte Pet Products, Hill's Pet Nutrition, Nestle Purina PetCare Company, P&G Pet Care, and Sunshine Mills.

In April 2007, the FDA announced that it had found a contaminant in a second pet food ingredient. Inspectors found melamine in an imported shipment of rice protein that had had been imported by Wilbur-Ellis, a San Francisco-based distributor of agricultural products. The shipment was traced back to Binzhou Futian Biological Technology of China. Wilbur-Ellis immediately initiated a recall of rice protein concentrate that could have contained melamine.

The discovery of the sources of the contamination led the FDA's Office of Criminal Investigations to pursue criminal charges against the companies responsible for the melamine being added to the products. In February 2008, a federal **grand jury** in Kansas City, Missouri handed down an indictment against three companies, including Xuzhou Anying Biologic Technology Development Co., Ltd. (XAC), Suzhou Textiles, Silk, Light Industrial Products, Arts and Crafts I/E Co., Ltd. (SSC), and ChemNutra. The president of SSC, Chen Zhen Hao, was also indicated along with Sally Qing Miller and Stephen Miller of ChemNutra.

According to the indictment, the companies added melamine to wheat gluten to make the protein content of the wheat gluten appear to be higher. SSC allegedly made false declarations to the Chinese government that the shipments of the contaminated wheat gluten were not subject to mandatory inspection by the Chinese government prior to exporting the products. A total of more than 800 tons of potentially contaminated wheat gluten was imported between November 2006 and February 2007.

The FDA never released an estimate of the total number of animal deaths that resulted from these contaminations. According to the indictment, though, as many as 1,950 cats and 2,200 dogs died after consuming the tainted food. Veterinarians have said that they believe tens of thousands of pets were affected by the products.

Warner-Lambert Co. v. Kent

During its 2007 term, the U.S. SUPREME COURT agreed to review a case to clarify the scope of one of its prior cases regarding federal **preemption** of certain state products liability laws. However, Chief Justice JOHN ROBERTS was forced to recuse himself from the decision because he owns stock in one of the litigants.

Without his vote, the Court remained tied 4–4, which allowed a Second **Circuit Court** of Appeals decision to stand.

In *Buckman Co. v. Plaintiffs' Legal Comm.*, 531 U.S. 341, 121 S. Ct. 1012, 148 L. Ed. 2d 854 (2001), the Court addressed the relationship between two federal statutes—the Food, Drug, and Cosmetic Act (FDCA), 21 U.S.C. §§ 301 **et seq.** and the Medical Device Act (MDA), 21 U.S.C. §§ 360e(b)(1)(A)-(B)—and state products liability laws. In *Buckman*, the plaintiffs had alleged that the manufacturer of orthopedic bone screws had obtained approval from the FOOD AND DRUG ADMINISTRATION (FDA) by making **fraudulent** representations to the agency. The plaintiffs sought to recover damages under California state law, arguing that but for the fraudulent representations, the FDA would not have approved the medical device.

By a 9–0 vote, the Court ruled against the original plaintiffs. In an opinion by the late Chief Justice WILLIAM REHNQUIST, the Court noted that "[p]olicing **fraud** against federal agencies is hardly a field which the States have traditionally occupied." Although the Court has established a general presumption against preemption when state laws govern matters of health and safety, the case did not present a simple matter of such a state law. Instead, the state law in question stood in contrast to a federal law governing a federal agency and an **entity** that the agency regulates.

Without a presumption against preemption, the Court determined that federal law impliedly preempted the state law in that situation. The Court noted, "The conflict stems from the fact that the federal **statutory** scheme amply empowers the FDA to punish and deter fraud against the [FDA], and that this authority is used by the [FDA] to achieve a somewhat delicate balance of statutory objectives." The Court determined that the state law in question did not predate the requirements of the federal statutes, but instead plaintiffs bringing an action under the California law would have to prove "fraud-on-the-FDA" as an element of their case. Given the conflict between state and federal law, the Court held that the FDCA and MDA preempted the federal law.

The case that came before the Court during the 2007 term arose when several Michigan residents allegedly suffered liver damage as a result of taking the drug Rezulin, which was manufactured by Warner-Lambert Co. and was used as a treatment for Type-2 diabetes. The FDA originally approved the drug in 1997 and then subsequently authorized label changes on four different occasions between 1997 and 1999. In 2000, Warner-Lambert removed the drug from the market. The plaintiffs originally brought the case in state courts in Michigan and California, but these claims were removed to federal court, and all of the claims were eventually transferred to Judge Lewis A. Kaplan of the Southern District of New York.

Prior to 1995, the Michigan products liability **statute** allowed a party to introduce evidence showing that a product complied with governmental or industry standards in a products liability action to prove that a certain standard of care had been met. In 1995, Michigan amended the statute by adding the following provision:

> In a **product liability** action against a manufacturer or seller, a product that is a drug is not defective or unreasonably dangerous, and the manufacturer or seller is not liable, if the drug was approved for safety and efficacy by the United States food and drug administration, and the drug and its labeling were in compliance with the United States food and drug administration's approval at the time the drug left the control of the manufacturer or seller.

The 1995 legislation also added an exception to this immunity provision. Under this exception, the immunity does not apply if a manufacturer does the following:

> Intentionally withholds from or misrepresents to the United States food and drug administration information concerning the drug that is required to be submitted under the federal food, drug, and cosmetic act and the drug would not have been approved, or the United States food and drug administration would have withdrawn approval for the drug if the information were accurately submitted.

The **district court** concluded that federal law preempted the exception to immunity provided under Michigan law. In support of his conclusion, Judge Kaplan cited both *Buckman* and the Sixth Circuit's decision in *Garcia v. Wyeth-Ayerst Labs.*, 385 F.3d 961 (6th Cir. 2004), the latter of which held that *Buckman* preempted the Michigan law.

On appeal, the Second Circuit Court of Appeals reversed the district court. The Second Circuit viewed the case as presenting a "very different set of circumstances" from those found in *Buckman*. The court concluded that case was based on long-standing **common law** claims, rather than a claim where fraud-on-the-FDA was an essential element of the plaintiff's claim. Accordingly, the Court determined that the presumption against preemption applied and ruled in favor of the original plaintiffs.

The manufacturer sought a review by the U.S. Supreme Court, and the Court agreed to hear the case. The Bush administration supported the manufacturers in the dispute, noting in a brief that "permitting lay juries to second-guess" the adequacy of a drug application would interfere with the agency's "exercise of its expert judgment." Commentators noted that *Kent* offered something of a preview for the broader preemption issues presented in *Wyeth v. Levine* (06-1249), which the Court will decide during its next term.

Chief Justice John Roberts has reported that he owns between $5,001 and $50,000 in stock in Pfizer Inc, the **parent company** of Warner Lambert. He therefore had to recuse himself from the case. In his absence, the Court found itself in a 4–4 deadlock. In such an instance, the Court must allow the lower court's decision to stand. The Court thus issued a *per curiam* decision affirming the Second Circuit's ruling. *Warner-Lambert Co. v. Kent*, ___ U. S. ___, 128 S. Ct. 1168, 170 L. Ed. 2d 51 (2008).

PROSTITUTION

The act of offering one's self for hire to engage in sexual relations.

N.Y. Governor Eliot Spitzer Linked to Prostitution Ring

New York Governor Eliot Spitzer became embroiled in a major controversy in 2008 when investigators determined that he had arranged to meet with a high-priced prostitute. The fallout from the scandal led to Spitzer's resignation as governor, probably ending the political career of an official who gained national prominence thanks to his investigation of Wall Street.

Spitzer graduated from Harvard Law School and worked as a corporate lawyer for several law firms in New York. He is the son of Bernard Spitzer, a famous real estate tycoon. In 1994, at the age of 35, Spitzer took a big gamble by quitting his law firm positions and running for attorney general of New York. He took out a large loan to finance the campaign and outspent each of the other Democratic hopefuls. Although he lost the election, he received a substantial number of votes.

New York governor Eliot Spitzer announces his resignation, with wife Silda at side, March 2008.
AP IMAGES

Four years later, he ran again and finally won the election. His use of his father's money, including an admission that his father had lent him money to finance a $4 million loan for the 1994 election, did not derail his efforts to win in 1998.

In 2001, Spitzer began an investigation that eventually led to the reshaping of America's financial markets. During an inquiry of emails from the financial analysis Merrill Lynch, Spitzer and his staff determined that the Merrill had downgraded an internet company because that company had refused to give Merrill its internet banking business. This discovery led to a wide-scale investigation that showed how common this practice had become. Spitzer's efforts led to new ethics rules that changed how analysts issue the reports on which the public relies for stock information.

In 2004, Spitzer announced his intention to run for governor of New York. He earned a solid national reputation among Democrats, with New Mexico Governor Bill Richardson touting Spitzer as the "future of the Democratic Party." Spitzer routed Thomas Suozzi in the Democratic primary with 81 percent of the vote. Spitzer then defeated Republican John Faso and other candidates with 69 percent of the vote. During his campaign, he pledged to tackle difficult issues, including alleged corruption in the New York state legislature and the legalization of gay marriage.

Less than a year after his election, suspicious bank records drew the attention of investi-gators. Spitzer reportedly made a number of wire transfers to two shell companies named QAT International and QAT Consulting Group. When bank employees attempted to contact these companies, the employees were unable to find any information in the form of documentation.

The bank filed some reports about the activity, which eventually led to an investigation by the INTERNAL REVENUE SERVICE. IRS agents determined that the shell companies were connected to an internet-based prostitution service called Emperor's Club V.I.P. Initially, the agents did not know the nature of the shell companies' businesses or how these companies had collected their revenues. However, they soon found Spitzer's name associated with some of these revenues.

Federal agents began to wiretap communications between the Emperor's Club and prospective clients. These communications revealed the nature of the business. The company had 50 prostitutes available in New York, Washington, Miami, London, and Paris. The leader of the company was Mark Brener of New Jersey, while the day-to-day operations were handled by Cecil Suwal, also of New Jersey. The company charged between $1,000 to $5,500 per hour for the services of one of the prostitutes. Clients could pay for the services through cash, credit card, wire transfer, or money orders. These clients could set appointments by telephone or through an online booking service.

Investigators worked with a woman who claimed to be a former Emperor's Club prostitute. An undercover agent posed as a client and arranged appointments through various means. In addition, other agents collected more than 5,000 telephone calls and text messages and about 6,000 email messages. Based on this investigation, federal prosecutors charged Brener and Suwal with prostitution and **money laundering**. Also prosecuted were two booking agents, who were accused of violating federal prostitution laws.

Three days after the initial reports about the prostitution ring emerged, further reports linked Spitzer with the investigation. One of the wiretaps captured a conversation on February 13 between someone identified as Client 9 and a booking agent, confirming that this client would meet one of the prostitutes at a Washington hotel room. A law enforcement officer later confirmed that Client 9 was Spitzer. Subsequent reports showed that Spitzer had reserved a room at the Mayflower Hotel in Washington under the name George Fox. Fox, who is one of Spitzer's donors, later denied that he knew anything about Spitzer's activities.

The prostitute that Spitzer met went by the name of "Kristen," who was later discovered to be 22-year-old Ashley Alexandra Dupre, an aspiring musician from New York. The *New York Times* quoted her as saying, "I just don't want to be thought of as a monster." She was featured on the cover of the *New York Post*, and her profile on MySpace.com was visited an estimated seven million times.

On March 12, 2008, Spitzer announced that he would step down as governor of New York. At a press conference, Spitzer stated, "I cannot allow for my private failings to disrupt the people's work. Over the course of my public life, I have insisted—I believe correctly—that people take responsibility for their conduct. I can and will ask no less of myself." Accordingly, Spitzer announced that his resignation would take effect March 17.

Upon Spitzer's resignation, Lieutenant Governor David Peterson became governor of New York. He is the state's first black governor and the fourth in U.S. history. As of July 2008, Spitzer had not been charged with any crimes by federal authorities.

PUBLIC UTILITIES

Businesses that provide the public with necessities, such as water, electricity, natural gas, and telephone and telegraph communication.

Morgan Stanley Capital Group Inc. v. Public Utility Dist. No. 1

In June 2008, the U.S. SUPREME COURT resolved a dispute that arose about energy contracts that California utilities and others signed during the state's energy crisis in 2000 and 2001. Officials in several states, including California, Washington, and Nevada, had asked officials with the Federal Energy Regulatory Commission (FERC) to allow utility companies to nullify or renegotiate deals that were struck when electricity prices were dramatically inflated due to illegal trading by Enron Corp. and other companies. The Court remanded the case so that FERC could reevaluate the contracts under standards that the Court established.

The Federal Power Act (FPA), 16 U.S.C. §§ 824 **et seq.** gives FERC (and its predecessor, the Federal Power Commission) the authority to regulate the sale of electricity in interstate commerce. Under the FPA, regulated utilities must file rate schedules, or tariffs, with FERC. FERC is also involved with setting the terms and prices for services to electricity purchasers. Utilities may additionally set rates with individual electricity purchasers through bilateral agreements. Both the rate schedules and the contracts must be filed with FERC.

Under the FPA, wholesale-electricity rates must be "fair and reasonable." When FERC considers a rate change, either through a new rate schedule or through a contract, FERC may take up to five months to investigate whether the rate is fair and reasonable. On the other hand, the commission may allow the rate to go into effect without making a determination that the rate is fair and reasonable. This occurrence does not prevent FERC from concluding later, in response to its own motion or in response to a complaint, that the rate is not fair and reasonable. The Supreme Court has traditionally given FERC and its predecessor great deference in setting the utility rates.

In 1956, the Supreme Court decided two cases that together establish the principles that apply when the commission considers modifications through rates established bilaterally by contract rather than unilaterally through a rate schedule. *United Gas Pipe Line Co. v. Mobile Gas Serv. Corp. (Mobile)*, 350 U.S. 332, 76 S. Ct. 373, 100 L. Ed. 373 (1956); *Fed. Power Comm'n v. Sierra Pac. Power Co. (Sierra)*, 350 U.S. 348, 76 S. Ct. 368, 100 L. Ed. 388 (1956). These cases resolved the question of how the commission may evaluate whether a contract rate is just and reasonable. According to the Court:

[W]hile it may be that the Commission may not normally impose upon a public utility a rate which would produce less than a fair return, it does not follow that the public utility may not itself agree by contract to a rate affording less than a fair return or that, if it does so, it is entitled to be relieved of its improvident bargain. . . . In such circumstances the sole concern of the Commission would seem to be whether the rate is so low as to adversely affect the public interest-as where it might impair the financial ability of the public utility to continue its service, cast upon other consumers an excessive burden, or be unduly discriminatory.

The Court, as well as lower **federal courts**, has further refined the *Mobile-Sierra* doctrine during the more than fifty years since it was decided. This doctrine stands for the principle that FERC must presume that an electricity rate established through a freely-negotiated, **bilateral contract** meets the "just and reasonable" requirement set forth in the FPA. This presumption may be overcome only if FERC determines that the contract causes serious harm to the public interest.

During the 1990s, California underwent a massive restructuring of its electricity market. This effort resulted in a program where the energy providers entered into short-term contracts (in a market known as the "spot" market), giving the providers only limited ability to enter into long-term agreements. The limitation on long-term contracts later caused problems when the State of California suffered through an energy crisis beginning in the summer of 2000. A variety of factors caused energy prices to skyrocket by as much as fifteen times their normal rates, and this price increase hit the spot market hard. The result was that utilities became buried in debt, and several parts of the state experienced rolling blackouts.

In response to the energy crisis, FERC effectively eliminated the reliance on the spot market and encouraged utilities to enter into long-term contracts. FERC likewise capped the price of wholesale electricity. Although prices fell to normal levels by June 2001, the long-term contracts that were executed prior to that time caused significant problems. Several utilities agreed to long-term contracts under which the utilities were required to pay several times the normal rate, even though these rates were much less than they were at peak times during the energy crisis. For example, one utility company purchased power from Morgan Stanley (the petitioner in the Supreme Court decision) at a rate of $105 per megawatt hour, compared with the historical average of $24 per megawatt hour.

After the energy crisis ended and the prices fell, several utilities were unhappy with the prices established in the long-term contracts. (The Supreme Court noted that "buyer's remorse set in"). The utilities asked FERC to modify the contracts, arguing that the commission should not presume the rates to be just and reasonable under the *Mobile-Sierra* doctrine. FERC determined that the *Mobile-Sierra* presumption applied and that the utilities were not entitled to have the contracts modified.

The Ninth **Circuit Court** of Appeals reviewed FERC's determination. A panel of the **appellate court** concluded that FERC had misapplied *Mobile-Sierra* because FERC had not provided sufficient oversight for the long-term contracts. Moreover, the court held that FERC had not properly considered the public interest of any of these long-term contracts. The court thus remanded the case to FERC for further consideration. *Public Utility Dist. No. 1 v. FERC*, 471 F.3d 1053 (9th Cir. 2006).

Morgan Stanley and other energy suppliers sought review from the U.S. Supreme Court, which granted a **writ** of **certiorari**. In a divided decision in which two justices did not participate, the Court disagreed with the Ninth Circuit's rationale but essentially agreed that the case should be remanded to FERC. Writing for a majority of four, Justice ANTONIN SCALIA concluded that the *Mobile-Sierra* doctrine required the Ninth Circuit to presume that the contracts were just and reasonable. According to Scalia, the only circumstance where FERC could set aside the type of contract at issue would be where the commission found "unequivocal public necessity" or "extraordinary circumstances." The Court's opinion directed FERC to review the contracts to determine whether unlawful market activity directly affected contract negotiations. If so, then the *Mobile-Sierra* presumption would not apply, and FERC could reform the contracts. *Morgan Stanley Capital Group Inc. v. Pub. Util. Dist. No. 1*, Nos. 06-1457, 2008 WL 2520522 (June 26, 2008).

Justice RUTH BADER GINSBURG agreed with the judgment but wrote a separate concurrence. She believed that the Court should have waited for FERC to reconsider the case before reviewing the commission's **final decision**. Justice JOHN PAUL STEVENS, joined by Justice

DAVID SOUTER, argued that the Court "mangle[d] both the governing **statute** and precedent" in reaching the decision. Chief Justice JOHN ROBERTS and Justice STEPHEN BREYER recused themselves from the case.

PUNITIVE DAMAGES

Monetary compensation awarded to an injured party that goes beyond that which is necessary to compensate the individual for losses and that is intended to punish the wrongdoer.

Exxon Shipping Co. v. Baker

Nearly two decades after the 1989 crash of the oil tanker *Exxon Valdez* on Bligh Reef off the Alaska coastline, spilling eleven million gallons of crude oil into the water, the legal battles over liability and damages were still going on. The U.S. Supreme Court's February 2008 decision in *Exxon Shipping Co. v. Baker*, No. 07-219, 554 U.S. ___, (with Justice Alito taking no part in deciding this issue because he owned Exxon stock), did little to put the remaining issues to rest. The Court split 4–4 on the question of whether maritime law permitted judges to award punitive damages for employee misdeeds (in this case, the tanker's Captain Hazelwood), leaving in place the decision of the Ninth Circuit Court of Appeals, which said yes. However, the Supreme Court, in letting the Ninth Circuit's decision stand, expressly indicated that this disposition did not constitute a precedent on the derivative liability question (see below).

Most of the facts leading up to the crash were no longer in dispute, having been stipulated to or proved in evidence in prior litigation. Icebergs had been visible on the ship's radar. In accordance with maritime custom, the ship informed the Coast Guard that it was going to navigate outside of normal shipping lanes. This alternate course took the ship near Bligh Reef. Captain Joseph Hazelwood did instruct Third Mate Gregory Cousins when to turn the ship to avoid the reef. However, in violation of Exxon's own written policies, Hazelwood then left the bridge, leaving Cousins to navigate alone. Cousins made the turn too late.

One important fact still in dispute was whether Captain Hazelwood, a known alcoholic, was under the influence of alcohol at the time of the disaster (he was found in an intoxicated condition several hours later). Witness testimony noted that Hazelwood had downed several vodka drinks at waterfront bars before the tanker left the port on the night of the disaster. Further, evidence proved that Exxon officials had known for years about Hazelwood's drinking problem, and in fact, Exxon officials had often joined Hazelwood in drinking sessions. Other evidence showed that Hazelwood was able to keep his job despite his alcoholism because an Exxon policy guaranteed that employees seeking alcohol treatment would not lost their jobs (evidence also showed that Hazelwood had stopped attending Alcoholics Anonymous sessions).

In the wake of the disaster, thousands of animals were killed and hundreds of thousands of birds died in the slick oil along the coastline. Several thousand people, including ordinary citizens as well as government and Exxon employees, attempted to contain the spill and clean up the oil. The official cleanup took three years, with residual damage to the ecosystem continuing through 2008.

Immediately after the spill, Exxon voluntarily paid $2.2 billion toward the cleanup. The State of Alaska sued Exxon for compensatory and punitive damages, and the United States government indicted Exxon for violations of the Clean Water Act, 33 USC § 1311(a) and other provisions. In settling these public suits, Exxon paid another $1 billion to Alaska and the United States governments. This money is being used for environmental studies and conservation programs for Prince William Sound.

Additionally, a large number of private sector persons and entities, including Alaska landowners, Native American groups, and commercial fishermen, filed suit against Exxon for economic harm and devaluation of property. In 1994, a jury in an Alaska district court awarded this group of plaintiffs $287 million in compensatory damages (later reduced to $20 million by the court to reflect settlements and released claims Exxon had reached during trial). The jury also found both Captain Hazelwood and Exxon were reckless, and awarded punitive damages (a penalty to punish the defendants and deter future misconduct). The punitive damages against Exxon were $5 billion.

Exxon appealed to the Ninth Circuit, contesting the basis as well as the amount of punitive damages. The Ninth Circuit upheld the award, but remanded the case to the district court with instructions to reduce the amount in light of recent Supreme Court decisions involving due process. The district court reduced the punitive damages to $4 billion, and Exxon appealed again. Again the case was remanded for consideration, but this time the trial court awarded $4.5 billion

Fisherman Steve Smith and Alaska Governor Sarah Palin as a news conference, February 26, 2008.
AP IMAGES

with interest. Exxon appealed a third time, and the Ninth Circuit ultimately reduced the amount to $2.5 billion. Exxon then appealed to the U.S. Supreme Court.

In amicus briefs filed in the appeal, concerns were articulated regarding the effect that such an award of punitive damages against the employer would have on the industry. It is well established that employers can be held vicariously liable for the wrongdoing of their employees with respect to compensatory damages, but punitive damages are generally not awarded against an employer.

Ultimately, the question before the Supreme Court was whether maritime law permitted judges to award punitive damages for employee misdeeds, particularly when Congress had not authorized them? As to the first part, the justices split 4–4, leaving in place (for now) the Ninth Circuit's conclusion that employers could be held to pay punitive damages for the misdeeds of their employees. As to the second part, the Court narrowly decided, 5–4 (with Justice Alito taking part in this more general question) that judges were free to create remedies in maritime cases where Congress had not legislated in that area. However, if Congress were to pass legislation, this would restrain such judicial activism.

The Court also found the punitive damages assessed against Exxon to be excessive as a matter of federal maritime common law, particularly finding that the punitive to compensatory damages ratio was extreme. The Court instead concluded that a ratio or "maximum multiple" should be used to assess such damages. The Court found that a punitive to compensatory ratio of 1:1 was most appropriate as a fair upper limit in maritime cases.

Justice Scalia, joined by Justice Thomas, wrote a concurring opinion that agreed with the Court's methodology of reviewing punitive damages precedent, but argued that those prior cases/decisions were erroneous. Justice Stevens, concurring in part and dissenting in part, opined that Congress and not the courts should be the sole entity entrusted with determining the permissibility of punitive damages. Justice Breyer also concurred in part, dissented in part, arguing that the punitive damages in this case should have been further reduced. Exxon's profits in 2007 were $40.6 billion, but this was not a factor in the Court's conclusions.

RAILROADS

CSX Transportation, Inc. v. Georgia State Board of Equalization

Since the introduction of railroads to the United States there have been ongoing legal disputes between railroad companies and the state governments over how much railroads should be taxed. By the 1970s, when the rail industry went into decline, the federal government stepped in to deal with discriminatory tax schemes imposed by the states. The Railroad Revitalization and Regulatory Act of 1976, 90 Stat. 31, gave railroads a tool to fight what they perceived as unfair taxation by the states. Railroads had been able to challenge the state's application of its valuation method, but there had been a split in the federal circuit courts of appeal over whether the law allowed railroads to challenge in court the state's valuation methods themselves. In *CSX Transportation, Inc. v. Georgia State Board of Equalization*, __U.S.__, 128 S. Ct. 467, 169 L. Ed. 2d 418(2007), the Supreme Court resolved the conflict, ruling that the act did permit the railroad to challenge the methods used to appraise their property.

CSX Transportation, Inc., a freight carrier with multiple routes across the state of Georgia, was subject to state taxes on its real property. Under Georgia law railroad property was initially valued by the Georgia State Board of Equalization, which then certified the proposed valuations to the county boards for adoption or modification. In 2001 the board valued CSX's tax liability at $4.6 million. In 2002 the figure increased dramatically to $6.5 million. The rise was caused by the state's appraiser using a differ-

ent combination of methods to calculate the value of SCSX property. The **market value** jumped by 47 percent in just one year due to the change in valuation method. CSX filed suit in federal **district court**, arguing that the 2002 tax assessment violated the 1976 railroad act. It contended that the state had grossly overestimated the market value of its in-state property, while accurately valuing other commercial and industrial property in Georgia. CSX claimed that its property was taxed more than 5 percent greater than the same ratio for the other property in the state.

CSX submitted the testimony of its own expert appraiser, who used a combination of valuation methods different from those used by the state appraiser. The CSX appraiser found the market value of the property to be $6 billion, not $7.8 billion as calculated by the state. The district court ruled in favor of Georgia, finding that the state had not violated the railroad act because it had used widely accepted methods to calculate market value. The court also held that the act did not permit a railroad to challenge the state's chosen method of valuation as long as the methods are rational and not motivated by discriminatory intent. The Eleventh **Circuit Court** of Appeals upheld this decision and the Supreme Court took CSX's appeal to resolve a split in the federal circuits over whether railroads could contest the methods of valuation.

In a unanimous decision, the Supreme Court reversed the Eleventh Circuit, ruling that CSX should have been allowed to demonstrate that the methods used by Georgia were flawed. Chief Justice JOHN ROBERTS, writing for the Court, stated that the purpose of the law, fair taxation, could not be achieved if the railroads were barred from suggesting alternative valuation methods that would reflect true market value. Reviewing the text of the law, Roberts could not find any language that distinguished between method and the application of a method. A district court's factfinding would be crippled if it was forced to accept the state's method as the starting point and then determine if the application of that method was discriminatory. In the Court's view the valuation of market value "is not a matter of mathematics" but more like "an applied science, even a craft."

Most appraisers use a combination of methods to estimate **fair market value**. These methods produce a range of possible market values that the appraiser uses to fix fair market value. In the present case the Georgia appraiser used three models, from which he derived five values that ranged from $8.1 billion to $12.3 billion. He selected a number at the low end of the ranged and subtracted $400 million to account for intangible property not covered by the railroad tax. Because chosen methods can affect the determination of value, it made no sense for the district court to accept the state's method, as it was one of the parties to the lawsuit.

Chief Justice Roberts dismissed Georgia's fear that allowing railroads to present alternative valuation methods would lead to a "futile clash of experts, which courts will have no reasonable way to settle." Congress was not troubled by this prospect when it passed the 1976 act and instructed the courts to find true market value. Moreover, the courts are used to dealing with issues of fair market value, which in the end is just "an issue of fact about possible market prices." In most cases the court will look at the two appraisals and determine which is more credible. The Court concluded that if Congress had meant to impose a limit on the types of evidence courts may consider it could have done so. The fact that the law was silent on this issue meant Congress had no objection. Georgia was free to use any mix of methods to ascertain fair market value but it had to realize a railroad could offer alternative methods to demonstrate a discriminatory tax.

RECALL

Recall on Chinese Products

It started in early 2007, when reports of sick and dying family pets caused further inquiry. Initially, pet owners were told that some food and treat products were contaminated with rat poison. Weeks later, the U.S. Food and Drug Administration (FDA) announced that it had found melamine, a chemical used to make plastic, in several pet foods. Ultimately, the FDA announced amid massive recalls of nearly 95 brands of pet food and treats, it was the wheat gluten found in these products that had been implicated in the pet casualties. The wheat gluten, containing melamine and other contaminants, was traced to China.

By May 2007, the Chinese government was acknowledging greater product quality control problems, and vowed to provide special monitoring of fertilizers, pesticides, and other additives to animal foods. The fear (well-founded) was that contaminated animal feed would travel through domesticated stock (cattle, sheep, hogs) and ultimately into human food consumption. The end-products were not Chinese-made, but rather, American manufactured products using Chinese wheat gluten in their ingredients.

By June, China was again in hot water with U.S. inspection officials who ordered a recall of 450,000 Chinese-made automobile tires. About this time, the FDA released a slew of recalls on Chinese-made toys tainted with lead paint, particularly those sold under the Mattel name. Several of the recalled toy products were popular household names, including SpongeBob Square Pants, Curious George, and Thomas the Tank Engine. By late September, the Starbucks-brand Coffee giant had to recall children's plastic drinking cups made in China.

In the end, nearly 70 percent of all products recalled by the independent Consumer Products Safety Commission in 2007 were Chinese-made or used Chinese-made ingredients or components. The list was expansive, from notebook computer batteries that burned up computers to faulty baby carriers, portable baby swings, and swimming pool ladders. Food products for human consumption included drug-laced frozen eel and juice made with toxic food coloring additives. Exploding air pumps, circular saws with faulty blade guards, baby cribs with incorrect assembly instructions resulting in babies falling out or becoming entrapped,—even books were contaminated. Even simple, inexpensive pinecone candles burned down homes when not just the wick but the flammable external coating caught on fire.

Of particular concern were electrical products, which represented a significant percentage of recalled items from China. These included counterfeit circuit breakers, power strips, and extension cords, batteries, and lights that all

Customers look at toys in Beijing, August 2007.

AP IMAGES

caused fires, explosions, shocks, and electrocutions. Also implicated were oil-filled electric heaters that burned down homes, oscillating tower fans with faulty wiring that resulted in fires, and massaging recliners that overheated and burned their users. Other Chinese recalls included Boy Scout badges, air purifiers, key chains, costume jewelry, and aluminum water bottles. The list was exhaustive.

Most frightening of all were the food products. Pet owners with massive veterinary bills or deceased animals were little comforted by being notified of recalled products for which they could receive "a full refund." Moreover, China was the leading exporter of seafood to the United States, but raised most of its fish products in water contaminated with raw sewage, and compensated by using dangerous drugs and chemicals banned by the FDA to conceal or contain the contamination.

How did all this happen? Jeff Rosensweig, professor of finance and Director of the Global Perspective Program at Emory University's Goizueta Business School, was quoted in an October 2007 *Forbes* magazine as placing the blame on China's burgeoning growth. "The eagerness to industrialize has caused the Chinese economy to grow rapidly, and the U.S. demand for low-priced goods has given them a niche in the consumer export market," he opined. He also believed that much of the quality control issues could be attributed to a decentralized China, making it difficult to regulate. "Much of China's manufacturing action is local, making it subject to bribery and conflicting interests. But even as local manufacturers were forced to tighten regulations, other southeast Asian like Vietnam were ready to step in and take up the slack.

Also interviewed in the *Forbes* article was Professor Marshall Meyer of the University of Pennsylvania's Wharton Business School. He noted that as quality went up, so would the prices. He predicted that consumer interests would "self-regulate," in that consumer markets would improve quality more than regulation. As the price of Chinese goods was expected to increase in response to more manufacturing regulation and inspection, or, alternatively, Chinese products continued to fail to meet safety standards, consumers would move to other emerging markets.

In September 2007, the U.S. and Chinese Product Safety agencies announced an agreement to improve the quality and safety of imported consumer goods. Notwithstanding, more products were recalled after that date, most already having been in the stream of commerce. The U.S. Consumer Product Safety Commission CPSC) and the FDA are primarily responsible for inspecting, rejecting imports, and administering recalls. The FDA blamed shortages in trained inspectors and other staffing deficiencies, while the CPSC announced in January 2008 that it was implementing a new surveillance inspection program for imported goods.

REPARATION

Compensation for an injury; redress for a wrong inflicted.

Legislative Efforts Increase for Wrongful Convictions

In December 2007, the Wrongful Convictions Tax Relief Act of 2007, S.B. 2421, was introduced in Congress by Senators Charles E. Schumer (D-NY) and Sam Brownback (R-KS). The bill was intended to provide certain tax relief benefits to wrongfully convicted, i.e., exonerated prisoners who had no prior **felony** convictions, and was initiated following published news about the plight of exoneree David Pope, who was incarcerated 15 years for a rape he did not commit and cleared by DNA in 2001. Upon release from prison, Pope was awarded $385,000 by the State of Texas for the wrongful conviction and set about starting a new life. After receiving letters from the U.S. INTERNAL REVENUE SERVICE (IRS), he learned that he owed $90,000 in federal taxes on the **reparation** compensation he had received from the state. By that time, he had spent the money on life's necessities.

Despite such good-faith efforts from both federal and state legislators, there were problems. The IRS had not yet declared a formula to calculate how much of any monetary reparation award should be applied to lost income, and how much should (or could) be allocated to other compensatory factors, such as emotional pain and suffering (for having been wrongfully convicted), loss of liberty and freedom, etc. As a result in Pope's case, the IRS simply taxed a standard percentage on the total monetary award ($385,000) according to which income bracket Pope fell into, treating all of it as "income."

Wrongful conviction reparation is generally referred to as "restorative," i.e., it is intended to help restore a person to where he or she would have stood (financially) if not wrongfully convicted. Such compensation parallels remedies available for other legal wrongs. For example, **wrongful death** awards generally include an amount for lost income estimated over the remainder of a victim's actuarial lifetime.

What complicated the federal taxation on wrongful conviction compensation was that some state statutes expressly broke down their awards to designate a specific sum as lost income, while the majority simply awarded a flat or straight amount of monetary reparation for each year of imprisonment. To address this concern, the Schumer/Brownback bill contained provisions that exempted wrongfully convicted

persons from federal tax liability on the first $50,000 of annual income received, for 15 years or the number of years incarcerated, whichever was less. State statutes rarely addressed tax consequences, if at all.

Reparation statutes enacted by states generally began to appear only since the 1990s, when newer DNA technology increasingly contributed to overturned convictions. Still, as of March 2008, only 22 states, the federal government, and the DISTRICT OF COLUMBIA had statutes providing for compensation to wrongfully convicted persons. Only three states, California, Massachusetts, and Vermont, exempted compensation received from state taxes. Further, the individual state laws presented a wide range in available compensation.

California law, for example, awarded $26,500 for each year a person was wrongfully imprisoned, while Ohio awarded $40,330 for each such year, plus attorney's fees and lost wages. Hawaii, Michigan, and Vermont all paid a maximum of $50,000 for each year served, but $50,000 was the minimum per year in Alabama. Tennessee had a cap of $1 million, irrespective of the number of years served. In Missouri, compensation was individually tailored on a number of subjective factors at the discretion of the state. In Texas, Senator Rodney Ellis (D-Houston) introduced 2007 legislation to increase the amount currently under Texas **statute** to match that offered for federal inmates, $50,000 per year (increased to $100,000 per year for wrongfully convicted death row inmates). The bill passed in the Senate but never made it to the House before expiration of the term.

In almost all states with such statutes, the compensation was not automatic and wrongfully convicted persons were required to file a petition or complaint for reparation. Moreover, the majority required the complainant to satisfy certain prerequisites to obtain compensation. Some states offered reparation only for felony convictions, while others required either felony or **misdemeanor** convictions. Five state statutes explicitly mandated a pardon from the governor on the basis of innocence, while the other statutes contained prerequisites that required either a pardon or judicial relief vacating, reversing, or dismissing the conviction on grounds that the claimant did not commit the crime. Most also required the claimant to prove that his or her own conduct did not contribute to the conviction, and this fact needed to be proven by clear and convincing evidence. At least four state statutes and the District of Columbia did not compensate persons who entered a plea of guilty to the offense for which they were wrongfully imprisoned. Applicable statutes of limitations for asserting a claim for reparation generally ranged from none to five years, the majority falling within the range of two to three years.

Although an increasing number of states without statutes were considering such measures, legislators were cognizant that careful and thoughtful provisions needed to be drafted. With the prospect of ever-increasing numbers of overturned convictions based on newer DNA technology, exposure for states could be substantial.

RICO

Chicago Mobsters Convicted of Decades-Old Murders

Three reputed Chicago mobsters were convicted in September 2007 for their involvement in a series of murders, some of which dated back to the 1970s. The convictions were the result of a lengthy operation by federal authorities trying to resolve these murders. The men face life sentences for these convictions.

In April 2005, following a massive federal investigation of organized crime activities in Chicago, federal authorities charged 14 alleged members of the Chicago mob with a variety of unsolved crimes, including 18 murders and one attempted murder. The list included Joey "The Clown" Lombardo, who had the reputation as one of Chicago's top gangsters.

"This unprecedented indictment puts a 'hit' on the mob," said Patrick J. Fitzgerald, U.S. Attorney. "After so many years, it lifts the veil of secrecy and exposes the violent underworld of organized crime." The FEDERAL BUREAU OF INVESTIGATION (FBI) and INTERNAL REVENUE SERVICE (IRS) ran the investigation, which was dubbed "Operation Family Secrets" by the investigators. The mob family targeted in the case is known as "The Outfit."

Among the crimes allegedly committed by the Chicago mob was the killing of Tony Spilotro and his brother Michael. Tony Spilotro was the top mob man in Las Vegas at the time of his death. The brothers' bodies were found buried in a cornfield in Indiana eight days after they went missing in 1986. Tony Spilotro was portrayed by actor Joe Pesci in the movie "Casino" in 1995.

In July 2005, prosecutors announced that they had 28,000 taped conversations involving several of the defendants. The recording, which had been reduced to several CDs, contained

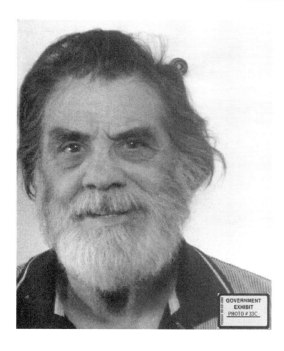

2006 photo of mobster Joseph "the Clown" Lombardo.
AP IMAGES

some 300,000 minutes of conversations. Most of these had been captured from a telephone wiretap during the prolonged investigation.

In November 2006, about seven months prior to trial, several of the defendants claimed that they were in bad health. At least two of the original fourteen defendants had died by that time, while the others complained of such ailments as back problems and bad teeth. One of the alleged crime bosses, Frank Calabrese, Sr., asked to be moved from the Metropolitan Correctional Center in downtown Chicago to another facility that would offer him more privacy while awaiting trial.

In January 2007, deputy U.S. marshal John Thomas Ambrose was charged with using his position to obtain information about Nicholas Calabrese, the brother of Frank Calabrese. Nicholas Calabrese was hidden as part of the U.S. Marshal's Witness Security Program and was a key witness for the prosecution. Ambrose allegedly passed on information about Calabrese to mob boss John "No Nose" DiFronzo in an effort by Ambrose to locate another defendant, Lombardo. After the indictments were sealed, Lombardo and alleged extortionist Frank "The German" Schweihs went missing, prompting a massive manhunt. Lombardo was later found when he set up a dentist appointment for a decaying tooth. Schweihs was found in the Kentucky hill country in December 2005.

The trial of the alleged mobsters began in June 2007. Facing trial in addition to Frank

Calabrese, Sr. and Lombardo were reported boss James Marcello and retired Chicago policeman Anthony Doyle. Doyle was alleged to have provided information about a prosecution witness to Calabrese. Others pleaded guilty to the charges, including Nicholas Calabrese, James Calabrese (brother of Nicholas and Frank Sr.), and Michael Marcello (brother of James Marcello). Schweihs was dropped from the trial for health reasons prior to the trial.

One of the more well-reported murders involved Tony Accardo, a powerful mob boss by the early 1970s. In 1977, some burglars decided to break into Accardo's home, which contained a vault in the basement. Accardo was less than amused, and members of The Outfit swiftly hunted down the burglars and killed each of them. Accardo died at the age of 86 in 1992.

Nicholas Calabrese served as one of the star witnesses in the case. In July, he testified about his murder of fellow hitman John Fecarotta. According to Calabrese, he took Fecarotta along on a mission under the guise that the two were going to bomb a dentist's office. Calabrese muffed the hit, and Fecarotta caught on that Calabrese was going to murder him. Calabrese accidentally shot himself during a scuffle between the two, and Fecarotta fled. Calabrese caught up and shot Fecarotta in the head. After the shooting, Calabrese dropped a pair of gloves he was wearing, and the gloves were later retrieved by police, who matched the blood with that of Calabrese. Another star witness was Frank Calabrese's son, Frank Jr. The son at one time wore a wiretap to help federal authorities collect evidence about the senior Calabrese. Frank Jr. testified about growing up in an organized crime household, including an incident where Frank Sr. told his son, "I'd rather have you dead than disobey me."

The trial consisted of two parts. The first part, which lasted from June until September, focused on racketeering charges. On September 11, 2007, a federal jury convicted Calebrese Sr., Lombardo, Marcello, and Schiro on the racketeering conspiracy charges. Doyle was also convicted on these charges, though he had not also been accused of murder. The racketeering charges alone could have led to life sentences for the defendants.

Less than three weeks after the initial verdicts were announced, the jury concluded that three of the defendants were guilty of 10 of the alleged murders. The three included Calabrese Sr., Marcello, and Lombardo. Schiro, best

known as a jewel thief, was acquitted on the murder charges.

Family members of several of the victims expressed relief about the verdicts. "Today was the anniversary of my dad's death so it was very sweet for us," said Joe Seifert, the son of businessman Daniel Seifert, who was gunned down just yards away from his wife and son in 1974. "It's a travesty I waited 26 years to hear this."

RIPARIAN RIGHTS

The rights, which belong to landowners through whose property a natural watercourse runs, to the benefit of such stream for all purposes to which it can be applied.

New Jersey v. Delaware

Rivers are often the dividing lines between nations and states. This is true in the United States, where legal disputes have arisen since the founding of the Republic over how much control a state has over a river that separates it from another state. Under the Constitution the U.S. SUPREME COURT has general, not **appellate** jurisdiction over federal lawsuits between the states. This means it serves as a trial court and must be the finder of fact. However, the Court always appoints a Special Master, who acts as the finder of fact and files a report with the Court as to these findings and to conclusions of law. Once the report is filed the Supreme Court reviews the report and the "exceptions" the states make to the report. Such was the case in *New Jersey v. Delaware*, ___ U.S. ___, 128 S. Ct. 1410, 170 L. Ed. 2d 315 (2008), where the Court reviewed the exceptions to the report the Special Master filed as to control of the Delaware River. The Court upheld the conclusions in the report and concluded that the boundary line fell in the state of Delaware's favor.

The controversy between the states over control of the Delaware reaches back to colonial times. The current controversy arose out of the planned construction in New Jersey of a large terminal to store and transport liquefied natural gas (LNG) that would extend some 2,000 feet into the Delaware River. The project would include a gasification plant, storage tanks, and other structures onshore in New Jersey. A pier and related structures would extend the 2,000 feet in the river and berth supertankers. Construction of the project would have required dredging over 1 million cubic yards of riverbed soil, which would have affected 29 acres of riverbed within Delaware's territory. In 2004,

British Petroleum, the operator of the proposed project, sought permission from Delaware's Department of Natural Resources and Environmental Control to construct the unloading terminal. The state refused, citing a state coastal **zoning** act that prohibits this type of offshore facility. Tempers flared on both sides of the Delaware River, with state officials threatening various actions and reprisals. In 2005 New Jersey decided to file the federal lawsuit that challenged Delaware's control of the river.

The Supreme Court, in a 5–3 decision (Justice STEPHEN BREYER did not participate), concluded that Delaware had title to part of the river where the terminal pier would have been located. Justice RUTH BADER GINSBURG, writing for the majority, noted that the two states had fought over control of the same portion of the river in a Supreme Court decision filed in 1934. In that case the Court had ruled that Delaware had title to "the river and the subaqueous soil" within a twelve-mile circle "up to the [low] mater mark on the easterly or New Jersey side." Ginsburg also looked to a 1905 Compact between the two states that dealt with the twelve-mile circle of water. The agreement permitted both states, on their own sides of the river, to exercise "riparian jurisdiction of every kind and nature." It also stated that nothing in the agreement affected the territorial limits, rights, or jurisdiction of either state concerning the Delaware river, or the soil underneath the river.

The Special Master's report contained a searching review of all prior legal disputes over the Delaware River. He concluded that Delaware had authority to regulate the proposed construction, concurrently with New Jersey, "to the extent that the project reached beyond New Jersey's border and extended into Delaware's territory. Justice Ginsburg and the majority accepted this recommendation and rejected New Jersey's exceptions to the report. The Court found that 1905 Compact did not grant New Jersey exclusive jurisdiction over all riparian improvements extending out-shore of the low-water mark. The Compact's use of the term "riparian jurisdiction" should be read as a limiting modifier and not as synonymous with "exclusive jurisdiction." In addition, a riparian dispute between Virginia and Maryland that the Court settled in 2004 did not support New Jersey's claim. That decision was based on a Maryland-Virginia boundary settlement that gave Virginia authority to build improvements on the shores of the Potomac River and to withdraw water from it. At the time of the 1905 Compact, when Delaware agreed to New Jersey's exercise of "riparian jurisdiction," the boundary was still disputed. The Compact did not recognize New Jersey's sovereign authority to the river. Finally, New Jersey accepted, until the present controversy, Delaware's claim to regulatory authority over "water and land within its domain to preserve the quality and prevent deterioration of the State's coastal areas."

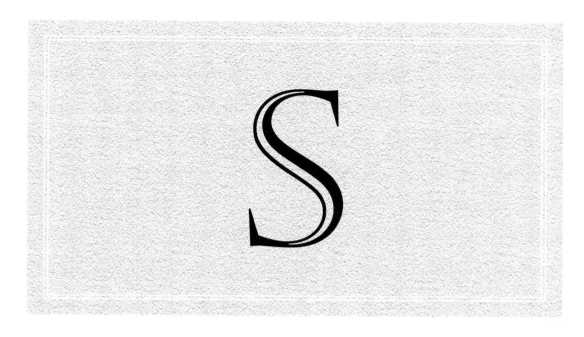

SECOND AMENDMENT

Virginia Tech Shootings Spur
Federal Gun Control Legislation

The debate in the United States over guns and gun control has gone on for decades. The periodic mass murder of individuals in public places by mentally ill persons wielding firearms typically reignites the debate. For the most part, however, horrific incidents have done little to change state and federal gun laws. An exception to this rule occurred following the shootings on the Virginia Tech University campus on April 16, 2007. Seung-Hui Cho, who killed 32 students and faculty at Virginia Tech before taking his own life, had been ordered to undergo outpatient mental health treatment and should have been prohibited from buying two guns he used in the killing spree. The state of Virginia never forwarded this information to the national background check system, allowing Cho to buy the weapons.

In 2005 a Virginia court found that Cho was mentally ill and a danger to himself. The court ordered him committed to a psychiatric facility. Federal law prohibits anyone who has been "adjudicated as a mental defective," as well as those who have been involuntarily committed to a mental health facility, from buying a gun. The state of Virginia did submit mental health records to the national background check system but its criteria were somewhat different than the federal government rules. Virginia reported only persons who were "involuntarily committed" or ruled mentally "incapacitated." Cho did not fit either of these categories, so his records were not entered into the national

database. Without this information, Cho appeared qualified to purchase the two firearms he used on April 16. A week after the killings, Virginia Governor Timothy Kaine, Democrat, signed an executive order that closed the reporting gap.

Some gun control advocacy groups, including the Brady Campaign to Prevent Gun Violence, and the NATIONAL RIFLE ASSOCIATION (NRA) supported the enactment of the first major piece of gun control legislation limiting the sale of assault weapons in 1994. The law was designed to improve the National Instant Criminal Background Check System (NICS), authorizing $250 million per year for the states to use to help pay the cost of providing the records to the national database. At the time of the Virginia Tech shootings, 17 states did not furnish mental health records to NCS. If states fail to act they may lose federal anti-crime funds.

The purpose of the NICS is to record the name of every criminal or person adjudicated as mentally ill, who are prohibited from possessing firearms. Firearms dealers must submit a customer's name to the system and receive approval before completing the purchase. The bases for these exclusions reach back to the assassinations of ROBERT F. KENNEDY and MARTIN LUTHER KING, JR, in 1968. Congress enacted a law that prohibits people from buying guns who have been convicted of a crime punishable by more than one year in prison, illegal drug users, those who have been adjudicated mentally disabled or mentally ill and illegal immigrants. Though some in Congress sought for several years to strengthen the NICS, which was created in 1998, there had no significant support.

Within weeks of the Virginia Tech shootings a bill was introduced by Rep. John Dingell, a Democrat from Michigan and an ardent supporter of gun rights, and Rep. Carolyn McCarthy, a Democrat from New York who is a strong gun-control advocate. (McCarthy ran for Congress after her husband was shot and killed by a crazed gunman on a Long island commuter train in 1993.)The NRA endorsed the general approach. Its executive vice president, Wayne LaPierre, did not believe the law amounted to gun control, stating that "We've always been vigilant about protecting the rights of law-abiding citizens to purchase guns, and equally vigilant about keeping the guns out of the hands of criminals and the mentally defective and people who shouldn't have them."

Though the Brady Campaign favored the bill, other gun-control groups expressed concerns about concessions the NRA obtained from legislators. The law automatically restores the gun-purchasing rights of veterans who were diagnosed with mental problems as part of the process of obtaining disability benefits. The NRA claimed that 80,000 veterans had been put into the NICS since the background check system had been created. Veterans may have their gun privileges restored if they can show they are not a threat to public safety or if they have received treatment and have recovered. In addition, the law established an appeals process for those who feel they have been wrongfully included in the system. The law also mandated that NICS funds are not used for other gun control purposes. Gun-control advocates unsuccessfully sought to include background checks for any gun sale, rather than just licensed dealers. The House of Representatives passed the bill on a voice vote, with only Rep. Ron Paul, Republican from Texas, speaking against it. In his view the law violated the Second Amendment's right to bear arms.

The bill was passed by the Senate in December 2007 and President GEORGE W. BUSH signed it into law on January 8, 2008.

District of Columbia v. Heller

In probably the most widely-anticipated decision of the 2007 term, the U.S. SUPREME COURT offered its first conclusive interpretation of the SECOND AMENDMENT with the Court's opinion in *District of Columbia v. Heller*, No. 07-290, 2008 WL 2520816 (June 26, 2008). The Court in a 5–4 decision affirmed a decision by the D.C. **Circuit Court** of Appeals to strike down a ban on handguns in the District of Columbia. Gun rights activists hailed the decision, while

critics argued that Justice ANTONIN SCALIA, who wrote the majority opinion, misread the words of the Amendment to reach the conclusion.

Concerned with widespread use of handguns in violent crimes, the District of Columbia in 1976 enacted a series of statutes that forbid or severely restricted the possession of firearms. Under these statutes, an applicant was required to register a handgun with the D.C. city police department, and in most instances, the registration was prohibited. The **statute** also generally prohibited a person from carrying a pistol without a license. For those with lawfully registered handguns, another statute required the owner to keep the firearm unloaded and disassembled or otherwise bound by a trigger lock.

The clear intention behind the statute was to decrease gun-related crime by limiting the number of guns on the street. However, data comparing the current crime rates with those in 1976 showed that the gun control law did not have the desired effect. One opponent of the gun control law noted that the homicide rate in the District of Columbia was 72 percent higher in 2001 than it was in 1976. On the other hand, at least one major public health study contradicted this result, concluding that the D.C. suicide and homicide rates dropped after the ban was adopted.

The Second Amendment provides, "A well-regulated Militia, being necessary to the security of a free state, the right of the people to keep and bear Arms, shall not be infringed." Historically, the Supreme Court focused its Second Amendment interpretation to allow states to maintain their own militias separate from federally-controlled militia. In *United States v. Cruikshank*, 92 U.S. 542, 23 L. Ed. 588 (1875), the Court declared that "the second amendment means no more than that [the right to bear arms] shall not be infringed by Congress, and has no other effect than to restrict the powers of the national government."

In more recent years, however, lower courts have reconsidered the scope of this right. Courts have provided extensive analysis of both the history and the text of the amendment to determine how this amendment should apply. For example, the Fifth Circuit Court of Appeals in *United States v. Emerson*, 270 F.3d 203 (5th Cir. 2001) determined that the right to bear arms was an individual right bestowed upon each citizen, rather than a collective right of the people through their states to maintain militias separate from the federal military. Other states and commentators have argued that the Founders only intended for the Second Amendment to apply to militias, since maintaining a state militia was a major issue at the time the Second Amendment was ratified.

Six residents of the District of Columbia challenged the law. Four of the plaintiffs wanted to have guns in their homes to provide self-defense. Another plaintiff wanted to keep a gun assembled in his home without a trigger lock. A final plaintiff, Dick Heller (the named plaintiff in the Supreme Court action), wanted to possess a gun both at home and in his position as a special police officer. The U.S. **District Court** for the District of Columbia ruled in 2004 that citizens do not have the right to challenge a law based on the Second Amendment. *Parker v. Dist. of Columbia*, 311 F. Supp. 2d 103 (D.D.C. 2004).

In 2007, the U.S. Court of Appeals for the District of Columbia sparked a major debate when it ruled that the D.C. restrictions on handguns violated the Second Amendment. In a lengthy opinion by Judge Laurence H. Silberman, the court ruled that the Second Amendment provided an individual right and that the D.C. statute violated this individual right. Silberman based his reasoning primarily on the text of the amendment itself. *Parker v. Dist. of Columbia*, 478 F.3d 370 (D.C. Cir. 2007).

The Supreme Court granted **certiorari** on November 20, 2007 to review the case. Nearly four dozen parties filed amicus briefs with the Court, arguing either in favor of gun rights or in favor of gun control laws. Justice ANTHONY KENNEDY asked a series of questions focused on the need to keep arms in a home for the purpose of self-protection. At one point in the discussion, Kennedy suggested that the amendment had in mind the right of the "remote settler to defend himself and his family against hostile Indian tribes and outlaws, wolves and bears and grizzlies. . . ." Other justices, including Justice STEPHEN BREYER, suggested that the ban on handguns might actually interfere with self-defense of a home, noting that the District of Columbia allows residents to keep rifles and shotguns in their homes for self-defense.

In a 5–4 decision, the Court affirmed the ruling of the D.C. Circuit. Justice Antonin Scalia's majority opinion focused heavily on the text of the amendment itself. Scalia wrote:

> The Second Amendment is naturally divided into two parts: its prefatory clause and its operative clause. The former does not limit the latter grammatically, but rather announces a purpose. The Amendment could be rephrased,

'Because a well regulated Militia is necessary to the security of a free State, the right of the people to keep and bear Arms shall not be infringed.' Although this structure of the Second Amendment is unique in our Constitution, other legal documents of the founding era, particularly individual-rights provisions of state constitutions, commonly included a prefatory statement of purpose.

Scalia noted that the Second Amendment is one of three places in the Bill of Rights where the phrase "the right of the people" is used. The two other instances include the Assembly-and-Petition Clause of the FIRST AMENDMENT and the Search-and-Seizure Clause of the FOURTH AMENDMENT. In each instance, Scalia noted, the phrase refers to an individual right, rather than a collective right. Moreover, Scalia noted that prior versions of the Second Amendment clearly referred to the right to bear arms as an individual right. Thus, the Court's first major conclusion was that the Second Amendment indeed provides individual, rather than collective, rights.

Based on this conclusion, the Court determined that the D.C. handgun ban and the trigger-lock requirement both violated the Second Amendment. The total handgun ban effectively prohibits an entire class of "arms" that citizens use for lawful self-defense, according to the Court. Moreover, the majority determined that the trigger-lock requirement makes it impossible for citizens to use guns for self-defense, thus rendering this restriction to be unconstitutional as well.

Dick Heller speaks to reporters outside U.S. Supreme Court, November 2007.
AP IMAGES

Justice JOHN PAUL STEVENS and Justice Stephen Breyer both dissented, and their dissents were joined by Justices DAVID SOUTER and RUTH BADER GINSBURG. Justice Stevens concluded that even though the Second Amendment protects individual rights, prior precedent establishes that the amendment "does not curtail the Legislature's power to regulate the non-military use and ownership of weapons. . . ." Justice Breyer agreed with Stevens, but also concluded that the Amendment's protections are not absolute and that the government may regulate the use of guns.

The Court's decision in *Heller* continued to spark controversy in the political arena after the opinion was announced. The NATIONAL RIFLE ASSOCIATION has viewed Democratic presidential candidate Barack Obama as a threat to gun-control rights and announced on July 1 that it would spend $15 million to portray Obama as a threat to the Court's decision in *Heller*. Other commentators have focused on the reality that half of the deaths in the U.S. that are attributed to guns are suicides.

SECURITIES

Evidence of a corporation's debts or property.

Supreme Court Dismisses Commodity Futures Case

The U.S. SUPREME COURT in December 2007 dismissed the case of *Klein & Co. Futures v. Board of Trade of NYC* (No. 06-1265) under Supreme Court Rule 46.1, which applies when the parties agree to a dismissal. The case, which had been argued before the Court in October 2007, involved the question of whether merchants could bring an action against a futures exchange under the Commodities Exchange Act (CEA), 7 U.S.C. § 25. The Second **Circuit Court** of Appeals concluded that a merchant could not bring such an action, and by dismissing the action, the Supreme Court allowed the Second Circuit's decision to stand.

The case of *Klein & Co. Futures v. Board of Trade of NYC* involved, in part, the different roles of various parties in commodities futures trading. A commodities futures market is one where customers buy and sell commodities that will be delivered or purchased at some time in the future. The commodities future itself is a contract to sell a particular commodity, such as corn, at a price established by the contract. Many of the customers who buy futures contracts do so with the anticipation that market prices will change so that the customers can then sell the contract to another purchaser for a profit.

Commodity futures contracts are sold at several commodity exchanges, which are governed by rules established by various boards of trade, such as the Board of Trade of the City of New York. Much of the actual trading at these exchanges is conducted by commodity futures merchants, who act as intermediaries for the customers who purchase the futures contracts.

Among the rules that the boards of trade must enact are those related to sales "on margin." Buying a futures contract on margin allows a customer to acquire a contract while only giving the merchant who makes the purchase a small percentage of the full cost. If the contract experiences fluctuation in value, the customer may be subject to a **margin call**, which requires the customer to pay the merchant more money to cover for the potential loss in value to the contract. The daily "settlement price," which is sometimes difficult to calculate, determines whether a customer must pay a margin call.

The boards are regulated under the CEA, which requires each board of trade to enact and enforce rules that govern the exchanges at those markets. Among other provisions, the CEA sets forth circumstances where a private litigant may bring a private **cause of action** for violating the CEA. The CEA specifically limits the types plaintiffs who may properly bring an action for violating the **statute**.

Norman Eisler was the Chairman of the New York Futures Exchange (NYFE). He was also a member of the NYFE's settlement committee for Pacific Stock Exchange Technology Index Futures Contract and Options. This committee's primary responsibility was to calculate the price of certain technology contracts for the purpose of calculating margin requirements for customer accounts, among other purposes. Eisler was moreover a customer of Klein & Co. Futures Inc., a merchant of commodity futures, and he was the principal of First West Trading Inc., which was also one of Klein's customers. Klein facilitated trading, along with other obligations, for customers that traded through the Board of Trade of the City of New York.

Acting as a member of the NYFE settlement committee, Eisler secretly manipulated the settlement prices for the technology contracts. While this manipulation benefited Eisler, it caused Klein to miscalculate the margin requirements. In March 2000, the Board of Trade began to receive complaints about irregularities in the settlement prices, but the board failed to make inquiries or place any of the parties on notice that there were any irregularities. During May 2000, Klein computed the margin for the First West account, but Klein based its computations on the incorrect settlement prices that Eisler had provided. After making this computation, Klein informed the Board of Trade that Eisler was unable to meet the margin call, along with other concerns. Klein reported then that if Eisler could not cover the margin deficit, it would impair Klein's net capital.

Klein and the Board of Trade soon discovered the extent of the problem. Eisler was removed from the NYFE settlement committee, and his membership privileges with the Board of Trade were suspended. The remaining settlement committee members recalculated the deficit and determined that First West's margin deficit had escalated to $4.5 million. First West could not meet this obligation, and after Klein took an immediate charge on its net capital to cover the difference, Klein soon collapsed.

Klein brought suit under the CEA against Board of Trade of the City of New York in the U.S. **District Court** for the Southern District of New York. Klein argued that the Board failed to enforce its own rules and that it violated antifraud provisions in the CEA. The Board of Trade responded by arguing that because Klein was not a purchaser or a seller of the futures, the company was not entitled to bring suit. The district court agreed, holding that because First West and not Klein owned the futures contracts, Klein was not entitled under CEA to bring suit. *Klein & Co. Futures v. Bd. of Trade*, NO. 00-CV-5563-GBD, 2005 WL 427713 (S.D.N.Y. Feb. 18, 2005). On appeal, the Second Circuit Court of Appeals agreed, noting that the CEA limits claims by private plaintiffs to those plaintiffs who actually traded in the commodities market. Since Klein was only a merchant that acted as an intermediary in the trading, the court agreed with the district court and held that Klein did not have standing to bring suit. *Klein & Co. Futures, Inc. v. Bd. of Trade*, 464 F.3d 255 (2d Cir. 2006).

The Supreme Court granted **certiorari** on May 17, 2007 and heard oral arguments in the case on October 29. Two months later, on December 28, the Court granted a dismissal of the case under Rule 46, which typically applies when the parties agree to drop an appeal so that the parties can settle the dispute out of court.

Stoneridge Investment Partners LLC v. Scientific-Atlanta, Inc.

Federal securities laws give the Security and Exchange Commission)SEC) the power to investigate and prosecute individuals and companies for misleading investors. In addition, the Supreme Court established a private **right of action** for individuals to sue companies for the financial losses that resulted from the distribution of misleading and **fraudulent** information about a company's financial health. In *Stoneridge Investment Partners LLC v. Scientific-Atlanta, Inc.*, __U.S.__, 128 S. Ct. 761, 169 L. Ed. 2d 627 (2008), investors in a cable company attempted to use this private right of action to sue the companies that helped the cable company manipulate its **balance sheet** to make it look more profitable that it was in fact. The Court, however, drew a line and found that this right to sue cannot be extended to corporate vendors and customers.

A **class action** lawsuit was filed by investors against Charter Communications, Inc. in Missouri federal **district court**, alleging that the cable company had illegally manipulated its quarterly financial statements to show Wall Street it would meet the market's expectations for cable subscriber growth and operating cash flow. Stonebridge Investment Partners, the lead plaintiff, also sued Charter's accounting firm and two manufacturers of digital cable converter boxes, Scientific-Atlanta and Motorola. The manufacturers were brought into the suit because of an alleged scheme in late 2000, when Charter executives realized that the company would miss projected operating cash flow numbers by $15 to $20 million. To help meet the shortfall, Charter arranged to overpay the two cable box companies $20 for each box it purchased until the end of the year. It was understood that the companies would return the overpayment by buying advertising from Charter.

The plaintiffs claimed this had no economic merit and was a way to record the advertising as revenue and **capitalize** its purchase of boxes; both actions violated generally accepted accounting principles. By doing so Charter tricked its auditor into approving a **financial statement** that showed the company had met its projected revenue and operating cash flow numbers. The cable-box manufacturers participated in the plan and drafted documents to make it appear the transactions were unrelated and made in the ordinary course of business and backdated other documents. The plaintiffs contended that Charter and the manufacturers were liable for damages, as they violated § 10(b) of the Securities Act of 1943 and SEC Rule 10-b5. The district court dismissed the two manufacturers from the lawsuit and the Eighth **Circuit Court** of Appeals affirmed the ruling. The appeals court noted that to violate § 10(b) a party must make misstatements that were relied upon by the public. In this case the cable-box companies had indeed aided and **abetted** Charter's fraudulent actions but there was no private right of action for aiding and **abetting** a § 10(b) violation. Because other circuit courts of appeals had permitted investors to sue aiders and abettors of stock **fraud**, the Supreme Court agreed to resolve the conflict.

The Court upheld the Eighth Circuit ruling in a 5–3 decision. (Justice STEPHEN BREYER did not participate in the case.) Justice ANTHONY KENNEDY, writing for the majority, noted a 1994 Supreme Court decision in which the Court ruled that the plaintiffs could not use § 10(b) to sue aiders and abettors. Though that case led to calls for amending the law to establish private claims against those aiding and abetting stock fraud, Congress declined to follow this course. Instead, in the Private Securities Litigation Reform Act of 1995 (PSLRA), 15 U.S.C. § 78t(e), it directed prosecution of aiders and abettors by the SEC. Therefore, for a plaintiff to prevail against a secondary actor, it must be shown that this actor met each element of the preconditions for liability under § 10(b).

Justice Kenney concluded that the plaintiffs could not show that the companies' "acts or statements" were relied upon by the investors in Charter stock. Reliance is an "essential element" of a § 10(b) private right of action yet the plaintiffs could not show that the companies had a duty to disclose their transactions with Charter. These deceptive acts were not communicated to the public, so no investor had either presumed or actual knowledge of these acts. Without knowledge there could be no reliance. The Court, though it had created a private right of action against primary actors, was reluctant to extend it to aiders and abettors. The practical consequences of an extension could allow plaintiffs with weak cases to "extort settlements from innocent companies," so those companies could avoid costly litigation. In addition, an expansion could lead to increased costs of **doing business** and to overseas firms "with no other exposure to our securities laws" declining to do business in the United States. The fact that Congress, in the PSLRA, gave the SEC the power to prosecute secondary actors, was a significant development.

The SEC has used this authority to good effect, collecting over $10 billion for distribution to injured investors.

SENTENCING

The postconviction stage of the criminal justice process, in which the defendant is brought before the court for the imposition of a penalty.

Begay v. U.S.

The U.S. SUPREME COURT in 2008 ruled that a charge for drunk driving did not constitute a "violent felony" that would impose a mandatory 15-year sentence under the Armed Career Criminal Act. As a result of this ruling, the Court ordered the reduction of the sentence of a man convicted of possessing and threatening his sister with a rifle.

Under federal law, a previously convicted felon may not possess a firearm. An ordinary offense provides a penalty of 10 years in prison under 18 U.S.C. § 922(g)(1). However, the Armed Career Criminal Act (ACCA), 18 U.S.C. § 924 provides for a heightened mandatory minimum sentence of 15 years where the offender has had three prior convictions "for a violent **felony** or a serious drug offense." Under the ACCA, a violent felony is defined as:

> any crime punishable by imprisonment for a term exceeding one year, or any act of juvenile delinquency involving the use or carrying of a firearm, knife, or destructive device that would be punishable by imprisonment for such term if committed by an adult, that—(i) has an element that the use, attempted use, or threatened use of physical force against the person of another; or (ii) is **burglary**, arson, or extortion, involves the use of explosives, or otherwise involves conduct that presents a serious potential risk of physical injury to another.

Larry Begay had been convicted in the past of 12 charges of driving while intoxicated (**DWI**) in New Mexico. In September 2004, Begay threatened to shoot his sister with a .22 caliber rifle if she would not give him money. After she told him she did not have any money, he repeatedly pulled the trigger of the unloaded weapon, though the gun obviously did not fire. His sister later called the Navajo Department of Law Enforcement while Begay was asleep. When the officers arrived, they found the rifle underneath his bed.

Begay pleaded guilty to being a felon in possession of a firearm after the state prosecuted him under the ACCA. Of his 12 convictions for DWI, three were considered felonies under New Mexico law. At sentencing, the U.S. **District Court** for the District of New Mexico determined that each of the three felonies for DWI constituted a "violent felony" under 18 U.S.C. § 922(g)(1). When taking into account Begay's acceptance of responsibility for his actions, the court determined that Begay's sentence should fall within a range of 188 to 235 months.

At the district court, Begay's counsel argued that he had been plagued by alcoholism "for the better part of his life" and stressed that Begay's only convictions were for drinking and driving. Begay's counsel also noted that Begay's father and brother had died in a car accident and that Begay had assumed responsibility as caretaker for his family. Begay argued that based on these factors, a sentence of 188 months was unreasonable. The trial judge, however, disagreed and sentenced him to 188 months.

Began appealed his sentence to the Tenth **Circuit Court** of Appeals. He argued there that a DWI is not considered to be a violent felony under the ACCA. The focus of Begay's argument was on the phrase "otherwise involves conduct that presents a serious potential risk of physical injury to another." According to Begay, the court should read that clause to include only those crimes similar to the others listed in the **statute**, including burglary, arson, extortion, or crimes that involve the use of explosives.

In a 2–1 decision, the court rejected Begay's argument and affirmed his sentence. The court concluded that Congress likely intended to include felony charges for drunk driving among the type of offenses covered by the statute. According to the court, "both the natural meaning of the **statutory** language and the apparent statutory purpose support a construction of the term *violent felony* to include felony DWI. Neither the legislative history nor **canons of construction** persuade otherwise." *United States v. Begay*, 470 F.3d 964 (10th Cir. 2006).

Circuit judge Michael McConnell dissented. He noted that the language of the statute did not have a plain meaning that could support only one conclusion. He determined that the offense covered in § 924 should only apply to offenses similar to those listed and that drunk driving was not a crime similar to those listed. Accordingly, he believed that a sentencing range of 41 to 51 months would have been appropriate.

The Supreme Court granted **certiorari** to review the case. Most of the arguments leading up the Court's decision focused on the appropriate tools of statutory construction that the Court should use to interpret the statute. The principle of *ejusdem generis* ("of the same kind") is a canon of statutory construction that applies when a statute lists two or more specific terms followed by a **general term**. Under the canon, the meaning of the general term is limited to the same class of items as the specific terms. Begay argued, as he did at the lower courts, that reading the statute in light of this principle would eliminate a DWI charge as a violent felony.

In an opinion by Justice STEPHEN BREYER, the Court agreed with Begay. The Court agreed with Judge McConnell that the crimes listed in the statute involve purposeful, violent, and aggressive conduct. "By way of contrast," Breyer wrote, "statutes that forbid driving under the influence, such as the statute before us, typically do not insist on purposeful, violent or aggressive conduct; rather, they are, or are more nearly comparable to, crimes that impose **strict liability**, criminalizing conduct in respect to which the offender need not have any criminal intent at all." After concluding that the Begay's crime did not amount to a violent felony, the Court reversed the lower court's ruling. *Begay v. United States*, 128 S. Ct. 1581 (2008).

Justice SAMUEL ALITO dissented. He noted that drunk driving causes about 15,000 alcohol-related crashes each year and that roughly 250,000 people are injured annually in alcohol-related incidents. In this case, a drunk driving charge in New Mexico is ordinarily a **misdemeanor**, but because of Begay's repeat offenses, the later incidents were elevated to felonies. Given these circumstances, Alito argued that his offenses should be considered violent felonies under the statute.

Crack Cocaine Sentencing Disparities Addressed

For 20 years the U.S. Sentencing Guidelines Commission has wrestled with the appropriate amount of prison time for individuals convicted of distributing and selling crack cocaine. Under the guidelines that were established in 1988, a crack cocaine dealer convicted of selling five grams of crack received a mandatory minimum sentence of five years in prison. In contrast, a dealer convicted of selling powder cocaine would have had to sell 500 grams of powder to receive the same five-year sentence. This sentencing disparity grew out of fears by Congress that the effects of crack cocaine were

U.S. Sentencing
Commission
Chairman Judge
Ricardo Hinojosa,
December 2007.

AP IMAGES

much worse than powder cocaine. The disparity was attacked from the beginning as being racially discriminatory, as most crack cocaine dealers were African American, while most powder cocaine dealers were white. Despite several efforts by the commission to address the issue, it was not until 2007 that it modified the guidelines and cut short the sentences of inmates convicted of dealing in crack cocaine. In addition, the Supreme Court addressed the issue in 2007, ruling that federal **district court** judges were entitled to find disparate crack cocaine sentences unreasonable.

When Congress created the Sentencing Guidelines Commission in 1984 it sought to reduce the discretion of federal judges when sentencing defendants. The commission was charged with developing point schemes based on the crime committed and the criminal history of the defendants. Judges were directed to impose mandatory minimum sentences. Judges could impose harsher sentences with little trouble but "downward departures" were discouraged. Crack cocaine and sentencing guidelines intersected for the first time in 1986, when Congress mandated that one gram of crack is equivalent to one hundred grams of powder cocaine. Congress justified tougher penalties on the general ground that physical and societal effects of crack were much worse than powder cocaine. The 100-to-1 formula was embodied in the 1998 cocaine guidelines, which led to lengthier prison sentences for low-level crack dealers than for powder cocaine wholesalers. Moreover, most of the states adopted sentencing guidelines and followed the federal guidelines on crack cocaine. Though racial disparities in cocaine sentencing

soon became apparent, most courts rejected claims by defendants that the guidelines violated the **Equal Protection** Clause.

By the mid-1990s, the commission attempted to reduce the disparity in sentencing. However, the commission's proposals, which included appeals to Congress to modify the formula, went nowhere. In 2005 the guidelines as a whole took a considerable blow when the Supreme Court, in *United States v. Booker*, 543 U.S. 220, 125 S.Ct. 738, 160 L.Ed.2d 621 (2005), ruled that the guidelines were not mandatory. Federal judges were to use them as advisory materials, with appeals courts judging sentences on a case-by-case basis using a "reasonableness" standard. Judges began to impose lighter sentences on crack cocaine dealers, which triggered appeals by prosecutors.

In April 2007 the commission modified the guidelines, reducing the sentence range for first-time offenders possessing 5 grams or more of crack cocaine to 51 to 63 months. The old range was 63 to 78 months. The new range for first-time offenders possessing at least 50 grams is 97 to 121 months in prison, decreasing from 121 to 151 months. A commission analysis estimated that changing the crack guidelines would reduce the size of the federal prison population by 3,800 in 15 years. The commission also asked Congress to **repeal** the mandatory prison term for simple possession and increase the amount of crack cocaine required to trigger 5-year and 10-year mandatory minimum prison terms. The commission argued that this was a way to focus on major drug traffickers. In November 2007 the commission applied the lower penalties retroactively to 19,500 crack cocaine offenders who were sentenced before the change. It was expected that up to 3,800 prisoners would be released from federal prisons by early 2008.

Less than a month later the the Supreme Court, in *Kimbrough v. United States*, ＿U.S.＿, 128 S.Ct. 558, 169 L.Ed.2d 481 (2007), upheld a lower court's decision not to impose the 100-to-1 crack cocaine sentence, which was now merely advisory. The Court found that because the 100-to-1 ratio was not mandatory, courts were free to consider, on a case-by-case basis, whether the disparity was unreasonable. In this case the district court judge made a considered review of all factors and the final result was "reasonable" under *Booker*.

Gall v. United States

In the wake of *United States v. Booker*, 543 U.S. 220, 125 S. Ct. 738, 160 L. Ed. 2d 621

(2005), in which the Supreme Court ruled that the U.S. Sentencing Guidelines are advisory rather than mandatory, the **federal courts** have wrestled with the standards that **appellate** courts must use in reviewing whether a sentence is reasonable. In the 2006 term the Court ruled that a sentence within the range recommended by the guidelines should be presumed by the court of appeals to be reasonable. A second case from the 2006 term was to address sentences that are below those recommended by the guidelines but the defendant died before the Court could consider the arguments. The Court deemed it important that this issue be addressed as soon as possible and selected another case with similar issues. In *Gall v. United States*, __U.S.__, 128 S.Ct. 586, 169 L.Ed.2d 445 (2007), the Supreme Court ruled that an appeals court cannot require "extraordinary circumstances" to justify a sentence outside the guidelines range. Most importantly, circuit courts of appeals must apply the **abuse of discretion** standard of review when examining sentences, regardless of whether the sentence is inside or outside the guidelines range.

In early 2000, Brian Gall, a second-year college student, was invited to join a group of fellow students that was distributing the controlled substances popularly known as "ecstasy." Gall, who used ecstasy, marijuana, and cocaine, accepted the invitation and, for the next seven months, delivered ecstasy pills to other members of the drug ring. In that seven months Gall made more than $30,000. At the end of the seventh month period he withdrew from the conspiracy and never sold illegal drugs again. He graduated from college in 2002 and moved to Arizona. He later moved to Colorado, where he worked as a master carpenter. While in Arizona, federal law enforcement officers questioned him about his involvement in the Iowa ecstasy ring. He admitted his participation and no further action was taken at that time. However, in 2004 he was indicted with the other seven members of the Iowa conspiracy with conspiring to sell illegal narcotics.

Gall moved back to Iowa, surrendered to authorities, and while free on his own **recognizance** started a business as a window installer that netted him over $2,000 per month. He entered into a plea agreement stating that he distributed at least 2,500 grams of ecstasy and at least 87.5 kilograms of marijuana. The probation officer recommended that Gall be sentenced to a prison, with a range of 30 to 37 months. Gall, with letters of support from family, friends, neighbors and business associates, sought probation. The prose-

cutor sought a prison term as recommended by the probation officer but the judge sentenced Gall to 36 months probation. The judge made a detailed sentencing memorandum explaining his decision. The fact that Gall had withdrawn from the conspiracy, stopped using drugs, graduated from college, had no other criminal history, and had started his own business justified probation. Any term of imprisonment "would be counter effective by depriving society of the contributions" of Gall.

The prosecutor appealed the sentence and the Eighth **Circuit Court** of Appeals vacated it, ruling that a sentence outside the sentencing guidelines range must be supported by a reason that is "proportional to the extent of the difference between the advisory range and the sentence imposed. The appeals court found the departure from the guidelines "extraordinary" because it amounted to a "100 percent downward variance. Such a variance must be supported by "extraordinary circumstances." The court then reviewed the justifications offered by the **district court** and attempted to quantify the value of them. It concluded that the sentence was not supported by the facts. Gall then appealed to the Supreme Court.

The Court, in a 7–2 decision, overturned the Eighth Circuit decision. Justice JOHN PAUL STEVENS, writing for the majority, noted that under the *Booker* ruling, a sentence outside the guidelines range must be evaluated in terms of reasonableness. Contrary to the Eighth Circuit, there is no appellate rule that requires extraordinary circumstances to justify a sentence outside the guidelines range. Stevens also rejected the use of a "rigid mathematical formula that uses the percentage of a departure as the standard for determining the strength of justifications required for a specific sentence." Instead, a judge must make an individualized assessment based on the facts presented and, in the case of a major departure, must provide a significant justification.

More importantly, the Court announced that appellate review of sentences must use the abuse of discretion standard of review. This restricts the ability of an **appellate court** from reviewing the facts anew and rendering a judgment. Instead, the appellate court can only overturn a decision if the district court committed a significant procedural error or if it made an unreasonable substantive conclusion that was unreasonable. If the sentence is within the guidelines range the appellate court may, but is not require to, apply a presumption of reasonableness. If the sentence is outside the guidelines range the court "may not apply a presumption of unreasonableness." It may consider the extent of the deviation but it must "give due deference to the district court's decision" that the factors, on the whole, justify the extent of the variance. An appellate court might well reasonably conclude that a different sentence was appropriate but that "is insufficient to justify reversal of the district court."

Kimbrough v. United States

The U. S. Supreme Court's landmark 2005 decision that turned the U.S. Sentencing Guidelines from a mandatory to an advisory document for federal **district court** judges has bred more litigation as judges have begun to use their discretion in shaping criminal sentences. The sentencing guidelines for crack cocaine have been a particularly contentious scheme, as the penalties for selling crack cocaine are much more severe than for selling powder cocaine. Under the 1986 crack cocaine criminal **statute**, a drug trafficker dealing in crack cocaine is subject to the same sentence as a trafficker dealing in 100 times more powder cocaine. The Sentencing Guidelines Commission adopted the same 100-to-1 ratio. Over the years criticism has mounted over the disparity between crack and powder cocaine sentences; the fact that the 85 percent of convicted crack cocaine dealers are black has raised the issue of race. Beginning in the 1990s the commission itself expressed misgivings at the crack cocaine sentencing scheme but it continued to enforce the 100-to-1 ratio. Once the guidelines became advisory, district court judges began addressing this issue at sentencing, reducing the amount of prison time for crack dealers. The Supreme Court, in *Kimbrough v. United States*, __U.S.__, 128 S. Ct. 558, 169 L. Ed. 2d 481 (2007), addressed how far courts could go in deviating from the crack cocaine guidelines in fashioning a sentence. The Court concluded that a district court was free to deviate from the 100-to-1 ratio when the disparity between crack cocaine and powder cocaine yields a sentence greater than necessary.

In 2004, Derrick Kimbrough was charged with three crack cocaine offenses and a firearms charge in Virginia federal district court. He pleaded guilty to all four charges. His plea subjected him to an aggregate 15 years to life in prison: 10 years to life for the drug offenses and a consecutive five years to life for the firearm offense. The district court used the now-advisory Sentencing Guidelines to calculate Kimbrough's sentence. He had possessed 56 grams of crack cocaine and 92 grams of powder cocaine. These amounts, along with Kim-brough's false testimony that no one else was involved in the criminal enterprise and the gun offense, yielded a guidelines range of 19 to 22.5 years imprisonment. The judge concluded that a sentence in this range would have been "greater than necessary" to accomplish the purposes of sentencing. The judge highlighted the disparity between crack and powder cocaine sentencing guidelines, noting that if Kimbrough had sold only powder cocaine his sentencing range would have declined of eight to nine years imprisonment, including the gun charge. Therefore, the judge sentenced Kimbrough to 15 years in prison, the **statutory** minimum sentence, and five years of supervised release. The Fourth **Circuit Court** of Appeals vacated the sentence, ruling that a sentence "outside the guidelines is per se unreasonable when it is based on a disagreement with the sentencing disparity for crack and powder cocaine offenses." The Supreme Court accepted Kimbrough's appeal to determine whether the crack/powder disparity adopted in the sentencing guidelines "has been rendered 'advisory' by" its 2005 decision making the guidelines as a whole advisory.

In a 7–2 decision the Court concluded that the crack/powder disparity was advisory and that the Fourth Circuit was in error to rule that a departure from the ratio was per se unreasonable. Justice RUTH BADER GINSBURG, writing for the majority, noted that in its 2005 decision, *United States v. Booker*, 543 U.S. 220, 125 S.Ct. 738, 160 L.Ed.2d 621 (2005), the Court instructed district courts to read the sentencing guidelines as "effectively advisory." The guidelines now served as one factor among several that courts must consider in determining an appropriate sentence. The *Booker* decision also instructed the courts that "reasonableness" is the standard controlling **appellate** review of district court sentences. Seen in this light, a judge may consider the disparity between crack and powder cocaine sentencing formulas.

Justice Ginsburg reviewed the history of crack cocaine sentencing that began in 1986. She noted that the 1986 crack cocaine criminal statute was enacted at a time when public opinion viewed this new drug as a "problem of overwhelming dimensions." Congress justified tougher penalties on the general ground that physical and societal effects of crack were much worse than powder cocaine. The Sentencing Guidelines Commission applied the 100-to-1 ratio as embodied by statute, but within 5 years the commission began to have second thoughts about this disparity. It was concerned because:

(1) studies had shown no support for the conclusion that crack was more harmful than powder cocaine; (2) retail crack dealers got longer sentences than the wholesale distributors of powder cocaine; and (3) the disparity fostered disrespect for and lack of confidence in the criminal justice system. Though the commission produced reports in 1997 and 2002 recommending that Congress lower the ratio, neither proposal was adopted. In 2007 the commission again asked Congress to lower the ratio but this time made an ameliorating change by reducing the base offense level for crack and powder cocaine offenses by two levels. This amendment produced sentences for crack cocaine between two and five times longer than sentences for equal amounts of powder cocaine.

The government, while acknowledging that the guidelines are now advisory in nature, contended that this was irrelevant. The 1986 act prohibited the commission or sentencing courts from departing from the 100-to-1 ratio. Any other deviation would be "logically incoherent." Justice Ginsburg rejected this argument, pointing out that it lacked grounding in the text of the law. The act only mandated minimum and maximum sentences. If Congress had wanted to impose the ratio it knew how to "direct sentencing practices in express terms." The government also contended that Congress' rejection of the commission's repeated recommendations to alter the ratio made clear that Congress believed the ratio was mandated by statute. Justice Ginsburg found no merit in this line of attack, as Congress only disapproved of a proposed 1 to 1 ratio. It did not explicitly state that the ratio must be 100 to 1. Because the 100 to 1 ratio is not mandatory, courts are free to consider, on a case-by-case basis, whether the disparity is unreasonable. In this case the district court judge made a considered review of all factors and the final result was "reasonable" under *Booker*.

Justices CLARENCE THOMAS and SAMUEL ALITO filed dissenting opinions, arguing that sentencing courts will return to the unbridled discretion that routinely produced sentencing disparities and that led to the movement for mandatory sentencing guidelines.

Logan v. United States

Federally mandated minimum sentences commenced in the 1980s and continue to the present. As a result, convicted felons have begun to concentrate legal efforts less on contesting guilt than on finding ways to avoid qualifying for a mandatory sentence. For example, the Armed Career Criminal Act of 1984 (ACCA), 18 U.S.C.

§ 924(e)(1), imposes a minimum 15-year prison term if the offender's prior criminal record includes at least three convictions for "violent felonies" or "serious drug offenses." For ACCA sentence-enhancement purposes, however, a prior conviction may be disregarded if the conviction "has been expunged, or set aside," or if the offender "has been pardoned or has had civil rights restored." Though this language seems unambiguous, the federal circuit courts of appeals have been divided over whether the phrase "civil rights restored" applied to convictions where the offender retained his civil rights at all times. If this phrase did apply to such convictions, offenders might be able to avoid having the convictions counted toward the ACCA mandatory minimum sentence. The U.S. SUPREME COURT, in *Logan v. United States*, __U.S.__, 128 S.Ct. 475, 169 L.Ed.2d 432 (2007), put an end to the conflict, finding that violent **misdemeanor** convictions, where the offender did not lose his civil rights, did not qualify under the "civil rights restored" exemption.

In 2005, James Logan had a domestic disturbance with his girlfriend, who filed a complaint against him. She told police that Logan kept a gun in his car. Logan agreed to a search of his car. Police found a 9-millimeter handgun in a hidden compartment behind the glove box. Logan pleaded guilty to the federal offense of possession of a firearm after having been convicted of a **felony**, as he had a 1991 Illinois drug offense conviction. At sentencing, the federal **district court** applied the ACCA minimum mandatory sentence when they imposed a 15-year prison term on Logan. The court took account of three Wisconsin misdemeanor **battery** convictions, each punishable by a maximum sentence of three years' imprisonment. Logan objected to the sentence, contending that the three Wisconsin convictions did not qualify as ACCA offenses because they caused no loss of his civil rights. In his view, rights retained were functionally equivalent to rights revoked but later restored. If the convictions did not qualify Logan would have been sentenced to a 10-year prison term. The district court rejected this argument, concluding that the ACCA exemption applied only to "defendants whose civil rights were both lost and restored pursuant to state statutes." The Seventh **Circuit Court** of Appeals affirmed this decision, finding that Logan's argument went "into the teeth" of the text of the ACCA. Because other circuit courts of appeals had adopted Logan's argument the Supreme Court agreed to hear the case to resolve the conflict.

The Supreme Court, in a unanimous decision, upheld the Seventh Circuit's reading of the ACCA exemption. Justice RUTH BADER GINSBURG, writing for the Court, acknowledged that Logan's three convictions did not result in his losing his civil rights, which include his right to vote, to serve on juries, and to hold public office. However, the ordinary meaning of the word "restored" did not help Logan, as the word means "to give back something that has been taken away." The context in which "restored" appeared in the ACCA provision counseled "adherence to the word's ordinary meaning," noting that words "in a list are generally known by the company they keep." The words "civil rights restored" appeared in a list of words that included "expunged," "set aside," and "pardoned." These terms each described ways in which the government "relieves an offender of some or all of the consequences of his conviction." This was in contrast to a defendant who retains his rights and is "simply left alone." In this situation the defendant does not receive a "status-altering dispensation" or a "token of forgiveness from the government."

In Justice Ginsburg's view there was no merit in looking beyond the plain meaning of the words Congress enacted. Logan relied on one major argument to overcome plain meaning: a literal reading of the provision could yield harsh results. Unless the retention of rights was treated as legally equivalent to restoration of rights, less serious offenders would be subject to ACCA's enhanced penalties, while more serious offenders in the same state, who have had their civil rights restored, might evade punishment. Justice Ginsburg rejected this argument because Logan's theory would "correct one potential anomaly, while creating others." For example, the most dangerous recidivist in a state that does not revoke any offender's civil rights could then qualify for the civil rights exemption. She pointed out that Maine does not deprive any offenders of their civil rights, so Logan's argument would allow a first-degree murder conviction to be exempted from a count of convictions. It was clear that Congress meant to cover the types of misdemeanors that Logan had been convicted under; a retention-of-rights exemption would defeat the intent of Congress.

U.S. v. Rodriquez

The Armed Career Criminal Act of 1984 (ACCA), 18 U.S.C. § 924(e)(1), imposes a minimum 15-year prison term if the offender's prior criminal record includes at least three convictions for "violent felonies" or "serious drug offenses." ACCA has generated numerous appeals concerning the scope of its application. For the second time in the 2007 term, the Supreme Court issued a decision clarifying an ACCA provision. In *U.S. v. Rodriquez*, ___U.S.___, 128 S. Ct. 1783, 170 L. Ed. 2d 719 (2008), the Court analyzed the meaning of the phrase "serious drug offense." The **statute** stated that a state drug-trafficking conviction will count as a "serious drug offense" if "a maximum term of imprisonment of ten years or more is prescribed by law" for the "offense." In this case the defendant was convicted of three drug offenses at one trial. Each offense occurred on a separate date. The state court sentenced the defendant to five years in prison for the first offense and imposed a maximum sentence of ten years for the other two offenses based on a state law that doubled the time served in prison for repeated convictions. This recidivist provision triggered the legal controversy. Were the two ten-year terms sufficient, in concert with a previous **burglary** conviction, to trigger ACCA's 15-year prison term when the defendant was convicted of another **felony**? The Supreme Court found that the enhanced prison terms were sufficient for ACCA purposes.

Gino Rodriquez, a felon, was convicted in federal court in the state of Washington for possessing a firearm. He had two prior convictions for burglary in California and three state convictions in Washington for delivering a controlled substance. The convictions were handed down on the same day but the drug deliveries took place on three separate dates. Though the base sentence for the drug offense was not more than five years in prison, another state law held that a person convicted of a second or subsequent offense could be imprisoned for a term up to twice the term otherwise authorized. Therefore, Rodriquez faced 10-year prison terms for the second and third drug convictions. The trial court's judgments of conviction for the second and third offenses listed the maximum term of imprisonment as ten years but sentenced Rodriquez to 48 months in prison on each count.

The federal prosecutor in Rodriquez's firearm possession conviction asked the federal **district court** to impose ACCA's 15-year minimum prison sentence on Rodriquez, arguing that the burglary convictions, coupled with the two 10-year prison terms for drug distribution, satisfied the ACCA requirements. The court agreed that the burglary convictions were violent felonies but rejected the contention that two 10-year sentences for drug offenses meant they qualified as "serious drug offenses." On the contrary, the drug offenses had a "maximum term of imprisonment" of five years for ACCA purposes. The recidivist enhancement statute's doubling of the terms of imprisonment would not be counted. The government appealed and the Ninth **Circuit Court** of Appeals upheld the trial court's interpretation of ACCA's "maximum term of imprisonment" provision. The Supreme Court accepted review because other circuit courts of appeals interpreted this provision to include enhanced sentences of imprisonment.

The Court, in a 6–3 decision, overruled the Ninth Circuit ruling. Justice SAMUEL ALITO, writing for the majority, stated that the government's reading of the provision was "compelled by the language of ACCA." Three **statutory** terms—"offense," "laws," and "maximum term"—made this reading clear. The "offense" in each of the drug-delivery cases violated a criminal drug law; the relevant state "laws" prescribed a "maximum term" of five years for a first "offense" and 10 years for a second or subsequent "offense." Therefore, the maximum term for two of Rodriquez's state drug offenses was 10 year. The Ninth Circuit's conclusion that the maximum term was five years "contorts ACCA's plain terms." Though Rodriquez was sentenced to just 48 months in prison, the law permitted a sentence of up to 10 years. It was sufficient that the law set a maximum term, regardless of whether the court applied the maximum.

Rodriquez had argued that the recidivist enhancement law should not be applied for ACCA purposes. But for his repeat crimes, the underlying drug offense was not "serious" because its maximum term was five years. Any portion of the punishment that was directed at his **recidivism** did not reflect the underlying offense. Justice Alito rejected this argument, finding that ACCA made no such distinction. Rodriquez also believed that the "manifest purpose" of ACCA would be subverted if the recidivist enhancement was counted. The seriousness of an offense is based on the elements of the offense and the conduct of the defendant and not on the status of the defendant as a recidivist. Justice Alito found no merit in this claim: "On the contrary, however, an offense committed by a repeat offender is often thought to reflect greater culpability and thus to merit greater punishment." In sum, prior convictions do bear on the serious of the offense. Therefore, ACCA must be read to include enhanced sentences.

Justice DAVID SOUTER, in a dissenting opinion joined by Justices JOHN PAUL STEVENS and

RUTH BADER GINSBURG, acknowledged that the reading of ACCA by the majority was not patently unreasonable. Instead, Souter focused on the many complexities involved with sentencing. Each state applied different laws and different levels of enhancement for repeat offenders. The work of the **federal courts** would increase in cases involving career criminals, as judges struggled to discern state sentencing schemes.

SEX OFFENSES

A class of sexual conduct prohibited by the law.

Human Rights Watch Report Critical of Sex Offender Laws

In what was touted as the first comprehensive study of sex offender laws and policies in the United States, the international HUMAN RIGHTS WATCH published its compiled findings and recommendations on the subject in September 2007, following two years of preparation. Human Rights Watch (HRW) is a non-governmental civil rights watchdog organization that conducts fact-finding investigations and publishes reports and findings for the international community.

The 146-page report, *No Easy Answers: Sex Offender Laws in the United States*, reviewed not only state and federal offender laws, but also the impact of such laws on the lives of victims, former offenders, and their families. HRW's report categorized the laws and policies into three main groups: those requiring registration of sex offenders with state authorities; those creating online registries of sex offenders accessible to the public; and those imposing residency restrictions on sex offenders, such as prohibitions against living near schools, playgrounds, or parks. Resources used in compiling the report included over 200 interviews with victims of sexual violence and their families, former offenders, treatment providers, law enforcement personnel and government officials, researchers, and child safety advocates.

The HRW report was generally critical of the plethora of sex offender laws enacted in many states during the 1990s, following several criminal cases sensationalized by the media. Those laws generally reflected public concern for children at risk for sexual abuse at the hands of sexual predators. However, as the report documented, government statistics showed that most sexual abuse of children was committed by family members or trusted authority figures, and not by repeat offenders who were strangers to the child.

The report found scant justification for—and questionable value in—a majority of the laws, concluding that they did little to protect victims, especially children. Moreover, overly-broad laws targeting offenders often ended up violating the rights of those offenders who posed little risk to the public, leading to harassment, ostracism, and sometimes violence directed against former offenders and their families. In the report, Human Rights Watch urged the reform of registration and community notification laws and the ultimate elimination of residency restriction laws. ". . . [C]urrent laws are ill-conceived and poorly crafted," the report concluded. "Protecting children requires a more thoughtful and comprehensive approach than politicians have been willing to support."

The report was most critical of residency restrictions, considering them among the most arbitrary and meaningless of all, and calling for their complete elimination. These laws generally prohibit sex offenders from living within a designated distance (e.g., 500 to 2,500 feet) from places where children may congregate, such as schools, playgrounds, and daycare centers. But the report showed that many of those restrictions applied to all sex offenders, even those never convicted of abusing children. It cited the example of a Georgia law that forced a 26-year-old woman to move from her residence because it was too close to a daycare center. The woman was listed as a sex offender because, at the age of 17, she had oral sex with a 15-year-old.

It found that offenders who were required to comply with local residency restrictions were often banished from their already-established homes, thus keeping them from residing with their own families. In some instances, residency in entire towns was prohibited, forcing offenders to live in isolated rural areas and keeping them from any gainful employment.

Even more troubling was the lack of evidence, according to the report, to support any connection between restrictions on where sex offenders could reside and the prevention or decrease in sexual crimes against children. The report noted that existing research to date suggested that child molesters who were potential repeat-offenders were as likely to choose a child far away from home as one who lived or played nearby. Moreover, forcing offenders from an area only caused them to move to other areas more favorable, including over state lines. Interviewed law enforcement officials found residency restrictions counterproductive, pushing away the persons most likely to need

family contact, professional treatment, and supervision.

With respect to registration policies, federal law and the laws in all 50 states required adults and some juveniles convicted of sexual misconduct to register their addresses with local law enforcement agencies. The laws were found to be overbroad in both scope and duration, resulting in the inclusion of individuals convicted on non-violent crimes such as consensual sex between teenagers, prostitution, and public urination. The report found that such registration policies not only strained the system, but also caused gross inequities and unfair treatment of many persons who posed no threat to society whatsoever. Because most states did not make individual risk assessments or provide former offenders with a way to get off the registry (e.g., upon a showing of rehabilitation or years of lawful behavior), offender registrations provided little justification for the burden it placed upon all offenders and their families.

Finally, the report criticized community notification laws, particularly those which included Internet online offender registries. Many of these provided to the public at large, without limitation, a former offender's full name and address as well as identifying photograph, criminal history, and other information such as vehicle license plate numbers. In its report, HRW concluded that the consequences of such unlimited access to personal information proved devastating to offenders and their families. Many were beaten, burned, stabbed, and/or had their children harassed at school, their houses vandalized (rocks through windows, feces left on doorsteps, signs posted in their front lawns, etc.) and employment prospects destroyed. For those offenders whose crimes were relatively harmless (e.g., consensual sex between teenagers, public urination as a high school prank), and who had already paid their debts to society for their wrongdoing, the harm caused by such online registries was unjustifiable, according to the HRW.

The report made several recommendations to state governments, including eliminating residency restriction laws, limiting registration requirements to persons convicted of serious crimes and individually assessed to pose a significant risk of re-offending, and eliminating unrestricted publicly-accessible online registries. It also urged states to refuse to adopt the federal Adam Walsh Act, passed in 2006, which forced states to increase the scope and duration of registration and community notification laws (including registration of youthful offenders as young as 14) or risk loss of federal enforcement grant money.

Originally created in 1978 as Helsinki Watch, HRW lacked legal authority to create or enforce laws, but its well-publicized findings carried international clout and have been effective in challenging governments to change currents laws, policies, or practices that it reviewed.

Judge Rules Federal Mental Health Commitment of Sex Offenders Unconstitutional

In 2006, Congress passed the Adam Walsh Child Protection and Safety Act, Pub. L. No. 109-248, which established a uniform National Sex Offender Registry to identify and track offenders. Congress also enacted several reforms affecting the correctional treatment of sex offenders. Section 4248 of the Act provided for civil mental health committals of offenders in the custody of the federal Bureau of Prisons. Specifically, it permitted officials to indefinitely commit sex offenders to a mental hospital following their prison terms.

In *U.S. v. Comstock*, 507 F. Supp. 2d 522 (E.D.N.C. 2007), U.S. **District Court** Judge Earl Britt of the U.S. Eastern District of North Carolina ruled that the civil commitment section of the Act was unconstitutional. The challenge to the law was brought by the North Carolina Public Defenders on behalf of Graydon Comstock, who served a 37-month prison sentence for receiving computer pornography via computer. After his prison term ended in November 2006, the government certified him as a "sexually dangerous person" and involuntarily confined him for mental health treatment.

The 59-page court order struck Section 4248 of the Act as violating the due process rights of offenders, in that it permitted federal prosecutors to request committal to a mental hospital upon "clear and convincing evidence" that the person was "sexually dangerous" (as defined under Section 4248 of the Act) and therefore likely to commit the crime in the future. (In most jurisdictions, **clear and convincing proof** is more than a preponderance but less than the criminal standard of "beyond a reasonable doubt.") The district court ruled that the Act's "failure to require a court to find, **beyond a reasonable doubt**, that a person has engaged or attempted to engage in sexually violent conduct or child molestation prior to permitting the individual's indefinite involuntary commitment as a sexually dangerous person constitutes a violation of [substantive] due process." The district court was also critical of the

fact that the Act permitted any federal prisoner to be certified as "sexually dangerous" irrespective of the nature of his or her crime or conviction. (Federal prosecutors had argued that the clear and convincing standard properly allocated the risk of an erroneous commitment between individual and state, and that post-commitment provisions existed for **redress** of any erroneous commitments.)

While the court noted that Section 4248 of the Act was aimed at preventing sexually violent conduct underlying various federal sex crimes, it held that Congress lacked the power to influence the outcomes of criminal proceedings that fell within the exclusive jurisdiction of state courts. The court based its ruling in part on the fact that most sex crimes and sexually violent conduct were regulated by state law. Judge Britt reasoned that where the federal government had no jurisdiction to prosecute a crime or class of crimes, it also lacked jurisdiction to act to prevent them. Wrote Judge Britt, "In sum, section 4248 unnecessarily and improperly deprives the states of *parens patriae* ["parent of the country" authority of states to act as guardians of persons under legal disability] and police powers and impermissibly intrudes upon an area historically regulated by the states."

Federal prosecutors also argued that the NECESSARY AND PROPER CLAUSE (Art. I, § 8 of the U.S. Constitution) permitted Congress to devise laws to confine persons until they were prosecuted. But the district court rejected this argument, finding that the authority did not extend to holding persons beyond their meted sentences, nor, e.g., to persons previously committed due to mental incompetence to stand trial, or to persons in federal custody and against whom all criminal charges had been dropped due to their mental condition. Likewise, the court rejected an argument that the law was justified under the **Commerce Clause** of the U.S. Constitution (Clause 3 of Art. I, § 8), which permits laws necessary for interstate commerce. In fact, noted the court, the federal government had no broad power generally to criminalize sexually dangerous conduct or child molestation.

In a separate but related May 2008 case, a federal district judge in Minnesota dismissed a petition by a federal prosecutor to prolong the confinement of a mentally disordered sex offender by having him declared a "sexually dangerous person" under the Act. As of May 2008, five district court judges across the nation had ruled on the Act's provisions, three finding them valid and two finding them unconstitutional. Although no circuit **court of appeal** had yet decided on the issue,

Esther Miller holds a quilt with pictures of proclaimed sex abuse victims of priests in San Diego, California.

AP IMAGES

challenges to the Adam Walsh Act under the Commerce Clause of the U.S. Constitution were pending in both 4th and 11th Circuit Courts of Appeals, including the *Comstock* ruling.

As of May 2008, 19 states had adopted civil commitment provisions for sex offenders. U.S. Senator Orrin Hatch (R-UT) had previously hailed the Act as "the most comprehensive child crimes and protection bill in our Nation's history."

SEXUAL ABUSE

Illegal sex acts performed against a minor by a parent, guardian, relative, or acquaintence.

San Diego Diocese Settles Clergy Abuse Cases for $198 Million

A steady flow of stories alleging sexual abuse of children by Roman Catholic priests first gar-

nered momentum in the early 2000s, with large numbers of lawsuits filed in 2002. In southern California, the erupting scandal centered on three primary areas or "dioceses" within the Catholic Church: the hierarchical Los Angeles Archdiocese and the smaller San Diego and San Bernardino Dioceses. In July 2007, the Los Angeles Archdiocese settled 508 abuse cases for $660 million.

In September 2007, the San Diego Diocese agreed to pay $198 million to 144 additional plaintiff-victims of clergy abuse, the second-largest settlement since the scandal erupted. The agreement ended four years of negotiations in both state and **federal courts**, and was nearly twice as much as that offered by the church six months prior.

The earlier settlement offer (of $95 million) occurred as part of **reorganization plan** after the diocese filed for bankruptcy to protect its assets, just hours before the first of 42 lawsuits was scheduled for trial. But U.S. Bankruptcy Court Judge Louise DeCarl Adler was unsympathetic, criticizing the church for poor bookkeeping, under-valuation of assets, and failure to disclose certain facts. Following her threat to dismiss the case if an agreement between the parties was not forthcoming during final negotiations before a federal **magistrate** judge, the settlement offer was announced.

Under its terms, the San Diego Diocese was to pay $153 million to settle 111 cases involving its own clergy, plus an additional $30 million to settle 22 other cases involving core members of other Catholic orders in its diocese. The San Bernardino Diocese, also a named defendant, contributed $15 million to settle the remaining 11 claims of clergy abuse that allegedly occurred after 1978, when San Bernardino split from the San Diego Diocese.

Various sources contributed to the settlement fund, including approximately $75 million in insurance, along with the sale of some land, loans to the diocese, and about $1 million raised by Catholic parishioners in the diocese.

Also negotiated in the settlement agreement was the public release of documents proving not only the validity of the abuse charges, but also the extent to which church officials were aware that sexual abuse was occurring.

On December 7, 2007, Los Angeles Superior Court Judge Peter D. Lichtman released his order distributing the settlement funds. Lichtman, who also oversaw the $100 million Orange County settlements as well as the $660 million Los Angeles settlement, stated that he actually wanted to award more, given the large number of egregious cases. "There was simply not enough money to compensate all of the high-end victims with a high-end dollar amount," the court order noted. "The range, extent and depth of abuse in the San Diego cases are unlike any that this court has previously seen." On average, the San Diego settlement gave $1.4 million to each claimant, but specific amounts for specific individuals was ordered under court seal. In deciding how to distribute the funds, Judge Lichtman reviewed investigative reports and notes and psychological evaluations provided by counsel (all of which would also remain under seal with the court), as well as considered the nature and extent of the abuse in each case. "The suffering experienced (and unending suffering which continues to this day) is truly life-altering and psychologically debilitating," the order noted. "At all times this court felt helpless and ineffective in trying to

assuage the grief, sorrow and unbearable weight of pain expressed by the victims."

In May 2008, the Salesian Society of Catholic Priests in California reached its own $19.5 million settlement in a sexual molestation lawsuit. It had been the only religious order that refused to join the $660 million settlement in the Los Angeles Diocese the previous year. The settlement was reached as a jury in Los Angeles County Superior Court had been seated to begin trial.

The lawsuit alleged that the Salesian Order knew a certain Father Titian Miani had been accused of abusing children at the time that the Order assigned him to St. John Bosco High School. Miani, 81, had previously been accused of molesting children in Italy and Canada before the Salesians transferred him to St. John Bosco in the 1960s, the lawsuit alleged. According to allegations in the complaint, Miani befriended a family whose father had died, then molested the son and two daughters while their widowed mother tried to work during the day and attend night school. Miani left the Order in 1974 but continued to serve as a priest until 1993. Defense counsel for the Salesians maintained that the Order did not know of Miani's alleged abuse prior to assigning him to the school. The $19.5 million settlement money was to be distributed to 17 victims.

SIXTH AMENDMENT

Indiana v. Edwards

On June 19, 2008, the U.S. SUPREME COURT decided that the State of Indiana could insist that a mentally ill defendant be represented by counsel at trial. Though the defendant in the case had been declared competent to stand trial, the state determined that the defendant was not competent to represent himself. The Indiana Supreme Court determined that the defendant could waive his right to counsel, but the Supreme Court disagreed in a 7–2 decision.

The SIXTH AMENDMENT to the U.S. Constitution provides, "In all criminal prosecutions, the accused shall enjoy the right to . . . have the Assistance **of Counsel** for his defence." Several prior Supreme Court cases have established some of the parameters with regard to the application of this right in the context of mentally ill defendants. Two cases established the principle that a mentally incompetent person cannot stand trial. Under *Dusky v. United States*, 362 U.S. 402, 80 S. Ct. 788, 4 L. Ed. 2d 824 (1960), the Court determined that to determine whether a defendant is competent to stand trial, a court must determine: (1) whether the defendant has "a rational as well as factual understanding of the proceedings against him;" and (2) whether the defendant "has sufficient present ability to consult with his lawyer with a reasonable degree of rational understanding." The Court also addressed the mental competency standard in *Drope v. Missouri*, 420 U.S. 162, 95 S. Ct. 896, 43 L. Ed. 2d 103 (1975). In *Drope*, the Court stated that it "has long been accepted that a person whose mental condition is such that he lacks the capacity to understand the nature and object of the proceedings against him, to consult with counsel, and to assist in preparing his defense may not be subjected to a trial."

Several other cases focus more directly on a defendant's right to self-representation. In *Faretta v. California*, 422 U.S. 806, 95 S. Ct. 2525, 45 L. Ed. 2d 562 (1975), the Court recognized that forcing a criminal defendant to accept representation from counsel "is contrary to his basic right to defend himself if he truly wants to do so." Accordingly, the Court held that a defendant has a constitutional right to proceed in a case without counsel if the defendant "voluntarily and intelligently elects to do so."

Yet another case further clarified the right to self-representation. In *Godinez v. Moran*, 509 U.S. 389, 113 S. Ct. 2680, 125 L. Ed. 2d 321 (1993), the Court addressed a case where a defendant had asked a state trial court to allow him to represent himself and to change his pleas from not guilty to guilty. A federal court of appeals determined that a defendant had to satisfy a heightened standard of competency to waive his right to counsel. The Supreme Court disagreed, holding that the *Dusky* standard applied both to competency to stand trial and to competency to waive the right to counsel.

The case of *Indiana v. Edwards* arose on July 12, 1999, when Ahmad Edwards fired three shots on a street in downtown Indianapolis. A security officer had seen Edwards steal a pair of shoes. One of the shots hit the security officer, while another struck a bystander. An agent of the FEDERAL BUREAU OF INVESTIGATION chased and eventually apprehended Edwards by shooting the suspect in the leg. The state charged Edwards with attempted murder, **battery** with a deadly weapon, criminal recklessness, and theft.

Edwards underwent a series of psychiatric evaluations. Two psychiatrists determined that Edwards was schizophrenic, and the trial court declared him to be incompetent. After two years of treatment and evaluation, another psychiatrist declared Edwards competent, but two other evaluators determined that he was not competent. Yet another psychiatrist in 2004 declared Edwards competent, and Edwards' trial finally proceeded.

Edwards made a motion to proceed **pro se** in the case, but the trial court denied the request because Edwards had indicted that he would raise the **insanity defense**. A jury in June 2005 convicted Edwards on charges of criminal recklessness and theft, but the jury was hung on the other charges. The judge ordered a new trial on two of the counts. Edwards again moved to proceed pro se, and his counsel moved to withdraw. Although the court allowed counsel to withdraw, the court twice denied Edwards' motions to proceed pro se. According to the trial court, Edwards had the competence to stand trial but lacked the additional capacity to conduct a defense. Edwards was subsequently convicted on counts of battery with a deadly weapon and attempted murder.

Edwards appealed his convictions to both an intermediate Indiana **appellate court** and the Indiana Supreme Court. The Indiana Supreme Court determined that the Supreme Court's precedents in *Faretta* and *Godinez* required the state courts to permit Edwards to represent himself. *Edwards v. State*, 866 N.E.2d 252 (Ind. 2007). The state sought a **writ** of **certiorari**, and the Supreme Court agreed to hear the case.

Justice ANTONIN SCALIA dominated a significant portion of the oral arguments, stressing a need for a simple rule for determining when a state can forbid a criminal defendant from representing himself. Scalia acknowledged that a pro se defendant may harm his own defense by representing himself, but this fact should not mean that the defendant does not have the right to waive this representation. "Surely [the pro se defendant's] total ignorance of all of the trial rules, the **hearsay** rule and the other details of conducting a trial, is a great disadvantage," Scalia said. "But we allow him to toss that away so long as he knows he's tossing it away."

Despite Scalia's efforts, the Court determined that the state could indeed restrict individuals who are competent to stand trial from defending themselves pro se. Justice STEPHEN BREYER wrote the majority opinion for the Court, which had voted 7–2 in favor of the state. According to Breyer's opinion, though the Court's precedent did not resolve the question before the Court, the prior cases suggested that the state should have the right to restrict self-representation based on mental competency. The

Court noted that mental illness can hinder a person's functioning in different ways at different times, meaning that the illness may have a different effect on the defendant's ability to defend himself as compared with the defendant's ability to stand trial. Moreover, forbidding a state from restricting a defendant from representing himself could undercut the ability of the defendant to receive a fair trial. The Court vacated the Indiana Supreme Court's decision and remanded the case for further proceedings. *Indiana v. Edwards*, No. 07-208, 2008 WL 2445082 (June 19, 2008).

In a dissent joined by Justice CLARENCE THOMAS, Scalia referred to the majority's opinion as "extraordinarily vague." Scalia argued that the Constitution does not permit a state to impose its own "perception of fairness" by limiting a "defendant's right to make his own case before the jury."

Rothgery v. Gillespie County

On June 29, 2007, the U.S. SUPREME COURT ruled that a Texas county was too slow in providing legal counsel to a man wrongfully arrested for **felony** weapon possession. The decision ended lengthy ordeal for Walter Rothgery, who was arrested due to a mistake in a computer database. The Court's decision reversed a ruling by the Fifth **Circuit Court** of Appeals.

The SIXTH AMENDMENT provides, "In all criminal prosecutions, the accused shall enjoy the right . . . to have the Assistance **of Counsel** for his defence." The Court has held on numerous occasions that this right is limited and that it does not commence until the commencement of a prosecution. In this context, the Court has determined that a prosecution has been commenced at "the initiation of adversary judicial criminal proceedings—whether by way of formal charge, **preliminary hearing**, indictment, information, or arraignment." At this point, the government has "committed itself to prosecute."

In two previous case, the Court has established that the right to counsel attaches at the time of a defendant's initial appearance before a judicial officer. In *Brewer v. Williams*, 430 U.S. 387, 97 S. Ct. 1232, 51 L. Ed. 2d 424 (1977), the Court addressed a case where a criminal defendant had been arraigned before a judge on an outstanding **arrest warrant**. After advising the defendant of his *Miranda* rights, the trial judge committed the defendant to jail. Though the defendant had not been provided counsel, police interrogated him and elicited information that led to an indictment and conviction for first-degree murder. The Supreme Court determined

that the proceedings had been initiated and that the defendant had the right to counsel when the police questioned him after the arraignment.

In a second case, *Michigan v. Jackson*, 475 U.S. 625, 106 S. Ct. 1404, 89 L. Ed. 2d 631 (1986), the Court revisited the question of whether the right to counsel attaches at the initial appearance of a criminal defendant before a **magistrate** or judge. The only distinction in *Jackson* was that in Michigan, the state had adopted a procedure under which a defendant went through two arraignments. The first arraignment was conducted immediately, while during the second arraignment, the defendant was given an opportunity to enter a plea with the court. A defendant who was not given counsel for the first arraignment argued that this procedure violated his right to counsel, and the Court agreed. The Court in that case rejected the state's argument that there was a distinction between the first arraignment and the arraignment on the indictment.

Rothgery's case arose on July 15, 2002, when police officers in Fredericksburg, Texas, arrested him without a warrant on suspicion that Rothgery was a felon in possession of a firearm. The crime is a third-degree felony in Texas. The arrest was based on an error in a computer database showing that Rothgery had a felony conviction in California. Felony charges against Rothgery had, in fact, been dismissed when he completed a diversionary program.

The officers took Rothgery to the Gillespie County jail. The following morning, he was brought before a **justice of the peace** to be informed of the accusations against him. Rothgery was also advised of his rights according to the requirements of Article 15.17 of the Texas Code of **Criminal Procedure** (these rights are generally equivalent to the required *Miranda* warnings). He could not afford a lawyer, and he was not provided appointed counsel despite making several oral and written requests for one. He was indicted in January 2003 for unlawful possession of a firearm by a felon. Once the court appointed counsel, the lawyer filed the appropriate paperwork showing that Rothgery had never been convicted of a felony. The district attorney subsequently dismissed the indictment. Rothgery had been arrested twice and spent three weeks in jail.

Rothgery brought an action under 42 U.S.C. § 1983 against Gillespie County. Rothgery alleged that the county violated his Sixth Amendment rights by not providing counsel in a timely fashion. According to Rothgery, had the county provided counsel within a reasonable time after the initial hearing. The county apparently adopted a policy here it would deny appointed counsel to an indigent defendant until at least the time of the entry of an information or an indictment.

The U.S. **District Court** for the Western District of Texas granted the county's motion for **summary judgment**. *Rothgery v. Gillespie County, Tex.*, 413 F. Supp. 2d 806 (W.D. Tex. 2006). Rothgery then appealed to the Fifth Circuit Court of Appeals, which affirmed the district court's ruling. According to the Fifth Circuit, Rothgery's right to counsel had not attached at the initial hearing because prosecutors were not involved at that stage. *Rothgery v. Gillespie County, Tex.*, 491 F.3d 293 (5th Cir. 2007). Rothgery then sought to appeal the case to the Supreme Court, which agreed to review the decision in 2007.

At oral argument, the justices focused much of their attention on the issue of how the Court could establish a rule that could give the states sufficient guidance regarding when counsel must be appointed. Counsel for Rothgery, Danielle Spinelli, argued that the Court's decisions in *Brewer* and *Jackson* controlled the case. However, several justices were concerned with the consequences of requiring states to provide counsel at too early of a juncture in a criminal proceeding.

In the **final decision**, eight of the justices disagreed with the Fifth Circuit and ruled in favor of Rothgery. Writing for the majority, Justice DAVID SOUTER noted that 43 of the states have adopted procedures where they appoint counsel before, at, or just after the initial appearance of a defendant. Texas is among a small minority of states that do not appoint counsel at this juncture, and the Court could not find any justification for this practice. Souter's overall opinion rested largely on the conclusion that *Brewer* and *Jackson* controlled the outcome.

Chief Justice JOHN ROBERTS and Justice SAMUEL ALITO filed concurring opinions, while Justice CLARENCE THOMAS dissented. Thomas argued that neither the history of the Sixth Amendment nor the Court's precedent supported the decision.

Wright v. Van Patten

The Sixth Amendment's right to effective legal counsel is a fundamental part of U.S. law. Given the state of technology at the time of its **ratification**, the SIXTH AMENDMENT does not explicitly state that the lawyer must be in the same courtroom as the defendant when a plea is taken. However, courts have allowed lawyers to participate by speaker phone in certain circumstances, which has raised Sixth Amendment concerns. This was illustrated in the case of *Wright v. Van Patten*, __U.S.__, 128 S. Ct. 743, 169 L. Ed. 2d 583 (2007), where the Supreme Court reviewed what legal precedent governed a petition of **habeas corpus** based on a claim of ineffective counsel. The Court rejected the more stringent precedent that would have presumed a lawyer's participation by speaker phone was a Sixth Amendment violation. Instead, the Court held that another precedent, which examined whether the defendant was actually prejudiced, was properly applied by the state supreme court.

Joseph Van Patten was charged in Wisconsin state court with first-degree intentional homicide and pleaded guilty to a reduced charge of first-degree reckless homicide. On the day of his plea hearing his lawyer was unable to be physically present in the courtroom, so the court allowed him to participate by speaker phone. During the hearing Van Patten stated that he had thoroughly discussed his case and plea decision with his lawyer and that he was satisfied with his legal representation. Van Patten was offered the opportunity to speak privately with his lawyer over the phone but he declined and proceeded to plead guilty to his crime.

After he was sentenced to 25 years in prison, Van Patten retained a new lawyer and asked the Wisconsin Court of Appeals to allow him to withdraw his plea. In his motion Van Patten argued that his Sixth Amendment right to counsel had been violated by his trial lawyer's physical absence from the plea hearing. The appeals court rejected his motion, finding that the lawyer's absence from Van Patten's hearing did not violate his right to counsel. The court noted Patten's statements on the record acknowledging and not objecting to the presence of his lawyer by phone. In addition, there was nothing in the plea hearing transcript that indicated he had been treated unfairly. The court applied the two-part test set out in *Strickland v. Washington*, 466 U.S. 668, 104 S.Ct. 2052, 80 L.Ed.2d 674 (1984), which requires a showing of deficient performance and prejudice to the defendant. Van Patten failed to meet this test. The Wisconsin Supreme Court refused to hear Van Patten's appeal, leading him to petition for a **writ** of habeas **corpus** in federal **district court**.

The district court denied relief but the Seventh **Circuit Court** of Appeals reversed this decision. The appeals court said Van Patten's

Sixth Amendment claims should not have been evaluated using the *Strickland* test. The proper standard to be used was to be found in *United States v. Cronic*, 466 U.S. 648, 104 S.Ct. 2039, 80 L.Ed.2d 657 (1984). Under that standard prejudice is presumed and the defendant does not need to establish actual prejudice.

The Supreme Court, in a unanimous decision, overruled the Seventh Circuit. In the Court's *per curiam* opinion (no justice takes credit for writing the decision) the justices framed the issue as one involving its habeas **jurisprudence** and the federal habeas **statute**, 28 U.S.C. § 2254. The key issue was whether a state court's **decision on the merits** was, under § 2254, "contrary to, or involved an unreasonable application of, clearly established Federal law, as determined by the Supreme Court of the United States." The Court reviewed the competing precedents of *Strickland* and *United States v. Cronic*, concluding that it had issued no decision that precisely addressed the issue in this case, and that it had never "clearly established" that *United States v. Cronic* should replace *Strickland* with this "novel factual content." *United States v. Cronic* could only be applied if an inquiry into the poor performance **of counsel** would "not be worth the time" because it was so obvious. Reviewing other Sixth Amendment decisions the Court concluded that there was no clear answer as to which precedent should be applied. Because there was no "clearly established Federal law" the Wisconsin Court of Appeals was free to apply *Strickland* and deny Van Patten habeas relief.

SOVEREIGN IMMUNITY

The legal protection that prevents a sovereign state or person from being sued without consent.

Ali v. Federal Bureau of Prisons

The federal government possesses **sovereign immunity**, a legal principle that makes the government immune from lawsuits seeking monetary damages. However, the government may, at its discretion, waive sovereign immunity in particular circumstances, while retaining immunity for other claims. The FEDERAL TORT CLAIMS ACT (FTCA), 28 U.S.C.A. § 1346, waives the federal government's sovereign immunity in certain circumstances to permit persons to sue it for damages. The act also contains a number of exceptions and limitations. The Supreme Court, in *Ali v. Federal Bureau of Prisons*, __U.S.__, 128 S.Ct. 831, __L.Ed.2d __ (2008), considered whether a federal prisoner could sue under the

FTCA for the value of personal possessions that he claimed were taken when his possessions were shipped to his new prison. A closely divided Court ruled that he could not sue because a provision of the FTCA (§ 2680(c)) that bars a claim arising in respect to "detention of any goods, merchandise, or other property by any officer of customs or **excise** or any other law enforcement officer." The majority held that the phrase "or any other law enforcement officer" immunized the government from any claims based on the negligence or wrongful acts of all federal law enforcement officers. The dissenting justices objected to the way the majority applied rules of **statutory** interpretation, believing that Congress only meant to immunize those employees who work in customs or excise positions.

The amount of money in question in this case was very small, but the impact of the ruling will be large. Abdus-Shahid M.S. Ali was a federal prisoner at the U.S. Penitentiary in Atlanta, Georgia. In December 2003 he was scheduled to be moved to the U.S. Penitentiary Big Sandy in Inez, Kentucky. Before his transfer Ali left two duffel bags containing his personal property in the Georgia facility's discharge unit, where it was to be inventoried, packaged, and shipped to the Kentucky prison. When his bags arrived Ali discovered that several items were missing. These items had religious and nostalgic significance, with Ali valuing the lost items as worth $177. The staff at the Kentucky prison said that he had been given everything that had been sent and said he could file a claim. Ali filed an administrative tort claim. Prison officials denied his claim, ruling that when he signed the receipt form he had certified the accuracy of the listed inventory items and had waived his right to make a claim. Ali then filed an action in U.S. **district court**, alleging that prison officials had violated the FTCA. The federal Bureau of Prisons (BOP) argued that his claim was barred by the exception in § 2680(c) for property claims against law enforcement officers. The district court agreed and dismissed the FTCA claim. The Eleventh **Circuit Court** of Appeals upheld the district court's interpretation of § 2680(c). The Supreme Court agreed to hear Ali's appeal because other circuit courts of appeals were in conflict over the proper scope of § 2680(c).

The Supreme Court, in a 5–4 decision, upheld the broad interpretation of § 2680(c) made by the Eleventh Circuit. Justice CLARENCE THOMAS, writing for the majority, stated that the case turned on whether the BOP officers who allegedly lost Ali's property qualified as "other law enforcement officer[s]" within the meaning of § 2680(c). Ali argued that the law enforcement officers referenced in the provision included only those who act in a customs or excise capacity. The law referenced customs and excise activities in the disputed provision as well as in the preceding clause, so the entire subsection focuses on preserving sovereign immunity only as to officers enforcing those laws.

Justice Thomas rejected this argument. The phrase "any other law enforcement officer" suggested a "broad meaning." He noted that the Court had previously read the word "any" to have an expansive meaning. Therefore, Congress' use of "any" to modify "other law enforcement officer" is "most naturally read to mean law enforcement officers of whatever kind." He acknowledged that the customs and excise references were meant to preserve immunity for claims against those who enforce custom and tax laws, but "there was no indication that Congress intended immunity for those claims to turn on the type of law being enforced."

Ali asserted that two **canons of construction** for the interpretation of statutes supported a narrow scope for § 2680(c) immunity. The canon known as *ejusdem generis* states that when a **general term** follows a specific term, the general term should be understood as a reference to subjects similar to the one with the specific term. Read this way, the "any other law enforcement officers" phrase was a general term that was tied to the customs and excise officers specific term. Justice Thomas disagreed, finding the canon inapplicable. There was no list of specific terms, separated by commas, and followed by a general or collective term. Instead, the clause contained one specific category and one general category. Ali also claimed that the canon known as *noscitur a sociis* supported his argument. This phrase states that "a word is known by the company it keeps." Justice Thomas dismissed this claim as well, finding that there were no strong contextual clues to prove that the provision was meant to focus exclusively on custom and excise officers.

Justice ANTHONY KENNEDY, in a dissenting opinion joined by Justices JOHN PAUL STEVENS, DAVID SOUTER, and STEPHEN BREYER, lamented the failure of the majority to properly use the canons of construction as interpretive tools. The Court's analytical framework would now be used by the lower courts when faced with "other cases in which a series of words operate in a clause similar to the one" in question. A proper application of the canons demonstrated that Congress never intended the

provision to grant immunity to all law enforcement officers.

35W Bridge Collapse Liability Issues

When the I-35W bridge collapsed into the Mississippi River and adjoining river banks in downtown Minneapolis, Minnesota on August 1, 2007, the immediate focus was on rescuing those unfortunate individuals who were on the span. In the days afterwards it became apparent that the victims of the bridge collapse and their families would seek compensation for their injuries and for the deaths of their loved ones. Thirteen people were killed that summer evening and 145 people suffered injuries. Not surprisingly, personal injury lawyers became involved almost immediately. However, within a short time, a group of prominent Minnesota lawyers agreed to represent bridge victims for no compensation.

The victims and their families faced a major problem in obtaining compensation: Minnesota law limits the state's liability for tort actions to $300,000 per victim and $1 million total for an incident, regardless of the number of victims. The state created these limitations under its tort claims statute, which waives sovereign immunity in some cases. Some lawyers continued to look into whether the architects, engineers and constructors, and private inspectors of the 35W bridge could be held liable for negligence. However, state investigators and the NATIONAL TRANSPORTATION SAFETY BOARD (NTSB) refused to share information with the lawyers. The victims and their families placed their energies in having the Minnesota legislature enact a victims' compensation fund.

The 35W bridge was an eight-lane steel truss arch bridge completed in 1967. Carrying 140,000 vehicles daily, the bridge was maintained by the Minnesota Department of Transportation (MnDOT). Since 1993, the bridge was inspected annually by MnDOT, although no inspection report was completed in 2007, as reconstruction of the bridge deck was underway. In the years prior to the collapse, several reports cited problems with the bridge structure. In 1990, the federal government gave the bridge a rating of "structurally deficient," pointing to significant corrosion in its bearings. "Structurally deficient" is a classification term which does not in itself indicate a lack of safety. Approximately 75,000 other U.S. bridges had this classification in 2007.

More troubling was a 2001 University of Minnesota study. Cracking had been previously

Wreckage of Interstate 35W bridge, St Paul, Minnesota, August 2007.

AP IMAGES

discovered in the cross girders at the end of the approach spans. The main trusses connected to these cross girders and resistance to motion at the connection point bearings was leading to stress cracking. MnDOT had addressed this issue prior to the study by drilling into the cracks to prevent further propagation and adding support struts to the cross girder. The university study also noted a concern about lack of redundancy in the main truss system: the bridge had a greater risk of collapse in the event of any single structural failure. In 2005, the federal government again rated the bridge as "structurally deficient" and in possible need of replacement. The day after the bridge collapsed, Minnesota Governor Tim Pawlenty revealed that the bridge had been scheduled to be replaced in 2020.

In January 2008 the NTSB announced that it had determined that the bridge's design-specified steel gusset plates, which were used to connect girders together in the truss structure, were undersized and inadequate to support the intended load of the bridge, a load which had increased over time. However, a final report from the NTSB was months away from completion.

The information surrounding MnDOT's inspection and maintenance of the bridge upset many state legislators, some of whom resolved to create a victims compensation fund. In May 2008 Governor Pawlenty signed a $38 million package to compensate victims for their injuries and losses. The law created two pools of money. The first pool covers everyone who was on the bridge when it fell. These individuals may be compensated up to $400,000. Individuals whose injuries and losses were more severe can apply for additional money from a pool of $12.6 million. A panel of three lawyers, appointed by the Chief Justice of the Minnesota Supreme Court, will serve as special masters and determine the exact amount for each victim. Victims who accept money from the funds must agree to waive all legal claims against the state.

Lawyers involved in the bridge litigation noted that victims were treated differently than victims who applied to the federal 9/11 compensation fund. Unlike the 9/11 victims, who had to waive all claims against third parties (private businesses) before receiving compensation, the 35W bridge victims did not. Second, bridge victims have the option of rejecting the award proposed by the three-lawyer panel. Bridge claimants must file by October 15, 2008 to be eligible for an award and all offers will be made by February 28, 2009. It is expected that most victims will accept compensation from the fund because of the state's sovereign immunity and the fact that the statutes of limitations have expired for most potential third-party.

In Re: Katrina Canal Breaches Consolidated Litigation

The devastation wrought by Hurricane Katrina to the city of New Orleans on August 29, 2005 was dramatically amplified when several of the levees that protected the city were breached. Thousands of families lost their homes and many businesses lost their buildings, equipment, and inventory. Many homeowners have sought to have their insurance **carriers** pay for the storm destruction but the insurance companies have, on the whole, persuaded state and **federal courts** that their policies did not cover the damages caused by the storm surge.

Other homeowners and businesses have filed claims against the federal government's Army Corps of Engineers, which built and maintains the levees, and against the city and the state of Louisiana. These plaintiffs have contended that negligence by government agencies at all levels led to the breaching of the levees and most of the destruction attributed to Katrina. However, lawsuits against state and federal governments are limited by the doctrine of **sovereign immunity**, which bars suits for damages against governmental entities. State and federal governments may, on their own, grant exceptions to sovereign immunity, such as the Federal Torts Claim Act, but they are not required to do so.

As part of the lawsuit named *In Re: Katrina Canal Breaches Consolidated Litigation*, plaintiffs alleged that the Corps of Engineers should be held liable for the breaches of the levees. Whether the Corps could be held liable was a significant legal issue. By January 2008, the Corps had received 489,000 claims forms. The forms provided notice to the Corps that the person planned to participate in a damage lawsuit against the federal agency. The claims totaled more than $3 quadrillion. The plaintiffs also sued the Orleans Parish Levee Board and the New Orleans Sewerage and Water Board. These boards are not automatically immune from damage lawsuits because they are part of municipal governments. However, they may be able to show a qualified immunity that will prevent a damages lawsuit from going forward.

The federal government sought to dismiss the Corps from the lawsuit, asserting that Congress had specifically granted immunity to the Corps for flood control projects. The plaintiffs argued that the three drainage canals in question, including the 17th Street Canal that allegedly accounted for 80 percent of the flooding in downtown New Orleans, had at one time been navigation channels. Judge Stanwood Duval of the federal **district court** in Louisiana, who oversees the consolidated litigation, issued a ruling in January 2008 that agreed with the government that the Corps of Engineers was immune. He noted that the Flood Control Act of 1928 gave the Corps and other federal agencies absolute immunity for actions involving flood projects. Duval cited 1986 and 2001 decisions by the Supreme Court that found the law "provides immunity, where, as here, a flood control project fails to control floodwaters because of the failure of the flood control project itself." As to the claim the canals had been used for navigation at one point, Duval ruled that once the canals and levee walls became part of the Lake Pontchartrain and Vicinity hurricane protection project, the 1928's immunity provision became effective.

Though Judge Duval ruled in the federal agencies favor, he did not disguise his anger at Congress and the Corps of Engineers for their actions over the last 50 years. He stated that "Millions of dollars were squandered in building a levee system with respect to these outfall canals which was known to be inadequate by the Corp's own calculations." The federal government, while immune for its actions, was not immune from "posterity's judgment concerning its failure to accomplish what was its task." The judge went on to note that sovereign immunity forgave any government action concerning the levees, whether it was a simple mistake or "gross incompetence." Duval suggested that Congress act to pay the victims of the levee failures.

Though the lawsuit could proceed against the local levee boards, other parts of the litigation continued to move forward. Judge Duval, in 2007, allowed plaintiffs from eastern New Orleans, the Lower 9th Ward, and St. Bernard Parish to sue the Corps of Engineers for defects in the Mississippi River-Gulf Outlet (MR-GO) navigation channel because the channel was a navigation channel not covered by the 1928 federal law. The lawsuit is scheduled for trial in September 2008. In addition, another **class action** suit is pending before the U.S. Court of Federal Claims in Washington, D.C. These plaintiffs contend that the construction of the MR-GO canal deprived St. Bernard Parish landowners of their land's value because of erosion and the increased effects of hurricanes.

Republic of the Philippines v. Pimentel

The U.S. SUPREME COURT in June 2008 concluded that a case involving millions of dollars invested in a New York account by former Philippine President Ferdinand Marcos could not proceed without the Philippines as a party to the case. The suit was originally brought by human rights victims who had received a $2 billion judgment against the Marcos family in 1995. The Philippine government reportedly expected a quick resolution of the dispute by its country's own courts.

Marcos became president of the Republic of the Philippines in 1965 after serving in the Philippine Senate for about six years. He remained in the office of the presidency for 21 years. Marcos was decried in both his own country and abroad due to his crimes and many acts of wrongdoing in the form of human rights violations. His ultimate undoing was caused in large part by his investment of hundreds of millions of dollars in the United States. During the so-called People Power Revolution, millions of Philippine citizens engaged in a series of nonviolent protests that ultimately resulting in overthrowing Marcos' regime in 1986.

Marcos was elected in national elections in 1965 and 1969. In 1972, however, Marcos used Communist and Muslim threats to justify his declaration of martial law, which effectively gave him complete power in the country. During the same year, he incorporated an **entity** named Arelma, S.A. Arelma subsequently opened an account with Merrill Lynch in New York and deposited a total of $2 million. By 2000, this account was worth between $35 and $37 million.

Once Marcos fled the Philippines in 1986, the Philippine government established a commission to recover property that Marcos had wrongfully taken during his presidency. One of the commission's first acts was to ask the Swiss government for its assistance in recovering assets that Marcos may have transferred to Switzerland. The Swiss government agreed to freeze assets, and in 1990, the Swiss Supreme Court upheld the freeze. The commission then asked a Philippine court of special jurisdiction known as the Sandiganbayan to declare that any money that Marcos obtained through misuse of his office to be forfeited to the Republic. The case has been pending in the Philippine court for more than a decade.

In 1995, a group of 9,539 human rights victims brought suit against Marcos' estate. The group brought a **class action** suit in the U.S. **District Court** for the District of Hawaii, and the court awarded the group a $2 billion judgment. In subsequent actions, the class was awarded the right to attach various assets, and the class sought to attach the assets of the Arelma account with Merrill Lynch. The Philippine commission, however, claimed that the Philippine government had a right to those assets by virtue of a 1955 law.

The Swiss government returned assets held in Switzerland to the Philippines, and the commission established an **escrow** account at the Philippine National **Banc** (PNB) to hold the funds until the Philippine court could determine who the rightful owner of the funds was. Both the Philippine government and the commission requested that Merrill Lynch also transfer funds to this escrow account, but Merrill Lynch refused. Merrill Lynch instead filed an **interpleader** action, naming as defendants the Philippine Republic, the commission, Arelma, the PNB, and the class of human rights victims.

The Judicial Panel on Multidistrict Litigation consolidated the various human rights complaints in the District of Hawaii. The panel appointed Judge Manuel Real of the U.S. District Court for the Central District of California to preside over the case. Both the Philippine government and the commission claimed that they were immune from suit under the Foreign **Sovereign Immunity** Act of 1976 (FSIA), 28 U.S.C. § 1604. The Republic and the commission sought to dismiss the action under Rule 19(b) of the Federal Rules of **Civil Procedure** (FRCP), which establishes the guidelines under which a court should dismiss an action when **joinder** of a required party is not feasible. The district court allowed the case to proceed, but the Ninth **Circuit Court** of Appeals reversed, ruling that the Republic and the commission were necessary parties to the case. *In re Republic of the Philippines*, 309 F.3d 1143 (9th Cir. 2002).

On remand, the district court again concluded that the case could proceed even without the Republic and the commission as parties. According to the district court, these parties had little chance to succeed in establishing their claims. On appeal, the Ninth Circuit affirmed the district court's decision, agreeing with the district court that the Republic and the commission would have difficulty prevailing at the trial. The **appellate court** thus held that even though these were required parties under Rule 19(a) of the FRCP, dismissal was not mandated under Rule 19(b).

The Republic sought a **writ** of **certiorari** with the U.S. Supreme Court. The U.S. government supported the petition, with the **Solicitor General** arguing that the Ninth Circuit's ruling had effectively deprived the Philippine government of the benefits of sovereign immunity. Moreover, the U.S. government stressed that the decision had raised difficult foreign policy questions. On December 3, 2007, the Court granted the petition to address the following issue: "Whether a foreign government that is a 'necessary' party to a lawsuit under Rule 19(a) and has successfully asserted sovereign immunity is, under Rule 19(b), an 'indispensable' party to an action brought in the courts of the United States to settle ownership of assets claimed by that government."

In an opinion by Justice ANTHONY KENNEDY, the Court reversed the Ninth Circuit. According to Kennedy, the Ninth Circuit did not give sufficient weight to all of the factors listed in Rule 19(b) of the FRCP. The Court determined that the Republic and the commission would be prejudiced if the case proceeded without these parties, and the Court concluded that the Ninth Circuit had not considered this factor carefully enough. The Court likewise concluded that the Ninth Circuit had failed to consider the appropriate facts when weighing other factors, such as whether the lower court could have lessened or avoided the prejudice by consider an alternative other than dismissal. Based on the Ninth Circuit's errors in applying Rule 19(b), the Court reversed the lower court's decision and remanded the case to the Ninth Circuit to instruct the district court to dismiss the action.

Justice JOHN PAUL STEVENS concurred in part and dissented in part. He agreed that the Ninth Circuit erred in its analysis under Rule 19(b), but he did not agree that the Court should order dismissal of the case. Justice DAVID

SOUTER likewise concurred in part and dissented in part, arguing that the Court should stay the proceedings in the U.S. court pending the outcome of the case in the Philippine court.

SPORTS LAW

Controversies Surround National Football League

The National Football League, which has developed into one of the most popular professional sports associations in the United States, faced a number of controversies in 2007 and 2008. Two players, including a Pro Bowl safety, suffered violent deaths. Several others became embroiled in legal problems involving a variety of crimes, including those involving weapons. Moreover, one of the most successful teams of the decade, the New England Patriots, was accused of cheating when evidence showed that the team had tape recorded opponents in an effort to steal play signals.

Roger Goodell was appointed as NFL commissioner in 2006, taking over for the highly-successful Paul Tagliabue, who had served in that post since 1989. Goodell is the son of a former U.S. senator and had been employed by the league in a variety of capacities since 1982. His responsibilities grew progressively as he gained experience, and he was named chief operating officer by the league in 2001. His first year as commissioner was marred by a number of off-the-field scandals involving players, and as a result Goodell in 2007 announced a new NFL Personnel Conduct Policy. This policy holds players to a higher standard and give the commissioner greater authority to suspend players who violate the rules.

Three players in particular ran into legal problems that prompted enforcement of the new policy. Perhaps the most notorious of these players was Adam "Pacman" Jones of the Tennessee Titans. After competing at West Virginia, Jones played his first season with Tennessee in 2005. He showed considerable promise during his first two seasons in the NFL, but he was also implicated in a number of major and minor criminal investigations. In two instances, he was questioned for his possible role in two shootings at strip clubs in Atlanta and Las Vegas. With regard to the Las Vegas incident, he was charged with two felonies but later accepted a plea bargain, under which he pleaded no contest to a charge of conspiracy to commit **disorderly conduct**. Goodell suspended Jones for the entire 2007 NFL season due to his legal problems, though Jones later signed to play with the Dallas Cowboys in 2008.

Another player who received a lengthy suspension was Tank Johnson of the Chicago Bears. Johnson was involved with several instances where he was charged with illegally carrying weapons. These incidents led Goodell to suspend Johnson for the first eight games of the 2007 season and also led the Bears to release Johnson. He signed with the Dallas Cowboys and played in the latter part of the season.

Like Johnson and Jones, Chris Henry of the Cincinnati Bengals has also had a lengthy list of altercations, including a charge in 2007 that he provided alcohol to minors. He also failed a drug test. These events led Goodell to suspend Henry for eight games in 2007. In April 2008, he was charged with assault and causing damage to property when he damaged a victim's car with a bottle and then punched the victim in the face. The Bengals released Henry the following day.

The off-the-field problems were far less tragic than the deaths of two young players. The first of these players was Denver Broncos cornerback Darrent Williams. He was killed while riding in a stretch Hummer following a dispute at a New Year's Eve party at a Denver nightclub. The car carrying the gunman drove up beside the Hummer that Williams was riding in and sprayed the side of the Hummer with bullets. Williams was hit in the neck and died instantly. Also riding with Williams was wide receiver Javon Walker. Police conducted a manhunt to identify the shooter, but the investigation stalled without producing any suspects.

Equally tragic was the death of Sean Taylor, a 24-year-old safety with the Washington Redskins. Taylor had been involved in a number of off-the-field events, but he had reportedly matured with the birth of a daughter. Eight days before his death, Taylor's mother called the police to report that someone had tried to break into Taylor's Miami home. Reports indicated that the intruders then had pried open a front window in the house and had rifled through dresser drawers. Police found a knife laying on the bed.

In the early morning hours of November 26, 2007, Taylor was at home with girlfriend Jackie Garcia (niece of actor Andy Garcia) and the couple's daughter. Taylor was startled by noises, and Garcia called 911. Taylor grabbed a machete for protection. An intruder broke through the bedroom door and fired two shots. One missed but the other struck Taylor in the upper leg. The bullet struck Taylor's femoral

NFL commissioner Roger Goodell speaks to reporters, Super Bowl trophy in foreground.
AP IMAGES

artery, resulting in an extreme loss of blood. Taylor was rushed to Jackson Memorial Hospital, where he underwent surgery. Although he showed some signs of life, such as clutching a nurse's finger, he remained in a coma and never regained consciousness. He died on November 27, one day after the shooting.

Three days after Taylor's death, police arrested four young men in connection with the break-in and the murder. The men, who were caught in Fort Myers included Venjah Hunte, Eric Rivera Jr., Jason Scott Mitchell, and Charles Kendrick Lee Wardlow. Three of the four men were under the age of 20 at the time of the shooting. In May 2008, police arrested a fifth suspect, 16-year-old Timothy Brown. All five men have been charged with murder, and all face life sentences for their participation in the crime if convicted.

In addition to the player problems, the league also faced embarrassment thanks to the revelation that the New England Patriots had video taped coaches of the New York Jets. The apparent intent of the taping was to steal defensive signals used the Jets on the sidelines, which would give the Patriots a strategic advantage over the Jets when the teams played again later in the season. Dubbed "Spygate," the event called into question whether the Patriots had used similar tactics when they won three Super Bowls during a four-year period between 2001 and 2004. As a result of the incident, Goodell docked the team a first-round draft pick in the 2008 draft.

The Patriots in 2008 became one of the very few teams in NFL history to complete a regular season undefeated and the first to do so in a 16-game season. Allegations continued to swirl, however, that additional evidence would surface that would show the extent of the Patriots' cheating. A former New England video assistant named Matt Walsh reportedly had a tape in his possession that would be especially damaging to the Patriots. However, his evidence revealed very little, and the case was effectively closed in May 2008.

Former Sen. George Mitchell Issues Report on Steroids in Baseball

Former U.S. Senator George Mitchell in December 2007 issued a report that detailed use of performance-enhancing drugs in the so-called "steroid era" of Major League Baseball (MLB). The report named several high-profile players, including pitcher Roger Clemens, as users of performance-enhancing substances. Clemens responded with strong denials, leading him to testify before Congress that he had not used steroids during his career. The report was issued shortly after star Barry Bonds was indicted for perjury and obstruction of justice for allegedly giving false testimony regarding steroid use.

Professional baseball has been at the center of attention regarding steroid use for some time. At his State of the Union Address in 2004, President GEORGE W. BUSH referred specifically to the steroid problem in sports, calling for this problem to end. Victor Conte, the former head of Bay Area Laboratory Cooperative (BALCO) was charged with distribution of illegal steroids, and the investigation into Conte's dealings revealed that Bonds was one of Conte's most well-known clients. The BALCO investigation led to a Congressional hearing in 2005, where former and current baseball stars Mark McGuire, Sammy Sosa, Rafael Palmeiro, and Curt Schilling appeared. The players either denied using performance enhancers or declined to speak on the subject.

In response to the swirling allegations, Major League Baseball Commissioner Bud Selig on March 30, 2006 established a committee to review use of steroids and similar drugs in baseball. Selig specifically told the committee to leave "no stone unturned" in its evaluation. He appointed Mitchell to lead the effort. Mitchell is a former federal prosecutor, former chairman of the Walt Disney Co., and a director of the Boston Red Sox.

For the first year of the investigation, Mitchell reportedly made little progress. Players refused to cooperate, and Mitchell did not have

power to subpoena them. Moreover, he could not access the results of MLB's drug-testing program. The breakthrough in the investigation came from Kirk Radomski, a former batboy and clubhouse attendant for the New York Mets. Radomski began working in the Mets' clubhouse during the 1980s before being officially hired in 1987. During the early 1990s, Radomski became involved with bodybuilding, which introduced him to the world of steroids.

In 1994, infielder David Segui became one of Radomski's first clients. Segui introduced Radomski to several other players, with led to the development of a network that was very lucrative for Radomski. "Segui stated that he still thinks highly of Radomski and that Radomski did not push drugs on any player," Mitchell reported. "According to Segui, Radomski was 'doing the players a favor' and they were 'lucky to have guys like Radomski,' because Radomski provided safe performance-enhancing substances, in contrast to what the players might receive from other sources."

The U.S. JUSTICE DEPARTMENT on April 27, 2007 announced that Radomski had pleaded guilty to steroid distribution. As part of his plea agreement, Radomski agreed to make himself available to Mitchell. Mitchell interviewed Radomski four times, and the information that Radomski provided led to additional sources. Radomski was able to back up his testimony with records of checks, money orders, and receipts, along with address books and telephone records. More than 60 percent of the players later named in the Mitchell report can be directly or indirectly linked to Radomski.

Amid intense media speculation, Mitchell released a 409-page report on December 13, 2007. The report was highly critical not only of the players, but also of team and MLB management. "For more than a decade there has been widespread illegal use of anabolic steroids and other performance enhancing substances by players in Major League Baseball, in violation of federal law and baseball policy," Mitchell wrote in the summary to the report. "Club officials routinely have discussed the possibility of such substance use when evaluating players. Those who have illegally used these substances range from players whose major league careers were brief to potential members of the Baseball Hall of Fame. They include both pitchers and position players, and their backgrounds are as diverse as those of all major league players."

The Mitchell Report showed the extent to which steroid abuse had become prevalent.

Former baseball player Roger Clemens testifying before Congress, February 2008.
AP IMAGES

"From hundreds of interviews and thousands of documents we learned enough to accurately describe that era," Mitchell wrote. "While this investigation was prompted by revelations about the involvement of players with Bay Area Laboratory Co-Operative, the evidence we uncovered indicates that this has not been an isolated problem involving just a few players or a few clubs. It has involved many players on many clubs. In fact, each of the thirty clubs has had players who have been involved with performance enhancing substances at some time in their careers."

The biggest shock in the report came from allegations that Clemens had used steroids for nearly a decade, dating back to his time with the Toronto Blue Jays in 1998. This information came from Clemens' former trainer, Brian McNamee. McNamee claimed that he injected Clemens with human growth hormones (HGH) for several years. Clemens quickly issued a public denial that he had taken any of these substances.

The debate between Clemens and McNamee took center stage during testimony before the House Committee on Oversight and Government Reform in February 2008. McNamee provided some evidence in support of his testimony in the form a beer can that contained needles that were allegedly used to inject substances into Clemens. Clemens countered that McNamee had manufactured evidence, with Clemens' lawyers branding McNamee as an unstable person with a vendetta against Clemens.

Because Clemens made statements about his steroid use under oath, it is possible that he could be charged with perjury if he were lying. This has been the fate of Bonds, who became baseball's all-time home run king in 2007. Bonds testified before a **grand jury** in December 2003 that he had not used performance-enhancing substances. However, government investigators later discovered that Bonds had tested positive for drugs. In November 2007, about one month before the release of the Mitchell Report, Bonds was indicted on charges of perjury and obstruction of justice.

Baseball has not been the only sport tarnished by allegations of steroids. In another high profile case in October 2007, track star Marion Jones pleaded guilty to charges that she had lied to investigators about using performance enhancers. She was later stripped of her Olympic metals, including three that she won at the Sydney Olympics in 2000.

STATUTE OF LIMITATIONS

A type of federal or state law that restricts the time within which legal proceedings may be brought.

John R. Sand & Gravel Company v. United States

Statutes of limitations are laws that place a time limit on filing lawsuits for a specific injury or claim. The amount of time varies by the type of law that is involved, be it contract, tort, or other legal fields. Because of the federalist system of government in the United States, there are both state and federal statutes of limitations. Courts usually enforce an untimely lawsuit by dismissing it. A defendant is most likely the person to bring it to a court's attention but a court could discover the late filing and dismiss the case of its own volition. Most statutes of limitations can be "tolled" (the time limit can be suspended for a time) if the plaintiff can show a compelling reason. However, there are certain statutes of limitations where there is no authority for a court to toll a **statute**. Moreover, if a court discovers that a case governed by such a hard-line limit is untimely, it must dismiss the case even if the defendant has waived the timeliness issue. The Supreme Court, in *John R. Sand & Gravel Company v. United States*, __U.S.__, 128 S. Ct. 750, 169 L. Ed. 2d 591(2008), reaffirmed these rules as applied to an action in the U.S. Court of Federal Claims, finding that case precedents reaching back to 1883 remained valid.

John R. Sand & Gravel Company held a 50-year mining lease on certain land. It filed suit in the Court of Federal Claims contending that the ENVIRONMENTAL PROTECTION AGENCY (EPA) had performed tasks on the land, such as building and moving fences, that constituted an unconstitutional taking of its **leasehold** rights. Congress established the Court of Federal Claims to hear property rights lawsuits involving the federal government. The federal **statute of limitations** for a Court of Federal Claims action is six years from the first time the claim accrues. The government first asserted that the company's claims were untimely, but as the litigation proceeded it conceded that certain claims were in fact timely. The government prevailed on the merits of the case and the company appealed to the Federal **Circuit Court** of Appeals, which hears all Court of Federal Claims cases. The government brief did not raise the statute of limitations argument but an *amicus's* (an interested person not a party to the lawsuit who files a legal brief on certain issues in the case) brief brought it to the court's attention. The appeals court believed it was obliged to address the issue and ruled that the action was untimely.

The Supreme Court, in a 7–2 decision, upheld the Federal Circuit's ruling. Justice STEPHEN BREYER, writing for the majority, noted the difference between the common form of statutes of limitations, which a defendant will waive if not asserted as an **affirmative defense**, and "jurisdictional" injunctions. Jurisdictional injunctions do not seek to protect a defendant's case specific interest in timeliness but rather are used to facilitate the administration of claims, limit the scope of a governmental waiver of **sovereign immunity**, or promote judicial efficiency. Courts have generally read the time limits in these statutes as more absolute. Justice Breyer pointed out that the Court had interpreted the **court of claims** limitations statute as a jurisdictional statute since the 1880s.

An 1883 Supreme Court decision on the court of claims statute barred a lawsuit as untimely, even though the CIVIL WAR made it impossible for the claimant to file within the six-year period. The Court refused to toll the statute due to the war, instead ruling that the statute did not permit tolling. In 1887 another decision by the Court reaffirmed the earlier one, stating that the Court of Claims could not waive a limitations period. A number of other cases in the 1890s followed this reasoning about the absolute nature of the court of claims limitations statute. Though the statute's language had been modified, Justice Breyer concluded that the changes were small and did not make a difference in the present case. Therefore, the company had to convince the Court to overturn this long-held precedent.

The company did not succeed. Justice Breyer dismissed the idea that the Court had already overturned the precedent in a 1990 case, ruling that it involved a different limitations statute. Moreover, the Court in that case said nothing about overturning the precedent. Breyer quipped that "Courts do not normally overturn a long line of earlier cases without mentioning the matter." As for taking a fresh look at the precedent, Justice Breyer declined. The importance of adhering to case precedents, *stare decisis*, obligated the Court to honor its previous rulings on the statute of limitations.

TAXATION

The process whereby charges are imposed on individuals or property by the legislative branch of the federal government and by many state governments to raise funds for public purposes.

Boulware v. United States

Federal tax law makes it a **felony** to willfully attempt "in any manner to evade or defeat any tax" imposed by the INTERNAL REVENUE CODE. A key element of tax evasion is the "existence of a tax deficiency," which the government must prove **beyond a reasonable doubt**. A question arose, however, as to whether a person charged with tax evasion who claimed he did not have a deficiency needed to prove that the funds he received from a corporation were nontaxable at the time the distribution occurred. The Supreme Court resolved this issue in *Boulware v. United States*, __U.S.__, __S.Ct. __, __ L.Ed.2d __ 2008 WL 552880 (2008), ruling that the defendant did not have to make such a showing. It was permissible for the defendant to introduce evidence that the income was nontaxable.

Michael Boulware was charged with tax evasion and filing a false income return, based on his diversion of funds from Hawaiian Isles Enterprises (HIE), a **closely held** corporation that he controlled as president, founder, and primary, but not sole, shareholder. The government claimed that Boulware had received **taxable income** by systematically diverting funds from HIE. At his trial the government showed that Boulware had given millions of dollars to his wife and to his girlfriend without reporting any of this money on his personal income tax returns. He diverted corporate funds by writing checks to employees and friends, who then returned the cash to him, by diverting payments by HIE customers, by submitting **fraudulent** invoices to HIE, and by laundering money through companies in Hong Kong and the Kingdom of Tonga.

Boulware fought these charges by seeking to introduce evidence that HIE had no retained or current earnings and profits in the taxable years in question. He contended that he had in effect received distributions of property that must have been returns of capital, up to his basis in his stock. In other words, he got back what he had put into the corporation, with no income derived from that original investment. The Internal Revenue Service Code states that the portion of any corporate distribution to a shareholder that is not earnings and profits is nontaxable. Boulware argued that because the return of capital was nontaxable, the government could not establish the tax deficiency required to convict him of tax evasion.

The government convinced the federal **district court** not to allow Boulware to introduce this line of argument, pointing to a 1976 Ninth **Circuit Court** of Appeals decision that held in a criminal tax evasion case, a diversion of funds may be considered a return of capital only after "some demonstration on the part of the taxpayer and/or the corporation that such [a distribution was] intended to be such a return." Boulware had not offered to make such a demonstration. A jury convicted Boulware on four counts of tax evasion and five counts of filing a false return. The Ninth Circuit upheld the verdict and its 1976 precedent that imposed an intent requirement on Boulware.

One judge concurred in the decision only because the court was required to follow precedent. He thought it illogical that a defendant "may be criminally sanctioned for tax evasion without owing a penny in taxes to the government." The precedent also contradicted the tax evasion **statute**, which requires a tax deficiency.

The Supreme Court, in a unanimous decision, vacated the criminal verdict and reversed the Ninth Circuit. Justice DAVID SOUTER, writing for the Court, found no merit in the 1976 Ninth Circuit case. There was no support for the view that a defendant had to show "contemporaneous intent" that the distribution was a return of capital. The tax consequences on such a distribution depend not on intent but on whether "the corporation had earnings and profits, and the amount of the taxpayer's basis for his stock." Agreeing with the concurring Ninth Circuit judge, Souter stated that there is "no criminal tax evasion without a tax deficiency, and there is no deficiency owing to a distribution" if the corporation "has no earnings or profits and the value distributed does not exceed the taxpayer-shareholder's basis for his stock." The Ninth Circuit precedent also failed to note that the contemporaneous intent requirement would be difficult to meet, as the corporation will not know until the end of its **fiscal** year whether there were earnings or profits. Therefore, Boulware had a right to make his defense based on the lack of a deficiency.

United States v. Clintwood Elkhorn Mining Company

On April 15, 2008, the U.S. SUPREME COURT issued a ruling where the Court held that coal exporters and producers were barred from recovering for past taxes beyond the period of time covered by the **statute of limitations** in the INTERNAL REVENUE CODE (I.R.C.). The case of *United States v. Clintwood Elkhorn Mining Co.*, ___ U.S. ___, 128 S. Ct. 1511, ___ L. Ed. 2d ___ (2008) resolved a potential conflict between the I.R.C. and the Tucker Act, which allows a private party to sue the government under some circumstances.

Congress first imposed the Coal **Excise** Tax in 1978 in order to finance the Black Lung Disability Trust Fund. The tax was rather unique in that it applied to all sales of coal, irrespective of whether the coal was sold domestically or was exported. Coal exporters brought suit against the United States, arguing that the tax violated the Constitution. More specifically, the companies pointed to the Export Clause of Article 1, Section 9 of the Constitution, which states that

"[n]o Tax or Duty shall be laid on **Articles** exported from any State." The U.S. **District Court** for the Eastern District of Virginia ruled that the Coal Excise Tax indeed violated the Export Clause, noting that the Supreme Court in the past had "broadly proscribed excise taxes levied on a variety of goods." *Ranger Fuel Corp. v. United States*, 33 F. Supp. 2d 466 (E.D. Va. 1998). Two years later, the INTERNAL REVENUE SERVICE (IRS) acquiesced in the decision in *Ranger Fuel*. IRS Notice 2000–28, 2000-1 Cumm. Bull. 1116.

Under the I.R.C., a taxpayer who seeks a refund of a tax that was erroneously or unlawfully assessed may file an action against the United States in either a U.S. district court or the U.S. Court of Federal Claims. Before filing such a suit, however, the taxpayer must comply with the I.R.C.'s tax refund scheme. I.R.C. § 7422. The claim must also be brought in a timely manner. Under I.R.C. § 6511, a taxpayer who seeks a "refund of an overpayment of any tax imposed by [the tax code] in respect of which tax the taxpayer is required to file a return" must file the return no later than three years from the time the return was filed, or two years from the time that the tax was paid (whichever is later). The section also states that "[n]o credit or refund shall be allowed or made" of the claim is not filed within the appropriate time limits.

Several coal producers and exporters, including Clintwood Elkhorn Mining Company, had paid excise taxes on their coal until the I.R.S. had acquiesced to the *Ranger Fuel* decision. In response to that decision, Clintwood Elkhorn and other companies in 2000 filed administrative claims with the I.R.S., requesting refunds for excise taxes. These claims could only cover the three-year period prior to this filing, due to the requirements of § 6511. The I.R.S. complied, refunding taxes for the years of 1997, 1998, and 1999.

In addition to the administrative claim filed with the I.R.S., the companies filed suit in the Court of Federal Claims, where they sought to recover a total of $1,065,936 for taxes paid in 1994, 1995, and 1996. The companies based their claim on the Tucker Act, which allows private citizens to sue the United States government. Under 28 U.S.C. § 1491, claims under the Tucker Act may be brought within six years of the time that the claim was filed.

The Court of Federal Claims relied on the Federal Circuit's decision in *Cyprus Amax Coal Co. v. United States*, 205 F.3d 1369 (Fed. Cir. 2000). In that case, the Federal Circuit held that the Excise Clause gave a party an independent **cause of action** under the Tucker Act, meaning that the party did not have to first file an administrative claim. The Court of Federal Claims allowed the companies to recover based on the Tucker Act, although the court would not allow recovery of interest. *Andalex Resources, Inc. v. United States*, 54 Fed. Cl. 563 (2002). On appeal, the Federal Circuit refused to revisit the holding of *Cyprus Amax* and held that the companies could bring their claims under the Tucker Act. Moreover, the **appellate court** reversed the Court of Federal Claims and held that the companies could recover interest. *Clintwood Elkhorn Mining Co. v. United States*, 473 F.3d 1373 (Fed. Cir. 2007).

The government sought an appeal from the Supreme Court, and the Court granted a **writ** of **certiorari**, and the Court agreed to hear the case. In a unanimous decision, the Court sided with the government, holding that the companies were barred from bringing suit for the taxes covering the period of 1994 to 1996. Writing for the Court, Chief Justice JOHN ROBERTS focused primarily on the **statutory** language of I.R.C. § 7422, which states that "[n]o suit . . . shall be maintained in any court for the recovery of any internal revenue tax alleged to have been erroneously or illegally assessed or collected, or of any penalty claimed to have been collected without authority, or of any sum alleged to have been excessive or in any manner wrongfully collected, until a claim for refund . . . has been duly filed with" the IRS. Commented Roberts, "Five 'any's' in one sentence and it begins to seem that Congress meant the **statute** to have expansive reach."

The companies tried to argue that the language regarding the I.R.C.'s requirements is ambiguous. The Court, however, flatly rejected this premise. "The companies argue that these statutory provisions are ambiguous . . . , but we cannot imagine what language could more clearly state that taxpayers seeking refunds of unlawfully assessed taxes much comply with the Code's refund scheme before bringing suit, including the requirement to file a timely administrative claim."

The companies focused much of their attention on their argument that the Tucker Act establishes an independent cause of action against the government. The Court refused to decide whether this was true, because the Court determined that it did not matter to the outcome of the case. The Court likewise rejected the companies' arguments that claims for refunds of taxes paid in violation of the Export Clause

should be treated any differently than other types of refund cases. Accordingly, the Court reversed the Federal Circuit's opinion.

Knight v. Commissioner of Internal Revenue

The intricacies and ambiguities of the INTERNAL REVENUE CODE keep legions of accountants and financial planners well-employed. The U.S. SUPREME COURT infrequently wades into tax law to settle disputes within the circuit courts of appeals on how to interpret a particular code provision. Such was the case in *Knight v. Commissioner of Internal Revenue*, __U.S.__, 128 S.Ct.782, __ L.Ed.2d __ (2008), where the legal debate was focused on the deductibility of certain trust expenses. The INTERNAL REVENUE SERVICE (IRS) ruled that the trust expenses were limited to an amount that exceeds 2 percent of gross adjusted income. The trust administrator argued that the trust was entitled to deduct the entire amount of the expense. The Court, in a case of **statutory** construction, ruled that the law clearly meant to limit the deductible amount.

Michael Knight was the **trustee** of the William Rudkin trust, which was established in Connecticut in 1967. In 2000, Knight hired a financial advising firm to provide its expertise on management of the trust. The trust paid the firm over $22,000 that year and its **fiduciary** income tax return for 2000 reported total income of $624,000. It deducted the entire $22,000 on the return but a later IRS audit found that these fees were miscellaneous itemized deductions subject to the 2 percent floor. The IRS allowed the trust to deduct the investment advising fees only to the extent that they exceeded 2 percent of **adjusted gross income**. This resulted in a tax deficiency of $4,448. Knight filed a petition in the U.S. **Tax Court** seeking review of this decision. He contended that under Connecticut state law he was required to obtain investment advisory services and therefore had to pay the associated fees. These fees, he argued, were unique to trusts and therefore were fully deductible under 26 U.S.C. § 67(e)(1). The Tax Court disagreed, ruling that this **statute** only applied to expenses that are not commonly incurred outside the trust setting. Investment advice is purchased by many individuals, so the trust expenses were subject to the 2 percent floor. The **Circuit Court** for the Second Circuit upheld the Tax Court decision.

The Supreme Court, in a unanimous decision, agreed that the fees were not fully deductible. Chief Justice John Robert, writing for the Court, noted that before 1986 itemized deductions were deductible in full. However, this system was complex and could be used, requiring extensive taxpayer record-keeping for small expenditures. Enforcing this part of the tax code was also taking a toll on IRS resources. The TAX REFORM ACT OF 1986, 100 Stat. 2085, changed this policy, placing the 2 percent floor on miscellaneous itemized deductions for any taxable year to the extent that aggregate of these deductions exceeds 2 percent of adjusted **gross income**. Investment advisory fees are deductible as miscellaneous itemized deductions, as the Code does note this as of one the categories that is fully deductible. Under § 67(e), trust expenses can be fully deductible if they "would not have been incurred if the property were not held in such trust or estate."

Knight had argued that this exception established a "straightforward causation test." The proper inquiry was whether a trust expense "was caused by the fact that the property was held in trust or estate." In this case the investment fees met the test because the costs were caused by the trustee's obligation to obtain financial advice in compliance with the trustee's fiduciary duties. Chief Justice Roberts was not persuaded. He pointed out that all or nearly all of a trust's expenses were incurred because the trustee has a duty to incur them: "otherwise, there would be no reason for the trust to incur the expense in the first place." The argument offered by Knight was circular: "Trust investment advice fees are caused by the fact the property is held in trust." If Knight's position was correct there would have been no need for Congress to insert the exception clause.

The Court ruled that the test adopted by Fourth and Federal Circuit Courts of Appeals was correct. Under this test costs incurred by trusts that escape the 2 percent floor are those that would not "commonly" or "customarily" be incurred by individuals. In this case Chief Justice Roberts noted that it was "not uncommon or unusual for individuals to hire an investment adviser." Therefore, the trust's financial advisory expenses were not fully tax-deductible.

MeadWestvaco v. Illinois Department of Revenue

The question before the U.S. Supreme Court in *MeadWestvaco Corp. v. Illinois Department of Revenue* No. 06-1413, 553 U.S. ___ (2008), was whether and under what circumstances a parent company may use a division as a non-taxable "investment" and thus avoid state tax consequences when the division is sold. An unanimous Supreme Court remanded the case to the Illinois Appellate Court for renewed analysis and determination under U.S. Supreme Court precedent.

MeadWestvaco, the petitioner, was the successor in interest to its wholly owned subsidiary known as the Mead Corporation (Mead), an Ohio company. In 1968, Mead bought Data Corporation. At that time, Mead dealt mainly in paper products and school supplies, and made the purchase because Data Corporation owned ink-jet printing technology that Mead was interested in acquiring. Data Corporation's business at that time also included an information technology component that ultimately developed into Lexis/Nexis, a leader in the field of electronic legal, business, and news research software tools.

In 1994, Mead sold Lexis/Nexis for approximately $1.5 billion and realized just over $1 billion in gain. However, it did not report any of this gain as business income on its Illinois tax return for 1994. Instead, it took the position that the gain qualified as non-business income that should be allocated to Mead's domiciliary state of Ohio, under Illinois's Income Tax Act (ITA)[Ill. Comp. Stat. Ch. 35, § 5/303(a)]. But according to the State of Illinois, after auditing Mead's return, the ITA required Mead to treat the capital gain from the sale as taxable business income. Mead paid the tax, then filed suit in state court.

The relevant provision in the ITA allows the state to tax a non-domiciliary corporation that conducts business in Illinois on business income that is derived from, or "apportioned to," its business in Illinois. Under the ITA, taxable business income includes income from intangible property, such as a corporation's subsidiaries. However, the "apportionment" referenced in the ITA is subject to constitutional limits of the Due Process and Commerce clauses. Accordingly, income from intangible property is only apportionable if the business and the intangible property are so closely related that they can be considered a singular entity (a "unitary business"). In the alternative, the intangible property must be necessary to the operation of the business (an "operational function").

The state trial court rejected Illinois' argument that Mead and Lexis/Nexis were a unitary business, but it found that, in the alternative, the gain was apportionable business income, because Lexis/Nexis served an operational function. Mead appealed to the Appellate Court of Illinois. That court upheld the apportionment tax and affirmed the judgment in the state's favor.

But the U.S. Supreme Court concluded that the state courts had "misapprehended the principles that we have developed for determining whether a multistate business is unitary . . ." The high court vacated the decision of the Appellate Court of Illinois and remanded for further proceedings consistent with prior Supreme Court precedent.

To wit, the Supreme Court had previously held that the Due Process and Commerce Clauses prohibited states to tax "extraterritorial values." *Container Corp. Of America v. Franchise Tax Bd.*, 463 U.S. 159 (1983). The "unitary business" language came from *Hunt-Wesson, Inc. v. Franchise Tax Bd. Of Cal.*, 528 U.S. 458 (2000), in which the Court held that a state may tax an apportioned share of the value generated by intrastate and extrastate activities of a multistate enterprise, if those activities form part of a unitary business.

Justice Alito delivered the opinion for an unanimous Supreme Court. Because in this case, Mead did business in Illinois, the inquiry shifted from whether Illinois may tax Mead, to what it may tax, wrote Alito. Under the unitary business principle, a state need not "isolate the intrastate income-producing activities from the rest of the business." Instead, it may "tax an apportioned sum of the corporation's multistate business if the business is unitary." (quoting from *Allied-Signal, Inc. v. Director, Div. Of Taxation*, 504 U.S. 768.

Justice Alito concluded that the Appellate Court of Illinois was misguided in applying an "operational function" test. Instead, said Alito, because in this case the "asset" was another business, the state appellate court should have looked for the existence of "functional integration, centralized management, and economies of scale." *Mobil Oil Corp. v. Commissioner of Taxes of Vt.*, 445 U.S. 425. This would be the proper examination to determine whether or not the two were a unitary business for tax purposes. Because the appellate court had relied on its operational function test instead, on remand, it should re-examine under the unitary business question, the Court concluded.

Justice Thomas wrote a separate opinion in which he concurred in the results but opined that the Court should refrain from jurisdiction over state tax cases.

TERRORISM

The unlawful use of force or violence against persons or property in order to coerce or intimate a government or the civilian population in furtherance of political or social objectives.

Jose Padilla Convicted On Terrorism Conspiracy Charges

The five-year legal saga involving a man once designated as an enemy combatant in the war on terrorism came to an end in a Miami, Florida federal courtroom in August 2007. A jury convicted Padilla, once designated and confined as an enemy combatant in the WAR ON TERRORISM, on terrorism conspiracy charges. Though convicted of conspiring with two other co-defendants to murder, kidnap, and maim people overseas, the government's most dramatic claim—that Padilla had sought to build a radioactive "dirty bomb" within the United States—was not part of the case. Though Padilla could have been sentenced to life in prison, U.S. **District Court** Judge Marcia Cooke reduced the penalty to 17 years and four months imprisonment. She did so in part because of the way Padilla had been treated during his confinement in a South Carolina Navy brig. In her view Padilla was subjected to "harsh conditions" and "extreme environmental stresses" while there.

The Padilla case arose in the aftermath of the September 11, 2001 terrorist attacks on the World Trade Towers and the Pentagon. Congress quickly enacted the USA Patriot Act and President GEORGE W. BUSH ordered suspected terrorists held as enemy combatants. On May 8, 2002, Padilla, a U.S. citizen, was arrested at Chicago's O'Hare Airport as he disembarked from a flight from Pakistan. He was arrested on a material witness warrant issued by the federal district court in New York City. Padilla was transported to New York and held in a local correctional facility. Attorney General JOHN ASHCROFT did not announce Padilla's arrest until June 10, alleging that Padilla had traveled in the Middle East, met with senior associates of al Qaeda's leader Osama Bid Laden, and proposed stealing radioactive material to make a "dirty bomb" within the United States. Ashcroft asserted that Padilla had undergone terrorist training and had arrived in Chicago to begin his terrorist activities.

A New York federal judge appointed a lawyer for Padilla but on June 9, 2002 President Bush signed an order designating Padilla as an enemy combatant. The order directed Secretary of Defense Donald Rumsfeld to take custody of Padilla, and Rumsfeld acted quickly in moving Padilla to a South Carolina military prison. On June 10 Ashcroft announced Padilla's apprehension and on June 11 the court held a hearing in which the warrant was dismissed and Padilla's lawyer filed a **habeas corpus** petition, demanding her client's release. The government refused

Court artist
portrait of Jose
Padilla,
January 2008.

AP IMAGES

had allegedly filled out to attend a terrorist training camp. The defense contended that the three men were passionate Muslims who voiced their beliefs and that they had no connection to Al Qaeda. Moreover, the defense claimed the charges were politically motivated. In the end the jury convicted the three men on all charges.

At Padilla's January 2008 sentencing hearing, Judge Cooke stated that as serious as the conspiracy was, there was "no evidence that these defendants personally maimed, kidnapped or killed anyone in the United States or elsewhere." In sentencing Padilla to 17 years in prison, the judge found that the conditions imposed on him while isolated and confined warranted consideration.

Federal District Courts Strike Down Parts of the Patriot Act

Within a three-week period in September 2007, two federal district courts struck down portions of the USA PATRIOT Act, which was originally enacted to provide law enforcement with greater tools to conduct counter-terrorism activities. In one case in a New York **district court**, a judge determined that parts of the act violated the FIRST AMENDMENT to the U.S. Constitution. In a second case arising in an Oregon district court, a judge determined that the Patriot Act was unconstitutional as applied to a U.S. citizen suspected of being involved with a bombing in Madrid, Spain.

Congress originally enacted the United and Strengthening of America by Providing Appropriate Tools Required to Intercept and Obstruct Terrorism Act (USA PATRIOT Act, or Patriot Act), Pub. L. No. 107-56, 115 Stat. 272 on October 26, 2001. Since its enactment, the Patriot Act has been the subject of extensive debate as well as judicial challenges. The AMERICAN CIVIL LIBERTIES UNION (ACLU) has been especially critical of the **statute**, arguing that many of its provisions violate a myriad of constitutional rights.

The provisions of 18 U.S.C.A. § 2709 was originally enacted in 1986 as part of the Electronic Communication Privacy Act, Pub. L. No. 99-508, 100 Stat. 1848. It was subsequently amended by the Patriot Act. This section applies to the issuance of National Security Letters (NSLs) by the FEDERAL BUREAU OF INVESTIGATION (FBI) to wire and electronic communication services providers (ECSPs). Under this section, the FBI may issue NSLs to request a wide range of information about subscribers to ECSPs. In addition to the contents of messages, the infor-

to allow the lawyer to meet or talk with Padilla, which led to a legal battle that culminated in a 2004 Supreme Court decision that allowed Padilla and his lawyer to meet but did not address the constitutionality of applying enemy combatant status to a U.S. citizen. Instead, the Court ruled that the case should have been brought in South Carolina rather than New York. The case was about to be heard on its merits by the Supreme Court in 2005 when the federal government announced that it was sending Padilla back into the criminal justice system on terrorism conspiracy.

The charges contained nothing about the alleged dirty-bomb plot, a plot to blow up apartment buildings, or even Padilla's presence in Afghanistan in late 2001. The government alleged that in the 1990s Padilla provided support to jihadists in Bosnia and Chechnya. Prior to trial Padilla's lawyers sought to have him declared mentally incompetent. For the three years when he was in the Navy brig he was subjected to extreme conditions: sleep deprivation, stress positions, and extreme temperatures. These conditions, coupled with solitary confinement and no exposure to natural light, had allegedly robbed Padilla of his mental competency. The government disagreed and claimed Padilla had never been mistreated. The judge agreed and the case proceeded to trial.

The trial lasted for three months. The government introduced recordings of the three defendants' phone conversations between 1993 and 2000, as well as an application that Padilla mation that may be subject to an NSL can also include a user's activity logs as well as information that can provide the identity of the user. For the FBI to send an NSL, the FBI director must certify that the information sought to be obtained is "relevant to an authorized investigation to protect against international terrorism or clandestine intelligence activities."

An unidentified Internet service provider, along with the ACLU, originally challenged the application of § 2709 in 2004. On September 28, 2004, the U.S. District Court for the Southern District of New York held in favor of the plaintiffs by ruling that § 2709 violated the First and Fourth Amendments to the U.S. Constitution. *Doe v. Ashcroft*, 334 F. Supp. 2d 471 (S.D.N.Y. 2004). A federal district court in Connecticut reached a similar conclusion shortly thereafter. *Doe v. Gonzales*, 386 F. Supp. 2d 66 (D. Conn. 2005).

While the appeals of these decisions were still pending, Congress amended the Patriot Act, including § 2709, in the USA Patriot Improvement and Reauthorization Act of 2005, Pub. L. No. 109-177, 120 Stat. 192. The reauthorization made a number of substantive changes to § 2709 and also added provisions regarding **judicial review** of NSLs. In light of these amendments, the Second Circuit remanded the original New York case to allow the trial court to review whether the statute was still unconstitutional. *Doe v. Gonzales*, 449 F.3d 415 (2d Cir. 2006).

The plaintiffs proceeded with their case, arguing that § 2709, along with the judicial review provisions contained in 18 U.S.C. § 3511, were unconstitutional. The plaintiffs' primary arguments focused on free speech concerns. The court acknowledged that while NSLs serve an important investigative function, the effect that these NSLs could have on free speech carried a heavy weight. Judge Victor Marreno wrote, "In light of the seriousness of the potential intrusion into the individual's personal affairs and the significant possibility of a chilling effect on speech and association—particularly of expression that is critical of the government or its policies—a compelling need exists to ensure that the use of NSLs is subject to the safeguards of public accountability, checks and balances, and separation of powers that our Constitution prescribes."

Of particular concern in the case was the provision that forbids the recipient of an NSL from disclosing receipt of the letter. The original version of the law contained a complete bar on disclosure, while the revised version requires the FBI to certify that disclosure may harm national security, criminal investigations, diplo-

macy, or someone's safety. Nevertheless, Marreno determined that the statute still curtails speech to an extent that it violates the First Amendment, noting that a recipient of an NSL is "effectively barred from engaging in any discussion regarding their experiences and opinions related to the government's use." Because the statute did not contain adequate procedural safeguards to protect free speech rights, the court determined that § 2709 in its entirety was unconstitutional. *Doe v. Gonzales*, 500 F. Supp. 2d 379 (S.D.N.Y. 2007).

The case in Oregon arose from the investigation of a terrorist bombing in Madrid in 2004. Within days of the bombings, FBI agents focused their attention on Brandon Mayfield, an Oregon lawyer who is also a former Army officer. FBI agents claimed that Mayfield's fingerprints matched those found on a plastic bag that contained explosive detonators. The FBI applied to the Foreign Intelligence Security Court (FISC) for authorization to place electronic listening devices on Mayfield's home and law office, and the court granted the request.

FBI tests had allegedly supported the claims that the fingerprints were Mayfield's, but other tests performed by police in Spain negated this proof. Nevertheless, based on the faulty fingerprint tests, the FBI obtained broad search warrants, and agents seized many of the personal items of both Mayfield and his family. Mayfield was eventually arrested, and his family was not told where he was being held. After two weeks of imprisonment, though, Spanish police captured a primary suspect from Algeria. Mayfield was then released.

Mayfield sought a **declaratory judgment** in federal court in the District of Oregon. He claimed that the FBI's motivation for pursuing him was due to his Muslim faith. Mayfield argued that the government's actions violated the FOURTH AMENDMENT, and Judge Ann Aiken agreed. Aiken rejected the government's argument that the FISC was sufficient to guarantee constitutional rights. "In place of the Fourth Amendment, the people are expected to defer to the executive branch and its representation that it will authorize such surveillance only when appropriate," wrote Aiken. "[The government] is asking this court to, in essence, amend the Bill of Rights, by giving it an interpretation that would deprive it of any real meaning. The court declines to do so." Accordingly, the court granted Mayfield's motion on September 26, 2007. *Mayfield v. United States*, 504 F. Supp. 2d 1023 (D. Or. 2007). In 2006, the government settled

Mayfield's financial claims by giving him $2 million, and allowed him to continue his challenge of the Patriot Act provisions discussed above.

United States v. Ressam

The U.S. SUPREME COURT in May 2008 upheld the conviction of the person known as the "Millennium Bomber" on federal explosive charges. The result of the 8–1 decision was that the defendant's prison sentence was increased by ten years. The case was noteworthy not only because it was the continuation of a well-known case on terrorism, but also because it marked the first appearance of Attorney General Michael B. Mukasey before the Supreme Court.

Ahmed Ressam was an Algerian citizen who spent time in France in the early 1990s. When he was arrested on a immigration-related charge in 1994, he obtained a passport with the name of Anjer Tahar Medjadi and moved to Montreal, Canada. He sought but was denied asylum in Canada, but was nevertheless allowed to remain there because Canada had imposed a moratorium on deportations to Algeria.

After he was recruited by an operative named Abderraouf Hannachi in 1998, he arranged to travel under the assumed name of Benni Antoine Noris to Pakistan and to Afghanistan to be trained by the al Qaeda as a terrorist. During a six-month period, he received training in using firearms and explosives. He also learned how to destroy certain infrastructure targets, including power plants, military installations, railroads, and airports.

In 1999, Mokhtar Haouari recruited Ressam to carry out a scheme to commit terrorist acts on United States soil. Also recruited as part of the plot was Abdel Ghani Meskini, a resident of Brooklyn, New York. One of the plots that the group planned to carry out was the bombing of Los Angeles International Airport on New Year's Eve in 1999. This plot earned Ressam, its mastermind, the nickname "Millennium Bomber."

Ressam returned to Canada in February 1999. When he returned to Montreal, he continued to work on the plot to bomb the L.A. airport. In November 1999, he and Abdelmajid Dahoumane traveled to Vancouver, British Columbia. The rented a car, and on December 14, 1999, loaded the trunk with explosives, electronic timing devices, detonators, fertilizer, and aluminum sulfate (these items were hidden in the spare tire well). Ressam and Dahoumane then boarded a ferry at Tswassen, British Columbia. Ressam thereafter boarded another ferry headed for Port Angeles, Washington,

while Dahoumane returned to Vancouver. Ressam used his passport with the name Benni Noris, and customs officials searched his vehicle, including the trunk, but did not find the explosives hidden in the tire well.

When the ferry arrived at Port Angeles, Ressam was stooped by inspector Diana Dean. He acted nervous and agitated, and so Dean asked Ressam to fill out a customs declaration form, which Ressam signed as Benni Noris. Upon their search of the vehicle, officials found the substances that could be used to make bombs. This included ingredients for primary explosives, which were contained in a pill bottle and a zinc lozenge case. The bombs that Ressam had planned to detonate at the L.A. Airport would have been twice as strong as normal TNT and would likely have killed and/or injured hundreds of people.

Ressam was indicted in 2001 on charges that he planned to commit acts of international terrorism against the United States. He was also charged with lying to customs officials as well as smuggling explosives. Prosecutors sought to impose the provisions of 18 U.S.C. § 844(h)(2), which punishes a person who "carries an explosive during the commission of any **felony** which may be prosecuted in a court of the United States" for a mandatory period of ten years in prison. The government argued that the felony that Ressam committed was lying on his customs form. Ressam argued that the section should not apply to him because his act of carrying the explosives did not play a part in making a false statement on the customs form. The trial court overruled Ressam's objection, and the court convicted Ressam on all counts.

Ressam had cooperated in the trial of Haouari, who was convicted of terrorist activities in 2002. Ressam's sentencing had been delayed because of his cooperation, but he stopped cooperating early in 2003. In 2005, four years after his conviction, the trial court imposed a sentence of 22 years in prison. Because of the relatively minimal sentence, the United States appealed to the Ninth **Circuit Court** of Appeals. Ressam, in turn, cross-appealed, arguing that he should not have been convicted under 18 U.S.C. § 844(h)(2).

The Ninth Circuit asked, rhetorically, "Does [the statute] criminalize carrying an explosive during the commission of another felony, or does it criminalize carrying an explosive during and *in relation* to that other felony?" The court then stress that "[t]he answer matters in this case because the government offered no evidence that Ressam's carrying the explosives in any way facilitated his falsifying the customs declaration form." On previous occasions, the Third Circuit and the Fifth Circuit courts of appeals had declined to hold that the explosives had to be carried in relation to the underlying felonies. Nevertheless, the Ninth Circuit disagreed with the other circuits and held that the **statutory** language implied that carrying the explosive had a relationship with the underlying felony for the second to apply. The court thus set aside Ressam's sentence. *United States v. Ressam*, 474 F.3d 597 (9th Cir. 2007).

The U.S. Supreme Court agreed to hear the case, and in an 8–1 decision, reversed the Ninth Circuit. According to the majority opinion written by Justice JOHN PAUL STEVENS, the legislative history of § 844(h)(2) supported a conclusion that Congress did not intend for the government to have to prove a relationship between the explosive that was carried and the underlying felony. According to Stevens, "There is no need to consult dictionary definitions of the word 'during' in order to arrive at the conclusion that **respondent** engaged in the precise conduct" that that federal **statute** described. *United States v. Ressam*, No. 07-455, 2008 WL 2078505 (2008).

The case gained as much attention for one of the lawyers arguing the case as it did for the substance. Mukasey, who assumed office at Attorney General in November 2007, argued the case on behalf of the United States. He admitted to reporters that he was nervous before his appearance, but he reportedly performed in a manner expected of a someone with more experience before the Court.

TOBACCO

Rowe v. New Hampshire Motor Transport Association

States often seek to fix problems by enacting **statutes** that may come into conflict with federal laws on the same subject. In many cases the state and federal laws peacefully coexist. However, when the federal government has drawn up a detailed regulatory scheme, it often inserts language stating that the law preempts any state law on the topic. When a state enacts a law in spite of a clear statement of federal **preemption**, the stage is set for a lawsuit challenging the legality of the state law. In *Rowe v. New Hampshire Motor Transport Association*, ___ U.S. ___, 128 S. Ct. 989, 169 L. Ed. 2d 933 (2008), the state of Maine's desire to prevent minors

from obtaining tobacco products ran up against the federal law that deregulated the trucking industry. Provisions of the state law placed obligations on trucking firms that the firms said placed unfair burdens on them. The Supreme Court agreed with several trucking associations who brought suit, ruling that the state law was invalid as it was preempted by the federal trucking law.

In 2003, Maine enacted a law that regulated the delivery and sale of tobacco products in an attempt to curtail the sale of tobacco products to minors. It provided that only Maine-licensed tobacco retailers could accept orders for delivery of tobacco. It required the retailer to use a delivery service that provided a special receipt-verification service. In addition, the law forbids any person to knowingly transport a tobacco product to a person in Maine unless the sender or receiver has a Maine license. A person is deemed to have known that the package contain tobacco product if the package is marked as containing tobacco or the person receives the package from someone whose name appears on a list of un-license tobacco retailers. Several interstate trucking associations challenged the law arguing that the 1994 federal law preempting state trucking regulations prohibited Maine from imposing these requirements on truckers. The federal **district court** agreed that the federal law preempted the Maine law. On appeal, the First **Circuit Court** of Appeals upheld the decision.

The Supreme Court, in a unanimous decision, agreed that the federal law preempted the state tobacco law. Justice STEPHEN BREYER, writing for the Court, noted that the 1994 federal trucking deregulation act prohibited the states from enacting any law "relating to" a motor carrier "price, router, or service." Congress believed it in the public interest to deregulate the trucking industry in 1980, as it has the airline industry in 1978, in an effort foster competition and allow market forces to work their will. In 1994 Congress enacted the ban on state regulation of trucking to remove the last impediment to free market forces. Justice Breyer first looked at the language of the 1978 airline deregulation law because Congress had copied the language of the air-carrier preemption provision into the 1994 act. Under rules of **statutory** interpretation the Court said that when one law replicates the language of another law, the judicial interpretations of the old law must apply to the new law. Therefore, the 1992 Supreme Court decision that preempted states from regulating airlines guided the Court in its analysis of the Maine law. The 1992 decision determined that state enforcement actions having a connection to carrier "rates, routes, or services" are preempted. Congress' desire to foster competition, improve service, and lower prices would be undercut by a quilt of regulations by the 50 states.

Justice Breyer concluded that the 1992 decision must be applied to the Maine law. The law would require "carriers to offer a system of services that the market does not now provide (and which the **carriers** would prefer not to offer.)" Therefore, the state law would produce the very effects that the 1994 federal law sought to avoid, i.e., the imposition of regulation rather than reliance on competitive market forces. In addition, the imposing of civil liability on a carrier for failing to examine every package and to consult the list of proscribed shippers would regulate "a significant aspect of the motor carrier's package pick-up and delivery service." Maine sought to justify the law on public health objectives. Justice Breyer acknowledged these objectives but held that the federal law did not make an exception for these objectives. Maine could take other actions that would not conflict with federal law, such as banning all non-face-to-face sales of tobacco. The state could also seek congressional approval of an amendment to the federal law, creating such an exception.

TORTURE

Waterboarding and Other Tactics

In 1988, the United States, along with several other nations, signed the declaration of the United Nations Convention Against Torture (reaffirmed in 1994), which defined torture as,

> "Any act by which severe pain or suffering, whether physical or mental, is intentionally inflicted on a person for such purposes as obtaining from him or a third person information or a confession, punishing him for an act he or a third person has committed . . . or intimidating or coercing him or a third person, or for any reason based on discrimination of any kind, when such pain or suffering is inflicted by or at the instigation of or with the consent or acquiescence of a public official or other person."

Twenty years later, in 2008, President George Bush vetoed a Congressional bill that banned "water boarding" and other allegedly cruel tactics contemplated for possible use on foreign detainees held outside the United States. President Bush explained his veto, stating that the ban "would take away one of the most valuable tools in the war on terror." The Bush Administration had consistently held that such tactics were neither torture nor illegal. As support, the Administration had consistently pointed to guidance received from the U.S. Department of Justice (DOJ) over the years.

Those "valuable tools" allegedly included, in addition to water boarding, extreme temperatures, head-slapping, and a number of combinations of the above. Water boarding is a technique involving the simulation of drowning. It involves binding a person to an inclined board, covering his or her head with cloth or cellophane, and pouring water repeatedly over the face and head. In some cases water actually enters the nose and mouth, but mostly, the sensation of water hitting the face (cloth or cellophane) causes a psychological reaction during which the brain processes information of drowning. This causes a gag reflex similar to choking.

The technique was brought to public attention in 2007, when certain internal memoranda of DOJ's Office of Legal Counsel (OLC) implied that military officials interrogating foreign detainees outside the United States answered to a different set of standards and definitions, especially those that explained what constituted prohibited "torture." The memoranda were prepared in response to a request for legal advice and guidance from the Department of Defense (DOD). Specifically, they werer intended to give legal guidance to DOD lawyers wrestling with a list of interrogation methods for prisoners at the military prison at Guantanamo Bay in Cuba.

In simpler terms, the memoranda gave the military broad latitude and discretion to use relatively harsh interrogation methods without fear of prosecution or violation of constitutional restraints. The legal logic contained within the memoranda conveyed that federal laws prohibiting assault were not applicable to military interrogators dealing with members of Al Qaeda because of Presidential powers during wartime. The memos also opined that many American and international laws would not apply to the treatment of detainees overseas.

According to the 2003 internal DOJ memoranda (not de-classified and released until 2008), a more narrow definition of torture applied to military interrogators. Similar to the memorandum written for the Central Intelligence Agency (CIA) in 2002, the 2003 memo offered the following definition of what constituted torture:

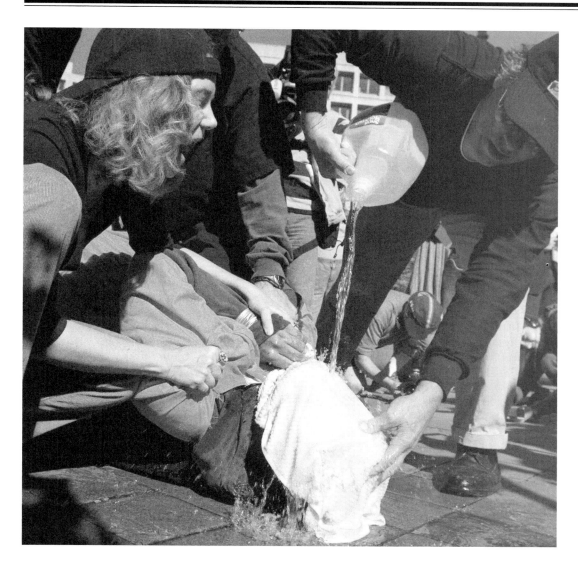

Protestors demonstrate the "water boarding" torture method on a volunteer in front of the Justice Department, Washington DC, November 2007.

AP IMAGES

"The victim must experience intense pain or suffering of the kind that is equivalent to the pain that would be associated with serious physical injury so severe that death, organ failure or permanent damage resulting in a loss of significant body functions will likely result. . . ."

The 2003 memorandum, authored by then-deputy counsel in the OLC, John Yoo, and finally released in April 2008, further advised,

"If a government defendant were to harm an enemy combatant during an interrogation . . . he would be doing so in order to prevent further attacks on the United States by the al Qaeda terrorist network. . . ."

Despite the wide latitude provided to interrogators under the memo's guidance, the OLC officially rejected the memos as containing "flawed reasoning," and DOJ and Pentagon officials never authorized some of the more harsh interrogation methods used by the CIA. Moreover, no Pentagon officials had since found any senior Bush Administration officials as having been complicit in any of the abuse at Abu Ghraib prison in Iraq. (Inhumane treatment by U.S. military personnel of prisoners at Abu Ghraib in 2004 was first revealed to the world through Internet photographs showing prisoners made to strip, wear leashes and hoods, chains, and be threatened by menacing attack dogs.) However, their investigations did find that for several years following the September 11, 2001 attacks, the Pentagon admittedly failed to set uniform standards for military interrogations worldwide. The Bush administration maintained that the CIA's water boarding against three top al Qaida detainees, Khalid Sheikh Mohammed, Abu

Zubaydah and Abd al-Rahim al-Nashiri was legal. The practice was halted in 2006.

Following this and other internal guidance and the debate it caused at the time, Congress passed the Detainee Treatment Act in 2005, requiring the DOD to restrict interrogation methods to those set out in the Army Field Manual, which banned coercive interrogations. In 2007, President Bush issued an executive order narrowing the list of approved techniques for the CIA. Although that list of authorized techniques remained classified, intelligence officials did state that water boarding was not on the list of approved techniques, but that President Bush could authorize it during an emergency.

Amid a new flurry of concern, White House Press Secretary Dana Perino responded to *The Times* report on October 4, 2007. Perino advised, "I am not going to comment on any specific alleged techniques. It is not appropriate for me to do so. And to do so would provide the enemy with more information on how to train against these techniques . . . but I will reiterate to you once again that we do not torture. . . ."

In December 2007, amid congressional inquiry, the CIA declared that it had destroyed video tapes of the interrogations of some key Iraqi detainees. This was met with much skepticism and criticism by Congress. In early 2008, the House Judiciary Committee conducted its fifth hearing into the meaning and parameters of "torture," particularly as applied to detainees held outside the United States. Called to testify, John Yoo declared executive privilege. David Addington, prior chief of staff to Dick Cheney, could not "recollect" matters of substance or interest. Former CIA Director George Tenet testified that the value of water boarding and other "enhanced" methods of interrogation "far exceeded" any other method(s). Former Attorney General John Ashcroft also testified in 2008 that water boarding was not torture, and had been approved by DOJ officials before being employed. All administration officials denied that any illegal "torture" was involved in military interrogations.

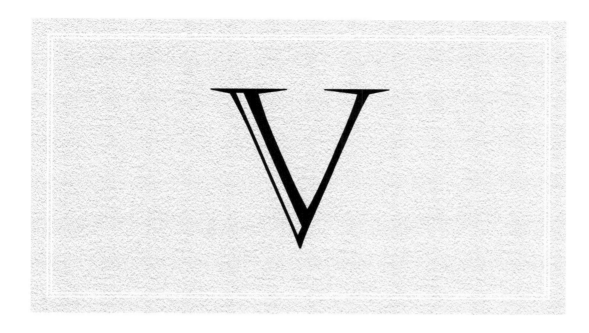

VOTING RIGHTS

Crawford v. Marion County Bd. Of Elections

Election law experts had long expressed hope that the U.S. Supreme Court would address the issue of voter ID requirements, especially photographic identification, found in many state laws. Appellate courts upheld such laws in Arizona, Georgia, and Indiana, but the Missouri Supreme Court had struck its voter identification statute in 2006. It was suggested that the inconsistency in state statutes could wreak havoc for the 2008 presidential elections.

But in *Crawford v. Marion County Bd. Of Elections* No. 7-21,553 U.S. ___, the U.S. Supreme Court affirmed the Seventh Circuit Court of Appeals' decision that upheld Indiana's state law requiring, with certain exceptions, in-person voters to present government-issued photo identification. The caveat that the photo ID be government-issued made Indiana's law one of the strictest in the nation. Still, the Supreme Court, by a 6–3 margin, concluded that the photo ID requirement was closely related to Indiana's legitimate interest in preventing voter fraud.

In 2005, the Indiana Legislature passed a new law prospectively requiring all voters in either state or federal elections to present photo identification issued by either the United States or the State of Indiana. Prior to this new enactment, voters had been permitted to sign the poll book and have their signatures compared to a photocopy record of their signatures on file. If their identification was challenged, they could sign an affidavit stating their identity. This would be coupled with an affidavit from the challenger, and a state prosecutor would investigate each incident.

Before the new law had gone into effect, a group of plaintiffs, including William Crawford and the Indiana Democratic Party, filed suit in U.S. District Court for the Southern District of Indiana. They argued that the new requirement denied them the right to vote and thus violated the First and Fourteenth Amendments to the U.S. Constitution, the Voting Rights Act of 1965, and the Help America Vote Act (HAVA) of 2002. The district court dismissed the case on summary judgment.

On appeal to the Seventh Circuit, a divided appellate court upheld the law and affirmed the district court. Judge Richard Posner, writing for the majority, found that the ID requirement did not severely burden the right to vote and was therefore within the state's regulatory power. He specifically addressed the underlying current of much contention: that the law favored one political party. "No doubt most people who don't have ID are low on the economic ladder and thus, if they do vote, are more likely to vote for Democratic than Republican candidates," he acknowledged. But the purpose of law, he continued, was to reduce voting fraud, "and voting fraud impairs the right of legitimate voters to vote by diluting their votes,—dilution being recognized to be an impairment of the right to vote."

The U.S. Supreme Court agreed in a plurality opinion. First, all nine justices rejected the argument that voter ID laws demanded the strictest scrutiny under judicial review, because those laws could potentially disenfranchise voters. Instead, the Court held that a state law's burden

213

must be justified by relevant and legitimate state interests "sufficiently weighty to justify the limitation." (quoting *Norman v. Reed*, 502 U.S. 279).

The Court then found that each of Indiana's asserted interests were unquestionably relevant to its interest in protecting the integrity and reliability of the electoral process. The Court noted that the relevant "burdens" were placed on a relatively small number of voters who lacked photo identification cards that complied with the requirement that they be issued by a governmental entity.

But, the Court noted, Indiana's cards were free, and the inconvenience of going to a Bureau of Motor Vehicles, bringing documents supporting identification, and posing for a photograph did not qualify as substantial burdens on most voters' right to vote. Even considering the severity of the burden on an even smaller number of voters, such as the elderly who were born out of state and who may have difficulty obtaining copies of their birth certificates, the Court found less than substantial burden. It noted the fact that otherwise eligible voters without photo ID could pass provisional ballots that would later be counted if they executed the required affidavit. In any event, the small number of voters affected, combined with the relatively small burden of meeting the state's requirements, were greatly offset by the state's burden of reducing fraud and diluting the results of legitimate voters.

Justice Scalia, joined by Justices Thomas and Alito, concurred but separately noted that he found as irrelevant any argument that the law imposed a special burden on some voters, if the law's overall burden was minimal and justified. However, his separate concurrence noted that the Supreme Court should defer such cases and issues (and the burdens of weighing "the costs and benefits of possible changes to their election codes" to state and local legislators. Justice Souter, joined by Justice Ginsburg, opined that the statute "imposes a disproportionate burden upon those without" government-issued photo IDs.

Michigan Upholds Voter Photo ID

Months before the U.S. Supreme Court held, in *Crawford v. Marion County Election Board*, No. 07-21, 553 U.S. ___ (2008) that requiring photo identification of in-person voters was constitutional, the Michigan Supreme Court had come to the same conclusion. In *Advisory Opinion 130589*, (July 18, 2007) with a 5–2 but contentious split in justices, the Michigan high court supported the constitutionality of Michigan's statute on the same issue, MCL

168.523, which required in-person voters to either produce photo identification or sign an affidavit attesting that they had none. The 1996 Michigan law had been "on the books" in some form (major revision 2005) since 1997, but the Secretary of State had never enforced it due to an opinion by the state's attorney general claiming that it was unconstitutional.

In House Resolution No. 199, dated February 22, 2006, the Michigan House of Representatives formally requested the state Supreme Court to issue an advisory opinion addressing the constitutionality of Section 523 of 2005 PA 71 (codified as MCL 168.523), which was scheduled to take effect on January 1, 2007. Section 523 required voters to produce an official state identification card, a driver's license, or "other generally recognized picture identification card" in order to vote. A voter unable to produce one of these items needed to sign an affidavit "to that effect" in order to vote.

However, in January 1997, then-Michigan Attorney General Frank J. Kelley issued an opinion which claimed that the 1996 provision violated the Equal Protection Clause of the Fourteenth Amendment. Since that opinion was issued, no Michigan secretary of state or any local official had enforced the photo identification requirement.

Then in 2002, the U.S. Congress passed the Help America Vote Act (HAVA), 42 U.S. 15301 *et seq.*, designed to "strengthen" the election process. In response to HAVA, in 2005, the Michigan Legislature reenacted the MCL 168.523 photo identification requirement. Following the request of House Resolution 199, the state Supreme Court agreed to issue an advisory opinion.

The major criticism of the photo ID requirement was that it essentially constituted a poll tax, a "tax" levied upon each person within a jurisdiction as a prerequisite to voting in elections. Poll taxes as a prerequisite to federal elections voting are prohibited by the 24th Amendment to the U.S. Constitution. Poll taxes as prerequisites for voting in state elections was deemed unconstitutional in *Harper v. Virginia Bd. Of Elections*, 383 U.S. 663. But critics of the Michigan requirement charged that it hit the poor, elderly, disabled, and minority populations the hardest, and tended to keep them away from the polls.

In July 2007, the Michigan Supreme Court issued its advisory opinion. More than 70 pages of its 121-page opinion were in the form of dissent from two of its five justices, Cavanaugh and Kelly. But the majority opinion, written by Justice Robert Young Jr., represented a deliberated analysis of case and constitutional issues, and those five justices found the statute constitutional.

The key factor considered by the court was the fact that the Michigan law allowed prospective voters who were unable to produce some form of photo identification to choose to sign an affidavit instead, basically swearing to their identities. Justice Young found the ID requirement "a reasonable, nondiscriminatory restriction designed to preserve the purity of elections and to prevent abuses of the electoral franchise."

Over the years and throughout the nation, division on this issue had often fallen along party lines, with Democrats generally opposing the requirement and Republicans supporting it. Michigan's opinion seemed to fall within that parameter as well. The original opinion that found the statute unconstitutional was by then-Michigan Attorney General Frank J. Kelley, a Democrat. In the final 5–2 advisory opinion, the two dissenting justices were both Democrats. The court's five Republicans voted to uphold the law.

Dissenting justices argued that the state had no compelling interest in requiring ID, noting that there was no evidence that in-person voter fraud existed in Michigan. Justice Marilyn Kelly opined that "history will judge us harshly for joining those states that have limited the precious constitutional right to vote." At the time of Michigan's advisory opinion, judges in Arizona and Indiana had upheld their states' voter ID laws, while such requirements were struck down in Missouri. In June 2007, the Georgia Supreme Court dismissed a challenge to that state's voter ID law.

In response to the anticipated hefty and lengthy dissent, the majority opinion in the Michigan opinion, noted that it would "pause . . . to briefly address some of the more inflammatory and emotional arguments made in Justice Cavanaugh's dissent." Then in six brief paragraphs, the majority accused the dissent of advancing "simply facetious," "overwrought," and "emotional" arguments. "When all other arguments are unavailing," noted the majority opinion, "resorting to a claim of racial discrimination is a frequent substitute. Unfortunately, the [sic] Justice Cavanaugh has chosen this tack."

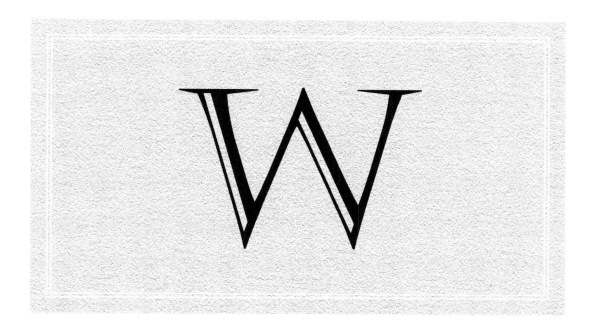

WIRETAPPING

2008 Amendments to FISA

On July 10, 2008, President George W. Bush signed into law sweeping new amendments to the Foreign Intelligence Security Act, 50 USC § 1801 *et seq.*, that the *The New York Times* referred to as "the biggest vamping of federal surveillance law in 30 years." H.R. 6304, the FISA Amendments Act of 2008, was signed into law shortly after passing in the Senate by a vote of 69 to 28. The biggest and most divisive of its provisions was the granting of legal immunity for telecommunications providers (e.g., telephone companies) that had cooperated in the National Security Agency's (NSA) wiretapping program following the September 11, 2001 terrorist attacks on the United States. The final bill ended nearly a year of debate in Congress over surveillance rules and the warrantless wiretapping program. In simplest terms, the measure provided for U.S. government agencies to intercept foreign telephone calls without court approval ("warrantless"). It also gave legal immunity (from lawsuits) to telephone companies who complied with requests pursuant to FISA. The immunity was both retroactive and prospective (for past and future cooperation).

Public disclosure of the warrantless wiretapping program was first made in late 2005 and ignited a fierce national debate over the balance of privacy and civil liberties against the need to protect the country against terrorist attacks. In the interim between public disclosure and the signing of the new amendments into law, approximately 40 lawsuits had been filed against telecommunications companies by groups and individuals. (In July 2007, a split panel of the U.S. Circuit Court of Appeals for the Sixth Circuit vacated the judgment of a federal district court and ruled that plaintiffs challenging government spying under the National Security Agency (NSA) lacked legal standing to sue. The NSA operated a program providing for interception (monitoring, wiretapping) of communications involving any individuals with suspected ties to al Qaeda (a terrorist organization widely held as being a key player in attacks against the United States) without first getting a court-issued warrant. In February 2008, the U.S. Supreme Court denied review of the appellate court's decision. *ACLU v. NSA*, 493 F.3d 644; cert. den., No. 07-468, 553 U.S. ___.)

FISA was established in 1978 following the Watergate scandal, to protect civil liberties against unwarranted government intrusion. It originally contained provisions prohibiting intentional electronic surveillance under the appearance of an official act, or the disclosure or use of information obtained by electronic surveillance, knowing that it was not authorized by statute. Wiretapping orders approved by secret orders under this prior version of the law were set to expire in August 2008 unless Congress acted.

The official amendments passed in the U.S. House of Representatives on June 20, 2008 by a vote of 293 to 129. A Senate vote was then delayed by filibuster efforts from Senators Russ Feingold (D-WI) and Chris Dodd (D-CT). Feingold argued that the bill threatened civil liberties, while Dodd called for an amendment to strike Title II (the immunity provisions), arguing that granting retroactive immunity

President George W Bush and attorney general Michael Mukasey speak about the FISA wiretapping act, March 2008.

AP IMAGES

would undermine the rule of law. Dodd's amendment was rejected by a 66 to 32 vote.

Supporters of the final bill argued that it contained several safeguards to protect Americans' civil liberties, and had been reviewed by several inspectors general. Senator Christopher Bond (R-MO), a lead negotiator, told *The New York Times* reporters that there was nothing to fear in the bill "unless you have Al Qaeda on your speed dial."

Support from key Democrats ensured passage of the final bill. Senator John D. Rockefeller IV(D-WV) agreed that modernizing FISA was necessary to provide intelligence officials with the necessary tools to deter attacks. E-mails, wireless telephones, and the Internet did not exist for consumers in 1978. But Rockefeller was quoted in *The New York Times* as stating that the plan "was made even more complicated by the president's decision, in the aftermath of Sep.11, 2001, to go outside of FISA rather than work with Congress to fix it."

The 2008 amendments essentially rendered moot the lawsuits against such telecommunications giants as AT&T, Verizon, and others that conducted wiretaps at the Bush Administration's direction without court order. New provisions included a narrow review by district courts to determine whether the companies being sued

received formal requests or directives from the administration to take part in the wiretapping. (The administration had acknowledged that such directives existed.) If such a finding is made, the lawsuits "shall be promptly dismissed," the new amendments stated.

"The new amendments also expanded the government's authority to invoke emergency wiretapping procedures. The NSA would be allowed to seek court orders for broad groups of foreign targets, but a new seven-day period for direct wiretaps without a court order could be exercised in "exigent" circumstances where important government security information would be lost. The amendments also expanded the existing three-day emergency wiretaps of Americans to seven days, if the attorney general certified there was probable cause to believe the target was linked to terrorism.

Immediately following the signing of the bill into law, the American Civil Liberties Union (ACLU) filed suit in federal district court, representing a coalition of attorneys, human rights activists, labor, and media organizations. The suit argued that the new law violated free speech and privacy under the First and Fourteenth Amendments to the U.S. Constitution. *Amnesty, et al., v. McConnell*, U.S] District Court for the Southern District of New York, filed July 10, 2008.

BIBLIOGRAPHY

AGE DISCRIMINATION

GOMEZ-PEREZ V. POTTER

Barnes, Robert and William Branigin, "Supreme Court Backs Workers Filing Bias Suits," *Washington Post*, May 29, 2008.

Sherman, Mark, "Court OKs Suits on Retaliation in Race, Age Cases," Associated Press, May 28, 2008.

KENTUCKY RETIREMENT SYSTEM V. EQUAL EMPLOYMENT OPPORTUNITY COMMISSION

Gregory, Raymond. *Age Discrimination in the American Workplace: Old at a Young Age.* Rutgers University Press, 2001.

Player, Mack. *Federal Law of Employment Discrimination in a Nutshell. 5th Ed.* West, 2004.

Sargeant, Malcom. *Age Discrimination in Employment.* Oxford University Press, 2006.

MEACHUM V. KNOLLS ATOMIC POWER LABORATORY

Greenhouse, Linda, "A Supreme Court Victory for Older Workers," *New York Times*, June 20, 2008.

Pender, Kathleen, "Age-Discrimination Ruling Ho-Hum in California," *San Francisco Gate*, June 22, 2008.

SPRINT/UNITED MANAGEMENT CO. V. MENDELSOHN

Gregory, Raymond. *Age Discrimination in the American Workplace.* Rutgers University Press, 2001.

Macnicol, John. *Age Discrimination: An Historical and Contemporay Analysis.* Cambridge University Press, 2006.

Sargeant, Malcom. *Age Discrimination in Employment.* Ashgate Publishing, 2007.

AGRICULTURE DEPARTMENT

POLLINATOR PROTECTION ACT OF 2007

"National Pollinator Week." The Xerces Society. Available at http://www.xerces.org/Pollinator_Insect_Conservation/pollinator_week_action.html as retrieved on 6 March 2008.

The Pollinator Partnership. "Farm Bill Pollinator Highlights." Available at www.pollinator.org/resources/house-passed-farm-bill-pollinator-highlightsv2.pdf

"Pollinator Protection Act Introduced in the Senate." The Xerces Society News, 26 June 2007. Available at http://lists.eco-farm.org/pipermail/ge_news/2007-August/000000.html as retrieved on 1 March 2008.

"Scientists Have an Official Name for the Disappearing Honeybees: Colony Collapse Disorder." Michigan Agricultural Education Services, Michigan State University. Available at http://www.maes.msu.edu/publications/futures/fall2007/ccd_fall2007.pdf.

Velasquez-Manoff, Moises. "Progress on 'Collapsing' Beehives." *Christian Science Monitor*, 8 November 2007. Available at http://www.csmonitor.com/2007/1108/p13s01-sten.html as retrived on 11 March 2008.

ARBITRATION

HALL STREET ASSOCIATES, L.L.C. V. MATTEL, INC.

Barett, Jerome. *A History of Alternative Dispute Resolution: The Story of a Political, Social, and Cultural Movement.* Hoboken, N.J.: Jossey-Bass. 2004.

Nolan-Haley, Jaqueline. *Alternative Dispute Resolution In A Nutshell.* Saint Paul, MN: Westgroup. Second Edition. 2001.

Ware, Stephen. *Alternative Dispute Resolution.* Saint Paul, MN: Westgroup. 2001.

PRESTON V. FERRER

Associated Press, "High Court Rules Against TV's 'Judge Alex'," CNN.com, February 20, 2008.

Slater, Dan, "High Court Nets Judge Alex; Scalia Opines on Preemption" *Wall Street Journal*, February 20, 2008.

ARMED ROBBERY

O.J. SIMPSON INDICTED FOR KIDNAPPING AND ARMED ROBBERY

"400 Jurors Could be Screened for O.J. Simpson Armed Robbery Trial." *FOX News* story, 16 January 2008. Available at http://www.foxnews.com/story/0,2933,357604,00.html

"D.A. Expects Simpson to be Charged With Seven Felonies." Associated Press news story, 18 September 2007, available at http://sports.espn.com/espn/?id=3022848

"O.J. Simpson Arrested, Faces Multiple Felony Charges." *USA Today*, 16 September 2007.

"O.J. Simpson's Robbery Trial to be Delayed Until September." Associated Press news story, 7 March 2008, available at http://sports.espn.com/espn/?id=328167

"Simpson Witnesses Offer Conflicting Testimony, but Agree Guns Were Involved." *FOX News* story, 9 November 2007. Available at http://www.foxnews.com

ATTORNEY GENERAL

GONZALES RESIGNS AS ATTORNEY GENERAL AMID CONTROVERSIES

Johnston, David, "Dismissed U.S. Attorneys Praised in Evaluations, *New York Times*, February 25, 2007.

Myers, Steven Lee and Philip Shenon, "Embattled Attorney General Resigns," *New York Times*, August 27, 2007.

"Schumer Calls for Gonzales's Resignation," *CBS News*, March 11, 2007.

ATTORNEY

THE VIRTUAL LAWYER AND THE ETHICS OF LAW BLOGS

Arias, Martha L. "U.S. Trends on Attorney Internet Advertisement Rules." Internet Business Law Services (IBLS), 5 February 2008. Available at http://ibls.com/cs/blogs/internet_law

Hilden, Julie. "Are Law Blogs Protected by the First Amendment?" *FINDLAW*, 16 October 2006.

"Lawyers Blogging on Cases: Good or Bad?" *The Wall Street Journal*, 1 May 2008.

Ward, Susan L. "Lawyers' Blogs Provide a Service." *njbiz*, 30 October 2006, Vol 19, Iss. 44.

Weiss, Debra Cassens. "At Virtual Law Firm, Lawyers Will Work at Home, Earn 85% of Billings." *ABA Journal*, 16 July 2008.

PROSECUTOR DISBARRED IN DUKE LACROSSE CASE

"Former Duke Lacrosse Players Sue Nifong, City." MSNBC News, 7 October 2007. Available at http://nbcsports.msnbc.com

"Judge Removes Ex-Durham DA Mike Nifong From Duke Lawsuit." FOXNews.com news story, 29 January 2008. Available at http://www.foxnews.com/story?id=0,3566,326479,00.html

Setrakian, Lara and Chris Francescani. "Duke Lacrosse Prosecutor Disbarred." ABC News, 16 June 2007. Available at http://abcnews.go.com/thelaw/story?id=3285862

Wilson, Duff. "Prosecutor in Duke Case is Disbarred for Ethics Breaches." *The New York Times*, 16 June 2007.

SEATTLE LAW FIRM REQUESTS ATTORNEY FEE AWARD IN PRO BONO CASE

Bronstad, Amanda. "Pro Bono Case Triggers a Fee Fight." *The National Law Journal*, 8 February 2008.

Heffter, Emily. "Billing in 'Pro Bono' Cases is Fodder for Ethics Debate." *Seattle Times*, 22 September 2007.

Westneat, Danny. "The Bill Just Keeps Going Up." *Seattle Times*, 19 September 2007.

Telephonic interview with Attorney Harry Korrell, Davis Wright Tremaine, at his office on 18 June 2008. (206) 757-8080.

CAPITAL PUNISHMENT

REPORT RENEWS CALL FOR A NATIONWIDE MORATORIUM ON THE DEATH PENALTY

"ABA Study: State Death Penalty Systems Deeply Flawed," Press Release, October 29, 2007, http://www.abanet.org/abanet/media/release/news_release.cfm?releaseid=209

Brouwer, Christine, "Lawyers Move to Kill Death Penalty," *ABC News*, October 28, 2007.

DEATH PENALTY DEVELOPMENTS

Banner, Stuart. *The Death Penalty: An American History.* Cambridge, Mass.: Harvard Univ. Press. 2003.

Bedau, Hugo and Cassell, Paul. *Debating the Death Penalty.* New York: Oxford Univ. Press. 2004.

Cohen, Stanley. *The Wrong Men: America's Epidemic of Wrongful Death Row Convictions.* New York: Carroll and Graf. 2003.

MISSOURI LAW SHIELDS IDENTITY OF EXECUTIONERS

Alper, Ty. "What Do Lawyers Know About Lethal Injection?" *Harvard Law & Pol'Y Review*, 3 March 2008.

"Inmates in Mo. Want Executioners Named." Associated Press News, 21 January 2008. Available at http://news.public.findlaw.com/ap/other/1110/01-21-2008/20080121055006_12.html

Kohler, Jeremy. "Inmates Seek More Details on Executioners." *St. Louis Post-Dispatch*, 20 January 2008.

"Lethal Injection Suit Moves Forward." *Daily Record and the Kansas City Daily News-Press*, 21 March 2008.

"New Mo. Law Bars Disclosure of Executioners' Names." Associated Press News, 7 July 2007. Available at http://www.firstmaendmentcenter.org/news/aspx?id=18754

STATE V. MATA

Bedau, Hugo and Cassell, Paul. *Debating the Death Penalty.* New York: Oxford Univ. Press. 2004.

Cohen, Stanley. *The Wrong Men: America's Epidemic of Wrongful Death Row Convictions.* New York: Carroll and Graf. 2003.

Banner, Stuart. *The Death Penalty: An American History.* Cambridge, Mass.: Harvard Univ. Press. 2003.

NEW YORK SENATE PASSES BILL TO REINSTATE DEATH PENALTY

Fever, Alan. "Aversion to Death Penalty, But No Lack of Cases." *New York Times*, 10 March 2008.

Schnittman, Suzanne. "Defacto National Moratorium Death on Penalty Ends." Press Release, New Yorkers Against the Death Penalty (NYADP), undated. Available at http://www.nyadp.org/main/home

"Senate Passes Bill to Establish Death Penalty for Cop Killers." New York State Senate Press Release dated 10 June 2008. Available at http://www .senate24/com/24/news/080610/senate_passes_bill_ to_establish_death_penalty_for_coop_killers.aspx

"Senate Passes Death Penalty Legislation." New York State Senate Press Release dated 20 June 2007. Available at http://www.senate.stat.ny.us

"Use of Federal Death Penalty Growing in New York State." Press Release, New Yorkers Against the Death Penalty (NYADP), undated. Available at http://www.nyadp.org/main/home

DIFFERENT RESULTS FOR THE MENTALLY ILL IN TENNESSEE AND SOUTH CAROLINA

"ACLU Successfully Challenges Conviction and Death Sentence of a Severely Mentally-Ill Man." 8 March 2008. www.aclu.org/capital/mentalillness/30356res 20070717.html

South Carolina v. Hill, No. 26477, April 28, 2008. Available at http://www.judicial.state.sc.us/opinions/ displayOpinion.cfm?caseNo=26477

Tennessee v. Taylor, No. M2005-01941-CCA-R3-DD, March 7, 2008. Available at www.aclu.org/capital/ mentalillness/30356res20070717.html

NO FIRST AMENDMENT RIGHT TO VIEW EXECUTIONS

"Ark. Journalists Seek Access to Entire Execution Process." Associated Press News, 26 July 2007. Available at http://www.firstamendmentcenter.org/ news,aspx?id=18846

Moritz, Rob. "Lawsuit Filed to Open Execution Process." *Arkansas News Bureau*, 26 July 2007.

Neil, Martha. "Court Finds No 1st Amendment Right To Witness Full Execution." *ABA Journal*, 11 January 2008.

Satter, Linda. "Judge Dismisses Lawsuit Seeking Full Access to Executions." *Arkansas Democrat-Gazette*, 9 January 2008.

"Witnesses Have No Right to View Entire Execution." Associated Press News Release, 10 January 2008.

CENTRAL INTELLIGENCE AGENCY (CIA)

CIA RELEASES ITS 'FAMILY JEWELS'

"The CIA's Family Jewels." National Security Archive, 26 June 2007, available at http://www.gwu.edu/

nsarchiv/NSAEBB/NSAEBB222/index.htm as retrieved on 28 April 2008.

DeYoung, Karen and Walter Pincus. "CIA Releases Files on Past Misdeeds." *Washington Post*, 27 June 2007.

"Files on Illegal Spying Show C.I.A. Skeletons From Cold War." *New York Times*, 26 June 2007.

Shane, Scott. "CIA to Release Documents on Decades-Old Misdeeds." *New York Times*, 22 June 2007.

CIVIL RIGHTS

THE JENA 6

Cammack, Mark and Garland, Norman. *Advanced Criminal Procedure in a Nutshell.* West Publishing Co. 2001.

Lewis, Jr., Harold and Norman, Elizabeth. *Civil Rights Law and Practice.* West Gropu. 2004.

Vieira, Norman. *Constitutional Civil Rights in a Nutshell.* West Group. 1998.

CLASS ACTION

STONERIDGE V. SCIENTIFIC ATLANTA

Rugaber, Christopher S. "High Court to Consider Liability of 'Secondary Actors' in Securities Fraud." Associated Press story, 27 March 2007, available at http://www.law.com

Stoneridge v. Scientific-Atlanta, Inc. 552 U.S. ___ ; No. 06-43 (2008). Available at www.supremecourtus .gov/docket/06-43.htm

Stoneridge v. Scientific-Atlanta, Inc. 552 U.S. ___ ; No. 06-43 (2008). The Oyez Project, available at http:// www.oyez.org/cases/2000-2009/2007/2007_06_43/

COMMERCE CLAUSE

Barron, Jerome, and Dienes, C. Thomas. *Constitution Law in a Nutshell.* West Group, 2005.

Chemerinsky, Erwin. *Constitutional Law: Principles and Policies. 3rd Ed.* Aspen Publishers, 2006.

Coenen, Dan. *The Commerce Clause.* Foundation Press, 2003.

COPYRIGHT

UNITED STATES LOSES COPYRIGHT PROTECTIONS TO ANTIGUA

Eldon, Eric. "U.S. Faces Challenge to Online Gambling Ban." *VentureBeat*, 23 August 2007.

Kanter, James and Gary Rivlin. "In Trade Ruling, Antigua Wins a Right to Piracy." *The New York Times*, 22 December 2007.

Vlaemminck, Philipe, et al. "Free Trade in a Regulated World: the United States Measures Affecting the Cross-Border Supply of Gambling and Betting Services in the WTO Dispute Settlement." *Public Gambling International*, January 2008.

CCIA REPORT ON 'FAIR USE'

Claburn, Thomas. "Fair Use Worth More to Economy Than Copyright, CCIA Says." *Information Week*, 12 September 2007.

"Fair Use Economy Represents One-Sixth of U.S. GDP." CCIA News Release, 12 September 2007. Available at http://www.ccianet.org/aartmanager/publish/news/First-Ever_Economic_Study_Calculates_Dollar_Value_of.shtml

Rogers, Thomas, et al. *Fair Use in the U.S. Economy*, CCIA Report, 2007. Available at http://www.ccia net.org

FIRST PERSON CONVICTED FOR ILLEGAL MUSIC DOWNLOADING

Miller, Arthur R., and Davis, Michael H. *Intellectual Property: Patents, Trademarks, and Copyright, 3rd Edition*. West Group, 2000.

Poltorak, Alexander, and Lerner, Paul. *Essentials of Intellectual Property*. Wiley, 2002.

Shaw, Russell, and Mercer, David. *Caution! Music & Video Downloading: Your Guide to Legal, Safe, and Trouble-Free Downloads*. Wiley, 2004.

"THE FAMILY GUY" SUBJECT TO THREE LAWSUITS FILED IN 2007

Associated Press, "It's 'Wish Upon a Star' vs. 'Family Guy'," CNN.com, October 4, 2007.

Hilden, Julie, "The Suit by Carol Burnett Against 'The Family Guy': Why Burnett Should Withdraw the Suit," Findlaw.com, April 2, 2007, http://writ.news.findlaw.com/hilden/20070402.html

11TH CIRCUIT SIDES WITH NATIONAL GEOGRAPHIC IN COPYRIGHT DISPUTE

McDonald, Robin, "11th Circuit Sides with National Geographic in Copyright Case," Law.com, July 2, 2008.

McDonald, Robin, "National Geographic Case Re-opens," Law.com, September 4, 2007.

AUTHOR SUES JERRY AND JESSICA SEINFELD OVER COOKBOOK

Hilden, Julie, "Seinfeld Sued: Will 'Sneaky Chef' Author Missy Chase Lapine Succeed in Her Suit Against Jerry and Jessica Seinfeld?," Findlaw.com, January 15, 2008, http://writ.news.findlaw.com/hilden/20080115.html

Rich, Motoko, "How to Get Junior to Eat His Veggies Turns Out to Be (Too) Common Knowledge," *New York Times*, October 19, 2007.

HEIRS RECLAIM SHARE OF 'SUPERMAN' COPYRIGHT

Cieply, Michael. "Ruling Gives Heirs a Share of Superman Copyright." *The New York Times*, 29 March 2008.

Okamoto, Sherri M. "Heirs of Co-Creator Reclaim 'Superman' Copyright." *Los Angeles Metropolitan News-Enterprise*, 2 April 2008.

Steele, Auric D. "Who Owns Suerman?" *The Brand*, 21 August 2006.

VIACOM V. YOUTUBE

Gill, Jay. "District Court Compels Disclosure of YouTube User Logging Records, Protects Source Code." *Harvard Journal of Law & Technology*, 12 July 2008.

"NY Court Orders YouTube User Records Released." Internet Business Law Services (IBLS), 9 July 2008. Available at http://ibls.com/cs

Viacom International Inc. v. YouTube, No. 07 Civ. 3582 Available at www.findlaw.com

CORRUPTION

THE RISE AND FALL OF BERNIE KERIK

"Bernard Kerik: From Hero to Tabloid Target." *ABC News*, 13 April 2005. Available at http://abcnews.com/print?id=667625

Druckman, Ed. "Election 2008: Rudy Guiliani Calls Bernard Kerik, 'Basically a Good Criminal'." 13 November 2007. Available at http://www.associatedcontent.com/article/443511

Gaskell, Stephanie. "Former Iraq Commander: Bernard Kerik Was a 'Waste of Time' in Iraq." New York *Daily News*, 5 May 2008.

Linzer, Dafna. "Kerik, Indicted on Corruption Charges, Pleads Not Guilty." *Washington Post*, 10 November 2007.

COURTS

CALIFORNIA SUPREME COURT IS NATION'S MOST INFLUENTIAL, ACCORDING TO REPORT

Dear, Jake and Edward W. Jessen, "'Followed Rates' and Leading State Cases, 1940-2005," *UC Davis Law Review*, Dec. 2007, 683.

Liptak, Adam, "Around the U.S., High Courts Follow California's Lead," *New York Times*, March 12, 2008.

CRIMINAL CONSPIRACY

NFL STAR MICHAEL VICK SENTENCED TO 23 MONTHS ON DOGFIGHTING CHARGES

Clayton, John, "Sentence Puts Vick's NFL Career in Jeopardy," ESPN.com, December 10, 2007.

Maske, Mark, "Falcons' Vick Indicted in Dogfighting Case," *Washington Post*, July 18, 2007, E1.

CRIMINAL LAW

U.S. V. KREISEL

Cammack, Mark and Garland, Norman. *Advanced Criminal Procedure in a Nutshell*. St. Paul, MN: West Publishing Co. 2001.

Dripps, Donald. *About Guilt and Innocence: The Origins, Development, and Future of Constitutional Criminal Procedure*. Praeger, 2002.

Sprack, John. *A Practical Approach to Criminal Procedure, 11th Edition*. Oxford University Press, 2006.

WATSON V. UNITED STATES

Cammack, Mark and Garland, Norman. *Advanced Criminal Procedure in a Nutshell*. St. Paul, MN: West Publishing Co. 2001.

Dripps, Donald. *About Guilt and Innocence: The Origins, Development, and Future of Constitutional Criminal Procedure.* Praeger, 2002.

Sprack, John. *A Practical Approach to Criminal Procedure, 11th Edition.* Oxford University Press, 2006.

CRIMINAL PROCEDURE

RELEASE OF DEPARTMENT OF JUSTICE INTERROGATION TACTICS MEMOS

Crawford-Greenburg, Jan and Ariane de Vogue, "Bush Administration Blocked Waterboarding Critic." ABC News Report, 2 November 2007. Available at http://abcnews.go.com/pring?id=3814076

"DOJ Memo Advised Military That Interrogations Not Limited by Criminal Law." *Paper Chase,* The Jurist, University of Pittsburgh School of Law, 2 April 2008.

"Democrats Demand DOJ Interrogation Memos." *Paper Chase,* The Jurist, University of Pittsburgh School of Law, 5 October 2007.

"DOJ Memos Supported 'Severe' Interrogation Tactics: NYT." *Paper Chase,* The Jurist, University of Pittsburgh School of Law, 4 October 2007.

Shane, Scott, et al. "Secret U.S. Endorsement of Severe Interrogations." *The New York Times,* 4 October 2007.

"'03 U.S. Memo Approved Harsh Interrogations." *The New York Times,* 2 April 2008.

DANFORTH V. MINNESOTA

Federman, Cary. *The Body And the State: Habeas Corpus And American Jurisprudence.* New York, NY: State University of New York Press. 2006.

Frank, Jerome. *Courts on Trial.* Princeton, NJ: Princeton University Press. 1973.

Freedman, Eric. *Habeas Corpus: Rethinking the Great Writ of Liberty.* New York: New York Univ. Press. 2003.

DISCRIMINATION

CBOCS WEST V. HUMPHRIES

CBOCS West, Inc. v. Humphries, No. 06-1431, 552 U.S. ___ Available at www.supremecourtus.gov/docket/06-43.htm

CBOCS West, Inc. v. Humphries, No. 06-1431, 552 U.S. ___ The Oyez Project, available at http://www.oyez.org/cases/2000-2009/2007/2007_06_1431/

Tilley, Cristina Carmody. "CBOCS West, Inc. v. Humphries." *On the Docket,* Northwestern School of Journalism, 27 May 2008.

DRUGS AND NARCOTICS

BURGESS V. U.S.

Doyle, Michael, "S.C. Inmate's Supreme Court Win Earns Him Criminal Probe," *McClatchy Newspapers,* March 24, 2008.

Kinnard, Meg, "Jailhouse Lawyer Gets Rare Nod from U.S. Supreme Court," Law.com, February 6, 2008.

DRUGS AND NARCOTICS

PURDUE FREDERICK PLEADS GUILTY TO MISBRANDING OXYCONTIN

Johnson, Carrie, "OxyContin Makers Admit Deception," *Washington Post,* May 11, 2007, A1.

Meier, Barry, "Big Part of OxyContin Profit Was Consumed by Penalties," *New York Times,* June 19, 2007.

NO RIGHT OF ACCESS TO UNAPPROVED DRUGS

Bailey, Ronald. "Whose Life is it Anyway?" *Reason,* 2 March 2007.

Patsner, Bruce. "Dying Patients and Their 'Right' to Unapproved Drugs: Did the D.C. Circuit Finally Get it Right in *Abigail Alliance?*" 2007.

Wang, Shirley S. "Supremes Back FDA on Limits for Unapproved Drugs." *Wall Street Journal,* 14 January 2008.

EDUCATION

SCHOOLS CRACK DOWN ON CANDY, SWEATERS

Associated Press, "School Clears Kids in Contraband Candy Caper," CNN.com, March 13, 2008.

Vogler, Mark E., "Student Suspended for Wearing Sweater," *The Eagle-Tribune,* March 14, 2008, http://www.eagletribune.com/archivesearch/local_story_073070943.html.

EDUCATION

BOARD OF EDUCATION OF THE CITY SCHOOL DISTRICT OF THE CITY OF NEW YORK V. TOM F.

Alexander, Kern, and Alexander, M. David. *The Law of Schools, Students and Teachers in a Nutshell. 3rd. Ed.* St. Paul: West Group, 2003.

Gerstein, Ralph, and Gerstein, Lois. *Law: An Essential Guide for Attorneys, Teachers, Administrators, Parents, and Students.* New York: Lawyers and Judges Publishing, 2007.

Gurney, Allen. *Special Education and the Law. 2nd Ed.* New York: Corwin Press, 2006.

EIGHTH AMENDMENT

BAZE V. REES

King, Gilbert, "Cruel and Unusual History," *New York Times,* April 23, 2008.

Savage, David G., "Supreme Court Finds Lethal Injections a Humane Means of Execution," *Los Angeles Times,* April 17, 2008.

ELDER LAW

JURY ACQUITS NURSING HOME OWNERS OF KATRINA DROWNINGS

"Editor's Page." *Surgical Rounds,* October 2006.

Gullette, Margaret Morganroth. "Tragic Toll of Age Bias."

Nossiter, Adam. "Nursing Home Owners Acquitted in Deaths." *New York Times*, 8 September 2007.

Rosen-Molina, Mike. "New Orleans Nursing Home Owners Found Not Guilty of Katrina Drowning Deaths." *The Jurist*, University of Pittsburgh School of Law, 7 September 2007.

Whoriskey, Peter. "Nursing Home Owners Acquitted in Katrina Deaths." *Washington Post*, 8 September 2007.

ELECTIONS

CRAWFORD V. MARION COUNTY ELECTION BOARD

Barnes, Robert, "Justices May Iron Out Compromise on Voter ID," *Washington Post*, January 10, 2008, A3.

Stout, David, "Supreme Court Upholds Voter Identification Law in Indiana," *New York Times*, April 29, 2008.

INTERNET BECOMES A MAJOR MEDIUM DURING 2008 CAMPAIGN

Associated Press, "2008 Candidates Gear Up for Internet Campaigning," CNN.com, June 8, 2007.

Garry, Stephanie, "Candidates Court Young Voters Online," *St. Petersburg Times*, June 8, 2007.

Pew Research Center for the People and the Press, *Social Networking and Online Videos Take Off: Internet's Broader Role in Campaign 2008* (January 11, 2008).

NEW YORK STATE BOARD OF ELECTIONS V. LOPEZ-TORRES

Carp, Robert. *Judicial Process in America*, 7th Edition. CQ Press, 2007.

Slotnick, Elliot. *Judicial Politics*, 3rd. Edition. CQ Press, 2005.

Streb, Matthew. *Running for Judge: The Rising Political, Financial, and Legal Stakes of Judicial Elections.* New York University Press, 2007.

EMPLOYMENT DISCRIMINATION

FEDERAL EXPRESS CORPORATION V. HOLOWECKI

Gregory, Raymond. *Age Discrimination in the American Workplace*. Rutgers University Press, 2001.

Macnicol, John. *Age Discrimination: An Historical and Contemporay Analysis*. Cambridge University Press, 2006.

Sargeant, Malcom. *Age Discrimination in Employment*. Ashgate Publishing, 2007.

EMPLOYMENT LAW

CALIFORNIA AND OREGON RULE ON EMPLOYER ACCOMMODATION OF MEDICAL MARIJUANA

"2007-2008 Bill 220: Marijuana." Available at http://www.scstatehouse.net/sess117_2007-2008/bills/220.htm

"California Assembly Votes to Protect Medical Marijuana Patients' Right to Work." Americans for Safe Access (ASA) Press Release, 28 May 2008. Available at http://www.safeaccessnow.org/article.php?id =5524

McCall, William. "Oregon Court of Appeals Protects Medical Marijuana." *The Seattle Times*, 11 June 2008.

ENVIRONMENTAL LAW

CALIFORNIA SUES THE EPA FOR WAIVER ON CAR EMISSIONS

Findley, Roger and Farber, Daniel. *Environmental Law in a Nutshell. 6th Ed.* West Publishing, 2006.

Freeman, Jody and Kulstad, Charles. *Moving to Markets in Environmental Regulation: Lessons from Twenty Years of Experience.* Oxford University Press, 2006.

McMahon, Robert. *The Environmental Protection Agency: Structuring Motivation In A Green Bureaucracy.* Sussex Academic Press, 2006.

ALL THINGS GREEN

Ball, Jeffrey. "Setting New Carbon Standards." *The Wall Street Journal*, 19 November 2007.

"Group Launches Voluntary Carbon Standard." *Environmental Leader*, 19 November 2007. Available at http://www.environmentalleader.com/2007/11/19/group-launches-voluntary.

Herrera, Tilde. "Adding the Enviroment to the Scales of Justice." 19 May 2008. Available at http://greenbiz.com.print/24302

"Markey Announces Revolutionary Global Warming Bill." Press Release, Office of Congressman Edward Markey, 28 May 2008.

"Mortgage Lenders Embrace Push for Green Buildings." *Greenbiz*, 17 September 2007. Available at http://www.greenerbuildings.com

Scherer, Ron. "Even as Economy Lags, Corporate 'Green' Push May Advance." *Christian Science Monitor*, 15 October 2007.

Shapiro, Sherri. "Green Building Law: Title IX of the House Energy Bill." 16 April 2007.

"Voluntary Carbon Market Tripled in 2007, Hit $331 Million." *Environmental Leader*, 19 November 2007.

ERISA

LaRUE V. DeWOLLF, BOBERG & ASSOCIATES, INC.

Conison, Jay. *Employee Benefits in a Nutshell, 3rd Ed.* West Group, 2003.

Rosenbloom, Jerry. *The Handbook of Employee Benefits, 6th Ed.* McGraw-Hill, 2005.

Ziesenheim, Ken. *Understanding ERISA: A Compact Guide to the Landmark Act.* Marketplace Books, 2002.

ESPIONAGE

NO STANDING TO CHALLENGE GOVERNMENT SPYING

ACLU v. NSA, 493 F.3d 644; cert. den., No. 07-468, 553 U.S. ___. Available at www.findlaw.com

"High Court Denies Review of Sixth Circuit Rejection of NSA-Telecom Spying Challenge." *Electronic Commerce & Law Report*, Published by BNA, Vol 13, No. 9, 27 February 2008.

"Recent Cases: Supreme Court Won't Hear Domestic Spying Challenge." *Harvard Law Review*, January 2008.

EXCLUSIONARY DOCTRINE

Virginia v. Moore

Eisman, Dale, "Portsmouth Case to Test Limits in Police Searches," *The Virginian-Pilot*, January 14, 2008.

Mears, Bill, "Supreme Court Broadens Police Searches," CNN.com, April 23, 2008.

EXECUTIVE PRIVILEGE

White House Visitor Logs are Public

Ashworth, Jennifer, and Cleveland, Bernita. *Freedom of Information Act Guide*. Washington, D.C.:Office of Information and Privacy, 2007.

Crenson, Matthew, and Ginsberg, Benjamin *Presidential Power: Unchecked and Unbalanced*. New York: Norton, 2007.

Rozell, Mark. *Executive Privilege: Presidential Power, Secrecy, and Accountability*. Lawrence, KS:University of Kansas, 2002.

FALSE CLAIMS ACT

Allison Engine Co. v. United States

Mauro, Tony, "Did Allison Engine Case Throw a Rod Before the U.S. Supreme Court?," Law.com, February 27, 2008.

Wehrman, Jessica, "Whistleblower Law Applies to Subcontractors, High Court Rules," *Dayton Daily News*, June 9, 2008.

FEDERAL COMMUNICATIONS COMMISSION

Fox Television Stations, Inc. v. Federal Communications Commission

Carter, T. Barton. *Mass Communications Law in a Nutshell*. 6th ed. West Group, 2006.

Tomlinson, Richard. *Tele-Revolution* Penobscot Press, 2000.

Zarkin, Kimberly and Zarkin, Michael. *The Federal Communications Commission*. Greenwood Press, 2006.

FCC Changes Media Ownership Rules

Carter, T. Barton. *Mass Communications Law in a Nutshell*. 6th ed. West Group, 2006.

Tomlinson, Richard. *Tele-Revolution*. Penobscot Press, 2000.

Zarkin, Kimberly and Zarkin, Michael. *The Federal Communications Commission*. Greenwood Press, 2006.

FOOD AND DRUG ADMINISTRATION

Merck Settles Vioxx Lawsuits

Epstein, Richard A. *Overdose: How Excessive Government Regulation Stifles Pharmaceutical Innovation*. Yale University Press, 2006.

Hawthorne, Fran. *Inside the FDA: The Business and Politics Behind the Drugs We Take and the Food We Eat*. Wiley, 2005.

Pina, Kenneth R. *A Practical Guide to Food and Drug Law and Regulation*. 2nd Ed. Food and Drug Law Institute, 2002.

FIRST AMENDMENT

Washington State Grange v. Washington State Republican Party

Cain, Bruce, and Gerber, Elizabeth, editors. *Voting at the Political Fault Line: California's Experiment with the Blanket Primary*. University of California Press, 2002.

Hershey, Marjorie. *Party Politics in America*. 13th ed. Longman, 2008.

Jewell, Malcom, and Morehouse, Sally. *Political Parties and Elections in American States*. 4th ed. CQ Press, 2000.

U.S. v. Williams

Barron, Jerome, Dienes, Thomas. *First Amendment Law in a Nutshell, 3rd ed*. West Group, 2004.

Farber, Daniel. *The First Amendment: Concepts and Insights*. Foundation Press, 2002.

Sunstein, Cass. *Democracy and the Problem of Free Speech*. Free Press, 1995.

FRAUD

Seventh Circuit Upholds Criminal Convictions of Conrad Black

Marek, Lynne. "Black Verdicts Are In, but the Case Is Far From Over." *The National Law Journal*, 24 July 2007.

Robinson, Mike. "7th Circuit Upholds Black's Fraud Conviction," 26 June 2008. Available at http://www.law.com/jsp/law/LawArticle.jsp?id=1202422548507

U.S. v. Black, Conrad, No. 07-4080 (7th Cir. 2008) Available at http://www.findlaw.com

Wisniewski, Mary. "Appeals Court Upholds Conrad Black's Conviction." *Chicago Sun-Times*, 25 June 2008.

David Chalmers and BAYOIL Companies Sentenced

"Texas Oil Executive Sentenced for Crimes Involving Illegal Kickbacks to Iraq Using Oil-for-Food Program." *Muncie Free Press*, 7 March 2008.

"Texas Oil Executive and Two Corporations Sentenced on Charges Involving A Scheme to Pay Secret Kickbacks . . ." U.S. Dept. of Justice Press Release, 7 March 2008.

"U.S. Announces Four Guilty Pleas in Oil-for-Food Case." Press Release, Office of the U.S. Attorney

Southern District of New York, 17 August 2007. Available at www.usdoj.gov/usao/nys/pressreleases/August07/chalmersdionissievbayoiloilforfoodpleaspr.pdf

U.S. v. Chalmers, No. Si-05-CR-59(DC). Available at www.findlaw.com

DEMOCRATIC FUNDRAISER NORMAN HSU SENTENCED AND CHARGED AGAIN

Cary, Lee. "Norman Hsu Who?" *American Thinker*, 14 April 2008.

Cote, Jon. "Ex-Fugitive Fundraiser Gets 3 Years in Glove Scam from 1990s." *San Francisco Chronicle*, 5 January 2008.

Dugan, Ianthe Jeanne. "What Made Norman Hsu Run?" *Wall Street Journal*, 8 September 2007.

Jordan, Lara Jakes. "Clinton to Return $850,000 Raised by Hsu." *New York Daily News*, 10 September 2007.

FREEDOM OF RELIGION

FIRST CIRCUIT UPHOLDS TEACHING ABOUT SAME-SEX FAMILIES

"Court Upholds Dismissal of David Parker Lawsuit Over School's Same-Sex Teaching." *Boston Globe*, 2 February 2008.

Haynes, Charles C. "Sexual Orientation and Public Schools: All or Nothing?" 17 February 2008. Available at www.firstamendmentcenter.org

Parker v. Hurley, No. 07-1528 (CA1 2008), Available at www.findlaw.com

CONNECTICUT SUPREME COURT UPHOLDS DENIAL OF BUDDHIST TEMPLE

"Buddhists Not Immune from Land-Use Regulation," *National Law Journal*, February 18, 2008, 17.

Tuohy, Lynne, "Denial of Buddhist Temple Upheld," *Hartford Courant*, January 31, 2008, A1.

FREEDOM OF SPEECH

NINTH CIRCUIT UPHOLDS ONLINE VOTE-SWAPPING

Porter v. Bowen, No. 06-55517 (9th Cir. 2007) Available at www.findlaw.com

Rosencrance, Linda. "Vote-swapping Over the Internet is Legal, Court Finds." *Computer World*, 7 August 2007.

Singer, Michael. "Vote Swap Site Gets Court O.K." Internet News Realtime, 7 February 2003. Available at www.internetnews.com/bus-news/article.php/1581161

WESTBORO BAPTIST CHURCH HELD LIABLE FOR PROTESTING MILITARY FUNERAL

Belzman, Josh, "Anti-Gay Church Sparks Free-Speech Fight," MSNBC.com, January 23, 2008.

Gomez, Alan, $11M Verdict in Funeral Protestors Case," *USA Today*, October 31, 2007.

GAMBLING

NBA REFEREE ADMITS TO BETTING ON GAMES

Associated Press, "Donaghy Pleads Guilty, Could Face Up to 25 Years in Prison," ESPN.com, August 15, 2007.

Munson, Lester, "Donaghy's Guilty Pleas Don't Answer All the Questions," ESPN.com, August 15, 2007.

STATE CONTINUE TO LOOK TO GAMBLING TO SOLVE BUDGET WOES

Bousquet, Steve, "Crist May Bet State Budget on Gambling," *St. Petersburg Times*, August 22, 2007.

Dreyfuss, Barbara T., "Politicians Bet the Farm," *American Prospect*, August 22, 2007.

Schultz, Randy, "Crist Plays the Same Old Bad Hand," *Palm Beach Post*, August 26, 2007.

GAY AND LESBIAN RIGHTS

MARTINEZ V. COUNTY OF MONROE

Gay Marriage. New York: Holt Paperbacks, 2004.

Gerstmann, Evan. *Same-Sex Marriage and the Constitution*. New York: Cambridge University Press, 2003.

Sullivan, Andrew. *Same-Sex Marriage: Pro and Con*. New York: Vintage, 2004.

CHAMBERS V. ORMISTON

Gay Marriage. New York: Holt Paperbacks, 2004.

Gerstmann, Evan. *Same-Sex Marriage and the Constitution*. New York: Cambridge University Press, 2003.

Sullivan, Andrew. *Same-Sex Marriage: Pro and Con*. New York: Vintage, 2004.

HABEAS CORPUS

ALLEN V. SIEBERT

Banner, Stuart. *The Death Penalty: An American History*. 2003. Cambridge: Harvard University Press.

Kurtis, Bill. *The Death Penalty on Trial: Crisis in American Justice*. 2004. New York: Public Affairs.

Zimring, Franklin. *The Contradictions of American Capital Punishment*. 2004. New York: Oxford University Press.

BOUMEDIENE V. BUSH

Barnes, Robert. "Court Says Guantanamo Detainees Have Right to Challenge Detention." *Washington Post*. June 12, 2008.

Savage, David. "Supreme Court Again Says Guantanamo Prisoners Should Have Rights." *Los Angeles Times*. June 12, 2008.

Stout, David. "Justices Rule Terror Suspects Can Appeal in Civilian Courts." *New York Times*. June 13, 2008.

MUNAF V. GERAN

"McCain's Challenge on Security." *The New York Observer*, 27 June 2008.

Munaf v. Geran, No. 06-1666; 553 U.S. ___, Available at www.supremecourtus.gov/docket/06-43.htm

"Munaf v. Geran," U.S. Supreme Court Media Publications, The Oyez Project, available at http://www.oyez.org/cases/2000-2009/2007/2007_06_1666

Vladeck, Stephen. "Deconstructing Hirota: Habeas Corpus, Citizenship, and Article III." *Georgetown Law Journal*, Vol 95:1497, 2007.

IDENTITY THEFT

FOURTH CIRCUIT UPHOLDS VERDICT AGAINST EQUIFAX

Cooper, Alan, "Virginia Court Rules Identity Theft Victim to Get $532,000 from Equifax," *Daily Record and Kansas City Daily News-Press*, September 23, 2006.

Sebok, Anthony J., "The Major Verdict in a Recent Identity Theft Case: How It Underlines the Risk for Financial Reporting Companies, and the Difficulty of Calculating Accurate Damages in This Area," Findlaw.com, January 7, 2008, http://writ.lp.findlaw.com/sebok/20080107.html

IMMIGRATION

NINTH CIRCUIT UPHOLDS ARIZONA'S BAN ON HIRING ILLEGAL IMMIGRANTS

"Arizona Law Banning the Hiring of Illegal Immigrants is Upheld." *New York Times*, 8 February 2008.

Archibold, Randal C. "Arizona Governor Signs Tough Bill on Hiring Illegal Immigrants." *New York Times*, 3 July 2007.

Gonzalez, Daniel. "Migrants Fleeing as Hiring Law Nears." *The Arizona Republic*, 26 August 2007.

Riccardi, Nicholas. "Appeals Court Denies Injunction Against Controversial Arizona Law." *The Los Angeles Times*, 29 February 2008.

Riccardi, Nicholas. "Arizona Slams Door on Illegal Iimmigrants." *Los Angeles Times*, 5 April 2008.

ILLEGAL IMMIGRATION WOES

"Bush Administration's Immigration Reform Fails." *American Law Yearbook*, 2007.

"Bush Urges Congress to Get Past Differences on Immigration Bill." FOXNews.com, 15 June 2007. Available at http://www.foxnews.com/story?id=0,3566,282772,00.html

Francis, David. "Election-year Politics: Why Immigration Reform Will Have to Wait." *Christian Science Monitor*, 11 February 2008.

Gaouette, Nicole. "Homeland Security Report Faults Care of Detained Immigrants." *Los Angeles Times*, 3 July 2008.

"Improving Border Security and Immigration." White House Press Release, 10 August 2007. Available at http://www.gov.news/relese/2007/08/20070810.html

Preston, Julia. "Employers Fight Tough Measures on Immigration." *The New York Times*, 6 July 2008.

INSURANCE

LOUISIANA ATTORNEY GENERAL SUES INSURANCE COMPANIES

Kunzelman, Michael. "Foti Files Lawsuit Against Insurance Companies, Alleges Price-Fixing." *The Southern Digest*, 7 November 2007.

"Louisiana Charges Price Fixing by Insurers." *New York Times*, 8 November 2007.

Mobray, Rebecca. "Louisiana Insurers Accused of Scheming to Reduce Storm Payouts." *New Orleans' Times-Picayune*, 10 November 2007.

Myers, Emily. "Attorney General's Office Files Suit Against Insurance Companies." National Association of Attorneys General News Release, 8 November 2007. Available at http://www.naag.org/attorney_general's_office_files_suit_against_insurance_companies.php

TUEPKER V. STATE FARM FIRE & CASUALTY COMPANY

Clarke, Malcolm. *Policies and Perceptions of Insurance Law in the Twenty First Century*. New York: Oxford University Press, 2007.

Dobbyn, John. *Insurance Law in a Nutshell. 4th Ed.* St. Paul, MN: West Group, 2003.

Keeton, Robert. *Insurance Law*. St. Paul: West Group, 1988.

INTERNATIONAL LAW

CANADIAN SUPREME COURT REFUSES ASYLUM APPEAL BY US ARMY DESERTER

Buergenthal, Thomas, and Muprhy, Sean. *Public International Law in a Nutshell. 4th ed.* Thomson West, 2006.

Jinks, Derek. *The Rules of War: The Geneva Conventions in the Age of Terror*. Oxford University Press, 2008.

Murphy, Sean. *Principles of International Law*. Thomson West, 2006.

JURIES

SNYDER V. LOUISIANA

Lieberman, Joel, and Sales, Bruce. *Scientific Jury Selection*. American Psychological Association, 2006.

Starr, V. Hale, and McCormick, Mark. *Jury Selection. Third Edition*. Aspen Law and Business Publishers, 2000.

Vidmar, Neil, and Hans, Valerie. *American Juries*. Prometheus Books, 2007.

LEGAL AID

CALIFORNIA JOINS STATES EXPANDING LEGAL AID FUNDS

"Assembly Bill No. 1723 Chapter 422 . . ." Courtesy California Bar Association. Available at bog.calbar.org/docs/agendaitem/agendaitem1000001056.pdf

"Bill Analysis." California Assembly Judiciary Committee, 13 June 2007. Available at http://info.sen.ca

.gov/pub/07-08/bill/asm/ab_1701-1750/ab_1723_cfa_20070628_113153_sen_floor.html

"Frequently Asked Questions." California State Bar Association. Available at http://www.calsb.org/state/calbar/calbar_generic.jsp?cid=10717&id=3248 as retrieved on Mar 30, 2008.

Ofgang, Kenneth. "Governor Signs Interst on Lawyer Trust Accounts Bill." *Metropolitan News-Enterprise*, 12 October 2007.

LEWDNESS

SENATOR LARRY CRAIG DISGRACED IN AIRPORT RESTROOM INCIDENT

Herszenhorn, David M. and Duff Wilson, "Craig Goes on Offensive, Angering G.O.P. Leaders," *New York Times*, September 6, 2007.

Yardley, William and Carl Hulse, "Craig Will Remain in Senate Until Judge Rules," *New York Times*, September 27, 2007.

MAGISTRATE

GONZALEZ V. UNITED STATES

Gonzalez v. United States, Cornell University School of Law Available at http://www.law.cornell.edu/supct/cert/06-11612.html

Gonzalez v. United States, No. 06-11612, 553 U.S. ___, Available at www.supremecourtus.gov/docket/06-43.htm

Gonzalez v. United States, Supreme Court Media, The Oyez Project, available at http://www.oyez.org/cases/2000-2009/2007/2007_06_11612/

MALICIOUS PROSECUTION

FRAMED MEN AWARDED $101.7 MILLION FROM FEDERAL GOVERNMENT

Associated Press, "U.S. Must Pay $101.7 Million to Men Framed by FBI," CNN.com, July 26, 2007.

Murphy, Shelley and Brian R. Ballou, "US Ordered to Pay $101.7m in False Murder Convictions," *Boston Globe*, July 26, 2007.

MALPRACTICE

REVISITING THE FERES DOCTRINE

"A Question Of Care: Military Malpractice?" CBS Evening News, 31 January 2007. Available at www.cbsnews.com/stories/2008/01/31/eveningnews/main3776580.shtml as retrieved on Apr 21, 2008.

"Feres Follies." *USA Today*, 12 April 2007.

Rosche, Walter F. Jr., "Military Medical Malpractice: Seeking Recourse." *Los Angeles Times*, 20 April 2008.

Stilman, Dale Frost. "Military Families Battle Feres Doctrine." New Jersey State Bar Foundation's *Legal Eagle*, 2007.

Turley, Jonathan. "What Our Soldiers Really Need: Lawyers." *USA Today*, 12 April 2007.

Veterans for Equal Justice Under Law (VERPA LLC) "VERPA Renewed National Petition To Reform

The Feres Doctrine Via The 'Military & Veterans Equal Rights Protection Act' or short title 'V'ERPA Act'." Available at http://www.ipetitions.com/petition/VERPA2008/ as retrieved on Feb 28, 2008.

MCCAIN, JOHN

"John Sidney McCain, III." Encyclopedia of World Biography Supplement, Vol. 25. Thomson Gale, 2005. Reproduced in Biography Resource Center. Farmington Hills, Mich.: Gale, 2008. http://galenet.galegroup.com/servlet/BioRC

MEDICARE

MERCK SETTLES WHISTLEBLOWER SUIT FOR $659 MILLION

Johnson, Carrie. "Merck to Pay $650 Million in Medicaid Settlement." *Washington Post*, 8 February 2008, p. A01.

McSherry, Robert Woodman. "Whistle-Blowers Share $92 Million in Medicaid Fraud Settlements." *Andrews Litigation Reporter*, Vol 13, Issue 8, 8 February 2008.

"Merck Pays $400 Million in National Medicaid Fraud Settlement." Taxpayers Against Fraud press release, 7 February 2008, available at www.drugfraudsettlement.com

Neil, Martha. "Merck Agrees to $650M Settlement in Medicaid Health Care Fraud." American Bar Association *ABA Journal*, 7 February 2008.

MERGERS AND ACQUISITIONS

WHOLE FOODS CEO TRASHES COMPETITOR PRIOR TO TAKE-OVER

Dubrow, Jon B. and Carla A.R. Hine. "How Did Whole Foods Ever Manage to Pull it Off?" *Daily Business Review*, 8 November 2007.

Federal Trade Commission, Plaintiff, v. Whole Foods Market, Inc., and Wild Oats Markets, Inc., (United States District Court for the District of Columbia) Civ. No. 07-cv-01021-PLF, FTC File No. 071 0114. Available at http://www.ftc.gov/os/caselist/0710114/0710114.shtm as retrieved on Apr 3, 2008.

Fineman, Josh and Oliver Staley. "FTC Will Try to Block Whole Foods, Wild Oats Merger." Bloomberg News. Available at http://www.bloomberg.com/apps/news?pid=20601087&id=aMdXMHXI2XOc&refer=home.

Moore, Angela. "Whole Foods to Acquire Wild Oats," *MarketWatch*, 22 February 2007.

"Whole Foods CEO's Anonymous Online Life." MSNBC News, 12 July 2007. Available at http://www.msnbc.msn.com/id/19718742

"Whole Foods Market Closes Acquisition of Wild Oats Markets, Secures $700 Million Senior Term Loan to Fund Merger and Signs New Five-Year $250 Million Revolver." Whole Foods Market Inc. Press Release, 28 August 2008. Available at http://www.wholefoodsmarket.com/investor/pr07_08-28.html

"Wild Oats Acquisition Causes Dip in Whole Foods' Bottom Line." *New Mexico Business World Weekly*, 20 February 2008.

MONEY LAUNDERING

CUELLAR V. UNITED STATES

Greenhouse, Linda, "Justices Weigh If Cash Hidden is Cash Laundered," *New York Times*, February 26, 2008.

Yost, Pete, "Court Rules for Defendants on Money Laundering," Associated Press, June 2, 2008.

MORTGAGE

THE 2007-2008 SUBPRIME CRISIS

Bajaj, Vikas and Louise Story. "Mortgage Crisis Spreads Past Subprime Loans." *The New York Times*, 12 February 2008.

Dodd, Randall and Paul Miller. "Outbreak: U.S. Subprime Contagion." *Finance & Development*, Vol. 45, No. 2, June 2008.

Labaton, Stephen. "Bush Offers Plan to Save Fannie Mae, Freddie Mac." *The New York Times*, 14 July 2008.

Labaton, Stephen and David M. Herszenhorn. "Opposition, From Both Parties, Over Bailout Plan." *The New York Times*, 16 July 2008.

Muolo, Paul and Mathew Padilla. *Chain of Blame: How Wall Street Caused the Mortgage and Credit Crisis*. Publisher: John Wiley & Sons, Inc., 2008.

Reinhard, Carmen M. and Kenneth S. Rogoff. "Is the 2007 U.S. Sub-Prime Financial Crisis So Different? An International Historical Comparison." Harvard Faculty Research Paper. Available at http://www.economics.harvard.edu/faculty/rogoff/files/Is_the_2007_U.S._Sub-Prime_Finaincial_Crisis_so_Different.pdf

"Michael B. Mukasey." Biography Resource Center Online. Gale, 2007. Reproduced in Biography Resource Center. Farmington Hills, Mich.: Gale, 2008. http://galenet.galegroup.com/servlet/BioRC

MURDER

MURDER-SUICIDE RULING IN PRO-WRESTLER BENOIT CASE

"Cops Eye 'roid Rage in Wrestler's Murder-Suicide." NBC News, 27 June 2007. Available at http://nbcsports.msnbc.com/id/19424899/site/21683474 as retrieved on March 30, 2008.

Dornin, Rusty and Adam Reiss. "'Roid Rage Questions Surround Benoit Murder-Suicide," CNN News, 26 June 2007. Available at http://www.cnn.com/2007/US/06/27/wrestler/index.html.

Mooneyham, Mike. "Benoit Incident Marred Pro-Wrestling in '07." Charleston *Post and Courier*, 30 December 2007.

"Police Paint Grisly Picture of Benoit Home." ABC News Report, 26 June 2007. Available at http://www.abcnews.com/Sports/story?id=3315501&page=1

"Steroids, Drugs Found in Benoit, Wife, Son." CBS News, 17 July 2007. Available at http://www.cbsnews.com/stories/2007/07/17/national/main3066550.shtml

NEW YORK MAN CONVICTED OF MURDER IN INTERNET HOAX CASE

Eltman, Frank, "NY Man on Trial in Slaying of White Teen," *USA Today*, December 18, 2007.

Chun, Susan, "Jury Deliberates Case of Internet Hoax That Led to Deadly Shooting," CNN.com, December 20, 2007.

SERIAL KILLER KRAJCIR ADMITS TO DECADES-OLD KILLINGS

"Confessed Killer Had Law Enforcement Degree." CNN News Report, 12 December 2007. Available at of http://www.cnn.com/2007/US/law/12/12/missouri.killings.ap/index.html as retrieved on 30 March 2008.

Gay, Malcolm. "Man Who Admits 6 Killings is Tied . . ." *New York Times*, 14 December 2007.

Salter, Jim. "Preliminary Hearing Set for Krajcir." *Chicago Tribune*, 13 March 2008

"Sex Offender Who Admitted to Killing 9 in Missouri, Illinois Studied Law Enforcement." FOX News Report, 17 December 2007. Available at http://www.foxnews.com/story/0,2933,316537,00.html as retrieved on 30 March 2008.

Suhr, Jim. "Inmate Sentenced in Killing Spree." WJLA Local News Report (ABC News), Marion, Illinois, 18 January 2008. Available at http://www.wjla.com/news/stories/0108/489133.html as retrieved on 30 March 2008.

KLANSMAN JAMES FORD SEALE CONVICTED FOR ROLE IN 1964 DEATHS

"Attorney General Alberto R. Gonzales Holds a Justice Department News Briefing on the Indictment of James Ford Seale." *FDCH Political Transcripts*, 25 January 2007.

"James Seale Suspected of Killing Black Teenagers; Indictment on Thursday." MSNBC News, 14 June 2007. Available at http://www.msnbc.msn.com/id/19234202/ as retrieved on Mar 31, 2008

Mudhar, Raju. "Cracking a Very Old Case." *Toronto Star*, 26 January 2007.

"Reputed Klansman Convicted in 1964 Deaths." MSNBC News, 14 June 2007. Available at http://www.msnbc.msn.com/id/19234202/ as retrieved on Mar 31, 2008

"Former Mississippi Klansman Sentenced to Three Life Terms in Prison for Role in 1964 Kidnapping and Murder of Two African-American Men." U.S. Dept. of Justice Press Release, 24 August 2007. Available at http://jackson.fbi.gov/dojpressrel/pressrel07/klansman082407.htm as retrieved on Apr 1, 2008.

MISTRIAL AND RETRIAL IN PHIL SPECTOR MURDER CASE

Booth, William, and Sara Geis. "Hung Jury for Phil Spector in Latest Case of Celeb Justice." *Washington Post*, 27 September 2007, Section C01.

"DA: Phil Spector Will Face Retrial." KNCB-TV News, Los Angeles, 27 September 2007. Available at http://www.knbc.com/entertainment/14208522/detail.html?dl = mainclick as

Deutsch, Linda. "Judge in Phil Spector Retrial Rebuffs Defense Motion to Disqualify Him for Prejudice." Minneapolis-St. Paul *Star Tribune*, 26 March 2008.

"Murder Retrial Penciled in for September 2008" Associated Press. December 10, 2007.

"Phil Spector Lawyer Needs Time for Retrial." *New York Daily News*, 8 December 2008.

"Phil Spector Wants LA Judge Dismissed From Murder Retrial." *San Francisco Gate*, 13 March 2008. Available at http://www.sfgate.com/cgi-bin/article .cgi?f = /n/a/2008/03/13/state/n121907D59 .DTL&tsp = 1 as retrieved on 3 April 2008.

NATIVE AMERICAN RIGHTS

COBELL V. KEMPTHORNE

Canby, William. *American Indian Law in a Nutshell.* St. Paul, MN: West. 2004 Fourth Edition.

Wilkins, David. *Uneven Ground: American Indian Sovereignty and Federal Law.* Norman, OK: University of Oklahoma Press. 2002.

Wilkins, David. *American Indian Sovereignty and the U.S. Supreme Court.* Austin, TX: University of Texas Press. 1997.

OBAMA, BARACK

"Barack Obama." Biography Resource Center Online. Gale, 2004. Reproduced in Biography Resource Center. Farmington Hills, Mich.: Gale, 2008. http://galenet.galegroup.com/servlet/BioRC

PARALEGAL

RICHLIN SECURITY SERVICE CO. V. CHERTOFF

Asimow, Michael, *A Guide to Federal Agency Adjudication*, Chicago, Ill.: Section of Administrative Law and Regulatory Practice, American Bar Association, 2003.

Coyle, Marcia, "Supreme Court to Hear Arguments Over Reimbursement of Paralegal Costs," *National Law Journal*, March 17, 2008.

PATENTS

MICROSOFT AND ALCATEL-LUCENT BATTLE OVER MP3 AND OTHER PATENTS IN COURT

Hansell, Saul, "MP3 Patents in Upheaval After Verdict," *New York Times*, February 23, 2007.

St. Onge, Jeff, "Microsoft, Dell Lose Bid to Void Alcatel Lawsuit" *Seattle Post-Intelligencer*, October 2, 2007.

PERJURY

DETROIT MAYOR KWAME KILPATRICK CHARGED WITH PERJURY

Ashenfelter, David, Joe Swickard, and Zachary Gorchow, "Kilpatrick and Beatty Surrender," *Detroit Free Press*, March 24, 2008.

Gorchow, Zachary, "Kilpatrick Vows to Stay Put After City Council Asks for Resignation," *Detroit Free Press*, March 18, 2008.

SCOOTER LIBBY CONVICTED OF PERJURY IN CIA LEAK CASE

Plame, Valerie. *Fair Game: My Life as a Spy, My Betrayal by the White House.* Simon and Schuster, 2007.

Weiner, Tim. *Legacy of Ashes: The History of the CIA* Anchor, 2008.

National Public Radio, "Timeline: The CIA Leak Case." Available at http://www.npr.org/templates/story/story.php?storyId = 4764919

PREEMPTION

CHAMBER OF COMMERCE V. BROWN

Associated Press, "Court Rejects California Union Law," *Chicago Tribune*, June 19, 2008.

Savage, David G., "Supreme Court Rejects California Law on Anti-Union Speech," *Los Angeles Times*, June 19, 2008.

PREEMPTION

RIEGEL V. MEDTRONIC, INC.

Epstein, Richard. *Federal Preemption.* AEI Press, 2007.

O'Reilly, James. *Federal Preemption of State and Local Law.* American Bar Association, 2006.

Zimmerman, Joseph. *Congressional Preemption.* State University of New York Press, 2006.

PRIVACY

FIFTH CIRCUIT STRIKES DOWN TEXAS BAN ON SEX TOYS

Brown, Angela K., "5th Circuit Overturns Texas Sex Toys Ban," Law.com, February 14, 2008.

Kreytak, Steven, "Court Overturns Texas Ban on Sex Toys," *Austin American-Statesman*, February 14, 2008.

PRODUCT LIABILITY

FDA ISSUES WARNINGS ABOUT BOTOX AND MYOBLOC

Ault, Alicia, "FDA Issues Warning on Botulinum Toxin Injections," *Internal Medicine News*, March 1, 2008.

Simons, John, "A Wrinkle in the Botox Story," CNNMoney.com, February 12, 2008.

CONTAMINATION LEADS TO MASSIVE PET FOOD RECALL

Associated Press, "Owners Watching Pets After Food Recall," MSNBC.com, March 21, 2007.

Thornton, Kim Campbell, "A Year After Pet Food Recall, Still Buyer Beware," MSNBC.com, March 17, 2008.

WARNER-LAMBERT CO. V. KENT

Greenhouse, Linda, "Court Allows Suit Against Drug Maker," *New York Times*, March 4, 2008.

Harris, Gardiner, "Court Considers Protecting Drug Makers From Lawsuits," *New York Times*, February 26, 2008.

PROSTITUTION

N.Y. GOVERNOR ELIOT SPITZER LINKED TO PROSTITUTION RING

Hakim, Danny and William K. Rashbaum, "Spitzer Is Linked To Prostitution Ring," *New York Times*, March 10, 2008.

Van Natta Jr., Don, and Jo Becker, "Spitzer Fall Began with Bank Reports," *New York Times*, March 13, 2008.

PUBLIC UTILITIES

MORGAN STANLEY CAPITAL GROUP INC. V. PUBLIC UTILITY DIST. NO. 1

Coyle, Marcia, "Energy Contracts Spark High-Stakes Supreme Court Case," Law.com, February 13, 2008.

Douglass, Elizabeth, "Supreme Court Deals Blow to States on Electricity," *Los Angeles Times*, June 27, 2008.

PUNITIVE DAMAGES

EXXON SHIPPING CO. V. BAKER

Exxon Shipping Co. v. Baker, No. 07-219, 554 U.S. ___ Available at www.supremecourtus.gov/docket/07_219.htm

Exxon Shipping Co. v. Baker, No. 07-219, 554 U.S. ___The Oyez Project, available at http://www.oyez.org/cases/2000-2009/2007/2007_07_219/

Loeb, Ellen and Ginger McCall, "Exxon Shipping v. Baker." Cornell University Law School Law Information Institute publication, available at http://law.cornell.edu/supct/cert/07-219.htmll/.

"Supreme Court Did Not Apply a Constitutional Standard in Exxon Shipping v. Baker." *The Conservation Report*, 26 June 2008.

RAILROADS

CSX TRANSPORTATION, INC. V. GEORGIA STATE BOARD OF EQUALIZATION

Appraisal Institute *The Appraisal of Real Estate, 12th ed.* Appraisal Institute, 2001.

Dooley, Frank. *Railroad Law a Decade After Deregulation.* Quorum Books, 1994.

Ely, James. *Railroads and American Law.* University of Kansas Press, 2001.

RECALL

RECALL ON CHINESE PRODUCTS

Lindner, Melanie. "Another China Recall, This Time for Starbucks." *Forbes* 10 October 2007.

National Public Radio (NPR), series of news reports, including, "Pet Food Deaths: FDA Blocks Gluten from China," 2 April 2007; "Chinese Inquiry Cites Need for Product Controls," 9 May 2007; "Thomas Tank Engine Toy Recall Angers Parents," 22 June 2007; and "Tires are Latest Chinese Recall in U.S.," 26 June 2007. Available at http://www.npr.org/templates/story/story.php?storyId =

"Toxic Trade: Guess Which Country Topped 2007 Recall List?" WorldNetDaily online magazine, 25 February 2008. Available at http://www.worldnetdaily.com/index.php?fa = 57069

REPARATION

LEGISLATIVE EFFORTS INCREASE FOR WRONGFUL CONVICTIONS

Berger, Vivian. "The Wrongful Convictions Tax Relief Act of 2007." From *National Law Journal* March 2008.

Browning, John G. "Legally Speaking: Compensating the Exonerated." *Southeast Texas Record*, 30 November 2007.

Radnofsky, Louise. "Compensating the Wrongly Convicted." *Prospect* 7 July 2007.

Santos, Fernanda. "Bill Would Give Tax Break to Exonerated Prisoners." *New York Times*, 7 December 2007.

Ward, Damin. "Compensation for the Wrongfully Convicted." *Minnesota Spokesman-Recorder*, 19 January 2007.

RICO

CHICAGO MOBSTERS CONVICTED OF DECADES-OLD MURDERS

Associated Press, "Will Fed Trial Put 'Hit' on Chicago Mob?," CBSNews.com, June 18, 2007.

Robinson, Mike, "Chicago Mob Trial Promises Drama," *Seattle Times*, June 18, 2007.

RIPARIAN RIGHTS

NEW JERSEY V. DELAWARE

Arnold, Craig, and Jewell, Leigh. Ed. *Beyond Litigation: Case Studies in Water Rights Disputes.* Environmental Law Institute, 2002.

Sherk, George. *Dividing the Waters: The Resolution of Interstate Water Conflicts in the United States.* Springer, 2000.

Wright, Kennth. Ed. *Water Rights of the Eastern United States.* American Water Works Association, 1998.

SECOND AMENDMENT

VIRGINIA TECH SHOOTINGS SPUR FEDERAL GUN CONTROL LEGISLATION

Jacobs, James. *Can Gun Control Work?* Oxford University Press, 2004.

Spitzer, Robert. *The Politics of Gun Control. 4th Ed.* CQ Press, 2007.

Young, Mitchell, Ed. *Gun Control.* Greenhaven Press, 2006.

DISTRICT OF COLUMBIA V. HELLER

Martin, Jonathan, "NRA Plans $40M Campaign Blitz," CBSNews.com, July 1, 2008.

Sherman, Mark, "Court Rules in Favor of Second Amendment Gun Right," Associated Press, June 26, 2008.

SECURITIES

SUPREME COURT DISMISSES COMMODITY FUTURES CASE

Lash, Steve, "Justices Weigh Fight Over Futures Law," *Chicago Daily Law Bulletin*, October 29, 2007.

Rummell, Nicholas, "Can a Futures Broker Sue an Exchange?," *Investment News*, November 19, 2007.

STONERIDGE INVESTMENT PARTNERS LLC V. SCIENTIFIC-ATLANTA, INC.

Hazen, Thomas. *Securities Regulation in a Nutshell, 9th Ed.* West Group, 2006.

Palmiter, Allen. *Security Regulation, 3rd Ed.* Aspen Publishers, 2005.

Soderquist, Larry, and Gabaldon, Theresa. *Securities Law: Concepts and Insights, 3rd Ed.* Foundation Press, 2006.

SENTENCING

BEGAY V. U.S.

Associated Press, "Court Rules DUI Does Not Count as Violent Felony," *Houston Examiner*, April 16, 2008.

Bamberger, Phylis Skloot and David J. Gottlieb, *Practice Under the Federal Sentencing Guidelines.* Gaithersburg, Md.: Aspen Law and Business, 2001.

SENTENCING

CRACK COCAINE SENTENCING DISPARITIES ADDRESSED

Branham, Lynm. *The Law of Sentencing and Corrections in a Nutshell.* West Group, 2005.

Stith, Kate. *Fear of Judging: Sentencing Guidelines in the Federal Courts.* University of Chicago Press, 1998.

Tonry, Michael. *Sentencing Matters.* Oxford University Press, 2004.

GALL V. UNITED STATES

Branham, Lynm. *The Law of Sentencing and Corrections in a Nutshell.* West Group, 2005.

Stith, Kate. *Fear of Judging: Sentencing Guidelines in the Federal Courts.* University of Chicago Press, 1998.

Tonry, Michael. *Sentencing Matters.* Oxford University Press, 2004.

KIMBROUGH V. UNITED STATES

Branham, Lynm. *The Law of Sentencing and Corrections in a Nutshell.* West Group, 2005.

Stith, Kate. *Fear of Judging: Sentencing Guidelines in the Federal Courts.* University of Chicago Press, 1998.

Tonry, Michael. *Sentencing Matters.* Oxford University Press, 2004.

LOGAN V. UNITED STATES

Branham, Lynm. *The Law of Sentencing and Corrections in a Nutshell.* West Group, 2005.

Stith, Kate. *Fear of Judging: Sentencing Guidelines in the Federal Courts.* University of Chicago Press, 1998.

Tonry, Michael. *Sentencing Matters.* Oxford University Press, 2004.

SEX OFFENSES

HUMAN RIGHTS WATCH REPORT CRITICAL OF SEX OFFENDER LAWS

Crary, David. "Report Faults Sex Offender Laws." Associated Press News Release, 12 September 2007. Available at http://abcnews.go.com/US/wireStory?id=3592687

"Human Rights News: Sex Offender Laws May Do More Harm Than Good." Human Rights Watch Press Release, 12 September, 2007. Available at http://hrw.org/english/docs/2007/09/06/usdom16819.htm

No Easy Answers: Sex Offender Laws in the United States, Available at http://hrw.org/reports/2007/us0907

JUDGE RULES FEDERAL MENTAL HEALTH COMMITMENT OF SEX OFFENDERS UNCONSTITUTIONAL

"Adam Walsh Act." Minnesota Dept. of Public Safety, Office of Justice Programs, *Commentary: Judicial Update,* Fall 2007.

Franklin, Karen. "Federal Court Strikes Down Portion of Adam Walsh Act." *Forensic Psychologist Newsletter,* 10 September 2007.

Oakes, Larry. "Minn. Judge Rules Federal Sex Offender Commitment Law Unconstitutional." Minnesota *Star-Tribune,* 29 May 2008.

U.S. v. Comstock, No. 507 F. Supp. 2d 522 (E.D.N.C. 2007)

SEXUAL ABUSE

SAN DIEGO DIOCESE SETTLES CLERGY ABUSE CASES FOR $198 MILLION

Figueroa, Teri. "Judge Divvies Up San Diego Clergy Abuse Settlement." *North County Times,* 7 December 2007.

Horsley, Scott. "San Diego Diocese Settles Abuse Claims." NPR News, *All Things Considered,* 22 May 2008.

"Settlement Reached in Catholic Clergy Sexual Abuse Lawsuits." Local 10 News, CNN Broadcasting System, San Diego. Available at http://www.10news.com/news/14065673/detail.html

"Settlement Reached in Salesian Priest Sex Abuse Case." *San Diego Union-Tribune*, 15 May 2008.

SIXTH AMENDMENT

INDIANA V. EDWARDS

Barnes, Robert, "High Court Weighs Self-Representation," *Washington Post*, March 27, 2008.

Biskupic, Joan, "High Court Hears Ind. Mental Illness Case," *USA Today*, March 26, 2008.

ROTHGERY V. GILLESPIE COUNTY

Graczyk, Michael, "Legal Help Too Slow in Texas Arrest, High Court Says," Associated Press, June 23, 2008.

Mauro, Tony, "Supreme Court Says Right to Counsel Begins with First Appearance Before Judge," Law.com, June 24, 2008.

WRIGHT V. VAN PATTEN

Federman, Cary. *The Body And the State: Habeas Corpus And American Jurisprudence.* New York, NY: State University of New York Press. 2006.

Frank, Jerome. *Courts on Trial.* Princeton, NJ: Princeton University Press. 1973.

Freedman, Eric. *Habeas Corpus: Rethinking the Great Writ of Liberty.* New York: New York Univ. Press. 2003.

SOVEREIGN IMMUNITY

ALI V. FEDERAL BUREAUS OF PRISONS

Chemerinsky, Erwin. *Federal Jurisdiction.* New York: Aspen Publishers. 2003. Fourth Edition.

Currie, David. *Federal Jurisdiction in a Nutshell.* Saint Paul, MN: West Group. 1999.

Wright, Charles Alan. *Law of Federal Courts.* Saint Paul, MN: West Group. 2002. Sixth Edition.

35W BRIDGE COLLAPSE LIABILITY ISSUES

Chemerinsky, Erwin. *Federal Jurisdiction, 4th Ed.* Aspen Publishers, 2003.

Currie, David. *Federal Jurisdiction in a Nutshell.* West Group, 1999.

Wright, Charles Alan. *Law of Federal Courts, 6th Ed.* West Group, 2002.

IN RE: KATRINA CANAL BREACHES CONSOLIDATED LITIGATION

Chemerinsky, Erwin. *Federal Jurisdiction.* New York: Aspen Publishers. 2003. Fourth Edition.

Currie, David. *Federal Jurisdiction in a Nutshell.* Saint Paul, MN: West Group. 1999.

Wright, Charles Alan. *Law of Federal Courts.* Saint Paul, MN: West Group. 2002. Sixth Edition.

REPUBLIC OF THE PHILIPPINES V. PIMENTEL

"Govt Wins Marcos Case in US High Court," *The Manila Times*, June 14, 2008.

Yost, Pete, "U.S. Supreme Court Takes Up Case of Marcos Millions," *Honolulu Advertiser*, March 17, 2008.

SPORTS LAW

CONTROVERSIES SURROUND NATIONAL FOOTBALL LEAGUE

Associated Press, "Redskins Safety Sean Taylor Dies One Day After Being Shot in Home," FoxNews.com, November 27, 2007.

Clayton, John, "Minus a Whistle-Blower, Spygate Will Expire Quietly," ESPN.com, May 8, 2008.

FORMER SEN. GEORGE MITCHELL ISSUES REPORT ON STEROIDS IN BASEBALL

Wilson, Duff and Michael S. Schmidt, "Baseball Braces for Steroid Report from Mitchell," *New York Times*, December 13, 2007.

Wilson, Duff and Michael S. Schmidt, "Clemens and McNamee Take Storites to the Hill," *New York Times*, February 8, 2008.

STATUTE OF LIMITATIONS

JOHN R. SAND & GRAVEL COMPANY V. UNITED STATES

Currie, David. *Federal Jurisdiction in a Nutshell.* West Group, 1999.

Lewis, Jr., Harold and Norman, Elizabeth. *Civil Rights Law and Practice.* West Group, 2004.

Vieira, Norman. *Constitutional Civil Rights in a Nutshell.* West Group, 1998.

TAXATION

BOULWARE V. UNITED STATES

Burke, Karen. *Federal Income Taxation of Corporations and Stockholders in a Nutshell. 5th Ed.* West Group, 2002.

Cammack, Mark and Garland, Norman. *Advanced Criminal Procedure in a Nutshell.* St. Paul, MN: West Publishing Co. 2001.

McNulty, John, and Lathrope, Daniel. *Federal Income Taxation of Individuals in a Nutshell. 7th Ed.* West Group, 2004.

UNITED STATES V. CLINTWOOD ELKHORN MINING COMPANY

"NFIB Weighs In on Tax Case Before the U.S. Supreme Court," *US Federal News*, February 21, 2008.

"Supreme Court Rules in Tax Cases" *Accounting Today*, May 19, 2008.

KNIGHT V. COMMISSIONER OF INTERNAL REVENUE

CCH Law. *The Federal Income Tax of Decedents, Estates and Trusts. 23rd Ed.* CCH Inc., 2007.

Mennell, Robert, and Burr, Sherri. *Wills and Trusts in a Nutshell.* West Pub., 2007.

McNulty, John, and McCouch, Grayson. *Federal Estate and Gift Taxation. 6th Ed.* West Pub., 2003.

MEADWESTVACO V. ILLINOIS DEPARTMENT OF REVENUE

MeadWestvaco Corp. v. Illinois Department of Revenue No. 06-1413, 553 U.S. ___ (2008) Available at www.supremecourtus.gov/docket/06-1413.htm

MeadWestvaco Corp. v. Illinois Department of Revenue No. 06-1413, 553 U.S. ___ (2008) The Oyez Project, available at http://www.oyez.org/cases/2000-2009/2007/2007_06_43/

Sarkar, Deepa and Joe Hashmall. "MeadWestvaco Corp. v. Illinois Department of Revenue." Legal Information Institute of the Cornell University School of Law, available at: http://www.law.cornell/edu/supct/cert/06-1413.html

TERRORISM

JOSE PADILLA CONVICTED ON TERRORISM CONSPIRACY CHARGES

Bovard, James. *Terrorism and Tyranny*. Palgrave Macmillan, 2003.

Martin, Clarence. *Understanding Terrorism: Challenges, Perspectives, and Issues. 2nd Ed.* Sage Publications, 2006.

Richardson, Louise. Ed. *The Roots of Terrorism.* Routledge, 2006.

FEDERAL DISTRICT COURTS STRIKE DOWN PARTS OF THE PATRIOT ACT

Associated Press, "Federal Judge Rules 2 Patriot Act Provisions Unconstitutional," CNN.com, September 26, 2007.

Eggen, Dan, "Patriot Act Provisions Voided," *Washington Post*, September 27, 2007, A2.

UNITED STATES V. RESSAM

Branigin, William, "High Court Affirms Terrorism Conviction," *Washington Post*, May 20, 2008.

Shenon, Philip, "Mukasey Goes to Court to Argue a Terrorism Case," *New York Times*, March 26, 2008.

TOBACCO

ROWE V. NEW HAMPSHIRE MOTOR TRANSPORT ASSOCIATION

Epstein, Richard. *Federal Preemption*. AEI Press, 2007.

O'Reilly, James. *Federal Preemption of State and Local Law*. American Bar Association, 2006.

Zimmerman, Joseph. *Congressional Preemption*. State University of New York Press, 2006.

TORTURE

WATERBOARDING AND OTHER TACTICS

"'03 U.S. Memo Approved Harsh Interrogations." *The New York Times*, 2 April 2008.

Crawford-Greenburg, Jan and Ariane de Vogue, "Bush Administration Blocked Waterboarding Critic." ABC News Report, 2 November 2007. Available at http://abcnews.go.com/pring?id=3814076

"DOJ Memo Advised Military That Interrogations Not Limited by Criminal Law." *Paper Chase*, The Jurist, University of Pittsburgh School of Law, 2 April 2008.

"Democrats Demand DOJ Interrogation Memos." *Paper Chase*, The Jurist, University of Pittsburgh School of Law, 5 October 2007.

"DOJ Memos Supported 'Severe' Interrogation Tactics: NYT." *Paper Chase*, The Jurist, University of Pittsburgh School of Law, 4 October 2007.

"Memo Reveals Bush Administration Legal Theory on Interrogation." PBS-The Online News Hour Extra, 9 April 2008. Available at http://www.pbs.org/news hour/extra

Robinson, Dan. "Former US Attorney General Tells Congress Waterboarding Isn't Torture." *Voice of America*, 17 July 2008.

Shane, Scott, et al. "Secret U.S. Endorsement of Severe Interrogations." *The New York Times*, 4 October 2007.

TRUSTS

KNIGHT V. COMMISSIONER

Newby, Laurel, "Supreme Court Argument Report: Can Trusts Deduct Fees for Investment Advice?," Law.com, February 20, 2008.

Notice 2008-32, *Internal Revenue Bulletin*, March 17, 2008.

VOTING RIGHTS

CRAWFORD V. MARION COUNTY BD. OF ELECTIONS

Burke, Victoria and Allison Condon. "Crawford v. Marion County Election Board." Cornell University School of Law, Law Information Institute, available at www.law.cornell.edu/supct/cert/07-21.html

Crawford v. Marion County Election Board, No. 7-21,553 U.S. ___, Available at www.supremecourtus.gov/docket/06-43.htm

Crawford v. Marion County Election Board No. 7-21, 553 U.S. ___, The Oyez Project, available at http://www.oyez.org/cases/2000-2009/2007/2007_07-21

Stout, David. "Supreme Court to Hear Case on Voter ID Law." *The New York Times*, 25 September 2007.

MICHIGAN UPHOLDS VOTER PHOTO ID

Advisory Opinion 130589, (July 18, 2007) Available at www.findlaw.com

Elmendorf, Christopher S. "Undue Burdens on Voter Participation." University of California at Davis Legal Studies Research Paper No. 128, January 2008.

Stout, David. "Supreme Court to Hear Case on Voter ID Law." *The New York Times*, 25 September 2007.

"The Nation: Michigan Voter ID Law OKd." *Los Angeles Times*, 19 July 2007.

WIRETAPPING

2008 AMENDMENTS TO FISA

"Congress Backs FISA, Hands Victory to Bush." *The Wahington York Times*, Available at www .washingtontimes.com/news/2008/jul/10/congress-backs-fisa-hands-victory-to-bush

Lichtblau, Eric. "Senate Approves Bill to Broaden Wiretap Powers." *The New York Times*, 10 July 2008.

Loven, Jennifer. "Bush Signs New Rules on Government Wiretapping." ABC News, 10 July 2008. Available at http://abcnes.go.com/story?id =5344932

"President Bush Signs H.R. 6304, FISA Amendments Act of 2008." White House Press Release, 10 July 2008. Available at http://www.whitehouse.gov/news/releases/2008/07/20080710-2.html

AGRICULTURE LAW

The Pollinator Protection Act of 2007

SECTION 1. SHORT TITLE.

This Act may be cited as the 'Pollinator Protection Act'.

SEC. 2. FINDINGS.

Congress finds the following:

(1) Many of the crops that humans and livestock consume rely on pollinators for healthy growth. More specifically, pollination by honey bees adds over $15,000,000,000 annually to the value of United States crops.

(2) One-third of our food supply depends on honey bee pollination, which makes the management and protection of pollinators an issue of paramount importance to the security of the United States food supply system.

(3) Colony Collapse Disorder is the name that has been given to the latest die-off of honey bee colonies, exacerbating the continual decline of pollinators in North America. Colonies in more than 23 states have been affected by this disorder.

(4) If the current rate of decline continues, the United States will be forced to rely more heavily on imported foods. Thus, American food security would be destabilized through adverse affects on availability, price, and quality of the many fruits, vegetables, and other products that depend on animal pollination.

(5) Enhanced funding for research on honey bees, parasites, pathogens, toxins, and other environmental factors affecting bees and pollination of cultivated and wild plants will yield responses to Colony Collapse Disorder and other factors causing the decline of pollinators in North America.

SEC. 3. SUSTAINED APICULTURAL RESEARCH AND COLONY COLLAPSE DISORDER WORKING GROUP.

(a) Agricultural Research Service- There is authorized to be appropriated to the Secretary of Agriculture, acting through the Agricultural Research Service, the following:

(1) $3,000,000 for each of the fiscal years 2008 through 2012 for new personnel, facilities improvement, and additional research at Department of Agriculture Apicultural Research Laboratories.

(2) $2,500,000 for each of fiscal years 2008 and 2009 for research on honey bee physiology, insect pathology, insect chemical ecology, and honey bee toxicology at other Department of Agriculture facilities in New York, Florida, California, and Texas.

(3) $1,750,000 for each of fiscal years 2008 through 2010 for an area-wide research program to identify causes and solutions for Colony Collapse Disorder in affected States.

(b) Cooperative State Research, Education, and Extension Service- There is authorized to be appropriated to the Secretary of Agriculture, acting through the Cooperative State Research, Education, and Extension Service, $10,000,000 for each of the fiscal years 2008 through 2012 to fund Department of Agriculture research grants to investigate—

(1) honey bee immunology;

(2) honey bee biology and ecology;

(3) pollination biology;

(4) honey bee genomics;

(5) honey bee bioinformatics;

(6) sublethal effects of insecticides, herbicides and fungicides on honey bees and other beneficial insects; and

(7) effects of genetically modified crops and their interaction with honey bees and other pollinators.

COPYRIGHT

Heirs Claim Share of 'Superman' Copyright: Ruling Excerpt

The following excerpt from the judge's ruling provides some of the background on the treatment of Superman's creators as they pursued remuneration for their work, and later the copyright.

After the conclusion of the 1970s Superman litigation, the New York Times "ran a story about how the two creators of Superman were living in near destitute conditions" . . .

Apparently in response to the bad publicity associated with this and similar articles, the parties thereafter entered into a further agreement, dated December 23, 1975. See id. ("'There is no legal obligation,' Mr. Emmett[, executive vice-president of Warner Communications, Inc.,] said, 'but I sure feel that there is a moral obligation on our part'"). In the agreement, Siegel and Shuster reacknowledged the Second Circuit's decision that "all right, title and interest in" Superman ("including any and all renewals and extensions of . . . such rights") resided exclusively with DC Comics and its corporate affiliates and, in return, DC Comics' now parent company, Warner Communications, Inc. ("WCI"), provided Siegel and Shuster with modest annual payments for the remainder of their lives; provided them medical insurance under the plan for its employees; and credited them as the "creators of Superman." In tendering this payment, Warner Communications, Inc. specifically stated that it had no legal obligation to do so, but that it did so solely "in consideration" of the pair's "past services . . . and in view of [their] present circumstances," emphasizing that the payments were "voluntary."

The 1975 agreement also made certain provisions for Siegel's spouse Joanne, providing her

with certain monthly payments "for the balance of her life if Siegel" died before December 31, 1985. Finally, Warner Communications, Inc. noted that its obligation to make such voluntary payments would cease if either Siegel or Shuster (or their representatives) sued "asserting any right, title or interest in the 'Superman' . . . copyright." As the years went by Warner Communications, Inc. increased the amount of the annual payments, and on at least two occasions paid the pair special bonuses.

As the time grew nearer to the December 31, 1985, cutoff date for surviving spouse benefits, Joanne Siegel wrote the CEO for DC Comics expressing her "terrible worry" over the company's refusal to provide Jerome Siegel life insurance in the 1975 agreement. (Decl. Michael Bergman, Ex. NN). She voiced her concern that, should anything happen to her husband after the cutoff date, she and their daughter "would be left without any measure of [financial] security." (Decl. Michael Bergman, Ex. NN). The parties thereafter agreed by letter dated March 15, 1982, that Warner would pay Joanne Siegel the same benefits it had been paying her husband if he predeceased her, regardless of the time of his death. (Decl. Michael Bergman, Ex. OO). Jerome Siegel died on January 28, 1996, and Joanne Siegel has been receiving these voluntary survival spouse benefits since that time.

In the meantime, changes in the law resurrected legal questions as to the ownership rights the parties had to the Superman copyright. With the passage of the Copyright Act of 1976 (the "1976 Act"), Congress changed the legal landscape concerning artists' transfers of the copyrights in their creations. First, the 1976 Act expanded by nineteen years the duration of the renewal period for works, like the initial release of Superman in Action Comics, Vol. 1, that were already in their renewal term at the time of the Act's passage. See 17 U.S.C. § 304(b). Second, and importantly for this case, the 1976 Act gave artists and their heirs the ability to terminate any prior grants of the rights to their creations that were executed before January 1, 1978, regardless of the terms contained in such assignments, e.g., a contractual provision that all the rights (the initial and renewal) belonged exclusively to the publisher. Specifically, section 304(c) to the 1976 Act provides that, "[i]n the case of any copyright subsisting in either its first or renewal term on January 1, 1978, other than a copyright in a work made for hire, the exclusive or nonexclusive grant of a transfer or license of the renewal copyright or any right under it, executed before January 1, 1978, . . . is subject to termination . . . notwithstanding any agreement to the contrary. . . ." It is this right of termination that Joanne Siegel and Laura Siegel Larson now seek to vindicate in this case.

FREEDOM OF SPEECH

Ninth Circuit Upholds Online Vote-swapping: Ruling Excerpt

Excerpted from the court's ruling:

Whatever the wisdom of using vote-swapping agreements to communicate these positions, such agreements plainly differ from conventional (and illegal) vote buying, which conveys no message other than the parties' willingness to exchange votes for money (or some other form of private profit). The Supreme Court held in Brown v. Hartlage, 456 U.S. 45, 55 (1982), that vote buying may be banned "without trenching on any right of association protected by the First Amendment." Vote swapping, however, is more akin to the candidate's pledge in Brown to take a pay cut if elected, which the Court concluded was constitutionally protected, than to unprotected vote buying. Like the candidate's pledge, vote swapping involves a "promise to confer some ultimate benefit on the voter, qua . . . citizen[ ] or member of the general public"—i.e., another person's agreement to vote for a particular candidate. Id. at 58-59. And unlike vote buying, vote swapping is not an "illegal exchange for private profit" since the only benefit a vote swapper can receive is a marginally higher probability that his preferred electoral outcome will come to pass. Id. at 55 (emphasis added); cf. Marc John 9358 PORTER v. BOWEN Randazza, The Other Election Controversy of Y2K: Core First Amendment Values and High-Tech Political Coalitions, 82 Wash. U.L.Q. 143, 221 (2004). ("There can be no . . . serious assertion, that anyone entered into a vote-swap arrangement for private profit or any other form of enrichment.")

Both the websites' vote-swapping mechanisms and the communication and vote swaps that they enabled were therefore constitutionally protected. At their core, they amounted to efforts by politically engaged people to support their preferred candidates and to avoid election results that they feared would contravene the preferences of a majority of voters in closely contested states. Whether or not one agrees with these voters' tactics, such efforts, when conducted honestly and without money changing hands, are at the heart of the liberty safeguarded by the First Amendment. Cf. Brown, 456 U.S. at 52-53; Buckley, 424 U.S. at 14-15; Monitor Patriot, 401 U.S. at 271-72; Mills, 384 U.S. at 218-19.12

We do not decide, however, whether the vote-swapping mechanisms and the communication and vote swaps they made possible were pure speech or expressive conduct. The distinction between the two concepts is often difficult to discern. See, e.g., FAIR, 126 S. Ct. at 1308-11 (considering law schools' policies toward military recruiters first as speech and then in the alternative as expressive conduct). It is also a distinction that makes no practical difference here, because our conclusion would be the same under the strict scrutiny that applies to restrictions of pure speech as it is under the intermediate scrutiny applicable to the burdening of expressive conduct that we employ below.

TERRORISM

Waterboarding and Other Tactics: Department of Justice "Torture Memo"

Excerpted from the Department of Justice "torture memo" that laid out reasoning allowing the president to make use of such techniques:

Section II.6. Commander-in-Chief Authority:

Even if these statutes were misconstrued to apply to persons acting at the direction of the President during the conduct of war, the Department of Justice could not enforce this law or all of the other criminal statutes applicable to the special maritime and territorial jurisdiction against federal officials acting pursuant to the President's constitutional authority to direct a war. Even if an interrogation method arguably were to violate a criminal statute, the Justice Department could not bring a prosecution because the statute would be unconstitutional as applied in this context. This approach is consistent with previous decisions of our Office involving the application of federal criminal law. For example, we have previously construed the congressional contempt statute not to apply to executive branch officials who refuse to comply with congressional subpoenas because of an assertion of executive privilege . . .

We have even greater concerns with respect to prosecutions arising out of the exercise of the President's express authority as Commander in Chief than we do with prosecutions arising out of the assertion of executive privilege. Any effort by Congress to regulate the interrogation of enemy combatants would violate the Constitution's sole vesting of the Commander-in-Chief authority in the President. There can be little doubt that intelligence operations, such as the detention and interrogation of enemy combatants and leaders, are both necessary and proper for the effective conduct of a military campaign. Indeed, such operations may be of more importance in a war with an international terrorist organization than one with the conventional armed forces of a nation-state, due to the former's emphasis on covert operations and surprise attacks against civilians. It may be the case that only successful interrogations can provide the information necessary to prevent future attacks upon the United States and its citizens. Congress can no more interfere with the President's conduct of the interrogation of enemy combatants than it can dictate strategic or tactical decisions on the battlefield. Just as statutes that order the President to conduct warfare in a certain manner or for specific goals would be unconstitutional, so too are laws that would prevent the President from gaining the intelligence he believes necessary to prevent attacks upon the United States.

Section II.C.2.b: "Severe Pain or Suffering"

The key statutory phrase in the definition of torture is the statement that acts amount to torture if they cause "severe physical or mental pain or suffering." In examining the meaning of a statute, its text must be the starting point. See INS v. Phinpathya, 464 U.S. 183, 189 (1984). Section 2340 makes plain that the infliction of pain or suffering per se, whether it is physical or mental, is insufficient to amount to torture. Instead, the pain or suffering must be "severe." The statute does not, however, define the term "severe." "In the absence of such a definition, we construe a statutory term in accordance with its ordinary or natural meaning." FDIC v. Meyer, 510 U.S. 471, 476 (1994). The dictionary defines "severe" as "[u]nsparing in exaction, punishment, or censure" or "[I]nflicting discomfort or pain hard to endure; sharp; afflictive; distressing; violent; extreme; as severe pain, anguish, torture." Webster's New International Dictionary 2295 (2d ed. 1935); see American Heritage Dictionary of the English Language 1653 (3d ed. 1992) ("extremely violent or grievous: severe pain") (emphasis in original); IX The Oxford English Dictionary 572(1978) ("Of pain, suffering, loss, or the like: Grievous, extreme" and "of circumstances . . . hard to sustain or endure"). Thus, the adjective "severe" conveys that the pain or suffering must be of such a high level of intensity that the pain is difficult for the subject to endure.

*This section includes difficult or uncommon legal terms (**bolded** in the essays) and their definitions from West's Encyclopedia of American Law (WEAL). Simple or common legal terms such as "lawsuit" and "plaintiff" are not **bolded** in the text and do not appear in this glossary; they do, however, have full entries in WEAL. Furthermore, terms that appear in SMALL CAPS within the essays—such as acts, cases, events, organizations, and persons—also appear in WEAL.*

A

Abet: To encourage or incite another to commit a crime. This word is usually applied to aiding in the commission of a crime. To abet another to commit a murder is to command, procure, counsel, encourage, induce, or assist. To facilitate the commission of a crime, promote its accomplishment, or help in advancing or bringing it about.

In relation to charge of aiding and abetting, term includes knowledge of the perpetrator's wrongful purpose, and encouragement, promotion or counsel of another in the commission of the criminal offense.

A French word, *abeter*—to bait or excite an animal.

Abuse of Discretion: A failure to take into proper consideration the facts and law relating to a particular matter; an arbitrary or unreasonable departure from precedents and settled judicial custom.

Adjudication: The legal process of resolving a dispute. The formal giving or pronouncing of a judgment or decree in a court proceeding; also the judgment or decision given. The entry of a decree by a court in respect to the parties in a case. It implies a hearing by a court, after notice, of legal evidence on the factual issue(s) involved. The equivalent of a determination. It indicates that the claims of all the parties thereto have been considered and set at rest.

Adjusted gross income: The term used for income tax purposes to describe gross income less certain allowable deductions such as trade and business deductions, moving expenses, alimony paid, and penalties for premature withdrawals from term savings accounts, in order to determine a person's taxable income.

Administrative Agency: An official governmental body empowered with the authority to direct and supervise the implementation of particular legislative acts. In addition to *agency*, such governmental bodies may be called commissions, corporations (e.g., FDIC), boards, departments, or divisions.

affirmative defense: A new fact or set of facts that operates to defeat a claim even if the facts supporting that claim are true.

Allocation: The apportionment or designation of an item for a specific purpose or to a particular place.

Annuity: A right to receive periodic payments, usually fixed in size, for life or a term of years that is created by a contract or other legal document.

Appellate: Relating to appeals; reviews by superior courts of decisions of inferior courts or administrative agencies and other proceedings.

Appellate Court: A court having jurisdiction to review decisions of a trial-level or other lower court.

Arbiter: [*Latin, One who attends something to view it as a spectator or witness.*] Any person who is given an absolute power to judge and rule on a matter in dispute.

Arrest warrant: A written order issued by authority of the state and commanding the seizure of the person named.

Articles: Series or subdivisions of individual and distinct sections of a document, statute, or other writing, such as the Articles of Confederation. Codes or systems of rules created by written agreements of parties or by statute that establish standards of legally acceptable behavior in a business relationship, such as articles of incorporation or articles of partnership. Writings that embody contractual terms of agreements between parties.

Attorney-Client Privilege: In law of evidence, client's privilege to refuse to disclose and to prevent any other person from disclosing confidential communications between the client and his or her attorney. Such privilege protects communications between attorney and client made for the purpose of furnishing or obtaining professional legal advice or assistance. That privilege that permits an attorney to refuse to testify as to communications from the client though it belongs to the client, not the attorney, and hence the client may waive it. In federal courts, state law is applied with respect to such privilege.

B

Balance sheet: A comprehensive financial statement that is a summarized assessment of a company's accounts specifying its assets and liabilities. A report, usually prepared by independent auditors or accountants, which includes a full and complete statement of all receipts and disbursements of a particular business. A review that shows a general balance or summation of all accounts without showing the particular items that make up the several accounts.

Banc: [*French, Bench.*] The location where a court customarily or permanently sits.

Battery: At common law, an intentional unpermitted act causing harmful or offensive contact with the person of another.

Bench Trial: A trial conducted before a judge presiding without a jury.

Beyond a Reasonable Doubt: The standard that must be met by the prosecution's evidence in a criminal prosecution: that no other logical explanation can be derived from the facts except that the defendant committed the crime, thereby over-coming the presumption that a person is innocent until proven guilty.

Bilateral contract: An agreement formed by an exchange of promises in which the promise of one party is consideration supporting the promise of the other party.

Blasphemy: The malicious or wanton reproach of God, either written or oral. In English law, the offense of speaking disparaging words about God, Jesus Christ, the Bible, or the Book of Common Prayer with the intent to undermine religious beliefs and promote contempt and hatred for the church as well as general immorality. In U.S. law, any maliciously intended written or oral accusation made against God or religion with the purpose of dishonoring the divine majesty and alienating mankind from the love and reverence of God.

Bona fide: [*Latin, In good faith.*] Honest; genuine; actual; authentic; acting without the intention of defrauding.

Burden of Persuasion: The onus on the party with the burden of proof to convince the trier of fact of all elements of his or her case. In a criminal case the burden of the government to produce evidence of all the necessary elements of the crime beyond a reasonable doubt.

Burglary: The criminal offense of breaking and entering a building illegally for the purpose of committing a crime therein.

C

Canons of construction: The system of basic rules and maxims applied by a court to aid in its interpretation of a written document, such as a statute or contract.

Capitalize: To regard the cost of an improvement or other purchase as a capital asset for purposes of determining income tax liability. To calculate the net worth upon which an investment is based. To issue company stocks or bonds to finance an investment.

Carriers: Individuals or businesses that are employed to deliver people or property to an agreed destination.

Cause of Action: The fact or combination of facts that gives a person the right to seek judicial redress or relief against another. Also, the legal theory forming the basis of a lawsuit.

Certiorari: [*Latin, To be informed of.*] At common law, an original writ or order issued by the Chancery of King's Bench, commanding officers of inferior courts to submit the record of a cause pending before them to give the party more certain and speedy justice.

A writ that a superior appellate court issues on its discretion to an inferior court, ordering it to produce a certified record of a particular case it has tried, in order to determine whether any irregularities or errors occurred that justify review of the case.

A device by which the Supreme Court of the United States exercises its discretion in selecting the cases it will review.

Chose: [*French, Thing.*] Chattel; item of personal property.

Circuit Court: A specific tribunal that possesses the legal authority to hear cases within its own geographical territory.

Civil Procedure: The methods, procedures, and practices used in civil cases.

Class Action: A lawsuit that allows a large number of people with a common interest in a matter to sue or be sued as a group.

Clear and convincing proof: A standard applied by a jury or by a judge in a nonjury trial to measure the probability of the truthfulness of particular facts alleged during a civil lawsuit.

Clemency: Leniency or mercy. A power given to a public official, such as a governor or the president, to in some way lower or moderate the harshness of punishment imposed upon a prisoner.

Closely held: A phrase used to describe the ownership, management, and operation of a corporation by a small group of people.

Collateral: Related; indirect; not bearing immediately upon an issue. The property pledged or given as a security interest, or a guarantee for payment of a debt, that will be taken or kept by the creditor in case of a default on the original debt.

Commerce Clause: The provision of the U.S. Constitution that gives Congress exclusive power over trade activities between the states and with foreign countries and Indian tribes.

Common Law: The ancient law of England based upon societal customs and recognized and enforced by the judgments and decrees of the courts. The general body of statutes and case law that governed England and the American colonies prior to the American Revolution.

The principles and rules of action, embodied in case law rather than legislative enactments, applicable to the government and protection of persons and property that derive their authority from the community customs and traditions that evolved over the centuries as interpreted by judicial tribunals.

A designation used to denote the opposite of statutory, equitable, or civil; for example, a common-law action.

Compensatory Damages: A sum of money awarded in a civil action by a court to indemnify a person for the particular loss, detriment, or injury suffered as a result of the unlawful conduct of another.

Corpus: [*Latin, Body, aggregate, or mass.*]

Correlative: Having a reciprocal relationship in that the existence of one relationship normally implies the existence of the other.

Court of Appeal: An intermediate federal judicial tribunal of review that is found in thirteen judicial districts, called circuits, in the United States.

A state judicial tribunal that reviews a decision rendered by an inferior tribunal to determine whether it made errors that warrant the reversal of its judgment.

Court of Claims: A state judicial tribunal established as the forum in which to bring certain types of lawsuits against the state or its political subdivisions, such as a county. The former designation given to a federal tribunal created in 1855 by Congress with original jurisdiction—initial authority—to decide an action brought against the United States that is based upon the Constitution, federal law, any regulation of the executive department, or any express or implied contracts with the federal government.

Criminal Law: A body of rules and statutes that defines conduct prohibited by the government because it threatens and harms public safety and welfare and that establishes punishment to be imposed for the commission of such acts.

Criminal Procedure: The framework of laws and rules that govern the administration of justice in cases involving an individual who has been accused of a crime, beginning with the initial investigation of the crime and concluding either with the unconditional release of the accused by virtue of acquittal (a judgment of not guilty) or by the imposition of a term of punishment pursuant to a conviction for the crime.

Cruel and Unusual Punishment: Such punishment as would amount to torture or barbarity, and cruel and degrading punishment not known to the common law, or any fine, penalty, confinement, or treatment so disproportionate to the offense as to shock the moral sense of the community.

D

De facto: [*Latin, In fact.*] In fact, in deed, actually.

Decision on the merits: An ultimate determination rendered by a court in an action that concludes the status of legal rights contested in a controversy and precludes a later lawsuit on the same cause of action by the parties to the original lawsuit.

declaratory judgment: Statutory remedy for the determination of a justiciable controversy where the plaintiff is in doubt as to his or her legal rights. A binding adjudication of the rights and status of litigants even though no consequential relief is awarded.

Disorderly Conduct: A broad term describing conduct that disturbs the peace or endangers the morals, health, or safety of a community.

Disposition: Act of disposing; transferring to the care or possession of another. The parting with, alienation of, or giving up of property. The final settlement of a matter and, with reference to decisions announced by a court, a judge's ruling is commonly referred to as disposition, regardless of level of resolution. In criminal procedure, the sentencing or other final settlement of a criminal case. With respect to a mental state, denotes an attitude, prevailing tendency, or inclination.

District Court: A designation of an inferior state court that exercises general jurisdiction that it has been granted by the constitution or statute which created it. A U.S. judicial tribunal with original jurisdiction to try cases or controversies that fall within its limited jurisdiction.

Doing business: A qualification imposed in state long-arm statutes governing the service of process, the method by which a lawsuit is commenced, which requires nonresident corporations to engage in commercial transactions within state borders in order to be subject to the personal jurisdiction of state courts.

DWI: An abbreviation for *driving while intoxicated*, which is an offense committed by an individual who operates a motor vehicle while under the influence of alcohol or drugs and narcotics.

An abbreviation for *died without issue*, which commonly appears in genealogical tables.

E

en banc: [*Latin, French. In the bench.*] Full bench. Refers to a session where the entire membership of the court will participate in the decision rather than the regular quorum. In other countries, it is common for a court to have more members than are usually necessary to hear an appeal. In the United States, the Circuit Courts of Appeal usually sit in panels of judges but for important cases may expand the bench to a larger number, when the judges are said to be sitting *en banc*. Similarly, only one of the judges of the U.S. Tax Court will typically hear and decide on a tax controversy. However, when the issues involved are unusually novel or of wide impact, the case will be heard and decided by the full court sitting *en banc*.

Entity: A real being; existence. An organization or being that possesses separate existence for tax purposes. Examples would be corporations, partnerships, estates, and trusts. The accounting entity for which accounting statements are prepared may not be the same as the entity defined by law.

Entity includes corporation and foreign corporation; not-for-profit corporation; profit and not-for-profit unincorporated association; business trust, estate, partnership, trust, and two or more persons having a joint or common economic interest; and state, U.S., and foreign governments.

An existence apart, such as a corporation in relation to its stockholders.

Entity includes person, estate, trust, governmental unit.

Equal Protection: The constitutional guarantee that no person or class of persons shall be denied the same protection of the laws that is enjoyed by other persons or other classes in like circumstances in their lives, liberty, property, and pursuit of happiness.

Escrow: Something of value, such as a deed, stock, money, or written instrument, that is put into the custody of a third person by its owner, a grantor, an obligor, or a promisor, to be retained until the occurrence of a contingency or performance of a condition.

Et seq.: "An abbreviation for the Latin *et sequentes* or *et sequentia*, meaning 'and the following.'"

Examiner: An official or other person empowered by another—whether an individual, business, or government agency—to investigate and review specified documents for accuracy and truthfulness.

A court-appointed officer, such as a master or referee, who inspects evidence presented to resolve controverted matters and records statements made by witnesses in the particular proceeding pending before that court.

A government employee in the Patent and Trademark Office whose duty it is to scrutinize the application made for a patent by an inventor to determine whether the invention meets the statutory requirements of patentability.

A federal employee of the Internal Revenue Service who reviews income tax returns for accuracy and truthfulness.

Excise: A tax imposed on the performance of an act, the engaging in an occupation, or the enjoyment of a privilege. A tax on the manufacture, sale, or use of goods or on the carrying on of an occupation or activity, or a tax on the transfer of property. In current usage the term has been extended to include various license fees and practically every internal revenue tax except the income tax (e.g., federal alcohol and tobacco excise taxes).

Executive Privilege: The right of the president of the United States to withhold information from Congress or the courts.

Exoneration: The removal of a burden, charge, responsibility, duty, or blame imposed by law. The right of a party who is secondarily liable for a debt, such as a surety, to be reimbursed by the party with primary liability for payment of an obligation that should have been paid by the first party.

F

Fair market value: The amount for which real property or personal property would be sold in a voluntary transaction between a buyer and seller, neither of whom is under any obligation to buy or sell.

Federal Courts: The U.S. judicial tribunals created by Article III of the Constitution, or by Congress, to hear and determine justiciable controversies.

Felony: A serious crime, characterized under federal law and many state statutes as any offense punishable by death or imprisonment in excess of one year.

Feres Doctrine: A doctrine that bars claims against the federal government by members of the armed forces and their families for injuries arising from or in the course of activity incident to military service.

Fiduciary: An individual in whom another has placed the utmost trust and confidence to manage and protect property or money. The relationship wherein one person has an obligation to act for another's benefit.

Final Decision: The resolution of a controversy by a court or series of courts from which no appeal may be taken and that precludes further action. The last act by a lower court that is required for the completion of a lawsuit, such as the handing down of a final judgment upon which an appeal to a higher court may be brought.

Financial statement: Any report summarizing the financial condition or financial results of a person or an organization on any date or for any period. Financial statements include the balance sheet and the income statement and sometimes the statement of changes in financial position.

First Impression: The initial presentation to, or examination by, a court of a particular question of law.

Fiscal: Relating to finance or financial matters, such as money, taxes, or public or private revenues.

Forensic: Belonging to courts of justice.

Fraud: A false representation of a matter of fact—whether by words or by conduct, by false or misleading allegations, or by concealment of what should have been disclosed—that deceives and is intended to deceive another so that the individual will act upon it to her or his legal injury.

Fraudulent: The description of a willful act commenced with the specific intent to deceive or cheat, in order to cause some financial detriment to another and to engender personal financial gain.

G

Gag Order: A court order to gag or bind an unruly defendant or remove her or him from the courtroom in order to prevent further interruptions in a trial. In a trial with a great deal of notoriety, a court order directed to attorneys and witnesses not to discuss the case with the media—such order being felt necessary to assure the defendant of a fair trial. A court order, directed to the media, not to report certain aspects of a crime or criminal investigation prior to trial.

General Jurisdiction: The legal authority of a court to entertain whatever type of case comes up within the geographical area over which its power extends.

General term: A sitting of the court en banc, with the participation of the entire membership of the court rather than the regular quorum. A phrase used in some jurisdictions to signify the ordinary session of a court during which the trial determination of actions occur.

Good Faith: Honesty; a sincere intention to deal fairly with others.

Grand Jury: A panel of citizens that is convened by a court to decide whether it is appropriate for the government to indict (proceed with a prosecution against) someone suspected of a crime.

Grantee: An individual to whom a transfer or conveyance of property is made.

Gross income: The financial gains received by an individual or a business during a fiscal year.

H

Habeas Corpus: "[*Latin, You have the body.*] A writ (court order) that commands an individual or a government official who has restrained another to produce the prisoner at a designated time and place so that the court can determine the legality of custody and decide whether to order the prisoner's release."

Hate Crime: A crime motivated by racial, religious, gender, sexual orientation, or other prejudice.

Hearsay: A statement made out of court that is offered in court as evidence to prove the truth of the matter asserted.

I

Implied warranty: A promise, arising by operation of law, that something that is sold will be merchantable and fit for the purpose for which it is sold.

in camera: In chambers; in private. A judicial proceeding is said to be heard *in camera* either when the hearing is had before the judge in his or her private chambers or when all spectators are excluded from the courtroom.

Insanity Defense: A defense asserted by an accused in a criminal prosecution to avoid liability for the commission of a crime because, at the time of the crime, the person did not appreciate the nature or quality or wrongfulness of the acts.

Interpleader: An equitable proceeding brought by a third person to have a court determine the ownership rights of rival claimants to the same money or property that is held by that third person.

Interrogatories: Written questions submitted to a party from his or her adversary to ascertain answers that are prepared in writing and signed under oath and that have relevance to the issues in a lawsuit.

J

Joinder: The union in one lawsuit of multiple parties who have the same rights or against whom rights are claimed as coplaintiffs or codefendants. The combination in one lawsuit of two or more causes of action, or grounds for relief. At common law the acceptance by opposing parties that a particular issue is in dispute.

Joint and several liability: A designation of liability by which members of a group are either individually or mutually responsible to a party in whose favor a judgment has been awarded.

Judicial Review: A court's authority to examine an executive or legislative act and to invalidate that act if it is contrary to constitutional principles.

Jurisprudence: "From the Latin term *juris prudentia*, which means 'the study, knowledge, or science of law'; in the United States, more broadly associated with the philosophy of law."

Justice of the Peace: A judicial officer with limited power whose duties may include hearing cases that involve civil controversies, conserving the peace, performing judicial acts, hearing minor criminal complaints, and committing offenders.

L

Leasehold: An estate, interest, in real property held under a rental agreement by which the owner gives another the right to occupy or use land for a period of time.

Ledger: The principal book of accounts of a business enterprise in which all the daily transactions are entered under appropriate headings to reflect the debits and credits of each account.

Legal Aid: A system of nonprofit organizations that provide legal services to people who cannot afford an attorney.

Lewdness: Behavior that is deemed morally impure or unacceptable in a sexual sense; open and public indecency tending to corrupt the morals of the community; gross or wanton indecency in sexual relations.

M

Magistrate: Any individual who has the power of a public civil officer or inferior judicial officer, such as a justice of the peace.

Mail Fraud: A crime in which the perpetrator develops a scheme using the mails to defraud another of money or property. This crime specifically requires the intent to defraud, and is a federal offense governed by section 1341 of title 18 of the U.S. Code. The mail fraud statute was first enacted in 1872 to prohibit illicit mailings with the Postal Service (formerly the Post Office) for the purpose of executing a fraudulent scheme.

Manslaughter: The unjustifiable, inexcusable, and intentional killing of a human being without deliberation, premeditation, and malice. The unlawful killing of a human being without any deliberation, which may be involuntary, in the commission of a lawful act without due caution and circumspection.

Margin call: A demand by a broker that an investor who has purchased securities using credit extended by the broker (on margin) pay additional cash into his or her brokerage account to reduce the amount of debt owed.

Market value: The highest price a willing buyer would pay and a willing seller would accept, both being fully informed, and the property being exposed for sale for a reasonable period of time. The market value may be different from the price a property can actually be sold for at a given time (market price). The market value of an article or piece of property is the price that it might be expected to bring if offered for sale in a fair market; not the price that might be obtained on a sale at public auction or a sale forced by the necessities of the owner, but such a price as would be fixed by negotiation and mutual agreement, after ample time to find a purchaser, as between a vendor who is willing (but not compelled) to sell and a purchaser who desires to buy but is not compelled to take the particular article or piece of property.

Mediation: A settlement of a dispute or controversy by setting up an independent person between two contending parties in order to aid them in the settlement of their disagreement.

Medicaid: A joint federal-state program that provides health care insurance to low-income persons.

Mental anguish: When connected with a physical injury, includes both the resultant mental sensation of pain and also the accompanying feelings of distress, fright, and anxiety. As an element of damages implies a relatively high degree of mental pain and distress; it is more than mere disappointment, anger, worry, resentment, or embarrassment, although it may include all of these, and it includes mental sensation of pain resulting from such painful emotions as grief, severe disappointment, indignation, wounded pride, shame, despair, and/or public humiliation. In other connections, and as a ground for divorce or for compensable damages or an element of damages, it includes the mental suffering resulting from the excitation of the more poignant and painful emotions, such as grief, severe disappointment, indignation, wounded pride, shame, public humiliation, despair, etc.

Misdemeanor: Offenses lower than felonies and generally those punishable by fine, penalty, forfeiture, or imprisonment other than in a penitentiary. Under federal law, and most state laws, any offense other than a felony is classified as a misdemeanor. Certain states also have various classes of misdemeanors (e.g., Class A, B, etc.).

Mistake of law: A misconception that occurs when a person with complete knowledge of the facts reaches an erroneous conclusion as to their legal effect; an incorrect opinion or inference, arising from a flawed evaluation of the facts.

Money Laundering: The process of taking the proceeds of criminal activity and making them appear legal.

Monopoly: An economic advantage held by one or more persons or companies deriving from the exclusive power to carry on a particular business or trade or to manufacture and sell a particular item, thereby suppressing competition and allowing such persons or companies to raise the price of a product or service substantially above the price that would be established by a free market.

Mutual mistake: An error of both parties to a contract, whereby each operates under the identical misconception concerning a post or existing material fact.

N

Natural law: The unwritten body of universal moral principles that underlie the ethical and legal norms by which human conduct is sometimes evaluated and governed. Natural law is often contrasted with positive law, which consists of the written rules and regulations enacted by government. The term *natural law* is derived from the Roman term *jus naturale*. Adherents to natural law philosophy are known as naturalists.

Of counsel: A term commonly applied in the practice of law to an attorney who has been employed to aid in the preparation and management of a particular case but who is not the principal attorney in the action.

Omnibus: [*Latin, For all; containing two or more independent matters.*] A term frequently used in reference to a legislative bill comprised of two or more general subjects that is designed to compel the executive to approve provisions that he or she would otherwise reject but that he or she signs into law to prevent the defeat of the entire bill.

Open court: "Common law requires a trial in open court; 'open court' means a court to which the public has a right to be admitted. This term may mean either a court that has been formally convened and declared open for the transaction of its proper judicial business or a court that is freely open to spectators."

Overbreadth doctrine: A principle of judicial review that holds that a law is invalid if it punishes constitutionally protected speech or conduct along with speech or conduct that the government may limit to further a compelling government interest.

P

Pander: To pimp; to cater to the gratification of the lust of another. To entice or procure a person, by promises, threats, fraud, or deception to enter any place in which prostitution is practiced for the purpose of prostitution.

Parent company: An enterprise, which is also known as a parent corporation, that owns more than 50 percent of the voting shares of its subsidiary.

Pension: A benefit, usually money, paid regularly to retired employees or their survivors by private business and federal, state, and local governments. Employers are not required to establish pension benefits but do so to attract qualified employees.

Peremptory Challenge: The right to challenge a juror without assigning, or being required to assign, a reason for the challenge.

Plurality: The opinion of an appellate court in which more justices join than in any concurring opinion.

The excess of votes cast for one candidate over those votes cast for any other candidate.

Polygamy: The offense of having more than one wife or husband at the same time.

Positive law: Those laws that have been duly enacted by a properly instituted and popularly recognized branch of government.

Preemption: A doctrine based on the Supremacy Clause of the U.S. Constitution that holds that certain matters are of such a national, as opposed to local, character that federal laws preempt or take precedence over state laws. As such, a state may not pass a law inconsistent with the federal law.

A doctrine of state law that holds that a state law displaces a local law or regulation that is in the same field and is in conflict or inconsistent with the state law.

Preliminary hearing: A proceeding before a judicial officer in which the officer must decide whether a crime was committed, whether the crime occurred within the territorial jurisdiction of the court, and whether there is probable cause to believe that the defendant committed the crime.

Preliminary Injunction: A temporary order made by a court at the request of one party that prevents the other party from pursuing a particular course of conduct until the conclusion of a trial on the merits.

Prevailing party: The litigant who successfully brings or defends an action and, as a result, receives a favorable judgment or verdict.

Price-Fixing: The organized setting of what the public will be charged for certain products or services agreed to by competitors in the marketplace in violation of the Sherman Anti-Trust Act (15 U.S.C.A. § 1 et seq.).

Pro Bono: Short for *pro bono publico* [*Latin, For the public good*]. The designation given to the free legal work done by an attorney for indigent clients and religious, charitable, and other nonprofit entities.

Pro se: For one's own behalf; in person. Appearing for oneself, as in the case of one who does not retain a lawyer and appears for himself or herself in court.

Probative: Having the effect of proof, tending to prove, or actually proving.

Procedural Law: The body of law that prescribes formal steps to be taken in enforcing legal rights.

Product Liability: The responsibility of a manufacturer or vendor of goods to compensate for injury caused by a defective good that it has provided for sale.

Profanity: Irreverence towards sacred things; particularly, irreverent or blasphemous use of the name of God. Vulgar, irreverent, or course language.

Proximate Cause: An act from which an injury results as a natural, direct, uninterrupted consequence and without which the injury would not have occurred.

Public Domain: Land that is owned by the United States. In copyright law, literary or creative works over which the creator no longer has an exclusive right to restrict, or receive a royalty for, their reproduction or use but which can be freely copied by the public.

Public Policy: A principle that no person or government official can legally perform an act that tends to injure the public.

Punitive Damages: Monetary compensation awarded to an injured party that goes beyond that which is necessary to compensate the individual for losses and that is intended to punish the wrongdoer.

Purview: The part of a statute or a law that delineates its purpose and scope.

R

Ratification: The confirmation or adoption of an act that has already been performed.

Recidivism: The behavior of a repeat or habitual criminal. A measurement of the rate at which offenders commit other crimes, either by arrest or conviction baselines, after being released from incarceration.

Recognizance: A recorded obligations, entered into before a tribunal, in which an individual pledges to perform a specific act or to subscribe to a certain course of conduct.

Redress: Compensation for injuries sustained; recovery or restitution for harm or injury; damages or equitable relief. Access to the courts to gain reparation for a wrong.

Reformation: A remedy utilized by the courts to correct a written instrument so that it conforms to the original intent of the parties to such an instrument.

Relevancy: The tendency of a fact offered as evidence in a lawsuit to prove or disprove the truth of a point in issue.

Reorganization plan: A scheme authorized by federal law and promulgated by the president whereby he or she alters the structure of federal agencies to promote government efficiency and economy through a transfer, consolidation, coordination, authorization, or abolition of functions.

Reparation: Compensation for an injury; redress for a wrong inflicted.

Repeal: The annulment or abrogation of a previously existing statute by the enactment of a later law that revokes the former law.

Rescind: To declare a contract void—of no legal force or binding effect—from its inception and thereby restore the parties to the positions they would have occupied had no contract ever been made.

Respondent: In equity practice, the party who answers a bill or other proceeding in equity. The party against whom an appeal or motion, an application for a court order, is instituted and who is required to answer in order to protect his or her interests.

Restitution: In the context of criminal law, state programs under which an offender is required, as a condition of his or her sentence, to repay money or donate services to the victim or society; with respect to maritime law, the restoration of articles lost by jettison, done when the remainder of the cargo has been saved, at the general charge of the owners of the cargo; in the law of torts, or civil wrongs, a measure of damages; in regard to contract law, the restoration of a party injured by a breach of contract to the position that party occupied before she or he entered the contract.

Retainer: A contract between attorney and client specifying the nature of the services to be rendered and the cost of the services.

Right of action: The privilege of instituting a lawsuit arising from a particular transaction or state of facts, such as a suit that is based on a contract or a tort, a civil wrong.

Robbery: The taking of money or goods in the possession of another, from his or her person or immediate presence, by force or intimidation.

Rule of law: Rule according to law; rule under law; or rule according to a higher law.

S

Solicitation: Urgent request, plea, or entreaty; enticing, asking. The criminal offense of urging someone to commit an unlawful act.

Solicitor General: An officer of the U.S. Department of Justice who represents the U.S. government in cases before the U.S. Supreme Court.

Solvency: The ability of an individual to pay his or her debts as they mature in the normal and ordinary course of business, or the financial condition of owning property of sufficient value to discharge all of one's debts.

Sovereign Immunity: The legal protection that prevents a sovereign state or person from being sued without consent.

State Action: A requirement for claims that arise under the **Due Process Clause** of the FOUR-TEENTH AMENDMENT and civil rights legislation, for which a private citizen seeks relief in the form of damages or redress based on an improper intrusion by the government into his or her private life.

Statute: An act of a legislature that declares, proscribes, or commands something; a specific law, expressed in writing.

Statute of Limitations: A type of federal or state law that restricts the time within which legal proceedings may be brought.

Statutory: Created, defined, or relating to a statute; required by statute; conforming to a statute.

Strict Liability: Absolute legal responsibility for an injury that can be imposed on the wrongdoer without proof of carelessness or fault.

Subcontractor: One who takes a portion of a contract from the principal contractor or from another subcontractor.

Subornation of perjury: The criminal offense of procuring another to commit perjury, which is the crime of lying, in a material matter, while under oath.

Substantive due process: The substantive limitations placed on the content or subject matter of state and federal laws by the Due Process Clauses of the FIFTH and FOURTEENTH AMENDMENTS to the U.S. CONSTITUTION.

Substantive law: The part of the law that creates, defines, and regulates rights, including, for example, the law of contracts, torts, wills, and real property; the essential substance of rights under law.

Summary Judgment: A procedural device used during civil litigation to promptly and expeditiously dispose of a case without a trial. It is used when there is no dispute as to the material facts of the case and a party is entitled to judgment as a matter of law.

Supremacy Clause: "The clause of Article VI of the U.S. Constitution that declares that all laws and treaties made by the federal government shall be the 'supreme law of the land.'"

Surcharge: An overcharge or additional cost.

Suspended sentence: A sentence given after the formal conviction of a crime that the convicted person is not required to serve.

T

Tax Court: A specialized federal or state court that decides cases involving tax-related controversies.

Taxable Income: Under the federal tax law, gross income reduced by adjustments and allowable deductions. It is the income against which tax rates are applied to compute an individual or entity's tax liability. The essence of taxable income is the accrual of some gain, profit, or benefit to a taxpayer.

Tort Law: A body of rights, obligations, and remedies that is applied by courts in civil proceedings to provide relief for persons who have suffered harm from the wrongful acts of others. The person who sustains injury or suffers pecuniary damage as the result of tortious conduct is known as the plaintiff, and the person who is responsible for inflicting the injury and incurs liability for the damage is known as the defendant or tortfeasor.

Trade name: Names or designations used by companies to identify themselves and distinguish their businesses from others in the same field.

Tribunal: A general term for a court, or the seat of a judge.

Trustee: An individual or corporation named by an individual, who sets aside property to be used for the benefit of another person, to manage the property as provided by the terms of the document that created the arrangement.

V

Voir Dire: [*Old French, To speak the truth.*] The preliminary examination of prospective jurors to determine their qualifications and suitability to serve on a jury, in order to ensure the selection of fair and impartial jury.

W

Wanton: Grossly careless or negligent; reckless; malicious.

Writ: An order issued by a court requiring that something be done or giving authority to do a specified act.

Wrongful Death: The taking of the life of an individual resulting from the willful or negligent act of another person or persons.

Z

Zoning: The separation or division of a municipality into districts, the regulation of buildings and structures in such districts in accordance with their construction and the nature and extent of their use, and the dedication of such districts to particular uses designed to serve the general welfare.

A.	Atlantic Reporter
A. 2d	Atlantic Reporter, Second Series
AA	Alcoholics Anonymous
AAA	American Arbitration Association; Agricultural Adjustment Act of 1933
AALS	Association of American Law Schools
AAPRP	All African People's Revolutionary Party
AARP	American Association of Retired Persons
AAS	American Anti-Slavery Society
ABA	American Bar Association; Architectural Barriers Act of 1968; American Bankers Association
ABC	American Broadcasting Companies, Inc. (formerly American Broadcasting Corporation)
ABM	Antiballistic missile
ABM Treaty	Anti-Ballistic Missile Treaty of 1972
ABVP	Anti-Biased Violence Project
A/C	Account
A.C.	Appeal cases
ACAA	Air Carrier Access Act
ACCA	Armed Career Criminal Act of 1984
ACF	Administration for Children and Families
ACLU	American Civil Liberties Union
ACRS	Accelerated Cost Recovery System
ACS	Agricultural Cooperative Service
ACT	American College Test
Act'g Legal Adv.	Acting Legal Advisor
ACUS	Administrative Conference of the United States
ACYF	Administration on Children, Youth, and Families
A.D. 2d	Appellate Division, Second Series, N.Y.
ADA	Americans with Disabilities Act of 1990
ADAMHA	Alcohol, Drug Abuse, and Mental Health Administration
ADC	Aid to Dependent Children
ADD	Administration on Developmental Disabilities
ADEA	Age Discrimination in Employment Act of 1967
ADL	Anti-Defamation League
ADR	Alternative dispute resolution
AEC	Atomic Energy Commission

AECB	Arms Export Control Board
AEDPA	Antiterrorism and Effective Death Penalty Act
A.E.R.	All England Law Reports
AFA	American Family Association; Alabama Freethought Association
AFB	American Farm Bureau
AFBF	American Farm Bureau Federation
AFDC	Aid to Families with Dependent Children
aff'd per cur.	Affirmed by the court
AFIS	Automated fingerprint identification system
AFL	American Federation of Labor
AFL-CIO	American Federation of Labor and Congress of Industrial Organizations
AFRes	Air Force Reserve
AFSC	American Friends Service Committee
AFSCME	American Federation of State, County, and Municipal Employees
AGRICOLA	Agricultural Online Access
AIA	Association of Insurance Attorneys
AIB	American Institute for Banking
AID	Artificial insemination using a third-party donor's sperm; Agency for International Development
AIDS	Acquired immune deficiency syndrome
AIH	Artificial insemination using the husband's sperm
AIM	American Indian Movement
AIPAC	American Israel Public Affairs Committee
AIUSA	Amnesty International, U.S.A. Affiliate
AJS	American Judicature Society
ALA	American Library Association
Alcoa	Aluminum Company of America
ALEC	American Legislative Exchange Council
ALF	Animal Liberation Front
ALI	American Law Institute
ALJ	Administrative law judge
All E.R.	All England Law Reports
ALO	Agency Liaison
A.L.R.	American Law Reports
ALY	*American Law Yearbook*
AMA	American Medical Association
AMAA	Agricultural Marketing Agreement Act
Am. Dec.	American Decisions
amdt.	Amendment
Amer. St. Papers, For. Rels.	American State Papers, Legislative and Executive Documents of the Congress of the U.S., Class I, Foreign Relations, 1832–1859
AMS	Agricultural Marketing Service
AMVETS	American Veterans (of World War II)
ANA	Administration for Native Americans
Ann. Dig.	Annual Digest of Public International Law Cases
ANRA	American Newspaper Publishers Association
ANSCA	Alaska Native Claims Act
ANZUS	Australia-New Zealand-United States Security Treaty Organization
AOA	Administration on Aging
AOE	Arizonans for Official English
AOL	America Online
AP	Associated Press
APA	Administrative Procedure Act of 1946
APHIS	Animal and Plant Health Inspection Service
App. Div.	Appellate Division Reports, N.Y. Supreme Court

Arb. Trib., U.S.-British	Arbitration Tribunal, Claim Convention of 1853, United States and Great Britain Convention of 1853
Ardcor	American Roller Die Corporation
ARPA	Advanced Research Projects Agency
ARPANET	Advanced Research Projects Agency Network
ARS	Advanced Record System
Art.	Article
ARU	American Railway Union
ASCME	American Federation of State, County, and Municipal Employees
ASCS	Agriculture Stabilization and Conservation Service
ASM	Available Seatmile
ASPCA	American Society for the Prevention of Cruelty to Animals
Asst. Att. Gen.	Assistant Attorney General
AT&T	American Telephone and Telegraph
ATFD	Alcohol, Tobacco and Firearms Division
ATLA	Association of Trial Lawyers of America
ATO	Alpha Tau Omega
ATTD	Alcohol and Tobacco Tax Division
ATU	Alcohol Tax Unit
AUAM	American Union against Militarism
AUM	Animal Unit Month
AZT	Azidothymidine
BAC	Blood alcohol concentration
BALSA	Black-American Law Student Association
BATF	Bureau of Alcohol, Tobacco and Firearms
BBS	Bulletin Board System
BCCI	Bank of Credit and Commerce International
BEA	Bureau of Economic Analysis
Bell's Cr. C.	Bell's English Crown Cases
Bevans	United States Treaties, etc. *Treaties and Other International Agreements of the United States of America, 1776–1949* (compiled under the direction of Charles I. Bevans, 1968–76)
BFOQ	Bona fide occupational qualification
BI	Bureau of Investigation
BIA	Bureau of Indian Affairs; Board of Immigration Appeals
BID	Business improvement district
BJS	Bureau of Justice Statistics
Black.	Black's United States Supreme Court Reports
Blatchf.	Blatchford's United States Circuit Court Reports
BLM	Bureau of Land Management
BLS	Bureau of Labor Statistics
BMD	Ballistic missile defense
BNA	Bureau of National Affairs
BOCA	Building Officials and Code Administrators International
BOP	Bureau of Prisons
BPP	Black Panther Party for Self-defense
Brit. and For.	British and Foreign State Papers
BSA	Boy Scouts of America
BTP	Beta Theta Pi
Burr.	James Burrows, *Report of Cases Argued and Determined in the Court of King's Bench during the Time of Lord Mansfield* (1766–1780)
BVA	Board of Veterans Appeals
c.	Chapter
C^3I	Command, Control, Communications, and Intelligence
C.A.	Court of Appeals
CAA	Clean Air Act
CAB	Civil Aeronautics Board; Corporation for American Banking

CAFE	Corporate average fuel economy
Cal. 2d	California Reports, Second Series
Cal. 3d	California Reports, Third Series
CALR	Computer-assisted legal research
Cal. Rptr.	California Reporter
CAP	Common Agricultural Policy
CARA	Classification and Ratings Administration
CATV	Community antenna television
CBO	Congressional Budget Office
CBS	Columbia Broadcasting System
CBOEC	Chicago Board of Election Commissioners
CCC	Commodity Credit Corporation
CCDBG	Child Care and Development Block Grant of 1990
C.C.D. Pa.	Circuit Court Decisions, Pennsylvania
C.C.D. Va.	Circuit Court Decisions, Virginia
CCEA	Cabinet Council on Economic Affairs
CCP	Chinese Communist Party
CCR	Center for Constitutional Rights
C.C.R.I.	Circuit Court, Rhode Island
CD	Certificate of deposit; compact disc
CDA	Communications Decency Act
CDBG	Community Development Block Grant Program
CDC	Centers for Disease Control and Prevention; Community Development Corporation
CDF	Children's Defense Fund
CDL	Citizens for Decency through Law
CD-ROM	Compact disc read-only memory
CDS	Community Dispute Services
CDW	Collision damage waiver
CENTO	Central Treaty Organization
CEO	Chief executive officer
CEQ	Council on Environmental Quality
CERCLA	Comprehensive Environmental Response, Compensation, and Liability Act of 1980
cert.	*Certiorari*
CETA	Comprehensive Employment and Training Act
C & F	Cost and freight
CFC	Chlorofluorocarbon
CFE Treaty	Conventional Forces in Europe Treaty of 1990
C.F. & I.	Cost, freight, and insurance
C.F.R	Code of Federal Regulations
CFNP	Community Food and Nutrition Program
CFTA	Canadian Free Trade Agreement
CFTC	Commodity Futures Trading Commission
Ch.	Chancery Division, English Law Reports
CHAMPVA	Civilian Health and Medical Program at the Veterans Administration
CHEP	Cuban/Haitian Entrant Program
CHINS	Children in need of supervision
CHIPS	Child in need of protective services
Ch.N.Y.	Chancery Reports, New York
Chr. Rob.	Christopher Robinson, *Reports of Cases Argued and Determined in the High Court of Admiralty* (1801–1808)
CIA	Central Intelligence Agency
CID	Commercial Item Descriptions
C.I.F.	Cost, insurance, and freight
CINCNORAD	Commander in Chief, North American Air Defense Command
C.I.O.	Congress of Industrial Organizations

CIPE	Center for International Private Enterprise
C.J.	Chief justice
CJIS	Criminal Justice Information Services
C.J.S.	Corpus Juris Secundum
Claims Arb. under Spec. Conv., Nielsen's Rept.	Frederick Kenelm Nielsen, *American and British Claims Arbitration under the Special Agreement Concluded between the United States and Great Britain, August 18, 1910* (1926)
CLASP	Center for Law and Social Policy
CLE	Center for Law and Education; Continuing Legal Education
CLEO	Council on Legal Education Opportunity; Chief Law Enforcement Officer
CLP	Communist Labor Party of America
CLS	Christian Legal Society; critical legal studies (movement); Critical Legal Studies (membership organization)
C.M.A.	Court of Military Appeals
CMEA	Council for Mutual Economic Assistance
CMHS	Center for Mental Health Services
C.M.R.	Court of Military Review
CNN	Cable News Network
CNO	Chief of Naval Operations
CNOL	Consolidated net operating loss
CNR	Chicago and Northwestern Railway
CO	Conscientious Objector
C.O.D.	Cash on delivery
COGP	Commission on Government Procurement
COINTELPRO	Counterintelligence Program
Coke Rep.	Coke's English King's Bench Reports
COLA	Cost-of-living adjustment
COMCEN	Federal Communications Center
Comp.	Compilation
Conn.	Connecticut Reports
CONTU	National Commission on New Technological Uses of Copyrighted Works
Conv.	Convention
COPA	Child Online Protection Act (1998)
COPS	Community Oriented Policing Services
Corbin	Arthur L. Corbin, *Corbin on Contracts: A Comprehensive Treatise on the Rules of Contract Law* (1950)
CORE	Congress on Racial Equality
Cox's Crim. Cases	Cox's Criminal Cases (England)
COYOTE	Call Off Your Old Tired Ethics
CPA	Certified public accountant
CPB	Corporation for Public Broadcasting, the
CPI	Consumer Price Index
CPPA	Child Pornography Prevention Act
CPSC	Consumer Product Safety Commission
Cranch	Cranch's United States Supreme Court Reports
CRF	Constitutional Rights Foundation
CRR	Center for Constitutional Rights
CRS	Congressional Research Service; Community Relations Service
CRT	Critical race theory
CSA	Community Services Administration
CSAP	Center for Substance Abuse Prevention
CSAT	Center for Substance Abuse Treatment
CSC	Civil Service Commission
CSCE	Conference on Security and Cooperation in Europe
CSG	Council of State Governments

CSO	Community Service Organization
CSP	Center for the Study of the Presidency
C-SPAN	Cable-Satellite Public Affairs Network
CSRS	Cooperative State Research Service
CSWPL	Center on Social Welfare Policy and Law
CTA	*Cum testamento annexo* (with the will attached)
Ct. Ap. D.C.	Court of Appeals, District of Columbia
Ct. App. No. Ireland	Court of Appeals, Northern Ireland
Ct. Cl.	Court of Claims, United States
Ct. Crim. Apps.	Court of Criminal Appeals (England)
Ct. of Sess., Scot.	Court of Sessions, Scotland
CTI	Consolidated taxable income
CU	Credit union
CUNY	City University of New York
Cush.	Cushing's Massachusetts Reports
CWA	Civil Works Administration; Clean Water Act
DACORB	Department of the Army Conscientious Objector Review Board
Dall.	Dallas's Pennsylvania and United States Reports
DAR	Daughters of the American Revolution
DARPA	Defense Advanced Research Projects Agency
DAVA	Defense Audiovisual Agency
D.C.	United States District Court; District of Columbia
D.C. Del.	United States District Court, Delaware
D.C. Mass.	United States District Court, Massachusetts
D.C. Md.	United States District Court, Maryland
D.C.N.D.Cal.	United States District Court, Northern District, California
D.C.N.Y.	United States District Court, New York
D.C.Pa.	United States District Court, Pennsylvania
DCS	Deputy Chiefs of Staff
DCZ	District of the Canal Zone
DDT	Dichlorodiphenyltricloroethane
DEA	Drug Enforcement Administration
Decl. Lond.	Declaration of London, February 26, 1909
Dev. & B.	Devereux & Battle's North Carolina Reports
DFL	Minnesota Democratic-Farmer-Labor
DFTA	Department for the Aging
Dig. U.S. Practice in Intl. Law	Digest of U.S. Practice in International Law
Dist. Ct.	D.C. United States District Court, District of Columbia
D.L.R.	Dominion Law Reports (Canada)
DMCA	Digital Millennium Copyright Act
DNA	Deoxyribonucleic acid
Dnase	Deoxyribonuclease
DNC	Democratic National Committee
DOC	Department of Commerce
DOD	Department of Defense
DODEA	Department of Defense Education Activity
Dodson	Dodson's Reports, English Admiralty Courts
DOE	Department of Energy
DOER	Department of Employee Relations
DOJ	Department of Justice
DOL	Department of Labor
DOMA	Defense of Marriage Act of 1996
DOS	Disk operating system
DOT	Department of Transportation
DPT	Diphtheria, pertussis, and tetanus
DRI	Defense Research Institute

DSAA	Defense Security Assistance Agency
DUI	Driving under the influence; driving under intoxication
DVD	Digital versatile disc
DWI	Driving while intoxicated
EAHCA	Education for All Handicapped Children Act of 1975
EBT	Examination before trial
E.coli	Escherichia coli
ECPA	Electronic Communications Privacy Act of 1986
ECSC	Treaty of the European Coal and Steel Community
EDA	Economic Development Administration
EDF	Environmental Defense Fund
E.D.N.Y.	Eastern District, New York
EDP	Electronic data processing
E.D. Pa.	Eastern-District, Pennsylvania
EDSC	Eastern District, South Carolina
EDT	Eastern daylight time
E.D. Va.	Eastern District, Virginia
EEC	European Economic Community; European Economic Community Treaty
EEOC	Equal Employment Opportunity Commission
EFF	Electronic Frontier Foundation
EFT	Electronic funds transfer
Eliz.	Queen Elizabeth (Great Britain)
Em. App.	Temporary Emergency Court of Appeals
ENE	Early neutral evaluation
Eng. Rep.	English Reports
EOP	Executive Office of the President
EPA	Environmental Protection Agency; Equal Pay Act of 1963
ERA	Equal Rights Amendment
ERDC	Energy Research and Development Commission
ERISA	Employee Retirement Income Security Act of 1974
ERS	Economic Research Service
ERTA	Economic Recovery Tax Act of 1981
ESA	Endangered Species Act of 1973
ESF	Emergency support function; Economic Support Fund
ESRD	End-Stage Renal Disease Program
ETA	Employment and Training Administration
ETS	Environmental tobacco smoke
et seq.	*Et sequentes* or *et sequentia* ("and the following")
EU	European Union
Euratom	European Atomic Energy Community
Eur. Ct. H.R.	European Court of Human Rights
Ex.	English Exchequer Reports, Welsby, Hurlstone & Gordon
Exch.	Exchequer Reports (Welsby, Hurlstone & Gordon)
Ex Com	Executive Committee of the National Security Council
Eximbank	Export-Import Bank of the United States
F.	Federal Reporter
F. 2d	Federal Reporter, Second Series
FAA	Federal Aviation Administration; Federal Arbitration Act
FAAA	Federal Alcohol Administration Act
FACE	Freedom of Access to Clinic Entrances Act of 1994
FACT	Feminist Anti-Censorship Task Force
FAIRA	Federal Agriculture Improvement and Reform Act of 1996
FAMLA	Family and Medical Leave Act of 1993
Fannie Mae	Federal National Mortgage Association
FAO	Food and Agriculture Organization of the United Nations
FAR	Federal Acquisition Regulations

FAS	Foreign Agricultural Service
FBA	Federal Bar Association
FBI	Federal Bureau of Investigation
FCA	Farm Credit Administration
F. Cas.	Federal Cases
FCC	Federal Communications Commission
FCIA	Foreign Credit Insurance Association
FCIC	Federal Crop Insurance Corporation
FCLAA	Federal Cigarette Labeling and Advertising Act
FCRA	Fair Credit Reporting Act
FCU	Federal credit unions
FCUA	Federal Credit Union Act
FCZ	Fishery Conservation Zone
FDA	Food and Drug Administration
FDIC	Federal Deposit Insurance Corporation
FDPC	Federal Data Processing Center
FEC	Federal Election Commission
FECA	Federal Election Campaign Act of 1971
Fed. Cas.	Federal Cases
FEHA	Fair Employment and Housing Act
FEHBA	Federal Employees Health Benefit Act
FEMA	Federal Emergency Management Agency
FERC	Federal Energy Regulatory Commission
FFB	Federal Financing Bank
FFDC	Federal Food, Drug, and Cosmetics Act
FGIS	Federal Grain Inspection Service
FHA	Federal Housing Administration
FHAA	Fair Housing Amendments Act of 1998
FHWA	Federal Highway Administration
FIA	Federal Insurance Administration
FIC	Federal Information Centers; Federation of Insurance Counsel
FICA	Federal Insurance Contributions Act
FIFRA	Federal Insecticide, Fungicide, and Rodenticide Act
FIP	Forestry Incentives Program
FIRREA	Financial Institutions Reform, Recovery, and Enforcement Act of 1989
FISA	Foreign Intelligence Surveillance Act of 1978
FISC	Foreign Intelligence Surveillance Court of Review
FJC	Federal Judicial Center
FLSA	Fair Labor Standards Act
FMC	Federal Maritime Commission
FMCS	Federal Mediation and Conciliation Service
FmHA	Farmers Home Administration
FMLA	Family and Medical Leave Act of 1993
FNMA	Federal National Mortgage Association, "Fannie Mae"
F.O.B.	Free on board
FOIA	Freedom of Information Act
FOMC	Federal Open Market Committee
FPA	Federal Power Act of 1935
FPC	Federal Power Commission
FPMR	Federal Property Management Regulations
FPRS	Federal Property Resources Service
FR	Federal Register
FRA	Federal Railroad Administration
FRB	Federal Reserve Board
FRC	Federal Radio Commission
F.R.D.	Federal Rules Decisions

FSA	Family Support Act
FSB	Federal'naya Sluzhba Bezopasnosti (the Federal Security Service of Russia)
FSLIC	Federal Savings and Loan Insurance Corporation
FSQS	Food Safety and Quality Service
FSS	Federal Supply Service
F. Supp.	Federal Supplement
FTA	U.S.-Canada Free Trade Agreement of 1988
FTC	Federal Trade Commission
FTCA	Federal Tort Claims Act
FTS	Federal Telecommunications System
FTS2000	Federal Telecommunications System 2000
FUCA	Federal Unemployment Compensation Act of 1988
FUTA	Federal Unemployment Tax Act
FWPCA	Federal Water Pollution Control Act of 1948
FWS	Fish and Wildlife Service
GAL	Guardian ad litem
GAO	General Accounting Office; Governmental Affairs Office
GAOR	General Assembly Official Records, United Nations
GAAP	Generally accepted accounting principles
GA Res.	General Assembly Resolution (United Nations)
GATT	General Agreement on Tariffs and Trade
GCA	Gun Control Act
Gen. Cls. Comm.	General Claims Commission, United States and Panama; General Claims United States and Mexico
Geo. II	King George II (Great Britain)
Geo. III	King George III (Great Britain)
GHB	Gamma-hydroxybutrate
GI	Government Issue
GID	General Intelligence Division
GM	General Motors
GNMA	Government National Mortgage Association, "Ginnie Mae"
GNP	Gross national product
GOP	Grand Old Party (Republican Party)
GOPAC	Grand Old Party Action Committee
GPA	Office of Governmental and Public Affairs
GPO	Government Printing Office
GRAS	Generally recognized as safe
Gr. Br., Crim. Ct. App.	Great Britain, Court of Criminal Appeals
GRNL	Gay Rights-National Lobby
GSA	General Services Administration
Hackworth	Green Haywood Hackworth, *Digest of International Law* (1940–1944)
Hay and Marriott	Great Britain. High Court of Admiralty, *Decisions in the High Court of Admiralty during the Time of Sir George Hay and of Sir James Marriott, Late Judges of That Court* (1801)
HBO	Home Box Office
HCFA	Health Care Financing Administration
H.Ct.	High Court
HDS	Office of Human Development Services
Hen. & M.	Hening & Munford's Virginia Reports
HEW	Department of Health, Education, and Welfare
HFCA	Health Care Financing Administration
HGI	Handgun Control, Incorporated
HHS	Department of Health and Human Services
Hill	Hill's New York Reports
HIRE	Help through Industry Retraining and Employment
HIV	Human immunodeficiency virus

H.L.	House of Lords Cases (England)
H. Lords	House of Lords (England)
HMO	Health Maintenance Organization
HNIS	Human Nutrition Information Service
Hong Kong L.R.	Hong Kong Law Reports
How.	Howard's United States Supreme Court Reports
How. St. Trials	Howell's English State Trials
HUAC	House Un-American Activities Committee
HUD	Department of Housing and Urban Development
Hudson, Internatl. Legis.	Manley Ottmer Hudson, ed., *International Legislation: A Collection of the Texts of Multipartite International Instruments of General Interest Beginning with the Covenant of the League of Nations* (1931)
Hudson, World Court Reps.	Manley Ottmer Hudson, ea., *World Court Reports* (1934–)
Hun	Hun's New York Supreme Court Reports
Hunt's Rept.	Bert L. Hunt, *Report of the American and Panamanian General Claims Arbitration* (1934)
IAEA	International Atomic Energy Agency
IALL	International Association of Law Libraries
IBA	International Bar Association
IBM	International Business Machines
ICA	Interstate Commerce Act
ICBM	Intercontinental ballistic missile
ICC	Interstate Commerce Commission; International Criminal Court
ICJ	International Court of Justice
ICM	Institute for Court Management
IDEA	Individuals with Disabilities Education Act of 1975
IDOP	International Dolphin Conservation Program
IEP	Individualized educational program
IFC	International Finance Corporation
IGRA	Indian Gaming Regulatory Act of 1988
IJA	Institute of Judicial Administration
IJC	International Joint Commission
ILC	International Law Commission
ILD	International Labor Defense
Ill. Dec.	Illinois Decisions
ILO	International Labor Organization
IMF	International Monetary Fund
INA	Immigration and Nationality Act
IND	Investigational new drug
INF Treaty	Intermediate-Range Nuclear Forces Treaty of 1987
INS	Immigration and Naturalization Service
INTELSAT	International Telecommunications Satellite Organization
Interpol	International Criminal Police Organization
Int'l. Law Reps.	International Law Reports
Intl. Legal Mats.	International Legal Materials
IOC	International Olympic Committee
IPDC	International Program for the Development of Communication
IPO	Intellectual Property Owners
IPP	Independent power producer
IQ	Intelligence quotient
I.R.	Irish Reports
IRA	Individual retirement account; Irish Republican Army
IRC	Internal Revenue Code
IRCA	Immigration Reform and Control Act of 1986
IRS	Internal Revenue Service
ISO	Independent service organization

ISP	Internet service provider
ISSN	International Standard Serial Numbers
ITA	International Trade Administration
ITI	Information Technology Integration
ITO	International Trade Organization
ITS	Information Technology Service
ITT	International Telephone and Telegraph Corporation
ITU	International Telecommunication Union
IUD	Intrauterine device
IWC	International Whaling Commission
IWW	Industrial Workers of the World
JAGC	Judge Advocate General's Corps
JCS	Joint Chiefs of Staff
JDL	Jewish Defense League
JNOV	Judgment *non obstante veredicto* ("judgment nothing to recommend it" or "judgment notwithstanding the verdict")
JOBS	Jobs Opportunity and Basic Skills
John. Ch.	Johnson's New York Chancery Reports
Johns.	Johnson's Reports (New York)
JP	Justice of the peace
K.B.	King's Bench Reports (England)
KFC	Kentucky Fried Chicken
KGB	Komitet Gosudarstvennoi Bezopasnosti (the State Security Committee for countries in the former Soviet Union)
KKK	Ku Klux Klan
KMT	Kuomintang (Chinese, "national people's party")
LAD	Law Against Discrimination
LAPD	Los Angeles Police Department
LC	Library of Congress
LCHA	Longshoremen's and Harbor Workers Compensation Act of 1927
LD50	Lethal dose 50
LDEF	Legal Defense and Education Fund (NOW)
LDF	Legal Defense Fund, Legal Defense and Educational Fund of the NAACP
LEAA	Law Enforcement Assistance Administration
L.Ed.	Lawyers' Edition Supreme Court Reports
LI	Letter of interpretation
LLC	Limited Liability Company
LLP	Limited Liability Partnership
LMSA	Labor-Management Services Administration
LNTS	League of Nations Treaty Series
Lofft's Rep.	Lofft's English King's Bench Reports
L.R.	Law Reports (English)
LSAC	Law School Admission Council
LSAS	Law School Admission Service
LSAT	Law School Aptitude Test
LSC	Legal Services Corporation; Legal Services for Children
LSD	Lysergic acid diethylamide
LSDAS	Law School Data Assembly Service
LTBT	Limited Test Ban Treaty
LTC	Long Term Care
MAD	Mutual assured destruction
MADD	Mothers against Drunk Driving
MALDEF	Mexican American Legal Defense and Educational Fund
Malloy	William M. Malloy, ed., *Treaties, Conventions International Acts, Protocols, and Agreements between the United States of America and Other Powers* (1910–1938)

Martens	Georg Friedrich von Martens, ea., *Noveau recueil général de traités et autres actes relatifs aux rapports de droit international* (Series I, 20 vols. [1843–1875]; Series II, 35 vols. [1876–1908]; Series III [1909–])
Mass.	Massachusetts Reports
MCC	Metropolitan Correctional Center
MCCA	Medicare Catastrophic Coverage Act of 1988
MCH	Maternal and Child Health Bureau
MCRA	Medical Care Recovery Act of 1962
MDA	Medical Devices Amendments of 1976
Md. App.	Maryland, Appeal Cases
M.D. Ga.	Middle District, Georgia
Mercy	Movement Ensuring the Right to Choose for Yourself
Metc.	Metcalf's Massachusetts Reports
MFDP	Mississippi Freedom Democratic party
MGT	Management
MHSS	Military Health Services System
Miller	David Hunter Miller, ea., *Treaties and Other International Acts of the United States of America* (1931–1948)
Minn.	Minnesota Reports
MINS	Minors in need of supervision
MIRV	Multiple independently targetable reentry vehicle
MIRVed ICBM	Multiple independently targetable reentry vehicled intercontinental ballistic missile
Misc.	Miscellaneous Reports, New York
Mixed Claims Comm., Report of Decs	Mixed Claims Commission, United States and Germany, Report of Decisions
M.J.	Military Justice Reporter
MLAP	Migrant Legal Action Program
MLB	Major League Baseball
MLDP	Mississippi Loyalist Democratic Party
MMI	Moslem Mosque, Incorporated
MMPA	Marine Mammal Protection Act of 1972
Mo.	Missouri Reports
MOD	Masters of Deception
Mod.	Modern Reports, English King's Bench, etc.
Moore, Dig. Intl. Law	John Bassett Moore, *A Digest of International Law*, 8 vols. (1906)
Moore, Intl. Arbs.	John Bassett Moore, *History and Digest of the International Arbitrations to Which United States Has Been a Party*, 6 vols. (1898)
Morison	William Maxwell Morison, *The Scots Revised Report: Morison's Dictionary of Decisions* (1908–09)
M.P.	Member of Parliament
MP3	MPEG Audio Layer 3
MPAA	Motion Picture Association of America
MPAS	Michigan Protection and Advocacy Service
MPEG	Motion Picture Experts Group
mpg	Miles per gallon
MPPDA	Motion Picture Producers and Distributors of America
MPRSA	Marine Protection, Research, and Sanctuaries Act of 1972
M.R.	Master of the Rolls
MS-DOS	Microsoft Disk Operating System
MSHA	Mine Safety and Health Administration
MSPB	Merit Systems Protection Board
MSSA	Military Selective Service Act
N/A	Not Available
NAACP	National Association for the Advancement of Colored People
NAAQS	National Ambient Air Quality Standards

NAB	National Association of Broadcasters
NABSW	National Association of Black Social Workers
NACDL	National Association of Criminal Defense Lawyers
NAFTA	North American Free Trade Agreement of 1993
NAGHSR	National Association of Governors' Highway Safety Representatives
NALA	National Association of Legal Assistants
NAM	National Association of Manufacturers
NAR	National Association of Realtors
NARAL	National Abortion and Reproductive Rights Action League
NARF	Native American Rights Fund
NARS	National Archives and Record Service
NASA	National Aeronautics and Space Administration
NASD	National Association of Securities Dealers
NATO	North Atlantic Treaty Organization
NAVINFO	Navy Information Offices
NAWSA	National American Woman's Suffrage Association
NBA	National Bar Association; National Basketball Association
NBC	National Broadcasting Company
NBLSA	National Black Law Student Association
NBS	National Bureau of Standards
NCA	Noise Control Act; National Command Authorities
NCAA	National Collegiate Athletic Association
NCAC	National Coalition against Censorship
NCCB	National Consumer Cooperative Bank
NCE	Northwest Community Exchange
NCF	National Chamber Foundation
NCIP	National Crime Insurance Program
NCJA	National Criminal Justice Association
NCLB	National Civil Liberties Bureau
NCP	National contingency plan
NCSC	National Center for State Courts
NCUA	National Credit Union Administration
NDA	New drug application
N.D. Ill.	Northern District, Illinois
NDU	National Defense University
N.D. Wash.	Northern District, Washington
N.E.	North Eastern Reporter
N.E. 2d	North Eastern Reporter, Second Series
NEA	National Endowment for the Arts; National Education Association
NEH	National Endowment for the Humanities
NEPA	National Environmental Protection Act; National Endowment Policy Act
NET Act	No Electronic Theft Act
NFIB	National Federation of Independent Businesses
NFIP	National Flood Insurance Program
NFL	National Football League
NFPA	National Federation of Paralegal Associations
NGLTF	National Gay and Lesbian Task Force
NHL	National Hockey League
NHRA	Nursing Home Reform Act of 1987
NHTSA	National Highway Traffic Safety Administration
Nielsen's Rept.	Frederick Kenelm Nielsen, *American and British Claims Arbitration under the Special Agreement Concluded between the United States and Great Britain, August 18, 1910* (1926)
NIEO	New International Economic Order
NIGC	National Indian Gaming Commission
NIH	National Institutes of Health

NIJ	National Institute of Justice
NIRA	National Industrial Recovery Act of 1933; National Industrial Recovery Administration
NIST	National Institute of Standards and Technology
NITA	National Telecommunications and Information Administration
N.J.	New Jersey Reports
N.J. Super.	New Jersey Superior Court Reports
NLEA	Nutrition Labeling and Education Act of 1990
NLRA	National Labor Relations Act
NLRB	National Labor Relations Board
NMFS	National Marine Fisheries Service
No.	Number
NOAA	National Oceanic and Atmospheric Administration
NOC	National Olympic Committee
NOI	Nation of Islam
NOL	Net operating loss
NORML	National Organization for the Reform of Marijuana Laws
NOW	National Organization for Women
NOW LDEF	National Organization for Women Legal Defense and Education Fund
NOW/PAC	National Organization for Women Political Action Committee
NPDES	National Pollutant Discharge Elimination System
NPL	National priorities list
NPR	National Public Radio
NPT	Nuclear Non-Proliferation Treaty of 1970
NRA	National Rifle Association; National Recovery Act
NRC	Nuclear Regulatory Commission
NRLC	National Right to Life Committee
NRTA	National Retired Teachers Association
NSA	National Security Agency
NSC	National Security Council
NSCLC	National Senior Citizens Law Center
NSF	National Science Foundation
NSFNET	National Science Foundation Network
NSI	Network Solutions, Inc.
NTIA	National Telecommunications and Information Administration
NTID	National Technical Institute for the Deaf
NTIS	National Technical Information Service
NTS	Naval Telecommunications System
NTSB	National Transportation Safety Board
NVRA	National Voter Registration Act
N.W.	North Western Reporter
N.W. 2d	North Western Reporter, Second Series
NWSA	National Woman Suffrage Association
N.Y.	New York Court of Appeals Reports
N.Y. 2d	New York Court of Appeals Reports, Second Series
N.Y.S.	New York Supplement Reporter
N.Y.S. 2d	New York Supplement Reporter, Second Series
NYSE	New York Stock Exchange
NYSLA	New York State Liquor Authority
N.Y. Sup.	New York Supreme Court Reports
NYU	New York University
OAAU	Organization of Afro American Unity
OAP	Office of Administrative Procedure
OAS	Organization of American States
OASDI	Old-age, Survivors, and Disability Insurance Benefits
OASHDS	Office of the Assistant Secretary for Human Development Services

OCC	Office of Comptroller of the Currency
OCED	Office of Comprehensive Employment Development
OCHAMPUS	Office of Civilian Health and Medical Program of the Uniformed Services
OCSE	Office of Child Support Enforcement
OEA	Organización de los Estados Americanos
OEM	Original Equipment Manufacturer
OFCCP	Office of Federal Contract Compliance Programs
OFPP	Office of Federal Procurement Policy
OIC	Office of the Independent Counsel
OICD	Office of International Cooperation and Development
OIG	Office of the Inspector General
OJARS	Office of Justice Assistance, Research, and Statistics
OMB	Office of Management and Budget
OMPC	Office of Management, Planning, and Communications
ONP	Office of National Programs
OPD	Office of Policy Development
OPEC	Organization of Petroleum Exporting Countries
OPIC	Overseas Private Investment Corporation
Ops. Atts. Gen.	Opinions of the Attorneys-General of the United States
Ops. Comms.	Opinions of the Commissioners
OPSP	Office of Product Standards Policy
O.R.	Ontario Reports
OR	Official Records
OSHA	Occupational Safety and Health Act
OSHRC	Occupational Safety and Health Review Commission
OSM	Office of Surface Mining
OSS	Office of Strategic Services
OST	Office of the Secretary
OT	Office of Transportation
OTA	Office of Technology Assessment
OTC	Over-the-counter
OTS	Office of Thrift Supervisors
OUI	Operating under the influence
OVCI	Offshore Voluntary Compliance Initiative
OWBPA	Older Workers Benefit Protection Act
OWRT	Office of Water Research and Technology
P.	Pacific Reporter
P. 2d	Pacific Reporter, Second Series
PAC	Political action committee
Pa. Oyer and Terminer	Pennsylvania Oyer and Terminer Reports
PATCO	Professional Air Traffic Controllers Organization
PBGC	Pension Benefit Guaranty Corporation
PBS	Public Broadcasting Service; Public Buildings Service
P.C.	Privy Council (English Law Reports)
PC	Personal computer; politically correct
PCBs	Polychlorinated biphenyls
PCIJ	Permanent Court of International Justice
	Series A-Judgments and Orders (1922–30)
	Series B-Advisory Opinions (1922–30)
	Series A/B-Judgments, Orders, and Advisory Opinions (1931–40)
	Series C-Pleadings, Oral Statements, and Documents relating to Judgments and Advisory Opinions (1923–42)
	Series D-Acts and Documents concerning the Organization of the World Court (1922 –47)
	Series E-Annual Reports (1925–45)
PCP	Phencyclidine

P.D.	Probate Division, English Law Reports (1876–1890)
PDA	Pregnancy Discrimination Act of 1978
PD & R	Policy Development and Research
Pepco	Potomac Electric Power Company
Perm. Ct. of Arb.	Permanent Court of Arbitration
PES	Post-Enumeration Survey
Pet.	Peters' United States Supreme Court Reports
PETA	People for the Ethical Treatment of Animals
PGA	Professional Golfers Association
PGM	Program
PHA	Public Housing Agency
Phila. Ct. of Oyer and Terminer	Philadelphia Court of Oyer and Terminer
PhRMA	Pharmaceutical Research and Manufacturers of America
PHS	Public Health Service
PIC	Private Industry Council
PICJ	Permanent International Court of Justice
Pick.	Pickering's Massachusetts Reports
PIK	Payment in Kind
PINS	Persons in need of supervision
PIRG	Public Interest Research Group
P.L.	Public Laws
PLAN	Pro-Life Action Network
PLC	Plaintiffs' Legal Committee
PLE	Product liability expenses
PLI	Practicing Law Institute
PLL	Product liability loss
PLLP	Professional Limited Liability Partnership
PLO	Palestine Liberation Organization
PLRA	Prison Litigation Reform Act of 1995
PNET	Peaceful Nuclear Explosions Treaty
PONY	Prostitutes of New York
POW-MIA	Prisoner of war-missing in action
Pratt	Frederic Thomas Pratt, *Law of Contraband of War, with a Selection of Cases from Papers of the Right Honourable Sir George Lee* (1856)
PRIDE	Prostitution to Independence, Dignity, and Equality
Proc.	Proceedings
PRP	Potentially responsible party
PSRO	Professional Standards Review Organization
PTO	Patents and Trademark Office
PURPA	Public Utilities Regulatory Policies Act
PUSH	People United to Serve Humanity
PUSH-Excel	PUSH for Excellence
PWA	Public Works Administration
PWSA	Ports and Waterways Safety Act of 1972
Q.B.	Queen's Bench (England)
QTIP	Qualified Terminable Interest Property
Ralston's Rept.	Jackson Harvey Ralston, ed., *Venezuelan Arbitrations of 1903* (1904)
RC	Regional Commissioner
RCRA	Resource Conservation and Recovery Act
RCWP	Rural Clean Water Program
RDA	Rural Development Administration
REA	Rural Electrification Administration
Rec. des Decs. des Trib. Arb. Mixtes	G. Gidel, ed., *Recueil des décisions des tribunaux arbitraux mixtes, institués par les traités de paix* (1922–30)

Redmond	Vol. 3 of Charles I. Bevans, *Treaties and Other International Agreements of the United States of America, 1776–1949* (compiled by C. F. Redmond) (1969)
RESPA	Real Estate Settlement Procedure Act of 1974
RFC	Reconstruction Finance Corporation
RFRA	Religious Freedom Restoration Act of 1993
RIAA	Recording Industry Association of America
RICO	Racketeer Influenced and Corrupt Organizations
RLUIPA	Religious Land Use and Institutionalized Persons Act
RNC	Republican National Committee
Roscoe	Edward Stanley Roscoe, ed., *Reports of Prize Cases Determined in the High Court Admiralty before the Lords Commissioners of Appeals in Prize Causes and before the judicial Committee of the Privy Council from 1745 to 1859* (1905)
ROTC	Reserve Officers' Training Corps
RPP	Representative Payee Program
R.S.	Revised Statutes
RTC	Resolution Trust Corp.
RUDs	Reservations, understandings, and declarations
Ryan White CARE Act	Ryan White Comprehensive AIDS Research Emergency Act of 1990
SAC	Strategic Air Command
SACB	Subversive Activities Control Board
SADD	Students against Drunk Driving
SAF	Student Activities Fund
SAIF	Savings Association Insurance Fund
SALT	Strategic Arms Limitation Talks
SALT I	Strategic Arms Limitation Talks of 1969–72
SAMHSA	Substance Abuse and Mental Health Services Administration
Sandf.	Sandford's New York Superior Court Reports
S and L	Savings and loan
SARA	Superfund Amendment and Reauthorization Act
SAT	Scholastic Aptitude Test
Sawy.	Sawyer's United States Circuit Court Reports
SBA	Small Business Administration
SBI	Small Business Institute
SCCC	South Central Correctional Center
SCLC	Southern Christian Leadership Conference
Scott's Repts.	James Brown Scott, ed., *The Hague Court Reports*, 2 vols. (1916–32)
SCS	Soil Conservation Service; Social Conservative Service
SCSEP	Senior Community Service Employment Program
S.Ct.	Supreme Court Reporter
S.D. Cal.	Southern District, California
S.D. Fla.	Southern District, Florida
S.D. Ga.	Southern District, Georgia
SDI	Strategic Defense Initiative
S.D. Me.	Southern District, Maine
S.D.N.Y.	Southern District, New York
SDS	Students for a Democratic Society
S.E.	South Eastern Reporter
S.E. 2d	South Eastern Reporter, Second Series
SEA	Science and Education Administration
SEATO	Southeast Asia Treaty Organization
SEC	Securities and Exchange Commission
Sec.	Section
SEEK	Search for Elevation, Education and Knowledge
SEOO	State Economic Opportunity Office
SEP	Simplified employee pension plan

Ser.	Series
Sess.	Session
SGLI	Servicemen's Group Life Insurance
SIP	State implementation plan
SLA	Symbionese Liberation Army
SLAPPs	Strategic Lawsuits Against Public Participation
SLBM	Submarine-launched ballistic missile
SNCC	Student Nonviolent Coordinating Committee
So.	Southern Reporter
So. 2d	Southern Reporter, Second Series
SPA	Software Publisher's Association
Spec. Sess.	Special Session
SPLC	Southern Poverty Law Center
SRA	Sentencing Reform Act of 1984
SS	*Schutzstaffel* (German, "Protection Echelon")
SSA	Social Security Administration
SSI	Supplemental Security Income
START I	Strategic Arms Reduction Treaty of 1991
START II	Strategic Arms Reduction Treaty of 1993
Stat.	United States Statutes at Large
STS	Space Transportation Systems
St. Tr.	State Trials, English
STURAA	Surface Transportation and Uniform Relocation Assistance Act of 1987
Sup. Ct. of Justice, Mexico	Supreme Court of Justice, Mexico
Supp.	Supplement
S.W.	South Western Reporter
S.W. 2d	South Western Reporter, Second Series
SWAPO	South-West Africa People's Organization
SWAT	Special Weapons and Tactics
SWP	Socialist Workers Party
TDP	Trade and Development Program
Tex. Sup.	Texas Supreme Court Reports
THAAD	Theater High-Altitude Area Defense System
THC	Tetrahydrocannabinol
TI	Tobacco Institute
TIA	Trust Indenture Act of 1939
TIAS	Treaties and Other International Acts Series (United States)
TNT	Trinitrotoluene
TOP	Targeted Outreach Program
TPUS	Transportation and Public Utilities Service
TQM	Total Quality Management
Tripartite Claims Comm., Decs. and Ops.	Tripartite Claims Commission (United States, Austria, and Hungary), Decisions and Opinions
TRI-TAC	Joint Tactical Communications
TRO	Temporary restraining order
TS	Treaty Series, United States
TSCA	Toxic Substance Control Act
TSDs	Transporters, storers, and disposers
TSU	Texas Southern University
TTBT	Threshold Test Ban Treaty
TV	Television
TVA	Tennessee Valley Authority
TWA	Trans World Airlines

UAW	United Auto Workers; United Automobile, Aerospace, and Agricultural Implements Workers of America
U.C.C.	Uniform Commercial Code; Universal Copyright Convention
U.C.C.C.	Uniform Consumer Credit Code
UCCJA	Uniform Child Custody Jurisdiction Act
UCMJ	Uniform Code of Military Justice
UCPP	Urban Crime Prevention Program
UCS	United Counseling Service
UDC	United Daughters of the Confederacy
UFW	United Farm Workers
UHF	Ultrahigh frequency
UIFSA	Uniform Interstate Family Support Act
UIS	Unemployment Insurance Service
UMDA	Uniform Marriage and Divorce Act
UMTA	Urban Mass Transportation Administration
U.N.	United Nations
UNCITRAL	United Nations Commission on International Trade Law
UNCTAD	United Nations Conference on Trade and Development
UN Doc.	United Nations Documents
UNDP	United Nations Development Program
UNEF	United Nations Emergency Force
UNESCO	United Nations Educational, Scientific, and Cultural Organization
UNICEF	United Nations Children's Fund (formerly United Nations International Children's Emergency Fund)
UNIDO	United Nations Industrial and Development Organization
Unif. L. Ann.	Uniform Laws Annotated
UN Repts. Intl. Arb. Awards	United Nations Reports of International Arbitral Awards
UNTS	United Nations Treaty Series
UPI	United Press International
URESA	Uniform Reciprocal Enforcement of Support Act
U.S.	United States Reports
U.S.A.	United States of America
USAF	United States Air Force
USA PATRIOT Act	Uniting and Strengthening America by Providing Appropriate Tools Required to Intercept and Obstruct Terrorism Act
USF	U.S. Forestry Service
U.S. App. D.C.	United States Court of Appeals for the District of Columbia
U.S.C.	United States Code; University of Southern California
U.S.C.A.	United States Code Annotated
U.S.C.C.A.N.	United States Code Congressional and Administrative News
USCMA	United States Court of Military Appeals
USDA	U.S. Department of Agriculture
USES	United States Employment Service
USFA	United States Fire Administration
USGA	United States Golf Association
USICA	International Communication Agency, United States
USMS	U.S. Marshals Service
USOC	U.S. Olympic Committee
USSC	U.S. Sentencing Commission
USSG	United States Sentencing Guidelines
U.S.S.R.	Union of Soviet Socialist Republics
UST	United States Treaties
USTS	United States Travel Service
v.	*Versus*
VA	Veterans Administration
VAR	Veterans Affairs and Rehabilitation Commission

VAWA	Violence against Women Act
VFW	Veterans of Foreign Wars
VGLI	Veterans Group Life Insurance
Vict.	Queen Victoria (Great Britain)
VIN	Vehicle identification number
VISTA	Volunteers in Service to America
VJRA	Veterans Judicial Review Act of 1988
V.L.A.	Volunteer Lawyers for the Arts
VMI	Virginia Military Institute
VMLI	Veterans Mortgage Life Insurance
VOCAL	Victims of Child Abuse Laws
VRA	Voting Rights Act
WAC	Women's Army Corps
Wall.	Wallace's United States Supreme Court Reports
Wash. 2d	Washington Reports, Second Series
WAVES	Women Accepted for Volunteer Service
WCTU	Women's Christian Temperance Union
W.D. Wash.	Western District, Washington
W.D. Wis.	Western District, Wisconsin
WEAL	*West's Encyclopedia of American Law*; Women's Equity Action League
Wend.	Wendell's New York Reports
WFSE	Washington Federation of State Employees
Wheat.	Wheaton's United States Supreme Court Reports
Wheel. Cr. Cases	Wheeler's New York Criminal Cases
WHISPER	Women Hurt in Systems of Prostitution Engaged in Revolt
Whiteman	Marjorie Millace Whiteman, *Digest of International Law*, 15 vols. (1963–73)
WHO	World Health Organization
WIC	Women, Infants, and Children program
Will. and Mar.	King William and Queen Mary (Great Britain)
WIN	WESTLAW Is Natural; Whip Inflation Now; Work Incentive Program
WIPO	World Intellectual Property Organization
WIU	Workers' Industrial Union
W.L.R.	Weekly Law Reports, England
WPA	Works Progress Administration
WPPDA	Welfare and Pension Plans Disclosure Act
WTO	World Trade Organization
WWI	World War I
WWII	World War II
Yates Sel. Cas.	Yates's New York Select Cases
YMCA	Young Men's Christian Association
YWCA	Young Women's Christian Association

INDEX
BY NAME AND SUBJECT

Page numbers appearing in boldface indicate major treatment
of entries. Italicized page numbers refer to photos.

ISBN-13: 978-1-4144-0899-6
ISBN-10: 1-4144-0899-4